The Capitalist System

PRENTICE-HALL, INC.
Englewood Cliffs, New Jersey

Written and Edited by

Richard C. Edwards
Michael Reich
and
Thomas E. Weisskopf

Harvard University
Cambridge, Massachusetts

The
Capitalist
System

A RADICAL ANALYSIS OF AMERICAN SOCIETY

ISBN: 0-13-113647-X

Library of Congress
Catalog number: 71-171840

10   9   8   7

Prentice-Hall International, Inc., *London*
Prentice-Hall of Australia, Pty. Ltd., *Sydney*
Prentice-Hall of Canada, Ltd., *Toronto*
Prentice-Hall of India Private Ltd., *New Delhi*
Prentice-Hall of Japan, Inc., *Tokyo*

*Printed in
The United States of America*

Contents

PART **III**

THE FUNCTIONING OF CAPITALISM IN AMERICA   203

Chapter 5.   Inequality   205

Preface

This book is only in the most immediate sense the result of our own work. It originated in the collective effort of a larger group of graduate students and junior faculty to develop a radical alternative to the Harvard Economics Department's standard fare of courses. Our alternative—a new course entitled "The Capitalist Economy: Conflict and Power"—was introduced into the undergraduate curriculum as Social Sciences 125 in 1968–69 and continues to be taught by a gradually evolving staff. In this book we have tried to organize, to extend, and to communicate the main themes of Social Sciences 125 so as to make available to others the results of our collective experience. In preparing the book we have drawn freely on the ideas and assistance of all the people associated with the course.

More generally, and more basically, this book owes its origins to the radical political movement. Political struggles for civil rights and against the Vietnam war—and the subsequent growth of a broader radical movement in opposition to imperialism, racism, inequality and other forms of social oppression associated with capitalism—have educated us all and have inspired many of us to study the economic and political structure of our society. Stimulated by the movement, students have brought increasing pressure upon universities to offer radical courses and have thereby created the opportunity for preparing courses such as Social Sciences 125 and books such as this one.

We three author-editors are in many ways typical of how the movement has affected individual lives. In the early and middle sixties, we were college students concerned with the need for social reform. It was a time when we blamed social evils on the outcome of elections, or on bureaucratic stupidity or incompetence. In the middle and late sixties we studied orthodox economics (Weisskopf at M.I.T., Edwards and Reich at Harvard), and at the same time participated in current struggles against racism, poverty, and the Vietnam war. This was perhaps the most fragmented period in our lives: we were studying a well-established and sophisticated discipline, but we became increasingly aware of its inadequacy. Not only did it deny or ignore most of our political concerns, but even worse, it constituted a system of belief that justified the *status quo* by defending the capitalist system.

Our work on Social Sciences 125, beginning in 1968, represented an effort to resolve this contradiction. In seeking to develop an analytical framework that would be relevant to our concerns, we recognized increasingly that social oppression is embedded in the basic economic and political institutions of capitalist society. Influenced by the writings of Paul Baran, Paul Sweezy, and Andre Gorz, to whom we are greatly indebted, we were attracted to a Marxist perspective. This is no coincidence: the Marxist tradition of social concern, critical analysis, and interdisciplinary theory is naturally congenial to the study of the complex issues confronting us.

We do not find everything that Marx or his followers have written to be useful, or even relevant or correct. On the contrary, readers familiar with the Marxist literature will notice (and may complain) that many strands of Marxist thought are not represented in this book. Nonetheless our primary intellectual debt is to Karl Marx. His approach to social problems has influenced us deeply. The following quotation by Ernesto (Che) Guevera best describes our position.[1]

> When asked whether or not we are Marxist, our position is the same as that of a physicist or a biologist when asked if he is a "Newtonian" or if he is a "Pasteurian."
>
> There are truths so evident, so much a part of people's knowledge, that it is now useless to discuss them. One ought to be "Marxist" with the same naturalness with which one is "Newtonian" in physics or "Pasteurian" in biology, considering that if facts determine new concepts, these new concepts will never divest themselves of that portion of truth possessed by the older concepts they have outdated. Such is the case, for example, of Einsteinian relativity or Planck's "quantum" theory with respect to the discoveries of Newton; they take nothing at all away from the greatness of the learned Englishman. Thanks to Newton, physics was able to advance until it had achieved new concepts in space. The learned Englishman provided the necessary steppingstone for them. . . .
>
> The merit of Marx is that he suddenly produces a qualitative change in the history of social thought. He interprets history, understands its dynamic, predicts the future, but in addition to predicting it (which would satisfy his scientific obligation), he expresses a revolutionary concept: the world must not only be interpreted, it must be transformed.

Explanation alone is not enough. The purpose of social and economic analysis should be to help to eradicate the current sources of oppression rather than merely to describe them, or—still worse—to obscure them. We want to place our analysis squarely on the side of the growing movement for radical social change. For, as a result of our studies and our association with the radical movement, it has become clear to us that to achieve a better society the capitalist system must be challenged.

This book is devoted to an analysis of the capitalist system in the *advanced* capitalist countries, especially the United States. We had first intended simply to reprint the most relevant material from the reading list of Social Sciences 125. As we began our work, however, we found that the unity and coherence of the book demanded rather extensive introductions as well as a variety of new essays to fill gaps in the literature. Thus we

[1]"Notes for the Study of the Ideology of the Cuban Revolution," *Studies on the Left*, Vol. 1, No. 3, 1960.

encouraged some of the members of the staff of Social Sciences 125 (including ourselves) to contribute new readings that would convey many of the ideas that had gone into the course but had not yet appeared in written form. The result is that approximately one-third of the readings in this book have been written by staff members of Social Science 125 or by other close friends and associates. Most of these are appearing here in print for the first time. Several of the new readings have been or will be published also in current issues of *The Review of Radical Political Economics.* *

We have edited judiciously most of the readings being reprinted. The editing, we trust, improves the clarity of exposition, avoids unnecessary repetition, and focuses on points that are most germane to our analysis. Deletions from the original text are indicated by elipses. Each source is cited in full so that readers can consult the original text as desired. In excerpting readings footnotes that are not essential to the understanding or documentation of the piece were removed and all footnotes and tables renumbered for continuity. Finally, we have included at the end of each chapter an annotated bibliography to refer both teachers and students to additional readings that we have found particularly useful.

The resulting book includes a variety of material selected and edited from the work of many different authors. It has been carefully woven into a logical sequence of twelve chapters, with extensive introductions to each chapter and to each reading to bind the diverse writings into a coherent whole. Though we have conceived the book as the basis for a radical course on American political economy, its applicability as a collection of readings supplementary to other courses in economics or in the social sciences is evident.

We have already mentioned our debt to all the other members of the staff of Social Sciences 125 during 1968–70. They are Keith Aufhauser, Peter Bohmer, Roger Bohmer, Samuel Bowles, Herbert Gintis, Carl Gotsch, Arthur MacEwan, Stephan Michelson, Ralph Pochoda, and Paddy Quick. We are grateful for the constructive criticism we received at several meetings of the weekly seminar of the Harvard chapter of the Union for Radical Political Economics, and we would like to thank specifically the following persons who have contributed in various ways to the book: Frank Ackerman, James Ault, James Campen, Margery Davies, Maria Delgado, Ellen Doughty, Carolyn Pope Edwards, Coburn Everdell, Elizabeth Fenton, Elizabeth Katz, Pamela Pacelli, Adria Reich, Janice Weiss, Susan Weisskopf, James Wetzler, and Andrew Zimbalist.

*Published by the Union for Radical Political Economics, 2503 Student Activities Building, University of Michigan, Ann Arbor, Michigan, 48104.

RICHARD C. EDWARDS
MICHAEL REICH
Cambridge, Mass.　　　THOMAS E. WEISSKOPF

The
Capitalist
System

Introduction

THIS BOOK HAS GROWN OUT OF A PROFOUND dissatisfaction with the society in which we live. We see a rich and powerful nation bombarding and decimating poor and much weaker nations on the opposite side of the globe. We see enormous wealth coexist with abject proverty; we see whites oppress blacks and men dominate women. We see our environment despoiled in the name of greater "productivity"; we see highways split communities and parking lots displace parks, fields, and meadows. And we see thousands upon thousands of men and women retreat from the boredom of their jobs into a stultifying color-TV land, or into liquor, or into destructive drugs.

Why do these problems occur? Are they simply the modern equivalents of age-old forms of oppression, to be expected in any society because people are inherently greedy, selfish, and power-seeking? Or are these problems, however formidable they seem at the moment, mere aberrations from the basically just and humane nature of Western industrial society? We reject both of these explanations. We believe that human behavior is significantly shaped by the institutional framework of a society. And we believe that oppression in its many forms is pervasive in and fundamental to Western industrial society.

Oppression has its roots in the basic economic institutions of a society. The forms of inequality, alienation, racism, sexism, irrationality, and imperialism that we observe in the United States today derive in large part from the existing capitalist institutions. The purpose of this book is to analyze the relationships between these forms of oppression and the capitalist system, and to examine the internal structure and dynamics of capitalism itself.

THE ORGANIZATION OF THE BOOK

We have divided this book into four parts and twelve chapters to follow the logical structure of its contents. The material to be presented has been organized into a sequence that we have found useful from a pedagogical point of view. Most of the essays in later chapters can be read with greater insight and understanding after a prior reading of earlier chapters.

Part I (Chapter 1),"Problems of Capitalism," presents a series of graphic accounts illustrating some of the forms of oppression that are so prevalent and intractable in the contemporary United States. These readings are intended to provide a glimpse of the range and the urgency of problems which, we shall argue, derive to a significant extent from the fundamental institutions of a capitalist system.

Part II (Chapters 2–4), "The Structure of the Capitalist System," is primarily theoretical in nature. We cannot understand the relationships between capitalism and the oppressive problems described in Chapter 1 without first examining what capitalism is and how it has developed. Chapter 2 considers the general place of economics in the analysis of social systems and examines the development of capitalism in England and the United States. In Chapter 3 we turn to a detailed analysis of the capitalist mode of production; Chapter 4 extends this basic analysis to examine the evolution of capitalist institutions in the contemporary United States.

In Part III (Chapters 5–10), "The Functioning of Capitalism in America," we turn to an analysis of the relationships between the oppressive problems described in Part I and the basic capitalist institutions examined in Part II. Each of the six chapters in Part III deals with one of the six important types of problems that we highlighted in Chapter 1: inequality, alienation, racism, sexism, irrationality (including militarism, consumerism, environmental destruction, and related problems), and imperialism. In each of these chapters we argue that the basic institutions that characterize the capitalist mode of production make it extremely difficult, if not

2

altogether impossible, to eliminate the problems at hand.

Nonetheless, we are by no means fatalistic about the persistence of oppression. We believe that there are good prospects for radical social change—the kind of fundamental change from capitalist to alternative institutions which would permit and encourage the development of a freer and more decent society. In Part IV (Chapters 11–12), "Toward an Alternative to the Capitalist System," we argue that the very process of capitalist development generates oppositional forces which, in the long run, may lead to a fundamental transformation of the capitalist system. Chapter 11 examines the contradictions which develop in contemporary capitalism—contradictions that cannot be resolved within the present social framework. Finally, Chapter 12 considers in broad outline some important aspects of an alternative, more desirable social system, which we shall call participatory socialism.

A FEW PRELIMINARY REMARKS

Throughout this book we will be criticizing the capitalist system that dominates the Western world today. In Part II we define quite explicitly what we mean by the capitalist mode of production and how it is to be distinguished from alternative modes. But since the meaning of capitalism is subject to considerable confusion, it may be useful at the outset to clarify a few points about our understanding and analysis of the capitalist system. In particular, we would like to explain our point of view on (1) the relationship between capitalism and industrialism, and (2) the relationship between capitalism and socialism.

Capitalism and Industrialism:

It is often alleged that many of the characteristics of the modern United States are inevitable in an advanced industrial society, with its complex and sophisticated technology, its cybernetic systems, and its massive scale. Technological society is seen as a system of domination, or as a machine out of control. In our view such arguments are fallacious and misplaced. To believe that industrialism by itself generates social problems is to fall prey to technological determinism. The villain is not the existing state of technology and productive capacity, but the power relations in society which, for example, dictate the ends of productive effort, the uses to which technology is to be put, and the very criteria by which some technologies are methodically developed and others left dormant and undeveloped.

As a specific example, consider the problem of pollution. We shall argue in Chapter 9 that in a capitalist society there are basic forces which operate to maximize the extent of environmental disruption that accompanies industrial production. These forces can in principle be curbed by state intervention, but such intervention is likely to be neither widespread nor effective because it goes counter to the natural logic of capitalism. A capitalist society cannot satisfactorily resolve environmental problems, but an alternative industrial society dependent on different basic institutions would not be so handicapped. In short, technology need not necessarily be destructive; under the appropriate conditions it can in fact become an instrument of liberation. Social theories that attribute every modern problem to industrialism are clearly inadequate.

Capitalism and Socialism:

Another common misconception is that the difference between capitalism and socialism depends solely upon the legal relations of ownership of the means of production. Capitalism is often equated with private ownership of capital, while socialism is equated with public or state ownership of capital.

In many advanced capitalist countries—

such as England, France, or Sweden—the state-owned branches of production have grown in importance in recent decades, and the state has taken on the responsibility of regulating and managing the entire economy. These countries are often said to be examples of mixed systems, in that they embody elements of both capitalism and socialism. However, the state-owned production sectors in these countries tend to differ only marginally, if at all, from the private sectors of the economy, inasmuch as the state employs capitalist-oriented criteria in organizing its activities. These countries are examples of what we would call *state capitalism*.

At the same time, in the Soviet Union and the Eastern European countries, virtually the entire economy is run by a centralized state apparatus. This system has resulted in a stratified, bureaucratic and hierarchical society in which the maximization of material goods production—subject to the constraint of preserving hierarchical control—is a primary objective. Such a society might best be called *state socialism*. In Serge Mallet's apt analogy, the state socialist societies of the Soviet Union and Eastern Europe are to true socialism what "the monsters of the paleolithic era are to present animal species: clumsy, abortive, prototypes."[1] It would be incorrect to equate mechanically state socialism and state capitalism, for the two systems do differ in significant respects. For example, the state socialist societies have gone much further toward equalizing the distribution of essential goods and services such as food, housing, medical care, and transportation. Yet state socialism and state capitalism are akin in many respects: neither are model societies of socialism to be emulated.

For us, socialism is more than a juridical change in the legal relations of ownership.

Socialism means democratic, decentralized, and *participatory* control for the individual: it means having a say in the decisions that affect one's life. Such a participatory form of socialism certainly requires equal access for all to material and cultural resources, which in turn requires the abolition of private ownership of capital and the redistribution of wealth. But it also calls for socialist men and women to eliminate alienating, destructive forms of production, consumption, education, and social relations. Participatory socialism requires the elimination of bureaucracies and all hierarchical forms, and their replacement, not by new state or party bureaucracies, but by a self-governing and self-managing people with directly chosen representatives subject to recall and replacement. Participatory socialism entails a sense of egalitarian cooperation, of solidarity of people with one another; but at the same time it respects individual and group differences and guarantees individual rights. It affords to all individuals the freedom to exercise human rights and civil liberties that are not mere abstractions but have concrete day-to-day meaning.[2]

Our vision of a radical social transformation of the United States clearly involves far more than formal changes in political and economic institutions. Such changes must be part of an ongoing process of change in social and cultural consciousness that will constitute a revolution of social relations among people. We do *not* regard men and women as inherently greedy, acquisitive, selfish, competitive, or aggressive. Human nature has shown enormous variation in time and space,

---

[1]"Bureaucracy and Technology in the Socialist Countries," *Socialist Revolution*, I, No. 3 (May/June, 1970), 45.

[2]By these criteria, no country has as yet achieved participatory socialism. China and Cuba, however, have tried to avoid individual, competitive material incentives by stressing social incentives for economic development; and to some extent they have also placed economic development in the proper context of overall balanced social development. Hence these countries can be contrasted favorably with the Soviet Union and Eastern Europe.

and it seems to be in large part a product of the social environment. We believe that changes in the environment can interact with changes in the individual to usher in a new era of human cooperation.

One final caveat is necessary; it will underscore the preceding points. Despite our critical perspective on the capitalist system, it is not our intention to imply that *all* forms of oppression are a result of capitalist institutions, though a great many are, or that *all* social problems will automatically wither away with the elimination of the basic institutions of capitalism. We have respect for the tenacity of such phenomena as male supremacy and military expansion, which predate the rise of capitalism and are not unique to capitalist societies today. Yet we do believe that in many cases capitalism makes use of and reinforces these forms of oppression and thereby precludes their eradication. Thus the elimination of basic capitalist institutions is necessary, though not sufficient, to eliminate the oppressive problems of the modern world. To achieve a decent society, the struggle against capitalism must be intimately linked to struggles against social oppression in all its forms.

PART I

PROBLEMS
OF
CAPITALISM

All chapter-opening art for this book prepared by Coburn Everdell.

What's
Wrong
in America?

1

NO ONE NEEDS TO BE TOLD IN THE 1970's that there is much that is wrong in America. If nothing else, the events of the past decade have brought home to every American the enormity and the variety of the problems that plague our society and our economy. These problems take different forms for different people, and some people suffer very much more than others. Yet no one can remain unaffected, for in the last analysis a society is an organic whole that is shaped by every component part.

To examine all of the problems in comprehensive fashion is an impossible task. War, poverty, alienation, racism, crime, destruction of the environment, waste, hypocrisy—all of these and more compete for headlines every day in the newspapers. Their combined effect is not only to oppress a great many people at home and abroad, but also to generate a widespread sense of anxiety among those who are not or do not perceive themselves to be oppressed.

In this book we attempt to analyze many of these problems by studying the basic social and economic institutions out of which they have arisen. Before beginning such an analysis, however, we believe that it is useful to focus directly on some of the problems themselves. For people who are not the most immediate victims, there is a persistent air of unreality about the disastrous news reports that appear on a printed page or flash across a television screen. The most shocking incidents in Vietnam can be absorbed without emotion by people who have almost become immune to the killing of innocent villagers and the destruction of their homes and land. Yet to undertake the study of serious social problems without an emotional sense of their urgency is to open oneself to irrelevant theorizing and intellectual gamesmanship.

In the readings in this chapter we draw attention to a few of the problems that are examined in greater detail in Part III. The choice of problems cannot be comprehensive; we have chosen to focus on some which we believe to be among the most significant in contemporary America. Furthermore, the selections we have chosen to depict these problems can necessarily only provide a glimpse of the overall situation. Thousands of books and articles have been written about various aspects of each of the problems we examine. The readings in this chapter aim simply to illustrate a problem and to motivate the reader to draw further from his own experience and from the extensive descriptive literature that already exists. Some of the best of this literature is noted in the bibliography at the end of the chapter.

The first six readings treat selectively the six major topics that are studied in Part III of the book. Inequality, alienation, racism, sexism, irrationality, and imperialism are illustrated briefly by descriptive accounts that are both personal and well informed.

It is an understandable fact of life that the most directly oppressed people are rarely in a position to articulate their oppression in written form. Instead, oppression is almost always described by sympathetic observers whose background and education have spared them from the most obvious forms of oppression and enabled them to communicate effectively in writing. The readings in this chapter do not depart significantly from this rule. However, by reprinting reports by persons directly or very closely involved with the problems described, we hope to convey some direct insight into what's wrong in America today.

The last reading in this chapter goes on to consider what's wrong with the way social scientists tend to analyze contemporary societies. The social problems that plague America today necessarily call for attention by intellectuals whose fields of learning are supposed to be relevant to these problems. Economists, political scientists, sociologists, etc., cannot wholly ignore the reality of contemporary American society. Yet as Blackburn points out in his "A Brief Guide to Bourgeois Ideology," the prevailing approach to social problems by Western social scientists tries to minimize the significance of these problems, to inhibit a thorough-going analysis of their origins, and to suppress the notion that preferable alternatives exist. This book represents an effort to move against the prevailing ideology of Western social science.

Before undertaking the task in the chapters to follow, it is useful to examine the nature of the prevailing ideology and the biases that pervade it.

1.1 *Inequality: Barbara Hayes*

In this first reading Studs Terkel interviews Mrs. Barbara Hayes, trapped near the bottom of the American ladder.

Source: The following is condensed from Part VI of *Division Street: America* by STUDS TERKEL. Copyright © 1967 by Studs Terkel. Reprinted by permission of Pantheon Books, a division of Random House, Inc.

Number 1510: a doorway facing out on the gallery.[1] An apartment in the world's largest public-housing project: the Robert Taylor Homes, on south State Street, extending from Pershing Road (39th Street) to 54th. We're in the kitchen of a six-room flat. Somewhere in the vague distance a child is whimpering. "The little one," murmurs Mrs. Hayes. "Her afternoon nap." A small boy of four or five is observing us.

She has eight children, four boys and four girls—including a set of twins—ranging in age from sixteen to the baby. She has recently been separated from her husband and is on ADC. She came to Chicago in 1954, and all these years she has lived in a project. . . .

It's about two in the afternoon. The place is in semidarkness, the electricity having been cut off. Fortunately, the battery of my tape-recorder was fully charged.

They said I hadn't paid my bills on time, and when you don't pay your bills on time, you get a black record. So they don't bother to send you a second notice. They send you your bill and then they send you a final

notice. This is the first time mine's been cut off. We're in darkness tonight.

If one of the kids wants to read a book. . . .

No, they can't read a book. They can't watch TV. They can't listen to the radio. If we didn't have a watch, we couldn't tell what time it was, because we have electric clocks.

In about three hours, it'll be totally dark. What happens?

They'll light a candle. We'll probably eat by candlelight. And just before it gets dark, they'll straighten up their rooms and change their clothes and lay out their school clothes for tomorrow. And this will be it. Then we'll sit in here, I suppose.

. . . I like children and I always thought that mothers needed a lot of understanding. I wanted to be a social worker because I realized people had so many problems that they needed somebody to listen to them, to talk to them, to help them. This was a busy world. People don't have too much time to listen. They have their own problems.

On a bus, it's easy to strike up a conversation. You don't have to say anything. Just look as though you'd listen and people start telling you, oh, something the boss did, or

[1]Gallery is the official name for the balcony that extends out on each story of the building. The words *porch* and *gallery* are used interchangeably.

somebody on the job, or what the landlord, say, or complain about prices—they might've just left a sale, you know. People want to talk; they don't have to know you.

But as far as life in public housing is concerned, I don't think it's a very good place to raise children. They can't make noise, they don't have freedom. They can't do like they can in a small town. They can't lay on the grass, they can't climb trees. . . .

The phone rings. It was the first of many such calls during the conversation.

That lady was not of this building. She's in the 5200. I'm chairman of this building's council. She called about the course in cashiering. The Joe Louis Milk Company is offering it. If we could get the people. I told them this is no problem. The women here would like to work. People think people on Aid won't work. If you have three or four children and you really care anything about them, you want to be sure when you go to work that they're taken care of. People will accept your money and say they're taking care of your children, but this is not always so. I think I've talked to about thirteen people who say they want to take the course. But one of the questions they ask: Where's the last place you worked and how long ago? If you haven't worked in six or seven years, who's gonna hire you? (*B-r-ring!*) Excuse me.

"She just got fired from the CHA—the Chicago Housing Authority. She was a janitress. Quite a thing going on here—among the row people, too. They have a tough supervisor and they don't want the employees to show any insubordination, whether they're right or wrong. There's a great deal of unemployment. Most people who do construction work, they're off quite a bit. It's seasonal. The others who work at the post office or at some stores don't have too much trouble— I don't think."

The people here want to do something. Last year, we had a garden project, seven acres. They raised their own vegetables and flowers. Quite a few of the ladies canned the vegetables. They were so pretty. Some of them had freezers and they had a whole family dinner. I think they enjoyed it because a lot of the people are from the South. They had done farming and this might have carried them back to, you know, memories.

I don't like the Taylor Homes. It's too crowded, there are not enough activities. Who does the child have to talk to at home? Mother's got other kids. If the father's there, he's working or on relief and this he doesn't appreciate. So who wants to be bothered with some kids? So they say: "Mama, what is this?" And: "I don't know, don't bother me. Go play." So they send them out on the porch or downstairs.

The kids have been shoved outside. So they break windows, destroy property, fight —anything to get some attention. That's how you get the gang leaders. Everybody wants recognition. You get it whichever way you can.

We had some teen-age boys around here that were pretty troublesome. Whenever we were going to have something, I'd ask those boys to keep order so that nobody would start any confusion. They were the ones who started the confusion, so by having them look out for the others, I didn't have any problems. They enjoyed this. And they respect you, too. I started out one evening for class and they were roughhousing downstairs and one of them said: "Cool it, here comes Miz Hayes." I hadn't gotten two feet away and they started again. But at least they let me pass. (Laughs.) This is the same group of boys that I would say: I need your help now.

You push them outdoors, out in the galleries: You can't play ball—no roller skating—you're making too much noise by the window. So they go downstairs: You can't sit on the benches—you're not supposed to be around here. Or somebody throws something down: You're not supposed to be hanging around out front. So what are they gonna do? You can push them so far. Then they're gonna push back. But if they had more to do. . . .

The turnover's so fast, you know. In a crowded place like this, you . . . oh, so what? You want to stay by yourself. You don't know about the people next door. You don't know what they're like. A lot of people are kinda suspicious. Maybe they resent conditions. A lot of them are on Aid, a lot of wrong things go on. So they stay to themselves and don't have to worry about it getting out.

Often the elevators don't work. I think we have one working today. It might be working at noon, two o'clock, it might be out of order. Three o'clock in the morning it might be out of order, you hear bells ringing. Children and adults get stuck in them. Sometimes they get frightened. Kids know how to stick the elevators. They make a game out of it. They find a kid who is afraid and they stick it.

I've walked fifteen flights quite frequently. When I first moved in, I did it for the exercise. I do it now when I have to. It's not too pleasant. You never know who you're gonna find on the stairs. People from off the street. The stairs are open. You might see people sleeping on the stairs, you might see people gambling on the stairs, you might see drinking on the stairs. You never know what you're gonna meet on the stairway. The light might be on, they might be off. If they're off, you're gonna come up those stairs, you know.

Suppose somebody gets sick, needs a doctor, and the elevator doesn't work?

They're just sick then. You have to take them down the stairs. Or, if somebody really gets sick, they'd just die, I suppose. I often wonder what's gonna happen when we have a fire?[2] I wonder what's gonna happen when they have a fire and the elevators don't work. It'll take 'em longer. We had one in Taylor when a couple of kids did die because they couldn't get an elevator.

They say kids play on 'em and people put 'em out of order; but if this is the case, certainly CHA should do something about it. Put some operators on. They have repairmen and electricians and maintenance men. Wouldn't it be less expensive for the CHA? Of course, it would be more convenient for the resident.

We can't get cooperation from management. Our council has gotten parents to say: We'll operate the elevators during the day, if they put some people on in the afternoon. We did this for two weeks. And they say you can't do anything with the kids. This is not so. After we had been on there for a week, the kids knew when to come down to the first floor instead of going to the third floor to get on. Came to the first floor, lined up and waited. In a matter of fifteen minutes, we had all the school kids home. It was working out.

We asked management to send some people up in the evenings. We were gonna help them, too. The kids had gotten used to seeing the parents down there, so they would straighten up, they wouldn't push. They'd get on and wouldn't touch the buttons. They'd tell you what floor. They didn't scream and just make a piano board out of the buttons as they do now. The management didn't object. They just didn't cooperate. They didn't care . . .

* * *

If kids come out of this environment stable, emotionally stable, they're lucky. It's very difficult. All the pressures, you know. Say, I live on the fifteenth floor. You can't

---

[2]From the Chicago *Daily News*, December 11, 1965: "Two children were killed Friday in a $200 fire in a Robert Taylor Homes building at 4352 S. State. The victims, Timothy Larde, 5, and his sister, Regina, 3, suffocated in their tenth-floor apartment, firemen said. Neighbors pulled Regina's body from the apartment. Timothy's body was found under a pile of clothes in a closet where he apparently sought refuge. The children's mother was at work, firemen said, and a girl who came to baby-sit discovered the fire. It was confined to the Larde apartment." This item appeared months after our conversation.

make too much noise, the people downstairs complain. You can't go out to play. You have to study, watch your little sister. Be careful, don't talk to a stranger. It's an open neighborhood, anybody can come through. The building is like a street. Not just your friends and your bill collectors, but everybody's you know . . . salesmen, anybody.

The people here don't know how to resist. They'll come by with something they know you want, or maybe you need it, you know, but you really can't afford it. And they high-pressure people into taking it. On the installment. No money down, or a dollar down, dollar a week, make it sound so simple. Yeah, they always pay more than what it's worth, you know. Sometimes they can't keep up with the bill and then comes this pressure from the company. They take it away or they pressure you about making a payment. So you have to take your food money or something else to pay them. They want to get paid, they don't really care. You pay for bein' poor.

*   *   *

What do you want most in life?

For my children to get a good education

—where they'll not have to be pitiful on public aid. And I hope to move from Taylor Homes into a place where I can have my own day-care center. Not just a baby-sitting thing. Expose them to the fine arts. And take them on trips.

Beauty. It's really all around. You just have to find it. Look around and see. Some think the sun and a bright day, that's beauty. Not necessarily. I'm quite sure *this* would be a scene of beauty to an artist. With his canvas. He can see so many things we don't see, you know.

POSTSCRIPT: *The elevator going down was crowded. A number of jerky stops. Two women, with Deep South accents, forlorn, lost. Their plaint: the obstinate elevator failed to stop at the fourteenth floor; they had pressed the button again and again; they had been going up and down, three times; yo-yos. "Lotsa time it don't work. I walk up fourteen floors, more'n I can count." One talking, the other nodding: " 'At's the truth, Lawd." Young Negro, in the hard hat of a construction worker, gets off at seventh floor. His departing comment over shoulder: "President's Physical Fitness Program." There was no laughter.*

1.2 *Alienation: Inside the New York Telephone Company*

As public utilities, the American telephone companies might be expected to differ in important respects from the large private corporations that dominate the economy. Yet as Elinor Langer so vividly describes from her own experience, the New York Telephone Company is as dedicated to the art of selling as the most profit-hungry private firm—with the same adverse consequences for the quality of work and life.

Source: The following is excerpted from "The Women of the Telephone Company" by Elinor Langer. From *The New York Review of Books* (March 12 and 26, 1970). Copyright © 1970 by *The New York Review*. Reprinted by permission of Elinor Langer; c/o International Fashion Agency.

From October to December 1969 I worked for the New York Telephone Company as a Customer's Service Representative in the Commercial Department. My office was one of several in the Broadway-City Hall area of lower Manhattan, a flattened, blue-windowed commercial building in which the telephone company occupies three floors. The room was big and brightly lit—like the city room of a large newspaper—with perhaps one hundred desks arranged in groups of five or six around the desk of a Supervisor. The job consists of taking orders for new equipment and services and pacifying customers who complain, on the eleven exchanges (although not the more complex business accounts) in the area between the Lower East Side and 23rd Street on the North and bounded by Sixth Avenue on the West.

My Supervisor is the supervisor of five women. She reports to a Manager who manages four supervisors (about twenty women) and he reports to the District Supervisor along with two other managers. The offices of the managers are on the outer edge of the main room separated from the floor by glass partitions. The District Supervisor is down the hall in an executive suite. A job identical in rank to that of the district supervisor is held by four other men in Southern Manhattan alone. They report to the Chief of the Southern Division, himself a soldier in an army of division chiefs whose territories are five boroughs, Long Island, Westchester, and the vast hinterlands vaguely referred to as "Upstate." The executives at ——— Street were only dozens among the thousands in New York Tel alone.

Authority in their hierarchy is parceled out in bits. A representative, for example, may issue credit to customers up to, say, $10.00; her supervisor, $25.00; her manager, $100.00; his supervisor, $300.00; and so forth. These employees are in the same relation to the centers of power in AT&T and the communications industry as the White House guard to Richard Nixon. They all believe that "The business of the telephone company is Service" and if they have ever heard of the ABM or AT&T's relation to it, I believe they think it is the Associated Business Machines, a particularly troublesome customer on the Gramercy-7 exchange.

I brought to the job certain radical interests. I knew I would see "bureaucratization," "alienation," and "exploitation." I knew that it was "false consciousness" of their true role in the imperialist economy that led the "workers" to embrace their oppressors. I believed those things and I believe them still. I know why, by my logic, the workers should rise up. But my understanding was making reality an increasing puzzle: Why didn't people move? What things, invisible to me, were holding them back? What I hoped to learn, in short, was something about the texture of the industrial system: what life within it meant to its participants.

I deliberately decided to take a job which was women's work, white collar, highly industrialized and bureaucratic. I knew that New York Tel was in a management crisis notorious both among businessmen and among the public and I wondered what effect the well-publicized breakdown of service was having on employees. Securing the position was not without hurdles. I was "overqualified," having confessed to college; I performed better on personnel tests than I intended to do; and I was inspected for symptoms of militance by a shrewd but friendly interviewer who noticed the several years' gap in my record of employment. "What have you been doing lately?" she asked me. "Protesting?" I said: "Oh, no, I've been married," as if that condition itself explained one's neglect of social problems. She seemed to agree that it did.

My problem was to talk myself out of a management traineeship at a higher salary while maintaining access to the job I wanted. This, by fabrications, I was able to do. I said: "Well, you see, I'm going through a divorce right now and I'm a little upset emotionally, and I don't know if I want a career with managerial responsibility." She said: "If anyone else said that to me, I'm afraid I wouldn't be able to hire them," but in the end she accepted me. I had the feeling it would have been harder for her to explain to her bosses why she had let me slip away, given my qualifications, than to justify to them her suspicions.

I nonetheless found as I began the job that I was viewed as "management material" and given special treatment. I was welcomed at length by both the District Supervisor and the man who was to be my Manager, and given a set of fluffy feminist speeches about "opportunities for women" at New York Tel. I was told in a variety of ways that I would be smarter than the other people in my class; "management" would be keeping an eye on me. Then the Manager led me personally to the back classroom where my training program was scheduled to begin.

. . .

LEARNING

The Representative's course is "programmed." It is apparent that the phone company has spent millions of dollars for high-class management consultation on the best way to train new employees. The two principal criteria are easily deduced. First, the course should be made so routine that any employee can teach it. The teacher's material—the remarks she makes, the examples she uses—are all printed in a loose-leaf notebook that she follows. Anyone can start where anyone else leaves off. I felt that I could teach the course myself, simply by following the program. The second criterion is to assure the reproducibility of results, to guarantee that every part turned out by the system will be interchangeable with every other part. The system is to bureaucracy what Taylor was to the factory: it consists of breaking down every operation into dis-

crete parts, then making verbal the discretions that are made.

At first we worked chiefly from programmed booklets organized around the principle of supplying the answer, then rephrasing the question. For instance:

> *It is annoying to have the other party to a conversation leave the line without an explanation.*
> *Before leaving, you should excuse yourself and——what you are going to do.*

Performing skillfully was a matter of reading, and not actual comprehension. . . .

Soon acting out the right way to deal with customers became more important than self-instruction. The days were organized into Lesson Plans, a typical early one being: How to Respond to a Customer if You Haven't Already Been Trained to Answer his Question, or a slightly more bureaucratic rendering of that notion. Sally [the instructor] explained the idea, which is that you are supposed to refer the call to a more experienced Representative or to the Supervisor. But somehow they manage to complicate this situation to the point where it becomes confusing even for an intelligent person to handle it. You mustn't say: "Gosh, that's tough, I don't know anything about that, let me give the phone to someone who does," though that in effect is what you do. Instead when the phone rings, you say: "Hello. This is Miss Langer. May I help you?" (The Rule is, get immediate "control of the contact" and hold it lest anything unexpected happen, like, for instance, a human transaction between you and the customer.)

He says: "This is Mr. Smith and I'd like to have an additional wall telephone installed in my kitchen."

You say: "I'll be very glad to help you, Mr. Smith (Rule the Second: Always express interest in the Case and indicate willingness to help), but I'll need more information. What is your telephone number?"

He tells you, then you confess: "Well, Mr.

Smith, I'm afraid I haven't been trained in new installations yet because I'm a new representative, but let me give you someone else who can help you." (Rule the Third: You must get his consent to this arrangement. That is, you must say: *May* I get someone else who can help you? *May* I put you on hold for a moment?)

The details are absurd but they are all prescribed. What you would do naturally becomes unnatural when it is codified, and the rigidity of the rules makes the Representatives in training feel they are stupid when they make mistakes. Another lesson, for example, was: What to Do if a Customer Calls And Asks for a Specific Person, such as Miss Smith, another Representative, or the Manager. Whatever the facts, you are to say "Oh, Miss Smith is busy but I have access to your records, may I help you?" A customer is never allowed to identify his interests with any particular employee. During one lesson, however, Sally said to Angela [another student]: "Hello, I'd like immediately to speak to Mrs. Brown," and Angela said, naturally, "Hold the line a minute, please. I'll put her on." A cardinal sin, for which she was immediately rebuked. Angela felt terrible.

Company rhetoric asserts that this rigidity does not exist, that Representatives are supposed to use "initiative" and "judgment," to develop their own language. What that means is that instead of using the precise words "Of course I'll be glad to help you but I'll need more information," you are allowed to "create" some individual variant. But you must always (1) express willingness to help and (2) indicate the need for further investigation. In addition, while you are doing this, you must always write down the information taken from the customer, coded, on a yellow form called a CF-1, in such a way as to make it possible for a Representative in Florida to read and translate it. "That's the point," Sally told us. "You are doing it the same way

a rep in Illinois or Alaska does it. We're one big monopoly."

The logic of training is to transform the trainees from humans into machines. The basic method is to handle any customer request by extracting "bits" of information: by translating the human problem he might have into bureaucratic language so that it can be processed by the right department. For instance, if a customer calls and says: "My wife is dying and she's coming home from the hopsital today and I'd like to have a phone installed in her bedroom right away," you *say,* "Oh I'm very sorry to hear that sir, I'm sure I can help you, would you be interested in our Princess model? It has a dial that lights up at night," meanwhile *writing* on your ever-present CF-1: "Csr wnts Prn inst bdrm immed," issuing the order, and placing it in the right-hand side of your workfile where it gets picked up every fifteen minutes by a little clerk.

. . .

SELLING

It is largely since World War II that the Bell System abandoned being a comparatively simple service organization and began producing such an array of consumer products as to rival Procter and Gamble. It is important to realize what contribution this proliferation makes both to creating the work and to making it unbearable. If the company restricted itself to essential functions and services—standard telephones and standard types of service—whole layers of its bureaucracy would not need to exist at all, and what did need to exist could be both more simple and more humane. The pattern of proliferation is also crucial, for among other things, it is largely responsible for the creation of the "new"—white collar—"working class" whose job is to process the bureaucratic desiderata of consumption.

In our classroom, the profit motivation behind the telephone cornucopia is not concealed and we are programmed to repeat its justifications: that the goods were developed to account for different "tastes" and the "need of variation." Why Touchtone Dialing? We learn to say that "it's the latest thing," "it dials faster," "it is easier to read the letters and numbers," and "its musical notes as you depress the buttons are pleasant to hear." We learn that a Trimline is a "spacesaver," that it has an "entirely new feature, a recall button that allows you to hang up without replacing the receiver," and that it is "featured in the Museum of Modern Art's collection on industrial design." Why a night-light? we were asked. I considered saying, "It would be nice to make love by a small sexy light," but instead helped to contribute the expected answers: "It gives you security in the bedroom," "it doesn't interfere with the TV."

. . .

Selling is an important part of the Representative's job. Sally introduced the subject with a little speech (from her program book) about the concept of the "well-telephoned home," how that was an advance from the old days when people thought of telephone equipment in a merely functional way. Now, she said, we stress "a variety of items of beauty and convenience." Millions of dollars have been spent by the Bell System, she told us, to find out what a customer wants and to sell it to him. She honestly believed that good selling is as important to the customer as it is to the company: to the company because "it makes additional and worthwhile revenue," to the customer because it provides services that are truly useful. We are warned not to attempt to sell when it is clearly inappropriate to do so, but basically to use every opportunity to unload profitable items. This means that if a girl calls up and asks for a new listing for a roommate, your job is to say: "Oh. Wouldn't your roommate prefer to have her own extension?"

The official method is to avoid giving the customer a choice but to offer him a total package which he can either accept or reject. For instance, a customer calls for new service. You find out that he has a wife, a teen-age daughter, and a six-room apartment. The prescription calls for you to get off the line, make all the calculations, then come back on and say all at once: "Mr. Smith, suppose we installed for you a wall telephone in your kitchen, a Princess extension in your daughter's room and one in your bedroom, and our new Trimline model in your living room. This will cost you only X dollars for the installation and only Y dollars a month."

Mr. Smith will say, naturally, "That's too many telephones for a six-room apartment," and you are supposed to "overcome his objections" by pointing out the "security" and "convenience" that comes from having telephones all over the place.

Every Representative is assigned a selling quota—so many extensions, so many Princesses—deducted and derived in some way from the quota of the next largest unit. In other words, quotas are assigned to the individual because they are first assigned to the five-girl unit; they are assigned to the unit because they are assigned to the twenty-girl section; and they are assigned to the section because they are assigned to the district: to the Manager and the District Supervisor. The fact that everyone is in the same situation— expected to contribute to the same total—is one of the factors that increase management-worker solidarity.

The women enact the sales ritual as if it were in fact in their own interest and originated with them. Every month there is a sales contest. Management provides the money—$25.00 a month to one or another five-girl unit—but the women do the work: organizing skits, buying presents, or providing coffee and donuts to reward the high sellers. At Thanksgiving the company raffled away turkeys: the number of chances one had depending on the number of sales one had completed.

SURVIVING

Daily life on the job at the New York Telephone Company . . . consists largely of pressure. To a casual observer it might appear that much of the activity on the floor is random, but in fact it is not. The women moving from desk to desk are on missions of retrieving and refiling customers' records; the tête-à-têtes that look so sociable are anxious conferences with a Supervisor in which a Representative is Thinking and Planning What to Do Next. Of course the more experienced women know how to use the empty moments that do occur for social purposes. But the basic working unit is one girl: one telephone, and the basic requirement of the job is to answer it, perhaps more than fifty times a day.

For every contact with a customer, the amount of paperwork is huge: a single contact can require the completion of three, four, or even five separate forms. No problems can be dispensed with handily. Even if, for example, you merely transfer a customer to Traffic or Repair you must still fill out and file a CF-1. At the end of the day you must tally up and categorize all the services you have performed on a little slip of paper and hand it in to the Supervisor, who completes a tally for the unit: it is part of the process of "taking credit" for services rendered by one unit vis-à-vis the others.

A Representative's time is divided into "open" and "closed" portions, according to a recent scientific innovation called FADS (for Force Administration Data System), of which the company is particularly proud; the innovation consists in establishing how many Representatives have to be available at any one moment to handle the volume of business anticipated for that month, that day, and that hour. Under this arrangement the contact with the customer and the processing of his request are carried out simultaneously: that is, the Representative does the paperwork needed to take care of a request

while she is still on the line. For more complex cases, however, this is not possible and the processing is left for "closed" time: a time when no further calls are coming in.

This arrangement tends to create a constant low-level panic. There is a kind of act which it is natural to carry to its logical conclusion: brushing one's teeth, washing a dish, or filling out a form are things one does not leave half done. But the company's system stifles this natural urge to completion. Instead, during "open" time, the phone keeps ringing and the work piles up. You look at the schedule and know that you have only one hour of "closed" time to complete the work, and twenty minutes of that hour is a break.

The situation produces desperation: How am I to get it done? How can I call back all those customers, finish all that mail, write all those complicated orders, within forty minutes? Occasionally, during my brief time at the job, I would accidentally press the wrong button on my phone and it would become "open" again. Once, when I was feeling particularly desperate about time, I did that twice in a row and both times the callers were ordering new telephone service —a process which takes between eight and ten minutes to complete.

My feeling that time was slipping away, that I would never be able to "complete my commitments" on time was intense and hateful. Of course it was worse for me than for the experienced women—but not much worse. Another situation in which the pressure of time is universally felt is in the minutes before lunch and before five o'clock. At those times, if your phone is open, you sit hoping that a complex call will not arrive. A "new line" order at five mintues to five is a source of both resentment and frustration.

Given the pressure, it becomes natural to welcome the boring and routine—the simple suspensions or disconnections of service— and dread the unusual or complex. The women deal with the pressure by quietly getting rid of as many calls as they can, transferring them to another department although the proper jurisdiction may be a borderline matter. This transferring, the lightening of the load, is the bureaucratic equivalent of the "soldiering" that Taylor and the early scientific managers were striving to defeat. It is a subtle kind of slowdown, never discussed, but quickly transmitted to the new Representative as legitimate. Unfortunately, it does not slow things down very much.

As Daniel Bell points out in his extraordinary essay, "Work and Its Discontents," the rhythm of the job controls the time spent off the job as well: the breaks, the lunches, the holidays; even the weekends are scarcely long enough to reestablish a more congenial or natural path. The work rhythm controls human relationships and attitudes as well. For instance: there was a Puerto Rican worker in the Schraffts downstairs whose job was to sell coffee-to-go to the customers: he spent his day doing nothing but filling paper cups with coffee, fitting on the lids, and writing out the checks. He was very surly and very slow and it looked to me as if the thoughts swirling in his head were those of an incipient murderer, not an incipient revolutionary. His slowness was very inconvenient to the thousands of workers in the building who had to get their coffee, take it upstairs, and drink it according to a precise timetable. We never had more than fifteen minutes to get there and back, and buying coffee generally took longer. The women resented him and called him "Speedy Gonzales," in tones of snobbery and hate. I know he hated us.

CONSUMING

The women of the phone company are middle class or lower middle class, come from a variety of ethnic backgrounds (Polish, Jewish, Italian, Irish, Black, Puerto Rican), mainly high-school graduates or with a limited college education. They live just about everywhere except in Manhattan: the Bronx, Brooklyn, Staten Island, or Queens. Their leisure time is filled, first of all, with the discussion of objects. Talk of shopping is endless, as is the pursuit of it in lunch hours, after work, and on days off. The women have a fixation on brand names, and describe every object that way: it is always a London Fog, a Buxton, a White Stag. This fixation does not preclude bargain-hunting: but the purpose of hunting a bargain is to get the brand name at a lower price. Packaging is also important: the women will describe not only the thing but also the box or wrapper it comes in. They are especially fascinated by wigs. Most women have several wigs and are in some cases unrecognizable from day to day, creating the effect of a continually changing work force. The essence of wiggery is escapism: the kaleidoscopic transformation of oneself while everything else remains the same. Anyone who has ever worn a wig knows the embarrassing truth: it *is* transforming.

Consumerism is one of the major reasons why these women work. Their salaries are low in relation to the costs of necessities in American life, ranging from $95.00 to $132.50 *before* taxes: barely enough, if one is self-supporting, to pay for essentials. In fact, however, many of the women are not self-supporting, but live with their families or with husbands who also work, sometimes at more than one job. Many of the women work overtime more than five hours a week (only for more than five extra hours do they get paid time and a half) and it seems from their visible spending that it is simply to pay for their clothes, which are expensive, their wigs, their color TV's, their dishes, silver, and so forth.

What the pressures of food, shelter, education, or medical costs contribute to their need to work I cannot tell, but it seems to me the women are largely trapped by their love of objects. What they think they need in order to survive and what they endure in order to attain it is astonishing. Why this is so is another matter. I think that the household appliances play a real role in the women's family lives: helping them to run their homes smoothly and in keeping with a (to them) necessary image of efficiency and elegance. As for the clothes and the wigs, I think they are a kind of tax, a tribute exacted by the social pressures of the work-place. For the preservation of their own egos against each other and against the system, they had to feel confident of their appearance on each and every day. Outside work they needed it too: to keep up, to keep their men, not to fall behind.

The atmosphere of passionate consuming was immeasurably heightened by Christmas, which also had the dismal effect of increasing the amount of stealing from the locker room. For a period of about three weeks nothing was safe: hats, boots, gloves. The women told me that the same happens every year: an overwhelming craving, a need for material goods that has to find an outlet even in thievery from one another.

The women define themselves by their consumerism far more than by their work, as if they were compensating for their exploitation as workers by a desperate attempt to express their individuality as consumers. Much of the consuming pressure is generated by the women themselves: not only in shopping but in constant raffles, contests, and so forth in which the prize is always a commodity— usually liquor. The women are asked to participate in these raffles at least two or three times a week.

But the atmosphere is also deliberately fostered by the company itself. The company gave every woman a Christmas present: a little wooden doll, about four inches tall, with the sick-humor look that was popular a few years ago and still appears on greeting cards. On the outside the doll says "Joy is . . . " and when you press down the springs a little stick pops up that says "Extensions in Color" (referring to the telephone extensions we were trying to sell). Under that label is another sticker, the original one, which says "Knowing I wuv you." The doll is typical of the presents the company distributes periodically: a plastic shopping bag inscribed with the motto "Colorful Extensions Lighten the Load"; a keychain with a plastic Princess telephone saying "It's Little, It's Lovely, It Lights"; plastic rain bonnets with the telephone company emblem, and so forth.

There were also free chocolates at Thanksgiving and, when the vending machine companies were on strike, free coffee for a while in the cafeteria. The women are disgusted by the company's gift-giving policies. Last year, I was told, the Christmas present was a little gold-plated basket filled with velour fruit and adorned with a flag containing a company motto of the "Extensions in Color" type. They think it is a cheap trick—better not done at all—and cite instances of other companies which give money bonuses at Christmas.

It is obvious that the gifts are all programmed, down to the last cherry-filled chocolate, in some manual of Personnel Administration that is the source of all wisdom and policy; it is clear from their frequency that a whole agency of the company is devoted to devising these gimmicks and passing them out. In fact, apart from a standard assortment of insurance and pension plans, the only company policy I could discover which offers genuine advantage to the employees and which is not an attempt at manipulation is a tuition support program in which the company pays $1000 out of $1400 of the costs of continuing education.

Going still further, the company, for example, sponsors a recruiting game among employees, a campaign entitled "People Make the Difference." Employees who recruit other employees are rewarded with points: 200 for a recommendation, an additional thousand if the candidate is hired. Employees are stimulated to participate by the circulation of an S&H-type catalogue, a kind of encyclopedia of the post-scarcity society. There you can see pictured a GE Portable Color Television with a walnut-grained polystyrene cabinet (46,000 points), a Silver-Plated Hors d'Oeuvres Dish By Wallace (3,900 points), and a staggering assortment of mass-produced candelabra, linens, china, fountain pens, watches, clothing, luggage, and—for the hardy—pup tents, power tools, air mattresses.

Similarly, though perhaps less crudely, the company has institutionalized its practice of rewarding employees for longevity. After every two years with the company, the women receive a small gold charm, the men a "tie-tac." These grow larger with the years and after a certain period jewels begin to be added; rubies, emeralds, sapphires, and eventually diamonds and bigger diamonds. The tie-tac evolves over the years into a tie-clasp. After twenty-five years you may have either a ceremonial luncheon or an inscribed watch: the watches are pre-fixed, pre-selected, and pictured in a catalogue.

The company has "scientifically structured" its rewards just as it has "scientifically structured" its work. But the real point is that the system gets the women as consumers in two ways. If consumption were less central to them, they would be less likely to be there in the first place. Then, the company attempts to ensnare them still further in the mesh by offering as incentives goods and images of goods which are only further way stations of the same endless quest.

.   .   .

1.3   Racism: The Way It Spozed to Be

James Herndon's observations at the 98 percent black George Washington Junior High provide some sobering insights into the effects of a racist society.

Source: The following is reproduced from Chapters 3 and 16 of *The Way It Spozed to Be* by JAMES HERNDON. Copyright © 1965, 1968 by James Herndon. Reprinted by permission of Simon & Schuster, Inc., and Sir Isaac Pitman and Sons Limited. Published in London by Pitman in 1970.

WELCOME BACK!

The first morning of the year at any school is bound to be pretty exciting and especially, it seems to me, at a junior high. You can stand around and watch the kids pour in, dressed as nicely as possible, all of them like yourself having forgotten momentarily what they're in for, yelling and laughing to each other, talking, asking questions—Whose room you got?—comparing summers and new shoes, all familiar and noisy and pleasant. Nothing is required of anyone so far.

I moved down through the kids to the end of the hall. There a huge new poster hung high on the wall above the stairs. WEL-

COME BACK! it said. Underneath these words a painted picture showed two kids, a boy and a girl, carrying lunch boxes and books, heading for school. An arrow sign painted in over on the side said

in case there was any doubt.

The only trouble with the poster was that these two life-sized painted kids didn't look like anybody I saw, or was likely to see, heading for old George Washington Junior High. The girl wore a blue sweater with buttons neatly painted down the front and a little round white collar on top; beneath that she wore a plaid skirt. The boy wore a white shirt, red tie and a green letterman's sweater with a big W on it. They both wore brown-and-white saddle shoes.

The girl was a blonde. Her hair hung in a nice long curl around her shoulders. The boy had brown hair, combed straight back. They were both white. Not just Caucasian. The butcher paper on which they'd been painted hadn't been white enough to suit the artist or artists, and they had carefully painted the arms, legs, and faces of their subjects with a thick, shiny, white paint. They were the whitest kids I ever saw, and there they were, headed for the first day of school at George Washington Junior High.

· · ·

THE UGLY STICK

As a kid of about fourteen I went to a high-school track meet with a friend of mine—I remember we went because Jesse Owens' brother was supposed to be there—and during the meet we were horsing around out on the grass when two Negro runners came

loping by. One of then slapped the other or something like that, and he said, Look out, man, I'll throw some white paint on you! Both of them laughed, running past, and we thought it was one of the most hilarious things we'd ever heard. It proved to us, also, that colored guys really didn't want to be white, just as our parents were always saying, and we didn't have to do any worrying about it.

It took quite a few visits to the art room before I asked Mr. Royal about that poster welcoming everyone back to school. What I wanted to know was whether the kids at GW had made it themselves. Yeah, they did, he told me. He didn't volunteer anything else. Well, I said, it was a pretty nice poster. He nodded. Yeah, it was, wasn't it? But what I wondered, I said, was why were the two kids painted white? There hadn't seemed any other way to state the question, which was what I really wanted to know.

Mr. Royal looked at me; he didn't say much at first. Just, they all try to paint what they see. He'd been teaching there a long time, although still a young guy, a small, dark, slightly popeyed man who looked a little like Baldwin. Warming up a little, he said, I mean, like all kids, they tend to paint like pictures they've seen. I don't mean they particularly copy—some do and some don't —but they're influenced, when they paint, by the paintings or posters they've seen, not by real life. They all want to paint pictures that look like real pictures, the kind they always see.

We left it at that; Malraux had said the same thing many times in many different ways, none better, and I was surprised I hadn't thought of it.

[Then there was the kids'] use of common American epithets applied to Negroes. . . . Not that they didn't know them or use them—the point was that they applied them to themselves. Every common derisive word, all the abusive nicknames, nouns and adjectives, all the big-lip, liver-lips, burr-heads, fuzzy-heads, kinky-haired, nappy-headed, big-leg, high-ass, apes, monkeys and too-blacks were dragged out daily and heaped on each other casually or furiously, continually and fanatically. The focal point of all this was the head and color of skin, and the point was ugliness. Nose, lips, hair, all counted, but nothing else could produce the real anger of a kid being called black, or the amount of derision in the cry of watermelon-head!

The Three C's alone among the kids I knew were immune from attack, being, as I say, whiter than anyone else and having fairly straight hair. The rest of the classes progressed through the traditional black, brown and beige, and the blacker a kid was, the kinkier his hair, the wider and flatter his nose, the larger and more everted his lips, the uglier he was and the more crap he had to take. Robert he got hit with the ugly stick, Mr. Hern-don, some kid would yell, and that was that for Robert. When it dark outside nobody can't even see Fletcher! Watch out somebody don't steal your head for a water-melon!

My own classes ran true to form. 7B rarely indulged in this sort of insult. 8B constantly, but surreptitiously, because they thought I'd disapprove and it would show up in their grades, 9D constantly and openly because their free gift was such that they did what they wanted to, and 7H whenever they could get their minds off their own problems long enough to remember to attack someone else. At first I was extremely surprised and shocked. I couldn't imagine how, with a whole white world ready and willing to call them all these names and always making the distinction between African-looking (ugly) Negroes and Caucasian-looking (handsome) Negroes, they could add to the situation themselves.

For a time I began to think that it was all a subtle way of finding out about me— if they said, for instance, that somebody was

big-lipped, fuzzy-headed, black and therefore ugly, was I going to somehow agree that he was uglier than the rest? Then I could be exposed as a racist, just another white mother, and could be dismissed. But as it kept on, day after day, all year long, even after they had in many cases ceased to pay any attention to me at all for long periods of time, I could see it wasn't for my benefit. It was for themselves.

It never stopped. It was a characteristic of The Tribe. They agreed that qualities which they all shared to some degree from birth were to add up to *bad*. It was crucial that they join the people most hostile to them all in order to establish relative degrees of ugliness, in order that some might be less ugly. I got over my surprise, got over trying to figure if it was meant for me, and it soon became only very boring, like slightly risqué jokes schoolkids are always telling you which you've heard a hundred times. You couldn't ever say anything about dark, black, brown, gray, shadow, night, head, nose, mouth, feet, legs, no raccoons, no dancing of jigs, no spades, no skin, without invoking hoots of laughter and a number of personal remarks. No one could read about any melons (your head look like one), no one could read about apes or monkeys (you look like one) . . . and if you somehow managed to avoid all that, the rhymes would get you. Say crack, back, track, Mac, hack, and you'd soon hear, Teacher, did you say black? or May, Mr. Herndon say you too black! Or there would be the bitter variation, Robert, go on leave me alone! You too white (quite, flight, bright, knight and right). Whooo-eee!

Times had changed, it seemed, since the track meet. White paint was now in favor. If I had imagined that the students of GW would present a united front on the question of their own (relative) blackness, it was a mistake. If I had supposed they were concerned with testing me, that was a mistake too. They weren't interested in degrees of liberal white attitudes like they spozed to be. No, just let the cry of *watermelon-head!* ring out through the classrooms of The Tribe and you knew that somebody was making a poster, painting himself white if only for a moment, even if only relatively . . . painting himself into the good, white side like any other artist.

1.4 Sexism: We Usually Don't Hire Married Girls

In recent years the Women's Liberation Movement has gained significant strength among American women; this reading suggests some of the reasons why.

Source: The following was written anonymously and first published in *Quicksilver Times* (Washington, D.C.).

I am 23 years old, I have a B.A. in Spanish literature, I am well traveled, I can speak Spanish and French, and I am a prostitute . . . I am a secretary, a wastebasket, a file-cabinet, a hostess, a messenger boy, and a slave. I am everything but a woman and a human being.

THE INTERVIEW

During my interview for this job my entire body was numbed. My interviewer kept looking at my legs and talking about how interesting he thought the job would be for me because I would be around men doing interesting work (not mentioning that my work would be boring).

He than looked at my legs again and looked up and gave me a very big paternalistic smile. "We usually don't hire married girls," he said. "We like to have young, pretty and available girls around the office. You know," he added, "it cheers things up a lot."

No wonder so many women fall apart in job interviews—our minds and our abilities are not questioned. It is our bodies and our smiles that are checked out to see if they will fit properly behind a mahogany desk.

I was hired and took the job because I was desperate. I was told I was awfully pretty and would most certainly be an asset to the office. For the first two weeks all the older women did was smile at me with their huge wide plastic smiles. They are not young, pretty or available anymore, so all they can offer is their smiles.

THE JOB

When I was hired I was told that two people constitute a team that would work on a specific project. "Teamwork" and "togetherness" were the key words used. It didn't take long to realize the real situation—racism, male supremacy, prejudice (you name it), all in one carpeted, IBM-filled office.

The "team" turned out to be a male, making around $15,000, and a female, making $6,000. Most girls have the same degrees as the men, or higher ones, but are still in the lower positions. The reason for this, I was told, was that most foreigners (whom the office deals with) don't "respect" women and would feel slighted if they had to deal with "one." (Wasn't that the reason given for not hiring blacks in offices and shops?—blacks would turn away customers!)

My job consists of serving coffee, answering the telephone, typing boring letters, and taking constant orders from my male "partner." I love "taking" letters for him. This gives him a chance to show me how really important he thinks he is. He leans back in his chair, takes a deep breath, and tries real hard to use the biggest words he knows. Dictating letters is a real ego-trip for these guys. It is incredible that the brainwashed females in this office will not admit that they have terrible jobs.

I have now been at this job for two months. My partner has never asked me anything about myself nor asked me to lunch. All he knows about me is that I type and take shorthand. Once in a while he will joke with me, but I am unable to respond. I would only be more of a whore if I did.

LUNCHTIME

We secretaries, nurses and administrative assistants have one hour to enjoy the day—lunchtime—and we usually are not even paid for that period. During the summer I attended a "Summer in the Parks" concert every Wednesday from 12 to 1 P.M. Sometimes the concert would run a little after the scheduled time. One could notice that exactly at 1 all the females would get up to go back to work. The males, who had no time clocks to punch, would stay to hear the rest of the concert.

There are few things we can do during that short time. It is too expensive and not easy to take a bus home to have lunch. A nice relaxing lunch would be nice—but at People's Drug or Linda's Cafeteria that is hardly possible. Have you ever gone to an expensive place at lunchtime? All men. How many working women can afford to spend more than $1 for lunch? How many restaurants are there that are cheap, relaxing, have good food and are not anxious to get rid of

you after you have swallowed the last bite?

I tried taking my lunch and a book and going to the park for lunch. A chance to be outside and read and enjoy the sunshine was very appealing. One day a man masturbated behind me in the bushes as I tried to read. The next day a guy asked me to come to his hotel. On different days I was told various parts of my body were "really fine." For four days I was followed, touched, and generally harassed. On the fifth day I ate lunch at my desk.

The only thing that is open for us to do during that time is shop—whether it's food, clothes or shoes, the stores are all waiting (and panting) with cash registers ready. These stores are the only places where we can be comfortably accommodated during that hour. The drawback is that we must buy.

In my office all the men go out to eat together and all the women go out to eat together. No one has ever broken that unwritten law. The three blacks in the mailroom eat inside. They are not permitted to go out to eat.

When I mention women's liberation to the men in my office they always reply that we women at least have to admit that things have gotten better—equal opportunity act, equal pay and all that. But when you are being oppressed so severely, $1,000 or even $2,000 extra a year doesn't mean very much. Because men are so hung up on money and titles on the door, they feel that we too should be appeased with a larger paycheck and a fancy title like "administrative assistant" instead of plain "secretary."

At the end of my working day I am tired and depressed. The entire day I have been used as an instrument. So I get on a pollution-emitting bus and go home. There I find the baby, the dishes in the sink, dinner to be made, and a husband who wants me to look like Twiggy. And people ask why women want to be liberated.

1.5   Irrationality: The Highway and the City

Lewis Mumford has spent a lifetime thinking and writing critically about
American society; here he turns his attention to the cult of the automobile.

Source: The following is excerpted from "The Highway and the City" by
LEWIS MUMFORD. From Lewis Mumford, *The Highway and the City*
(New York: Harcourt Brace & World, Inc., 1958). Copyright © 1958
by Lewis Mumford. Reprinted by permission of Harcourt Brace Jovanovich, Inc., and Secker & Warburg, Limited.

When the American people, through their
Congress, voted [in 1957] for a twenty-six-
billion-dollar highway program, the most
charitable thing to assume about this action
is that they hadn't the faintest notion of
what they were doing. Within the next fifteen
years they will doubtless find out; but by
that time it will be too late to correct all the
damage to our cities and our countryside, not
least to the efficient organization of industry
and transportation, that this ill-conceived and
preposterously unbalanced program will
have wrought.

Yet if someone had foretold these consequences before this vast sum of money was
pushed through Congress, under the spe-
cious, indeed flagrantly dishonest, guise of a
national defense measure, it is doubtful
whether our countrymen would have listened
long enough to understand; or would even
have been able to change their minds if they
did understand. For the current American
way of life is founded not just on motor
transportation but on the religion of the motorcar, and the sacrifices that people are prepared to make for this religion stand outside
the realm of rational criticism. Perhaps the
only thing that could bring Americans to
their senses would be a clear demonstration
of the fact that their highway program will,
eventually, wipe out the very area of freedom
that the private motorcar promised to retain
for them.

As long as motorcars were few in number, he who had one was a king: he could

go where he pleased and halt where he
pleased; and this machine itself appeared as
a compensatory device for enlarging an ego
which had been shrunken by our very success
in mechanization. That sense of freedom and
power remains a fact today only in low-
density areas, in the open country; the pop-
ularity of this method of escape has ruined
the promise it once held forth. In using the
car to flee from the metropolis the motorist
finds that he has merely transferred congestion to the highway and thereby doubled it.
When he reaches his destination, in a distant
suburb, he finds that the countryside he
sought has disappeared: beyond him, thanks
to the motorway, lies only another suburb,
just as dull as his own. To have a minimum
amount of communication and sociability in
this spread-out life, his wife becomes a taxi
driver by daily occupation, and the sum of
money it costs to keep this whole system running leaves him with shamefully overtaxed
schools, inadequate police, poorly staffed
hospitals, overcrowded recreation areas, ill-
supported libraries.

In short, the American has sacrificed his
life as a whole to the motorcar, like someone
who, demented with passion, wrecks his
home in order to lavish his income on a capricious mistress who promises delights he
can only occasionally enjoy.

For most Americans, progress means accepting what is new because it is new, and
discarding what is old because it is old. This
may be good for a rapid turnover in busi-

ness, but it is bad for continuity and stability in life. Progress, in an organic sense,
should be cumulative, and though a certain
amount of rubbish-clearing is always necessary, we lose part of the gain offered by a
new invention if we automatically discard all
the still valuable inventions that preceded it.

In transportation, unfortunately, the old-
fashioned linear notion of progess prevails.
Now that motorcars are becoming universal,
many people take for granted that pedestrian
movement will disappear and that the railroad system will in time be· abandoned; in
fact, many of the proponents of highway
building talk as if that day were already here,
or if not, they have every intention of making it dawn quickly. The result is that we
have actually crippled the motorcar, by placing on this single means of transportation the
burden for every kind of travel. Neither our
cars nor our highways can take such a load.
This overconcentration, moreover, is rapidly
destroying our cities, without leaving anything half as good in their place.

What's transportation for? This is a question that highway engineers apparently never
ask themselves: probably because they take
for granted the belief that transportation
exists for the purpose of providing suitable
outlets for the motorcar industry. To increase the number of cars, to enable motor-
ists to go longer distances, to more places,
at higher speeds, has become an end in itself. Does this overemployment of the motorcar not consume ever larger quantities of gas,
oil, concrete, rubber, and steel, and so provide the very groundwork for an expanding
economy? Certainly, but none of these make
up the essential purpose of transportation.
The purpose of transportation is to bring
people or goods to places where they are
needed, and to concentrate the greatest variety of goods and people within a limited
area, in order to widen the possibility of
choice without making it necessary to travel.
A good transportation system minimizes un-

necessary transportation; and in any event,
it offers a change of speed and mode to fit
a diversity of human purposes.

.   .   .

Perhaps our age will be known to the future historian as the age of the bulldozer and
the exterminator; and in many parts of the
country the building of a highway has about
the same result upon vegetation and human
structures as the passage of a tornado or the
blast of an atom bomb. Nowhere is this bull-
dozing habit of mind so disastrous as in the
approach to the city. Since the engineer regards his own work as more important than
the other human functions it serves, he does
not hesitate to lay waste to woods, streams,
parks, and human neighborhoods in order to
carry his roads straight to their supposed
destination.

The fatal mistake we have been making
is to sacrifice every other form of transportation to the private motorcar—and to offer,
as the only long-distance alternative, the airplane. But the fact is that each type of transportation has its special use; and a good
transportation policy must seek to improve
each type and make the most of it. This cannot be achieved by aiming at high speed or
continuous flow alone. If you wish casual opportunities for meeting your neighbors, and
for profiting by chance contacts with ac-
quaintances and colleagues, a stroll at two
miles an hour in a concentrated area, free
from needless vehicles, will alone meet your
need. But if you wish to rush a surgeon to a
patient a thousand miles away, the fastest
motorway is too slow. And again, if you wish
to be sure to keep a lecture engagement in
winter, railroad transportation offers surer
speed and better insurance against being
held up than the airplane. There is· no one
ideal mode or speed: human purpose should
govern the choice of the means of transportation. That is why we need a better transportation *system*, not just more highways.

The projectors of our national highway program plainly had little interest in transportation. In their fanatical zeal to expand our highways, the very allocation of funds indicates that they are ready to liquidate all other forms of land and water transportation. The result is a crudely over-simplified and inefficient method of mono-transportation: a regression from the complex many-sided transportation system we once boasted.

In order to overcome the fatal stagnation of traffic in and around our cities, our highway engineers have come up with a remedy that actually expands the evil it is meant to overcome. They create new expressways to serve cities that are already overcrowded within, thus tempting people who had been using public transportation to reach the urban centers to use these new private facilities. Almost before the first day's tolls on these expressways have been counted, the new roads themselves are overcrowded. So a clamor arises to create other similar arteries and to provide more parking garages in the center of our metropolises; and the generous provision of these facilities expands the cycle of congestion, without any promise of relief until that terminal point when all the business and industry that originally gave rise to the congestion move out of the city, to escape strangulation, leaving a waste of expressways and garages behind them. This is pyramid building with a vengeance: a tomb of concrete roads and ramps covering the dead corpse of a city.

But before our cities reach this terminal point, they will suffer, as they do now, from a continued erosion of their social facilities: an erosion that might have been avoided if engineers had understood [the] point that a motorway, properly planned, is another form of railroad for private use. Unfortunately, highway engineers, if one is to judge by their usual performance, lack both historic insight and social memory: accordingly, they have been repeating, with the audacity of confident ignorance, all the mistakes in urban planning committed by their predecessors who designed our railroads. The wide swaths of land devoted to cloverleaves, and even more complicated multi-level interchanges, to expressways, parking lots, and parking garages, in the very heart of the city, butcher up precious urban space in exactly the same way that freight yards and marshalling yards did when the railroads dumped their passengers and freight inside the city. These new arteries choke off the natural routes of circulation and limit the use of abutting properties, while at the points where they disgorge their traffic they create inevitable clots of congestion, which effectively cancel out such speed as they achieve in approaching these bottlenecks.

.   .   .

Just as highway engineers know too little about city planning to correct the mistakes made in introducing the early railroad systems into our cities, so, too, they have curiously forgotten our experience with the elevated railroad—and unfortunately most muncipal authorities have been equally forgetful. In the middle of the nineteenth century the elevated seemed the most facile and up-to-date method of introducing a new kind of rapid transportation system into the city; and in America, New York led the way in creating four such lines on Manhattan Island alone. The noise of the trains and the overshadowing of the structure lowered the value of the abutting properties even for commercial purposes; and the supporting columns constituted a dangerous obstacle to surface transportation. So unsatisfactory was elevated transportation even in cities like Berlin, where the structures were, in contrast to New York, Philadelphia, and Chicago, rather handsome works of engineering, that by popular consent subway building replaced elevated railroad building in all big cities, even though no one could pretend that riding in a tunnel was nearly as pleasant to the rider as was travel in the open air. The destruction of the old elevated railroads in New York was, ironically, hailed as a triumph of progress precisely at the moment that a new series of elevated highways was being built to repeat on a more colossal scale the same errors.

Like the railroad, again, the motorway has repeatedly taken possession of the most valuable recreation space the city possesses, not merely by thieving land once dedicated to park uses, but by cutting off easy access to the waterfront parks, and lowering their value for refreshment and repose by introducing the roar of traffic and the bad odor of exhausts, though both noise and carbon monoxide are inimical to health. Witness the shocking spoilage of the Charles River basin parks in Boston, the arterial blocking off of the Lake Front in Chicago (after the removal of the orignal usurpers, the railroads), the barbarous sacrifice of large areas of Fairmount Park in Philadelphia, the partial defacement of the San Francisco waterfront, even in Paris the ruin of the Left Bank of the Seine.

One may match all these social crimes with a hundred other examples of barefaced highway robbery in every other metropolitan area. . . . [And] the vast sums of money that go into such enterprises drain necessary public monies from other functions of the city, [making] it socially if not financially bankrupt.

.   .   .

While federal funds and subsidies pour without stint into highway improvements, the two most important modes of transportation for cities—the railroad for long distances and mass transportation, and the subway for shorter journeys—are permitted to languish and even to disappear. This is very much like what has happened to our postal system. While the time needed to deliver a letter across the continent has been reduced, the time needed for local delivery has been multiplied. What used to take two hours now sometimes takes two days. As a whole our postal system has been degraded to a level that would have been regarded as intolerable even thirty years ago. In both cases, an efficient system has been sacrificed to an overfavored new industry, motorcars, telephones, airplanes; whereas, if the integrity of the system itself had been respected, each of these new inventions could have added enormously to the efficiency of the existing network.

.   .   .

1.6   Imperialism: The American Impact on Vietnam

No single event has so torn at the fabric of American life in recent times as the Vietnam War. Yet the damage done in the United States cannot begin to match the havoc wreaked in Vietnam itself. Some of the most destructive effects of the American presence in Vietnam are described in the following reading by Ngo Vinh Long, a Vietnamese student in the United States.

Long's account is excerpted from a longer speech in which he began by tracing the history of the anticolonial struggle of the Vietnamese up to the point where the French—in spite of substantial aid from the United States—were defeated by the Viêt Minh at Dien Bien Phu. There followed the Geneva Conference on Indochina, at which the territory of Vietnam was temporarily partitioned and general elections were scheduled to be held in

1956. But the United States refused to sign the Geneva Agreements, and instead turned for an alternative "solution" to Ngô Dinh Diêm.

Source: The following is excerpted from "The Vietnam War and Its Implications for Southeast Asia" by NGO VINH LONG, a speech given on March 27, 1970, at the Conference of Southeast Asian Students at Indiana University and first published in *Thoì-Báo Ga*, No. 9 (April 1970). Reprinted by permission of the author.

. . .

Ngô Dinh Diêm, who had been sent back to [South] Vietnam by the United States to be the premier under Emperor Bao Dai, deposed the latter in a sham plebiscite of October 23, 1955, with the aid of American dollars and with the influence of the American organizing genius, especially as reflected in a large secret police force. Diêm got 98 percent of the votes in spite of the fact that the Americans had told him 60 percent would be O.K.,[1] and he became the first "President of the Republic of Vietnam," ruling over the zone to the south of the 17th parallel. Earlier in the year, on July 16, 1955, with the support of the United States, Ngô Dinh Diêm had already announced that his government would refuse to participate in the scheduled conferences to discuss the unification of Vietnam or in the free elections called for in 1956. The reason behind this refusal was the same as that which President Eisenhower later referred to in his book, *Mandate for Change*, in which he tells us that, as of 1954, he had met nobody informed on Vietnam who did not agree that "possibly 80 percent" of the Vietnamese people would have chosen Hô Chí Minh in a free election.[2] Columnist Joseph Alsop wrote in August, 1954, after a trip through

Vietnam, that, "In the area I visited, the Communists have scored a whole series of political, organizational, military—and one has to say it—moral triumphs. . . . What impressed me most, alas, was the moral fervor they had inspired among the non-Communist cadres and the strong support they had obtained from the peasantry.."[3]

. . .

There was not much that the United States and Ngô Dinh Diêm could do except to refuse to have the election and to cut off every kind of communication between the two zones as they did in 1955. The *Viêt Minh* was constantly referred to by American leaders as "The Communists," and as Communists they could not be allowed to take over the country even through fair and free elections. After sealing off the border between the two zones and after cutting off communications in order to contain the "Communists" in the North, Ngô Dinh Diêm began to try to root out the "Communists" in the South. A nationwide "Communist Denunciation Campaign" (*Phong Trào Tô Cóng*) was started in 1955, in which people were forced to denounce those who had been members of the Resistance against the French. By 1956, the term "Viet Cong," which literally means "Vietnamese Communists," was being used by Diêm to mean anybody at all who opposed his regime.

During this time, peasant unrest was evident in the countryside as a result of a so-called "land reform," by which the Diêm government sent landlords back to the coun-

[1]*Life* Magazine, May 13, 1957, writes that American advisers had told Diêm that a 60 percent "success" would have been quite sufficient, but Diêm "insisted on 98 percent." In fact, in Saigon, Diêm got 605,025 votes from a total of 450,000 registered voters.

[2]Dwight D. Eisenhower, *Mandate for Change* (Garden City, N.Y.: Doubleday & Co., 1963), p. 372.

[3]New York Herald Tribune, August 1, 1954.

tryside to reclaim their land, and to collect land rents, averaging about 50 percent of the yearly harvest, for as many years back as the landlords could lay claim to. As for those lands previously owned by French landlords, the peasants were made to *buy* them from the Diêm government in six annual installments. These installments amounted to between 40 and 50 percent of the crops. All of the land claimed by landlords had originally either been expropriated from the peasants or ceded by the court to the French during the French colonization period. During their fight with the French, however, the *Viêt Minh* took the land away from the landlord in the reconquered areas, and redistributed it to the local people. It was only then, for the first time since the French conquest, that these peasants had some land of their own, on which they had to pay at most 15 percent in tax. To carry out a Diêm-style "land reform" was, therefore, to invite unrest in the countryside. When there was unrest in the countryside, the Diêm government blamed it all on the "Communists." Thus, a "pacification program," which involved wholesale resettlement of the resident population, was forcefully carried out in order to separate the "Communists" from the "non-Communists." American and British "experts" were brought in. As for the Vietnamese majority living in the lowlands, by February, 1959, according to one American expert, "Relocation of families within communities had begun and, in contrast to land development and refugee activities, these relocations were often forced!"[4]

The earliest form of relocation was based on a division of the population into so-called "loyal" and "disloyal" groups. Those suspected of having contacts with the *Viêt Minh*, or known to have relatives in the North, were placed in one type of area known as *qui-khu*, while those considered loyal were

placed in other areas known as *qui-âp*.[5] The program, according to many observers, was devoid of any economic or social considerations.[6] People were taken from their plots of ground, on which their houses, their rice fields, their ancestral tombs, etc., were located, and moved to totally unsuitable areas where they were supposed to be "protected." It is not surprising that the relocated families were not wholly enthusiastic in their response. Moreover, since it often happened that many loyal families were grouped together with "suspect" families for no reason other than the fact that they might have relatives in the North, this settlement technique brought protests even from the ranks of senior government officials.

In April of 1959, more "sophisticated" relocation sites were planned, with barbed wire fences and spiked moats around them. These were euphemistically called "agrovilles." "The application of the plan," wrote William Nighswonger, a senior AID advisor for the Pacification Program, "involved enormous demands on the peasants: [such as] *corvee* labor well beyond the ten-day assessment and long commuting distances to their fields. . . ."[7] In many cases, when the houses and fields of those who had been relocated were considered too distant from the newly constructed "agrovilles" and their smaller satellites (the so-called "agro-hamlets"), they were simply burnt down to deny their use to the "Viet Cong." Resentment ran high among the population, but the "agrovilles" were simply too big for the Saigon government to effectively control the population. So in 1961 the program was discontinued, to be taken over by the "strategic hamlet" pro-

[4]W. A. Nighswonger, *Rural Pacification in Vietnam* (New York: Praeger, 1966), p. 46.

[5]M. E. Osborne, *Strategic Hamlets in South Vietnam* (Ithaca, N.Y.: Cornell University, 1965), p. 22.

[6]Nguyên Khac Nhân, "Policy of Key Rural Agrovilles," *Asian Culture*, III, Nos. 3-4 (July-Dec., 1961), 32.

[7]Nighswonger, *Rural Pacification in Vietnam*, p. 46.

gram. The only difference between the "agro-ville" and the "strategic hamlet" was that the latter was smaller, with about 100 families per hamlet. The families were divided into groups of five, which went by the name of *liên-gia.* One family was put in charge of the other four, and the group as a whole was responsible for individual behavior and for reporting on each other to the government. The basic strategy as stated by both the American and the Vietnamese authorities was that of "isolating the Viet Cong from his contacts in the hamlets and winning village support through relatively just and effective government programs. . . ."[8] The first thing the just government mentioned by the Americans did was to force the peasants to labor on the fences and the moats without any compensation, while their houses and their fields outside the hamlets were burnt down, again without any compensation.

From 1959 till early 1963, I was part of a land survey expedition which was involved in making detailed military maps (of scale 1/25,000) of the whole of South Vietnam, and thus I had occasion to be, at one time or another, in virtually every hamlet and village in the country. As a result of this experience, I was able to witness, at close hand, the living conditions of the Vietnamese rural population in both the "agrovilles" and the "strategic hamlets."

In 1961, after the American defoliation program had begun against jungle growth along highways, railways, and in places considered to be Viet Cong areas, the Diêm regime came up with still other uses for the chemicals: Seymour Hersh, in an article entitled "Our Chemical War" published in the *New York Review of Books* on April 25, 1968, quoted *Newsweek* Magazine in saying that by the end of November, 1961, the American special warfare troops had begun teaching Vietnamese fliers how to spray "Communist-held areas with a chemical that

turns the rice-fields yellow, killing *any* crop being grown in rebel strongholds." What *Newsweek* failed to say is that the Diêm regime in fact began putting this training into practice before the end of the same year. The so-called "rebel strongholds" referred to by *Newsweek* were more often than not, as I have witnessed personally, simply ordinary communities, usually located in sparsely populated areas, where the Diêm government found it expedient to kill crops as a means of driving the population more quickly into the "strategic hamlets," which had replaced abortive "agrovilles" earlier in the year. It proved easier to order fliers to spray crops from the air than to send in ground troops to force the people out by setting fire to their fields and houses. For one thing, it had been discovered that government soldiers, on coming face to face with the misery and the tearful entreaties of those who were to be relocated, could not always be trusted to carry out orders. In any case, the combined effect of regrouping the population in totally unsuitable areas and of killing their crops brought hunger and starvation to thousands upon thousands of people. Starvation ravaged almost all of the strategic hamlets that I visited in the whole central part of Vietnam. In many hamlets, up to a hundred persons died monthly. Many of them had not eaten anything decent in months, and as a result, their anal muscles had become so dilated that whenever they would eat or drink something, it passed through them in just a couple of minutes or so.

.   .   .

The misery inflicted upon the population, and the repression of the Buddhists and of students, among other factors, finally led to the downfall of the Diêm regime. The AID advisor, Nighswonger, wrote: "The fall of the Ngo regime was accompanied by a complete collapse of the pacification efforts in many areas, and vast regions that had been under government control quickly came un-

[8]*Ibid.,* p. 58.

der the influence of the Viet-Cong."[9] In September, 1963, Rufus Phillips reported to the President of the United States, "giving [him] the estimates of USOM Rural Affairs that the Delta was falling under Viet Cong control in areas where pacification was supposedly complete."[10] Thus, after the Saigon regime had declared that 8,544 hamlets, involving 85 percent of the rural population, had been constructed, the strategic hamlet program failed miserably.[11] By January, 1964, the pacification program against the rural population was being carried on under another name, that of "New Life Hamlets" (*Ấp Tân Sinh*). The U.S. military had by that time completely taken into their own hands the task of spraying crops in what they referred to as "Viet Cong territory."[12]

However, the situation in Vietnam became increasingly worse, and in 1965 the United States had to send in American troops in great numbers. Beginning in 1965, the American military initiated still another version of "pacification" by sending in the Marines to "secure villages" and to root out "Viet Cong infra-structures." Typical techniques, as described by Nighswonger, run as follows:

> *Before the operation to secure a village, leaflets are dropped asking the people to get into the open fields for safety, so they can freely hit the Viet Cong in tunnels around the houses and in hedgerows.*[13]

As I well know, the tunnels around the houses were most often bomb shelters of the villagers, and the people hiding in them were not likely to be V.C. cadres as the Americans claim.

What was the result of these American tactics? After more than two years of con-

tinuous effort by American combat troops, a *New York Times* report of August 7, 1967, in citing official United States data on the loyalties of the hamlets, stated that out of 12,537 hamlets, the number of hamlets under total Saigon government control was a mere 168. On the other hand, those totally controlled by the Viet Cong was 3,978. The rest of the hamlets were listed as "contested" or partially controlled by both sides. The hamlets under total Viet Cong control were declared "free strike zones," which meant that they could be bombed, shelled or gassed at any time. The total population in the 3,978 hamlets totally controlled by the Viet Cong was given as just under three million persons. As for the contested areas, the Americans had by then formulated another new program which they called "The Other War: The War to Win the Hearts and Minds of the People." The name was invented in an attempt to differentiate it from the military war, which involved tactics of search and destroy. There were different ways to carry out the Other War, all depending on how the population in the "contested areas" were regarded by the Americans. One way was to send out American troops with bulldozers and bombers to raze the villages to the ground, and then to transport the inhabitants to the so-called "camps for refugees fleeing from Communism" in and around the larger towns and cities where they could be "protected." Some American intellectuals have called this a process of "urbanization." The American military, however, have been more frank about it: A high U.S. field commander was reported from Saigon in 1966 to have said that, "If the people are to the guerrillas as the oceans are to the fish, then . . . we are going to dry up that ocean."[14]

Another way was the intensified use of chemicals, much in the same way that the Diêm regime had used them before. In his

[9]*Ibid.*, p. 62.

[10]*Ibid.*, p. 64.

[11]*Ibid.*, pp. 61–63.

[12]Seymour M. Hersh, "Our Chemical War," *The New York Review of Books*, April 25, 1968, pp. 1–2 of the article.

[13]Nighswonger, *Rural Pacification in Vietnam*, p. 115.

[14]U.P.I. dispatch, quoted in *New Statesman*, March 11, 1966.

article already cited, Seymour M. Hersh writes:

> By early 1967, Presidential advisers had a different reason for using herbicides, one that wasn't directly linked to cutting off Viet Cong food supplies. The rationale was presented to a group of scientists who met in February with Donald Hornig, President Johnson's chief scientific adviser, to protest the use of anticrop chemicals. According to one scientist who attended the session, Hornig explained that the anticrop program was aimed chiefly at moving the people.

Mr. Hersh further states that the Pentagon used 60 million dollars worth of defoliants and herbicides, or 12 million gallons, in Viet Nam in 1967, which was enough to cover "nearly half of the arable land in South Viet Nam." He also writes that, since Pentagon officials were arguing that the herbicides were more effective in killing crops than in stripping foliage:

> ... by the end of 1966 more than half of the C-123 missions were admittedly directed at crops, and it is probable that any effort at a trebling of capability in 1967 was aimed not at the jungles of South Vietnam but at its arable crop land.

In a study of American anticrop and defoliation methods, Yōichi Fukushima, head of the Agronomy Section of the Japan Science Council, claims that American chemical attacks by 1967 had ruined more than 3.8 million acres (or one-half) of the arable land in South Vietnam and were a direct cause of death for nearly 1,000 peasants and more than 13,000 head of livestock. The impact of the U.S. anticrop program upon those peasants who have escaped being taken to the camps for "refugees fleeing from Communism" is not known for sure. As for the "refugees," their situation was (and is) so bad that the editorial staffs of Saigon newspapers, in spite of the harsh government censorship,

felt compelled to run long articles on the misery endured by these people.

. . .

By 1969, Saigon government statistics proudly showed that they had been successful in getting 4 million refugees "urbanized." During 1968 and 1969, the U.S. Air Force sprayed about 10 million gallons of herbicides yearly over South Vietnam. Ten million gallons is enough to treat four million acres, and one-third of the land treated has been crop land. The denial of foodstuffs to the rural population in order to drive the people into the government-controlled camps and the effort to starve the so-called "enemy" through the use of herbicides have produced terrible side effects in the form of diseases and hideously deformed babies, as well as dangerous long-term effects on Vietnam's ecology. All these have been amply documented. But let me not go into these matters here.

My point so far has been this: From the very start, the enemy that the United States wanted to crush has been termed as "The Communists" or "Communism." But in the frantic search for this enemy, who has the United States bumped up against? It has been the Vietnamese peasants which the Americans have bumped into at every turn. At first, the United States thought that the reason for the peasants' disapproval of the Diêm regime and its policies was because of "Communist propaganda." So the United States tried to devise means to separate the peasants from the so-called "Communists." But afterwards, when the United States learned it was the peasants which furnished most of the enemy's manpower, food and information, the United States began to carry out a virtually unrestrained warfare *against the entire Vietnamese peasantry.* . . . The tonnage of bombs dropped on the countryside in South Vietnam alone, when added together, exceeds by far the total amount used against the Japanese and the Germans on all fronts during the Second World War.

Well, in spite of all this, the so-called "enemy" survived and became even more numerous. When the United States saw that it could not weaken the enemy in the South, it was decided that the enemy's real strength must lie in the North. So the United States went north after it. After two years of intense bombing of North Vietnam, enemy forces occupied most of the cities in South Vietnam in early 1968. What was most surprising to many Americans was that even though the city people knew of the planned attack beforehand, few of them, if not to say none, reported it to the Americans or to the Saigon authorities!

The Americans had known for a long time that no matter how hard they might try to starve out the enemy soldiers with their anti-crop programs, American rice from the cities was finding its way into enemy areas. But they merely supposed that it was somehow being exacted from the city people by "enemy" trickery and deceit. But now, with the occupation of the cities, there was no longer any doubt that much of the city population had given in to "Communist" propaganda too. Keeping this newly appraised fact in mind, the Americans, instead of trying to take back the towns and cities with ground troops (which they realized would be a near impossibility), made the decision that the cities of the South were to join the countryside as targets for American bombs and shells. On the average, about 50 percent of every major town was destroyed by the American bombardment. In many cases the area of destruction was as much as 90 per-

cent. Thus we see that, in spite of saying repeatedly that they are in Vietnam to help the Vietnamese people and to protect their freedom, the Americans have by their actions proved that their real enemy has all along been the Vietnamese people—except, of course, for the collaborators whom they call "The South Vietnamese."

What has been the reaction of this "enemy"? Here is one example. On the occasion of Moratorium Day, i.e., October 15, 1969, ninety-three Catholic priests and intellectuals now residing in France, together with "a great number of Catholics in Vietnam" (whose names were not published for fear of retaliation by the Saigon government) sent an open letter to American Christians, in which there appear the following words:

> *How can the U.S.A. be wicked enough to wish to exterminate all of our people to defend an idea, a theory, which time has adequately demonstrated to have only been a myth and never a reality? . . . Those whom the U.S.A. accuses in its ignorance as Communists, are in reality our relatives, our brothers, our sisters, our friends dispersed in villages and hamlets. They are only peasants, workers, peddlers, hairdressers, and herdsmen. They ask only one thing: to be masters of their own home and to gain a livelihood by the sweat of their brow.*

Meanwhile, the "silent majority" in Vietnam, who perhaps find it difficult to make public their views in so many words, have chosen to express themselves by continuing to fight.

·   ·   ·

1.7   *A Brief Guide to Bourgeois Ideology*

Having looked very briefly into some aspects of the problems that plague contemporary American society, we turn now to an examination of the way in which such problems are typically approached by Western social scientists. In the final reading of the chapter, Robin Blackburn describes and criticizes the bourgeois ideology that prevails not only in his own country (Great Britain) but in all of the advanced capitalist nations of the world. Blackburn's lucid essay on the inadequacy of orthodox social science provides a useful point of departure for the effort in the rest of this book to develop a more fruitful approach to the study of capitalist societies.

Source: The following is excerpted from "A Brief Guide to Bourgeois Ideology" by ROBIN BLACKBURN. From *Student Power*, edited by Alexander Cockburn and Robin Blackburn (Baltimore: Penguin Books, Inc., 1969). Copyright © 1969 by the *New Left Review*. Reprinted by permission of the *New Left Review*.

.   .   .

My intention here is to try to identify the prevailing ideology in the field of the social sciences as taught in British universities and colleges. This ideology, I hope to show, consistently defends the existing social arrangements of the capitalist world. It endeavors to suppress the idea that any preferable alternative does, or could exist. Critical concepts are either excluded (e.g., "exploitation," "contradiction") or emasculated (e.g., "alienation," "class"). It is systematically pessimistic about the possibilities of attacking repression and inequality: on this basis it constructs theories of the family, of bureaucracy, of social revolution, of "pluralist" democracy, all of which imply that existing social institutions cannot be transcended. Concepts are fashioned which encapsulate this determinism (e.g., "industrial society") and which imply that all attempts to challenge the *status quo* are fundamentally irrational (e.g., "charisma"). In short, bourgeois social science tries to mystify social consciousness by imbuing it with fatalism and by blunting any critical impulse. Those aspects of this social science which are not directly aimed at consecrating the social order are concerned with the techniques of running it. They are providing vocational training for future market researchers, personnel managers, investment planners, etc. And all this in the name of "value neutral" social science.

.   .   .

THE ASSUMPTIONS OF CAPITALIST ECONOMICS

Let us begin where the capitalist system itself begins, with the exploitation of man by man. We shall see that capitalist economics refuses to consider even the possibility that exploitation lies at the root of inequality or poverty—one can acquire a first class degree in economics in Britain without ever having studied the causes of these phenomena. It is now a well established (though not so well known) fact that economic inequality within most capitalist countries has remained roughly constant for many decades. In Britain, for example, the share of national income going to wages and the share going as profits has remained more or less the same since the statistics were first collected towards the end of the nineteenth century: the richest 2 percent of British adults own 75 percent of all private wealth, while the income of the top one percent of incomes is in sum about the same as that shared out among the poorest third of the population. Marx and the classical economists tried to explore the causes of such phenomena in sharp distinction to their neglect by most modern bourgeois economics. The shift in emphasis is stated as follows by a recent historian of the subject:

Marx inherited both the strengths and the weaknesses of his classical forerunners. In both theoretical systems, the central ana-

*lytical categories were moulded to illumin-
ate the causes and consequences of long
term economic change and the relationship
between economic growth and income distribution. The tools useful for these purposes were not, however, well adapted (nor
were they intended to be) to a systematic
inspection of other matters: e.g., the process
through which market prices are formed
and the implications of short term economic
fluctuations.*[1]

It is these latter questions which have for
so long preoccupied the main bourgeois
economists and all too often the conceptual
tools developed in these inquiries are then
used to tackle the larger issues with predictable lack of success. Thus in the age of attempted "incomes policies" economic theory
is quite incapable of accounting for the share
of national income represented by profits. In
the most recent edition of a now standard
textbook we read:

*We conclude by raising the interesting ques-
tion of the share of profits in the national
income. We have no satisfactory theory of
the share of national income going as profits
and we can do little to explain past behaviour of this share, nor do we have a
body of predictions about the effect on this
share of occurrences like the rise of unions,
wage freezes, profits taxes, price controls,
etc.*[2]

In his conclusion on theories of income distribution as a whole Professor Lipsey con-
fesses: "We must, at the moment, admit defeat; we must admit that we cannot at all
deal with this important class of problems."
His solution to the impasse is a little lame,
faced with all this: "There is a great deal of
basic research that needs to be done by students of this subject."

A re-examination of the tradition of Marx
and the classical economists would have
given these researchers the analytical cate-

gories they so evidently need. In fact the
most promising work in this field is being
done on precisely this basis but without acknowledgement from the mainstream of
bourgeois economics.[3] For Marx, the tendency of capitalism to generate wealth at one
pole and poverty at the other, whether on the
national or international scale, was a consequence of the exploitive social relations on
which it was based. For bourgeois social science, the very concept of "exploitation" is
anathema since it questions the assumed underlying harmony of interests within a capitalist society. But of course the rejection of
this concept is carried out in the name of the
advance of science not the defense of the
status quo. For example, the whole question
is disposed of in the following fashion by
Samuelson in the other main economics textbook: "Marx particularly stressed the labor
theory of value that labor produces all value
and if not exploited would get it all. . . .
Careful critics of all political complexions
generally think this is a sterile analysis. . . ."[4]
The tone of this remark is characteristic with
its reference to the academic consensus
which the student is invited to join. A more
recent work on this subject makes greater
concessions to the "sterile analysis" but preserves the essential taboo on the key concept:
the author writes that we must "retain the
germ of truth in Marx's observation of the
wage bargain as one of class bargaining or
conflict without the loaded formulation of the
concept 'exploitation'."[5] By excluding *a
priori* such ways of analysing economic relationships, modern bourgeois economics ensures that discussion will never be able to
question the capitalist property system. Thus
Lipsey writes:

*Various reasons for nationalizing industries
have been put forward and we can only*

[1]W. J. Barber, *A History of Economic Thought,*
Penguin, UK, 1967, p. 161.
[2]R. G. Lipsey, *An Introduction to Positive Economics,* UK, 1967, p. 481.

[3]The work of Piero Straffa and his school.
[4]P. A. Samuelson, *Economics,* Fifth Edition,
USA, 1961, pp. 855–56.
[5]Murray Wolfson, *A Reappraisal of Marxian
Economics,* USA, 1966, p. 117.

give very brief mention to these. I. to con-
fiscate for the general public's welfare instead of the capitalist's. *In so far as nationalized industries are profitable ones and in
so far as they are not any less efficient
under nationalization than in private hands
this is a rational object. Quantitively however it is insignificant besides such redistributive devices as the progressive income
tax.*[6]

Lipsey is to be congratulated for sparing a
few lines to such thoughts in his eight hundred page tome—most bourgeois economists
simply ignore the idea altogether. However,
his argument is patently ideological. Firstly,
his confidence in the redistributive effects of
taxation is in striking contrast to his statements made a few pages earlier, and quoted
above, that he cannot with current theory say
anything useful about income distribution or
the effects on it of taxation. More important
is the implicit assumption that capitalists'
profits are being confiscated but they are being compensated for the take-over of their
property. Nationalization without compensation would have an immediate, massive and
undeniable effect on distribution. Even when
the bourgeois economist steels himself to
consider the prospect of socialism being installed in an advanced capitalist country, he
usually finds it impossible to imagine the
complete elimination of property rights. In
Professor J. E. Meade's *Equality, Efficiency
and the Ownership of Property*, he constructs
a model where we find that the fledgling
"Socialist State" is burdened from the outset
with a huge national debt. It seems that the
mind of the bourgeois social scientist is quite
impervious to any idea that "property is
theft" or that the expropriators should be
expropriated. Instead the only "rational" objectives for him are ones defined by the
rationality of the system itself. A good example of this is provided by Samuelson's discussion of the problems raised by redundancy
in a capitalist economy.

*Every individual naturally tends to look
only at the immediate economic effects
upon himself of an economic event. A
worker thrown out of employment in the
buggy industry cannot be expected to reflect that new jobs may have been created
in the automobile industry! but we must
be prepared to do so.*[7]

The "we" here is all aspirant or practising
economists. Nobody, it seems will be encouraged to reflect that workers should not
individually bear the social costs of technological advance, that their standard of living
should be maintained until alternative employment is made available to them where
they live, etc. For the bourgeois economist
the necessities of the social system are unquestionable technological requirements. The
passage quoted is dedicated to informing the
student that: "the economist is interested in
the workings of the economy *as a whole*
rather than in the viewpoint of any one
group."[8]

*. . . an elementary course in economics does
not pretend to teach one how to run a business or a bank, how to spend more wisely,
or how to get rich quick from the stock
market. But it is to be hoped that general
economics will provide a useful background
for many such activities.*[9]

The one activity to which this brand of economics certainly does not provide a useful
background is that of critical reflection on
the economy "as a whole" and the social contradictions on which it is based.

Classical economics could analyse class relationships because it was a constitutive part
of "political economy," the study of social
relations in all their aspects. In contemporary
social science the economic, political and sociological dimensions of society are split up

[6]Lipsey, *An Introduction to Positive Economics*, p. 532.

[7]Samuelson, *Economics*, p. 10. The complex
nature of capitalist rationality is admirably discussed in Maurice Godelier's *Rationalité et Irra-
tionalité en Economie*, Paris, 1967.
[8]Samuelson, *Ibid.*, p. 10.
[9]*Ibid.*, p. 10.

and parcelled out among the different academic departments devoted to them. This process itself helps to discourage consideration of the nature of the economic system on other than its own terms. The whole design is lost in the absorption with details.

. . .

IMPERIALISM AND SOCIAL SCIENCE

The ideological character of a sociology which assumes on principle a harmonious economic system is particularly evident when the relations between advanced and backward countries are being examined. It is now widely acknowledged that the gap between them is growing and it should be equally evident that the relations between them involve the domination and exploitation of poor capitalist nations by rich ones. . . . Yet we are informed by Professor Aron that "In the age of the industrial society there is no contradiction between the interests of the underdeveloped countries and those of advanced countries."[10] Talcott Parsons is also determined to ignore what he calls "irrational accusations of imperialism." He writes,

> My first policy recommendation, therefore, is that every effort be made to promulgate carefully considered statements of value commitments which may provide a basis for consensus among both have and have-not nations. This would require that such statements be disassociated from the specific ideological position of either of the polarized camps.[11]

Parsons' notorious obsession with values is patently ideological in such a context—especially since he goes on to assert that in creating this consensus atmosphere "the proper application of social science should prove useful." Nowhere in this essay on the "world social order" does Parsons discuss the

[10]Raymond Aron, *The Industrial Society*, UK, 1917, p. 24.
[11]Talcott Parsons, *Sociological Theory and Modern Society*, UK, 1968, p. 475.

role of the capitalist world market or the US Marine Corps as forces acting to maintain the *status quo*. Further, note the sheer fatuousness of Parsons' belief that anything would be changed by the promulgation of carefully considered statements, etc. Even Parsons' undoubted intellectual distinction is no protection against the feebleness imposed on its devotees by bourgeois ideology.

. . .

[A] striking instance of the excessive value emphasis encouraged by Parsonian theory is *The Politics of Developing Areas* by G. Almond and J. S. Coleman. This book, published in 1960, so persistently ignored Mao's dictum that "power grows out of the barrel of a gun" that the index contains no reference for "army," "armed forces," etc, and its discussions have been completely bypassed by the subsequent wave of military coups throughout the underdeveloped zone. The assumption usually made in such writings is that the "West" provides the model for the development of the underdeveloped world. The fact that the Western capitalist powers were plundering the rest of the world at the time of their industrialization, whereas the underdeveloped world is in the reverse position, is rarely considered. The profits of the slave trade, the sales of opium to China, the plantations of the Americas, etc. (not to speak of the expropriation of the common lands of the European peasantry and the grazing grounds of the American Indian) all contributed to the early capital accumulation of the Western Imperialist powers quite as much as their devotion to a "universalistic" value system. Curiously enough, bourgeois economists do not recommend underdeveloped countries to follow the Western model in this respect. In all the mountains of literature devoted to the strategy of economic development, writers who urge the poor countries to nationalize the investments of the rich are very rare. Martin Bronfenbrenner's excellent article on "The Appeal of Confiscation in Economic Development," first published in 1955, has evoked almost no response and most textbooks on development strategy ignore the question altogether.

Not surprisingly the best allies of foreign capital in the underdeveloped regions are the remaining traditional elites and the feeble local capitalist class. At one time it was hoped by Western strategists that the "middle sectors" could carry through the process of economic development in their respective countries. This ignored the fact that the context provided by the imperialist world market invariably poses an insuperable obstacle to the underdeveloped bourgeoisie of the poor capitalist countries. As a consequence they have usually sought enrichment through battening on a corrupt government or sponsoring a military coup rather than producing the hoped-for economic advance.[12] All this creates most unpleasant dilemmas for the bourgeois social scientist and accounts for the growing acceptance of development strategies based on an analysis such as the following:

> *I am trying to show how a society can begin to move forward as it is, in spite of what it is. Such an enterprise will involve a systematic search along two closely related lines: first, how acknowledged, well entrenched obstacles to change can be neutralized, outflanked and left to be dealt with decisively at some later stage; secondly and perhaps more fundamentally, how many among the conditions and attitudes that are widely considered as inimical to change have a hidden positive dimension and can therefore unexpectedly come to serve and nurture progress.*[13]

This fantasy enables the bourgeois social scientist to ignore the fact that the main obstacles to development are either directly provided by imperialist domination or buttressed by it.

[12]The writings of Frantz Fanon, Régis Debray, André Gunder Frank and José Nun, explore different aspects of this process.
[13]Albert O. Hirschman, *Journeys Towards Progress*, USA, 1963, pp. 6–7.

The attraction of the Hirschman approach is increased as earlier illusions about "underdevelopment" are eroded. The economists, in particular, have often acted as if economic development can be induced as soon as a few well-meaning tax reforms are enforced. The fiasco of Nicolas Kaldor's policies in India, Ceylon, Ghana, Guyana, Mexico and Turkey illustrate this well.

> *Since I invariably urged the adoption of reforms which put more of the burden of taxation on the privileged minority of the well-to-do, and not only on the broad masses of the population, it earned me (and the governments I advised) a lot of unpopularity, without, I fear, always succeeding in making the property-owning classes contribute substantial amounts to the public purse. The main reason for this . . . undoubtedly lay in the fact that the power, behind the scenes, of the wealthy property-owning classes and business interests proved to be very much greater than . . . suspected.*[14]

On the whole, bourgeois economists only achieve such revelations in connexion with remote places whose local "privileged minority" appear to impede imperialist penetration. Even then they usually persist in believing that their technical nostrums can be made to work:

> *In most underdeveloped countries, where extreme poverty coexists with great inequality in wealth and consumption, progressive taxation is, in the end, the only alternative to complete expropriation through violent revolution. . . . The progressive leaders of underdeveloped countries may seem ineffective if judged by immediate results; but they are the only alternatives to Lenin and Mao Tse Tung.*[15]

The political exclusion of expropriation could scarcely be more unabashed.

· · ·

[14]Nicolas Kaldor, *Essays on Economic Policy,* UK, 1964, Vol. 1, pp. xvii–xx.
[15]*Ibid.*

"INDUSTRIAL" SOCIETY AND TECHNOLOGICAL DETERMINISM

The category "industrial society" has now become the accepted definitional concept for modern capitalism. Raymond Aron, who has done much to promote it, makes clear its intention: it is, he writes, "a way of avoiding at the outset the opposition between socialism and capitalism and of considering them as two species of the same genus: industrial society."[16] This way of thinking in sociology owes much to Weber. It contains a large dose of technological determinism since it suggests that the industrial nature of technology dominates social organization as a whole. For pre-industrial societies' values may act as an independent variable capable of re-shaping society itself in important ways. But once a society has industrialized, the range of significant institutional alternatives available to it is very narrow. Thus the unavoidable concomitant of modern industry will be bureaucratic organization, the "nuclear" form of the family (i.e., the family system of the modern American middle class), etc. By deducing social organization from industrial technology bourgeois sociology can portray capitalist society as void of contradictions. In the "industrial society" there is no possibility of a clash between the forces of production and the institutions of the property system since they form a harmonious, non-antagonistic unity. Capitalist social relations cannot be rejected without abandoning modern technology. Nor with such a view can capitalist relations of production (private property, the sale of labour power as a commodity, etc.) act as a fetter on the development of the forces of production (technology, natural resources, etc.).

According to Talcott Parsons, Weber regarded "capitalism," including bureaucratic organization, both private and governmental, as essentially the "fate" of Western society:

> . . . clearly to him capitalism in some sense had to be accepted; but equally on a variety of grounds scientific and ethical, the prevailing interpretations were on the one hand inadequate to the phenomena itself, on the other out of accord with his feelings of rightness and appropriateness . . . with respect to my own country I have long felt that the designation of its social system as "capitalistic," even in Weber's highly sophisticated sense, was grossly inadequate.[17]

Parsons eschews the term capitalist, no doubt because its critical overtones are out of accord with his "feelings of rightness and appropriateness" as well as Weber's. But at the same time he manages to smuggle back the distinctive features of capitalist society in his theory of "evolutionary universals," that is the universal aspects of all societies as they evolve into modern industrial states. These evolutionary universals, according to Parsons, include "money and markets" and "bureaucracy." The sociological theory of bureaucracy deriving from Weber has marked fatalistic overtones, as Gouldner has noted.[18] It will be convenient to examine this theory in some detail as it is most often cited as one of the forms of social organization made inescapable by modern industrial society. Indeed the more alert defenders of bureaucratic domination, wherever it is found, draw on these ideas.

BUREAUCRACY AND BOURGEOIS FATALISM

For Weber bureaucratic organization represented a superior and necessary form of rationality. He recognized that the historical

---

[16]Raymond Aron, *Eighteen Lectures on Industrial Society*, UK, 1967, p. 42. The term "industrial society" can be used descriptively, without the intention here acknowledged by Aron, in which case its function need not be ideological.

[17]Parsons, *Sociological Theory and Modern Society*, pp. 99–101.

[18]Alvin Gouldner, "The Metaphysical Pathos of Bureaucracy," in *Complex Organizations*, edited by A. Etzione, USA, 1964.

origin of modern bureaucracy was to be found in the internal organization of the early capitalist enterprise, and he further claimed that this type of organization was the general destiny of any society which developed an industrial economy. Indeed to some extent it was a prerequisite for industrial development. The bureaucratic mode of organization was characterized as follows:

(1) All official actions are bound by rules with the official subject to strict and systematic control from above.
(2) Each functionary has a limited and defined sphere of competence.
(3) The organization of offices follows a principle of hierarchy with each lower one subordinate to each higher one.
(4) Candidates are selected only from the basis of technical qualification: "they are appointed, not elected."
(5) Officials are salaried and have no right of ownership over their job: "The salary scale is graded according to rank in the hierarchy: but in addition to this criterion . . . the requirements of incumbents' social status may be taken into account."
(6) The office is the sole, or at least primary, occupation of the incumbent and it constitutes a career: "Promotion is dependent on the judgement of superiors."[19]

For Weber the style of work originating in the bureaucratic enterprise would inevitably generalize itself through society in all other institutions (army, church, political parties, state machine, etc.). In this ideal type Weber mixes together some organizational rules which may, in determinate historical conditions, encourage efficient administration, together with others which can only foster the negative effects for which bureaucracies are so notorious (impersonality, manipulation of the administered, evasion of responsibility, empire-building, stifling working conditions, etc.). The whole is then presented as a pack-

[19]Max Weber, *Economic and Social Organization,* edited by Talcott Parsons, USA, 1947, pp. 333–39.

age which it is fruitless to reject since its imperatives are unavoidable. . . .

Weber was aware that the type of bureaucratic organization he was analysing was intimately linked to the existence of a market economy. Thus he argued that the absence of a developed market produced a structural weakness in the traditional type of Chinese Bureaucracy—the taxation crisis. Simply to finance the on-going operation of the bureaucracy a money economy was necessary: without adequate funds a bureaucracy will begin to allow officials to make money on the side by exploiting their official position. In some ways the bureaucracy outlined by Weber is an institutionalization of the imperatives of market society with its consequent alienations. The capitalist market reduces quality to quantity, makes human labour power a commodity and ensures that the exchange value of a commodity dominates its individual use value. In the same way a bureaucracy reduces both its own workers and the public it administers to a set of abstract characteristics (age, formal qualifications, sex, race, etc.). Just as the market organizes human behavior according to unquestionable economic laws, so the bureaucracy imposes man-made rules as if they had some impersonal necessity. For Weber all this was part of the formal, abstract efficiency which bureaucracy provides. Such efficiency can only serve the powers that be; its formal rationality is dependent on the rationality of the capitalist system, of which it is a part.

·   ·   ·

CHARISMA—A PSEUDO-CONCEPT

If Weber expels innovation from his concept of bureaucracy where does he find room for it in his sociology? In practice it seems that Weber identified social innovation and creativity with the irrational: they are subsumed under the category "charisma." This category has become very popular in later sociological writing and tends to be used by leader writers, pundits and social commentators of all types who wish to discredit popular movements of any sort. Historically "charisma" was the "gift of grace" which early Christian saints were supposed to receive from God. Weber used it to describe the source of the attraction wielded by great popular leaders. As such it seems to be a survival in modern bourgeois social science of the medieval doctrine of essences. This doctrine held, for example, that fire as a physical phenomenon was to be explained by the fact that every combustible object contained a substance, phlogiston, which was released when it caught fire. In similar fashion the ascendancy of every popular leader who rebels against things as they are is "explained" in terms of his possession of charismatic qualities. In addition to absolving the social scientist from any real examination of the social forces and circumstances which produce popular movements it also enables him to lump together quite disparate types of leaders. For Weber, Napoleon and St. Augustine were both charismatic figures: for the modern bourgeois sociologist a typical amalgam might be Hitler and Mao Tse Tung. Here is an example of how the concept is used:

> Cuba did not prove that a Latin American nation could deliberately choose Communism; it proved, if proof were still needed, that a charismatic leader can make a nation choose almost anything even in the act of denying he is choosing it for them. . . . Castro's charisma . . . cut across all classes; he established a mass relationship primarily with his person, not with his ideas.[20]

The term charisma is invariably used in this way, namely to imply that support for a popular leader is not to be explained by reference to his ideas, programme or actions,

but rather, exclusively, by some quality of personal magnetism.

.   .   .

THE SOCIOLOGY OF REVOLUTION AS PHILOSOPHY OF COUNTER-REVOLUTION

We have seen that the drift of much bourgeois social theory is to undermine the idea that men can ever transform society—its function is to induce a morbid paralysis of social will. In the twentieth century revolutionary disturbances have affected most parts of the world and in areas inhabited by one third of humanity the prevailing order has been completely overturned. Such events have only filtered relatively slowly into the consciousness of mainstream bourgeois sociology. . . .

The technique adopted by bourgeois social science to deal with the consequences of successful revolution can be reduced to one basic theme. Basically revolutions change very little. This is often a variation of the bureaucracy argument discussed above. In his accustomed professional manner Raymond Aron has announced:

> We have all become intensely aware of power as the major phenomenon in all societies, and as a problem which no reforms in the property system or in the functioning of the economy can solve.[21]

Crane Brinton, in "Anatomy of Revolutions," talks of the "universality of Thermidorean reaction" as a law of revolution. For Talcott Parsons the only aspect of revolutions on which he dwells is the necessity after the "ascendancy of the charismatic revolutionary movement" for a process of "concession" to the development of "adaptive structures." Of course, this approach is not wholly invalid. As Georg Lukacs has observed, all false consciousness has its own truth: but this truth is partial and inserted

[20]Theodor Draper, *Castroism*, USA, 1965, p. 127.

[21]Raymond Aron, *German Sociology*, p. 131.

into a false overall perspective. In this instance, for example, the one-sided approach of bourgeois sociology renders it blind to the process of radicalization which often occurs in revolution (e.g., the Cultural Revolution, Soviet collectivization, etc.).[22] Carrying out a revolution is a momentous experience of effective social action: if anything it is likely, at one point, to encourage voluntarism rather than a policy of concessions. The post-revolutionary history of Russia, China and Cuba certainly do not substantiate any unilateral adaptive concession theory. In short, bourgeois sociology only begins to understand modern revolutions in so far as they fail—

and this is undoubtedly because they want them to fail. The bourgeois social scientists' attempt to deny the efficacy of social revolution by no means inhibits them from proclaiming the existence or necessity of all other sorts of "revolution." Indeed revolutions are discovered everywhere: the "industrial revolution," the "revolution of rising expectations," the "technological revolution," etc. This oblique homage to potency of the notion is also to be found in the writings of those who seek to avert them. Nicolas Kaldor, writing on "underdeveloped" countries, puts the matter thus: "The problem which has to be solved, and to which no one has yet found a satisfactory answer, is how to bring about that change in the balance of power which is needed to avert revolutions without *having* a revolution."[23]

[22]A variant of this approach acknowledges this radicalization but considers it only as an irrational "totalitarian" phenomenon. . . . Many such studies of post-revolutionary societies argue that revolutions do not so much change them as intensify their basic characteristics: see for example, Karl Wittfogel, *Oriental Despotism.*

[23]Kaldor, *Essays on Economic Policy*, Vol. I, p. 265.

SELECTIVE BIBLIOGRAPHY

Further reading is recommended in Blackburn, "A Brief Guide to Bourgeois Ideology," as cited in the source line for Section 1.7. In addition, the following books are suggested as representative of the broad range of descriptive literature on the problems of contemporary American society.

Inequality

[1] Harrington, Michael, *The Other America.* Baltimore: Penguin, 1963.*

[2] Lundberg, Ferdinand, *The Rich and the Super-Rich.* New York: Bantam, 1968.*

Alienation

[3] Chinoy, Eli, *Automobile Workers and the American Dream.* Boston: Beacon, 1965.*

[4] Slater, Philip, *The Pursuit of Loneliness.* Boston: Beacon, 1970.*

Racism

[5] Brown, Claude, *Manchild in the Promised Land.* New York: Macmillan, 1965.*

[6] Conot, Robert, *Rivers of Blood, Years of Darkness.* New York: Bantam, 1967.*

Sexism

[7] Lessing, Doris, *The Golden Notebook.* New York: Bantam/Ballantine, 1968.*

[8] Woolf, Virginia, *A Room of One's Own.* New York: Harbinger/Harbrace, 1957.*

Irrationality

[9] Goodman, Paul "Like a Conquered Province," in his *People or Personnel: Like a Conquered Province.* New York: Random House, 1963.*

[10] Packard, Vance, *The Waste-Makers.* New York: Pocket Book/Simon & Schuster, 1963.*

PART

THE
STRUCTURE
OF THE
CAPITALIST SYSTEM

The Study of Historical Change:
The Emergence
of Capitalism

diffused throughout every part of

IN THIS BOOK WE SHALL ARGUE THAT MANY of the pervasive social problems that we see around us—inequality, alienation, racism, sexism, militarism, destruction of the environment, consumerism, imperialism, etc.— are significantly and systematically related to the economic institutions that make up a capitalist society. To understand how to deal with these problems and to achieve a better society, we must understand the internal structure and the dynamics of modern capitalism. Therefore, in this and the two succeeding chapters we concentrate on analyzing the social system that we call capitalism, devoting relatively little direct attention to the manifest, contemporary social problems that were described in Chapter 1.

In this chapter we examine in a general way the importance of economic forces and the relationship between economic and noneconomic forces in the structure of a social system and in the dynamics of social change. A central theme of the chapter is that the analysis of the production relations of a society is the key which unlocks the nature of that social system.

Why start from production relations rather than somewhere else? We argue that the general character of a social system, as well as the historical evolution of a society, is governed primarily by the social relations which people enter into in connection with production. Consider questions such as the following: How did capitalism come into being? What are its long-run tendencies? How might it ultimately be transformed? Or, on an even more general plane: What are the historical forces which lead to the replacement of one social order by another fundamentally different one? At what point do growing economic, political, or social changes within the framework of one social order fundamentally alter the characteristics of that order? To analyze these questions, we shall in this chapter introduce the conceptual approach developed by Marx known as historical materialism,[1] and apply it to the analysis of the

dynamics of capitalist development.

We begin with several important concepts: forces of production, social surplus, social class, social relations of production, and the mode of production. The *forces of production* consist of the tools, buildings and equipment used to carry out production, as well as the existing state of science and technology, know-how, organizational techniques, etc. The simplest definition of *social surplus* is as follows: the social surplus is that part of the total material product of a society that is left over after the basic requirements needed to maintain the people at a subsistence level of living have been met.[2]

With historical progress in the development of the forces of production, the potential social surplus that can be produced gradually increases. Societies then increasingly tend to divide into two groups: those who *produce* the surplus, on the one hand, and those who *appropriate* the surplus, on the other. We shall define a *social class* in terms of its common relationship to the production or appropriation of surplus. The *social relations of production* are precisely the relationships between those who produce the social surplus and those who control or appropriate it.[3] Finally, we define the *mode of production* as consisting of both the existing forces of production and the existing social relations of production.

Examples from slave, feudal, and capitalist societies may help to clarify the concept of the social relations of production. Each of these societies is characterized by fundamentally different social relations of produc-

[1]We use the term materialism to suggest the importance of social and physical factors, but not to imply the reduction of all phenomena to economic factors.

[2]For a more extensive discussion of the surplus, see Weisskopf, Section 9.1, p. 364.

[3]Here we have reduced the concept of the mode of production to its barest essentials; as Baran and Hobsbawm point out in Section 2.2, p. 53, it is a much more complex concept when actually applied.

tion. In slave societies, the producer (the slave) is attached to his master by force and does not own or control the instruments or means of production (land, machinery, tools, factories, etc.). The master owns the slave as a piece of property, but he is also responsible for providing the slave with basic subsistence; the master is free to sell the slave if he so desires. By contrast, in feudal societies, the producer (the serf) owns the means of production but is forced by his lord to provide annually certain economic services. In return, the lord provides basic military protection and security. The serf is tied to the land and ordinarily cannot be sold by the lord.

In a capitalist society the social relations of production are characterized by separation of the producers (laborers) from the means of production. In this respect capitalism resembles slavery and differs from feudalism. The land, factories, machines, offices, etc. are owned privately, by a small group of people who use their control to organize the work process and sell goods and services in order to make profits for themselves. Workers sell their labor-power to the owners of the means of production (capitalists) in exchange for a wage. The employer is free to discharge any workers he does not need, and the worker is free to change employers if he so desires. Capitalism thus differs from both slavery and feudalism in that the relationship between the worker and the owner of the means of production is purely contractual; no additional obligations by either party are incurred.[4]

While the mode of production is crucial in governing the general character of a society, the connection between the economic base (or foundation) of the society and other spheres of life is not simple or unidirectional in causation. A purely *economic* his-

tory of any society would by itself be grossly inadequate. Social custom and tradition, culture, ideology, kinship system, religion, form of government, judicial forms—each of these certainly has a historical life of its own and conditions to some extent the basic production relations.

But the important thing is to see the social system *as a whole*. A lack of correspondence between the economic structure and the remaining aspects of society cannot long endure. In this sense, the relations between the other spheres of life and the economic foundation are *asymmetrical*. As Engels put it, economic factors are determining, but only "in the last instance." Baran and Hobsbawm carefully point out that "simplistic economic determinism" was never a part of the Marxian conception of history. Marx himself once wrote that "Men make their own history, but they do not make it just as they please. They do not make it under circumstances chosen by themselves."[5]

How is the mode of production related to historical change? The key point is that the means or forces of production are continually developing (here, technological change plays a key role), leading sooner or later to a non-correspondence or contradiction with the prevailing social relations of production and the prevailing superstructure of society. Such a contradiction can manifest itself in either of two ways: (1) the existing relations of production may become a *fetter* on the further development of the productive forces, or (2) the position of some class may become increasingly compromised or unbearable. For example, the development in England of the factory as a new form of economic organization was predicated on the dissolution of traditional feudal ties and guild restrictions, thus placing the rising capitalist class in direct conflict with the landed aristocracy and the guild masters.

[handwritten margin note: To restrain Confine]

---

[4]The characterization of capitalism in this paragraph can serve temporarily as our definition of capitalism. The defining characteristics of capitalism are further discussed in Dobb, Section 2.3, p. 56 and are examined in detail in Chapter 3.

[5]Engels, Letter to Bloch, September 21, 1890; Marx, *The Eighteenth Brumaire of Louis Bonaparte* (New York: International Publishers, 1963).

But a dominant class, i.e., those who control the surplus and most benefit from the prevailing relations of production, is unlikely to give up its previleged status peacefully. The contradiction tends to grow in severity and eventually produces tensions throughout society. A generalized social crises develops, and only a decisive, often violent rupture with the *status quo* can resolve the contradiction. Historical examples of such ruptures include the French Revolution (1789), the American Civil War (1861-1865), and the Russian Revolution (1917).

The first three readings in this chapter explore the analysis of social systems and the dynamics of social change from the perspective of historical materialism. In the remaining three readings this approach is applied to examine the development of the capitalist mode of production both in England and in the United States.[6]

[6]For examples of the application of historical materialism to analyze relationships between economic and noneconomic factors and changes which occurred *within* the capitalist mode of production, see Chapter 4, especially Weinstein, Section 4.7, p. 188. and O'Connor, Section 4.8, p. 192.

2.1   *The Materialist Conception of History*

In the following classic reading, Karl Marx summarizes his principal thesis. The reading, although short and rather complex, contains many important ideas and should be read carefully and then read again.

> Source: The following is excerpted from the preface to *A Contribution to the Critique of Political Economy* by KARL MARX (first published in 1859).

I was led by my studies to the conclusion that legal relations as well as forms of state could neither be understood by themselves, nor explained by the so-called general progress of the human mind, but that they are rooted in the material conditions of life, which are summed up by Hegel after the fashion of the English and French of the eighteenth century under the name "civic society"; the anatomy of that civic society is to be sought in political economy. . . . The general conclusion at which I arrived and which, once reached, continued to serve as the leading thread in my studies, may be briefly summed up as follows.

In the social production which men carry on they enter into definite relations that are indispensable and independent of their will; these relations of production correspond to a definite stage of development of their material powers of production. The sum total

of these relations of production constitutes the economic structure of society—the real foundation, on which rise legal and political superstructures and to which correspond definite forms of social consciousness. The mode of production in material life determines the general character of the social, political and spiritual processes of life. It is not the consciousness of men that determines their existence, but, on the contrary, their social existence determines their consciousness. At a certain stage of their development, the material forces of production in society come in conflict with the existing relations of production, or—what is but a legal expression for the same thing—with the property relations within which they had been at work before. From forms of development of the forces of production these relations turn into their fetters. Then comes the period of social revolution. With the change of the economic foundation the entire immense superstructure is more or less rapidly transformed. In considering such transformations the distinction should always be made between the material transformation of the economic conditions of production which can be determined with the precision of natural science, and the legal, political, religious, esthetic or philosophic —in short ideological forms in which men become conscious of this conflict and fight it out. Just as our opinion of an individual is not based on what he thinks of himself, so can we not judge of such a period of transformation by its own consciousness; on the contrary, this consciousness must rather be explained from the contradictions of material life, from the existing conflict between the social forces of production and the relations of production. No social order ever disappears before all the productive forces, for which there is room in it, have been developed; and new higher relations of production never appear before the material conditions of their existence have matured in the womb of the old society. Therefore, mankind always takes up only such problems as it can solve; since, looking at the matter more closely, we will always find that the problem itself arises only when the material conditions necessary for its solution already exist or are at least in the process of formation. In broad outlines we can designate the Asiatic, the ancient, the feudal, and the modern bourgeois methods of production as so many epochs in the progress of the economic formation of society. The bourgeois relations of production are the last antagonistic form of the social process of production—antagonistic not in the sense of individual antagonism, but of one arising from conditions surrounding the life of individuals in society; at the same time the productive forces developing in the womb of bourgeois society create the material conditions for the solution of that antagonism. This social formation constitutes, therefore, the closing chapter of the prehistoric stage of human society. . . .

. . .

2.2 The Method of Historical Materialism

A common but erroneous approach to Marx views his concept of historical materialism as a form of naive economic determinism in which everything depends upon economic forces alone. But, as Paul Sweezy has put it, "Marx was not trying to reduce everything to economic terms. He was rather attempting to uncover the *true* interrelationship between the economic and the noneconomic factors in the totality of social existence."[1] In the following reading, Paul Baran and Eric Hobsbawm emphasize that historical materialism is above all a method of approaching social questions, not a set of mechanical formulas. The kernel of the approach is the examination of the unfolding contradiction between the forces of production and the relations of production.

[1]*The Theory of Capitalist Development* (New York: Monthly Review Press, 1942), p. 15.

Source: The following is excerpted from "The Stages of Economic Growth" by PAUL BARAN and ERIC HOBSBAWM. From *Kyklos*, 14, No. 2 (1961). Reprinted by permission of *Kyklos*.

[What is] the nature of the engine which propels economic, social, and political evolution in the course of history? To this fundamental question, historical materialism provides a comprehensive and sophisticated answer. . . . What historical materialism . . . claim[s] is to have discovered an indispensable *approach* to the understanding of historical constellations and to have focused attention on the nature of the principal energies responsible for their emergence, transformation, and disappearance. To put it in a nutshell: these energies are to be traced back to the always present tension between the degree of development of the forces of production on one side, and the prevailing relations of production on the other. To be sure, neither "forces of production" nor "relations of production" are simple notions. The former encompasses the existing state of rationality, science, and technology, the mode of organization of production and the degree of development of man himself, that "most important productive force of all" (Marx). The latter refers to the mode of appropriation of the products of human labor, the social condition under which production takes place, the principles of distribution, the modes of thought, the ideology, the *Weltanschauung* which constitute the "general ether" (Marx) within which society functions at any given time. The conflict between the two—sometimes dormant and sometimes active—is due to a fundamental difference in the "laws of motion" of forces and relations of production respectively. The forces of production tend to be highly dynamic. Driven by man's quest for a better life, by the growth and expansion of human knowledge and rationality, by increasing population, the forces of production tend continually to gain in strength, in depth and in scope. The relations of production on the other hand tend to be sticky, conservative. Prevailing systems of appropriation and social organization, and political institutions favor some classes and discriminate against, frustrate, oppress other classes.

They give rise to vested interests. Modes of thought freeze and display a tenacity and longevity giving rise to what is sometimes referred to as "cultural lags." When the forward movement of the forces of production becomes stymied by the deadweight of dominant interests and the shackles of dominant thought, one or the other has to yield. And since a dominant class never willingly relinquishes its time-honored privileges (partly for reasons of self-interest and partly because its own horizon is more or less narrowly circumscribed by the prevailing ideology sanctifying those very privileges), the clash tends to become violent. This is not to say that obsolete, retrograde relations of production are *always* burst asunder and swept away by revolutions. Depending on the circumstances prevailing in each indivdual case, the process unfolds in a wide variety of ways. Violent upheavals "from below" and relatively peaceful transformations "from above" are as much within the range of possibilities as periods of protracted stagnation in which the political, ideological, and social power of the ruling classes is strong enough to prevent the emergence of new forms of economic and social organization, to block or to slow a country's economic development.

Marx's historical materialism insists, however, that the development of the forces of production has thus far been *the* commanding aspect of the historical process. Whatever may have been its vicissitudes, whatever may have been the setbacks and interruptions that it has suffered in the course of history, in the long run it has tended to overcome all obstacles, and to conquer all political, social and ideological structures subordinating them to its requirements. This struggle between the forces of production and the relations of production proceeds unevenly. Dramatic conquests are less frequent than long periods of siege in which victories remain elusive, imperfect, and impermanent. Different countries display different patterns which depend on their size, location, the strength and cohesion of their ruling classes, the courage, determination and leadership of the underprivileged; on the measure of foreign influence and support to which both or either are exposed; on the pervasiveness and power of the dominant ideologies (e.g., religion). Moreover, the course taken by this struggle and its outcome differ greatly from period to period. Under conditions of capitalism's competitive youth they were different from what they have become in the age of imperialism; in the presence of a powerful socialist sector of the world, they are not the same as they were or would have been in its absence. No bloodless schema of 5 (or 3 or 7) "stages" can do justice to the multitude and variety of economic, technological, political, and ideological configurations generated by this never-ceasing battle between the forces and relations of production. What Marx and Engels and Lenin taught those whose ambition it was to learn rather than to make careers by "refuting" is that these historical configurations cannot be dealt with by "a generalization from the whole span of modern history," but have to be studied *concretely*, with full account taken of the wealth of factors and forces that participate in the shaping of any particular historical case.

To forestall a possible misunderstanding: the foregoing is not intended to advocate renunciation of theory in favor of plodding empiricism. Rather it suggests the necessity of an interpenetration of theory and concrete observation, of empirical research illuminated by rational theory, of theoretical work which draws its life blood from historical study. Consider for instance any one of the many existing underdeveloped countries. . . . [For] an understanding of the country's economic and social condition or . . . the country's developmental possibilities and prospects . . . [what is required] . . . is as accurate as possible an assessment of the social and political forces in the country pressing for change and for development (the economic condition and the stratification of

the peasantry, its political traditions and its ideological make-up, the economic and social status, internal differentiation and political aspirations of the bourgeoisie, the extent of its tie-up with foreign interests and the degree of monopoly prevailing in its national business, the closeness of its connection with the landowning interests and the measure of its participation in the existing government; the living and working conditions and the level of class consciousness of labor and its political and organizational strength). Nor is this by any means the entire job. On the other side of the fence are the groups, institutions, relations, and ideologies seeking to preserve the *status quo*, obstructing efforts directed towards its overturn. There are wealthy landowners and/or rich peasants; there is a segment of the capitalist class firmly entrenched in monopolistic positions and allied with other privileged groups in society; there is a government bureaucracy interwoven with and resting upon the military establishment; there are foreign investors supported by their respective national governments and working hand in hand with their native retainers. Only a thorough historical-materialist analysis, piercing the ideological fog maintained by the dominant coalition of interests and destroying the fetishes continually produced and reproduced by those concerned with the preservation of the *status quo*, only such historical-materialist analysis can hope to disentangle the snarl of tendencies and countertendencies, forces, influences, convictions and opinions, drives and resistances which account for the pattern of economic and social development.

. . .

Far from asserting that "history is uniquely determined by economic forces," and far from ignoring the "significant links between economic and non-economic behavior," the theory of historical materialism advanced by Marx and his followers is nothing if not a powerful effort to explore the manifold, and historically changing connections between the development of the forces and relations of production and the evolution of the consciousness, emotions, and ideologies of men. So much so that the Marxian theory of ideology has served as the point of departure and as a guide to an entire discipline known under the name of "sociology of knowledge," with all analytical history of religion, literature, art and science deriving its inspiration from the same source. Marx's theory of alienation, anticipating much of the subsequent development of social psychology, is in the center of modern study and criticism of culture. Marx's political theory has served as a conceptual basis for most that is valuable in modern European and American historical scholarship. And *The Eighteenth of Brumaire of Louis Bonaparte*—to name only one unsurpassed gem of historical and sociological study—still shines as a model of a comprehensive and penetrating analysis of the "significant links between economic and non-economic behavior" in one particular historical case. . . .

The problem of the "links between economic and non-economic behavior," or for that matter of the explanation of any human activity, economic or other, is not and never has been whether or not man "balances alternatives" or "adheres to the principle of maximization" (which terms, incidentally, if they mean anything at all, amount to exactly the same), no more than there is meaning to the question whether man does or does not have "freedom of will." No one in his right mind —Marxist, mechanical materialist, or idealist —has ever denied that men make choices, exercise their wills, balance alternatives, or, for that matter, move their legs when they walk. The problem is and always has been to discover what determines the nature of the alternatives that are available to men, what accounts for the nature of the goals which they set themselves in different periods of historical development, what makes them will what they will in various societies at various times. To this fundamental question there have been several answers. The theologian's solution has been that all human acts and decisions are governed by the omnipotent and inscrutable will of God. The idealist who substituted the human spirit for the Deity arrives at a very similar position, unable as he is to explain what accounts for the actions and transactions of the spirit. The adherents of "psychologism" view human activity as an emanation of the human psyche, itself an aspect of an eternally constant human nature. The historical materialist considers human actions and motivations to be complex results of a dialectical interaction of biotic and social processes, the latter continually propelled by the dynamism of the forces and relations of production as well as by the ideological evolutions deriving from them and influencing them in turn.

·   ·   ·

2.3   *The Essence of Capitalism*

How should we define capitalism? What are its distinguishing features? In the following reading Maurice Dobb argues that capitalism can be characterized as a particular mode of production in which labor becomes a commodity like any other object of exchange; with this definition, capitalism can be identified as a distinct historical epoch. The prerequisite for the capitalist mode of production was the separation of producers from the means of production and the concentration of the latter in a few hands.

Dobb further argues that it is instructive to divide history into periods, each of which is characterized by a different mode of production; the (antagonistic) social classes of each stage are defined by the manner in which surplus product is appropriated. The process whereby one mode of production replaces another is thus intimately bound up with changing relationships between social classes. In the last 500 years the central tendency of history has been the growing separation of producers from the means of production and their transformation into proletarians, i.e., sellers of their labor power in exchange for a wage.

The analysis of the capitalist mode of production which Dobb begins in this selection is continued in greater detail in Chapter 3.

Source: The following is excerpted from Chapter 1 of *Studies in the Development of Capitalism* by MAURICE DOBB. Revised edition copyright © 1963 by Maurice Dobb. Reprinted by permission of International Publishers, Inc.

I

It is perhaps not altogether surprising that the term Capitalism, which in recent years has enjoyed so wide a currency alike in popular talk and in historical writing, should have been used so variously, and that there should have been no common measure of agreement in its use. What is more remarkable is that in economic theory, as this has been expounded by the traditional schools, the term should have appeared so rarely, if at all. There is even a school of thought, numbering its adherents both among economists and historians, which has refused to recognize that Capitalism as a title for a determinate economic system can be given an exact meaning. . . .

To-day, after half a century of intensive research in economic history, this attitude is rarely regarded by economic historians as tenable, even if they may still hold the origin of the term to be suspect. . . . The prevailing view of those who have studied the economic development of modern times is summed up by Professor Tawney in a well-

known passage. "After more than half a century of work on the subject by scholars of half a dozen different nationalities and of every variety of political opinion, to deny that the phenomenon exists, or to suggest that if it does exist, it is unique among human institutions in having, like Melchizedek, existed from eternity, or to imply that, if it has a history, propriety forbids that history to be disinterred, is to run wilfully in blinkers. . . . An author . . . is unlikely to make much of the history of Europe during the last three centuries if, in addition to eschewing the word, he ignores the fact." But if to-day Capitalism has received authoritative recognition as an historical category, this affords no assurance that those who claim to study this system are talking about the same thing. . . . If it is the pattern which historical events force upon us, and not our own predilections, that is decisive in our use of the term Capitalism, there must then be one definition that accords with the actual shape which historical development possesses, and others which, by contrast with it, are wrong. Even a believer in historical relativism must, surely, believe that there is one picture that is right from the standpoint of any given homogeneous set of historical observations.

. . .

We [accept] the meaning originally given by Marx, who sought the essence of Capitalism neither in a spirit of enterprise nor in the use of money to finance a series of exchange transactions with the object of gain, but in a particular mode of production. By mode of production he did not refer merely to the state of technique — to what he termed the state of the productive forces — but to the way in which the means of production were owned and to the social relations between men which resulted from their connections with the process of production. Thus Capitalism was not simply a system of production for the market — a system of commodity-production as Marx termed it — but a system under which labour-power had "itself become a commodity" and was bought and sold on the market like any other object of exchange. Its historical prerequisite was the concentration of ownership of the means of production in the hands of a class, consisting of only a minor section of society, and the consequential emergence of a propertyless class for whom the sale of their labour-power was their only source of livelihood. Productive activity was furnished, accordingly, by the latter, not by virtue of legal compulsion, but on the basis of a wage-contract. It is clear that such a definition excludes the system of independent handicraft production where the craftsman owned his own petty implements of production and undertook the sale of his own wares. Here there was no divorce between ownership and work; and except where he relied to any extent on the employment of journeymen, it was the purchase and sale of inanimate wares and not of human labour-power that was his primary concern. What differentiates the use of this definition from others is that the existence of trade and of money-lending and the presence of a specialized class of merchants or financiers, even though they be men of substance, does not suffice to constitute a capitalist society. Men of capital, however acquisitive, are not enough: their capital must be used to yoke labour to the creation of surplus-value in production.

. . .

II

If it be right to maintain that the conception of socio-economic systems, marking distinct stages in historical development, is not merely a matter of convenience but an obligation—not a matter of suitable chapter-headings but something that concerns the essential construction of the story if the story is to be true—then this must be because there is a quality in historical situations which both makes for homogeneity of pattern at any given time and renders periods of transition, when there is an even balance of discrete elements, inherently unstable. It must be because society is so constituted that conflict and interaction of its leading elements, rather than the simple growth of some single element, form the principal agency of movement and change, at least so far as major transformations are concerned. If such be the case, once development has reached a certain level and the various elements which constitute that society are poised in a certain way, events are likely to move with unusual rapidity, not merely in the sense of quantitative growth, but in the sense of a change of balance of the constituent elements, resulting in the appearance of novel compositions and more or less abrupt changes in the texture of society. To use a topical analogy: it is as though at certain levels of development something like a chain-reaction is set in motion.

Clearly the feature of economic society which produces this result, and is accordingly fundamental to our conception of Capitalism as a distinctive economic order, characteristic of a distinctive period of history, is that history has been to-date the history of *class societies*: namely, of societies divided into classes, in which either one class, or else a coalition of classes with some common interest, constitutes the dominant class, and stands in partial or complete antagonism to another class or classes. The fact that this is so tends to impose on any given historical period a certain qualitative uniformity; since the class that is socially and politically dominant at the time will naturally use its power to preserve and to extend that particular mode of production—that particular form of relationship between classes—on which its income depends. If change within that society should reach a point where the continued hegemony of this dominant class is seriously called in question, and the old stable balance of forces shows signs of being disturbed, development will have reached a critical stage, where either the change that has been proceeding hitherto must somehow be halted, or if it should continue the dominant class can be dominant no longer and the new and growing one must take its place. Once this shift in the balance of power has occurred, the interest of the class which now occupies the strategic positions will clearly lie in accelerating the transition, in breaking up the strongholds of its rival and predecessor and in extending its own. The old mode of production will not necessarily be eliminated entirely; but it will quickly be reduced in scale until it is no longer a serious competitor to the new.[1] For a period the new mode of production, associated with new productive forces and novel economic potentialities, is likely to expand far beyond the limits within which the old system was destined to move; until in turn the particular class relations and the po-

litical forms in which the new ruling class asserts its power come into conflict with some further development of the productive forces, and the struggle between the two is fought to a climax once again.

The common interest which constitutes a certain social grouping, a class in the sense of which we have been speaking, does not derive from a quantitative similarity of income, as is sometimes supposed: a class does not necessarily consist of people on the same income level, nor are people at, or near, a given income level necessarily united by identity of aims. Nor is it sufficient to say simply that a class consists of those who derive their income from a common source; although it is source rather than size of income that is here important. In this context one must be referring to something quite fundamental concerning the roots which a social group has in a particular society: namely to the relationship in which the group as a whole stands to the process of production and hence to other sections of society. In other words, the relationship from which in one case a common interest in preserving and extending a particular economic system and in the other case an antagonism of interest on this issue can alone derive must be a relationship with a particular mode of extracting and distributing the fruits of surplus labour, over and above the labour which goes to supply the consumption of the actual producer. Since this surplus labour constitutes its life-blood, any ruling class will of necessity treat its particular relationship to the labour process as crucial to its own survival; and any rising class that aspires to live without labour is bound to regard its own future career, prosperity and influence as dependent on the acquisition of some claim upon the surplus labour of others. "A surplus of the product of labour over and above the costs of maintenance of the labour," said Friedrich Engels, "and the formation and enlargement, by means of this surplus, of a social production and reserve fund, was and is the

---

[1]It is not necessary to assume that this is done as part of a conscious long-term plan; although, in so far as the dominant class pursues a definite political policy, this will be so. But it assumes at least that members of a class take common action over particular questions (e.g., access to land or markets or labour), and that greater strength enables them to oust their rivals.

basis of all social, political and intellectual progress. In history up to the present, this fund has been the possession of a privileged class, on which also devolved, along with this possession, political supremacy and intellectual leadership."[2]

The form in which surplus labour has been appropriated has differed at different stages of society; and these varieties of form have been associated with the use of various methods and instruments of production and with different levels of productivity. Marx spoke of Capitalism itself as being, "like any other definite mode of production, conditioned upon a certain stage of social productivity and upon the historically developed form of the productive forces. This historical prerequisite is itself the historical result and product of a preceding process, from which the new mode of production takes its departure as from its given foundation. The conditions of production corresponding to this specific, historically determined, mode of production have a specific, historical passing character."[3] At a stage of social development when the productivity of labour is very low, any substantial and regular income for a leisured class, living on production but not contributing thereto, will be inconceivable unless it is grounded in the rigorous compulsion of producers; and in this sense, as Engels remarked, the division into classes at a primitive stage of economic development "has a certain historical justification."[4] In a predominantly agricultural society the crucial relationships will be connected with the holding of land; and since the division of labour and exchange are likely to be little developed, surplus labour will tend to be performed directly as a personal obligation or to take the form of the delivery of a certain quota of his produce by the cultivator as tribute in natural form to an overlord. The growth of industry, which implies the inven-

tion of new and varied instruments of production, will beget new classes and by creating new economic problems will require new forms of appropriating surplus labour for the benefit of the owners of the new instruments of production. Mediæval society was characterized by the compulsory performance of surplus labour by producers: producers who were in possession of their own primitive instruments of cultivation and were attached to the land. Modern society, by contrast, is characterized, as we have seen, by a relationship between worker and capitalist which takes a purely contractual form, and which is indistinguishable in appearance from any of the other manifold free-market transactions of an exhange society. The transformation from the mediæval form of exploitation of surplus labour to the modern was no simple process that can be depicted as some genealogical table of direct descent. Yet among the eddies of this movement it is possible for the eye to discern certain lines of direction of the flow. These include, not only changes in technique and the appearance of new instruments of production, which greatly enhanced the productivity of labour, but a growing division of labour and consequently the development of exchange, and also a growing separation of the producer from the land and from the means of production and his appearance as a proletarian. Of these guiding tendencies in the history of the past five centuries a special significance attaches to the latter; not only because it has been traditionally glossed over and decently veiled behind formulas about the passage from status to contract, but because into the centre of the historical stage it has brought a form of compulsion to labour for another that is purely economic and "objective"; thus laying a basis for that peculiar and mystifying form whereby a leisured class can exploit the surplus labour of others which is the essence of the modern system that we call Capitalism.

[2]*Anti-Dühring*, 221.
[3]*Capital*, Vol. III, 1023–24.
[4]*Anti-Dühring*, 316.

. . .

2.4   *The Transition from Feudalism to Capitalism*

According to Karl Marx, the emancipation of the serfs and the destruction of the guild restrictions, the separation of freemen from the land, and the concentration of the means of production into a few hands were preconditions for the rise of capitalism. The forcible, violent process by which these preconditions were achieved illustrates the historical perspective from which Marx concluded that revolutionary action is necessary to bring about such changes. As he notes in the next reading, the original accumulation of capital on which capitalism was based was achieved through the use of force: enslavement, exploitation of colonies, outright plunder, etc.

Source: The following is excerpted from Chapters 27–31 of *Capital, Volume I* by KARL MARX (first published in 1867).

· · ·

The economic structure of capitalistic society has grown out of the economic structure of feudal society. The dissolution of the latter set free the elements of the former.

The immediate producer, the laborer, could only dispose of his own person after he had ceased to be attached to the soil and ceased to be the slave, serf, or bondman of another. To become a free seller of labor-power, who carries his commodity wherever he finds a market, he must further have escaped from the regime of the guilds, their rules for apprentices and journeymen, and the impediments of their labor regulations. Hence, the historical movement which changes the producers into wage-workers, appears, on the one hand, as their emancipation from serfdom and from the fetters of the guilds, and this side alone exists for our bourgeois historians. But, on the other hand, these new freedmen became sellers of themselves only after they had been robbed of all their own means of production, and of all the guarantees of existence afforded by the old feudal arrangements. And the history of this, their expropriation, is written in the annals of mankind in letters of blood and fire.

The industrial capitalists, these new potentates, had on their part not only to displace the guild-masters of handicrafts, but also the feudal lords, the possessors of the sources of wealth. In this respect their conquest of social power appears as the fruit of a victorious struggle both against feudal lordship and its revolting prerogatives, and against the guilds and the fetters they laid on the free development of production and the free exploitation of man by man.

· · ·

In the history of primitive accumulation, all revolutions are epoch-making that act as levers for the capitalist class in course of formation; but, above all, those moments when great masses of men are suddenly and forcibly torn from their means of subsistence, and hurled as free and "unattached" proletarians on the labor-market. The expropriation of the agricultural producer, of the peasant, from the soil, is the basis of the whole process. This history of this expropriation, in different countries, assumes different aspects, and runs through its various phases in different orders of succession, and at different periods. In England alone, which we take as our example, has it the classic form.

THE EXPROPRIATION OF THE AGRICULTURAL POPULATION FROM THE LAND

In England, serfdom had practically disappeared in the last part of the 14th century. The immense majority of the population consisted then, and to a still larger extent, in the 15th century, of free peasant proprietors, whatever was the feudal title under which their right of property was hidden. In the larger seignorial domains, the old bailiff, himself a serf, was displaced by the free farmer. The wage-laborers of agriculture consisted partly of peasants, who utilized their leisure time by working on the large estates, partly of an independent special class of wage-laborers, relatively and absolutely few in numbers. The latter also were practically at the same time peasant farmers, since, besides their wages, they had allotted to them arable land to the extent of 4 or more acres, together with their cottages. Besides they, with the rest of the peasants, enjoyed the usufruct of the common land, which gave pasture to their cattle, furnished them with timber, fire-wood, turf, &c. . . .

The prelude of the revolution that laid the foundation of the capitalist mode of production, was played in the last third of the 15th, and the first decade of the 16th century. A mass of free proletarians was hurled on the labor-market by the breaking-up of the bands of feudal retainers, who, as Sir James Steuart well says, "everywhere uselessly filled house and castle." Although the royal power, itself a product of bourgeois development, in its strife after absolute sovereignty forcibly hastened on the dissolution of these bands of retainers, it was by no means the sole cause of it. In insolent conflict with king and parliament, the great feudal lords created an incomparably larger proletariat by the forcible driving of the peasantry from the land, to which the latter had the same feudal right as the lord himself, and

by the usurpation of the common lands. The rapid rise of the Flemish wool manufacturers, and the corresponding rise in the price of wool in England, gave the direct impulse to these evictions. The old nobility had been devoured by the great feudal wars. The new nobility was the child of its time, for which money was the power of all powers. Transformation of arable land into sheep-walks was, therefore, its cry. Harrison, in his "Description of England, prefixed to Holinshed's Chronicles," describes how the expropriation of small peasants is ruining the country. "What care our great encroachers?" The dwellings of the peasants and the cottages of the laborers were razed to the ground or doomed to decay. "If," says Harrison, "the old records of euerie manour be sought . . . it will soon appear that in some manour seventeene, eighteene, or twentie houses are shrunk . . . that England was never less furnished with people than at the present. . . . Of cities and townes either utterly decaied or more than a quarter or half diminished, though some one be a little increased here or there; of towns pulled downe for sheepe-walks, and no more but the lordships now standing in them. . . . I could saie somewhat." The complaints of these old chroniclers are always exaggerated, but they reflect faithfully the impression made on contemporaries by the revolution in the conditions of producing.

. . .

The process of forcible expropriation of the people received in the 16th century a new and frightful impulse from the Reformation, and from the consequent colossal spoliation of the church property. The Catholic church was, at the time of the Reformation, feudal proprietor of a great part of the English land. The suppression of the monasteries, &c., hurled their inmates into the proletariat. The estates of the church were to a large extent given away to rapacious royal favorites, or sold at a nominal price to speculating farmers and citizens, who drove out, *en masse*, the hereditary sub-tenants and threw their holdings into one. The legally guaranteed property of the poorer folk in a part of the church's tithes was tacitly confiscated. . . . These immediate results of the Reformation were not its most lasting ones. The property of the church formed the religious bulwark of the traditional conditions of landed property. With its fall these were no longer tenable.

. . .

After the restoration of the Stuarts, the landed proprietors carried, by legal means, an act of usurpation, effected everywhere on the Continent without any legal formality. They abolished the feudal tenure of land, *i.e.*, they got rid of all its obligations to the State, "indemnified" the State by taxes on the peasantry and the rest of the mass of the people, vindicated for themselves the rights of modern private property in estates to which they had only a feudal title. . . .

The "glorious Revolution" brought into power, along with William of Orange, the landlord and capitalist appropriators of surplus-value. They inaugurated the new era by practicing on a colossal scale thefts of state lands, thefts that had been hitherto managed more modestly. These estates were given away, sold at a ridiculous figure, or even annexed to private estates by direct seizure. All this happened without the slightest observation of legal etiquette. The Crown lands thus fraudulently appropriated, together with the robbery of the Church estates, as far as these had not been lost again during the republican revolution, form the basis of the to-day princely domains of the English oligarchy. The bourgeois capitalists favored the operation with the view, among others, to promoting free trade in land, to extending the domain of modern agriculture on the large farm-system, and to increasing

their supply of the free agricultural proletarians ready to hand. Besides, the new landed aristocracy was the natural ally of the new bankocracy, of the newly-hatched *haute finance*, and of the large manufacturers, then depending on protective duties.

. . .

The last process of wholesale expropriation of the agricultural population from the soil is, finally, the so-called clearing of estates, *i.e.*, the sweeping men off them. All the English methods hitherto considered culminated in "clearing." . . . Where there are no more independent peasants to get rid of, the "clearing" of cottages begins; so that the agricultural laborers do not find on the soil cultivated by them even the spot necessary for their own housing. But what "clearing of estates" really and properly signifies, we learn only in the promised land of modern romance, the Highlands of Scotland. There the process is distinguished by its systematic character, by the magnitude of the scale on which it is carried out at one blow (in Ireland landlords have gone to the length of sweeping away several villages at once; in Scotland areas as large as German principalities are dealt with), finally by the peculiar form of property, under which the embezzled lands were held.

. . .

The spoliation of the church's property, the fraudulent alienation of the State domains, the robbery of the common lands, the usurpation of feudal and clan property, and its transformation into modern private property under circumstances of reckless terrorism, were just so many idyllic methods of primitive accumulation. They conquered the field for capitalistic agriculture, made the soil part and parcel of capital, and created for the town industries the necessary supply of a "free" and outlawed proletariat.

. . .

THE GENESIS OF INDUSTRIAL CAPITALISM

Now that we have considered the forcible creation of a class of outlawed proletarians, the bloody discipline that turned them into wage-laborers, the disgraceful action of the State which employed the police to accelerate the accumulation of capital by increasing the degree of exploitation of labor, the question remains: whence came the capitalists originally?

. . .

Doubtless many small guild-masters, and yet more independent small artisans, or even wage-laborers, transformed themselves into small capitalists, and (by gradually extending exploitation of wage-labor and corresponding accumulation) into full-blown capitalists. In the infancy of capitalist production, things often happened as in the infancy of mediaeval towns, where the question, which of the escaped serfs should be master and which servant, was in great part decided by the earlier or later date of their flight. The snail's pace of this method corresponded in no wise with the commercial requirements of the new world-market that the great discoveries of the end of the 15th century created.

. . .

The discovery of gold and silver in America, the extirpation, enslavement and entombment in mines of the aboriginal population, the beginning of the conquest and looting of the East Indies, the turning of Africa into a warren for the commercial hunting of blackskins, signalized the rosy dawn of the era of capitalist production. These idyllic proceedings are the chief momenta of primitive accumulation. On their heels treads the commercial war of the European nations, with the globe for a theatre. It begins with the revolt of the Netherlands from Spain, assumes giant dimensions in England's Anti-Jacobin War, and is still going on in the opium wars against China, etc.

The different momenta of primitive accumulation distribute themselves now, more or less, in chronological order, particularly over Spain, Portugal, Holland, France, and England. In England at the end of the 17th century, they arrive at a systematical combination, embracing the colonies, the national debt, the modern mode of taxation, and the protectionist system. These methods depend in part on brute force, *e.g.*, the colonial system. But they all employ the power of the State, the concentrated and organized force of society, to hasten, hothouse fashion, the process of transformation of the feudal mode of production into the capitalist mode, and to shorten the transition. Force is the midwife of every old society pregnant with a new one. It is itself an economic power. . . .

The history of the colonial administration of Holland—and Holland was the head capitalistic nation of the 17th century—"is one of the most extraordinary relations of treachery, bribery, massacre, and meanness." Nothing is more characteristic than their system of stealing men, to get slaves for Java. The men stealers were trained for this purpose. The thief, the interpreter, and the seller, were the chief agents in this trade, native princes the chief sellers. The young people stolen, were thrown into the secret dungeons of Celebes, until they were ready for sending to the slave-ships. An official report says: "This one town of Macassar, *e.g.*, is full of secret prisons, one more horrible than the other, crammed with unfortunates, victims of greed and tyranny fettered in chains, forcibly torn from their families." To secure Malacca, the Dutch corrupted the Portuguese governor. He let them into the town in 1641. They hurried at once to his house and assassinated him, to "abstain" from the payment of £21,875, the price of his treason. Wherever they set foot, devastation and depopulation followed. Banjuwangi, a province of Java, in 1750 numbered over 80,000 inhabitants, in 1811 only 18,000. Sweet commerce!

The English East India Company, as is well known, obtained besides the political rule in India, the exclusive monopoly of the tea-trade, as well as of the Chinese trade in general, and of the transport of goods to and from Europe. But the coasting trade of India and between the islands, as well as the internal trade of India, were the monopoly of the higher employes of the company. The monopolies of salt, opium, betel and other commodities, were inexhaustible mines of wealth. The employes themselves fixed the price and plundered at will the unhappy Hindus. The Governor-General took part in this private traffic. His favorites received contracts under conditions whereby they, cleverer than the alchemists, made gold out of nothing. Great fortunes sprang up like mushrooms in a day; primitive accumulation went on without the advance of a shilling. The trial of Warren Hastings swarms with such cases. Here is an instance. A contract for opium was given to a certain Sullivan at the moment of his departure on an official mission to a part of India far removed from the opium district. Sullivan sold his contract to one Binn for £40,000; Binn sold it the same day for £60,000, and the ultimate purchaser who carried out the contract declared that after all he realised an enormous gain. According to one of the lists laid before Parliament, the Company and its employes from 1757–1766 got £6,000,000 from the Indians as gifts. Between 1769 and 1770, the English manufactured a famine by buying up all the rice and refusing to sell it again, except at fabulous prices.

. . .

The treasures captured outside Europe by undisguised looting, enslavement, and murder, floated back to the mother-country and were there turned into capital. Holland, which first fully developed the colonial system, in 1648 stood already in the acme of its commercial greatness. It was "in almost exclusive possession of the East Indian trade and the commerce between the south-east and north-west of Europe. Its fisheries, marine, manufactures, surpassed those of any other country. The total capital of the Republic was probably more important than that of all the rest of Europe put together." Gulich forgets to add that by 1648, the people of Holland were more over-worked, poorer and more brutally oppressed than those of all the rest of Europe put together.

To-day industrial supremacy implies commercial supremacy. In the period of manufacture properly so called, it is, on the other hand, the commercial supremacy that gives industrial predominance. Hence the preponderant role that the colonial system plays at that time.

. . .

The birth of Modern Industry is [also] heralded by a great slaughter of the innocents. Like the royal navy, the factories were recruited by means of the press-gang. Blasé as Sir F. M. Eden is as to the horrors of the expropriation of the agricultural population from the soil, from the last third of the 15th century to his own time; with all the self-satisfaction with which he rejoices in this process, "essential" for establishing capitalistic agriculture and "the due proportion between arable and pasture land"—he does not show, however, the same economic insight in respect to the necessity of child-stealing and child-slavery for the transformation of manufacturing exploitation into factory exploitation, and the establishment of the "true relation" between capital and labor-power. He says: "It may, perhaps, be worthy the attention of the public to consider, whether any manufacture, which, in order to be carried on successfully, requires that cottages and workhouses should be ransacked for poor children; that they should be employed by turns during the greater part of the night and robbed of that rest which, though indispensable to all, is most required by the young; and that numbers of both sexes, of different ages and disposition, should be collected together in such a manner that the contagion of example cannot but lead to profligacy and debauchery; will add to the sum of individual or national felicity?"

"In the counties of Derbyshire, Nottinghamshire, and more particularly in Lancashire," says Fielden, "the newly-invented machinery was used in large factories built on the sides of streams capable of turning the water-wheel. Thousands of hands were suddenly required in these places, remote from towns; and Lancashire, in particular, being, till then, comparatively thinly populated and barren, a population was all that she now wanted. The small and nimble fingers of little children being by very far the most in request, the custom instantly sprang up of procuring *apprentices* from the different parish workhouses of London, Birmingham, and elsewhere. Many, many thousands of these little, hapless creatures were sent down into the north, being from the age of 7 to the age of 13 or 14 years old. The custom was for the master to clothe his apprentices and to feed and lodge them in an 'apprentice house' near the factory; overseers were appointed to see to the works, whose interest it was to work the children to the utmost, because their pay was in proportion to the quantity of work that they could exact. Cruelty was, of course, the consequence. . . . In many of the manufacturing districts, but particularly, I am afraid, in the guilty county to which I belong [Lancashire], cruelties the most heart-rendering was practised upon the unoffending and friendless creatures who were thus consigned to the charge of master-manufacturers; they were harassed to the brink of death by excess of labor . . . were flogged, fettered and tortured in the most exquisite refinement of cruelty; . . . they were in many cases starved to the bone while flogged to their work and . . . even in some instances . . . were driven to commit suicide. . . . The beautiful and romantic valleys of Derbyshire, Nottinghamshire and Lancashire, secluded from the public eye, became the dismal solitudes of torture, and of many a murder. The profits of manufacturers were enormous; but this only whetted the appetite that it should have satisfied, and therefore the manufacturers had recourse to an expedient that seemed to secure to them those profits without any possibility of limit; they began the practice of what is termed 'night-working,' that is, having tired one set of hands, by working them throughout the day, they had another set ready to go on working throughout the night; the day-set getting into the beds that the night-set had just quitted, and in their turn again, the night-set getting into the beds that the day-set quitted in the morning. It is a common tradition in Lancashire, that the beds *never get cold*."

. . .

Such a task it was to establish the "eternal laws of Nature" of the capitalist mode of production, to complete the process of separation between laborers and conditions of labor, to transform, at one pole, the social means of production and subsistence into capital, at the opposite pole, the mass of the population into wage-laborers, into "free laboring poor," that artificial product of modern society. If money, according to Augier, "comes into the world with a congenital blood-stain on one cheek," capital comes dripping from head to foot, from every pore, with blood and dirt.

[handwritten: an essential Characteristic coming from Birth.]

2.5 The Rise of the Bourgeoisie

The capitalists, having stripped away the cobwebs of feudalism, were able to achieve tremendous advances in the development of the material forces of production. There are few paeans so eloquently praiseworthy of capitalism's accomplishments as the following classic reading from Karl Marx and Friedrich Engels' *Communist Manifesto*. The bourgeoisie dominates an ever-increasing proportion of social activity and draws into itself an ever-increasing proportion of the globe. In the process it creates a proletariat and begins to draw this proletariat together. The internal dynamic of capitalism is described as contained in the contradiction between (1) the increasing centralization and private control of the means of production on the one hand, and (2) the increasingly social character of the production process on the other.

Source: The following is excerpted from *The Communist Manifesto* by KARL MARX and FRIEDRICH ENGELS (first published in 1848).

The history of all hitherto existing society is the history of class struggles.

Freeman and slave, patrician and plebeian, lord and serf, guild-master and journeyman, in a word; oppressor and oppressed, stood in constant opposition to one another, carried on an uninterrupted, now hidden, now open fight, a fight that each time ended, either in a revolutionary re-constitution of society at large, or in the common ruin of the contending classes.

In the early epochs of history, we find almost everywhere a complicated arrangement of society into various orders, a manifold graduation of social rank. In ancient Rome we have patricians, knights, plebeians, slaves; in the Middle Ages, feudal lords, vassals, guild-masters, journeymen, apprentices, serfs; in almost all of these classes, again, subordinate gradations.

The modern bourgeois society that has sprouted from the ruins of feudal society, has not done away with class antagonisms. It has but established new classes, new conditions of oppression, new forms of struggle in place of the old ones.

Our epoch, the epoch of the bourgeoisie, possesses, however, this distinctive feature; it has simplified the class antagonisms. Society as a whole is more and more splitting up into two great hostile camps, into two great classes directly facing each other: Bourgeoisie and Proletariat.

From the serfs of the Middle Ages sprang the chartered burghers of the earliest towns. From these burgesses the first elements of the bourgeoisie were developed.

The discovery of America, the rounding of the Cape, opened up fresh ground for the rising bourgeoisie. The East-Indian and Chinese markets, the colonization of America, trade with the colonies, the increase in the means of exchange and in commodities, generally, gave to commerce, to navigation, to industry, an impulse never before known, and thereby, to the revolutionary element in the tottering feudal society, a rapid development.

The feudal system of industry, under which industrial production was monopolized by closed guilds, now no longer sufficed for the growing wants of the markets. The manufacturing system took its place. The guild-masters were pushed on one side by the manufacturing middle-class; division of labor between the different corporate guilds vanished in the face of division of labor in each single workshop.

Meantime the markets kept ever growing, the demand, ever rising. Even manufacturing no longer sufficed. Thereupon, steam and machinery revolutionized industrial production. The place of manufacture was taken by the giant, Modern Industry, the place of the industrial middle-class, by industrial millionaires, the leaders of whole industrial armies, the modern bourgeoisie.

Modern Industry has established the world-market, for which the discovery of America paved the way. This market has given an immense development to commerce, to navigation, to communication by land. This development has, in its turn, reacted on the extension of industry; and in proportion as industry, commerce, navigation, railways extended in the same proportion the bourgeoisie developed, increased its capital, and pushed into the background every class handed down from the Middle Ages.

We see, therefore, how the modern bourgeoisie is itself the product of a long course of development, of a series of revolutions in the modes of production and of exchange.

Each step in the development of the bourgeoisie was accompanied by a corresponding political advance of that class. An oppressed class under the sway of the feudal nobility, an armed and self-governing association in the medieval commune, here independent urban republic (as in Italy and Germany), there taxable "third estate" of the monarchy (as in France), afterwards, in the period of manufacturing proper, serving either the semi-feudal or the absolute monarchy as a counterpoise against the nobility, and in fact, cornerstone of the great monarchies in general, the bourgeoisie has at last, since the establishment of Modern Industry, and of the world-market, conquered for itself, in the modern representative State, exclusive political sway. The executive of the modern State is but a committee for managing the common affairs of the whole bourgeoisie.

The bourgeoisie, historically, has played a most revolutionary part.

The bourgeoisie, wherever it has got the upper hand, has put an end to all feudal, patriarchal, idyllic relations. It has pitilessly torn asunder the motley feudal ties that bound man to his "natural superiors," and has left remaining no other nexus between man and man than naked self-interest, than callous "cash payment." It has drowned the most heavenly ecstasies of religious fervor, of chivalrous enthusiasm, of philistine sentimentalism, in the icy water of egotistical calculation. It has resolved personal worth into exchange value, and in place of the numberless indefeasible chartered freedoms, has set up that single, unconscionable freedom—Free Trade. In one word, for exploitation, veiled by religious and political illusions, it has substituted naked, shameless, direct, brutal exploitation.

The bourgeoisie has stripped of its halo every occupation hitherto honored and looked up to with reverent awe. It has converted the physician, the lawyer, the priest, the poet, the man of science, into its paid wage-laborers.

The bourgeoisie has torn away from the family its sentimental veil, and has reduced the family relation to a mere money relation.

The bourgeoisie has disclosed how it came to pass that the brutal display of vigor in the Middle Ages, which Reactionists so much admire, found its fitting complement in the most slothful indolence. It has been the first to show what man's activity can bring about. It has accomplished wonders far surpassing Egyptian pyramids, Roman aqueducts, and Gothic cathedrals; it has conducted expeditions that put in the shade all former Exoduses of nations and crusades.

The bourgeoisie cannot exist without constantly revolutionizing the instruments of production, and thereby the relations of production, and with them the whole relations of society. Conservation of the old modes of production in unaltered form, was, on the contrary, the first condition of existence for all earlier industrial classes. Constant revolutionizing of production, uninterrupted disturbance of all social conditions, everlasting uncertainty and agitation distinguish the bourgeois epoch from all earlier ones. All fixed, fast-frozen relations, with their train of ancient and venerable prejudices and opinions, are swept away, all newly-formed ones become antiquated before they can ossify. All that is solid melts into air, all that is holy is profaned, and man is at last compelled to face with sober senses, his real conditions of life, and his relations with his kind.

The need of a constantly expanding market for its products chases the bourgeoisie over the whole surface of the globe. It must nestle everywhere, settle everywhere, establish connections everywhere.

The bourgeoisie has through its exploitation of the world-market given a cosmopolitan character to production and consumption in every country. To the great chagrin of Reactionists, it has drawn from under the feet of industry the national ground on which it stood. All old-established national industries have been destroyed or are daily being destroyed. They are dislodged by new industries, whose introduction becomes a life and death question for all civilized nations, by industries that no longer work up indigenous raw material, but raw material drawn from the remotest zones; industries whose products are consumed, not only at home, but in every quarter of the globe. In place of the old wants, satisfied by the productions of the country, we find new wants, requiring for their satisfaction the products of distant lands and climes. In place of the old local and national seclusion and self-sufficiency, we have intercourse in every direction, universal interdependence of nations. And as in material, so also in intellectual production. The intellectual creations of individual nations become common property. National one-sidedness and narrow-mindedness become more and more impossible, and from the numerous national and local literatures there arises a world-literature.

The bourgeoisie, by the rapid improvement of all instruments of production, by the immensely facilitated means of communication, draws all, even the most barbarian, nations into civilization. The cheap prices of its commodities are the heavy artillery with which it batters down all Chinese walls, with which it forces the barbarians' intensely obstinate hatred of foreigners to capitulate. It compels all nations, on pain of extinction, to adopt the bourgeois mode of production; it compels them to introduce what it calls civilization into their midst, i.e., to become bourgeois themselves. In a word, it creates a world after its own image.

The bourgeoisie has subjected the country to the rule of the towns. It has created enormous cities, has greatly increased the urban population as compared with the rural, and has thus rescued a considerable part of the population from the idiocy of rural life. Just as it has made the country dependent on the towns, so it has made barbarian and semi-barbarian countries dependent on the civilized ones, nations of peasants on nations of bourgeois, the East on the West.

The bourgeoisie keeps more and more doing away with the scattered state of the population, of the means of production, and of property. It has agglomerated population, centralized means of production, and has concentrated property in a few hands. The necessary consequence of this was political centralization. Independent, or but loosely connected provinces, with separate interests, laws, governments and systems of taxation, became lumped together in one nation, with one government, one code of laws, one national class-interest, one frontier and one customs-tariff.

The bourgeoisie, during its rule of scarce one hundred years, has created more massive and more colossal productive forces than have all preceding generations together. Subjection of Nature's forces to man, machinery, application of chemistry to industry and agriculture, steam-navigation, railways, electric telegraphs, clearing of whole continents for cultivation, canalization of rivers, whole populations conjured out of the ground—what earlier century had even a presentiment that such productive forces slumbered in the lap of social labor?

We see then: the means of production and of exchange on whose foundations the bourgeoisie built itself up, were generated in feudal society. At a certain stage in the development of these means of production and of exchange, the conditions under which feudal society produced and exchanged, the feudal organization of agriculture and manufacturing industry, in one word, the feudal relations of property became no longer compatible with the already developed productive forces; they became so many fetters. They had to be burst asunder; they were burst asunder.

Into their places stepped free competition, accompanied by a social and political constitution adapted to it, and by the economical and political sway of the bourgeois class.

A similar movement is going on before our own eyes. Modern bourgeois society with its relations of production, of exchange and of property, a society that has conjured up such gigantic means of production and of exchange, is like the sorcerer, who is no longer able to control the power of the nether world whom he has called up by his spells. For many a decade past the history of industry and commerce is but the history of the revolt of modern productive forces against modern conditions of production, against the property relations that are the condition for the existence of the bourgeoisie and of its rule. It is enough to mention the commercial crises that by their periodical return put on trial, each time more threateningly, the existence of the entire bourgeois society. In these crises a great part not only of the existing products, but also of the previously created productive forces, are periodically destroyed. In these crises there breaks out an epidemic that, in all earlier epochs, would have seemed an absurdity—the epidemic of over-production. Society suddenly finds itself put back into a state of momentary barbarism; it appears as if a famine, a universal war of devastation had cut off the supply of every means of subsistence; industry and commerce seem to be destroyed; and why? Because there is too much civilization, too much means of subsistence, too much industry, too much commerce. The productive forces at the disposal of society no longer tend to further the development of the conditions of bourgeois property; on the contrary, they have become too powerful for these conditions, by which they are fettered, and so soon as they overcome these fetters, they bring disorder into the whole of bourgeois society, endangering the existence of bourgeois property. The conditions of bourgeois society are too narrow to comprise the wealth created by them. And how does the bourgeoisie get over these crises? On the one hand by enforced destruction of a mass of productive forces; on the other, by the conquest of new markets, and by the more thorough exploitation of the old ones. That is to say, by paving the way for more extensive and more destructive crises, and by diminishing the means whereby crises are prevented.

The weapons with which the bourgeoisie felled feudalism to the ground are now turned against the bourgeoisie itself.

But not only has the bourgeoisie forged the weapons that bring death to itself; it has also called into existence the men who are to wield those weapons—the modern working-class—the proletarians.

In proportion as the bourgeoisie, i.e., capital, is developed, in the same proportion is the proletariat, the modern working-class, developed, a class of laborers, who live only so long as they find work, and who find work only so long as their labor increases capital. These laborers, who must sell themselves piecemeal, are a commodity, like every other article of commerce, and are consequently exposed to all the vicissitudes of competition, to all the fluctuations of the market.

Owing to the extensive use of machinery and to division of labor, the work of the proletarians has lost all individual character, and, consequently, all charm for the workman. He becomes an appendage of the machine, and it is only the most simple, most monotonous, and most easily acquired knack that is required of him. Hence, the cost of production of a workman is restricted, almost entirely, to the means of subsistence that he requires for his maintenance, and for the propagation of his race. But the price of a commodity, and also of labor, is equal to its cost of production. In proportion, therefore, as the repulsiveness of the work increases, the wage decreases. Nay more, in proportion as the use of machinery and division of labor increases, in the same proportion the burden of toil also increases, whether by prolongation of the working hours, by increase of the work enacted in a given time, or by increased speed of the machinery, etc.

Modern Industry has converted the little workshop of the patriarchal master into the great factory of the industrial capitalist. Masses of laborers, crowded into the factory, are organized like soldiers. As privates of the industrial army they are placed under the command of a perfect hierarchy of officers and sergeants. Not only are they the slaves of the bourgeois class, and of the bourgeois State, they are daily and hourly enslaved by the machine, by the over-looker, and, above all, by the individual bourgeois manufacturer himself. The more openly this despotism proclaims gain to be its end and aim, the more petty, the more hateful and the more embittering it is.

The less the skill and exertion or strength implied in manual labor, in other words, the more modern industry becomes developed, the more is the labor of men superseded by that of women. Differences of age and sex have no longer any distinctive social validity for the working-class. All are instruments of labor, more or less expensive to use, according to their age and sex.

No sooner is the exploitation of the laborer by the manufacturer so far at an end, that he receives his wages in cash, than he is set upon by the other portions of the bourgeoisie, the landlord, the shopkeeper, the pawnbroker, etc.

The low strata of the middle-class—the small tradespeople, shopkeepers, and retired tradesmen generally, the handicraftsmen and peasants—all these sink gradually into the proletariat, partly because their diminutive capital does not suffice for the scale on which Modern Industry is carried on, and is swamped in the competition with the large capitalists, partly because their specialized skill is rendered worthless by new methods of production. Thus the proletariat is recruited from all classes of the population.

The proletariat goes through various stages of development. With its birth begins its struggle with the bourgeoisie. At first the contest is carried on by individual laborers, then by the workpeople of a factory, then by the operatives of one trade, in one locality, against the individual bourgeois who directly exploits them. They direct their attacks not against the bourgeois conditions of production, but against the instruments of production themselves; they destroy imported wares that compete with their labor, they smash to pieces machinery , they set factories ablaze, they seek to restore by force the vanished status of the workman of the Middle Ages.

At this stage the laborers still form an incoherent mass scattered over the whole country, and broken up by their mutual competition. If anywhere they unite to form more compact bodies, this is not yet the consequence of their own active union, but of the union of bourgeoisie, which class, in order to attain its own political ends, is compelled to set the whole proletariat in motion, and is moreover yet, for a time, able to do so. At this stage, therefore, the proletarians do not fight their enemies, but the enemies of their enemies, the remnants of absolute monarchy, the landowners, the non-industrial bourgeoisie, the petty bourgeoisie. Thus the whole historical movement is concentrated in the hands of the bourgeoisie; every victory so obtained is a victory for the bourgeoisie.

2.6   *The Crisis of the Slave South*

One of the most important chapters in the history of social change in the United States was the transformation of the South from a slaveholders' regime to a social system based on the *capitalist* mode of production. The midwife of this great social transformation was force—a long and bloody Civil War.

What was the nature of the social system of the slave South? What were the factors that precluded a peaceful negotiated settlement of the conflicts between the North and the South? In a lucid application of the Marxian approach to historical change, Eugene Genovese argues in the following reading that both internal contradictions within the slave South and external conflicts with the capitalist North combined to produce a crisis of the South's entire social system. This crisis was economic and political, as well as ideological and psychological.

Genovese points out how the slave mode of production governed the general social character of the South. The slaveholders were more than a random collection of individuals with common interests. Welded together by a common culture and a well-articulated ideology (or world view) which regarded slavery as morally superior to capitalism, the slaveholders formed a dominant social class, highly conscious of its own existence, and whose culture pervaded the South's entire social system. Furthermore, as Genovese argues, the nature of the master-slave relationship placed limits on the material growth of the South, i.e., the relations of production became a fetter on the further development of the productive forces. This argument is worth summarizing here.

First, in order that they work efficiently, slaves required close supervision; therefore, technological improvements which would have raised productivity had to be ruled out because they involved complex and varied operations. Moreover, the slaveholders' need to keep the slaves stupid so that they would not rebel—in some areas slaves were forbidden by law to learn to read or write—further limited the productivity of the slave mode of production. Second, unlike capitalists, the slaveholders could not adjust the size of their labor force with varying needs. Third, also unlike capitalism with its spirit of accumulation, the culture of the slaveholders favored conspicuous luxury consumption; thus, less surplus was reinvested in the plantation economy, reducing the rate of material growth. Finally, the high concentration of wealth and the political dominance of the slaveholders precluded the development of a dynamic industrial base in the South.

Meanwhile, the capitalist North was rapidly expanding its material base and, as a proponent of natural rights philosophy, becoming ideologically opposed to any restrictions on the market in free labor. Eventually, both the ideologies and the economic interests of the Southern slaveholders and the Northern bourgeoisie clashed head-on, placing the slaveholders in an untenable position in the Union. Both the existence and *raison d'être* of the slaveholding class were threatened by the ensuing social crisis of the South. It is precisely because the slaveholders formed a self-conscious class that the North was unable to negotiate a peaceful agreement with the slave-holders. The slaveholders were willing to use force to defend what they considered to be a superior way of life; no material compensation from the North would have been sufficient to co-opt them.

In reading this essay, it is especially instructive to note Genovese's brilliant use of Marxian methodology to show how (1) the social relations of production governed the character of the South and became a fetter on the further development of production in the South; (2) the ideology and the economic interests of the slaveholders and the Northern bourgeoisie clashed; and (3) the social classes were antagonistic: each dominant class was ready to use force and did use force to defend its position in society.

Source: The following is condensed from the introduction to and Chapter 1 of *The Political Economy of Slavery* by EUGENE GENOVESE. Copyright © 1961, 1963, 1965, by Eugene Genovese. Reprinted by permission of Pantheon Books, a division of Random House, Inc.

INTRODUCTION

. . . Slavery gave the South a social system and a civilization with a distinct class structure, political community, economy, ideology, and set of psychological patterns. . . . [A]s a result, the South increasingly grew away from the rest of the nation and from the rapidly developing sections of the world. That this civilization had difficulty in surviving during the nineteenth century—a bourgeois century if any deserves the name—raises only minor problems. The difficulty, from this point of view, was neither economic, nor political, nor moral, nor ideological; it was all of these, which constituted manifestations of a fundamental antagonism between modern and premodern worlds.

The premodern quality of the Southern world was imparted to it by its dominant slaveholding class. Slavery has existed in many places, side by side with other labor systems, without producing anything like the civilization of the South. Slavery gave the South a special way of life because it provided the basis for a regional social order in which the slave labor system could dominate all others. Southern slavery was not "mere slavery"—to recall Louis Hartz's luckless term—but the foundation on which rose a powerful and remarkable social class: a class constituting only a tiny portion of the white population and yet so powerful and remarkable as to try, with more success than our neo-abolitionists care to see, to build a new, or rather to rebuild an old, civilization.

[This study] sketches the main features of antebellum Southern civilization, which it describes as having been moving steadily into a general crisis of society as a whole and especially of its dominant slaveholding class. The slaveholders' economic and political interests, as well as ideological and psychological commitments, clashed at many points with those of Northern and European capitalists, farmers, and laborers. The successful defense of slavery presupposed an adequate rate of material growth, but the South could not keep pace with an increasingly hostile North in population growth, manufacturing, transportation, or even agricultural development. The weaknesses of Southern agriculture were especially dangerous and galling to the regime—dangerous because without adequate agricultural progress other kinds of material progress were difficult to effect; galling because Southerners prided themselves on their rural society and its alleged virtues.

.   .   .

The War for Southern Independence, from the viewpoint [of this study], arose naturally from the long process of the development of the slaveholders' regime. Since this viewpoint is not generally accepted, it would be proper to give some account of the contending interpretations. Historians fall into two broad camps: the traditionalists have seen the war as an irrepressible or inevitable conflict, whereas the revisionists have seen it as an unnecessary bloodbath that could have been prevented by good will or statesmanship. Until about thirty years ago the lines were firmly drawn.

In recent decades a great shift has occurred. The revisionists have scored a series of stunning victories over their opponents and forced them to abandon most of their ground. They have done hard digging into source materials, whereas since the appearance of Arthur C. Cole's admirable *The Irrepressible Conflict* (1934) the traditionalists have largely contended themselves with writing essays. Originally, the traditionalist argument posited a wide area of antagonism between the North and South, viewing slavery as a moral issue but also as the basis of intense material differences. Their notion of material differences contained two debilitating tendencies: it centered on narrow economic issues like the tariff, which hardly added up to a reasonable cause for a bloody war; and it assumed, in accordance with a rigid theoretical model, a slavery-engendered soil exhaustion and territorial expansionism which empirical research did not establish.

The revisionists have offered a great many monographs which argue that slavery did not necessarily prevent soil reclamation and agricultural adjustment; they have investigated the conditions for Southern expansionism and

concluded that slavery neither needed nor had prospects for additional territory. As a result of their work, the traditional or irrepressible-conflict interpretation has come to rest almost entirely on moral grounds: the conscience of the nation could not tolerate forever the barbarism of slavery. The question of a profound material antagonism has thereby virtually been laid to rest.

If we had to choose between the two positions narrowed to embrace the moral question alone, it would be difficult to avoid choosing some variation of the revisionist, especially since such neo-revisionist historians as Allan Nevins and David Donald have avoided the more naive formulations of earlier writers and offered attractive alternatives. In effect, they each deny that North and South represented hostile civilizations and stress the inability of American institutional structure to cope with problems and disagreements that were in themselves negotiable. Against such an interpretation, continued harping on the moral issue becomes trying. Moral issues do have their place, as do the irrational actions with which they are sometimes associated, but to say that slavery was merely an immoral way to command labor and that it produced no special society is to capitulate before the revisionists' thrust. They maintain simply and forcefully that time and good will would have removed slavery had a holier-than-thou attitude not prevailed in the North and had there not been so much room for the demagogy of scheming politicians in both sections. The best that the recent traditionalists have been able to offer as a reply is the assertion that Southern immorality proved too profitable to be dispensed with. This is no answer. The notion that the values of the South's ruling class, which became the values of the South as a whole, may be dismissed as immoral is both dubious and unenlightening, but we may leave this point aside. If the commitment of the slaveholders to slavery was merely a matter of dollars and cents, a national effort could have paid them to become virtuous. The answer, I suppose, is that the North could not be expected to pay to free slaves when it believed slave-holding immoral in the first place. As a matter of fact, it could have, and there is not much evidence of such high-mindedness in the North outside of a small band of abolitionists. Either the revisionists are essentially right or the moral question existed as an aspect of something much deeper.

I begin with the hypothesis that so intense a struggle of moral values implies a struggle of world views and that so intense a struggle of world views implies a struggle of worlds —of rival social classes or of societies dominated by rival social classes. In investigating this hypothesis I have rejected the currently fashionable interpretation of slavery as simply a system of extra-economic compulsion designed to sweat a surplus out of black labor. Slavery was such a system, but it was much more. It supported a plantation community that must be understood as an integrated social system, and it made this community the center of Southern life. It extruded a class of slaveholders with a special ideology and psychology and the political and economic power to impose their values on society as a whole. Slavery may have been immoral to the world at large, but to these men, notwithstanding their doubts and inner conflicts, it increasingly came to be seen as the very foundation of a proper social order and therefore as the essence of morality in human relationships. Under the circumstances the social conflict between North and South took the form of a moral conflict. We need not deny the reality of the moral issue to appreciate that it represented only one aspect of a many-sided antagonism. These studies seek to explore the material foundations of that irrepressible antagonism.

Let us make our bows to the age: I do not believe in inevitability in the everyday meaning of the word, nor in a mechanical determinism that leaves no place for man's will,

nor in sin. I do say that the struggle between North and South was irrepressible. From the moment that slavery passed from being one of several labor systems into being the basis of the Southern social order, material and ideological conflict with the North came into being and had to grow worse. If this much be granted, the question of inevitability becomes the question of whether or not the slaveholders would give up their world, which they identified quite properly with slavery itself, without armed resistance. The slaveholders' pride, sense of honor, and commitment to their way of life made a final struggle so probable that we may call it inevitable without implying a mechanistic determinism against which man cannot avail.

I have attempted to demonstrate that the material prerequisites for the slaveholders' power were giving way before internal and external pressures; that the social system was breaking on immanent contradictions; that the economy was proving incapable of adapting itself to reforms while slavery existed; that slavery was naturally generating territorial expansion; and that therefore secession and the risk of war were emerging as a rational course of action. I have, in other words, tried to rebuild the case on which a materialist interpretation of an irrepressible conflict may rest.

.   .   .

THE PROBLEM

The uniqueness of the antebellum South continues to challenge the imagination of Americans, who, despite persistent attempts, cannot divert their attention from slavery. Nor should they, for slavery provided the foundation on which the South rose and grew. The master-slave relationship permeated Southern life and influenced relationships among free men. A full history would have to treat the impact of the Negro slave and of slaveless as well as slaveholding whites, but a first approximation, necessarily concerned with essentials, must focus on the slaveholders, who most directly exercised power over men and events. The hegemony of the slaveholders, presupposing the social and economic preponderance of great slave plantations, determined the character of the South. These men rose to power in a region embedded in a capitalist country, and their social system emerged as part of a capitalist world. Yet, a nonslaveholding European past and a shared experience in a new republic notwithstanding, they imparted to Southern life a special social, economic, political, ideological, and psychological content.

To dissolve that special content into an ill-defined agrarianism or an elusive planter capitalism would mean to sacrifice concern with the essential for concern with the transitional and peripheral. Neither of the two leading interpretations, which for many years have contended in a hazy and unreal battle, offers consistent and plausible answers to recurring questions, especially those bearing on the origins of the War for Southern Independence. The first of these interpretations considers the antebellum South an agrarian society fighting against the encroachments of industrial capitalism; the second considers the slave plantation merely a form of capitalist enterprise and suggests that the material differences between Northern and Southern capitalism were more apparent than real. These two views, which one would think contradictory, sometimes combine in the thesis that the agrarian nature of planter capitalism, for some reason, made coexistence with industrial capitalism difficult.

The first view cannot explain why some agrarian societies give rise to industrialization and some do not. A prosperous agricultural hinterland has generally served as a basis for industrial development by providing a home market for manufactures and a source of capital accumulation, and the prosperity of farmers has largely depended on the growth of industrial centers as markets for foodstuffs. In a capitalist society agriculture is

one industry, or one set of industries, among many, and its conflict with manufacturing is one of many competitive rivalries. There must have been something unusual about an agriculture that generated violent opposition to the agrarian West as well as the industrial Northeast.

The second view, which is the more widely held, emphasizes that the plantation system produced for a distant market, responded to supply and demand, invested capital in land and slaves, and operated with funds borrowed from banks and factors. This, the more sophisticated of the two interpretations, cannot begin to explain the origins of the conflict with the North and does violence to elementary facts of antebellum Southern history.

SLAVERY AND THE EXPANSION OF CAPITALISM

The proponents of the idea of planter capitalism draw heavily, wittingly or not, on Lewis C. Gray's theory of the genesis of the plantation system. Gray defines the plantation as a "capitalistic type of agricultural organization in which a considerable number of unfree laborers were employed under a unified direction and control in the production of a staple crop." Gray considers the plantation system inseparably linked with the international development of capitalism. He notes the plantation's need for large outlays of capital, its strong tendency toward specialization in a single crop, and its commercialism and argues that these appeared with the industrial revolution.

In modern times the plantation often rose under bourgeois auspices to provide industry with cheap raw materials, but the consequences were not always harmonious with bourgeois society. Colonial expansion produced three sometimes overlapping patterns: (1) the capitalists of the advanced country simply invested in colonial land—as illustrated even today by the practice of the United

Fruit Company in the Caribbean; (2) the colonial planters were largely subservient to the advanced countries—as illustrated by the British West Indies before the abolition of slavery; and (3) the planters were able to win independence and build a society under their own direction—as illustrated by the Southern United States.

In alliance with the North, the planter-dominated South broke away from England, and political conditions in the new republic allowed it considerable freedom for self-development. The plantation society that had begun as an appendage of British capitalism ended as a powerful, largely autonomous civilization with aristocratic pretensions and possibilities, although it remained tied to the capitalist world by bonds of commodity production. The essential element in this distinct civilization was the slaveholders' domination, made possible by their command of labor. Slavery provided the basis for a special Southern economic and social life, special problems and tensions, and special laws of development.

THE RATIONALITY AND IRRATIONALITY OF SLAVE SOCIETY

Slave economies normally manifest irrational tendencies that inhibit economic development and endanger social stability. Max Weber, among the many scholars who have discussed the problem, has noted four important irrational features. First, the master cannot adjust the size of his labor force in accordance with business fluctuations. In particular, efficiency cannot readily be attained through the manipulation of the labor force if sentiment, custom, or community pressure makes separation of families difficult. Second, the capital outlay is much greater and riskier for slave labor than for free. Third, the domination of society by a planter class increases the risk of political influence in the market. Fourth, the sources of cheap labor usually dry up rather quickly,

and beyond a certain point costs become excessively burdensome. Weber's remarks could be extended. Planters, for example, have little opportunity to select specifically trained workers for special tasks as they arise.

There are other telling features of this irrationality. Under capitalism the pressure of the competitive struggle and the bourgeois spirit of accumulation direct the greater part of profits back into production. The competitive side of Southern slavery produced a similar result, but one that was modified by the pronounced tendency to heavy consumption. Economic historians and sociologists have long noted the high propensity to consume among landed aristocracies. No doubt this difference has been one of degree. The greater part of slavery's profits also find their way back into production, but the method of reinvestment in the two systems is substantially different. Capitalism largely directs its profits into an expansion of plant and equipment, not labor; that is, economic progress is qualitative. Slavery, for economic reasons as well as for those of social prestige, directs its reinvestments along the same lines as the original investment—in slaves and land; that is, economic progress is quantitative.

In the South this weakness proved fatal for the slaveholders. They found themselves engaged in a growing conflict with Northern farmers and businessmen over such issues as tariffs, homesteads, internal improvements, and the decisive question of the balance of political power in the Union. The slow pace of their economic progress, in contrast to the long strides of their rivals to the north, threatened to undermine their political parity and result in a Southern defeat on all major issues of the day. The qualitative leaps in the Northern economy manifested themselves in a rapidly increasing population, an expanding productive plant, and growing political, ideological, and social boldness. The slaveholders' voice grew shriller and harsher as they contemplated impending disaster and sought solace in complaints of Northern aggression and exploitation.

Just as Southern slavery directed reinvestment along a path that led to economic stagnation, so too did it limit the volume of capital accumulated for investment of any kind. We need not reopen the tedious argument about the chronology of the plantation, the one-crop system, and slavery. While slavery existed, the South had to be bound to a plantation system and an agricultural economy based on a few crops. As a result, the South depended on Northern facilities, with inevitably mounting middlemen's charges. Less obvious was the capital drain occasioned by the importation of industrial goods. While the home market remained backward, Southern manufacturers had difficulty producing in sufficient quantities to keep costs and prices at levels competitive with Northerners. The attendant dependence on Northern and British imports intensified the outward flow of badly needed funds.[1]

Most of the elements of irrationality were irrational only from a capitalist standpoint. The high propensity to consume luxuries, for example, has always been functional (socially if not economically rational) in aristocratic societies, for it has provided the ruling class with the façade necessary to control the middle and lower classes. Thomas R. Dew knew what he was doing when he defended the high personal expenditures of Southerners as proof of the superiority of the slave system. Few Southerners, even few slaveholders, could afford to spend lavishly and effect an aristocratic standard of living, but those few set the social tone for society. One wealthy

planter with a great house and a reputation for living and entertaining on a grand scale could impress a whole community and keep before its humbler men the shining idea of plantation magnificence. Consider Pascal's observation that the habit of seeing the king accompanied by guards, pomp, and all the paraphernalia designed to command respect and inspire awe will produce those reactions even when he appears alone and informally. In the popular mind he is assumed to be naturally an awe-inspiring being. In this manner, every dollar spent by the planters for elegant clothes, a college education for their children, or a lavish barbecue contributed to the political and social domination of their class. We may speak of the slave system's irrationality only in a strictly economic sense and then only to indicate the inability of the South to compete with Northern capitalism on the latter's grounds. The slaveholders, fighting for political power in an essentially capitalist Union, had to do just that.

CAPITALIST AND PSEUDO-CAPITALIST FEATURES OF THE SLAVE ECONOMY

The slave economy developed within, and was in a sense exploited by, the capitalist world market; consequently, slavery developed many ostensibly capitalist features, such as banking, commerce, and credit. These played a fundamentally different role in the South than in the North. Capitalism has absorbed and even encouraged many kinds of precapitalist social systems: serfdom, slavery, Oriental state enterprises, and others. It has introduced credit, finance, banking, and similar institutions where they did not previously exist. It is pointless to suggest that therefore nineteenth-century India and twentieth-century Saudi Arabia should be classified as capitalist countries. We need to analyze a few of the more important capitalist and pseudo-capitalist features of Southern slavery and

---

[1]This colonial dependence on the British and Northern markets did not end when slavery ended. Sharecropping and tenantry produced similar results. Since abolition occurred under Northern guns and under the program of a victorious, predatory outside bourgeoisie, instead of under internal bourgeois auspices, the colonial bondage of the economy was preserved, but the South's political independence was lost.

especially to review the barriers to industrialization in order to appreciate the peculiar qualities of this remarkable and anachronistic society.

The defenders of the "planter-capitalism" thesis have noted the extensive commercial links between the plantation and the world market and the modest commercial bourgeoisie in the South and have concluded that there is no reason to predicate an antagonism between cotton producers and cotton merchants. However valid as a reply to the naive arguments of the proponents of the agrarianism-versus-industrialism thesis, this criticism has unjustifiably been twisted to suggest that the presence of commercial activity provides the predominance of capitalism in the South. Many precapitalist economic systems have had well-developed commercial relations, but if every commercial society is to be considered capitalist, the word loses all meaning. In general, commercial classes have supported the existing system of production. As Maurice Dobb observes, their fortunes are bound up with those of the dominant producers, and merchants are more likely to seek an extension of their middlemen's profits than to try to reshape the economic order.

We must concern ourselves primarily with capitalism as a social system, not merely with evidence of typically capitalistic economic practices. In the South extensive and complicated commercial relations with the world market permitted the growth of a small commerical bourgeoisie. The resultant fortunes flowed into slaveholding, which offered prestige and economic and social security in a planter-dominated society. Independent merchants found their businesses dependent on the patronage of the slaveholders. The merchants either became planters themselves or assumed a servile attitude toward the planters. The commercial bourgeoisie, such as it was, remained tied to the slaveholding interest, had little desire or opportunity to invest capital in industrial expansion, and

adopted the prevailing aristocratic attitudes.

The Southern industrialists were in an analogous position, although one that was potentially subversive of the political power and ideological unity of the planters. The preponderance of planters and slaves on the countryside retarded the home market. The Southern yeomanry, unlike the Western, lacked the purchasing power to sustain rapid industrial development. The planters spent much of their money abroad for luxuries. The plantation market consisted primarily of the demand for cheap slave clothing and cheap agricultural implements for use or misuse by the slaves. Southern industrialism needed a sweeping agrarian revolution to provide it with cheap labor and a substantial rural market, but the Southern industrialists depended on the existing, limited plantation market. Leading industrialists like William Gregg and Daniel Pratt were plantation-oriented and proslavery. They could hardly have been other.

.   .   .

If for a moment we accept the designation of the planters as capitalists and the slave system as a form of capitalism, we are then confronted by a capitalist society that impeded the development of every normal feature of capitalism. The planters were not mere capitalists; they were precapitalist, quasi-aristocratic landowners who had to adjust their economy and ways of thinking to a capitalist world market. Their society, in its spirit and fundamental direction, represented the antithesis of capitalism, however many compromises it had to make. The fact of slave ownership is central to our problem. This seemingly formal question of whether the owners of the means of production command labor or purchase the labor power of freeworkers contains in itself the content of Southern life. The essential features of Southern particularity, as well as of Southern backwardness, can be traced to the relationship of master to slave.

THE BARRIERS TO
INDUSTRIALIZATION

If the planters were losing their economic and political cold war with Northern capitalism, the failure of the South to develop sufficient industry provided the most striking immediate cause. Its inability to develop adequate manufactures is usually attributed to the inefficiency of its labor force. No doubt slaves did not easily adjust to industrial employment, and the indirect effects of the slave system impeded the employment of whites.[2] Slaves did work effectively in hemp, tobacco, iron, and cotton factories but only under socially dangerous conditions. They received a wide variety of privileges and approached an elite status. Planters generally appreciated the potentially subversive quality of these arrangements and looked askance at their extension.

Slavery concentrated economic and political power in the hands of a slaveholding class hostile to industrialism. The slaveholders feared a strong urban bourgeoisie, which might make common cause with its Northern counterpart. They feared a white urban working class of unpredictable social tendencies. In general, they distrusted the city and saw in it something incongruous with their local power and status arrangements. The small slaveholders, as well as the planters, resisted the assumption of a heavy tax burden to assist manufacturers, and as the South fell further behind the North in industrial development more state aid was required to help industry offset the Northern advantages of scale, efficiency, credit relations, and business reputation.

Slavery led to the rapid concentration of land and wealth and prevented the expansion of a Southern home market. Instead of providing a basis for industrial growth, the Southern countryside, economically dominated by a few large estates, provided only a limited market for industry. Data on the cotton textile factories almost always reveal that Southern producers aimed at supplying slaves with the cheapest and coarsest kind of cotton goods. Even so, local industry had to compete with Northern firms, which sometimes shipped direct and sometimes established Southern branches.

· · ·

THE GENERAL FEATURES OF
SOUTHERN AGRICULTURE

The South's greatest economic weakness was the low productivity of its labor force. The slaves worked indifferently. They could be made to work reasonably well under close supervision in the cotton fields, but the cost of supervising them in more than one or two operations at a time was prohibitive. Slavery prevented the significant technological progress that could have raised productivity substantially. Of greatest relevance, the impediments to technological progress damaged Southern agriculture, for improved implements and machines largely accounted for the big increases in crop yields per acre in the Northern states during the nineteenth century.

Slavery and the plantation system led to agricultural methods that depleted the soil. The frontier methods of the free states yielded similar results, but slavery forced the South into continued dependence upon exploitative methods after the frontier had passed further west. It prevented reclamation of worn-out lands. The plantations were much too large to fertilize easily. Lack of

---

[2]Slavery impeded white immigration by presenting Europeans with an aristocratic, caste-ridden society that scarcely disguised its contempt for the working classes. The economic opportunities in the North were, in most respects, far greater. When white labor was used in Southern factories, it was not always superior to slave labor. The incentives offered by the Northern economic and social system were largely missing; opportunities for acquiring skills were fewer; in general, productivity was much lower than in the North.

markets and poor care of animals by slaves made it impossible to accumulate sufficient manure. The low level of capital accumulation made the purchase of adequate quantities of commercial fertilizer unthinkable. Planters could not practice proper crop rotation, for the pressure of the credit system kept most available land in cotton, and the labor force could not easily be assigned to the required tasks without excessive costs of supervision. The general inefficiency of labor thwarted most attempts at improvement of agricultural methods.

. . .

THE IDEOLOGY OF THE MASTER CLASS

The planters commanded Southern politics and set the tone of social life. Theirs was an aristocratic, antibourgeois spirit with values and mores emphasizing family and status, a strong code of honor, and aspirations to luxury, ease, and accomplishment. In the planters' community, paternalism provided the standard of human relationships, and politics and statecraft were the duties and responsibilities of gentlemen. The gentleman lived for politics, not, like the bourgeois politician, off politics.

The planter typically recoiled at the notions that profit should be the goal of life; that the approach to production and exchange should be internally rational and uncomplicated by social values; that thrift and hard work should be the great virtues; and that the test of the wholesomeness of a community should be the vigor with which its citizens expand the economy. The planter was no less acquisitive than the bourgeois, but an acquisitive spirit is compatible with values antithetical to capitalism. The aristocratic spirit of the planters absorbed acquisitiveness and directed it into channels that were socially desirable to a slave society: the accumulation of slaves and land and the

achievement of military and political honors. Whereas in the North people followed the lure of business and money for their own sake, in the South specific forms of property carried the badges of honor, prestige, and power. Even the rough parvenu planters of the Southwestern frontier—the "Southern Yankees"—strove to accumulate wealth in the modes acceptable to plantation society. Only in their crudeness and naked avarice did they differ from the Virginia gentlemen. They were a generation removed from the refinement that follows accumulation.

Slavery established the basis of the planter's position and power. It measured his affluence, marked his status, and supplied leisure for social graces and aristocratic duties. The older bourgeoisie of New England in its own way struck an aristocratic pose, but its wealth was rooted in commercial and industrial enterprises that were being pushed into the background by the newer heavy industries arising in the West, where upstarts took advantage of the more lucrative ventures like the iron industry. In the South few such opportunities were opening. The parvenu differed from the established planter only in being cruder and perhaps sharper in his business dealings. The road to power lay through the plantation. The older aristocracy kept its leadership or made room for men following the same road. An aristocratic stance was no mere compensation for a decline in power; it was the soul and content of a rising power.

. . .

At their best, Southern ideals constituted a rejection of the crass, vulgar, inhumane elements of capitalist society. The slaveholders simply could not accept the idea that the cash nexus offered a permissible basis for human relations. Even the vulgar parvenu of the Southwest embraced the plantation myth and refused to make a virtue of necessity by glorifying the competitive side of slavery as civilization's highest achievement. The slaveholders generally, and the planters in particular, did identify their own ideas with the essence of civilization and, given their sense of honor, were prepared to defend them at any cost.

This civilization and its ideals were antinational in a double sense. The plantation offered virtually the only market for the small nonstaple-producing farmers and provided the center of necessary services for the small cotton growers. Thus, the paternalism of the planters toward their slaves was reinforced by the semipaternal relationship between the planters and their neighbors. The planters, in truth, grew into the closest thing to feudal lords imaginable in a nineteenth-century bourgeois republic. The planters' protestations of love for the Union were not so much a desire to use the Union to protect slavery as a strong commitment to localism as the highest form of liberty. They genuinely loved the Union so long as it alone among the great states of the world recognized that localism had a wide variety of rights. The Southerners' source of pride was not the Union, nor the nonexistent Southern nation; it was the plantation, which they raised to a political principle.

THE INNER REALITY OF SLAVEHOLDING

The Southern slaveholder had "extraordinary force." In the eyes of an admirer his independence was "not as at the North, the effect of a conflict with the too stern pressure of society, but the legitimate outgrowth of a sturdy love of liberty." This independence, so distinctive in the slaveholders' psychology, divided them politically from agrarian Westerners as well as from urban Easterners. Commonly, both friendly and hostile contemporaries agreed that the Southerner appeared rash, unstable, often irrational, and that he turned away from bourgeois habits toward an aristocratic pose.

Americans, with a pronounced Jeffersonian bias, often attribute this spirit to agra-

rians of all types, although their judgment seems almost bizarre. A farmer may be called "independent" because he works for himself and owns property; like any grocer or tailor he functions as a petty bourgeois. In Jefferson's time, when agriculture had not yet been wholly subjected to the commanding influences of the market, the American farmer perhaps had a considerable amount of independence, if we choose to call self-sufficient isolation by that name, but in subsequent days he has had to depend on the market like any manufacturer, if not more so. Whereas manufacturers combine to protect their economic interests, such arrangements have proved much more difficult, and until recently almost impossible, to effect among farmers. In general, if we contrast farmers with urban capitalists, the latter emerge as relatively the more independent. The farmer yields constantly to the primacy of nature, to a direct, external force acting on him regardless of his personal worth; his independence is therefore rigorously circumscribed. The capitalist is limited by the force of the market, which operates indirectly and selectively. Many capitalists go under in a crisis, but some emerge stronger and surer of their own excellence. Those who survive the catastrophe do so (or so it seems) because of superior ability, strength, and management, not because of an Act of God.

The slaveholder, as distinct from the farmer, had a private source of character making any mythmaking—his slave. Most obviously, he had the habit of command, but there was more than despotic authority in this master-slave relationship. The slave stood interposed between his master and the object his master desired (that which was produced); thus, the master related to the object only mediately, through the slave. The slaveholder commanded the products of another's labor, but by the same process was forced into dependence upon this other.

Thoughtful Southerners such as Ruffin, Fitzhugh, and Hammond understood this dependence and saw it as arising from the general relationship of labor to capital, rather than from the specific relationship of master to slave. They did not grasp that the capitalist's dependence upon his laborers remains obscured by the process of exchange in the capitalist market. Although all commodities are products of social relationships and contain human labor, they face each other in the market not as the embodiment of human qualities but as things with a seemingly independent existence. Similarly, the laborer sells his labor-power in the way in which the capitalist sells his goods—by bringing it to market, where it is subject to the fluctuations of supply and demand. A "commodity fetishism" clouds the social relationship of labor to capital, and the worker and capitalist appear as mere observers of a process over which they have little control. Southerners correctly viewed the relationship as a general one of labor to capital but failed to realize that the capitalist's dependence on his laborers is hidden, whereas that of master on slave is naked. As a Mississippi planter noted:

I intend to be henceforth stingy as far as unnecessary expenditure—as a man should not squander what another accumulates with the exposure of health and the wearing out of the physical powers, and is not that the case with the man who needlessly parts with that which the negro by the hardest labor and often undergoing what we in like situation would call the greatest deprivation. . . .

This simultaneous dependence and independence contributed to that peculiar combination of the admirable and the frightening in the slaveholder's nature: his strength, graciousness, and gentility; his impulsiveness, violence, and unsteadiness. The sense of independence and the habit of command developed his poise, grace, and dignity, but the less obvious sense of dependence on a despised other made him violently intolerant of anyone and anything threatening to expose the full nature of his relationship to his slave. Thus, he had a far deeper conservatism than that usually attributed to agrarians. His in-

dependence stood out as his most prized possession, but the instability of its base produced personal rashness and directed that rashness against any alteration in the status quo. Any attempt, no matter how well meaning, indirect, or harmless, to question the slave system appeared not only as an attack on his material interests but as an attack on his self-esteem at its most vulnerable point. To question either the morality or the practicality of slavery meant to expose the root of the slaveholder's dependence in independence.

THE GENERAL CRISIS OF THE SLAVE SOUTH

The South's slave civilization could not forever coexist with an increasingly hostile, powerful, and aggressive Northern capitalism. On the one hand, the special economic conditions arising from the dependence on slave labor bound the South, in a colonial manner, to the world market. The concentration of landholding and slaveholding prevented the rise of a prosperous yeomanry and of urban centers. The inability to build urban centers restricted the market for agricultural produce, weakened the rural producers, and dimmed hopes for agricultural diversification. On the other hand, the same concentration of wealth, the isolated, rural nature of the plantation system, the special psychology engendered by slave ownership, and the political opportunity presented by the separation from England, converged to give the South considerable political and social independence. This independence was primarily the contribution of the slaveholding class, and especially of the planters. Slavery, while it bound the South economically, granted it the privilege of developing an aristocratic tradition, a disciplined and cohesive ruling class, and a mythology of its own.

Aristocratic tradition and ideology intensified the South's attachment to economic backwardness. Paternalism and the habit of command made the slaveholders tough stock, determined to defend their Southern heritage. The more economically debilitating their way of life, the more they clung to it. It was this side of things—the political hegemony and aristocratic ideology of the ruling class— rather than economic factors that prevented the South from relinquishing slavery voluntarily.

As the free states stepped up their industrialization and as the westward movement assumed its remarkable momentum, the South's economic and political allies in the North were steadily isolated. Years of abolitionist and free-soil agitation bore fruit as the South's opposition to homesteads, tariffs, and internal improvements clashed more and more dangerously with the North's economic needs. To protect their institutions and to try to lessen their economic bondage, the slaveholders slid into violent collision with Northern interests and sentiments. The economic deficiencies of slavery threatened to undermine the planters' wealth and power. Such relief measures as cheap labor and more land for slave states (reopening the slave trade and territorial expansion) conflicted with Northern material needs, aspirations, and morality.[3] The planters faced a steady deterioration of their political and social power.

Even if the relative prosperity of the 1850s had continued indefinitely, the slave states would have been at the mercy of the free, which steadily forged ahead in population growth, capital accumulation, and economic development. Any economic slump threatened to bring with it an internal political disaster, for the slaveholders could not rely on their middle and lower classes to remain permanently loyal.[4]

When we understand that the slave South developed neither a strange form of capitalism nor an undefinable agrarianism but a special civilization built on the relationship of master to slave, we expose the root of its conflict with the North. The internal contradictions in the South and the external conflict with the North placed the slaveholders hopelessly on the defensive with little to look forward to except slow strangulation. Their only hope lay in a bold stroke to complete their political independence and to use it to provide an expansionist solution for their economic and social problems. The ideology and psychology of the proud slaveholding class made surrender or resignation to gradual defeat unthinkable, for its fate, in its own eyes at least, was the fate of everything worth while in Western civilization.

[3]These measures met opposition from powerful sections of the slaveholding class for reasons that cannot be discussed here. The independence of the South would only have brought the latent intraclass antagonisms to the surface.

[4]The loyalty of these classes was real but unstable. For our present purposes let us merely note that Lincoln's election and federal patronage would, if Southern fears were justified, have led to the formation of an antiplanter party in the South.

SELECTIVE BIBLIOGRAPHY

Further reading is recommended in Dobb, *Studies in the Development of Capitalism*, in Marx, *Capital*, Vol. I, Part 8, and in Genovese, *The Political Economy of Slavery*, as cited in the source lines for Sections 2.3, 2.4, and 2.6. Selsam and Martel [6], Part 5, and Feuer [2] contain basic statements by Marx and by Engels on the methodology of historical materialism. Bendix and Lipset [1] have assembled many of Marx's comments on social classes together with a discussion of the role of classes in Marx's theory. A summary of recent anthropological evidence on the relationship between the development of a social surplus and the rise of class divisions in primitive society is in Mandel [4], chapters 1 and 2. The usefulness of a Marxian framework has been highlighted in a number of recent excellent general histories of the development of capitalism in England and in the United States. Hobsbawm [3] is a highly readable account of the Industrial Revolution in England. For a view of the actual experiences of working people during the Industrial Revolution, and the ways in which the handling of these experiences involved the historical formation of a class, Thompson [7] is an indispensable classic. Chapter 1 in Moore [5] on England is an interesting analysis of the process by which the capitalist class came to power; Chapter 3 on the Civil War in the United States nicely complements the Genovese work cited above. Finally, Williams [8] is a bold attempt to reconceptualize all of United States history from a radical perspective.

[1] Bendix, Reinhard, and Seymour Lipset, "Karl Marx's Theory of Classes," in *Class Status and Power* (2nd ed.), Bendix and Lipset. New York: Free Press, 1966.

[2] Feuer, Lewis S., ed., *Marx and Engels: Basic Writings on Politics and Philosophy*. Garden City, N.Y.: Doubleday, 1959.*

[3] Hobsbawm, Eric J., *Industry and Empire*. Baltimore: Penguin, 1969.*

[4] Mandel, Ernest, *Marxist Economic Theory*. New York: Monthly Review Press, 1968.*

[5] Moore, Barrington, Jr., *The Social Origins of Dictatorship and Democracy*. Boston: Beacon, 1966.*

[6] Selsam, Howard, and Harry Martel, eds., *A Reader in Marxist Philosophy*. New York: International Pub., 1963.*

[7] Thompson, Edward P., *The Making of the English Working Class*. New York: Vintage, 1966.*

[8] Williams, William A., *The Contours of American History*. Chicago: Quadrangle, 1966.*

*Available in paperback editions.

The

Capitalist Mode

of Production 3

THE CAPITALIST MODE OF PRODUCTION PROvides the key to understanding the character of capitalist society. The mode of production determines the context within which a society's social structure—its laws, race relations, schools, class structure, government, etc.—develops. Limits are set on the possible ways in which these elements of a society can develop, and possibilities incompatible with the mode of production are excluded. Further, the mode of production creates conditions conducive to the development of some particular social outcomes rather than others.

This description may suggest a harmonious society in which people accept their fate and capitalist institutions function smoothly. But capitalist institutions confer power and wealth differentially among different groups of people. And so the relations of production are antagonistic: the economic process generates conflict between groups in society who have contradictory needs and interests. These conflicts are decided by the power relations embedded in the mode of production.

Further, capitalism does not continue unchanged, but is itself subject to historical processes. As the mode of production develops, the concrete historical form which it assumes necessarily changes. For example, the unit of capitalist production has changed from the small independent producer of the nineteenth century to the large multinational corporation of today, and production has become highly complex and interdependent on a worldwide scale. This historical unfolding of the "internal logic" of the mode of production at the same time intensifies the conflicts within society—conflicts which induce people actively to oppose the existing relations of production. Under capitalism, the increasingly social character and consequences of production increasingly conflict with the existing *private* control and ownership of production, which have become more concentrated than ever before. These "contradictions" within the society continue to intensify; they can be resolved only by transforming or "revolutionizing" society, i.e., by changing the mode of production.

These propositions were the subject of Chapter 2, which introduced the analytic method for study of societies called "historical materialism"; to illustrate that analysis, it examined the transition from precapitalist to capitalist societies. The purpose of this chapter is to apply the historical materialist method in detail by turning directly to the analysis of capitalism and the capitalist mode of production. In this chapter we shall attempt to explain what is meant by "capitalism" and how capitalist institutions function.

THE INSTITUTIONS OF CAPITALISM

The essays in this chapter describe certain institutions of capitalism which we consider to be the *basic* or *fundamental* economic institutions. They are "basic" in a triple sense. First, as Dobb argued[1] in Chapter 2, the emergence of these institutions defines the historical period of capitalism; hence these institutions provide the *historical* delineation of capitalism. Second, these institutions are basic in the *logical* sense: they initiate the analysis by defining what we mean by "capitalism." Third, they are basic in an *empirical* sense; as the following chapters show, these institutions are the most important for understanding capitalist society.

In the previous chapter we defined the mode of production in terms of the "productive forces" and the "social relations of production." Within any particular society, these productive forces and social relations are embodied in, or take specific historical form in, a set of economic institutions—that is, those institutions which surround and govern the production, distribution, and consumption of material goods and valuable

[1]See Dobb, Section 2.3, p. 56.

services.[2] Therefore, to understand the capitalist mode of production we need first to describe the basic capitalist economic institutions.

We must be careful to define precisely what we mean by "an institution." An institution is simply a *social process* whereby individual people or groups of people interact with one another in a commonly understood, typical, and patterned way. An institution, then, consists of two parts. First, there must be commonly understood guidelines (like rules in a game) which point out what is considered acceptable behavior, and on which people base their expectations of how other people will act. For example, consider as an institution the free market in labor: the "rules of the game" declare that workers must compete against each other for jobs and employers must compete against each other for workers. Any other behavior (for example, using violence to force an employer to hire you) is contrary to the rules of the free market.

Second, such institutional rules must be accompanied by people actually acting according to those rules; that is, there must be normal and patterned behavior consistent with the "rules of the game." A set of institutional "rules" does not constitute an institution unless people behave according to those rules.[3]

What, then, are the basic institutions of capitalism? We will identify four such institutions. We must emphasize, however, that

these four institutions simply characterize different aspects of what is historically one unified process: capitalist production. The institutions therefore do not exist and cannot be analyzed independently of each other: each exists only in the context of the others.

(1) The Market in Labor

Throughout the centuries, people of many different cultures and economic systems have traded a wide variety of goods with each other, so markets in physical goods existed long before the appearance of capitalism. Sometimes these markets even included people, as for example, trading in wives and slaves. However, only with the emergence of capitalism has production been based on the transformation of free men and women into commodities in a market. For the purposes of a market, people are transformed into wage-laborers who "own" their labor-power. Labor is then treated as any market commodity: it must follow the dictates of supply and demand; and it is assigned or allocated to various employments on the basis of whichever buyer offers the highest wage bid.

(2) Private Property and the Legal Relations of Ownership

Property rules establish the rights of a particular person, the owner, with respect to property such as a physical object, a service, or a valuable claim (e.g., money). In general these rights grant to the owner the exclusive right to control the use of the object, enjoy the benefits from it, dispose of it, consume it, sell it, and so forth. For personal items (e.g., household items for personal use) these rules usually just reflect patterns of use: the "ownership" of beds among people in a family only identifies the way in which the beds will be used. However, *for social objects* (e.g., factories, schools, labor services, recreation areas, land in a commu-

---

[2]By "material goods and valuable services" (or the term "commodities" which we introduce below), we simply mean all those things produced for sale in a market.

[3]This definition of institutions as social processes should be contrasted with the popular use of the term. Sometimes people use "institution" to signify a group or collectivity of people. In this sense they speak of a "financial institution" (i.e., a bank), a "mental institution" (a mental hospital), an "educational institution" (a school), and so forth. In our use of the term, a bank, a hospital, or a school does not constitute an institution.

nity) *property rules also establish relations among people.* But no matter how social in character "private" property may be, the legal relations of ownership under capitalism still provide to the owner the legal right to control the property's use and disposition.

The legal relations of ownership entail as an inevitable consequence that people receive income only in return for selling something—that is, as the result of a market exchange.[4] Workers sell their labor-power for wages or salaries; the more highly the market values their labor-power, the higher their income. Capitalists—the owners of the physical means of production—derive income in the form of profits.[5] A capitalist's income (i.e., his profit) is simply the difference between the amount that his firm receives for selling its products and the amount it must pay out to hire labor, buy its required raw materials, and so forth. His profit depends on the ability of his firm to sell its goods for more than it cost the firm to produce these goods. The bigger the gap between labor and other input costs and the firm's sales revenues, then the bigger profits will be.

The vast majority of people own very little or no property, aside from personal property such as their own homes. In particular, they do not own *income-earning* property. Most of the income-earning property is owned by a few people. Since people can derive income only from a market exchange, most people can therefore earn income only by selling their labor services as workers in the market.

The income which people receive, that is, the price of the particular type of labor (skilled, blue-collar, managerial, etc.) which they have to sell, as well as the amount of profits which capitalists can make, is largely determined by supply-and-demand conditions. Hence the legal relations of ownership imply that the distribution of income is determined primarily on the basis of market criteria.

(3) Private Ownership and Control of the Means of Production

The factories, machines, and other instruments of production are privately owned by capitalists, and ownership is highly concentrated. Capitalists, by virtue of their private property rights to the means of production, possess the ultimate legal right to control production. The other side of private ownership and control of the means of production is that, as part of the wage bargain, the worker relinquishes control over the disposition of his labor during the stipulated workday; he also has no say in the disposition of the thing he produces, his product. Hence the worker is separated or "alienated" from control over both his work activities and his work product.

Vesting ownership and ultimate control of the society's economic apparatus in the hands of capitalists ensures that they will use that control in their own interests. Hence, decisions about what technology to use, what to produce, what to do with the goods that are produced, and so forth, will reflect their needs and interests. In particular, capitalist control takes two forms: (a) capitalists set the overall goals of the firm (profit-making) and the dominant capitalist ideology creates the cultural context within which people who control the day-by-day operation of the firm must operate; (b) capitalists determine the organizational framework within which people work in an enterprise. In particular, capitalists have instituted highly *hierarchical* work structures, establishing enterprises with many different layers and levels of employees, from production and clerical workers through "middle management" to the high-

---

[4]To the extent that people receive income from welfare agencies, criminal activities, gifts, etc., they do so outside the institutional context of capitalism. If large numbers of people received significant amounts of income in this manner, it would tend to undermine capitalist institutions.

[5]Rent and interest income, as a return to property, are a form of profits.

level managers and executives. They have organized production along these lines in order to maintain overall control of the large firm as well as to contribute to the efficiency of production. Hierarchy in production means that managers and executives, whether they own the means of production or not, control and direct the day-to-day activities of the workers. Thus the social relations of production take highly hierarchical forms under capitalism.

(4) Homo Economicus ("economic man")

In order for these economic institutions to work effectively, the people who participate in them must be motivated to act and respond in certain ways. The primary ideological assertion of capitalism is that the most important method of increasing an individual's happiness and welfare is by increasing how much money he has or earns. Despite occasional references to the "unhappy rich," the powerful dictum of which capitalism must convince its citizens is that "no matter how happy you are now, you would be even happier with more income." That is,

> ...the cultural system of corporate capitalism must, and does, induce the view that nearly any subjectively felt need can be met by some form of goods-and-services consumption. If your life is empty, earn more money and experience "the good life." If your body sags, get an exercise machine, or a television set and live through the bodies of others. If your sex life wanes, buy a ballsy new car, take a Hawaiian vacation, or buy new decorated sheets and pillowcases. If you feel you are nothing, at least you can live through your belongings.[6]

More specifically, capitalists by and large must wish to remain capitalists, strive to maximize profits, and perform their social

[6]Herb Gintis, "Activism and Counter-Culture" in Raymond Franklin (ed.), *Party and Class-State and Revolution* (forthcoming).

functions as production organizers. For example, capitalism would collapse if capitalists followed Christ's command: "If you would be perfect, go, sell what you possess and give to the poor" (Matthew, 19:21). Likewise, workers must respond to the system of individual-gain incentives; if they didn't pursue higher wages, or if they didn't accept the capitalist proposition that the way to greater happiness is more money, the system would not function.

It is important to note here that we are *not* saying that people are inevitably motivated by economic self-interest or the other characteristics of *homo economicus*. Nor are we saying that *homo economicus* is "rational" or "good." *Nor* are we saying that people in a capitalist society act only according to the dictates of *homo economicus*. Indeed, much of the rest of this book is devoted to describing the tension which results from the need of capitalist institutions to have people behave *as if* they were *homo economicus* when in reality they are not— when they feel many needs and have many aspects and are not the single-mindedly greedy, materialistic people posited by *homo economicus*.

We should also note here, however, that the limited options open to the individual within capitalist society are a mighty impetus toward behaving as *homo economicus*. While it may be true that "you can't buy everything," so much of social life in capitalist society has become subordinated to the market that you can buy *almost* everything. And living as a person who is free and integrated with his community, which is the alternative to acting as *homo economicus*, requires precisely what cannot be bought—a meaningful community, an unpolluted environment, an unalienated job.

These four basic institutions of capitalism operate so that the worker who sells labor-power in the market does not meet on equal terms with the capitalist employer. The wage bargain is not a free and voluntary exchange between equals. Since capital ownership is concentrated, a large number of people as workers confront a small number of potential employers. Although the worker does not have to sell his labor to any particular firm, nonetheless he is forced to sell it to some firm, as a simple necessity of survival. Capitalists enter the wage bargain only to increase profits, that is, to survive and enhance their privileges *as capitalists*. Since the capitalist as owner of the means of production also ultimately controls the work process, the wage bargain incorporates the surrender of the workers' control over the disposition of their labor services; that is, the wage bargain is the means by which the capitalist firm maintains control of the work process.

3.1   *The Role of Markets in Capitalist Society*

We now turn in more detail to an analysis of how capitalist institutions operate. In the following reading Karl Polanyi argues that capitalist institutions (he prefers the term "market economy") organize production by linking all of the elements of the production process—including man himself—together by means of markets. The work process, rather than being determined on the basis of tradition, force, or collective decision, gets determined according to profitability or market criteria. The market system is therefore fundamental to the capitalist mode of production.

An important characteristic of Polanyi's conclusions is that they are based on *anthropological* evidence. To an extent not adequately evident in this reading, Polanyi has drawn from his studies of other cultures his conclusions about the powerful influence of institutions in shaping behavior.[1] These studies demonstrate the great variety of both societies and patterns of human behavior; hence they go far toward disproving the often-heard assertion that the way people act in capitalist society (that is, *homo economicus*) is simply "human nature."

Polanyi notes that under capitalism the economic system begins to dominate the rest of society rather than being submerged in it. *Homo economicus* faces the market alone, deprived of the counteracting supportive traditions of community and kinship ties. The possibility of individual starvation amid group plenty replaces the previous assurance of an individual's "just" share of the community's collective material resources, even in the face of a threat of group starvation. Polanyi also notes the powerful transforming effect of the creation of a "market economy" on other social institutions and on society in general. This is a theme we shall pursue later.[2] The important point to note here is that as capitalist society develops, it becomes in-

---

[1]See Polanyi's essays in George Dalton, (Ed.), *Primitive, Archaic, and Modern Economies: Essays of Karl Polanyi* (New York: Doubleday & Co., 1968). See also Ernest Mandel, *Marxist Economic Theory* (New York: Monthly Review Press, 1968), Volume I, Chapters 1 and 2 for a wide-ranging review of anthropological studies.

[2]See, for example, Morton, Section 3.6, p. 119.

creasingly an *economic* society; that is, a greater portion of the society becomes determined by the market or measured in market terms.[3]

[3]Polanyi contrasts the "market system" with "mercantilism." Mercantilism is the
name for the economic philosophy that was dominant in Western European nations
during the period 1500-1800. The principal tenet of mercantilism was that the central government (in most cases a king) should intervene in the economy to help
manufacturers prosper, especially capitalists who exported their goods for sale
abroad. For example, the king might charter a monopoly (i.e., outlaw any competition), subsidize the cost of transporting goods, provide a bounty for every
article sold abroad, and so forth.

Source: Part I of the following is excerpted from Chapter 6 of *The Great
Transformation* by KARL POLANYI. Copyright © 1944 by Karl Polanyi.
Reprinted by permission of Holt, Rinehart and Winston, Inc. Part II is
excerpted from "Our Obsolete Market Mentality" by KARL POLANYI.
From *Primitive Archaic, and Modern Economies*, edited by George
Dalton. (Garden City, N.Y.: Anchor Books, Doubleday and Co., Inc.,
1968). Reprinted by permission of Marie Helen Polanyi.

I

. . .

A market economy is an economic system
controlled, regulated, and directed by markets alone; order in the production and
distribution of goods is entrusted to this self-
regulating mechanism. An economy of this
kind derives from the expectation that human beings behave in such a way as to
achieve maximum money gains. It assumes
markets in which the supply of goods (including services) available at a definite price
will equal the demand at that price. It assumes the presence of money, which functions as purchasing power in the hands of its
owners. Production will then be controlled
by prices, for the profits of those who direct
production will depend upon them; the distribution of the goods also will depend upon
prices, for prices form incomes, and it is
with the help of these incomes that the goods
produced are distributed amongst the members of society. Under these assumptions order in the production and distribution of
goods is ensured by prices alone.

Self-regulation implies that all production
is for sale on the market and that all incomes
derive from such sales. Accordingly, there
are markets for all elements of industry, not
only for goods (always including services)
but also for labor, land, and money, their
prices being called respectively commodity
prices, wages, rent, and interest. The very
terms indicate that prices form incomes: interest is the price for the use of money and
forms the income of those who are in the
position to provide it; rent is the price for
the use of land and forms the income of
those who supply it; wages are the price for
the use of labor power, and form the income
of those who sell it; commodity prices, finally, contribute to the incomes of those who
sell their entrepreneurial services, the income
called profit being actually the difference between two sets of prices, the price of the
goods produced and their costs, i.e., the price
of the goods necessary to produce them. If
these conditions are fulfilled, all incomes will
derive from sales on the market, and incomes
will be just sufficient to buy all the goods
produced.

. . .

To realize fully what this means, let us
return for a moment to the mercantile system and the national markets which it did
so much to develop. Under feudalism and the

guild system, land and labor formed part of the social organization itself. . . . Land, the pivotal element in the feudal order, was the basis of the military, judicial, administrative, and political system; its status and function were determined by legal and customary rules. Whether its possession was transferable or not, and if so, to whom and under what restrictions; what the rights of property entailed; to what uses some types of land might be put—all these questions were removed from the organization of buying and selling, and subjected to an entirely different set of institutional regulations.

The same was true of the organization of labor. Under the guild system, as under every other economic system in previous history, the motives and circumstances of productive activities were embedded in the general organization of society. The relations of master, journeyman, and apprentice; the terms of the craft; the number of apprentices; the wages of the workers were all regulated by the custom and rule of the guild and the town. What the mercantile system did was merely to unify these conditions either through statute as in England, or through the "nationalization" of the guilds as in France. As to land, its feudal status was abolished only insofar as it was linked with provincial privileges; for the rest, land remained *extra commercium*, in England as in France. . . .

Mercantilism, with all its tendency toward commercialization, never attacked the safeguards that protected these two basic elements of production—labor and land—from becoming the objects of commerce. . . .

That mercantilism, however emphatically it insisted on commercialization as a national policy, thought of markets in a way exactly contrary to market economy, is best shown by its vast extension of state intervention in industry. On this point there was no difference between mercantilists and feudalists, between crowned planners and vested interests, between centralizing bureaucrats and conservative particularists. They disagreed only on the methods of regulation: guilds, towns, and provinces appealed to the force of custom and tradition, while the new state authority favored statute and ordinance. But they were all equally averse to the idea of commercializing labor and land—the precondition of market economy. . . .

Not before the last decade of the eighteenth century was, in either country, the establishment of a free labor market even discussed; and the idea of the self-regulation of economic life was utterly beyond the horizon of the age. . . .

A self-regulating market demands nothing less than the institutional separation of society into an economic and political sphere. Such a dichotomy is, in effect, merely the restatement, from the point of view of society as a whole, of the existence of a self-regulating market. It might be argued that the separateness of the two spheres obtains in every type of society at all times. Such an inference, however, would be based on a fallacy. True, no society can exist without a system of some kind that ensures order in the production and distribution of goods. But that does not imply the existence of separate economic institutions; normally, the economic order is merely a function of the social, in which it is contained. Neither under tribal, nor feudal, nor mercantile conditions was there, as we have shown, a separate economic system in society. Nineteenth-century society, in which economic activity was isolated and imputed to a distinctive economic motive, was indeed, a singular departure.

Such an institutional pattern could not function unless society was somehow subordinated to its requirements. A market economy can exist only in a market society. We reached this conclusion on general grounds in our analysis of the market pattern. We can now specify the reasons for this assertion. A market economy must comprise all elements of industry, including labor, land,

and money. (In a market economy the last also is an essential element of industrial life and its inclusion in the market mechanism has, as we will see, far-reaching institutional consequences.) But labor and land are no other than the human beings themselves of which every society consists and the natural surroundings in which it exists. To include them in the market mechanism means to subordinate the substance of society itself to the laws of the market.

We are now in the position to develop in a more concrete form the institutional nature of a market economy, and the perils to society which it involves. We will, first, describe the methods by which the market mechanism is enabled to control and direct the actual elements of industrial life; second, we will try to gauge the nature of the effects of such a mechanism on the society that is subjected to its action.

It is with the help of the commodity concept that the mechanism of the market is geared to the various elements of industrial life. *Commodities are here empirically defined as objects produced for sale on the market*; markets, again, are empirically defined as actual contacts between buyers and sellers. Accordingly, every element of industry is regarded as having been produced for sale, as then and then only will it be subject to the supply-and-demand mechanism interacting with price. In practice this means that there must be markets for every element of industry; that in these markets each of these elements is organized into a supply and a demand group; and that each element has a price, which interacts with demand and supply. These markets—and they are numberless—are interconnected and form One Big Market.

The crucial point is this: labor, land, and money are essential elements of industry; they also must be organized in markets; in fact, these markets form an absolutely vital part of the economic system. But labor, land,

and money are obviously *not* commodities; the postulate that anything that is bought and sold must have been produced for sale is emphatically untrue in regard to them. In other words, according to the empirical definition of a commodity they are not commodities. Labor is only another name for a human activity that goes with life itself, which in its turn is not produced for sale but for entirely different reasons, nor can that activity be detached from the rest of life, be stored or mobilized; land is only another name for nature, which is not produced by man; actual money, finally, is merely a token of purchasing power which, as a rule, is not produced at all, but comes into being through the mechanism of banking or state finance. None of them is produced for sale. The commodity description of labor, land, and money is entirely fictitious.

Nevertheless, it is with the help of this fiction that the actual markets for labor, land, and money are organized; they are being actually bought and sold on the market; their demand and supply are real magnitudes; and any measures or policies that would inhibit the formation of such markets would *ipso facto* endanger the self-regulation of the system. The commodity fiction, therefore, supplies a vital organizing principle in regard to the whole of society affecting almost all its institutions in the most varied way, namely, the principle according to which no arrangement or behavior should be allowed to exist that might prevent the actual functioning of the market mechanism on the lines of the commodity fiction.

Now, in regard to labor, land, and money such a postulate cannot be upheld. To allow the market mechanism to be sole director of the fate of human beings and their natural environment, indeed, even of the amount and use of purchasing power, would result in the demolition of society. For the alleged commodity "labor power" cannot be shoved about, used indiscriminately, or even left unused, without affecting also the human individual who happens to be the bearer of this peculiar commodity. In disposing of a man's labor power the system would, incidentally, dispose of the physical, psychological, and moral entity "man" attached to that tag. Robbed of the protective covering of cultural institutions, human beings would perish from the effects of social exposure; they would die as the victims of acute social dislocation through vice, perversion, crime, and starvation. Nature would be reduced to its elements, neighborhoods and landscapes defiled, rivers polluted, military safety jeopardized, the power to produce food and raw materials destroyed.

.   .   .

II

. . . By buying and selling labor and land freely, the mechanism of the market was made to apply to them. There was now supply of labor, and demand for it; there was supply of land, and demand for it. Accordingly, there was a market price for the use of labor power, called wages, and a market price for the use of land, called rent. Labor and land were provided with markets of their own, similar to the commodities proper that were produced with their help. The true scope of such a step can be gauged if we remember that labor is only another name for man, and land for nature. The commodity fiction handed over the fate of man and nature to the play of an automaton running in its own grooves and governed by its own laws.

.   .   .

Market economy thus created a new type of society. The economic or productive system was here entrusted to a self-acting device. An institutional mechanism controlled human beings in their everyday activities as well as the resources of nature. This instrument of material welfare was under the sole control of the incentives of hunger and gain

—or, more precisely, fear of going without the necessities of life, and expectation of profit. So long as no propertyless person could satisfy his craving for food without first selling his labor in the market, and so long as no propertied person was prevented from buying in the cheapest market and selling in the dearest, the blind mill would turn out ever-increasing amounts of commodities for the benefit of the human race. Fear of starvation with the worker, lure of profit with the employer, would keep the vast establishment running.

In this way an "economic sphere" came into existence that was sharply delimited from other institutions in society. Since no human aggregation can survive without a functioning productive apparatus, its embodiment in a distinct and separate sphere had the effect of making the "rest" of society dependent upon that sphere. This autonomous zone, again, was regulated by a mechanism that controlled its functioning. As a result, the market mechanism became determinative for the life of the body social. No wonder that the emergent human aggregation was an "economic" society to a degree previously never even approximated. "Economic motives" reigned supreme in a world of their own, and the individual was made to act on them under pain of being trodden under foot by the juggernaut market. Such a forced conversion to a utilitarian outlook fatefully warped Western man's understanding of himself.

This new world of "economic motives" was based on a fallacy. Intrinsically, hunger and gain are no more "economic" than love or hate, pride or prejudice. No human motive is per se economic. There is no such thing as a *sui generis* economic experience in the sense in which man may have a religious, aesthetic, or sexual experience. These latter give rise to motives that broadly aim at evoking similar experiences. In regard to material production these terms lack self-evident meaning.

The economic factor, which underlies all social life, no more gives rise to definite incentives than the equally universal law of gravitation. Assuredly, if we do not eat, we must perish, as much as if we were crushed under the weight of a falling rock. But the pangs of hunger are not automatically translated into an incentive to produce. Production is not an individual, but a collective affair. If an individual is hungry, there is nothing definite for him to do. Made desperate, he might rob or steal, but such an action can hardly be called productive. With man, the political animal, everything is given not by natural, but by social circumstance. What made the nineteenth century think of hunger and gain as "economic" was simply the organization of production under a market economy. . . .

Aristotle was right: man is not an economic, but a social being. He does not aim at safeguarding his individual interest in the acquisition of material possessions, but rather at ensuring social good will, social status, social assets. He values possessions primarily as a means to that end. His incentives are of that "mixed" character which we associate with the endeavor to gain social approval— productive efforts are no more than incidental to this. *Man's economy is, as a rule, submerged in his social relations*. The change from this to a society which was, on the contrary, submerged in the economic system was an entirely novel development.

.   .   .

At no time prior to the second quarter of the nineteenth century were markets more than a subordinate feature in society. . . .

Markets through which otherwise self-sufficient householders get rid of their surplus neither direct production nor provide the producer with his income. This is only the case in a market economy where *all* incomes derive from sales, and commodities are obtainable exclusively by purchase.

.   .   .

The market mechanism, moreover, created the delusion of economic determinism as a general law for all human society. Under a market economy, of course, this law holds good. Indeed, the working of the economic system here not only "influences" the rest of society, but determines it—as in a triangle the sides not merely influence, but determine, the angles. Take the stratification of classes. Supply and demand in the labor market were *identical* with the classes of workers and employers, respectively. The social classes of capitalists, landowners, tenants, brokers, merchants, professionals, and so on, were delimited by the respective markets for land, money, and capital and their uses, or for various services. The income of these social classes was fixed by the market, their rank and position by their income. This was a complete reversal of the secular practice. In Maine's famous phrase, "contractus" replaced "status"; or, as Tönnies preferred to put it, "society" superseded "community"; or, in terms of the present article, *instead of the economic system being embedded in social relationships, these relationships were now embedded in the economic system.*

While social classes were directly, other institutions were indirectly determined by the market mechanism. State and government, marriage and the rearing of children, the organization of science and education, of religion and the arts, the choice of profession, the forms of habitation, the shape of settlements, the very aesthetics of private life— everything had to comply with the utilitarian pattern, or at least not interfere with the working of the market mechanism. But since very few human activities can be carried on in the void, even a saint needing his pillar, the indirect effect of the market system came very near to determining the whole of society. It was almost impossible to avoid the erroneous conclusion that as "economic" man was "real" man, so the economic system was "really" society.

.   .   .

3.2   *The Logic of Capitalist Expansion*

Polanyi's "market economy," or more precisely, the capitalist mode of
production, has grown to be a powerful mechanism for developing production. Ever greater quantities of individual consumption goods reach
the market, and continued prosperity requires that they be sold.[1] The
following essay by Richard C. Edwards shows how the capitalist institutions outlined in the introduction to this chapter necessarily generate a
continually expanding output.

The pressure created by the necessity to find markets for expanded production constitutes one of the most fundamental characteristics of capitalism. As Edwards explains, competition induces capitalists to expand sales
and production of goods in order to realize profits. Greater output leads to
expanded profits and capital accumulation (that is to investment in more
factories, larger machines, etc.), but in order to realize profits on the
newly accumulated capital, even greater sales of output are required. The
pressure to find new buyers for these goods leads to exaggerated advertising campaigns stressing personal consumption, and indeed the creation of
a whole commodity fetishist culture; it leads to militarism as a means of
justifying immense arms sales; and it leads to imperialism, as capitalists
attempt to find new markets abroad. When these goods are sold, new
profits are realized and the whole cycle is repeated.

Thus it is not merely an individual capitalist's greed for profits that is
important. Instead, the inexorable pressure for greater profits and expanded
sales is created by the entire economic *system*, by the capitalist mode of
production. And it is this system-produced, never-ending, increasingly intensified pressure for profits that drives capitalist society.

Several qualifications must be kept in mind in this discussion of the
"productivity" of capitalism. First, the growth process described below
does not apply to those capitalist countries which constitute the underdeveloped part of the worldwide capitalist system.[2] Second, everything
produced for the market is counted as "productive" economic output,
whether or not it increases the "standard of living"—nuclear weapons,
moon rockets, and TV commercials are included, to name a few. Many
aspects of society important to the quality of life are excluded—wisdom,
community, justice, the opportunity for friendship. Further, the benefits
from increased production have been very unequally distributed. Finally,
measures of economic output do not take account of the widespread pollution and ecological damage resulting from production. So the pressures
to produce more marketable output often lead to *socially* irrational production priorities: building supersonic jets (which sell) while real malnutrition (which has no potential for profit) exists in many American homes;
producing 50 million cars and 40,000 miles of interstate highways, but
no mass transit; urban sprawl around decayed inner cities; and so forth.

[1]Rates of economic growth for several capitalist countries are given in Table 9.A,
p. 365.
[2]See Weisskopf, Section 10.5, p. 442.

Hence while greater quantity of production *may* contribute to a generally higher "standard of living," it by no means necessarily does so.[3]

[3]See Chapter 9.

Source: The following essay was written by RICHARD C. EDWARDS for this book. Copyright © 1972 by Richard C. Edwards.

The capitalist period as an historical epoch has been characterized by a rapid expansion of production in the advanced countries.[1] The material productiveness of advanced capitalist societies was noted by Marx and Engels, writing in 1848:[2]

> The bourgeoisie, during its rule of scarce one hundred years, has created more massive and more colossal productive forces than have all preceding generations together. Subjection of nature's forces to man, machinery, application of chemistry to industry and agriculture, steam navigation, railways, electric telegraphs, clearing of whole populations conjured out of the ground—what earlier century had even a presentiment that such productive forces slumbered in the lap of social labor?

If the statement seemed true in 1848, how much truer it appears from the affluent perspective of another hundred years.

The purpose of this essay is to show how the basic capitalist institutions described at the beginning of this chapter have fostered such a tremendous expansion of economic capacity. How has capitalism led to the development of what Marx and Engels called "colossal productive forces"?

The argument presented below is divided into two parts. The first section deals with those motivations and pressures which induce capitalists to strive to expand output; we note both "internal" motivations (the capitalist's

[1]Note that we are talking only about the *advanced* countries; the *failure* to generate such growth in the outlying areas is one of the aspects of this growth in advanced countries.

[2]The quote is from *The Communist Manifesto*, excerpted in Section 2.5, p. 66.

own desire to accumulate) and "market pressures" (the necessity for the capitalist to maintain a competitive market position). The second section outlines the way in which workers enter the production process under capitalism, leading to the market allocation of labor resources according to profit criteria.

THE CAPITALIST AS OWNER

The capitalist mode of production is historically unique in that it concentrates the means of production in the hands of a few people —capitalists—whose *only* role in the society is to make profits; they stand to gain personally, directly, and in large measure from the expansion of profits. Their interest in production, then, is not in the social merit or intrinsic value of what they produce, but only in their product's potential profitability.

This social justification places the capitalist in contrast to the feudal lord, the ancient slave-owner, or the eastern potentate, all of whom controlled the production process as firmly as the capitalist does today. However, these earlier dominant classes rested their ideological superiority and their right to rule on claims other than economic prowess. Some classes had religious claims (the Hebrew priests, the medieval church, "divinely" appointed kings); others had military claims (medieval lords, Roman emperors, Indian war chiefs); still others had political, cultural, or other claims. Only the capitalist class bases its claim to dominance and privilege directly on its ability to make profits by selling goods on the market.

Hence it is understandable that previous dominant classes should have had less interest in expanding production, and that the capitalist class, whose single rationale is making and accumulating profits, should have been the historical agent for creating growth in material production.

The fundamental characteristic of capitalist production is that it is organized, controlled, and motivated by capitalists and their firms to make profits. The capitalist firm *realizes* profits only by producing goods and selling them on the market. Firms therefore attempt to sell as much as possible at as high a price as possible. The motivation to capture profits leads the capitalist firm to produce huge quantities of goods for sale on the market if it thinks it can sell them.

The question, then, is what motivates the capitalist to strive so diligently to make and accumulate profits? First, of course, the profits which are generated in a firm *belong* to the owner-capitalist. So undoubtedly the primary motivation is simply the *personal* one: the capitalist, by increasing profits, increases his own wealth and ability to consume, expands his own power and sphere of control, and enhances his own privileges and status. In capitalist society, power and status are gained primarily through one's control over commodities, especially ownership of wealth; so the incentive to accumulate is correspondingly stronger. Furthermore, these attributes are measured *relative* to other people's situations, so the desire to expand profits (and hence increase one's wealth, power and status) continues indefinitely.

Second, we have already noted the ideological basis for capitalists' need to maximize profits. The social rationale for putting capitalists in charge (rather than, say, running firms democratically or letting communities operate local firms) is that capitalists *own* as private property the means of production, and therefore they have the *right* to determine its use.

But the efficacy of this claim for *private* control of what is after all the *social* means

of production, while it rests in the first instance on the inviolability of private property, ultimately reflects a deeper ideological assertion: that the whole society benefits by granting capitalists the right to control production. Everyone benefits, the argument goes, because property-owning capitalists organize society's production efficiently. The magnitude of his profits provides the evidence demonstrating the capitalist's social usefulness; for he realizes profits only to the extent that he efficiently produces what people want and need. This reasoning thus transforms the capitalist's act of making profits for himself into a socially essential and useful act. The *raison d'être* of the capitalist is his ability to expand production for the good of all. This ideological justification reinforces the capitalists' personal stake in expanding profits.

Capitalists' personal and ideological interest in expanding profits would by itself lead us to expect a powerful dynamic within capitalism for expansion of output. But they are driven to expand profits not only because they *want* to, but also because if they are to remain capitalists, the market *forces* them to do so. Capitalists do not operate independently; they sell goods in a market and buy labor and raw materials in other markets and must therefore face the constraints of supply and demand and market competition.

The choice of technology, the need to expand production, and the organization of the work process are determined primarily by the structure of the market system, and only in small part by the particular characteristics of individual capitalists. A particularly greedy or insensitive capitalist may exacerbate the oppressive conditions of the workplace, for example, but he cannot alter the basic situation. Neither can a particularly kind and humane capitalist change matters. *Capitalists act as capitalists because, if they are to survive as capitalists, the market forces them to act that way.* For example, suppose a certain capitalist decided on his own to pay higher wages, not to introduce oppressive kinds of new technology, and to distribute the product to the community at a lower price. He would be successful for a while, making smaller profits than other capitalists, but nonetheless remaining in business.

But sooner or later other capitalists would enter the scene. They would realize that they could make higher profits if they simply paid the market wage rate, not the higher rate that our "humane" capitalist voluntarily decided to pay. They would also realize that they could make higher profits if they were unafraid to introduce more efficient technology, which our "humane capitalist" refused to do because of the alienating characteristics of that technology. Finally, with the savings gained by paying lower wages and using more efficient technology, these new capitalists would realize that they could reduce the price even a bit further than the humane capitalist did, and still make profits. By doing so, they would underprice the "humane capitalist's" profits and drive his goods from the market.

Since he can no longer sell his products, the "humane capitalist" is now faced with a dilemma: either emulate the other capitalists, reduce wages, and introduce the new technology—in short, act as a "nonhumane" capitalist—or quit being a capitalist altogether. The conclusion is that no matter how much he might wish to act differently, if he is to remain a capitalist, he must act within the constraints set by competition in the market.[3] Marx described this process as follows:[4]

[3]Notice that only certain decisions are made by the market and that there is tremendous scope left in capitalists' hands for control of work. The capitalist decides what products to produce, who shall work for him, where and at what hours work shall be performed, when new factories shall be built, what the authority relations among the workers shall be, and so forth. The market merely places *constraints* on his options, requiring him, for example, to pay the market wage, to avoid inefficient technologies, to ignore ecological damage, etc. For an excellent historical discussion, see S. A. Marglin, "What Do Bosses Do? The Origins and Function of Hierarchy in Capitalist Production" (Harvard University, 1971, Mimeo).

[4]Karl Marx, *Wage Labour and Capital.*

The method of production and the means of production are constantly enlarged, revolutionized, division of labor necessarily draws after it greater division of labor, the employment of machinery greater employment of machinery, work upon a large scale work upon a still greater scale. This is the law that continually throws capitalist production out of its old ruts and compels capital to strain ever more the productive forces of labor for the very reason that it has already strained them—the law that grants it no respite, and constantly shouts in its ear, March! March! ...

No matter how powerful the means of production which a capitalist may bring into the field, competition will make their adoption general; and from the moment that they have been generally adopted; the sole result of the greater productiveness of his capital will be that he must furnish at the same price, ten, twenty, one hundred times as much as before. But since he must find a market for, perhaps, a thousand times as much, in order to outweigh the lower selling price by the greater quantity of the sales; since now a more extensive sale is necessary not only to gain a greater profit, but also in order to replace the cost of production (the instrument of production itself grows always more costly, as we have seen), and since this more extensive sale has become a question of life and death not only for him, but also for his rivals, the old struggle must begin again, and it is all the more violent the more powerful the means of production already invented are. The division of labor and the application of machinery will therefore take a fresh start, and upon an even greater scale.

Whatever be the power of the means of production which are employed, competition seeks to rob capital of the golden fruits of this power by reducing the price of commodities to the cost of production; in the same measure in which production is cheapened, i.e., in the same measure in which more can be produced with the same amount of labor, it compels by a law which is irresistible a still greater cheapening of production, the sale of ever greater masses of product for smaller prices. Thus the capitalist will have gained nothing more by his efforts than the obligation to furnish a greater product in the same labor time; in a word, more difficult conditions for the profitable employment of his capital. While competition, therefore, constantly pursues him with its law of the cost of production and turns against himself every weapon that he forges against his rivals, the capitalist continually seeks to get the best of competition by restlessly introducing further subdivision of labor and new machines, which, though more expensive, enable him to produce more cheaply, instead of waiting until the new machines shall have been rendered obsolete by competition.

If we now conceive this feverish agitation as it operates in the market of the whole world, *we shall be in a position to comprehend how the growth, accumulation, and concentration of capital bring in their train an ever more detailed subdivision of labor, an ever greater improvement of old machines, and a constant application of new machines—a process which goes on uninterruptedly, with feverish haste, and upon an ever more gigantic scale.*

Thus, not only does the capitalist firm *want* to expand production and profits, it is *forced* to expand production and cut costs to *retain* profits. The firm cannot stand still. It must push on.

This pressure to keep up with the market and to maintain one's competitive position also induces firms to seek new products, entirely new markets, and new technologies. Often this search for new sources of profits is carried on within the domestic economy as new products are promoted by advertising, or old markets are entered by new firms. But since the motivation is simply realization of profits, capitalist firms have increasingly turned to the cultivation of foreign markets. So a powerful tendency towards geographic expansion and extension of market control on an international scale has likewise characterized capitalism.[5]

This dynamic competition, in addition to the more routine price competition Marx described, poses both opportunities and constant threats to all firms. According to Schumpeter:[6]

[5]See MacEwan, Section 10.1, p. 409.
[6]Joseph Schumpeter, *Capitalism, Socialism and Democracy* (New York: Harper & Row Publishers, Inc., 1950), pp. 82-85.

The essential point to grasp is that in dealing with capitalism we are dealing with an evolutionary process. . . . Capitalism is by nature a form or method of economic change and not only never is, but never can be stationary. And this evolutionary character of the capitalist process is not merely due to the fact that economic life goes on in a social and natural environment which changes and by its change alters the data of economic action; this fact is important and these changes (wars, revolutions, and so on) often condition industrial changes, but they are not its prime movers. Nor is this evolutionary character due to a quasi-automatic increase in population and capital or to the vagaries of monetary systems of which exactly the same thing holds true. The fundamental impulse that sets and keeps the capitalist engine in motion comes from the new consumer goods, the new methods of production or transportation, the new markets, the new forms of industrial organization that capitalist enterprise creates. . . . In capitalist reality as distinguished from its textbook picture, it is not price competition or a small cost advantage which counts but the competition from the new commodity, the new technology, the new source of supply, the new type of organization (the largest-scale unit of control for instance)—competition which commands a decisive cost or quality advantage and which strikes not at the margins of the profits and the outputs of the existing firms but at their foundations and their very lives.

It is hardly necessary to point out that competition of the kind we now have in mind acts not only when in being but also when it is merely an ever-present threat. It disciplines before it attacks. The businessman feels himself to be in a competitive situation even if he is alone in his field or if, though not alone, he holds a position such that investigating government experts fail to see any effective competition between him and any other firms in the same or a neighboring field and in consequence conclude that his talk, under examination, about his competitive sorrows is all make-believe. In many cases, though not in all, this will in the long run enforce behavior very similar to the perfectly competitive pattern.

Most industries have become so concentrated that one or a few firms dominate the entire national industry. In the United States a few firms in each industry account for most of the market in automobile, steel, food processing, computers, oil, drugs, aviation, chemicals, and most other goods. In these industries collusion and price agreements among the large firms have largely eliminated price competition.

But even the largest firms do not escape the market pressure for reducing costs, introducing more productive technologies, expanding one's market, increasing profits, and repeating the whole cycle. Large firms face *international* competition from similarly large firms in other advanced countries. Likewise *nonprice* competition continues in both domestic and foreign markets. Baran and Sweezy describe the situation well:[7]

The abandonment of price competition in monopolistic industries does not mean the end of all competition: it takes new forms and rages on with ever increasing intensity. Most of these new forms of competition come under the heading of what we call the sales effort. . . . Here we confine attention to those forms of competition which have a direct bearing on costs of production and hence on the magnitude of the surplus.

There are, it seems to us, two aspects of non-price competition which are of decisive importance here. The first has to do with what may be called the dynamics of market sharing. The second has to do with the particular form which the sales effort assumes in the producer goods industries. . . .

To begin with, the firm with lower costs and higher profits enjoys a variety of advantages over higher-cost rivals in the struggle for market shares. (This fact seems to have been largely overlooked by economists, but it is perfectly clear to businessmen.) The firm with the lowest costs holds the whip hand; it can afford to be aggressive even to the point of threatening, and in the limiting case precipitating, a price war. It can get away with tactics (special discounts, favorable credit terms, etc.) which if adopted by a weak firm would provoke retaliation.

[7]Paul Baran and Paul Sweezy, *Monopoly Capital*, (New York: Monthly Review Press, 1966) pp. 67-70.

It can afford the advertising, research, development of new product varieties, extra services, and so on, which are the usual means of fighting for market shares and which tend to yield results in proportion to the amounts spent on them. Other less tangible factors are involved which tend to elude the economist's net but which play an important part in the business world. The lower-cost, higher-profit company acquires a special reputation which enables it to attract and hold customers, bid promising executive personnel away from rival firms, and recruit the ablest graduates of engineering and business schools. For all these reasons, there is a strong incentive for the large corporation in an oligopolistic industry not only to seek continuously to cut its costs but to do so faster than its rivals. . . .

There is an additional reason, in our judgement as important as it is neglected, why a tendency for costs of production to fall is endemic to the entire monopoly capitalistic economy, including those areas which if left to themselves would stagnate technologically. It stems from the exigencies of non-price competition in the producer goods industries. Here, as in industries producing consumer goods, sellers must be forever seeking to put something new on the market. But they are not dealing with buyers whose primary interest is the latest fashion or keeping up with the Joneses. They are dealing with sophisticated buyers whose concern is to increase profits. Hence the new products offered to the prospective buyers must be designed to help them increase their profits, which in general means to help them reduce their costs. If the manufacturer can convince his customers that his new instrument or material or machine will save them money, the sale will follow almost automatically.

As we noted earlier, the firm only *realizes* profits by *selling* its products in a market. So the drive for greater profits leads inevitably to the drive to expand marketed output. In many industries, especially the more monopolistic ones, unlimited expansion of sales (and profits) may be ruled out, because demand has been satisfied as much as the profit criterion allows. However, if sales cannot be expanded, profits can nonetheless be increased by reducing costs; that is, by reducing the amount of labor and other inputs which the firm must buy. The resources released by reducing inputs are then available for production elsewhere. Likewise, if output cannot be profitably expanded in one's own market, this simply increases the incentive for the firm to enter new markets—either markets in different goods or geographically new markets. In either event, the result is the same: expanding profits directly or indirectly require and hence lead to the expansion of production.[8]

But output (and hence profits) are expanded only by reinvesting previous profits to make more profits. To this end, the firm will attempt to expand its factory or build a new one, buy new and better machines, or do whatever it thinks best to increase output, capture a price advantage from its competitors, develop new markets, or invade new industries—all in the pursuit of turning its previously earned profits into more profits.

Now of course the capitalist firm will reinvest its profits only if it expects to get in return not only the amount reinvested but also a dividend, the interest on the capital, or put simply, more profits than it invested. Otherwise, there would be no reason for it to invest—it could as well put the money in a safe mattress.

Hence there is an ever-expanding volume of profits seeking opportunities for reinvestment. Every time profits are created, they must be reinvested. And reinvestment means precisely creating more output, reducing

costs (thus freeing resources for employment elsewhere), and expanding profits. Then the cycle is repeated. This expanding volume of profits therefore impels the firm to look for new markets, search for new products to be produced, and create more output to sell.[9]

This process ensures that production will become increasingly efficient or market-rationalized; i.e., the capitalists will produce whatever brings the highest market value using resources for which the capitalist had to pay the least. Hence a new technology is introduced, people are thrown out of work, transferred, etc. when the savings of inputs from the new method promises higher profits.

Both "internal" motivations and competitive market pressures drive the capitalist toward more profits. Capitalists therefore have the *motivation* to expand profits. With ownership and legal control of the means of production, they have the *power* required to institute and carry out this drive for expanded profits. Finally, their accumulated profits, their control over the social surplus, provides them with the material *resources* needed to expand production. *The capitalist has therefore gathered into his own hands all of the elements required for him, in his social role as production organizer, to structure and restructure the workplace to suit his drive for profits.*

THE WORKER AS ALIENATED LABOR

The market in labor is an important link in this process of market-rationalizing production. The wage contract is viewed as a voluntary exchange of labor services for wages. The capitalist is then free to hire, fire, and reemploy workers at will and without regard for the social consequences. In medieval

---

[8]In industries where only a few firms dominate the market, the prices are presumably set by an agreement among the firms at the level which they think will yield the greatest profits. Further expansion of sales would require reduction of the artificially high monopoly price, and if the price decline was large enough, would reduce profits. It is sometimes claimed that since in this case firms *restrict* output, the existence of monopoly refutes the tendency described in the text for capitalism to generate ever-greater output. But it should be clear that while output may be restricted in particular industries, the continuing incentive to reduce costs simply requires the expansion mechanism to operate indirectly and does not change the result.

[9]This expansion of profits particularly occurs when governmental policy is able to avert depressions, since in this case the capitalist firm can sell its products and thereby translate its output *capacity* into profit *realization*. See Weisskopf, Section 9.1, p. 364.

society, production was carried out with the workforce on the manor. The entire workforce—serfs, artisans, bailiffs, and lord—all shared the vicissitudes of the crops. They shared unequally, of course, the lord getting many times the portion due the serf. Yet no one was fired in bad times; each person had a claim to his "just" part of the product, and everyone had a right to participate in the tradition-determined organization of work.

In a labor market, however, the capitalist firm makes its decisions about whom to hire and how many to hire strictly on the basis of profitability. Labor is treated as a commodity like any other raw material required for production. The capitalist firm is not tied to its workers by traditional obligations, as the feudal lord was to his serf. The capitalist need not consider workers' lives or rights when choosing a work force.[10] Hence the allocation of people among various jobs is determined by the market criterion of profitability. Each worker, as the commodity "labor," is assigned to that job where he has the highest productivity, for that employment will produce the greatest profit for the capitalist.

The size of the wage which a capitalist is willing to pay depends on how valuable a worker is to the firm—or more precisely, how much his work adds to the profits of the firm. For example, a skilled worker is more valuable than an unskilled worker. Consequently, when a skilled worker enters the labor market, capitalist firms will compete to hire him and will be willing to pay a higher wage.

Capitalists will bid against each other for workers, and will quit bidding when they perceive that the wage they pay the worker would be greater than the additional profits realized from his being hired. The winner in the bidding will be that capitalist who has

organized production in the most profitable manner, hence who can offer the most "productive" (i.e., profitable) employment. Labor therefore tends to be "efficiently" allocated among various uses.

The individual worker is given tremendous incentive to obtain those skills which make him valuable to the production process. Most people own no wealth assets which could provide a large enough income to support them without working. Consequently, for survival, they must sell their labor power in the market. Since a worker's labor power will be more highly valued in the market if he has productive skills, the incentive is created for him to obtain those skills. The worker goes to school, learns vocational skills, learns to be a "respectful" and disciplined worker, and so forth, in the hopes that he can earn a higher wage.

The market allocation of labor thus directly reinforces the tendency towards expansion of output under capitalism. Greater production occurs because workers are assigned to their most productive employments and because workers themselves strive to become more productive to gain higher wages.

The major theme of this essay is perhaps best restated by Baran and Sweezy:[11]

We have come a long way since the historical dawn of capitalist production and even since Karl Marx wrote Das Capital. *Nowadays the avaricious capitalist, grasping for every penny and anxiously watching over his growing fortune, seems like a stereotype out of a nineteenth-century novel. The company man of today has a different attitude. To be sure, he likes to make as much money as he can, but he spends it freely, and the retirement benefits and other perquisites which he gets from his company enable him to take a rather casual attitude towards his personal savings. Noting the contrast between the modern businessman and his earlier counterpart, one might jump to the conclusion that the old drive has*

[10]See the description of the first "mass firing," i.e., the expulsion of the peasants from their land, in Marx, Section 2.4, p. 61.

[11]Baran and Sweezy, *Monopoly Capital*, pp. 43-44.

gone out of the system, that the classical picture of capitalism restlessly propelled forward by the engine of accumulation is simply inappropriate to the conditions of today.

This is a superficial view. The real capitalist today is not the individual businessman but the corporation. What the businessman does in his private life, his attitude toward the getting and spending of his personal income—these are essentially irrelevant to the functioning of the system. What

counts is what he does in his company life and his attitude toward the getting and spending of the company's income. And here there can be no doubt that the making and accumulating of profits hold as dominant a position today as they ever did. Over the portals of the magnificent office building of today, as on the wall of the modest counting house of a century or two ago, it would be equally appropriate to find engraved the motto: "Accumulate! Accumulate! That is Moses and the Prophets!"

3.3   *Alienated Labor*

So far in this chapter we have provided a preliminary view of the operation of basic capitalist institutions. We now return in more depth to private property and its crucial defining role in the fundamental social relationship of capitalism, the relation between worker and capitalist.

As Karl Marx argues in the following classic essay, the worker produces the product but the capitalist owns it. This estrangement or alienation of labor from its product is fundamental to capitalism, because "*private property* is . . . the product, the necessary result of *alienated labor*. . . ."

Since the capitalist takes charge of work, the capitalist mode of production requires that the workers surrender control over their work activities; that is, workers are excluded from decisions about what product should be produced, how it should be produced, or how it should be used once it is produced. Compliance in this exclusion (or "alienation") from control is part of the wage bargain, in which the individual worker exchanges control over his own work activities for a wage.

These decisions are instead made by capitalists and high-level managers, within the constraints of the market.[1] Decisions are taken according to the owners' interests, that is, to realize profits. Capitalists choose the most profitable product to produce, the most profitable way (technology) to produce that product, and the most profitable market to sell that product to. Work itself is organized to make a profit (exchange value) for the firm rather than directly to satisfy people's needs (use value).

The alienation of workers from control of the work process has consequences both for the individual worker and for the society as a whole. Individual workers face the consequences of capitalist organization every

[1]The ability of unions to set certain limits on the capitalists' control (e.g., by work rules, grievance procedures, etc.) is only a minor qualification to this statement. Union demands are generally *defensive maneuvers*, seeking to alleviate the very worst aspects of capitalist control. On the question of introducing technology, for example, unions at best can delay implementation of obnoxious forms of new technology. For further discussion of the role of unions in the United States, see Reich, Section 4.5, p. 174.

day at their jobs. They can take little satisfaction or pride in knowing that their work is important to the community or themselves, or in deciding how the work activity should relate to their community. They work only to earn wages. For the *society*, the alienation of the workers means that work will be *privately* rationalized (i.e., most profitable) rather than *socially rational* (most useful), as indeed the irrationalities in capitalist society indicate.

The alienation of workers from their work product is in the first instance *not* a psychological condition of workers, but rather the *social* and *objective* fact that the workers produce the work product but the capitalist owns it. Workers therefore have no control over (are alienated from) their *product*.

In exactly the same way, workers are alienated from the work process, not in the psychological sense of not liking the activities of work (though that may be true as well), but rather in the sense that the workers perform the work activities but the managers control and direct them. Workers therefore do not themselves establish (they are alienated from) the *process* of work.

The following reading by Marx describes these characteristics of the capitalist workplace.

Source: The following is excerpted from the section on "Alienated Labor" in Economic and Philosophical Manuscripts, First Manuscript, of *Karl Marx Early Writings* translated and edited by T. B. Bottomore. Copyright © 1963 by T. B. Bottomore. Used by permission of McGraw-Hill Book Company and C. A. Watts & Co., Limited.

· · ·

This fact simply implies that the object produced by labor, its product, now stands opposed to it as an *alien being*, as a *power independent* of the producer. The product of labor is labor which has been embodied in an object and turned into a physical thing; this product is an *objectification* of labor. The performance of work is at the same time its objectification. The performance of work appears in the sphere of political economy as a *vitiation* of the worker, objectification as a *loss* and as *servitude to the object*, and appropriation as *alienation*.

· · ·

All these consequences follow from the fact that the worker is related to the *product of his labor* as to an *alien* object. For it is clear on this presupposition that the more the worker expends himself in work the more powerful becomes the world of objects which he creates in face of himself, the poorer he becomes in his inner life, and the less he belongs to himself. It is just the same as in religion. The more of himself man attributes to God the less he has left in himself. The worker puts his life into the object, and his life then belongs no longer to himself but to the object. The greater his activity, therefore, the less he possesses. What is embodied in the product of his labor is no longer his own. The greater this product is, therefore, the more he is diminished. The *alienation* of the worker in his product means not only that his labor becomes an object, assumes an *external* existence, but that it exists independently, *outside himself*, and alien to him, and that it stands opposed to him as an autonomous power. The life which he has given to the object sets itself against him as an alien and hostile force.

. . .

So far we have considered the alienation of the worker only from one aspect; namely, *his relationship with the products of his labor*. However, alienation appears not only in the result, but also in the *process*, of *production*, within *productive ability* itself. How could the worker stand in an alien relationship to the product of his activity if he did not alienate himself in the act of production itself? The product is indeed only the *résumé* of activity, of production. Consequently, if the product of labor is alienation, production itself must be active alienation—the alienation of activity and the activity of alienation. The alienation of the object of labor merely summarizes the alienation in the work activity itself.

What constitutes the alienation of labor? First, that the work is *external* to the worker, that it is not part of his nature; and that, consequently, he does not fulfill himself in his work but denies himself, has a feeling of misery rather than well being, does not develop freely his mental and physical energies but is physically exhausted and mentally debased. The worker therefore feels himself at home only during his leisure time, whereas at work he feels homeless. His work is not voluntary but imposed, *forced labor*. It is not the satisfaction of a need, but only a *means* for satisfying other needs. Its alien character is clearly shown by the fact that as soon as there is no physical or other compulsion it is avoided like the plague. External labor, labor in which man alienates himself, is a labor of self-sacrifice, of mortification. Finally, the external character of work for the worker is shown by the fact that it is not his own work but work for someone else, that in work he does not belong to himself but to another person.

Just as in religion the spontaneous activity of human fantasy, of the human brain and heart, reacts independently as an alien activity of gods or devils upon the individual, so the activity of the worker is not his own spontaneous activity. It is another's activity and a loss of his own spontaneity.

We arrive at the result that man (the worker) feels himself to be freely active only in his animal functions—eating, drinking and procreating, or at most also in his dwelling and in personal adornment—while in his human functions he is reduced to an animal. The animal becomes human and the human becomes animal.

Eating, drinking and procreating are of course also genuine human functions. But abstractly considered, apart from the environment of other human activities, and turned into final and sole ends, they are animal functions.

We have now considered the act of alienation of practical human activity, labor, from two aspects: (1) the relationship of the worker to the *product of labor* as an alien object which dominates him. This relationship is at the same time the relationship to the sensuous external world, to natural objects, as an alien and hostile world; (2) the relationship of labor to the *act of production* within *labor*. This is the relationship of the worker to his own activity as something alien and not belonging to him, activity as suffering (passivity), strength as powerlessness, creation as emasculation, the *personal* physical and mental energy of the worker, his personal life (for what is life but activity?) as an activity which is directed against himself, independent of him and not belonging to him. This is *self-alienation* as against the above-mentioned alienation of the *thing*.

. . .

Labor, *life activity, productive life*, now appear to man only as *means* for the satisfaction of a need, the need to maintain his physical existence. Productive life is, however, [the distinguishing characteristic of human life]. It is life creating life. In the type of life activity resides the whole character of a species, its species-character; and free, conscious activity is the species-character of human beings. Life itself appears only as a *means of life.*

The animal is one with its life activity. It does not distinguish the activity from itself. It is *its activity.* But man makes his life activity itself an object of his will and consciousness. He has a conscious life activity. It is not a determination with which he is completely identified. Conscious life activity distinguishes man from the life activity of animals. . . .

Only for this reason is his activity free activity. Alienated labor reverses the relationship, in that man because he is a self-conscious being makes his life activity, his *being,* only a means for his *existence.*

The practical construction of an *objective world,* the *manipulation* of inorganic nature, is the confirmation of man as a conscious . . . being. Of course, animals also produce. They construct nests, dwellings, as in the case of bees, beavers, ants, etc. But they only produce what is strictly necessary for themselves or their young. They produce only in a single direction, while man produces universally. They produce only under the compulsion of direct physical need, while man produces when he is free from physical need and only truly produces in freedom from such need. Animals produce only themselves, while man reproduces the whole of nature. The products of animal production belong directly to their physical bodies, while man is free in face of his product. Animals construct only in accordance with the standards and needs of the species to which they belong, while man knows how to produce in accordance with the standards of every species and knows how to apply the appropriate standard to the object. Thus man constructs also in accordance with the laws of beauty.

. . .

A direct consequence of the alienation of man from the product of his labor, from his life activity and from his species life is that *man is alienated* from other *men.* When man confronts himself he also confronts *other* men. What is true of man's relationship to his work, to the product of his work and to himself, is also true of his relationship to other men, to their labor and to the objects of their labor.

. . .

We have so far considered this relation only from the side of the worker, and later on we shall consider it also from the side of the non-worker.

Thus, through alienated labor the worker creates the relation of another man, who does not work and is outside the work process, to this labor. The relation of the worker to work also produces the relation of the capitalist (or whatever one likes to call the lord of labor) to work. *Private property* is therefore the product, the necessary result, of *alienated labor,* of the external relation of the worker to nature and to himself.

Private property is thus derived from the analysis of the concept of *alienated labor*; that is, alienated man, alienated labor, alienated life, and estranged man.

We have, of course, derived the concept of *alienated labor (alienated life)* from political economy, from an analysis of the *movement of private property.* But the analysis of this concept shows that although private property appears to be the basis and cause of alienated labor, it is rather a consequence of the latter, just as the gods are *fundamentally* not the cause but the product of confusions of human reason. At a later stage, however, there is a reciprocal influence.

. . .

We also observe, therefore, that *wages* and *private property* are identical, for wages, like the product or object of labor, labor itself remunerated, are only a necessary consequence of the alienation of labor. In the wage system labor appears not as an end in itself but as the servant of wages. We shall develop this point later on and here only bring out some of the consequences.

An enforced *increase in wages* (disregarding the other difficulties, and especially that such an anomaly could only be maintained by force) would be nothing more than a *better remuneration of slaves*, and would not restore, either to the worker or to the work, their human significance and worth.

Even the *equality of incomes* which Proudhon demands would only change the relation of the present day worker to his work into a relation of all men to work. Society would then be conceived as an abstract capitalist.

From the relation of alienated labor to private property it also follows that the emancipation of society from private property, from servitude, takes the political form of the *emancipation of the workers*; not in the sense that only the latter's emancipation is involved, but because this emancipation includes the emancipation of humanity as a whole. For all human servitude is involved in the relation of the worker to production, and all the types of servitude are only modifications or consequences of this relation.

3.4 *Commodities and Commodity Fetishism*

To this point we have described how the work process is organized in capitalist society: how the worker becomes transformed into the commodity labor and sells his services on the market; how the capitalist (or capitalist firm) organizes the work process to make profits for himself (or itself); how the entire process of producing society's material needs becomes directed and motivated by the firm's drive for profits; and how the basis of this system, private property, is the worker's alienation from his work product and his work activities.

Growing out of the capitalist mode of production is a consequence directly related to production itself: what Marx called "commodity fetishism." The concept of commodities—goods which are produced for exchange on a market—assumes enormous importance in a society in which all material products (and even man and nature as the "fictitious commodities, labor and land") are commodities. Since the only relationship between commodities recognized by the market is their relative worth, their *exchange relationship*, all relationships within capitalist society begin to assume the character of exchange relationships.

The exaggerated role which commodities and commodity relations assume within capitalist society was hinted at by Polanyi in an earlier reading. Commodities and commodity relations are important on the production side and the consumption side of the economy.

On the production side, men and women as producers do not relate to each other as people, but rather as commodities. All production relationships are reduced to the character of exchange relationships. For example, the relationship between capitalist and worker is not the human relationship based on a cooperative work activity; instead it is an exchange relationship: the worker asks, "How much can I obtain in wages from this capitalist?" and the capitalist asks, "How much in extra profits can be realized if I hire this worker?"

On the consumption side, the status of commodities is likewise inflated. Instead of commodities serving as *instruments* for worthwhile human activities, commodities themselves become *ends*: the accumulation of commodities and the exaggerated consumption of commodities replace rational use.

In the next reading Paul Sweezy discusses the basis for this "commodity fetishism" and points out some of the consequences for the production relationships which people enter into. A later reading will demonstrate some of the consumption aspects.[1]

[1]See Fromm, Section 6.3, p. 265.

Source: The following is excerpted from Chapter 2 of *The Theory of Capitalist Development* by PAUL SWEEZY. Copyright © 1942 by Paul Sweezy. Reprinted by permission of Monthly Review Press.

The first chapter of *Capital* is entitled "Commodities." It has already been pointed out that a commodity is anything that is produced for exchange rather than for the use of the producer; the study of commodities is therefore the study of the economic relation of exchange.

. . .

Commodity production . . . is not the universal and inevitable form of economic life. It is rather one possible form of economic life, a form, to be sure, which has been familiar for many centuries and which dominates the modern period, but none the less a historically conditioned form which can in no sense claim to be a direct manifestation of human nature. The implications of this view are striking. Commodity production itself is withdrawn from the realm of natural phenomena and becomes the valid subject of socio-historical investigation. No longer can the economist afford to confine his attention to the quantitative relations arising from commodity production; he must also direct his attention to the character of the social relations which underlie the commodity form. We may express this by saying that the tasks of economics are not only quantitative, they are also qualitative. More concretely, in the case of exchange value there is, as Adam Smith saw, the quantitative relation between products; hidden behind this, as Marx was the first to see, there is a specific, historically conditioned, relation between producers.

. . .

USE VALUE

"Every commodity," Marx wrote, "has a twofold aspect, that of use value and exchange value."

In possessing use value a commodity is in no way peculiar. Objects of human consumption in every age and in every form of society likewise possess use value. Use value is an expression of a certain relation between the consumer and the object consumed.

. . .

EXCHANGE VALUE

In possessing exchange value relative to one another, commodities show their unique characteristic. It is only as commodities, in a society where exchange is a regular method of realizing the purpose of social production, that products have exchange value. At first sight it might seem that even less than in the case of use value have we here to do with a social relation. Exchange value appears to be a quantitative relation between things, between the commodities themselves. In what sense, then, is it to be conceived as a social relation and hence as a proper subject for the investigation of the economist? Marx's answer to this question is the key to his value theory. The quantitative relation between things, which we call exchange value, is in reality only an outward form of the *social* relation between the commodity owners, or, what comes to the same thing in simple commodity production, between the producers themselves. The exchange relation as such, apart from any consideration of the quantities involved, is an expression of the fact that individual producers, each working in isolation, are in fact working for each other. Their labor, whatever they may think about the matter, has a social character which is impressed upon it by the fact of exchange. In other words, the exchange of commodities is an exchange of the products of the labor of individual producers. What finds expression in the form of exchange value is therefore the fact that the commodities involved are the products of human labor in a society based on division of labor in which producers work privately and independently.

· · ·

THE FETISH CHARACTER OF COMMODITIES

Our analysis of commodities has led us to see in exchange value a relation between producers in a definite system of division of labor, and in the particular labor of individuals a component part of the aggregate labor force of society. In other words, we have looked beneath the forms of social organization to discover the substance of social relations. That we are able to do this, however, is no indication that the forms are unimportant. On the contrary, they are of the greatest importance. Reality is perceived in terms of form. Where, as here, there is a gap between form and substance which can be bridged only by critical analysis, the understanding plays queer tricks. Error and fantasy are readily accepted as obvious common sense and even provide the basis for supposedly scientific explanation. An incapacity to comprehend, a false consciousness, permeates, to a greater or lesser extent, the structure of thought. This principle applies with peculiar force to commodities and commodity production. The thinking to which this form of social organization gives rise frequently bears only a remote and perverted relation to the real social relations which underlie it. In his doctrine of Commodity Fetishism, Marx was the first to perceive this fact and to realize its decisive importance for the ideology of the modern period.

In commodity production, the basic relation between men "assumes in their eyes, the fantastic form of a relation between things."[1] This reification of social relations [that is, treating as objects or things what are really relations between people—Ed.] is the heart and core of Marx's doctrine of Fetishism.

In the mist-enveloped regions of the religious world . . . the productions of the human brain appear as independent beings endowed with life, and entering into relation both with one another and with the human race. So it is in the world of commodities with the products of men's hands. This I call the Fetishism which attaches itself to the products of labor, so soon as they are produced as commodities, and which is therefore inseparable from the production of commodities.

This fetish character of the commodity

[1] Karl Marx, *Capital* (Chicago: Charles Kerr and Company, 1933), Volume I, p. 83. "Fantastic" is, of course, meant in its literal sense.

world has its origin . . . in the peculiar social character of the labor which produces commodities.

As a general rule, articles of utility become commodities only because they are products of private individuals or groups of individuals who carry on their work independently of each other. The sum total of the labor of all these private individuals forms the aggregate labor of society. Since the producers do not come into contact with each other, the specific social character of each producer's labor does not show itself except in the act of exchange. In other words, the labor of the individual asserts itself as a part of the labor of society only through the relations which the act of exchange establishes directly between the products and indirectly, through them, between the producers. To the latter, therefore, the social relations between the labor of private individuals appear for what they are, i.e., not as the direct social relations of persons in their work, but rather as material relations of persons and social relations of things.

In earlier periods of history, when the relations of production had a direct personal character, such a reification of social relations was obviously impossible. Even in the early stages of commodity production itself "this mystification is as yet very simple" and is therefore easily seen through. It is, in fact, only when commodity production becomes so highly developed and so widespread as to dominate the life of society that the phenomenon of reification of social relations acquires decisive importance. This occurs under conditions of relatively advanced capitalism such as emerged in Western Europe during the seventeenth and eighteenth centuries. Here the impersonalization of productive relations is brought to its highest pitch of development. The individual producer deals with his fellow men only through "the market," where prices and amounts sold are the substantial realities and human beings merely their instruments. "These quantities vary continually, independently of the will, foresight, and action of the producers. To them their own social movement takes the form of the movement of things which rule the producers instead of being ruled by them." This is, indeed, "a state of society in which the process of production has the mastery over man instead of being controlled by him, "[2] and in which, therefore, the real character of the relations among the producers themselves is both distorted and obscured from view.

Once the world of commodities has, so to speak, achieved its independence and subjected the producers to its sway, the latter come to look upon it in much the same way as they regard that other external world to which they must learn to adjust themselves, the world of nature itself. The existing social order becomes in the apt expression of Lukacs, a "second nature" which stands outside of and opposed to its members.

The consequences for the struggle of thought are both extensive and profound. Here we shall have to be content with a few suggestions which may serve to illustrate the possibilities for critical interpretation which are opened up by the doctrine of Fetishism.

. . .

Reification of social relations has exercised a profound influence on traditional economic thinking in at least two further important respects. In the first place, the categories of the capitalist economy—value, rent, wages, profit, interest, et cetera—have been treated as though they were the inevitable categories of economic life in general. Earlier economic systems have been looked upon as imperfect or embryonic versions of modern capitalism and judged accordingly. It requires but little reflection to see that this procedure slurs over significant differences between social forms, encourages an unhistorical and sterile taxonomy, and leads to misleading and at times even ludicrous judg-

[2]*Ibid.*, p. 86.

ments. Thus, it has been common for economists to denounce medieval prohibitions of usury as irrational and misguided because (in modern capitalism) interest plays an important part in regulating the productive mechanism. Or, to take another example, we find Keynes evaluating pyramid building in ancient Egypt and cathedral building in medieval Europe in terms appropriate to a public-works program in twentieth-century England. It cannot, of course, be denied that certain features are common to all forms of social economy, but to comprehend them all in a single set of categories and hence to ignore their specific differences is in a very real sense a negation of history. That modern economics has consistently pursued this course is the best evidence of its subordination to the fetishism inherent in commodity production.

In the second place, the attribution of independent power to things is nowhere more clear than in the traditional division of "factors of production" into land, labor, and capital, each of which is thought of as "producing" an income for its owners. Here, as Marx expressed it,

> we have the complete mystification of the capitalist mode of production, the transformation of social conditions into things, the indiscriminate amalgamation of the material conditions of production with their historical and social forms. It is an enchanted, perverted, topsy-turvy world in which Monsieur le Capital and Madame la Terre carry on their goblin tricks as social characters and at the same time as mere things.[3]

. . .

Turning from political economy in a narrow sense, it is apparent that the commodity-producing form constitutes the most effective possible veil over the true class character of capitalist society. Everyone appears first of all as a mere commodity owner with some-

thing to sell—this is true of landowners, capitalists, and laborers alike. As commodity owners they all stand on a perfectly equal footing; their relations with each other are not the master-servant relations of a regime of personal status, but the contractual relations of free and equal human beings. It does not appear to the worker that his own lack of access to the means of production is forcing him to work on terms dictated by those who monopolize the means of production, that he is therefore being exploited for the benefit of others just as surely as the serf who was forced to work a certain number of days on the lord's land in return for the privilege of working a strip of land for himself. On the contrary, the world of commodities appears as a world of equals. The labor power of the worker is alienated from the worker and stands opposed to him as any commodity to its owner. He sells it, and so long as true value is paid all the conditions of fair and equal exchange are satisfied.

This is the appearance. Those who regard capitalist forms as natural and eternal—and, generally speaking, this includes most of those who live under capitalist forms—accept the appearance as a true representation of social relations. On this foundation there has been erected the whole vast superstructure of ethical and legal principles which serve at once to justify the existing order and to regulate men's conduct towards it. It is only by means of a critical analysis of commodity production, an analysis that goes beneath the superficial forms to the underlying relations of man to man, that we can see clearly the historically relative character of capitalist justice and capitalist legality, just as it is only by such an analysis that we can see the historical character of capitalism itself. This illustration, while it cannot be pursued further here, shows that the doctrine of Fetishism has implications which far transcend the conventional limits of economics and economic thinking.

If commodity production has fostered the

[3] Ibid., Volume III, p. 966.

illusion of its own permanence and hidden the true character of the social relations which it embodies, it has at the same time created the economic rationality of modern times without which a full development of society's productive forces would be unthinkable. Rationality, in the sense of a deliberate adaptation of means to ends in the economic sphere, presupposes an economic system which is subject to certain objective laws which are not altogether unstable and capricious. Given this condition, the individual can proceed to plan his affairs in such a way as to achieve what is, from his own standpoint and from the standpoint of prevailing standards, an optimum result.

That this condition is fulfilled by commodity production does not mean that the system is to be regarded as a planned or rational whole. On the contrary, the development of commodity production under capitalist conditions displays on the one hand an intense rationalization of its part-processes and an ever increasing irrationality in the behavior of the system as a whole. It is clear that we have to do here with one of the most comprehensive contradictions of the capitalist order. A social system which has sway over man educates him to the point where he has the capacity to control his own destiny. At the same time it blinds him to the means of exercising the power which is within his grasp and diverts his energies increasingly into purely destructive channels. . . .

3.5 *Bureaucratic Organization in the Capitalist Firm*

Since capitalists own the firms and other productive enterprises under capitalism, they control production itself. One aspect of this control is the particular organizational form of the capitalist firm. Historically capitalists have chosen a *bureaucratic* structure, within which employees work and by which employees' day-to-day activities are "managed" or controlled. This bureaucratic structure has become increasingly stratified as firms have developed and expanded. General Motors and other large corporations are examples of the most advanced development of this form.

In this essay on the bureaucratic organization of production, Richard C. Edwards focuses on the organizational aspect of capitalist control.

Source: The following essay was written by RICHARD C. EDWARDS for this book. Copyright © 1972 by Richard C. Edwards.

Bureaucratic organization of firms and other places of work (e.g., the state apparatus) has become a pervasive characteristic of capitalist society. Indeed, it has become so common that people often have difficulty imagining other forms of organization. But the dominance of bureaucratic forms is not inevitable in an industrial society; it derives instead directly from capitalists' need to control production.

Bureaucratic forms provide the means by which the owners and managers of a firm can retain overall direction of the firm's activities. A hierarchical structure is instituted so that some employees can watch over other employees, and the entire firm assumes the shape of a giant pyramid. The owners at the top of the pyramid control the activities of all those below them. Their "control" is less than perfect, of course, since workers in the pyramid have some power as well (for example, they can withhold information or simply "work to rules," thus diminishing efficiency). But the workers' power is mainly defensive, and open opposition always brings into play the most basic power relation: the capitalist's legal right to fire the worker. So capitalists at the top of the bureaucratic firms define the main goals and activities of their firms and see to it that no large deviations from their decisions are permitted.

Bureaucratic organization permits firms to extend their operations without the owners losing control. Bureaucratic growth in firms paralleled historically the growth in the overall size of leading firms such as the top 50 corporations.[1] Growth in overall size brought increased complexity of a firm's operations, increasing as well the difficulty of coordination. But coordinating different divisions within the expanded firm is essential for its overall profit position. Over the past several decades business activities involving sales work, advertising, marketing, financial and legal deals, tax "management," product "research," and cost accounting controls have increasingly supplemented physical, assembly-line production as a means of *realizing* larger profits.[2] These aspects of a firm's operations lend themselves well to bureaucratic organization.

THE NATURE OF BUREAUCRATIC

ORGANIZATION OF PRODUCTION

Bureaucratic organization is founded upon hierarchical control. The most basic hierarchical distinction in capitalist firms is of course the distinction between the capitalist owners, who have ultimate control in determining the goals of the firms (and in whose interest the firms exist), and the nonowning and noncontrolling workers. In this respect

all capitalist production is hierarchical. But organizing production bureaucratically extends and intensifies this basic hierarchy by placing the workers themselves in a hierarchical ordering. In the modern firm one finds "workers" (i.e., nonowners) as production workers, foremen, and managers. Hierarchical relations have therefore been extended throughout the capitalist firm.

Hierarchical control in production is nothing new. It existed in feudal times, for example, in the relations between apprentice, journeyman, and master.[3] Likewise, capitalists directly supervised workshops and factories in the early days of capitalism. But bureaucratic organization systematically applies hierarchical principles: it rigidly structures the right and authority of employees, permitting owners and managers to retain control over vastly expanded operations, where more direct supervision would be impossible.

In a bureaucratic organization work activities are carried on at many different levels within the firm. Specific tasks or activities of work are performed at the different levels, depending on the nature of the work and the "qualifications" required for its accomplishment. For example, the actual physical production of goods is performed by those at the lowest levels, whose work requires the manual or mechanical skills associated with operating machinery; the upper levels do work depending more heavily on strictly cognitive processes. The duties and responsibilities of each level are carefully delegated, each

---

[1]See Hymer, Section 4-2, p. 156.
[2]For evidence, note the growth of white-collar workers relative to blue-collar workers documented in Table 4-L, p. 178.

[3]But as S.A. Marglin points out, there are two essential differences between feudal and capitalist hierarchy. The feudal hierarchy was linear, not pyramidal, with nearly as many positions at the top as at the bottom; therefore every apprentice had a reasonable expectation of one day becoming a master. Furthermore, overall control remained in the hands of the producers; the master worked alongside the apprentice in producing the product. There was therefore no intermediary between producers and market, so the producer controlled both his product and work process. See S.A. Marglin, "What Do Bosses Do? The Origins and Function of Hierarchy in Capitalist Production," (Cambridge, Mass.: Harvard University, 1971), mimeo.

person being responsible for certain tasks.

An essential feature of bureaucratic organization is that it is highly stratified, with each level being responsible *for* the levels below it and accountable *to* the higher strata. The organization's rules grant to each person a certain degree of authority (the right to direct other people's activities) in order that he can perform his assigned duties. Naturally, the few at the top direct many people's activities and have a great deal of authority, while the many at the bottom have very little authority. People at the bottom usually work with some kind of machine.

While an individual in a bureaucracy is granted sufficient authority to carry out his assigned duties, he at the same time is deprived of any right to participate in other decisions, since those decisions are someone else's assigned responsibility. So the reverse side of delegating authority to one individual is the systematic limitation of everyone else's participation in the firm's decisions. In this way, specific individuals can be held accountable if a decision is taken contrary to the firm's profit interests.

CONTROL AND MOTIVATION

Bureaucratic organization developed in response to the need for a significant change in the mechanisms of control within capitalist firms. In a small firm the capitalist himself, alone or with the aid of a few managers at most, could oversee the activities of the workers; control was direct and based on the owner's legal authority—for example, his right to dismiss a worker. Likewise in piecework industries, each worker performs a certain discrete task, e.g., mounting individual parts to assemble a radio, and he is paid on the basis of how many radios he assembles. In this situation as well, control is direct, open, and easily administered.

But the nature of work has been changing: it has become more interdependent, more indivisible, and in this sense, more so-

cial. Contributing to this change in the nature of work has been the growth of sales, advertising, marketing, and other nonproduction "white-collar" jobs—jobs involving communication and the manipulation of ideas and requiring primarily cognitive processes rather than—or in addition to—mechanical or manual skills.

Unlike piece-rate work, these jobs are not conducive to direct, external control or direction. It is usually impossible to identify discrete tasks by which to judge the worker's performance. Feedback on the quality of an employee's work, directly and immediately available in piece-rate work, must await more long-run evaluation. Furthermore, since the work does not produce simple, standardized products, determining whether the task has been performed "correctly" becomes more ambiguous.[4] In this situation a new mechanism for enforcing proper work activities became necessary; bureaucratic organization has been the response. "Good" workers in these jobs must be capable of some self-direction and initiative, since it is not feasible to give workers specific instructions for every situation that may arise. To function adequately, such workers must *internalize* the values, outlook, and goals of the firm, especially when the job depends significantly on cognitive processes. For example, consider what is involved in responding to a business letter, or taking purchasing orders from customers, or making out voucher payments, or interviewing prospective new personnel. If the employee is to do his job properly, he must put himself in the position of the firm (that is, assume the firm's values, criteria, and goals), and then interpret what from that perspective would be the appropriate response. But since the firm's goals

[4]There exists a continuum of jobs, from those that involve purely standardized, piece-rate type production to those that involve much individual interpretation of the firm's values. Yet even in certain jobs (e.g., secretaries in a typing pool) where the work itself is more like piece-rate work, the organization of the work tends to follow bureaucratic lines.

reflect the capitalist's interests, not the worker's own interests, bureaucratic organization encounters a problem of worker motivation.

The fundamental problem of motivation results from alienated labor: where the workers have no control over work activities or the product of their labor, they can be motivated to work only by the external reward of wages, including the threat of having no income. This source of motivation continues in bureaucratic firms. But bureaucratic organization, by requiring greater reliance on the worker's internalization of the firm's (i.e., the capitalist's) goals, exacerbates the motivation problem.

Both the firm's rewards (higher pay, status, promotions) and penalties (threats of being fired, demotions, actual dismissal) are geared to the quality of an individual's work performance. But the internal social relations of bureaucratic firms—the fine degree of stratification, the multiple levels of authority and subordinacy, the isolation from participation in overall decision-making, and especially the need for workers to internalize the firm's values—require much of the worker. Attaining the firm's rewards and avoiding its penalties—that is, being successful in a bureaucratic firm—requires a particular cluster of behavioral or personality characteristics: workers must be "disciplined" and their behavior predictable; they must respect the authority of those higher in the hierarchy; they must be able to assume the firm's values and outlook; they must divorce their motivation from the intrinsic content of the work and instead must value highly the external reward of wages. Workers are "successful" to the extent that they incorporate these characteristics.

The personality requirements placed on workers by bureaucratic organization of production create contradictions both within and outside of the firm. First, there is a growing contradiction internally between the need to involve individual workers in particular decisions of the firm (evidenced by the increasing demand to have workers internalize the

firm's values) and their exclusion from participation in overall decision-making in the firm. Second, the burden of training or "socializing" young people for adult work roles has been imposed on both the family and the schools, and their development in response to this need has produced internal conflicts in both those institutions. This conflict is particularly apparent in the rebellion of workers and students from being perfectly "socialized" (i.e., from being molded to fit harmoniously into the system).[5]

ECONOMIC RATIONALITY

We will conclude our discussion with some observations on the alleged efficiency of bureaucratic organization of work. Bureaucratic organization is often linked with economic rationality; it is argued that eliminating the "human element" from production also eliminates inefficiencies.[6] This claim is no doubt true. But it is true in the strictly limited sense that bureaucratic organization promotes efficiency or rationality only *within the context of managerial control*. Bureaucratic organization, with its reliance on multiple levels of authority and supervision and its emphasis on discipline and predictability, is probably the only way of ensuring efficient production using alienated labor. In this respect, "efficiency" becomes a synonym for "successful control." Once the need to maintain managerial control is accepted, bureaucratic production becomes "efficient."

That bureaucratic production is efficient only within the confines of managerial control is indicated by both historical and con-

[5]For a more thorough analysis of these and other contradictions, see Chapter 11.

[6]As Max Weber put it: "[bureaucracy] develops the more completely it succeeds in eliminating from official business love, hatred, and all purely personal, irrational, and emotional elements which escape calculation. Max Weber, "On Bureaucracy," in Hans Gerth and C. Wright Mills, (editors), *From Max Weber: Essays in Sociology* (New York: Oxford University Press, 1958). That is, bureaucracy develops the more completely it succeeds in repressing the human side of its workers.

temporary evidence. S.A. Marglin suggests from historical evidence that hierarchical relations of control were instituted not to improve efficiency, but rather to provide an essential place in the production process for the capitalist.[7] It was only *within* the constraints of maintaining hierarchical control that changes in technology or work activities were introduced. Thus current technology, which embodies and may require hierarchical control, must itself be seen as a product of capitalist development, rather than an exogenous, neutral force.

Marglin argues that hierarchical firms achieved a certain *dynamic* advantage from the concentration in capitalists' hands of control over the social surplus. The capitalists accumulated this surplus, and reinvested it to reduce costs and produce greater output. The advantage of bureaucratic production, therefore, was in its ability to produce capital accumulation, not in its inherent "rationality" or "efficiency."[8]

Contemporary evidence also suggests the limited rationality of bureaucratic organization of production. Gintis draws on the findings of recent studies in industrial psychology to argue that bureaucratic organization is chosen "because it is the only means of maintaining and stabilizing control over the profit generated in production, and of avoiding workers' gaining enough general expertise and initiative to embark on cooperative production on their own.[9] He cites in particular one careful review of the industrial psychology literature which concludes:

> *There is scarcely a study in the entire literature which fails to demonstrate that satisfaction in work is enhanced or ... productivity increases accrue from a genuine increase in worker's decision-making power. Findings of such consistency, I submit, are rare in social research ... the participative worker is an involved worker, for his job becomes an extension of himself and by his decisions he is creating his work, modifying and regulating it.[10]*

That genuine work participation has rarely been tried, and then only for brief periods, suggests that bureaucratic hierarchy has been instituted and is maintained primarily so that capitalists can retain control.

---

[7]"What Do Bosses Do? The Origins and Function of Hierarchy In Capitalist Production" (Harvard University, 1971, Mimeo).

[8]This is not to say that hierarchical control is the *only* method for accumulating capital. One can conceive of a democratic decision-making process by which people as a group could jointly decide the best savings rate. However, in the early capitalist period there was no material basis on which to build the collective consciousness required for an alternative, collective, and democratic system of capital accumulation; hence there was no real historical alternative to the hierarchical firms. As long as the basic economic insti-

tutions of capitalism remained, the dynamic advantage of hierarchical firms which exploited the workers and reinvested the surplus would have eliminated by market competition any other forms of production.

[9]See Gintis, Section 6.5, p. 274.
[10]Quoted in Gintis, *ibid.*

3.6   *Supportive Institutions: The Family and the Schools*

The previous readings have argued that capitalist society becomes increasingly an "economic society." Economic institutions come to dominate other social institutions in such a way as to subject the entire society to market values and needs. In fact, the *precondition* for "rationalizing" social life according to market criteria is that other spheres of society (state, family, schools, media, etc.) not stand in the way of such rationalization. These other spheres of life become subordinated to, and hence develop in accordance with, the primacy of the economic sphere.

One reason for economic institutions' assuming such an important and dominating position within capitalist society is the power of capitalism's drive for accumulation and expansion. The demand for new cost-reducing technology, the struggle to gain new markets and expand old ones, and the drive to accumulate and concentrate capital require continual change in and expansion of the economic sphere. And this continual change and expansion produce fragmentation and ferment in the rest of society.

The family and the schools are two institutions which have developed in such a way as to reinforce the capitalist mode of production. Of course, their development cannot be explained solely on the basis of their relation to economic institutions, and conflicting pressures have produced important contradictions both within these institutions and between them and the economic institutions. The following reading points out some of the connections between the needs of capitalist institutions and the development of family structure and schools.

In Part I ("The Evolution of the Family Under Capitalism") Peggy Morton links changing family structure to the requirements of capitalist institutions. In Part II ("Economic Rationality and the Function of Schooling") Herbert Gintis concentrates on the ways in which schooling serves capitalist institutions.

Family life and schools "socialize" the young. They are the places where children are taught how to behave "properly"—in particular, how they are supposed to act when they become adults. As the demands upon adult behavior change, so must the socialization process, if that process is to produce adults who function effectively in the new environment. For example, as the factory system was introduced, adults (and even children) were expected to work long hours at fatiguing and monotonous work; Morton points out that this change in the nature of work required changes in family structure to prepare people for such work. Likewise, bureaucratic production in capitalist firms required the inculcation of certain personality characteristics among workers; Gintis shows how schools responded to meet this need.

In later chapters we shall examine the functioning of the family and the school system in greater detail.[1] The importance of the present reading is that it illustrates the relationship between social institutions and the basic institutions of capitalism and shows in particular how social institutions reinforce and support the capitalist mode of production.

[1]See especially Cohen and Lazerson, Section 4.6, p. 183; Bowles, Section 5.2, p. 218; Gintis, Section 6.5, p. 274; and Chapter 8.

Source: Part I of the following is excerpted from "A Woman's Work Is Never Done" by PEGGY MORTON. From *Leviathan*, 2, No. 1 (March 1970). Reprinted by permission of the author. Part II is excerpted from "New Working Class and Revolutionary Youth" by HERBERT GINTIS. From *Socialist Revolution* 1, No. 3 (May/June, 1970). Reprinted by permission of *Socialist Revolution*.

Part I: The Evolution of the
Family Under Capitalism

There has been a great deal of debate over the past few years about the function of the family in capitalist society. Discussion has generally focused on the role of the family as the primary unit of socialization; the family is the basic unit in which authoritarian personality structures are formed, particularly the development of authoritarian relationships between parents and children and between men and women: the family is necessary to the maintenance of sexual repression in that sexuality is allowed legitimate expression only in marriage; through the family men can give vent to feelings of frustration, anger and resentment that are the products of alienated labor, and can act out the powerlessness which they experience in work by dominating the other members of the family; and within the family little girls learn what is expected of them and how they should act.

. . .

[How has] the family developed in different stages of capitalism as the requirements for the maintenance and production of labor power change? The essence of the position I want to argue in this paper is as follows. . . . The family is a unit whose function is the *maintenance of and reproduction of labor power*, i.e., that the structure of the family is determined by the needs of the economic system, at any given time, for a certain kind of labor power. . . .

By "reproduction of labor power" we mean simply that the task of the family is to maintain the present work force and provide the next generation of workers, fitted with the skills and values necessary for them to be productive members of the work force. When we talk about the evolution of the family under capitalism, we have to understand both the changes in the family among the proletariat, and the changes that come from the increasing proletarianization of the labor

force, and the urbanization of the society.

The pre-capitalist family functioned (as does the farm family in capitalist society) as an integrated economic unit; men, women and children took part in production work in the fields, the cottage industry and production for the use of the family. There was a division of labor between men and women, but a division within an integrated unit. There was much brutality in the old system (the oppression of women, harsh ideas about child-raising, and a culture that reflected the limitations of peasant life) but the family also served as a structure for the expression and fulfillment of simple human emotional needs.

THE FAMILY IN THE FIRST STAGES
OF CAPITALISM

For those who became the urban proletariat, this was all ruthlessly swept away with the coming of factories. The function of the family was reduced to the most primitive level; instead of skilled artisans, the factories required only a steady flow of workers with little or no training, who learned what they needed on the job, and who could easily be replaced. Numbers were all that mattered and the conditions under which people lived were irrelevant to the needs of capital. The labor of women and children took on a new importance.

The result was a drastic increase in the exploitation of child labor (in Britain, in the period 1780–1840). Even small children worked 12–18 hour days, death from overwork was common, and despite a series of Factory Acts which made provisions for the education of child labourers, the education was almost always mythical—when teachers were provided, they themselves were often illiterate. The report on Public Health, London, 1864, documents that in industrial districts, infant mortality was as high as one death in four in the first year of life, as compared to one in ten in non-industrial districts. As many as half the children died in the first five years of life in the industrial slums—not because of a lack of medical knowledge but because of the conditions under which the urban proletariat were forced to live. Girls who had worked in the mills since early childhood had a characteristic deformation of the pelvic bones which made for difficult births; women worked until the last week of pregnancy and would return to the mills soon after giving birth for fear of losing their jobs; children were left with those too young or too old to work, were given opiates to quiet them, and often died from malnutrition resulting from the absence of the mother and the lack of suitable food.

> *On what foundation is the present family, the bourgeois family, based? On capital, or private gain. In its completely developed form this family exists only among the bourgeoisie. But this state of things finds its complement in the practical absence of the family among the proletarians, and in public prostitution. . . . The bourgeois clap-trap about the family and education, about the hallowed correlation of parent and child, become all the more disgusting, the more, by the action of Modern Industry, all family ties among the proletarians are torn asunder and their children transformed into simple articles of commerce and instruments of labour.* (The Communist Manifesto)

The need of capitalism in the stage of primitive accumulation of capital for a steady flow of cheap and unskilled labor primarily determined the structure of the family. In contrast, the prevailing ideology was used in turn to prepare the working class for the new drudgery. The repressive Victorian morality, brought to the working class through the Wesleyan sects, clamped down harder on the freedom of women, and perpetrated the ideology of hard work and discipline. The Victorian concept of the family was both a reflection of the bourgeois family, based on private property, and an ideal representing

a status to which the proletarian would like to rise.

Colonized nations within imperialist nations have experienced this destruction of the family almost permanently. During slavery, the black family was systematically broken up and destroyed. Because black people have been used as a reserve army of unskilled labor, there has been no need for a family structure that would ensure that the children received education and skills. And direct oppression and repression (racism) eliminated the need for more subtle social control through the socialization process in the family. Often the women were the breadwinners because they were the only ones who could find jobs, and when there were no jobs the welfare system further discouraged the maintenance of the family by making it more difficult to get welfare if the man was around. The bourgeois family has never existed for the black colony; instead children were seen not as individual property but as belonging to the whole community.

For white North Americans, the family developed differently for those who first settled the continent and for industrial workers. "Frontier life" required the family in an even stronger form than in Europe, because all members of the family had to function as a production unit in the back-breaking work of clearing land, ploughing and harvesting. At the same time, the need for co-operation between family units meant that a strong community developed. For industrial workers, conditions were similar to those of Europe in the early stages of capitalism, i.e., the family system was weakened by the employment of all members of the family in the mines and the mills.

The evolution of the family is affected both by the proletarianization of the work force engaged in agriculture and resulting urbanization, and by changes in the kind of labor power required which changed the form of the family among the proletariat itself.

The constant need of each capitalist to increase the productivity of his enterprise in order to remain competitive was secured both by increasing the level of exploitation of the workers and by the continual introduction of new, more complex and more efficient machinery. Thus a new kind of worker was required as the production process became more complex—workers who could read instructions and blueprints, equipped with skills that required considerable training. As the need for skilled labor increases the labor of women and children tends to be replaced by that of men—workers involve a capital investment and therefore it makes more sense to employ those who can work steadily throughout their lives.

At the same time, the growth of trade unions and the increasing revolutionary consciousness of the working class forced the ruling class to meet some of their demands or face full-scale revolt. The rise in material standards of living accommodated both the need to restrain militancy, to provide a standard of living that would allow for the education of children as skilled workers, and the need for consumers to provide new markets for the goods produced. The abolition of child labor and the introduction of compulsory education were compelled by the need for a skilled labor force.

REPRODUCTION OF LABOR POWER IN ADVANCED CAPITALISM

The transformation in the costs of educating and training the new generation of workers is fundamental to the changes that have taken place and are still taking place in the family structure. A fundamental law of capitalism is the need for constant expansion. Automation is required for the survival of the system. Workers are needed who are not only highly skilled but who have been trained to learn new skills. Profits depend more and more on the efficient organization of work and on the "self-discipline" of the workers

rather than simply on speed-ups and other direct forms of increasing the exploitation of the workers. The family is therefore important both to shoulder the burden of the costs of education, and to carry out the repressive socialization of children. The family must raise children who have internalized hierarchical social relations, who will discipline themselves and work efficiently without constant supervision. The family also serves to repress the natural sexuality of its members —an essential process if people are to work at jobs which turn them into machines for eight or more hours a day. Women are responsible for implementing most of this socialization.

. . .

Part II: Economic Rationality and the Function of Schooling

It would be strange indeed if the [needs of economic institutions did not have an impact] beyond the economic sphere. In any society economic activity establishes parameters for the major non-economic institutions —the worker's basic consumption unit (be it nuclear or extended family, clan, or commune), the residential community, the work-environment, education, the cultural system, and the formation of individual personalities as well. These institutions are intertwined with the economic system, and mold the psychological make-up of individuals in such a manner as to facilitate its operation. The development of economic institutions along the lines of maximal production implies that economic rationality governs the development of society as a whole.

. . .

[Schooling is an example of how other institutions support and reinforce the basic institutions of capitalism.] The function of education in any society is the socialization of youth into the prevailing culture. On the one hand, schooling serves to integrate individuals into society by institutionalizing dominant value, norm, and belief systems. On the other hand, schooling provides the individual competencies necessary for the adequate performance of social roles. Thus educational systems are fundamental to the stability and functioning of any society.

In a society devoted to economic rationality, education must be separated from the family and the community. Citizens are developed in isolation from the general pattern of social activity; the educational process is segregated into a separate and jurisdictionally distinct sphere—schools. This shrinkage follows from the more fundamental removal of economic functions from family and community for two reasons. First, the rationalization of production places ever-increasing demands on the isolated individual. Production relations are not part of the "normal social relations" of the family and the community and hence cannot be developed through the gradual integration of the child into family and society. Second, technologies develop over time in response to the criterion of maximal efficiency, and thus the requisites for adequate job performance—the very competencies which must be developed in the child—change from generation to generation. An eduactional system imbedded in the fabric of family and community cannot respond rapidly enough to changing demands imposed by developing capitalist technology.

An independent educational system provides the flexibility necessary to the operation of capitalism. The functions of this system include: (a) the preservation of social status along class lines; (b) the transmission and preservation of cultural norms, attitudes and values to the degree that they remain compatible with an increasingly materially-oriented economy; (c) the training of a stratum capable of developing new technologies favorable to capitalist development; and (d) the generation of an educated work-force, with competence to perform in complex, alienated work-environments. I shall focus on

the last of these functions, one central to the question of educated labor as a class, and the role of (potentially) revolutionary youth.

The problem of developing individual competence for adequate job-performance reduces to the need for a structure of individual motivation compatible with capitalist organization, and the technical capability and personality traits necessary for the execution of bureaucratic tasks. These requirements limit the ability of the educational system to foster the "human development" of the individual in two basic ways. First, many personality types are incompatible with prerequisites of individual motivation and capacity for adequate job performance. Thus a truly spiritual individual or an individual who values aesthetic, physical, or interpersonal activities may be incapable of adjusting to an alienating work-environment. In this sense, non-capitalist values are incompatible with competence for job performance. Second, the time and energy required for the development of economic motivations and capacities may be so great as to severely limit the time and energy that an individual has to develop other interests and skills. As capitalist technologies become ever more highly developed, the time and energy required for competence are correspondingly increased, so that the dimensions of individual personality development become severely limited. *In this situation, the educational system tends to become functionally reduced to its role in generating labor for the economy, and the development of the individual becomes more or less fully tailored to the needs of "economic rationality."*

. . .

The personality traits rewarded and penalized in the classroom seem admirably suited to the generation of workers who fit harmoniously in a system of hierarchical authority, and the concomitant personality changes induced through schooling represent a central element in the contribution of schooling to individual productivity. Just as subordination is required for adequate functioning in bureaucratic organization, so is a proper worker discipline.

Another aspect of adequate functioning in bureaucratic roles involves the modes of thought typically required of the worker. Roughly, advancement within a bureaucratic organization requires the employment of a more cognitive, as opposed to affective, mode of thought. . . . To what extent is this emphasis on cognitive, as opposed to affective, modes of personal organization developed in the classroom? According to Robert Dreeben, the very structure of the social relations in education is conducive to cognitive orientation.

The bureaucratization of work is a result of the capitalist control of the work process, as bureaucracy seems to be the sole organizational form compatible with capitalist hegemony. If bureaucracy in the factory is a "given," it follows that the development of increasingly cost-minimizing technologies will be limited to those technologies compatible with bureaucratic organization. Potentially "efficient" technologies that are destructive of bureaucratic organization will not be introduced; technology will not develop in these directions. Bureaucracy itself is thus not necessarily "economically rational," but is only a necessary instrument for profit-maximization. As a result, we cannot say whether the personality characteristics associated with adequate job-performance in a bureaucracy are required directly by efficiency criteria in production, or only indirectly as a concomitant of capitalist hegemony. In either case, *the educational system must act as a repressive force in the production of workers who fit harmoniously in an alienating and bureaucratic work-environment*, and in either case *education is productive only insofar as it is repressive.*

3.7   *Capitalism and Inequality*

The existence of an economic surplus makes possible an unequal distribution of income and wealth among people in a society. Great economic inequalities have characterized most societies that have generated a surplus in the past, including slave, feudal, and other precapitalist societies. In these societies a small but dominant class appropriated most of the economic surplus, thereby creating for itself the privileges of unequal status.

The capitalist mode of production has generated an unprecedented expansion of the productive capacity of advanced capitalist nations and a correspondingly huge economic surplus. As in earlier class societies, this surplus has been divided very unequally, so that capitalist societies have also been characterized by great inequalities in income and wealth.

In the following reading Thomas E. Weisskopf shows that a significant degree of income inequality is functionally necessary to the capitalist mode of production. Furthermore, he identifies strong forces in a capitalist society that tend to prevent the equalization of incomes over time and to transmit inequalities from generation to generation.

1. INTRODUCTION

The rise of capitalism has engendered a tremendous increase in the productive capacity of the capitalist economies of North America, Western Europe, Japan, Australia, and New Zealand. Yet this tremendous growth in the forces of production has been accompanied by vast inequalities in the distribution of the fruits of that production. The disparity in income and wealth between the industrialized nations at the center of the world capitalist system and the underdeveloped areas on the periphery has been increasing continuously since the early days of colonial plunder. Moreover, *within* each capitalist nation tremendous fortunes coexist with indescribable poverty in spite of the growth of the modern "welfare state."

Capitalism has historically always been characterized by great inequalities in the distribution of income and wealth. I shall argue in this essay that inequality under capitalism is no mere historical accident; rather, a significant degree of income inequality is functionally essential to the capitalist mode of production. Furthermore, I shall argue that there are dynamic forces at work in a capitalist system that tend to perpetuate if not to exacerbate the degree of income inequality over time.

Income *inequality* must be distinguished conceptually from income *immobility*. The existence of a hierarchy of income levels at any one point in time need not imply that the same families continue to occupy the same position in the hierarchy from one generation to the next. In principle, a high degree of income inequality in a society could be accompanied by a high degree of intergenerational income mobility, such that opportunities to receive income were equalized for all children irrespective of family background. However, I shall argue that a capitalist society is necessarily characterized not only by a substantial degree of income inequality but also by considerable income immobility, for much of the income inequality in one gen-

eration is passed directly on to the next generation.

In Section 2 I will discuss the fundamental characteristics of the process of income distribution under capitalism and argue that income inequality is functionally essential to the capitalist mode of production. The argument abstracts from historical and political forces in order to concentrate on the *institutional* constraints on income distribution imposed by the capitalist system. In Section 3 I will turn to the dynamics of income distribution and argue that there are strong forces inherent in a capitalist system that tend to prevent the reduction of income inequality over time from any initial historically determined level. Some of these same forces in turn limit mobility between income classes and thereby perpetuate income inequality from one generation to the next. In Section 4 I provide a brief summary of the conclusions to be drawn from the analysis of the preceding sections.

2. THE NECESSITY OF INCOME INEQUALITY

The most fundamental characteristic of the distribution of income under capitalism is that it is tied directly to the production process. The ethical principle used to justify the capitalist method of distributing income is "to each according to what he and the instruments he owns produces."[1] Thus under the capitalist mode of production the only legitimate claim to income arises from the possession of one's own labor-power and from the ownership of physical means of production.[2]

[1] Milton Friedman, *Capitalism and Freedom* (Chicago: University of Chicago Press, 1962), pp. 161–62.

[2] There are other sources of income from which some people do receive a limited amount of income in capitalist societies, e.g., welfare agencies, gifts, prizes, crime, etc. However such sources are always treated as exceptions to the normal capitalist rules of the game—exceptions that arise from unusually distressing or pathological circumstances.

Each individual receives income in the form of payments for the use of his "factors of production"—the labor-power and the physical means of production that he owns. The amount of these payments depends upon how "valuable" his factors are in the production process, i.e., how much they contribute to the market value of production. The income received by any individual thus depends both on the quantity of the factors of production he owns and on the price which these factors command in the market. Inequalities in income can result either from unequal ownership of factors of production or from unequal prices paid for those factors.

For the purposes of this analysis, I shall distinguish only the two basic factors of production: labor-power and capital. Labor-power includes all of the productive attributes of individuals, from the most elementary manual capacity to the most highly valued personality characteristics and managerial and technical skills. Capital includes all physical means of production: land, natural resources, buildings, plant, and equipment. Capital is thus defined to include all forms of productive property, but to exclude such possessions as residential housing, automobiles, etc., insofar as they are owned only for personal use.

Income from labor-power and income from capital together account for the overall income of any individual. I shall show that income from each of these sources is necessarily unequally distributed in a capitalist society in such a way as to result in overall income inequality.

In the advanced capitalist nations, labor income typically accounts for about three-quarters and property (capital) income for about one-quarter of total national income.[3] The distribution of capital ownership in a capitalist society is necessarily unequal, for if every individual shared equally in the

[3]For evidence on this point, see Simon Kuznets, *Modern Economic Growth* (New Haven: Yale University Press, 1966), pp. 167–86.

ownership of capital, the fundamental distinction between capitalist and worker would vanish. Each individual would be equally capable of controlling the production process, and no individual would be compelled to relinquish control over his or her labor-power to someone else. But the operation of a capitalist economy is predicated upon the existence of a labor market in which workers are obliged to exchange control over their labor-power in return for wages and salaries. If this obligation were removed, there would no longer be any basis for control of the production process by a limited class of capitalists. Hence equality of capital ownership is incompatible with some of the basic institutions of the capitalist mode of production itself.

If *income* from capital could be separated from *ownership* of capital, the inequality in the latter would not necessarily imply inequality in the former. But to divorce the two would be contrary to the basic capitalist principle that an individual is entitled to income from property as well as from labor. Thus the necessity of unequal income from capital in a capitalist society follows directly from the functional necessity of unequal capital ownership.

The capitalist mode of production likewise requires that the possession of labor-power and the earnings from labor income be distributed highly unequally among workers. For if the labor market is to operate efficiently in developing and allocating labor throughout an economy, there must be a significant degree of inequality in labor earnings. Since workers under capitalism relinquish most control over the process or product of their work, they are not likely to acquire and develop productive attributes for their own sake nor to be motivated to work by intrinsic aspects of the work process. So long as work itself is perceived as a burden to be endured rather than a creative endeavor, workers must be motivated to increase their labor-power and to work hard by extrinsic rewards such as income with which they can purchase material goods and services.

In principle, nonmonetary status rewards could substitute for income rewards and provide an extrinsic psychic rather than material motivation for work. But the *homo economicus* of capitalist society[4] is socialized to value quantitative and "objective" monetary success much more highly than qualitative and "subjective" status achievement. Hence status rewards unrelated to monetary success cannot be expected to play a significant motivational role under capitalism. Instead, material gain incentives are generally necessary to encourage the development of productive attributes and to call forth the energies of workers who do not control the work process.

The productivity of a worker depends on certain relevant personality characteristics, on manual skills, and on certain cognitive skills; the required mix of these types of productive attributes depends upon the nature of the job. The development of these attributes depends to a significant degree on family background and socialization, but later education and job training can also have an impact, especially on the acquisition of cognitive skills. Under the circumstances described above, individuals will be motivated to acquire needed skills through education and job training mainly insofar as this leads to the prospect of higher incomes. Similarly, workers are likely to apply themselves more productively and energetically on the job only insofar as this qualifies them for bonus pay or for promotions to higher-paying positions. In order for this incentive system to operate effectively, it is essential to maintain a hierarchy based upon the differential possession of labor-power and the corresponding differential receipt of labor earnings.

The argument of the preceding paragraphs is not intended to suggest that *no* work would be done in a capitalist society in the absence

[4]See the introduction to Chapter 3, p. 88.

of significant income differentials. The point is rather that the capitalist mode of production is characterized by a serious conflict between income equality on the one hand and economic efficiency and growth on the other. A high degree of income equality could be attained in a capitalist society only at a very high cost in productive efficiency. In order to remain economically viable, the capitalist mode of production therefore requires significant inequalities in the distribution of labor income.

The inequalities in income from capital and income from labor-power combine to generate an unequal distribution of overall income. In order for the labor market to function effectively, most workers must have little or no capital and correspondingly low capital incomes. The necessary differentials in the labor incomes of workers will therefore be reflected in corresponding inequalities in overall incomes. On the other hand, the necessary concentration of capital ownership will result in inequalities of capital income that are not offset by any contrary inequalities in labor income. Thus it can be concluded that overall income inequality is indeed functionally essential to the capitalist mode of production. No amount of political intervention short of a complete transformation of the mode of production could eliminate income inequality under capitalism.

3. THE DYNAMICS OF INCOME INEQUALITY

I have argued in Section 2 that a certain degree of income inequality is inherent in any capitalist society. But the actual extent of this income inequality may well be greater than would be strictly essential to the capitalist mode of production. Current inequality in capitalist societies is in part the result of a historical legacy, but it is also attributable to dynamic forces operating within the process of capitalist growth itself. To analyze the impact of capitalist growth on income distribution, it is useful to examine first how the supply of factors of production owned by an individual is determined and how that supply can be increased over time. This requires a study of the *inheritance* and the *accumulation* of factors of production. Such a study in turn will shed light on the question of income mobility under capitalism, for income mobility depends upon the extent of intergenerational transmission of income-earning opportunities through the process of inheritance.

The amount of capital that a person owns depends on how much he inherits from his parents and how much he accumulates himself. Since there is no limit to the amount of capital one person can own, capital can be amassed into vast fortunes. The ownership of capital in all capitalist societies is in fact highly unequal.[5] I shall argue in this section that the process of capital accumulation within a generation tends to increase the concentration of capital ownership, while the process of capital inheritance from one generation to the next fails to arrest this tendency.

Capital is accumulated by an individual when he saves—refrains from consuming—a part of his income and invests these savings in the purchase of new capital to add to his existing stock. The ability to increase one's capital ownership thus depends upon how much surplus income one receives in excess of basic consumption needs. The higher one's overall income, the greater is the surplus available for investment and hence the greater is the opportunity for capital accumulation. Since basic consumption needs do not vary as greatly as overall income, the distribution of surplus income among households is necessarily far more unequal than the distribution of overall incomes. Large owners of capital are clearly favored over small owners because they receive correspondingly greater incomes from their capital. Their advantage is due both to the greater size of their holdings and to the fact that they tend to get higher rates of profit on their capital because of better access to relevant information and to profitable opportunities. As a result, large holders tend to save and invest much more than small holders of capital, and inequalities in capital ownership are thus likely to increase over time.

Since capital consists of material objects (or titles thereto), the inequalities of capital ownership that exist in one generation can be passed directly on to the next. Whether the process of inheritance tends to increase or decrease the dispersion of property ownership depends upon the extent of selective mating and on the relative reproduction rates of the rich and the poor. So long as the wealthy marry among themselves and the poor do likewise, the existing degree of inequality in property ownership is perpetuated. To the extent that the wealthy tend to have fewer heirs than the poor, the inequality is actually increased. On the other hand, anything short of a perfect match of wealth between husband and wife tends to reduce the disparities of ownership in the next generation.[6] On balance, it appears that the process of inheritance in a capitalist society is unlikely to increase or decrease significantly the degree of inequality of capital ownership over time.

It emerges quite clearly from the preceding discussion, however, that inheritance contributes heavily to intergenerational immobility in capital ownership. Perfect mobility would require that each individual have an

---

[5]For evidence from the United States, see Lundberg, Section 4.4, page 169. For evidence from England, see J. E. Meade, *Efficiency, Equality and the Ownership of Property* (Cambridge, Mass.: Harvard University Press, 1964), Chapter 2.

[6]See J. E. Meade, *Efficiency, Equality and the Ownership of Property*, for a more detailed and rigorous discussion of the points raised in the last two paragraphs.

equal opportunity to accumulate capital. Obviously, differential inheritance of capital transmits much of the inequality of capital ownership from one generation to the next. So long as property can be transferred readily from parents to children through family inheritance, the children of large holders will enjoy great privileges relative to the children of small holders. Only a drastic curtailment or abolition of the rights of inheritance could prevent the transmission of inequalities in capital ownership from one generation to the next. Yet to interfere seriously with inheritance rights would be incompatible with the capitalist mode of production because it would undermine the fundamental capitalist institutions of private property and the legal relations of ownership. As Milton Friedman has appropriately pointed out, "it seems illogical to say that a man is entitled . . . to the produce of the wealth he has accumulated, but that he is not entitled to pass any wealth on to his children."[7]

Like capital, the amount of labor-power that an individual possesses depends both on how much he inherits from his parents and on how much he accumulates himself. But the processes of inheritance and accumulation take on rather different forms in the case of labor-power. As noted earlier, marketable labor-power involves several kinds of productive attributes of an individual: personality characteristics, manual skills and cognitive skills. These attributes are acquired in part at birth (through biological inheritance), in part during early childhood (through family socialization), in part during school age (through the educational system), and in part on the job (through job training, experience, etc.). Labor-power can be inherited—directly or indirectly—at birth and in the process of family socialization; and it can be accumulated—to some extent —through education and job training.

[7]Milton Friedman, *Capitalism and Freedom*, p. 164.

The accumulation of labor-power during an individual's lifetime through investment in education and training is in many respects similar to the accumulation of capital through investment in productive property. The process whereby labor-power is accumulated is also likely to be disequalizing because those individuals with the greatest initial advantages—e.g., personality characteristics or cognitive abilities inherited at birth or developed through the family socialization process—are likely to be the best able to acquire even more. Tracking systems in high schools, competitive admissions procedures in colleges and universities, and the overall emphasis on promoting the "highest achievers" in educational institutions contribute to highly unequal educational opportunities. Such inequalities are further reinforced by the interaction of the possession of labor-power with monetary wealth. Parents who earn substantial labor incomes can use some of their money to invest in a longer and better education for their children than the children of the poor, thereby contributing further to the differential acquisition of productive attributes by the next generation.

There is only one major constraint on the accumulation of labor-power that does not apply to capital. This constraint is due to the embodiment of productive attributes in individual human beings and the fact that every individual life is finite. In order for the accumulation of labor-power to "pay off," an individual must work during part of his life. This means that the time during which he can profitably acquire productive attributes is limited, and hence the extent to which labor-power will be accumulated by any one individual is also limited. Because of this constraint, inequalities of labor-power are unlikely to become as vast as inequalities of capital ownership, and the forces tending toward an increase in the degree of inequality over time are less powerful in the case of labor-power than capital ownership.

The extent to which the inheritance of

labor-power accentuates and/or perpetuates inequalities over time depends primarily on the degree of selective mating in a society and to a lesser extent on differential rates of reproduction. Unlike property, which is precisely defined in quantity and must be divided among heirs, personality characteristics and cognitive skills are diffused in a more general way through biological inheritance and the family environment. The greater the tendency of men and women of the same social class to intermarry, the more disequalizing is the inheritance of labor-power. There are clearly very powerful social forces that favor marriage among relative equals in social and educational background, most notably educational channeling and class segregation of neighborhoods. Whether or not this effect is strong enough actually to exacerbate the degree of inequality over time, it is clearly a powerful force working to perpetuate the existing hierarchy of labor-power from one generation to the next.

Having considered separately the patterns of accumulation of the two basic factors of production within and between generations, it remains to examine their interaction to determine their overall impact on the time trend of income inequality and the extent of income immobility under capitalism. Whether increasing inequality in the distribution of labor-power and of capital leads also to increasing inequality in overall income depends upon (1) the extent to which the ownership of labor-power is correlated among individuals with the ownership of capital, and (2) the extent to which the relative shares of labor and capital in overall incomes change over time. Finally, it is important also to examine the impact of technological change on the overall distribution of income in a capitalist society.

The more highly correlated is the ownership of labor-power and capital, the more surely does the perpetuation of inequality in each contribute to the perpetuation of inequality in overall income. In fact, the own-

ership of and earnings from each of the two sources tend naturally to be associated with one another. People with high incomes from their labor-power are better able to save and to acquire income-yielding capital than are people with low labor incomes. And people with high incomes from their capital ownership are better able to purchase the educational services that can help to increase their marketable labor-power than are people with little capital income. Thus there is a significant degree of correlation of ownership of labor-power and capital that contributes to the existence and perpetuation of an unequal distribution of total incomes among individuals or family units.

Even if the degree of inequality in both labor and capital incomes were increasing over time, and if the two were perfectly correlated among individuals, there still *might not* be an increase in the degree of overall income inequality. This would be the case if the percentage share of total income represented by income from the more unequally distributed factor were diminishing over time. Income from capital is typically much more unequally distributed than income from labor. If the inequality in both types of income is increasing, but if an ever larger share of income represents returns to labor rather than to capital, then the increasing significance of labor incomes could result in a decline in the degree of inequality in overall income. There is, in fact, some evidence of a long-run increase in the share of labor income in the rich capitalist nations.[8] This increase probably reflects the decline in importance of independent proprietors and the growth of the white-collar working class; more people now rely on the sale of their labor-power as their main source of income.[9] The apparent rise in the share of labor in-

---

[8]See Simon Kuznets, *Modern Economic Growth,* pp. 177–86.

[9]For thorough documentation on the changing occupational structure of the labor force in the United States, see Reich, Section 4.5, p. 174.

come has a dampening effect on tendencies toward increased income inequality over time.

Thus far we have proceeded with the simplifying assumption that all income could be attributed directly to the ownership of factors of production. But the growth of an economy derives not only from the accumulation of factors of production but also through technological changes in the productive process that arise out of the development of new products and new methods of production. Such changes generate income that is received ultimately in the form of higher capital or labor incomes by the individuals involved, but the income really represents a return to technological innovation or entrepreneurial initiative.

Inequalities arising from and perpetuated by the differential ownership of labor-power and capital tend to be exacerbated by the impact of technological changes in a capitalist economy. It is generally those who own capital and/or control the work process who are best able to introduce new technologies and new products and thereby to reap the initial and very important monetary gains associated with their introduction. Likewise, it is the highly educated groups in society who are best able to adapt themselves to the new requirements of technical change and to seek out the most remunerative outlets for their labor. And, conversely, it is the least educated who are the least mobile geographically and occupationally, and therefore the least able to protect themselves by adapting to rapid technical and economic change.

CONCLUSION

In summary, there are important dynamic forces at work in the process of capitalist growth that tend to accentuate the degree of overall income inequality over time. There are also forces working in the opposite direction, whose strength will vary with the his-

torical context. One cannot therefore predict that a capitalist society will necessarily always tend towards greater income inequality over time. One can say, however, that there are very serious constraints on the reduction of existing income inequality in a capitalist society.

Some of the constraints which inhibit the reduction of income inequality under capitalism act as formidable barriers to intergenerational income mobility. The inheritance of capital ownership and of labor-power precludes equality of income-earning opportunity and assures that the hierarchy of income inequality will be transmitted to a significant degree from one generation to the next. Intergenerational income immobility remains an inherent characteristic of a capitalist society no matter what the precise trend in the degree of income inequality over time.

Although equality of income and equality of opportunity to earn income (income mobility) cannot be achieved in a capitalist society, some of the pressures for further inequality and further immobility might in principle be countered by deliberate state interference with the natural processes involved. For example, the state could redistribute income by taxing the rich much more than the poor; it could redistribute capital by levying high inheritance taxes; it could redistribute labor-power by providing for compensatory education, etc. Whether such actions are in fact undertaken depends upon the forces that act upon the state—the direct influence of the most powerful groups in the society, the indirect influence of the prevailing ideology, and the pressures exerted by the poor and the weak.[10] In most capitalist societies, the evidence suggests that relatively little redistribution has in fact been achieved by state action.[11] And it remains fundamen-

[10]For a discussion of the role of the state in capitalist society, see Sweezy, Section 3.8, p. 133, and Edwards and MacEwan, Section 3.9, p. 135.

[11]For evidence from the United States, see Ackerman *et al.*, Section 5.1, p. 207.

tally true that a significant degree of inequality and immobility is functionally essential to the institutions of a capitalist society. No amount of political intervention short of a complete transformation of these institutions—i.e., a change in the mode of production—could eradicate such inequalities under capitalism.

3.8 The Primary Function of the Capitalist State

We have now completed the general description of the capitalist mode of production outlined in the introduction to this chapter. One question which remains to be addressed is: What about the government? Central governments have become vast and powerful in modern society,* and many of capitalism's most blatant irrationalities seem to involve the failure of governments to act in a beneficial manner. No social theory can claim to be adequate or relevant unless it explains the operation of the state.

The question of state power will recur throughout this book.[1] In this reading Paul Sweezy introduces the subject with a theoretical analysis of the role of the capitalist state.

[1]See especially Weinstein, Section 4.7, p. 188, and O'Connor, Section 4.8, p. 192, for a discussion of the evolution of the role of the state in the United States.

Source: The following is excerpted from The Theory of Capitalist Development by PAUL M. SWEEZY (New York: Monthly Review Press, 1942), Chapter XIII. Copyright © 1942 by Paul M. Sweezy. Reprinted by permission of Monthly Review Press.

. . .

There is a tendency on the part of modern liberal theorists to interpret the state as an institution established in the interests of society as a whole for the purpose of mediating and reconciling the antagonisms to which social existence inevitably gives rise. This is a theory which avoids the pitfalls of political metaphysics and which serves to integrate in a tolerably satisfactory fashion a considerable body of observed fact. It contains, however, one basic shortcoming, the recognition of which leads to a theory essentially Marxian in its orientation. A critique of what may be called the class-mediation conception of the state is, therefore, perhaps the best way of introducing the Marxian theory.

The class-mediation theory assumes, usually implicitly, that the underlying class structure, or what comes to the same thing, the system of property relations is an immutable datum, in this respect like the order of nature itself. It then proceeds to ask what arrangements the various classes will make to get along with each other, and finds that an institution for mediating their conflicting interests is the logical and necessary answer. To this institution, powers for maintaining order and settling quarrels are granted. In the real world what is called the state is identified as the counterpart of this theoretical construction.

The weakness of this theory is not difficult to discover. It lies in the assumption of an immutable and, so to speak, self-maintaining class structure of society. The superficiality of this assumption is indicated by the most cursory study of history. The fact is that many forms of property relations with their concomitant class structures have come and gone in the past, and there is no reason to assume that they will not continue to do so in the future. The class structure of society is no part of the natural order of things; it is the product of past social development, and it will change in the course of future social development.

Once this is recognized it becomes clear that the liberal theory goes wrong in the manner in which it initially poses the problem. We cannot ask: Given a certain class structure, how will the various classes, with their divergent and often conflicting interests, manage to get along together? We must ask: How did a particular class structure come into being and by what means is its continued existence guaranteed? As soon as an attempt is made to answer this question, it appears that the state has a function in society which is prior to and more fundamental than any which present-day liberals attribute to it. Let us examine this more closely.

A given set of property relations serves to define and demarcate the class structure of society. From any set of property relations one class or classes (the owners) reap material advantages; other classes (the owned and the non-owners) suffer material disadvantages. A special institution capable and willing to use force to whatever degree is required is an essential to the maintenance of such a set of property relations. Investigation shows that the state possesses this characteristic to the fullest degree, and that no other institution is or can be allowed to compete with it in this respect. This is usually expressed by saying that the state, and the state alone, exercises sovereignty over all those subject to its jurisdiction, It is, therefore, not difficult to identify the state as the guarantor of a given set of property relations.

If now we ask where the state comes from, the answer is that it is the product of a long and arduous struggle in which the class which occupies what is for the time the key positions in the process of production gets the upper hand over its rivals and fashions a state which will enforce that set of property relations which is in its own interest. In other words any particular state is the child of the class or classes in society which benefit from the particular set of property relations which it is the state's obligation to enforce. A moment's reflection will carry the conviction that it could hardly be otherwise. As soon as we have dropped the historically untenable assumption that the class structure of society is in some way natural or self-enforcing, it is clear that any other outcome would lack the prerequisites of stability. If the disadvantaged classes were in possession of state power, they would attempt to use it to establish a social order more favorable to their own interests, while a sharing of state power among the various classes would merely shift the locale of conflict to the state itself.

That such conflicts within the state, corresponding to fundamental class struggles outside, have taken place in certain transitional historical periods is not denied. During those long periods, however, when a certain social order enjoys a relatively continuous and stable existence, the state power must be monopolized by the class or classes which are the chief beneficiaries.

As against the class-mediation theory of the state, we have here the underlying idea of what has been called the class-domination theory. The former takes the existence of a certain class structure for granted and sees in the state an institution for reconciling the conflicting interests of the various classes; the latter, on the other hand, recognizes that classes are the product of historical development and sees in the state an instrument in the hands of the ruling classes for enforcing and guaranteeing the stability of the class itself.

It is important to realize that, so far as capitalist society is concerned, "class domination" and "the protection of private property" are virtually synonymous expressions. Hence when we say with Engels that the highest purpose of the state is the protection of private property, we are also saying that the state is an instrument of class domination. This is doubtless insufficiently realized by critics of the Marxian theory who tend to see in the notion of class domination something darker and more sinister than "mere" protection of private property. In other words they tend to look upon class domination as something reprehensible and the protection of private property as something meritorious. Consequently, it does not occur to them to identify the two ideas. Frequently, no doubt, this is because they have in mind not capitalist property, but rather private property as it would be in a simple commodity-producing society where each producer owns and works with his own means of production. Under such conditions there are no classes at all and hence no class domination. Under capitalist relations, however, property has an altogether different significance, and its protection is easily shown to be identical with the preservation of class dominance.

Capitalist private property does not consist in things—things exist independently of their ownership—but in a social relation between people. Property confers upon its owners freedom from labor and the disposal over the labor of others, and this is the essence of all social domination whatever form it may assume. It follows that the protection of property is fundamentally the assurance of social domination to owners over nonowners. And this, in turn, is precisely what is meant by class domination, which it is the primary function of the state to uphold.

The recognition that the defense of private property is the first duty of the state is the decisive factor in determining the attitude of genuine Marxist socialism towards the state. "The theory of the Communists," Marx and Engels wrote in the *Communist Manifesto*, "can be summed up in the single sentence: Abolition of private property." Since the state is first and foremost the protector of private property, it follows that the realization of this end cannot be achieved without a head-on collision between the forces of socialism and the state power.

3.9   *Ruling Class Power and the State*

In the previous reading Sweezy argued that the primary function of the capitalist state is to defend capitalist institutions. This view of the state is essential for understanding its role in capitalist society.

The state cannot be held accountable for the failure to "solve" the irrationality and oppression of capitalist society, for it did not create the problems in the first place. The problems result from the capitalist mode of production. Insofar as the state helps to maintain the capitalist mode of production, it perpetuates—but does not cause—the attendant social problems. An important implication of this theory of the state is that transforming the state alone is insufficient to end the irrationality of capitalism.

In the following reading Richard C. Edwards and Arthur MacEwan discuss the exercise of political power in the capitalist state. They argue that the state is dominated—through a series of direct and indirect mechanisms—by the capitalist class, and that this domination implies that the state's activities will reflect and be responsive to the needs of that class.

This view of the state therefore builds directly on the interpretation given by Sweezy; according to both readings the top priority of the capitalist state is to defend and to facilitate the operation of capitalist institutions.

Note that Edwards and MacEwan claim that political power is only dominated—but not monopolized—by the capitalist class. It is possible that in any given situation, other groups can win concessions. Furthermore, preserving the entire system may on occasion require concessions within the capitalist institutional framework. But what this theory leads us to predict is that on fundamental issues, i.e., those involving the operation of the basic economic institutions, no concessions are possible.

In this chapter we wish to establish only a general theoretical view of the state. In later chapters we will consider in more detail the operation and impact of governmental institutions.[1]

[1]See in particular Weinstein, Section 4.7, p. 188; O'Connor, Section 4.8, p. 192; Edwards, Section 5.5, p. 244; Weisskopf, Section 9.1, p. 364; and MacEwan, Section 10.1, p. 409.

Source: The following is excerpted from "A Radical Approach to Economics: Basis for a New Curriculum" by RICHARD C. EDWARDS, ARTHUR MACEWAN et al. From the *American Economic Review* LX, No. 2 (May 1970). Reprinted by permission of the *American Economic Review*.

CLASS DIVISIONS IN CAPITALIST SOCIETY

The development and operation of capitalist institutions divides society into classes. First, class division is a prerequisite for the effective organization of the institutions: most of the population must be reduced to worker status while simultaneously a capitalist elite is created and its existence justified. Second, the basic institutions function so as to augment the wealth, power, and privilege of that elite.

The analysis of economic institutions which leads to these conclusions provides a basis for examining the exercise of power—the ability of groups to resolve the outcomes of social conflict processes in their own favor. First, the analysis provides the working hypothesis that economic organization is the basis of power. Second, the analysis emphasizes that the different classes have conflicting interests with regard to the maintenance of the existing social relations. Together, these statements would lead us to hypothesize that power in a capitalist society is dominated by the capitalist class, and since social conflict may lead to instability in the institutions themselves, the class exercises power primarily to maintain the institutions which function in its favor. The intervention of power—to deflect political threats, depoliticize class conflict, and so forth—assures the smooth functioning of capitalism.[1]

[1]While we argue that power is dominated by the capitalist class, that is not to say that it monopolizes power or that its rule is unrestricted. Furthermore, capitalists need not monopolize decision-making positions nor must they operate according to an articulated schema in order to be dominant. The existence of an ideology which favors capitalist interests and a sufficiently pervasive common set of objective self-interests among capitalists serves to assure that decisions will be in their favor. It is in this sense that we can identify the capitalist class as a ruling class. The dichotomous division of society into workers and capitalists obviously involves a simplification. Other groups (e.g., highly paid professionals, land-

THE OPERATION OF RULING
CLASS POWER—THE STATE

An example of the interaction between the operation of institutions and the exercise of power is provided by the recent history of welfare programs. [As was pointed out earlier in this chapter,] an unequal income distribution results from the functioning of the labor market, the system of individual gain incentives, and the linking of income to ownership and sale of productive factors. There are, however, several secondary forces which exacerbate inequality, and the reality of capitalism is even worse than the model. First, there are many family units which own no salable labor or other factors of production: the sick, the aged, the disabled. Second, there are those who own labor power but who are discriminated against in the labor market: blacks, other non-whites, and women. Third, income inequalities are exacerbated by unequal access to activities through which labor quality is "improved" (e.g., schooling and apprenticeship). Fourth, unemployment is always present in a capitalist system, and its incidence falls heaviest on the groups already at the bottom of the income ladder.

This situation poses a threat to capitalism. Those affected have no stake in maintaining the system and become unruly. The preservation of capitalism requires that the misery of poverty be alleviated, or at least that something be done about its appearance. Yet an attack on the basic causes of the problem, the functioning of the basic economic institutions, is ruled out. For example, an adequate welfare program would interfere with

work incentives; it would conflict with the principle that income is a payment for productive factors. Therefore, political power is focused on the secondary factors and symptoms, but the basic processes remain unaffected. Old age pension programs are established; equal opportunity employment regulations are legislated; manpower training programs are set up; unemployment compensation schemes are developed. Even if such programs were successful on their own terms, they could eliminate only the most severe aspects of inequality and poverty. In fact, most of these programs fail to achieve their own modest objectives.

Opposition to system-preserving welfare programs derives not only from their conflict with the institutions. Often, interest groups within the capitalist class or powerful professional groups are hurt by welfare legislation. Thus, the A.M.A. battles against medical care; housing developers oppose public housing programs and city planning; the automobile companies work to keep public transit facilities inadequate; textile employers subvert equal employment opportunity legislation. These are cases where class interests and self-interest seem to conflict. While the ruling class as a whole would benefit by establishing an ameliorative program and thereby securing its position, some of its members would be hurt. Thus because ruling class solidarity (see below) is at least as important for the preservation of that system as is preventing disruption by the poor, inadequate welfare programs are the outcome.

Welfare programs are but one example of ruling-class functioning—taking action, compromising within itself, absorbing discontent —carried out through the state. Other revealing examples are public education, tariff policies, financing of research programs, agriculture and transportation subsidies, and the structure of taxation. We believe that these operations of the state are best understood if the state is viewed as basically operating in the interests of the capitalist class.

---

owning farmers, etc.) exist who cannot readily be identified directly with either class. However, we use the term "worker" broadly to identify all who sell their labor power on a market and therefore the class categories extend to most of the population. Furthermore, our preceding analysis of capitalist institutions and our analysis below of the exercise of power lead us to the conclusion that these are the most important groups to study for understanding social change.

THE PRIORITIES OF THE STATE

If, as according to our hypothesis, the state is dominated by the capitalist class, then the operations of the state should reflect the needs of the capitalist class. In modern capitalist states, when the basic institutions have been thoroughly established, the maintenance and preservation of these institutions upon which the structure of class and privilege depends is of the greatest importance to the capitalist class. The uninhibited operation of the economic institutions will continue to bestow power, wealth, and prestige upon the capitalists. They do not need the state to enhance their position, only to assure it.

The system-preserving function of the state is evident in several areas. A continued threat to capitalism has been the failure of the economy autonomously to generate adequate aggregate demand. This failure has brought recurring crises with substantial unemployment. In spite of once seemingly inviolable ideological objections to the contrary, the state has assumed the function of demand regulator. Such regulation does not eliminate unemployment but simply reduces it to levels which are not system threatening.

A second system-preserving function of the state has been its decisive role in obfuscation and suppression of class conflict. This is accomplished through suppressing system-threatening groups (e.g., the Wobblies, Black Panthers), by deflecting their demands for structural changes into acceptable material demands (e.g., labor union economism, black capitalism), or through ameliorative programs. If we may modify the jargon of public finance, state actions such as suppression or amelioration may be viewed as "class goods." When the challenge posed by workers becomes severe, no single capitalist can protect himself. Were he to give concessions to his workers, his competitive position would be endangered. To employ private armies has been possible but highly inefficient. Thus, action by the capitalists as a class is necessary.

The enormous military establishment provides another example of system-preserving state operations; as such, it performs a dual function. First, it provides the rationale for huge expenditures which serve to maintain aggregate demand without threatening the security or position of any group in the ruling class. For example, social welfare measures often do threaten such groups. Second, as the capitalist system becomes increasingly an international system, the military directly protects the far-flung parts of that system.

The response of the state to changes in the process of production which require more highly developed labor, illustrates a second priority of the state; namely, the creation of new institutions. The rise of mass education in the United States has occurred in response to the need by industry for a skilled work force. Because workers are not tied to particular employment, individual capitalists cannot invest in the general training of workers and expect to appropriate the returns. Thus, capitalists turn to the state to provide a skilled work force. When education is handled by the state and portrayed as social welfare, it is paid for by general tax revenue rather than by the capitalists themselves.

The structure of the educational system betrays its class-oriented genesis. Mass education in the United States covers a vast quality range, and a positive association has been established between parents' incomes or class and the quality of public education which children receive. If, as seems reasonable, the benefits of education are correlated with the quality of that education, then the class bias of U.S. education is obvious. Thus the educational system operates to reinforce the class bias of the core economic institutions.[2]

There is a further aspect of the educational function which reveals its class bias; namely, its role in transmitting ideology. Students are taught a view of society which justifies the *status quo* and which poses efforts for change as unnecessary or futile.

[2]See Bowles, Section 5.2, p. 218.

The primacy of the roles of the state in preserving the system and in developing new institutions to meet changing circumstances should not obscure the fact that the state also intervenes directly in the economy to benefit immediate interests of capitalists. The most significant realm—in quantitative terms —where the state intervenes is in military and space spending, which we discussed above.

Another example of direct intervention, one which illustrates the case particularly well, is the government's relation to the agricultural sector. The general picture of what has happened in agriculture is well known. Wages in agriculture have remained low and unemployment high. Subsistence farmers have been unable to survive. The rural poor have been forced into the urban ghettos, supplying the low-cost labor force for industrial expansion. All the while, large farmers have received subsidies, price supports, and protection.

Furthermore, the very process which creates the agricultural problem is exacerbated by government programs. Government expenditure on agricultural research and extension has played a significant role in raising agricultural productivity at a more rapid rate than general productivity and has thereby contributed to the mass dislocation of rural workers and subsistence farmers. Those statistical studies which are available confirm casual empiricism: the overall impact of the government in its agricultural programs has been to increase inequality within the agricultural sector.[3]

The point is, however, not only that the process has worked toward increasing inequality but that it is the large owners of property—of the agricultural means of production—who benefit. Their benefit is derived directly from the programs which have been developed for "helping agriculture." Payment for unused land is of no help to rural laborers. Price supports for marketable

[3]See Bonnen, Section 5.4, p. 235.

surplus is of no help to subsistence farmers. Government subsidies for capital-augmenting technical change have the same class bias.

Military spending, agricultural subsidies, and other such programs provide ample ammunition for the muckraker. However, in terms of their importance in the overall operations of the state, we believe they are not of highest priority. Their position is behind the system-preserving and secondary-institutions-creating roles of the state. Nonetheless, when studied as a group, these actions of the state which directly enhance the privilege of the capitalist class reveal the basic character of the state in a capitalist society and provide a useful starting point for the analysis of power.

COHESION OF THE RULING CLASS

The term "ruling class" may evoke the image of a small, conspiratorial group which coldly calculates the oppression of the poor and its own gain. The actual functioning of the capitalist ruling class in the United States cannot, however, be well understood in such terms.

A class operates as a class in a number of ways. First, the class can be conscious of itself as a group with common objective interests, and can function cohesively on the basis of that consciousness. Second, the class can hold in common a value system or ideology which justifies the class's position and serves as a guide to action. Third, the class can coalesce on specific issues which serve the interests of some of its members if the favor is returned when the special interests of other members are at issue.

In general, it is difficult to distinguish which of these three mechanisms is at work at any given time. In the case of the United States, all three mechanisms operate. For example, elite schools, class-segregated neighborhoods, and social clubs tend to instill in ruling class members a sense of identity and of their separateness from the rest of society.

Thus, they become aware of their special stake in the *status quo* social relations and consciously work for the stability of the system. Obviously, if aware of their own position and if working toward a common goal, the members of the ruling class need not "conspire" to assure behavior in their common interest.

On the other hand, the very strong capitalist ideology in the United States tends to make class consciousness per se less important. A set of values that justify the position of the capitalist class, the basic institutions of capitalism, and the *status quo* in general provides a guide to action. Indeed, the prevalence of the capitalist ideology not only assures common action by members of the capitalist class but means that others will cooperate to serve capitalist interests above their own. This is the case, for example, when white workers accept racism and reject a working-class consciousness.

On many issues, logrolling furthers the class interest. This occurs when each group within the capitalist class structures its own policies so that they do not come into conflict with other groups within the class, expecting (and receiving) such cooperation in return. . . .

These mechanisms which tie a class together should not be confused with the objective identity of the class itself. The capitalist class in the United States is a ruling class. The degree to which it has consciousness, a strong ideology, and internal cooperation determines how successfully it can rule.

SELECTIVE BIBLIOGRAPHY

Further reading is recommended in Sweezy, *The Theory of Capitalist Development*, especially Chapters 1 to 4 and Chapter 13, and in Edwards and MacEwan, "A Radical Approach to Economics," as cited in the source lines for Sections 3.4 and 3.9. The original expression of many of these ideas is scattered throughout Karl Marx's writings, for which the classic and most comprehensive source, though very difficult and diffuse reading, is Marx [4]; see especially Vol. I, Part 1 for a basic discussion of commodity relations under capitalism, and Vol I, Part 8 for an excellent historical description of "The So-Called Primitive Accumulation." Nicolaus [7] reviews Marx's analysis of exchange relationships under capitalism in light of some important manuscripts of Marx which have only recently been published. An important book relating ideology and the development of particular character or personality types (elements of the Marxist "superstructure") to the requirements of economic institutions (the "base") is Reich [8], especially Chapter 1; Reich describes the mechanism creating the historical lag between changes in the base and the resulting ideology and personality changes. Merton *et al.* [5] gives a useful introduction to the dimensions of bureaucratic forms; see especially the essay by Merton, "Bureaucratic Structure and Personality," for an analysis of how the requirements of bureaucracy restrict personality development compatible with bureaucracy. Weber, "On Bureaucracy" and "The Meaning of Discipline" in [2], provides the classic definition of bureaucracy and statement of its operating rules. On the state, Bachrach [1] traces how bourgeois theorists have redefined "democracy" to be more consistent with political scientists' empirical observations of ruling elites. Lenin [3], especially Part 1, is a good exposition of the basic position that the capitalist state is dominated by, and acts in the interests of, the capitalist class; Miliband [6] is a more recent treatment of many of these issues, including a critique of pluralism, the role of the state in defending private property, and the state's new responsibilities for avoiding depressions.

[1] Bachrach, Peter, *The Theory of Democratic Elitism*. Boston: Beacon, 1968.

[2] Gerth, Hans, and C. Wright Mills, eds., *From Max Weber: Essays in Sociology*. New York: Oxford U. P., 1958.*

[3] Lenin, V. I., *State and Revolution*. New York: International Pub., 1939.* First published 1918.

[4] Marx, Karl, *Capital*, 3 vols. New York: International Pub., 1967.* First English edition, 1887.

[5] Merton, Robert K., Alisa P. Gray, Barbara Hockey, and Hanan C. Selvin, *Reader in Bureaucracy*. New York: Free Press, 1952.

[6] Miliband, Ralph, *The State in Capitalist Society* New York Basic Books, 1967.

[7] Nicolaus, Martin, "The Unknown Marx," *New Left Review*, No. 48, March-April, 1968; reprinted in Carl Oglesby, *The New Left Reader*, New York: Grove Press, 1969.

[8] Reich, Wilhelm, *The Mass Psychology of Fascism*, trans., Vincent R. Carfagno. New York: Farrar, Straus & Giroux, 1970.

*Available in paperback editions.

The Evolution
of American
Capitalism

No social system is ever completely stagnant. There are always forces at work—external or internal, equilibrating or disequilibrating—that contain the possibility of change over time. In Chapter 2 we examined some of the ways in which a combination of forces could lead to dynamic changes in the basic mode of production; the method of historical materialism was introduced as an analytical tool for studying such changes.

In Chapter 3 we focused upon the capitalist mode of production and the institutions that define it, since capitalism is the social system that has dominated the Western world for the past few centuries, and its domination has only recently begun to be seriously challenged. But during the period of its growth and maturity the capitalist system has undergone many changes. The form of capitalism that characterizes the modern American economy differs from earlier stages of capitalism as a result of a variety of forces that have been at work during this period.

Just as the method of historical materialism can be used to illuminate fundamental changes in the mode of production, so it provides a basis for examining evolutionary changes within the confines of a particular mode of production. The purpose of this chapter is to shed light on the nature of the changes that have occurred in American capitalism over the past century. In particular, it will be argued that these changes have largely represented the response of the economy and the society to the requirements of the capitalist mode of production in an age of increasing economic and industrial complexity.

The various changes that have occurred within the American capitalist system have had a significant impact upon the three major sectors of American society: business, labor, and the state. The readings in this chapter are devoted to each of these sectors. In each case material is presented to describe some of the salient aspects of the changes that have taken place and to evaluate the significance of those changes for the capitalist mode of production. Before turning to the readings, it may be helpful to outline briefly the major changes with which we are concerned.

The most striking development in American business over the past century has been the rise of the giant corporation. Most major industries are characterized by a very high concentration of economic activity among a few large corporations. The large corporations as a group dominate the American economy and are increasingly expanding to dominate the world capitalist economy as a whole. American capitalism has clearly come a long way since the days in which small family businesses were the typical unit of enterprise. The increase in size and the increasingly hierarchical structure of the typical firm have both responded to and helped to shape the development of an increasingly complex productive technology. In this chapter we shall be particularly concerned with the impact of these changes on the behavior of the firm and on its role within the economy as a whole.

The changes in the structure of the American labor force have been just as dramatic; it too has responded to changes in the forces of production. The decline in significance of the small firm has been accompanied by a similar decline in importance of the old middle class of independent proprietors. In their wake there has arisen a "new middle class" of white-collar workers whose numbers have grown much more rapidly than the blue-collar proletariat. We shall examine the extent to which white-collar workers themselves constitute a new educated proletariat, and the increasing role of the educational system in preparing workers to function efficiently in large hierarchical organizations.

Finally, we turn to the steadily increasing role of the state in the modern American economy. As the capitalist system has become more and more complex, increasing demands have been placed upon the state not only to protect the system itself, but also to regulate, to manage, and to intervene in various ways directly in the functioning of the system. Thus we observe the rise of regulatory agencies, the increasing use of fiscal policy to ensure economic stability, and increasing control and/or subsidization of activities such as education, transportation, the space program, etc., by the American government. We shall be particularly interested in analyzing the relationship between the increasing role of the state and the interests of the dominant capitalist class.

It is sometimes contended that the major changes discussed in this chapter constitute in themselves a fundamental change in the mode of production. However, we conclude that this assertion is false. We shall argue that the changes in business organization represent changes in form but not in substance: the giant corporation continues to pursue the capitalist objectives of profits and growth just as the old family firm did—in fact it is much better equipped to do so. The increasing stratification of the labor force has not eroded the distinction between capitalist and worker, for the educated white-collar workers are no less proletarian than their less educated blue-collar counterparts. In fact the decline of independent proprietors has led to an increase in the relative size of the proletariat, who remain sharply differentiated from the small number of wealthy capitalists and their managers who control the large corporations. Finally, we shall argue that the increasing role of the state is largely a response to the needs of the dominant capitalist class. Where there is conflict between individual capitalists and the capitalist class as a whole, the state is the key instrument which can and does represent the collective class interest. In sum, American society remains fundamentally capitalist in spite of—and because of—the major changes that have occurred in its recent history.

Although the readings that follow relate specifically to the evolution of capitalism within the United States, most of the conclusions are generally applicable to all of the advanced capitalist nations. In the first place, many of the changes that have taken place in the United States are matched by similar changes in other capitalist countries. Secondly, since the United States is the major power within an increasingly integrated capitalist system, what happens in the United States has an important impact on the evolution of capitalism throughout the world.

4.1   Business Concentration in the American Economy

The most obvious and at the same time the most important trend in American business organization has been the growth of the modern corporation and the domination of the economy by a small number of huge corporations. Although there are some 5 million individual business units in the United States today,[1] the top 150 corporations are so big and powerful that their removal "would effectively destroy the American economy."[2]

[1]Richard Caves, *American Industry: Structure, Conduct, Performance* (Englewood Cliffs, N.J.: Prentice-Hall, Inc., 1967), p. 1.

[2]Robert Heilbroner, *The Limits of American Capitalism* (New York: Harper and Row, Publishers, 1965), p. 13.

In the following reading, Gardiner Means assembles the available statistical information to assess the degree of concentration in the economy
as a whole and in the manufacturing sector (where the most data are available). Not only does he document the high degree of current concentration, but he shows that concentration has been increasing over time—
although in recent decades more slowly than in the beginning of this
century.

The reasons for which large-scale business tends to drive out small-
scale business are varied. Among the more important factors are: (1) technological economies of scale, where large-scale production is more efficient
and less costly than small-scale production; (2) financial economies of
scale, where large firms are better able to raise money, to absorb losses,
to take risks, etc., than small firms; (3) market economies of scale, where
large firms are better able to capture markets with sales promotion campaigns based on widely known brand names, etc. Such advantages can
often be translated into political as well as economic power, which helps
to reinforce the dominant position of large over small firms. In recognition of such tendencies toward greater concentration in private industry,
the U.S. government has legislated and implemented a series of antitrust
measures designed to curb excessive monopolistic power. Yet the legal
restrictions imposed on economic concentration have served merely to restrain but not to offset the natural forces at work in the opposite direction.[3]

A statistical appendix is included after Means's essay to provide further
documentation on the concentration of corporate power in the United
States.

[3]For a more detailed exposition of the issues raised in this paragraph, see Joe S.
Bain, *Industrial Organization* (New York: John Wiley & Sons, 1959).

Source: The following is excerpted from "Economic Concentration" by
GARDINER MEANS. From *Hearings Before the Subcommittee on Antitrust
and Monopoly of the Committee on the Judiciary*, United States Senate,
88th Congress, 2nd Session, pursuant to S. Res. 262, Part 1: Overall and
Conglomerate Aspects (Washington D.C.: U.S. Government Printing
Office, 1964).

. . .

CONCENTRATION IN THE
ECONOMY AS A WHOLE

Let me take you back a century to the economic conditions which prevailed just before
the Civil War. Then there was little concentration. Two-thirds of the labor force was
engaged in agriculture where the family farm
was the usual form of organization and
flexible farm prices were determined by the
interaction of a considerable number of
buyers and sellers in the market. There were
no telephones or electric power companies
then and the railroads were just beginning
to be consolidated. . . .

Likewise, with manufacturing, most production was in small local plants or in small
shops. The clothing industry was just coming
out of the home with the invention of the
sewing machine. The shoe industry was just
being brought into factories and shoes were
still made by handsewing or by pegging.

American ironmasters had only just shifted from the old method of hammering out bar iron in a forge fired by charcoal to the newer methods of rolling. The Bessemer steel furnace, invented in 1856, had not yet been put into practical operation and the open-hearth furnace was still to be developed.

At that time, ours was indeed an economy of small-scale enterprise. For practical purposes there was little concentration. For theoretical purposes even such concentration as existed could be disregarded. National economic policy could be decided on the basis of a body of economic theory which assumed that all production was carried on under conditions of classical competition; that is, competition in which no producer or consumer had significant pricing power; one in which the laws of supply and demand determined prices; and one in which most prices could not be administered and such administered prices as existed were not significant.

The next 70 years saw a complete change in the character of our economy. Mass production and big corporate enterprises took over much of manufacturing; the railroads were consolidated into a few great systems; public utility empires and the big telephone system developed; and, even in merchandising, the big corporation played a part.

By 1929, the economy of this country had become one in which the big modern corporation was the outstanding characteristic. Only a fifth of the labor force was engaged in agriculture. Railroads, public utilities, over 90 percent of manufacturing, and much of merchandising was conducted by corporations. In the year 1929, the 200 largest corporations legally controlled 48 percent of the assets of all nonfinancial corporations, that is, of all corporations other than banks, insurance companies, and similar financial companies. If we focus on land, buildings, and equipment—the instruments of physical production—the 200 largest corporations had legal control of 58 percent of the net

capital assets reported by all nonfinancial corporations. Thus, by 1929, the dominantly small-enterprise economy which prevailed in 1860 had been largely replaced by one in which the huge corporation was the most characteristic feature.

.   .   .

Since 1929, there have been forces working both against and for greater concentration in the American economy as a whole. In the 1930's, legislation against holding companies was passed and many of the big utility systems were broken up or forced to reorganize; further concentration in railroading was kept to a minimum; and the automobile, bus, and truck, took business away from the railroads so that, today, transportation, as a whole, is probably less concentrated than in 1929; in manufacturing, there was greater resistance to mergers among big companies than prevailed in the 1920's; and a larger proportion of national effort has gone into producing services such as health and recreation, which tend to be less concentrated activities. All of these tend to reduce or limit concentration.

On the other hand, there have been developments which have tended to increase the degree of concentration. Today, less than 7 percent of the gainfully employed are engaged in agriculture as compared with 20 percent in 1929; manufacturing is more concentrated than it was in 1929; the chain supermarket and other chain stores have increased in relative importance. . . .

I have tried to make an estimate of the proportion of corporate assets legally controlled by the 200 largest corporations comparable to that we made for 1929. The results are too crude to be worth publishing but they suggest that if a careful study were made . . . it would show [that] the [largest] 200 corporations legally controlled somewhat more than the 58 percent of the net capital assets controlled by the 200 that were largest in 1929. However, the most that I can say with reasonable certainty is that concentration for the economy as a whole is not significantly less than it was in 1929.

. . .

CONCENTRATION IN MANUFACTURING

Though manufacturing employs less than a quarter of the gainfully employed persons in this country, it is the field in which unregulated competition has been, *par excellence,* the instrument relied on to convert the actions of self-seeking individuals into actions which serve the public interest. . . . What has been the trend of concentration in manufacturing?

I have already pointed out that, in 1860, most of manufacturing was carried on in small-scale unincorporated enterprises. In the major industrial center of Pittsburgh, with 17 foundries, 21 rolling mills, 76 glass factories, and 47 other manufactories, not a single manufacturing enterprise was incorporated. The only industry in which the modern type of corporation played an important role was the cotton textile industry. The big integrated cotton mills of Lowell, Lawrence, and some other New England towns were incorporated with characteristics that today look quite modern. Indeed, they were known throughout New England as "the corporations." But apart from these cotton mills, big corporate business was almost nonexistent in manufacturing before the Civil War. Altogether it is doubtful if as much as 6 or 8 percent of manufacturing activity at that time was carried on by corporations and a much smaller proportion by what could be called in these days big corporations.

Between the Civil War and the turn of the century, there was a great increase in corporate manufacturing so that by 1900, close to two-thirds of manufacturing output was produced by corporations.[1]

[1] U.S. Bureau of Census, Historical Statistics of the United States (Washington, D.C.: U.S. Government Printing Office, 1960), p. 413.

Also toward the end of the century there was the first great merger movement culminating in the formation of the United States Steel Corp. as a merger of mergers in 1901. The pattern of mergers in this period is shown in Figure 4-A, which indicates the number of mergers reported in the *Commercial and Financial Chronicle* year by year from 1895 to 1914. It does not include all the mergers but presumably includes all the important mergers.

As you can see, there was a great burst of mergers from 1898 to 1902. All of this led to a great increase in manufacturing concentration even though a third of manufacturing output was still produced by unincorporated enterprises.

A very sharp peak in 1899, a heavy volume of mergers in 1900, 1901, and 1902, and then a fall off.

But the drive for monopoly created a strong public reaction. When Theodore Roosevelt became President in 1901, he was responsible for vigorous enforcement of the Sherman Act. The *Northern Securities* decision by the Supreme Court in 1904 outlawed the holding company as a device for achieving monopoly and other cases were brought which led to the breakup of the Standard Oil monopoly and the Tobacco Trust. Also some of the early combinations proved to be less successful than had been expected. As Figure 4-A shows, the wave of mergers came to an end as the goal of monopoly was clearly established as illegal. Between 1902 and the First World War, reported mergers averaged only a hundred a year. Whether there was an actual decline in manufacturing concentration in this period or a very slow growth is far from clear.

A second merger movement occurred after World War I, culminated in 1929, and was followed after the great depression by a quiescent period under a second President Roosevelt. This pattern of mergers is shown in Figure 4-B.

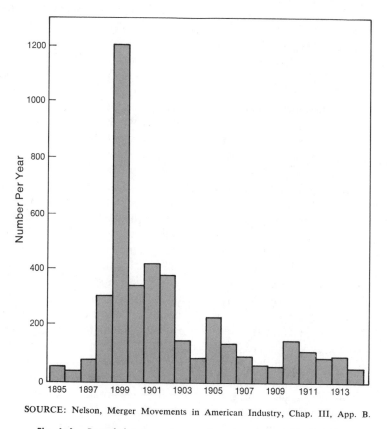

SOURCE: Nelson, Merger Movements in American Industry, Chap. III, App. B.

Fig. 4—A. Recorded mergers in manufacturing and mining, 1895–1914.

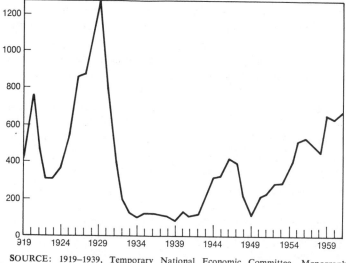

SOURCE: 1919–1939, Temporary National Economic Committee, Monograph No. 27, 1940–1961, Federal Trade Commission.

Fig. 4—B. Number of mergers and acquisitions in manufacturing and mining, 1919–1961

149

In this second merger movement, the aim of combination appears to have been quite different from that in the first. Particular big companies sought to strengthen their organization by acquiring companies which supplies raw materials or used their products or carried on similar—but not identical—types of manufacturing. Instead of monopoly-seeking horizontal merging we had vertical merging to obtain efficiencies in production and the merging of related products to obtain economies in management and merchandising.

Since World War II, there has been a renewal of the merging process but not on the scale of the earlier monopoly movement. The pattern of this third period also is indicated in Figure 4–B and includes all types of merging. These figures come from the Federal Trade Commission and are more comprehensive in their coverage than those covered by the first figure, but probably fail to include a significant number of small mergers. However, their inclusion would not change the general pattern though they would alter the actual number of mergers in particular years.

It is fair to assume that the greatest increases in manufacturing concentration have come in the three periods of greatest mergering. But increased concentration can also come from internal growth either through the reinvestment of earnings or from the sale of new securities, provided, of course, that the growth from these sources is more rapid for larger companies than for smaller companies. In a 6-year period in the 1920's more than four-fifths of the growth of large companies came from internal growth and only a fifth from mergers.[2] Presumably the present day concentration has come partly from mergers and partly from more rapid internal growth.

What has been the actual trend of manufacturing concentration and how far has concentration progressed?

Clearly a peak in the rate of concentration was reached just after 1900. It would be nice if we had reliable concentration data for that period but we don't. Certainly some lines of manufacturing such as steel were more concentrated at the turn of the century than they are today and some product lines such as cotton textiles are more concentrated today. But this is not the issue when we are considering concentration for manufacturing as a whole since mergers have been to a much greater extent either vertical or conglomerate and their effect on concentration is not fully reflected in separate product or narrow industry figures. Much careful research will be needed before we can determine the relative change in manufacturing concentration since 1900. And in this connection it is important to remember that, in 1900, only about two-thirds of manufacturing was carried on by corporations while today, 95 percent is corporate.[3]

The most reliable figures we have on concentration in manufacturing are those reported in the study made by the National Resources Committee for 1929. Among the 200 largest corporations in that year, the Resources Committee report included 82 manufacturing corporations. It included the Western Electric Co. along with the assets of its parent, the American Telephone & Telegraph Co., and it presented unconsolidated data for 107 large industrial corporations in 1935. From these data I have derived two concentration estimates for the 100 largest manufacturing corporations in 1929. According to these figures, 100 large companies in 1929 had legal control of approximately 40 percent of the total assets of all manufacturing corporations and 44 percent of their net capital assets. (See Table 4–A.)

[2]Adolf A. Berle, Jr. and Gardner C. Means, *The Modern Corporation and Private Property,* (New York: The Macmillan Co., 1933).

[3]U.S. Bureau of Census, *Historical Statistics of the United States* (Washington, D.C.: U.S. Government Printing Office, 1960), p. 413.

Let me explain just what these figures mean. The figures for legal control by the 100 largest mean that these companies either own the assets directly or control them through owning or controlling more than 50 percent of the stock of the corporations that do own the assets.[4]

By restricting the figures to legal control, the practical degree of concentration tends to be somewhat understated, partly because the figures exclude joint ventures in which each of two or more of the big companies owns 50 percent or less of a smaller company but in combination have legal control, and partly because practical or working control of one company can often be exercised with a holding of stock which is not sufficient to give legal control.

[4]Where two or more of the 100 largest corporations have a combined stock holdings of more than 50 percent in another corporation which would otherwise be included in the 100 largest, its assets are combined with the assets of the 100 largest as if it were legally controlled by one of them.

The figures for "total assets" include total current assets such as inventories, accounts receivable, and government securities and the fixed assets such as land, buildings and equipment after depreciation and depletion, but exclude the estimated holdings of securities of other corporations. The latter are excluded since they represent, in large degree, double counting. This still leaves some duplication in the figures due to intercorporate debt between parent and subsidiary but complete consolidation would probably not affect the concentration percentages significantly.

The figures for net capital assets include only the net property—the land, buildings, and equipment less depreciation and depletion. They constitute the instruments of production and provide the material basis for corporate power. A corporation is not industrially powerful because it has a large amount of bills receivable. It is not industrially powerful because it has large inventories. It is not industrially powerful because it has large holdings of government securities.

TABLE 4–A ASSETS OF 100 LARGEST MANUFACTURING CORPORATIONS IN 1929:

	Total Consolidated Assets (millions)	Ratio to All Manufacturing (percent)	Net Capital Assets (millions)	Ratio to All Manufacturing (percent)
82 largest (excluding Western Electric)	$23,641	37.0	$11,803	41.4
Western Electric	309	.5	70	.2
17 next largest	1,350	2.1	605	2.1
100 largest manufacturing corporations	25,300	39.6	12,478	43.7
All manufacturing corporations (including Western Electric)	63,955	100.0	28,531	100.0

SOURCE: For 82 largest: Gardner C. Means, *The Structure of the American Economy* (Washington, D.C.: National Resources Committee, 1939). For Western Electric, *Moody's Manual.* For total consolidated assets of 17 next largest, the partially consolidated figures given in the *Structure of the American Economy*, pp. 274–75—complete consolidation might increase the figures slightly. For net capital assets of 17 next largest, the ratio of net capital assets to total assets for all corporations (44.8 percent), was applied to the total assets of the 17 next largest. For all manufacturing corporations, *The Structure of the American Economy*, p. 285 plus Western Electric.

Its industrial power must rest on its control of factories or natural resources. For this reason, the 44 percent of net capital assets legally controlled by the 100 largest manufacturing corporations in 1929 would appear to be a more significant figure of concentration than the 40 percent of total assets held by the 100 largest. It has the added advantage that the figures for net capital assets do not involve any double counting.

Whether we consider total assets or net capital assets, the 40 percent or more controlled by the largest 100 corporations indicates that a very considerable degree of concentration existed in manufacturing in 1929.

What has happened since 1929? We have no figures for manufacturing concentration which are as reliable as those for 1929. However, I have attempted to make estimates for concentration in 1962 as nearly comparable with the 1929 figures as published data will allow. Because these estimates are less reliable, I want to indicate just how they were made.

The big problem in making such estimates arises from incomplete consolidation in the published figures of the large corporations. A few, like Standard Oil of New Jersey, publish balance sheets in which they consolidate the assets of all corporations in which they control more than 50 percent of the voting stock. More often corporations consolidate only those subsidiaries in which they have a 95 to 100 percent stock interest, reporting the stocks of corporations over which they have legal control by a smaller percent as "investments in subsidiaries" or in the larger category of "other noncurrent assets." As a result, the assets over which they have legal control exceed the assets reported in their balance sheets to the extent that the assets of controlled companies exceed the value of their stocks on the books of the controlling company. To get a clear picture of concentration, it is necessary to approximate a more complete consolidation. In

making the study for 1929 back in the 1930's, a small staff and I were sworn into the Bureau of Internal Revenue and had direct access to the actual tax returns of corporations. We selected what appeared to be the biggest 200 companies and then for all other corporations with 14 million assets or more and for a sample of still smaller companies, several thousand companies in total, we searched the standard reference books to discover all cases in which more than 50 percent of the stock was controlled by one of the big companies. While we undoubtedly missed some subsidiaries, we probably picked up most of the important ones. . . .

Today much more information is publicly available than in 1929 but it would still be necessary to go into the detailed information in the hands of Government to make an estimate as reliable as that which we made in 1929. For my present estimates I have done the best I could with the information that has been made public. . . . I [have compiled a list of] what appear to be the 100 largest manufacturing corporations in 1962, giving their total assets, including investments, and their net capital assets. . . . [I have also adjusted] the total assets and

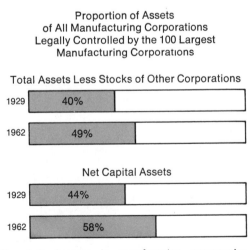

Proportion of Assets
of All Manufacturing Corporations
Legally Controlled by the 100 Largest
Manufacturing Corporations

Total Assets Less Stocks of Other Corporations

| 1929 | 40% |
| 1962 | 49% |

Net Capital Assets

| 1929 | 44% |
| 1962 | 58% |

Fig. 4—C. Increase in manufacturing concentration measured by assets, 1929–1962.

property of these 100 companies for inter-corporate stockholding, [comparing] the result with the adjusted assets of all manu-facturing corporations to [obtain] ratios of concentration comparable to those for 1929.

On this basis, I estimate that the 100 larg-est manufacturing corporations in 1962 con-trolled at least 49 percent of the assets of all manufacturing corporations (excluding stocks in other corporations) and 58 percent of the net capital assets—the net land, build-ings and equipment—of all manufacturing corporations.

These estimates, though less reliable than those for 1929, suggest that there has been a very considerable increase in concen-tration in manufacturing as a whole in the last 33 years. The difference is shown in Fig-ure 4–C, which compares the estimates for the 2 years.

The top panel shows the increase in the proportion of total assets held by the 100 largest from 40 to 49 percent, the area in black. The lower panel shows the corre-sponding increase for net capital assets from 44 to 58 percent. This is a very sizable in-crease in concentration since 1929.

Just when this increase in concentration took place is debatable. There is little ques-tion that there was a considerable increase in concentration from 1929 to 1933 as business activity declined in the great depression. How much of this was a temporary depression effect which would be reversed with recov-ery and how much it was a part of the long run trend in manufacturing concentration is not clear. Certainly some of it was reversi-ble. The net capital assets of the big com-panies declined only 6 percent in that pe-riod while the net capital assets of smaller companies declined 24 percent. Some of this was the result of big companies acquiring the assets of smaller companies. But to a greater extent it reflected the simple closing down of many smaller companies which would be reopened or replaced in the period

of recovery. In measuring trends in concen-tration as in measuring trends in so many other economic factors, I believe the only valid comparisons are between years which are reasonably comparable in the rate of business activity.

The question of whether—and the extent to which—events during and after World War II contributed to this overall increase is a subject on which I am not commenting here. . . . What I can testify to is that man-ufacturing concentration, whether measured by total assets or by net capital assets, has increased greatly since 1929 and that, with-out taking account of joint ventures or com-panies controlled through less than a ma-jority ownership, somewhere in the close vicinity of 58 percent of the net capital as-sets of manufacturing are controlled by 100 companies. . . .

Statistical Appendix
(by the editors)

THE CONCENTRATION OF CORPORATE POWER IN THE UNITED STATES

The degree of concentration of corporate economic power in the United States is fur-ther illuminated in the following tables. Ta-ble 4–B lists the top 25 industrial corpora-tions in the United States in 1969 ranked by sales volume. For each of these firms, the level of sales and the level of after-tax prof-its are shown along with the corresponding rank listings. In addition, the cumulative sales and profits totals of the top 10, the top 25, the top 50, and the top 100 firms are tabulated and expressed as a percentage of the corresponding figure for all industrial corporations.

The extent of industrial concentration

TABLE 4–B SALES AND PROFITS OF THE LARGEST INDUSTRIAL CORPORATIONS IN THE U.S., 1969 (all figures in millions of dollars)

Corporation	Rank	Sales Level	%	Rank	After-Tax Profits Level	%
General Motors	1	$24,925		1	$1,711	
Standard Oil (N.J.)	2	14,930		2	1,048	
Ford Motor	3	14,756		6	547	
General Electric	4	8,448		13	278	
IBM	5	7,197		3	934	
Chrysler	6	7,052		58	89	
Mobil Oil	7	6,621		8	435	
Texaco	8	5,868		4	770	
ITT	9	5,475		15	234	
Gulf Oil	10	4,953		5	611	
TOP 10		99,595	14.4			23.9
Western Electric	11	4,883		17	227	
U.S. Steel	12	4,754		18	217	
Standard Oil (Calif.)	13	3,825		7	454	
Ling-Temco-Vought	14	3,750		500	−38	
DuPont	15	3,655		10	356	
Shell Oil	16	3,537		12	292	
Westinghouse Electric	17	3,509		33	150	
Standard Oil (Indiana)	18	3,469		11	321	
Gen. Telephone & Electronics	19	3,262		14	237	
Goodyear	20	3,215		27	158	
RCA	21	3,188		32	151	
Swift	22	3,108		225	22	
McConnell-Douglas	23	3,024		44	118	
Union Carbide	24	2,933		20	186	
Bethlehem Steel	25	2,928		29	157	
TOP 25		152,995	22.0		9,665	34.7
TOP 50		209,838	30.2		12,407	44.4
TOP 100		280,751	40.6		16,287	58.2
TOTAL		692,512	100.0		27,931	100.0

SOURCES: 1. Individual corporation data: *Fortune*, May 1970 (Directory of the top 500 industrial corporations) 2. Total corporation data: U.S. Dept. of Commerce, *Survey of Current Business*, July 1970, Table 6-15 (data for mining, manufacturing and rest of world) and Table 6-19 (data for mining and manufacturing).

TABLE 4–C PROFIT RATES OF ALL U.S. CORPORATIONS BY ASSET SIZE

	Asset class (lower limit)							
Year	$0	$50,000	$100,000	$250,000	$500,000	$1,000,000	$5,000,000	$10,000,000	$50,000,000
1931	−21.6	−8.9	−6.3	−4.4	−3.6	−2.7	−1.5	−0.2	2.4
1937	−8.2	1.8	3.9	4.9	5.3	6.0	6.0	6.9	5.4
1943	14.6	15.9	18.0	20.5	22.1	22.6	22.8	22.0	17.0
1949	−3.4	7.4	10.5	12.9	13.5	14.3	13.9	14.6	13.9
1955	−1.6	7.9	10.3	11.1	12.9	14.1	14.1	16.0	17.2
1961	−4.9	6.4	8.2	8.1	9.4	9.8	10.2	10.6	11.2

*Total profits or losses before taxes were divided by equity to obtain the profit rate, which is expressed as a percentage; the data are from U.S. Treasury Department, Internal Revenue Service, *Statistics of Income: Tax Returns*, vols. for 1916-1961 (Washington, D.C.: U.S.G.P.O., 1919-1965).

SOURCE: Excerpted from Howard J. Sherman: *Profits in the United States: An Introduction to a Study of Economic Concentration and Business Cycles*, pp. 231-32. Copyright © 1968 by Cornell University. Used by permission of Cornell University Press.

emerges plainly from the figures. The top 10 firms account for fully one-seventh of total industrial sales and almost one-quarter of total industrial after-tax profits. The top 100 firms account for more than 40 percent of total sales and almost 60 percent of total profits. Profits are evidently even more highly concentrated than sales or assets; of the three measures, the level of profits is probably the best indicator of the power of a firm.

The data in Table 4–B suggest that larger firms not only make a higher absolute level of profits than smaller firms, but that they also make a higher percentage *rate* of profit. A recent study by Howard Sherman[1] confirms the hypothesis that profit rates tend to increase with the size of a firm as measured by the value of its assets. Table 4–C reports

[1]*Profits in the United States* (Ithaca, N.Y.: Cornell University Press, 1968).

TABLE 4–D   CONCENTRATION IN MANUFACTURING INDUSTRIES

Percentage of Sales, Total Assets,
Net Capital Assets, and Profits after Taxes Accounted for by the
4 Largest Firms in Each Industry for 28 Selected Industry Groups,
4th Quarter, 1962

	Percent of total			
Industry	Sales	Total Assets	Net Capital Assets	Profits
Motor vehicles	80.8	79.7	83.1	89.1
Aircraft	47.3	41.9	32.6	46.6
Other transportation equipment	30.3	44.2	59.9	51.6
Electrical machinery	34.4	35.6	41.5	44.4
Metalworking machinery	14.5	16.3	18.5	19.1
Other machinery	20.6	24.3	31.5	39.6
Primary iron and steel	40.2	48.0	48.8	44.3
Primary nonferrous metals	27.3	41.1	47.7	37.1
Other fabricated metal products	14.7	19.9	30.3	17.7
Stone, clay, and glass products	18.1	19.9	19.8	23.4
Furniture and fixtures	5.2	8.4	9.6	5.3
Lumber and wood products	21.2	31.0	41.5	48.6
Instruments	37.9	41.2	50.2	56.6
Miscellaneous manufacturing	16.3	33.1	34.3	25.2
Dairy products	42.9	48.8	47.4	73.9
Bakery products	33.6	39.6	38.2	52.8
Other food	12.5	13.2	14.9	20.1
Textile mill products	22.0	26.1	25.7	30.5
Apparel	4.9	7.7	11.4	7.4
Paper	20.7	23.2	22.3	35.0
Basic industrial chemicals	42.0	45.5	44.6	64.6
Drugs and medicines	31.0	29.2	33.3	32.6
Other chemicals	28.5	30.0	33.6	35.8
Petroleum refining	50.3	50.1	47.7	54.3
Rubber	48.1	55.0	56.4	51.6
Leather	26.7	32.1	35.4	28.8
Alcoholic beverages	41.4	47.2	30.8	58.3
Tobacco	70.9	72.7	69.8	72.5

SOURCE: Bureau of Economics, Federal Trade Commission.

the key results of Sherman's study: it shows annual profit rates by asset classes for all corporations in selected years from 1931 to 1961.

The degree of concentration of corporate power varies considerably among different industries. Table 4-D shows the percentage of total sales, assets, and profits accounted for by the four largest firms in 28 different industry groups. Among the most highly concentrated are the transportation equipment industries—motor vehicles, aircraft, and other transportation equipment—and such basic raw material industries as iron and steel, industrial chemicals, rubber, and petroleum. The least concentrated industries tend to be relatively light consumer good industries, e.g., apparel, furniture, and "other food" products. The list of the top 25 corporations in Table 4–B confirms that the most powerful firms in the United States are predominantly in the core industrial sectors of the economy.

4.2 The Evolution of the Multinational Corporation

The increasing concentration of capitalist enterprise has gone hand in hand with a steady increase in the size of the representative firm. In the following reading Stephen Hymer analyzes the changes in the scope and structure of the individual firm that have accompanied its growth from the small workshop to the international corporation. One of the most significant points that emerges from Hymer's analysis is that, with the passage of time, it becomes less and less meaningful to analyze the capitalist system as contained within the borders of a single country and more and more important to recognize it as a worldwide system dominated by a set of multinational corporations. In chapter 10 we pursue the analysis of the multinational corporation as it contributes to imperialist expansion.[1]

[1]See especially MacEwan, Section 10.1, p. 409, and Baran and Sweezy, Section 10.4, p. 435.

. . .

Since the beginning of the Industrial Revolution, there has been a tendency for the representative firm to increase in size from the *workshop* to the *factory* to the *national corporation* to the *multidivisional corpora-**tion* and now to the *multinational corporation*. This growth has been qualitative as well as quantitative. With each step business enterprise acquired a more complex administrative structure to coordinate its activities and a larger brain to plan for its survival and growth. . . . [T]his essay traces the evolution of the corporation, stressing the development of a hierarchical system of authority and control.

. . .

THE MARSHALLIAN FIRM AND THE MARKET ECONOMY

Giant organizations are nothing new in international trade. They were a characteristic form of the mercantilist period when large joint-stock companies, e.g., The Hudson's Bay Co., The Royal African Co., The East India Co., to name the major English merchant firms, organized long-distance trade with America, Africa and Asia. But neither these firms, nor the large mining and plantation enterprises in the production sector, were the forerunners of the multinational corporation. They were like dinosaurs, large in bulk, but small in brain, feeding on the lush vegetation of the new worlds (the planters and miners in America were literally *Tyrannosaurus rex*).

The merchants, planters and miners laid the groundwork for the Industrial Revolution, but the driving force came from the small-scale capitalist enterprises in manufacturing, operating at first in the interstices of the feudalist economic structure, but gradually emerging into the open and finally gaining predominance. It is in the small workshops, organized by the newly emerging capitalist class, that the forerunners of the modern corporation are to be found.

The strength of this new form of business enterprise lay in its power and ability to reap the benefits of division of labor. Without the capitalist, economic activity was individualistic, small-scale, scattered and unproductive. But a man with capital, i.e., with sufficient funds to buy raw materials and advance wages, could gather a number of people into a single shop and obtain as his reward the increased productivity that resulted from specialization and cooperation. The reinvestment of these profits led to a steady increase in the size of capital, making further division of labor possible, and creating an opportunity for using machinery in production. A phenomenal increase in productivity and production resulted from this process, and entirely new dimensions of human existence were opened. The growth of capital revolutionized the entire world and, figuratively speaking, even battered down the Great Walls of China.

The hallmarks of the new system were *the market* and *the factory*, representing the two different methods of coordinating the division of labor. In the factory, entrepreneurs consciously plan and organize cooperation, and the relationships are hierarchical and authoritarian; in the market, coordination is achieved through a decentralized, unconscious, competitive process.

To understand the significance of this distinction, the new system should be compared to the structure it replaced. In the pre-capitalist system of production, the division of labor was hierarchically structured at the *macro* level, i.e., for society as a whole, but unconsciously structured at the *micro* level, i.e., the actual process of production. Society as a whole was partitioned into various castes, classes and guilds, on a rigid and authoritarian basis so that political and social stability could be maintained and adequate numbers assured for each industry and occupation. Within each sphere of production, however, individuals by and large were independent and their activities only loosely coordinated, if at all. In essence, a guild was composed of a large number of similar individuals, each performing the same task in roughly the same way with little cooperation or division of labor. This type of organization could produce high standards of quality and workmanship but was limited quantitatively to low levels of output per head.

The capitalist system of production turned

this structure on its head. The macro system became unconsciously structured, while the micro system became hierarchically structured. The market emerged as a self-regulating coordinator of business units as restrictions on capital markets and labor mobility were removed. (Of course the State remained above the market as a conscious coordinator to maintain the system and ensure the growth of capital.) At the micro level, that is, the level of production, labor was gathered under the authority of the entrepreneur capitalist.

Marshall, like Marx, stressed that the internal division of labor within the factory, between those who planned and those who worked (between "undertakers" and laborers), was "the chief fact in the form of modern civilization, the 'kernel' of the modern economic problem."[1] Marx, however, stressed the authoritarian and unequal nature of this relationship based on the coercive power of property and its anti-social characteristics. He focused on the irony that concentration of wealth in the hands of a few and its ruthless use were necessary historically to demonstrate the value of cooperation and the social nature of production.[2]

· · ·

THE CORPORATE ECONOMY

The evolution of business enterprise from the small workshop (Adam Smith's pin factory) to the Marshallian family firm represented only the first step in the development of business organization. As total capital accumulated, the size of the individual concentrations composing it increased continuously, and the vertical division of labor grew accordingly.

It is best to study the evolution of the corporate form in the United State environment, where it has reached its highest stage. In the 1870s, the United States industrial structure consisted largely of Marshallian type, single-function firms, scattered over the country. Business firms were typically tightly controlled by a single entrepreneur or small family group who, as it were, saw everything, knew everything, and decided everything. By the early twentieth century, the rapid growth of the economy and the great merger movement had consolidated many small enterprises into large national corporations engaged in many functions over many regions. To meet this new strategy of continent-wide, vertically integrated production and marketing, a new administrative structure evolved. The family firm, tightly controlled by a few men in close touch with all its aspects, gave way to the administrative pyramid of the corporation. Capital obtained new powers and new horizons. The domain of conscious coordination widened, and that of market-directed division of labor contracted.

According to Chandler[3] the railroad, which played so important a role in creating the national market, also offered a model for new forms of business organization. The need to administer geographically dispersed operations led railway companies to create an administrative structure which distinguished field offices from head offices. The field offices managed local operations; the head office supervised the field offices. According to Chandler and Redlich, this distinction is important because "it implies that the executive responsible for a firm's affairs had, for the first time, to supervise the work of other executives."[4]

[1] Alfred Marshall, *Principles of Economics,* 8th ed. (London: Macmillan, 1920), p. 75.
[2] Karl Marx, *Capital*, Vol. I (Moscow: Foreign Language Publishing House, 1961), p. 356.

[3] Alfred D. Chandler, *Strategy and Structure* (New York: Doubleday & Co., 1961).
[4] Alfred D. Chandler and Fritz Redlich, "Recent Developments in American Business Administration and Their Conceptualization," *Business History Review*, Spring, 1961, pp. 103–28.

This first step towards increased vertical division of labor within the management function was quickly copied by the recently formed national corporations, which faced the same problems of coordinating widely scattered plants. Business developed an organ system of administration, and the modern corporation was born. The functions of business administration were subdivided into *departments* (organs)—finance, personnel, purchasing, engineering, and sales—to deal with capital, labor, purchasing, manufacturing, etc. This horizontal division of labor opened up new possibilities for rationalizing production and for incorporating the advances of physical and social sciences into economic activity on a systematic basis. At the same time a brain and nervous system, i.e., a vertical system of control, had to be devised to connect and coordinate departments. This was a major advance in decision-making capabilities. It meant that a special group, the Head Office, was created whose particular function was to coordinate, appraise, and plan for the survival and growth of the organism as a whole. The organization became conscious of itself as organization and gained a certain measure of control over its own evolution and development.

The corporation soon underwent further evolution. To understand this next step we must briefly discuss the development of the United States market. At the risk of great oversimplification we might say that by the first decade of the twentieth century, the problem of production had essentially been solved. By the end of the nineteenth century, scientists and engineers had developed most of the inventions needed for mass producing at low cost nearly all the main items of basic consumption. In the language of systems analysis, the problem became one of putting together the available components in an organized fashion. The national corporation provided *one* organizational solution, and by the 1920s it had demonstrated its great power to increase material production.

. . .

[But] the uneven growth of per capita income [that characterized economic development under capitalism] implied unbalanced growth and the need on the part of business to adapt to a constantly changing composition of output. Firms in the producers' goods sectors had continuously to innovate labor-saving machinery because the capital/output ration was increasing steadily. In the consumption goods sector, firms had to continuously introduce new products since, according to Engel's Law, people do not generally consume proportionately more of the same things as they get richer, but rather reallocate their consumption away from old goods and towards new goods. This non-proportional growth of demand implied that goods would tend to go through a life-cycle, growing rapidly when they were first introduced and more slowly later. If a particular firm were tied to only one product, its growth rate would follow this same life-cycle pattern and would eventually slow down and perhaps even come to a halt. If the corporation was to grow steadily at a rapid rate, it had continuously to introduce new products.

Thus, product development and marketing replaced production as a dominant problem of business enterprise. To meet the challenge of a constantly changing market, business enterprise evolved the multidivisional structure. The new form was originated by General Motors and DuPont shortly after World War I, followed by a few others during the 1920s and 1930s, and was widely adopted by most of the giant U.S. corporations in the great boom following World War II. As with the previous stages, evolution involved a process of both differentiation and integration. Corporations were decentralized into several *divisions*, each concerned with one product line and organized with its own head office. At a higher level, a *general office* was created to coordinate the divisions and to plan for the enterprise as a whole.

The new corporate form has great flexibility. Because of its decentralized structure, a multidivisional corporation can enter a new market by adding a new division while leaving the old divisions undisturbed. (And to a lesser extent it can leave the market by dropping a division without disturbing the rest of its structure.) It can also create competing product-lines in the same industry, thus increasing its market share while maintaining the illusion of competition. Most important of all, because it has a cortex specializing in strategy, it can plan on a much wider scale than before and allocate capital with more precision.

The modern corporation is a far cry from the small workshop, or even from the Marshallian firm. The Marshallian capitalist ruled his factory from an office on the second floor. At the turn of the century, the president of a large national corporation was lodged in a higher building, perhaps on the seventh floor, with greater perspective and power. In today's giant corporation, managers rule from the top of skyscrapers; on a clear day, they can almost see the world.

U.S. corporations began to move to foreign countries almost as soon as they had completed their continent-wide integration. For one thing, their new administrative structure and great financial strength gave them the power to go abroad. In becoming national firms, U.S. corporations learned how to become international. Also, their large size and oligopolistic position gave them an incentive. Direct investment became a new weapon in their arsenal of oligopolistic rivalry. Instead of joining a cartel (prohibited under U.S. law), they invested in foreign customers, suppliers and competitors. For example, some firms found they were oligopolistic buyers of raw materials produced in foreign countries and feared a

monopolization of the sources of supply. By investing directly in foreign producing enterprises, they could gain the security implicit in control over their raw material requirements. Other firms invested abroad to control marketing outlets and thus maximize quasi rents on their technological discoveries and differentiated products. Some went abroad simply to forestall competition.

The first wave of U.S. direct foreign capital investment occurred around the turn of the century, followed by a second wave during the 1920s. The outward migration slowed down during the depression but resumed after World War II and soon accelerated rapidly. Between 1950 and 1969, direct foreign investment by U.S. firms expanded at a rate of about 10 percent per annum.[5] At this rate it would double in less than 10 years, and even at a much slower rate of growth, foreign operations will reach enormous proportions over the next 30 years.

Several important factors account for this rush of foreign investment in the 1950s and the 1960s. First, the large size of the U.S. corporations and their new multidivisional structure gave them wider horizons and a global outlook. Secondly, technological developments in communications created a new awareness of the global challenge and threatened established institutions by opening up new sources of competition. For reasons noted above, business enterprises were the first to recognize the potentialities and dangers of the new environment and to take active steps to cope with it.

A third factor in the outward migration of U.S. capital was the rapid growth of Europe and Japan. This, combined with the slow growth of the United States economy in the 1950s, threatened the dominant position of American corporations. Firms confined to the U.S. market found themselves falling behind in the competitive race and losing ground to

[5]See Table 10–B, p. 429.

European and Japanese firms, which were growing rapidly because of the expansion of their markets. Thus, in the late 1950s, United States corporations faced a serious "non-American" challenge. Their answer was an outward thrust to establish sales production and bases in foreign territories. This strategy was possible in Europe, since governments there provided an open door for United States investment, but was blocked in Japan, where the government adopted a highly restrictive policy. To a large extent, United States business was thus able to redress the imbalances caused by the Common Market, but Japan remained a source of tension to oligopoly equilibrium.

What about the future? The present trend indicates further multinationalization of all giant firms, European as well as American. In the first place, European firms, partly as a reaction to the United States penetration of their markets, and partly as a natural result of their own growth, have begun to invest abroad on an expanded scale and will probably continue to do so in the future, and even to enter the United States market. This process is already well underway and may be expected to accelerate as time goes on. The reaction of United States business will most likely be to meet foreign investment at home with more foreign investment abroad. They, too, will scramble for market positions in underdeveloped countries and attempt to get an even larger share of the European market, as a reaction to European investment in the United States. Since they are large and powerful, they will on balance succeed in maintaining their relative standing in the world as a whole—as their losses in some markets are offset by gains in others.

4.3   *The Behavior of the Large Corporation*

The preceding readings have shown that the large corporation is now the representative and the dominant type of firm in the American economy. The large corporation is typically characterized by (1) great power and considerable financial independence and (2) a nominal separation of ownership and control, where ownership is vested in a large number of stockholders and control is exercised by top-level management executives. These characteristics have suggested to some observers that the modern corporation is capable of pursuing—and often does pursue—policies that serve socially desirable goals rather than the narrow private objective of profit maximization.

In the following reading, Paul Baran and Paul Sweezy begin by examining some of the arguments in support of the proposition that the large corporation has become a "soulful" one. They acknowledge the major differences between the modern corporation and the individually owned business enterprise of an earlier era, but go on to conclude on the basis of both theoretical and empirical evidence that "the economy of large corporations is more, not less, dominated by the logic of profit-making than the economy of small entrepreneurs ever was."

In a careful statistical study,[1] Robert J. Larner has provided further

---

[1]Robert J. Larner, "The Effect of Management-Control on the Profits of Large Corporations," in Maurice Zeitlin (ed.), *American Society, Inc.* (Chicago: Markham Publishing Co., 1970).

support for the proposition that the management-controlled corporation typical of the modern American economy is just as much oriented to the maximization of profits as the more old-fashioned owner-controlled firm. Larner separated 128 management-controlled corporations from 59 owner-controlled firms (all in the top 500) and found that there are no significant differences between the profit rates of the two types of firms. He attributes this result in part to the financial stake that management executives have in their own companies. His evidence on 93 chief executives from the corporations he studied shows that the corporations' dollar profit and rate of return on equity were the major variables affecting the overall level of executive compensation. Like Baran and Sweezy, Larner concludes that the nominal separation of ownership and control in modern corporations has made no significant difference to the behavior of the capitalist firm.

The analysis in this reading by Baran and Sweezy involves the application to the contemporary American economy of many of the points introduced in a more general context by Edwards in Chapter 3.[2] The profit-maximizing orientation of the American corporation is related specifically to five significant factors: (1) that alternative goals of growth, size, status, etc., are highly dependent on profit-making itself; (2) that managers themselves are typically also stockholders and derive significant property incomes from the corporations they control; (3) that there is great competitive pressure to cut costs even in industries dominated by relatively few firms; (4) that large corporations in fact devote much time and money to systematic methods of profit maximization and are therefore extremely well equipped to maximize profits; and most fundamentally (5) that the maximization of profits is the criterion of success defined and imposed by a social system—the capitalist mode of production—and its dominant class—the capitalists—because otherwise the *raison d'être* of both the system and the class would be undermined.

[2]See Edwards, Section 3.2, p. 98.

Source: The following is excerpted from Chapter 2 of *Monopoly Capital* by PAUL BARAN and PAUL SWEEZY. Copyright © 1966 by Paul Sweezy. Reprinted by permission of Monthly Review Press.

. . .

What pattern of behavior can we expect from huge, management-controlled, financially independent corporations?

Formal economic theory has largely ignored this question, continuing to operate with the assumption of the profit-maximizing individual entrepreneur who has occupied the central role in theories of the capitalist system since well before the time of Adam Smith. Retaining this assumption amounts in effect to making another: that in all respects that matter to the functioning of the system the corporation acts like an individual entrepreneur.

If one stops to think about it, this seems unlikely on the face of it. Furthermore, while economic theorists have largely ignored the corporation, other social scientists have devoted much time and energy to its study. So far as we know, none of them has ever supported the proposition that the modern corporation is merely an enlarged version of the classical entrepreneur. On the other hand, there is a voluminous literature dating back to the turn of the century and reaching its culmination in the famous work of Berle and Means which argues most emphatically that the modern corporation represents a qualitative break with the older form of individual enterprise and that radically different types of behavior are to be expected from it. According to Berle and Means:

It is conceivable—indeed it seems almost inevitable if the corporate system is to survive—that the "control" of the great corporations should develop into a purely neutral technocracy, balancing a variety of claims by various groups in the community and assigning to each a portion of the income stream on the basis of public policy rather than private cupidity.[1]

What Berle and Means described as "conceivable" a quarter of a century ago is taken for granted as an accomplished fact by many present-day observers of the business scene. Thus Carl Kaysen, in a paper delivered at the 1956 annual meeting of the American Economic Association, speaks of "the wide-ranging scope of responsibility assumed by management" as one of the "characteristic features of behavior" of the modern corporation, and proceeds as follows:

No longer the agent of proprietorship seeking to maximize return on investment, management sees itself as responsible to stockholders, employees, customers, the general public, and, perhaps most important, the firm itself as an institution. . . . From one point of view, this behavior can be termed responsible: there is no display of greed or

[1]*The Modern Corporation and Private Property* (New York: The Macmillan Co., 1933), p. 356.

graspingness; there is no attempt to push off onto workers or the community at large part of the social costs of the enterprise. The modern corporation is a soulful corporation.[2]

According to this view, which is certainly very widespread nowadays, the maximization of profits has ceased to be the guiding principle of business enterprise. Corporate managements, being self-appointed and responsible to no outside group, are free to choose their aims and in the typical case are assumed to subordinate the old-fashioned hunt for profits to a variety of other, quantitatively less precise but qualitatively more worthy, objectives.

The implications of this doctrine of the "soulful corporation" are far-reaching. The truth is that if it is accepted, the whole corpus of traditional economic theory must be abandoned and the time-honored justification of the existing social order in terms of economic efficiency, justice, etc., simply falls to the ground. This has been most effectively pointed out by Edward S. Mason:

But if profit maximization is not the directing agent, how are resources allocated to their most productive uses, what relation have prices to relative scarcities, and how do factors get remunerated in accordance with their contribution to output? Assume an economy composed of a few hundred large corporations, each enjoying substantial market power and all directed by managements with a "conscience." Each management wants to do the best it can for society

[2]Carl Kaysen, "The Social Significance of the Modern Corporation," *American Economic Review*, May 1957, pp. 313–314. See also M. J. Rathbone, President of Standard Oil of New Jersey, in the *Saturday Review*, April 16, 1960: "Managements of large companies must harmonize a wide span of obligations: to investors, customers, suppliers, employees, communities and the national interest. Thus the large organization may actually have a narrower range for its decision-making than the small, closely held corporation which is not so much in the public eye and hence not so exposed to criticism."

consistent, of course, with doing the best it can for labor, customers, suppliers, and owners. How do prices get determined in such an economy? How are factors remunerated, and what relation is there between remuneration and performance? What is the mechanism, if any, that assures effective resource use, and how can corporate managements "do right by" labor, suppliers, customers, and owners while simultaneously serving the public interests?[3]

Economists have made no attempt to answer these questions, and indeed it is doubtful whether it even makes sense to ask them in relation to an economy such as Mason postulates, that is to say, one made up of or dominated by a few hundred soulful corporations. Prices and incomes would be indeterminate, and there would be no theoretically definable tendencies toward equilibrium. To be sure, economic life in such a society might settle down into routines and patterns which could be analyzed by historians, sociologists, and statisticians, but it seems reasonably clear that today's economic theorists would be out of a job.

One school of thought, associated especially with the name of Herbert A. Simon of Carnegie Institute of Technology, seems already to have drawn these conclusions and is attempting to study the big corporation and its implications by means of what Simon calls "organization theory." According to this theory, corporations do not try to maximize anything but merely to achieve "satisfactory" results. Thus, to the maximizing behavior which was assumed to characterize the old-fashioned entrepreneur, Simon contrasts what he calls the "satisficing" behavior of modern corporate managements. At the annual meetings of the American Economic Association in 1956, a paper by Simon expounding this view was answered by James Earley of the University of Wisconsin who had been engaged for a number of years on

[3]Edward S. Mason, "The Apologetics of 'Managerialism,'" *The Journal of Business,* January, 1958, p. 7.

a study of the management policies of a sample of large and successful American corporations. Summing up a wealth of carefully collected and analyzed empirical material, Earley had little difficulty in disposing of Simon's theory; what is more significant from our point of view is that he went on to give a most useful and illuminating description of how modern corporate managements really behave. This statement is so good that it seems worthwhile to rescue large parts of it from the untitled obscurity of the Economic Association's *Papers and Proceedings.* After noting some points of agreement and others of minor disagreement with Simon, Earley proceeds as follows:

I have more serious reservations concerning what appears to be the major economic theorem Simon arrives at; namely, that the business enterprise looks for merely satisfactory solutions of its problems and specifically seeks merely satisfactory profits. That his approach has led so directly to this conclusion is one of the facts that makes me especially doubt that it is a satisfactory one. Whatever may be true of individuals or of other types of organization, I cannot square Simon's "satisficing" behavior with the behavior of the large-scale American business firm. I agree that the conventional notion of profit maximization and of general "optimization" must be modified. I contend this is carrying the change much too far. Let me briefly catalogue the main types of evidence that lead me to reject the "satisficing" postulate.

(1) As a part of my research, I have made a study of recent management literature, both general and specialized, one of my hypotheses in doing so being that this literature will reveal the frames of reference and mores of advanced business management. A striking characteristic of this literature (except where public relations is an evident objective) is its systematic focus on cost reduction, the expansion of revenue, and the increase of profits. There is, of course, much reference to standards and to the need of remedying unsatisfactory situations. The drive is always toward the better and frequently the best, not just the good. Like Samuel Gompers' ideal union

leader, the exemplary man of management seems to have "More!" for at least one of his mottoes.

(2) Secondly, my questionnaire studies of the practices and policies of leading so-called "excellently managed" companies lead me toward generally similar conclusions. I have published the major results of the first of these studies and will not review them here.[4]

(3) The third fact that makes me doubt Simon's postulate as applied to the firm is the rapidly growing use of economists, market analysts, other types of specialists, and management consultants by our larger businesses. The main function of most of these people is to help the firm reduce costs, find superior methods, choose the most profitable alternatives, and uncover new profit opportunities. As these sophisticated gentlemen gain in influence in business councils—and I confidently believe they will—profit-oriented rationality is likely to be more and more representative of business behavior.

(4) Most of all I am impressed by the rapid development of analytical and managerial techniques that both stimulate and assist the business firms to find the least costly ways of doing things and the most profitable things to do. Operations research and mathematical programming are only the more fancy of this growing genus. There are also greatly improved forms of accounting and budgeting, improved methods of market analysis, refinements in business forecasting, and interesting types of nonmathematical programming. The unifying character of these new techniques is that they seek to apply the principles of rational problem-solving to business planning and decision making.

Let me conclude by briefly sketching the notion of business behavior that seems to be emerging from my own studies. It falls somewhere between the old postulate of profit maximization and Simon's "satisfactory profit." It fully recognizes the limited informational and computational resources of the firm. It also incorporates his suggested concept of the "aspiration level" and a modified principle of "viability." My

behavioral postulate could best be briefly described as "a systematic temporal search for highest practicable profits."

The theory underlying it runs, very briefly, as follows:

The major goals of modern large-scale business are high managerial incomes, good profits, a strong competitive position, and growth. Modern management does not view these goals as seriously inconsistent but rather, indeed, as necessary, one to the other. Competitive strength and even survival, management believes, require large innovative and substantial growth expenditures in the rapidly changing technical and market conditions of the present day. Since growth by merger is hazardous and frequently impossible, large and more or less continuous capital expenditures are necessary. For well-recognized reasons, management wishes to minimize outside financing, so the funds for most of these expenditures must be internally generated. This requires high and growing profits above dividend levels. So, too, do high managerial rewards. High and rising profits are hence an instrument as well as a direct goal of great importance.

With these goals and needs in view, advanced management plans for profit through time, using coordinated programs stretching as far ahead as practicable. The profit targets incorporated in these programs are sufficient to finance not only good dividends but also desired innovative and growth expenditures. The programs are revised frequently, as experience accrues and new opportunities are discovered.

The tendency toward profit maximization (i.e., highest practicable profit) appears in this system along several dimensions. In the process of revising and reformulating programs, more expensive and less profitable activities are pruned or dropped and cheaper or more profitable ones are added. Less costly processes and the more profitable product and market sectors serve as the standards toward which others are expected to converge or be replaced. By steadily selecting those methods and sectors that promise better returns, these standards are kept high and, if possible, rising. Finally, the overall profit and growth targets of the enterprise as a whole are raised through time, unless adversity prevents.

These goals and programs and standards, it is true, represent at any time "aspira-

[4]The author's reference here is to James S. Earley, "Marginal Policies of 'Excellently Managed' Companies," The American Economic Review, March, 1956.

tion levels," and the efforts to satisfy them receive prime attention. But the two major points about them are that (1) they are to be hard to reach and (2) they will ordinarily recede (i.e., grow larger) through time. Even in good times the firm's aspiration levels, therefore, are fairly taut, and they are highly elastic upward. On the other hand, there is great resistance to adjusting profit and other standards downward, so that in bad times the business firm tries even harder to make the highest practicable profits.

I readily agree that I have sketched the behavior of what might be called the "exemplary firm" rather than the firm that is quantitatively representative of the present business population. But my main point is that the management techniques and the expertise that can validate my notion are developing rapidly, are increasingly being made available to business, and are being rapidly adopted by leading firms. Consequently, I suspect, the exemplary firm will be the representative firm of the future. If so, its behavior will be more rather than less appropriately analyzed by some of our time-honored theoretical notions, such as profit maximization. . . .[5]

Two aspects of this admirable statement call for comment. First, it introduces a healthy corrective to what Earley calls "the conventional notion of profit maximization and general 'optimization.' " This conventional notion has been tied to a more or less explicitly stated assumption that the maximizing entrepreneur has complete knowledge of all alternatives open to him and of the consequences of choosing any combination of them. Given this assumption, he can always select the combination of alternatives which yields an absolute maximum. Further, if it is assumed that his knowledge remains equally complete in the face of changing conditions, it follows logically that he can always make instantaneous and appropriate adjustments to new circumstances.

[5]*American Economic Review*, May, 1957, pp. 333–35.

What is involved here is an assumption of omniscience on the part of the entrepreneur, which, far from being a useful abstraction, is of course an absurdity. In practice, to be sure, economists have usually given a more sensible meaning to the maximization principle, but by failing expressly to repudiate the omniscience postulate, by failing to spell out what is and what is not involved in the assumption of profit maximization, they have left themselves vulnerable to attacks of the kind mounted by Simon. It is therefore valuable to have Earley's carefully considered statement. By stressing the "limited informational and computational resources of the firm," he makes clear that no assumption of complete knowledge is involved, and his entire argument is based on the rejection of any idea of an absolute maximum or optimum. The firm (whether individual entrepreneur or corporation makes no difference) always finds itself in a given historical situation, with limited knowledge of changing conditions. In this context it can never do more than improve its profit position. In practice, the search for "maximum" profits can only be the search for the greatest *increase* in profits which is possible in the given situation, subject of course to the elementary proviso that the exploitation of today's profit opportunities must not ruin tomorrow's. This is all there is to the profit maximization principle, but it also happens to be all that is necessary to validate the "economizing" behavior patterns which have been the very backbone of all serious economic theory for the last two centuries.

The second aspect of Earley's statement which we want to emphasize, and the one most relevant to our present purpose, is the convincing demonstration that the big corporation, if not more profit-oriented than the individual entrepreneur (he quite properly leaves this question open), is at any rate better equipped to pursue a policy of profit maximization. The result is much the same:

the economy of large corporations is more, not less, dominated by the logic of profit-making than the economy of small entre-preneurs ever was.

. . .

Big corporations . . . are run by company men. What kind of people are they? What do they want and why? What position do they hold in the class structure of American society?

There is a widespread impression, and much literature to support and propagate it, that the managements of big corporations form some sort of separate, independent, or "neutral" social class. This view we have already encountered in an elementary form in the "neutral technocracy" of Berle and Means and the "soulful corporation" of Carl Kaysen; it is developed more elaborately in such works as James Burnham's *The Managerial Revolution* and Berle's *The 20th-Century Capitalist Revolution*. Most of the variants of this theory have interesting and enlightening insights to contribute, but in our view they all share a common defect: the basic idea is wrong.

The fact is that the managerial stratum is the most active and influential part of the propertied class. All studies show that its members are largely recruited from the middle and upper reaches of the class structure; they overlap with what C. Wright Mills calls the "very rich"; with few and negligible exceptions, they are wealthy men in their own right, quite apart from the large incomes and extensive privileges which they derive from their corporate connections.[6] It is of course true, as we have emphasized, that in the typical big corporation the management is not subject to stockholder control, and in this sense the "separation of

[6]By far the best treatment of these subjects will be found in C. Wright Mills, *The Power Elite* (New York: Oxford University Press, 1956), especially Chapters 6, 7, and 8.

ownership from control" is a fact. But there is no justification for concluding from this that managements in general are divorced from ownership in general. Quite the contrary, managers are among the biggest owners; and because of the strategic positions they occupy, they function as the protectors and spokesmen for all large-scale property. Far from being a separate class, they constitute in reality the leading echelon of the property-owning class.

This is not to argue that managers have no distinctive interests *qua* managers. Like other segments of the propertied class, they do. But the conflicts of interest that arise in this way are between managers and small property owners rather than between managers and large property owners.

. . .

The company man is dedicated to the advancement of his company. This does not mean, however, that he is any more or less *homo economicus*, any more or less selfish, any more or less altruistic than either the tycoon or the individual owner-entrepreneur before him. All of these conceptions are at best irrelevant and at worst misleading. The problem is not one of "psychology" of any kind but of the selective and molding effects of institutions on the personnel that operates them. It might seem that this is too elementary to require mention, but unfortunately it is not possible to take for granted such a degree of enlightenment among economists. Economic theory is still heavily permeated by the "psychologizing" tradition of nineteenth-century utilitarianism, and economists need continually to be reminded that this tradition leads only to confusion and obscurantism.

To be a going concern, a social order must instill in its members the ambition to be a success in its own terms. Under capitalism the highest form of success is business success, and under monopoly capitalism the highest form of business is the big corporation. In this system the normal procedure for an ambitious young man must be to work himself up to as near the top as possible of as big a corporation as possible.[7] Once he enters a given corporation, he devotes himself to two ends: ascending the managerial ladder and advancing the relative status of his company in the corporate world. In practice these two ends are indistinguishable: the young man's rise in the company depends on his contribution to improving the position of the company. This is the crux of the matter, and this is why we can say without qualification that the company man is dedicated to the advancement of his company: he is dedicated to the advancement of his company precisely to the extent that he is dedicated to advancing himself.

This remains true even after he has reached the top of a given company. If he makes a good record, he may be "called" to a larger company. And even if he is not, or has no hope of being, he is still just as much interested in improving the position of the company he heads; for standing, prestige, and power in the business world are not personal attributes but rather are conferred on the individual businessman by the standing, prestige, and power of his company and by his position in that company.

·   ·   ·

But size is not the only index of corporate status: this is an oversimplification. Other important indexes are rate of growth and "strength" as measured by such standards as credit rating and the price of a company's securities. Thus, assuming equal size, one company will rank ahead of others if it is stronger and growing more rapidly;

[7]"The way to achieve and retain greatness is always to be striving for something more." Osborn Elliott, *Men at the Top*, New York, 1959, p. 40. This book contains much useful information on American business leaders.

and strength and rapid growth may even offset a big size differential if the larger company is stagnant or declining. The primary objectives of corporate policy—which are at the same time and inevitably the personal objectives of the corporate managers —are thus strength, rate of growth, and size. There is no general formula for quantifying or combining these objectives—nor is there any need for one. For they are reducible to the single common denominator of profitability. Profits provide the internal funds for expansion. Profits are the sinew and muscle of strength, which in turn gives access to outside funds if and when they are needed. Internal expansion, acquisition, and merger are the ways in which corporations grow, and growth is the road to size. Thus profits, even though not the ultimate goal, are the necessary means to all ultimate goals. As such, they become the immediate, unique, unifying, quantitative aim of corporate policies, the touchstone of corporate rationality, the measure of corporate success. Here is the real—the socio-structural as distinct from individual-psychological—explanation of the kind of profit-maximizing behavior so ably described by Earley in the passage quoted on pages 164–66.

·   ·   ·

To sum up: Business is an ordered system which selects and rewards according to well understood criteria. The guiding principle is to get as near as possible to the top inside a corporation which is as near as possible to the top among corporations. Hence the need for maximum profits. Hence the need to devote profits once acquired to enhancing financial strength and speeding up growth. These things become the subjective aims and values of the business world because they are the objective requirements of the system. The character of the system determines the psychology of its members, not vice versa.

4.4   The Concentration of Wealth and Power in America

The previous readings have focused on the concentration of business enterprise and on the evolution and behavior of the large corporation in the United States. Although most such corporations are directed by salaried managers, they tend to be operated so as to maximize the long-run profits of their owners—the property-owning capitalists. In the next reading we inquire into the distribution of property ownership in the United States in order to identify more closely the class of wealthy capitalists who exercise ultimate control over most of the productive strength of the American economy.

Ferdinand Lundberg examines here the evidence on the distribution of wealth in the United States presented in two recent studies by Robert J. Lampman and by Dorothy Projector and Gertrude Weiss. Both studies reveal a tremendously high degree of concentration of overall personal wealth. Furthermore, the distribution of productive property (i.e., income-earning wealth such as investment assets) is even more highly concentrated: some 200,000 families held almost one-third of all investment assets in 1962. As Lundberg points out, this elite class of big capitalists holds effective power over essentially all of America's corporate wealth.

Source: The following is excerpted from Chapter 1 of *The Rich and the Super-Rich* by FERDINAND LUNDBERG. Copyright © 1968 by Ferdinand Lundberg. Reprinted by permission of Lyle Stuart, Inc.

THE LAMPMAN FINDINGS

What Lampman found was as follows:[1]

1. More than 30 percent of the assets and equities of the personal sector of the economy (about 20 percent of all wealth in the country being government-owned) in 1953 was held by 1.6 percent of the adult population of 103 million.[2]

2. This group of 1.6 percent owned 32 percent of all privately owned wealth, consisting of 82.2 percent of all stock, 100 percent of state and local (tax-exempt) bonds, 38.2 percent of federal bonds, 88.5 percent of other bonds, 29.1 percent of the cash, 36.2 percent of mortgages and notes, 13.3 percent of life insurance reserves, 5.9 percent of pension and retirement funds, 18.2 percent of miscellaneous property, 16.1 percent of real estate and 22.1 percent of all debts and mortgages.[3]

3. [Table 4–E] shows the percentage of national wealth-holdings for the top ½ of 1 percent and 1 percent for the indicated years.[4]

[Editors' note: Table 4–F, drawn directly from Lampman's study, documents the share of personal property of different types held by the top 1 percent of wealth-holders in

[1]All of Lampman's results were published in his detailed study: Robert J. Lampman, *The Share of Top Wealth-Holders in National Wealth, 1922–1956*, A Study by the National Bureau of Economic Research (Princeton, N.J.): Princeton University Press, 1962).
[2]*Ibid.*, p. 23.

[3]*Ibid.*, pp. 23, 192–93.
[4]*Ibid.*, pp. 202, 204, 209.

different years. Note especially the high and increasing concentration of coporate stock ownership, which belies the notion that investment assets are widely and democratically distributed among the people of the United States.]

4. The estimated gross estate size for the total adult population in 1953, obtained by extension of the same methods, [was as shown in Table 4–G].[5]

[5]*Ibid.*, p. 213.

TABLE 4–E CONCENTRATION OF WEALTH

	½ of 1 Percent of Adult Population (percent)	1 Percent of Adult Population (percent)
1922	29.8	31.6
1929	32.4	36.3
1933	25.2	28.3
1939	28.0	30.6
1945	20.9	23.3
1949	19.3	20.8
1953	22.7	24.2
1954	22.5	. . .
1956	25.0	26.0

TABLE 4–F PERCENTAGE OF PROPERTY HELD BY TOP 1 PERCENT OF WEALTH-HOLDERS

Type of Property	1922	1929	1939	1945	1949	1953
Real estate	18.0	17.3	13.7	11.1	10.5	12.5
U.S. govt. bonds	45.0	100.0	91.0	32.5	35.8	31.8
State and local bonds	88.0	*	*	*	77.0	*
Other bonds	69.2	82.0	75.5	78.5	78.0	77.5
Corporate stock	61.5	65.6	69.0	61.7	64.9	76.0
Cash	—	—	—	17.0	18.9	24.5
Mortgages and notes	—	—	—	34.7	32.0	30.5
Cash, mortgages, and notes	31.0	34.0	31.5	19.3	20.5	25.8
Pension and retirement funds	8.0	8.0	6.0	5.9	5.5	5.5
Insurance	35.3	27.0	17.4	17.3	15.0	11.5
Miscellaneous property	23.2	29.0	19.0	21.4	15.0	15.5
Gross estate	32.3	37.7	32.7	25.8	22.4	25.3

*In excess of 100 percent.

SOURCE: Robert J. Lampman, *The Share of Top Wealth-Holders in National Wealth, 1922-1956* (Princeton, N.J.: Princeton University Press, 1962), Table 97, p. 209 (only the part of the table dealing with assets and gross estate is reproduced here). Reprinted by permission of the National Bureau of Economic Research.

TABLE 4–G GROSS ESTATE SIZE FOR ADULT POPULATION, 1953

Gross Estate Size (dollars)	Persons Aged 20 and Over (millions)	Percentage	Average Estate Size (dollars)	Total Gross Estate (billion dollars)	Percentage
0 to 3,500	51.70	50.0	1,800	93.1	8.3
3,500–10,000	19.00	18.4	6,000	114.0	10.2
10,000–20,000	21.89	21.2	15,000	328.4	29.3
20,000–30,000	6.00	5.8	25,000	150.0	13.4
30,000–40,000	2.00	1.9	35,000	70.0	6.3
40,000–50,000	0.80	0.8	45,000	36.0	3.2
50,000–60,000	0.35	0.3	55,000	19.3	1.7
All under 60,000	101.74	98.4	7,900	810.8	72.4
60,000–70,000	0.18	0.1	61,000	10.5	0.9
60,000 and over	1.66	1.6	186,265	309.2	27.6
All estate sizes	103.40	100.0	10,800	1,120.0	100.0
Median estate size			3,500		

In [Table 4–G] is found one verification of my initial paragraph. It shows that 50 percent of the people, owning 8.3 percent of the wealth, had an average estate of $1,800 —enough to cover furniture, clothes, a television set and perhaps a run-down car. Most of these had less; many had nothing at all. Another group of 18.4 percent, adding up to 68.4 percent of the population, was worth $6,000 on the average, which would probably largely represent participation in life insurance or emergency money in the bank. Perhaps this percentage included some of the select company of "people's capitalists" who owned two or three shares of AT&T.

Another 21.2 percent of adults, bringing into view 89.6 percent of the population, had $15,000 average gross estates—just enough to cover a serious personal illness. This same 92-plus percent of the population all together owned only 47.8 percent of all assets.

TOP WEALTH-HOLDERS

The number of persons in the top 1 percent of wealth-holders through the decades was as [shown in Table 4–H]:[6]

But the top 11 percent of persons in the magic 1 percent (or 0.11 percent) held about 45 percent of the wealth of this particular group while the lower half (or 0.50 percent) held only 23 percent.[7]

Says Lampman: "The personally owned wealth of the total population in 1953 amounted to about $1 trillion. This means that the average gross estate for all 103 million adults was slightly less than $10,000. The median would, of course, be considerably lower. In contrast the top wealth-holder group had an average gross estate of $182,-000. The majority of this top group was clustered in estate sizes below that average.

TABLE 4–H   TOP 1 PERCENT OF WEALTH-HOLDERS

Years	Number of Persons (thousands)	Percentage Share of Gross Estates
1922	651	32
1929	744	38
1939	855	33
1945	929	26
1949	980	22
1953	1,030	25

Of the 1.6 million top wealth-holders, over half had less than $125,000 of gross estate and less than 2 percent (27,000 persons) had more than $1 million."[8]

There were, then, in excess of 27,000 millionaires in the country in 1953—not only the greatest such aggregation at one time in the history of the world but a number greater than the aggregation throughout all of history before 1875 (as of 1966, millionaires numbered about 90,000). If consumer prices had remained stable from 1944 to 1953 there would have been fewer. "In 1944 there were 13,297 millionaires," says Lampman. "In 1953 there were 27,502 millionaires in 1953 prices, but only 17,611 in 1944 prices."[9]

What of the 1965–67 year-span? As the prices of stocks advanced tremendously in the preceding dozen years, one can only conclude that the proportion of wealth of the top wealth-holders also advanced impressively. For this small group, as we have seen, owns more than 80 percent of stocks. The Dow-Jones average of 65 industrial stocks stood at 216.31 at the end of 1950; at 442.72 in 1955; at 618.04 in 1960; and at 812.18 in March, 1964. As of May, 1965, it was well over 900. The less volatile Securities and Exchange Commission index of 300 stocks shows the same quadrupling in value, standing at 41.4 in 1950; 81.8 in 1955; 113.9 in 1960; and 160.9 in March, 1964. How many employees have experi-

[6]*Ibid.*, p. 220.
[7]*Ibid.*, pp. 86–87.

[8]*Ibid.*, p. 84.
[9]*Ibid.*, pp. 84, 276.

enced a fourfold increase in salaries in the same period?

The rise in value of stocks, however, surely invalidates one of Lampman's speculations, to this effect: "Our finding that the share of wealth held by the top 2 percent of families fell from about 33 to 29 percent from 1922 to 1953, or about one-eighth, would seem compatible with . . . the general belief that there has been some lessening of economic inequality in the United States in recent decades."[10] The more recent rise in stock prices and in corporation earnings shatters even that slight concession.

Professor A. A. Berle, Jr., has rushed forward to hail the Lampman showing that the upper 1 percent saw its participation reduced from 32 percent of all wealtn in 1922 to 25 percent in 1953; but his celebration was premature and he did not fully report Lampman, who indicated that the participation had been reduced from 1922 to 1949 but thereafter was again increasing.[11]

The Lampman findings were extended to 1958 in an extremely sophisticated statistical critique presented in 1965 to the American Statistical Association by James D. Smith and Staunton K. Calvert of the Statistics Division of the Internal Revenue Service.[12]

After reviewing Lampman, revising him in a minor particular, Smith and Calvert conclude that "top wealth-holders owned 27.4 percent of gross and 28.3 percent of net prime wealth in 1953, but increased their share to 30.2 and 32.0 percent respectively by 1958. These data support Lampman's conclusion that the share of top wealth-holders has been increasing since 1949." Prime wealth, as they explain, is total wealth less the value of assets in trust funds and pension reserves.

This is where the question rests on the basis of the most recent data supplied by leading authorities in the field: Concentration of wealth in a few hands is intensifying.

. . .

DEFINITIVE DATA FROM THE FEDERAL RESERVE

In a complex and comprehensive study prepared for the Board of Governors of the Federal Reserve System on the basis of Census Bureau data under the title *Survey of Financial Characteristics of Consumers*,[13] the cold figures are officially presented on asset holdings as of December 31, 1962, removing the entire subject from the realm of pettifogging debate.

On that date the number of households in the country worth $500,000 or more was carefully computed at about 200,000. The number of millionaires at the year-end was more than 80,000, compared with Lampman's 27,000 as of 1953. Only 39 percent of these 200,000 had no inherited assets. These 200,000 at the time held 22 percent of all wealth, while 57 percent of the wealth was held by 3.9 million individual consumer units worth $50,000 or more.

The panorama of wealth-holding throughout the populace was as shown in Table 4–I (in millions of units).[14]

In stating that 200,000 households held 22 percent of the wealth there is some danger of suggesting that the power of these 200,000 is less than it actually is. The nature of the wealth held is of determining impor-

[10]*Ibid.*, p. 217.

[11]A. A. Berle, Jr., *The American Economic Republic* (New York: Harcourt, Brace & World, 1963), p. 221.

[12]James D. Smith and Staunton K. Calvert, "Estimating the Wealth of Top Wealth-Holders from Estate Tax Returns," Proceedings of the American Statistical Association, Philadelphia, September, 1965.

[13]Dorothy Projector and Gertrude Weiss, *Survey of Financial Characteristics of Consumers* (Washington, D.C.: Federal Reserve Board, 1966).
[14]*Ibid.*, p. 151.

TABLE 4–1   DISTRIBUTION OF WEALTH BY SIZE

All consumer units (households)	Millions	Percentage of Households
	57.9	100.0
Size of wealth:		
Negative	1.0	1.8
Zero	4.7	8.0
$1–$999	9.0	16.0
$1,000–$4,999	10.8	18.0
$5,000–$9,999	9.1	16.0
$10,000–$24,999	13.3	23.0
$25,000–$49,999	6.2	11.0
$50,000–$99,999	2.5	5.0
$100,000–$199,999	.7	1.25
$200,000–$499,999	.5	Less than 1.0
$500,000 and up	.2	Less than 0.4

tance here. In general, the lower wealth-holders mostly own inert assets such as automobiles, small amounts of cash and some residential equity, while the upper wealth-holders mostly own corporate equities in an aggregate amount sufficient to show that they are in full control of the productive side of the economic system.

Households in the number of 200,000 worth $500,000 and more held 32 percent of all investment assets and 75 percent of miscellaneous assets, largely trust funds, while 500,000 worth $200,000 to $499,999 held 22 percent of investment assets. The 700,000 households worth $100,000 to $199,999 held 11 percent of investment assets.[15]

CENTER OF ECONOMIC POLITICAL CONTROL

We see, then, that 1.4 million households owned 65 percent of investment assets, which are what give economic control. Automobile and home ownership and bank deposits do not give such control. The economic power of the upper 200,000 is greater

[15]*Ibid.*, p. 136.

than indicated by their ownership of 22 percent of all assets; it amounts to 32 percent of investment assets.

Experts concede that a 5 percent ownership stake in a large corporation is sufficient in most cases to give corporate control. It is my contention that *general* corporate control lies in this group of 200,000 very probably, and almost certainly lies in the combined group of 700,000 wealthiest households, slightly more than 1 percent owning assets worth $200,000 and more.

There is a danger here, as the erudite will recognize, of perpetrating the logical fallacy of division—that is, arguing that what is true of a whole is true of its individual parts. That argument here would be that because 200,000 households own 32 percent of investment assets they each hold a stake of exactly 32 percent in the corporate system. I do *not* make such a ridiculous argument. First, this upper group concentrates its holdings for the most part in leading corporations, bypassing the million or so paper-tiger corporations of little or no value. Again, as just noted, far less than 32 percent of ownership in any individual corporation is required to control it. *Control*, as we shall see, is the relevant factor where power is concerned. Usually comparatively little ownership is necessary to confer complete corporate control which, in turn, extends to participation in political control.

A man whose entire worth lies in 5 percent of the capital stock of a corporation capitalized at $2 billion is worth only $100 million. But as this 5 percent—and many own more than 5 percent—usually gives him control of the corporation, his actual operative *power* is of the order of $2 billion. Politically his is a large voice, not only because of campaign contributions he may make but by reason of all the legislative law firms, congressional and state-legislative, under retainer by his corporation; for every national corporation has law firms in every state. There is additionally to be reckoned with all the advertising his corporation has to dispense among the mass media as a tax-free cost item, the lobbyists his corporation puts into the field and the cultural-charitable foundations both he and the corporation maintain.

Such a man, worth only $100 million net, is clearly a shadowy power in the land, his ownership stake vastly multiplied by what he controls—other people's property as well as his own. And there are more than a few such.

On the other hand, many intelligent citizens today complain, in the face of the alleged complexity of affairs, of feelings of powerlessness. Their feelings are justified. For they are in fact politically powerless.

The actual power of such concentrated ownership, therefore, is much greater than its proportion in the total of investment assets. The corporate power of the top 200,-000, and certainly of the top 700,000, is ac-tually 100 percent. The *power* of this top layer corporatively would be no greater if it owned 10 percent of invested assets. Actually, it might be less: It would then receive no support from many tremulous small holders but would probably find them in political opposition.

As to distribution of investment assets among smaller property holders, 1 percent are owned by the $5,000 to $9,999 group, 7 percent by the $10,000 to $24,999 group, 11 percent by the $25,000 to $49,999 group and 15 percent by the $50,000 to $99,999 group, or 34 percent in all. In this group of comparatively modest means one finds some of the most voluble supporters of the established corporate way. Within their own terms they are all winners, certainly hold some financial edge. Most of them, as their expressions at stockholders meetings show, greatly admire the larger stockholders. In their eyes, a divinity doth hedge the large stockholders.

4.5   The Evolution of the United States Labor Force

Just as the organization and concentration of business enterprise have changed over time, so the structure of the labor force has undergone profound changes since the early days of capitalism in the United States. In the following reading Michael Reich documents the changing occupational structure of the American population and the changes that have òccurred in the character of the labor force. The proportion of wage and salary earners in the population has steadily increased since the American Revolution, but in recent decades white-collar workers have become more important than blue-collar workers as a proportion of wage and salary earners. Although this trend might suggest that the proletarian character of the labor force is weakening, Reich argues that the nature of modern white-collar work is increasingly indistinguishable from blue-collar work and no less proletarian. Despite changing conditions of work, all workers are still obliged to sell their labor in the marketplace and almost all are denied any participation in the control or direction of their work. Reich concludes his essay with a brief discussion of the role of unions, stressing their failure to challenge or affect the basic capitalist rules of the game.

Source: The following essay was written by MICHAEL REICH for this book. Copyright © 1972 by Michael Reich.

THE DEVELOPMENT OF A
PROLETARIAT

In 1780, just after the American Revolution, about four-fifths of the nonslave labor force in the United States were independent property owners or professionals—farmers, merchants, traders, craftsmen and artisans, businessmen, lawyers, doctors, etc.[1] A century later, after slavery was abolished and as the United States was developing into a highly industrial economy, only one-third of the adult working population was classified in the category of "independent enterprisers." The destruction and disappearance of small shopkeepers, small-scale family farms, independent professionals and artisans continued unabated with the further advance of large-scale industry. As a result,

[1]Slaves totaled 20 percent of the population. An extended examination of the class structure in this period is contained in Jackson T. Main, *The Social Structure of Revolutionary America* (Princeton, N.J.: Princeton University Press, 1965).

by 1969 more than 80 percent of all adults in the labor force were non-managerial wage and salary employees, sellers of their labor-power on the labor market. In short, the labor force has been undergoing a dramatic and continuing transformation over time from professionals and independent owners of small capital into mere sellers of labor-power—i.e., the process of proletarianization —is clearly indicated in Table 4–J.

The growth of the wage and salary proletariat is even more dramatic when one considers the transformed role of women and blacks in the economy. As a result of both the growth of demand for labor in occupations traditionally open to women and the decline in household production, an increasing proportion of women work as wage and salary earners, many of them on a full-time year-round basis.[2] In 1890, 18 percent of all women of working age were in the

[2]For a more detailed explanation of the change in women's work, see Davies and Reich, Section 8.4, p. 348.

TABLE 4–J   THE PROLETARIANIZATION OF THE U.S. LABOR FORCE[a]

Year	Percent Wage and Salaried Employees[b]	Percent Self-Employed Entrepreneurs[c]	Percent Salaried Managers and Officials	Total
1780[d]	20.0	80.0	—	100.0
1880	62.0	36.9	1.1	100.0
1890	65.0	33.8	1.2	100.0
1900	67.9	30.8	1.3	100.0
1910	71.9	26.3	1.8	100.0
1920	73.9	23.5	2.6	100.0
1930	76.8	20.3	2.9	100.0
1939	78.2	18.8	3.0	100.0
1950	77.7	17.9	4.4	100.0
1960	80.6	14.1	5.3	100.0
1969	83.6	9.2	7.2	100.0

Notes: [a] Defined as all income recipients who participate directly in economic activity; unpaid family workers have been excluded. [b] Excluding salaried managers and officials. [c] Business entrepreneurs, professional practicioners, farmers and other property owners. [d] Figures for 1780 are rough estimates. Slaves, who comprised one-fifth of the population, are excluded; white indentured servants are included in the wage and salaried employees category.

SOURCES: Data for 1780 from Jackson T. Main, *The Social Structure of Revolutionary America* (Princeton, N.J.: Princeton University Press, 1965), pp. 270-77. Data for 1880-1939 from Spurgeon Bell, *Productivity, Wages and National Income* (Washington, D.C.: Brookings Institution, 1940), p. 10. Data for 1950-1969 computed from U.S. Dept. of Labor, *Manpower Report of the President*, various years; and U.S. Dept. of Commerce, Bureau of the Census, *Census of Population*, 1950 and 1960, and *Current Population Reports*, Series P-60, various years.

paid labor force; this proportion rose steadily to 29 percent by the eve of World War II, jumped to 38 percent during the war as male labor shortages developed, and fell to 31 percent by 1947 as shortages eased. After 1947 the proportion began rising again: by 1969, 43 percent of all adult women were active members of the paid labor force, most of them wage and salary employees. By 1969 women comprised 38 percent of the total civilian labor force.[3]

Furthermore, working for a wage or salary has become more of a permanent feature of life for many women. The 18 percent of adult women who were working in the market economy in the late nineteenth century were mostly unmarried and under 25 and most left the labor force never to return once they were married. By contrast, current projections indicate that women born in 1960 will spend, on the average, twenty years of their life as wage or salary workers.[4]

The most startling transformation of working status has occurred among blacks. After the Civil War some ex-slaves became artisans, some became wage earners in urban areas or on reorganized plantations, and a few obtained land of their own to farm. But most ex-slaves eked out an existence as farm tenants or sharecroppers, dependent on the white landlord for credit, tools, work animals, and feed. Beginning about the turn of the century, however, and particularly since 1940, blacks have left agriculture and sharecropping in large numbers and joined the wage and salary proletariat. By 1969, 75 percent of adult black males and 49 percent of adult black females were members of the labor force, most as nonmanagerial wage and salary workers.[5]

Most wage and salary employees in the United States are dependent on their jobs

for their livelihood; few have alternative sources of substantial income or control over productive assets. A recent survey (see Table 4–K) indicated that in 1962, apart from a car, a house, household possessions, and a small ($500 or less) savings account and pension fund, 45 percent of all households owned absolutely no income-producing assets (stocks, bonds, bank accounts, real estate, etc.), while an additional 40 percent of households owned income-producing assets of $10,000 or less (assuming a rate of return of 8 percent, an asset worth $10,000 would bring in $800 per year in income). By contrast, 1 percent of all adults own over three-quarters of the corporate stock and the corporate bonds in America.[6]

In short, the United States has become a nation of wage and salary employees, who have virtually no access to income from property or control over the production process, and whose economic welfare is determined by the vicissitudes of the labor market. The term "proletarians" applies to all such employees and not only to assembly-line industrial day laborers. Interestingly, the process by which capitalist development progressively reduces more adults to the status of seller of labor-power has taken place in all capitalist countries; for example, data for France and Germany also indicate a steadily increasing proportion of wage and salary earners.[7]

At the same time, the old capitalist class has also been changing. While the traditional image of a leisure class of rentiers who live by clipping coupons of stocks and bonds was never very accurate, it has become particularly obsolete under modern capitalism. More common today is the large capital-owner who also participates in production, for a high salary, as director, manager, trustee, or executive. With the increasing complexity of modern corporate organizations

---

[3]*1969 Handbook on Women Workers*, U.S. Department of Labor, Women's Bureau, p. 10, Table 1.

[4]V. Perella, "Women and the Labor Force," *Monthly Labor Review*, February, 1968, p. 2.

[5]U.S. Department of Labor, *Manpower Report of the President*, 1970.

[6]See Table 4–G, p. 170.

[7]Data for France and Germany are reported in E. Mandel, *Marxist Economic Theory* (New York: Monthly Review Press, 1968), pp. 164–65.

TABLE 4–K   THE DISTRIBUTION OF INCOME-PRODUCING ASSETS* DECEMBER 31, 1962

Size of portfolio (in dollars)	Number of consumer units (millions)	Percent of consumer units
0	11.8	20.4
1–500	14.5	24.9
500–2,000	10.2	17.7
2,000–5,000	7.4	12.8
5,000–10,000	4.9	8.9
10,000–25,000	5.2	9.0
25,000–50,000	2.1	3.6
50,000 and above	1.8	3.1
Total	57.9	100.0

*bank accounts, stocks and bonds of all types, real estate, mortgage assets, etc.

SOURCE: Dorothy Projector and Gertrude Weiss, *Survey of Financial Characteristics of Consumers*, Washington, D.C., Federal Reserve Board, 1966, Table A-36, p. 15. Percentages may not add to total because of rounding.

and bureaucracies, managers have become increasingly numerous in the labor force (see Table 4–L). A large proportion of high-level managers and executives in the largest corporations and banking institutions have substantial personal holdings in the stocks and bonds of those companies.[8]

THE STRUCTURE OF THE PROLETARIAT

The growth of production on a large scale has led to important structural changes within the wage and salary labor force. Along with a growing hierarchy in the production process, a pyramidal social structure has developed as white-collar workers, many of whom occupy intermediate positions in the occupational structure, have grown in number. C. Wright Mills was fond of referring to such workers as the *new middle class* since, unlike the small farmers and shopkeepers of the old middle class, most of these white-collar workers do not own property which is significant in the production process. In what follows we trace the

changing composition of the labor force and indicate how the character of white-collar jobs is being transformed.

The importance in the economy of blue-collar labor in industry (mining, manufacturing, and construction) increased continuously in the United States until about the 1930's, as industry displaced the family farm and the farm laborer. Since about the 1930's, however, white-collar and service employment have replaced industrial blue-collar employment as the most rapidly expanding occupations in the economy. The proportion of white-collar workers in the labor force grew from 6.7 percent in 1870 to 33 percent in 1940 and 47 percent in 1969. By contrast, blue-collar employees in mining, manufacturing and construction accounted for 37 percent of the total labor force in 1940 and have remained near this proportion since.[9]

These long-run changes in the occupational structure reflect (1) advances in the technology of production, (2) changes associated with the growth of corporate bureauc-

[8]See Robert J. Larner, "The Effect of Management-Control on the Profits of Large Corporations," in Maurice Zeitlin (ed.), *American Society, Inc.* (Chicago: Markham Publishing Co., 1970).

[9]Service workers comprise the remaining 12 percent of employment. Unless otherwise noted, all data in this paper are taken from official U.S. government sources; for a fuller account and detailed references see Victoria Bonnell and Michael Reich, "Workers and the American Economy," New England Free Press pamphlet, 1969.

TABLE 4–L   THE CHANGING OCCUPATIONAL STRUCTURE OF THE LABOR FORCE

Occupational Group	1910	1920	1930	1940	1950	1960	1967*	1975*,†
Managers, Officials and Proprietors (except farm)	*6.6%*	*6.6%*	*7.4%*	*7.3%*	*8.8%*	*8.5%*	*10.1%*	*10.4%*
White-Collar Workers	*14.7*	*18.3*	*22.0*	*23.8*	*27.7*	*33.8*	*36.0*	*38.1*
Professional and Technical	4.7	5.4	6.8	7.5	8.5	11.4	13.3	14.8
Clerical	5.3	8.0	8.9	9.6	12.3	15.0	16.6	16.9
Sales	4.7	4.9	6.3	6.7	6.9	7.4	6.1	6.4
Blue-Collar Workers	*38.2*	*40.2*	*39.6*	*39.8*	*41.2*	*39.5*	*36.7*	*34.0*
Craftsmen and Foremen	11.6	13.0	12.8	12.0	14.5	14.3	13.2	13.0
Semi-skilled	14.6	15.6	15.8	18.4	20.9	19.7	18.7	16.9
Unskilled	12.0	11.6	11.0	9.4	6.8	5.5	4.8	4.1
Service Workers	*9.6*	*7.8*	*9.8*	*11.8*	*10.3*	*11.7*	*12.5*	*13.8*
Private Household (e.g., Maids)	5.0	3.3	4.1	4.7	2.5	2.8	2.4	
Other service	4.6	4.5	5.7	7.1	7.8	8.9	10.1	
Agricultural Workers	*30.9*	*27.0*	*21.2*	*17.4*	*11.8*	*6.3*	*4.7*	*3.6*
Farmers and Farm Managers	16.5	15.3	12.4	10.4	7.5	3.9	2.6	
Farm Laborers	14.4	11.7	8.8	7.0	4.3	2.4	2.1	
TOTAL‡	100.0	100.0	100.0	100.0	100.0	100.0	100.0	100.0

NOTES: * Data for 1967 and 1975 refer to employed persons only. † Projected figures. ‡ Individual items are rounded independently and therefore may not add up to totals.

SOURCES: Data for 1910-1940 from U.S. Dept. of Commerce, Bureau of the Census, *Historical Statistics of the United States, Colonial Times to 1957*, Table D 72-122; data for 1950-1960 from U.S. Dept. of Commerce, Bureau of the Census, *U.S. Census of Population, 1960*, Table 201; data for 1967 and 1975 from U.S. Dept. of Labor, *Manpower Report of the President, 1968*, Tables A-9 and E-8.

racies, and (3) shifts in the sectoral composition of goods and services produced in the economy.

(1) With technical improvements related primarily to mechanization and automation, fewer industrial workers are needed to produce increasing quantities of output. For example, in manufacturing total output increased 79 percent between 1950 and 1965, with only a 7 percent increase in production workers; in mining, output increased 38 percent in the same period, while blue-collar production employment declined nearly 40 percent.[10]

(2) In the same period, white-collar nonproduction employment increased by 70 per-

cent in manufacturing and by more than 60 percent in mining. As Hymer points out elsewhere in this chapter,[11] modern corporate enterprises have become increasingly complex in their organizational structure. With the development of far-flung corporate sales and distribution networks and corporate divisions specializing in research and development and overall corporate coordination, more white-collar workers—managerial, professional, technical, clerical, and sales —are needed. Research and development activities have become particularly important in many military-related sectors in American industry. These high-technology industries, such as electronics, telecommunications, and missile guidance systems, employ large num-

[10]U.S. Department of Labor, Bureau of Labor Statistics, Bulletin 1599, p. 15.

[11]See Hymer, Section 4.2, p. 156.

bers of scientists, engineers, designers, and technicians. Thus, white-collar workers are becoming an increasing proportion of the total labor force within the manufacturing sector of the economy. We can expect this trend to continue; nonmanagerial white-collar workers comprised less than 10 percent of employment in manufacturing in 1899, 20 percent of total manufacturing employment in 1952, and are expected to be 27 percent by 1975.[12]

(3) The changes in the sectoral composition of goods and services produced in the economy have also contributed to the growth of white-collar employment. The service sectors—wholesale and retail trade; finance, insurance and real estate; professional, business, and personal and repair services; institutions (private hospitals, universities, foundations, etc.); and government—become increasingly important at higher levels of gross national product. These service sectors tend to employ a high percentage of white-collar workers.

A large proportion of the increased employment in the service sector is concentrated in increased state and local government employment in education, health, and local public administration. For example, "the *increase* in employment in the field of education between 1950 and 1960 was

greater than the total number employed in the steel, copper, and aluminum industries in either year. The *increase* in employment in the field of health between 1950 and 1960 was greater than the total number employed in automobile manufacturing in either year."[13]

THE NATURE OF WHITE-COLLAR EMPLOYMENT

As the number of white-collar jobs has grown, the character of these jobs has been transformed. First, the greatest increases (in absolute numbers) in white-collar jobs have occurred in the low-level clerical and sales categories. Second, the growth of bureaucracies and the increasing importance of machinery of various types in modern offices —copying machines, new varieties of dictating equipment, improved typewriters, key punch machines, and other accessories to electronic data processing—have made much work in the modern office resemble factory and assembly-line labor. The work of a telephone operator or of a secretary in a typing pool is similar in many ways to the work of a machine operator in a textile factory. Hierarchy, barriers to advancement, extreme specialization, and lack of control more and more characterize many white-collar jobs. Several recent national surveys have pointed

[12]The 1899 estimate is cited in Chinoy, *Automobile Workers and the American Dream*, p. 5; 1952 and 1975 figures are taken from BLS Bulletin 1599.

[13]Victor Fuchs, *The Service Economy* (New York: National Bureau for Economic Research, 1968), p. 1.

TABLE 4–M   SELECTED WHITE COLLAR OCCUPATIONS AS A PERCENT OF TOTAL MANUFACTURING EMPLOYMENT

	1940	1952	1963	1975 (projected)
Professional and Technical	3.0	5.3	9.3	11.2
Clerical	14.1	11.8	12.2	12.2
Sales		2.8	3.3	3.6
Total	17.1	19.9	24.8	27.0

SOURCE: U.S. Census of Population, 1940; Bureau of Labor Statistics Bulletin 1599; unpublished BLS data presented in E. Kassalow, "White Collar Unionism in the United States," in A. Sturmthal, Ed., *White Collar Trade Unions* (Urbana: University of Illinois Press, 1966), p. 318.

to increasing job dissatisfaction among white-collar workers as a result of such changes.[14]

Furthermore, the independent status of many once elite professional white-collar jobs has been steadily eroded. Scientists, engineers, architects, teachers, nurses, university professors, technicians, etc., find that they work in ever larger organizations where the content of their jobs, as well as their working conditions, are narrowly defined and set down from above. In recent years many professional and technical white-collar workers have become subject to layoffs, a long-time hallmark of blue-collar employment.

Even doctors and lawyers have not escaped some loss of independence. For example, an increasing percentage of all doctors are employed on a salary basis in the large, urban, often university-connected hospitals, clinics, and research institutes. Fewer lawyers are engaged primarily in their own practice; many now work for large law firms or are employed directly by corporations and governments on an annual salary basis.

Finally, the salaries of white-collar workers have not risen as fast as those of blue-collar workers. In 1890, white-collar workers received on the average about double the average wage of the blue-collar manufacturing worker.[15] Today most white-collar clerical and sales workers earn less than many blue-collar workers. While female clerical and sales workers receive the lowest pay, the average income of male clerical and sales workers alone is below the average income of skilled blue-collar workers.[16]

The relative position on the income scale of professional white-collar workers has also fallen. For example, in 1904, high school teachers in large cities earned nearly three times the wage of an average manufacturing production worker.[17] Today, high school teachers earn only about 50 percent more than the average manufacturing wage earner.

If we look at the blue-collar component of the labor force, we can also discern dramatic shifts within it. With mechanization and automation, unskilled labor jobs have been rapidly disappearing and will continue to do so. Semi-skilled blue-collar workers and skilled craftsmen, particularly the latter, increasingly dominate the blue-collar category. More blue-collar jobs involve the use of power machinery and fewer require brute physical strength. In short, many of the old distinctions between blue- and white-collar work are breaking down.

THE ROLE OF UNIONS

Although the first workers' organizations in the United States were formed before 1800 (Philadelphia printers conducted a strike in 1786), as late as 1933 less than three million workers—about 5 percent of the total labor force—were organized into unions.[18] These unions were predominantly structured along craft lines, i.e., only skilled craftsmen were eligible for membership. Very few semi-skilled or unskilled workers, and few blacks, belonged to these craft unions.

Before the 1930's, ethnic and racial an-

---

[14]For a summary of several recent studies, see "Psychological Impact of Work," *Manpower Report of the President, 1968*, pp. 47–55.

[15]In 1890, average annual earnings for clerical workers in manufacturing and steam railroads were $848, compared to $439 for blue-collar wage earners in manufacturing; see *Historical Statistics of the United States from Colonial Times to the Present* (Washington, D.C.: U.S. Government Printing Office), p. 92.

[16]Bonnell and Reich, "Workers and the American Economy," Table 25.

[17]P.G. Keat, "Long-Run Changes in the Occupational Wage Structure," *Journal of Political Economy*, December, 1960.

[18]Figures cited on union membership are based on official U.S. Department of Labor estimates. See *Handbook of Labor Statistics 1967*, BLS Bulletin 1600, 1968.

tagonisms, an open frontier, and above all, organized employer resistance (often violent and repressive and backed by the military and police power of the state) combined in blocking numerous attempts to organize industrial-wide unions. But during the decade of the Thirties, industrial unionism became a mass movement: four million workers, many of them semi-skilled or unskilled, were organized into the Congress of Industrial Organization (CIO) between 1934 and 1938 alone. The movement reached a crescendo in the massive sit-down strikes of 1936–1937, when tens of thousands of workers successfully occupied factories, often for weeks, until their unions were recognized as legitimate bargaining agents by the employers. The CIO solidified its success during World War II when it organized an additional four million workers into unions.

By 1947, union membership had reached 14.8 million, or about 24 percent of the total labor force, and about 34 percent of the nonfarm labor force. In 1960, about half of all blue-collar workers were members of unions, and four-fifths of all union members were in the mining, manufacturing, and construction industries. By contrast, in 1960 only 8 percent of service workers and 13 percent of white-collar workers were unionized. Thus the decline in blue-collar production employment and the rise of white-collar and service employment have led to a decline in the proportion of the nonfarm labor force which is unionized: 34 percent in 1947 versus 28 percent in 1966 (see Table 4–N).

The degree of unionization varies considerably by industry, region, sex, and race. In 1966, while approximately half of all manufacturing workers were organized, the proportion unionized was even higher in the more concentrated and heavy industries, reaching 89 percent in primary metals (steel, copper, etc.), 80 percent in rubber, and 90 percent in transportation equipment (auto-

mobiles, aircraft, etc.). Many of the remaining unorganized workers in these industries were in the smaller scattered plants. As for regional differences, union organization tends to be less extensive in the South. Women and blacks are underrepresented in the unions: about 18 percent of union members are women, although they comprise nearly 30 percent of the labor force; similarly, blacks comprise only 11 percent of all union members, although they are one-fifth of the highly organized blue-collar occupations. Recently, unions have grown rapidly among white-collar public employees— clerks, teachers, social workers, etc.

What has been the impact of the unions? Have the unions modified traditional employer control over the process of production, or the conditions surrounding the workers' sale of their labor-power? The overall picture is complex and we cannot here present a comprehensive and detailed answer, but a few generalizations can be made.

Unions were originally primarily defensive organizations trying to resist layoffs and firings as well as employer attempts to reduce wages or the quality of working conditions. Once both illegal and radical, unions have been recognized by legislation and become a conservative force. As Andre Gorz points out, the legitimacy of the unions in the eyes of employers and the state is dependent on two conditions:

1. First, that unions must voice only demands that are realistic, and that do not call capitalism into question; demands that are *negotiable*.
2. Second, that once an agreement has been bargained out, unions must stick to it and prevent the workers from breaking it.[19]

The first of these conditions has tended to channel unions to concentrate on quantitative wage demands and place less emphasis on qualitative demands relating to working conditions, since quantitative wage

[19]See Gorz, Section 11.4, p. 478.

TABLE 4–N   UNION MEMBERSHIP AS A PROPORTION OF THE LABOR FORCE, 1930–1966

Year	Total Union Membership (millions)	Percent of Total Labor Force	Percent of Non-agricultural Labor Force
1930	3.40	6.8	11.6
1933	2.69	5.2	11.3
1934	3.09	5.9	11.9
1936	3.99	7.4	13.7
1937	7.01	12.9	22.6
1938	8.03	14.6	27.5
1940	8.72	15.5	26.9
1942	10.38	17.2	25.9
1944	14.15	21.4	33.8
1946	14.40	23.6	34.5
1947	14.79	23.9	33.7
1950	14.27	22.0	31.5
1952	15.89	23.9	32.5
1954	17.02	25.1	34.7
1958	17.03	24.2	33.2
1962	16.59	22.6	29.8
1964	16.84	22.2	28.9
1966	17.89	22.7	28.0

SOURCE: U.S. Department of Labor, *Handbook of Labor Statistics, 1968.*

demands both are easily negotiable and relate only to how the pie is to be cut, not to whether management has the prerogative to cut it.

This is not to deny the importance of union struggles for higher wages. In fact, unions have probably had some upward impact on real wages of workers, though it is difficult to estimate how much. By promoting the idea of "equal pay for equal work," unions have succeeded to a certain extent in reducing some wage differentials and establishing standard wage rates for production workers in all plants of a given industry. But insofar as unionism has been concentrated among the oligopolistic, capital-intensive industries which are capable of absorbing wage increases by passing on higher product prices to the consumer, part of the wage gains won by unions may have come at the expense of employees in unorganized sectors rather than at the expense of employers.

Unionism has also generally resulted in a systematized, formalized "web of rules" governing labor-management relations, both in the hiring process and within the workplace. Uniform, structured procedures are developed to handle seniority, promotions, transfers, layoffs, employee grievances, etc., thus reducing arbitrary and inequitable treatment of workers by foremen and employers. In return unions fulfill the second condition mentioned by Gorz and enforce no-strike clauses in contracts and otherwise discipline reluctant members to submit to the authority of the collective bargaining contract. The advantages of such well-administered grievance procedures have been summarized by a panel of collective bargaining experts as follows:

A major achievement of collective bargaining . . . is the creation of a system of industrial jurisprudence . . . under which employer and employee rights are set forth in contractual form and disputes over the meeting of the contract are settled through a rational grievance process. . . . This system helps prevent arbitrary action on the questions of discipline, lay-off, promotion and transfer, and sets up orderly proce-

dures *for the handling of grievances.* Wild-cat strikes and other disorderly means of protest have been curtailed and effective work discipline generally established.[20] (*italics added*)

Trade unions, operating within the confines of capitalist institutions, have never challenged management's perogatives in deciding what to produce and have only marginal impact in deciding how to produce it. As Professors Bok and Dunlop, two well-known labor mediators and academicians, have written,

Some writers have contended that collective bargaining is a process of joint decision-making or joint management. It is true that many rules are agreed to by the parties and

[20]*The Public Interest and National Labor Policy* (New York: Committee for Economic Development, 1961), p. 32. Cited in D. Bok and J. Dunlop, *Labor and the American Community* (New York: Simon & Schuster, 1970), p. 221.

written into the collective agreement, but many other functions are left exclusively to management. ... Although management may consider it wise to consult with the union before taking certain types of action, it is normally not obligated to seek advanced consent from the union. It is misleading to equate collective bargaining with joint management by union and employers.[21]

We see that unions have had a dual character. Some wage and working condition improvements have been obtained, but only in exchange for the service of providing a disciplined labor force to the employer. Thus, the unions and collective bargaining system have only marginally modified the basic character of the capitalist free market in labor and capitalist control over the production process.

[21]Bok and Dunlop, *Labor and the American Community,* p. 223.

4.6 *Education and the Labor Force*

With the advance of technology and the increasing complexity of productive techniques, the demand for labor has undergone a qualitative change. Not only a disciplined labor force but also an increasingly skilled labor force is required by the industrial system. As a result of these developments, education has become increasingly important as a factor of production in the economy, and no analysis of modern capitalism can afford to ignore its role.

David Cohen and Marvin Lazerson in the following essay discuss the way in which the development of the American educational system has responded to the changing needs of the industrial capitalist economy. The basic capitalist criterion of profit maximization in the market environment determines the structure of production and hence also the nature and requirements of jobs. Individual people must fit the requirements of these jobs in order to find work; thus they need an education that will train them appropriately.

The expanding educational system was often promoted as a means for achieving social mobility and eliminating class distinctions. In fact, as Cohen and Lazerson point out, the increasing differentiation of job requirements has led to a corresponding differentiation of educational offerings

that serves to reinforce the existing class structure. This point is developed
further by Bowles in Chapter 5.[1]

1See Bowles, Section 5.2, p. 218.

Source: The following is an excerpted and revised version of "Education
and the Corporate Order" by DAVID K. COHEN and MARVIN LAZERSON.
From *Socialist Revolution* 2, No. 3 (May/June, 1971). Copyright ©
1971 by David K. Cohen and Marvin Lazerson. Reprinted by permission
of the authors and *Socialist Revolution*.

In our view the main developments in education since the late nineteenth century involve the schools' adaptation to industrialism and the conflicts this engendered. The period's dominant motif was infusing the schools with the values of industrialism and reorganizing them in ways thought to be consistent with the new economic order. The aims of education were closely tied to production—schooling was justified as a way of increasing wealth, improving industrial output, and making management more effective.

The schools' role was to socialize economically desirable values and behavior, teach vocational skills, and provide education consistent with students' expected occupational attainment. As a result, the schools' culture became closely identified with the ethos of the workplace. Schooling came to be seen as work or the preparation for work; schools were pictured as factories, educators as industrial managers, and students as the raw materials to be inducted into the production process. The ideology of school management was recast in the mold of the business corporation, and the character of education was shaped after the image of industrial production.

THE INDUSTRIAL SYSTEM OF SCHOOLING

The most prominent feature of the industrial system of schooling is the idea that education is essentially an economic activity;

schooling is justified as a way to expand wealth by improving production. The mechanisms to accomplish this are skill and behavior training, selecting students for occupational strata based on ability, and matching students to occupations through counseling and training. Education has been fashioned into an increasingly refined training and selection mechanism for the labor force. These ideas were nicely reflected in the formulation of a Michigan educator in 1921:

We can picture the educational system as having a very important function as a selecting agency, a means of selecting the men of best intelligence from the deficient and mediocre. All are poured into the system at the bottom; the incapable are soon rejected or drop out after repeating various grades and pass into the ranks of unskilled labor.... The more intelligent who are to be clerical workers pass into the high school; the most intelligent enter the universities, whence they are selected for the professions.[1]

Such ideas had important implications for the conception and organization of schooling. If schools were the primary occupational training and selection mechanism, then the criteria of merit within schools had to conform to the criteria of ranking in the occupational structure. The schools' effectiveness could then be judged by how well

1W. B. Pillsbury, "Selection—An Unnoticed Function of Education," *Scientific Monthly*, XII (January, 1921), 71.

success in school predicted success at work. The criteria for these predictions were work behavior and academic ability.

From the late nineteenth century onward, schoolmen's concern with student behavior was justified in terms of training for work. In 1909 the Boston School Committee described the program of instruction in an elementary school given over to "prevocational" classes—i.e., a school for children expected to become factory workers:

> Everything must conform as closely as possible to actual industrial work in real life. The product must be not only useful, but must be needed, and must be put to actual use. It must be something which may be produced in quantities. The method must be practical, and both product and method must be subjected to the same commercial tests, as far as possible, as apply to actual industry.[2]

Typically, school officials stressed that classroom activities should inculcate the values thought to make good industrial workers— respect for authority, discipline, order, cleanliness, and punctuality—and the schools developed elaborate schemes for grading, reporting, and rewarding student behavior. "One great benefit of going to school, especially of attending regularly for eight or ten months each year for nine years or more," argued A. E. Winship, editor of the *Journal of Education* in 1900, "is that it establishes a habit of regularity and persistency in effort." "Indeed," Winship claimed, "the boy who leaves school and goes to work does not necessarily learn to work steadily, but often quite the reverse."[3] Going to school, then, was better preparation for becoming a good worker than work itself!

If schooling is conceived as a preparation for work, it is only natural to organize it on the model of the factory. School superin-

tendents conceived themselves as plant managers, and proposed to treat education as a production process in which children were the raw materials.[4] It was equally natural to evaluate schooling in terms of economic productivity. Indeed, if education is work then the only suitable criterion for determining its effects is extrinsic—income returns to schooling. This tendency to use market criteria in evaluating education first flowered around the turn of the century: between 1880 and 1910 scores of studies of income returns to education appeared.[5] Superintendents, plant managers, and teachers' associations published reports which sought to show that the more education students received, the greater their later earnings would be. This was reflected in the schools' internal evaluation systems, as grades and school retention were justified as strategies for raising later earnings. The justification for learning had itself become an explicit form of money fetishism.

The ability criterion was no less important. Indeed, since the turn of the century the notion that adult success depended on school achievement has attained the status of religious dogma. As Ellwood Cubberley revealed in 1909, this idea is closely linked to the view that as production grows more technological workers require greater education:

> Along with these changes [industrialism] there has come not only a tremendous increase in the quantity of our knowledge, but also a demand for a large increase in the amount of knowledge necessary to enable one to meet the changed conditions of modern life. The kind of knowledge needed, too, has fundamentally changed. The ability to read and write and cipher no longer distinguishes the educated from the uneducated man. A man must have better, broader, and

---

[2]Boston, *Documents of the School Committee,* 1908, #7, pp. 48–53.

[3]A. E. Winship, *Jukes-Edwards* (Harrisburg, Pa., 1900), p. 13.

[4]See Raymond Callahan, *Education and the Cult of Efficiency,* (Chicago, 1962).

[5]A. C. Ellis, *The Money Value of Education,* Bulletin #22, U.S. Bureau of Education (Washington, D.C., 1917).

a different kind of knowledge than did his parents if he is to succeed under modern conditions.[6]

The idea that knowledge is power dates back to the scientific revolution, but here Cubberley was articulating a new version. It was not simply that knowledge was power, but that trained technological ability was the key to personal success.

These themes became explicit with the appearance of the differentiated curriculum. The differentiation of educational offerings emerged out of the new ideology of meritocracy—the notion that individuals would choose the educational program most suited to their particular abilities. But multiple curricula offerings also arose out of the increasing differentiation of work, the demand of business and industrial leaders for trained and disciplined workers, and the need to protect educational opportunities for children from advantaged families, something which seemed incompatible when the common curriculum was turned to mass schooling. Under the pressure of these forces the older curriculum had begun to give way at the turn of the century and was being replaced with a multiplicity of course offerings geared to the major strata of the occupational structure. The National Education Association's 1910 *Report of the Committee on the Place of Industries in Public Education* summarized the rationale for educational differentiation:

1. Industry, as a controlling factor in social progress, has for education a fundamental and permanent significance.
2. Educational standards, applicable in an age of handicraft, presumably need radical change in the present day of complex and highly specialized industrial development.
3. The social aims of education and the psychological needs of childhood alike

require that industrial (manual-constructive) activities form an important part of school occupations. . . .

4. The differences among children as to aptitudes, interests, economic resources, and prospective careers furnish the basis for a rational as opposed to a merely formal distinction between elementary, secondary, and higher education.[7]

The last point is important, for the inventory of differences among children clearly reveals the frank class character of educational differentiation. The point was not only that the children of the poor should get a different sort of schooling, but also that they should get less. The movement to differentiate educational offerings at first centered on temporal differences. Working class children were leaving school without completing the elementary grades: industrial elementary schools, prevocational programs, and junior high schools all were offered as ways of assuring that such pupils would stay in school and receive what was conceived to be appropriate training.[8] Cleveland's school superintendent, for example, argued that working class children would neither continue their education beyond the compulsory minimum, nor learn very much if they did stay. He proposed that their schooling be limited to the elementary years, with a curriculum which imparted basic literacy, good behavior, and rudimentary vocational skills.[9] As time wore on, however, differentiation centered more and more on curricular differences within secondary schools. In part this resulted from the considerations expressed in the NEA report, but it was also due to the gradual increases in schools'

---

[6]Ellwood Cubberley, *Changing Conceptions of Education* (Cambridge, Mass., 1909) pp. 18–19.

[7]National Education Association, *Report of the Committee on the Place of Industry in Public Education*, 1910, pp. 6–7.

[8]See Frank M. Leavitt and Edith Brown, *Prevocational Education in the Public Schools* (Boston, 1915).

[9]Sol Cohen, "The Industrial Education Movement, 1906–1917," *American Quarterly*, Fall, 1969, pp. 105–6.

holding power. As the high schools became less and less the preserves of children from advantaged families, curricular differentiation was necessary to maintain differences in educational opportunity. At the turn of the century special business and commercial courses already had been established in the high schools; by the second decade many cities had created vocational, business, and academic curricula. The school board president in the Lynds' [book] *Middletown* summarized the change succinctly, in the mid-1920's: "For a long time all boys were trained to be President. Then for a while we trained them all to be professional men. Now we are training boys to get jobs."[10]

The differentiation of educational offerings ran across the grain of established ideas about equality in education. As in so many things, Cubberley characterized the situation bluntly in 1909:

> *Our city schools will soon be forced to give up the exceedingly democratic idea that all are equal, and our society devoid of classes ... and to begin a specialization of educational effort along many lines in an attempt to adapt the school to the needs of these many classes ... industrial and vocational training is especially significant of the changing conception of the school and the classes in society which the school is in the future expected to serve.*[11]

Although some schoolmen insisted that differentiation implied no change in the reigning ideas of equal opportunity, a greater number embraced both differentiation and its implications for equality. The NEA juxtaposed "equality of opportunity as an abstraction" to the idea that education should be based on "the reality of opportunity as measured by varying needs, tastes, and abilities."[12] Although such formulations were

offered to support differentiation of educational offerings along class lines, this was rarely seen as inconsistent with the idea that "education should give to all an equal chance to attain any distinction in life."[13] The reason for this lay in the ready identification of ability with inherited social and economic status, an idea which the early testing movement only reinforced. In theory, at least, there was no tension between the differentiation of school offerings and the academic meritocracy.

The appeal of the meritocratic idea extended far beyond a rationale for curricular differentiation. Educators and social reformers at the turn of the century were not insensible to the accumulation of a large, heavily immigrant industrial proletariat in the cities; they feared the prospect of class warfare, and found in educational opportunity a ready formula for remedy. The academic meritocracy was thought to promise a remedy for poverty and inequality. Schools would provide a mechanism whereby those who were qualified could rise on the basis of ability. Even the greatest skeptics about the influences of environment on ability— E. L. Thorndike, for example—agreed that the schools should provide avenues for mobility based on selection of talent.[14] And liberals maintained that schools ought to remedy deficiencies which the environment inflicted upon children. Frank Tracy Carleton wrote in 1907 that the schools should reduce crime and dependency by providing special education for disadvantaged children. If schools compensated for environmental deficiencies, they would improve children's chances for success in later life.[15]

This faith in the transforming power of education has been the basis for compensatory education and social welfare programs

---

[10]Robert and Helen Lynd, *Middletown* (New York, 1956 edition) p. 194.

[11]Ellwood Cubberley, *Changing Conceptions of Education*, pp. 53–57.

[12]National Education Association, *Report*, p. 7.

[13]*Ibid.*, pp. 21–22.

[14]E. L. Thorndike, *Educational Psychology* (New York, 1903), pp. 44–46.

[15]Frank Carleton, "The School as a Factor in Industrial and Social Problems," *Education*, XXVIII (October, 1907), 77–79.

since the late nineteenth century. Schooling was conceived as an engine of social reform, a mechanism whereby injustice could be remedied by distributing rewards on the basis of talent rather than inheritance. It was, of course, an idea peculiarly suited to bourgeois liberalism. The redistribution of social and economic status promised through schooling was neither an attack on property nor an effort to weaken the class structure. Far from promising to eliminate inequalities in the distribution of privilege, schooling would only insure that they were consistent with qualification rather than birth. The notion that schools were a mechanism of social reform rested on the idea that individual redistribution of wealth based on achievement was preferable to across-the-board redistribution. The great appeal of social reform through education was that all issues of distributive social justice were translated into matters of individual ability and effort in school and marketplace.

These developments did not occur all at once, nor was the industrial system of schooling monolithic. Educators who sought

to model their schools on industrialism frequently seemed to have little idea of how industrial corporations worked.[16] Efforts to articulate the curriculum with the occupational structure did not mean that educators knew, or tried to find out, what the society's labor needs actually were. For the most part it meant little more than embodying the differences between blue-collar, clerical, and professional jobs in schools' curricula and offerings.

As the economy shifted toward increasingly technological forms of production, the schools slowly followed suit. The old model of the schools as factories is slowly being replaced, as manpower needs change. But the commitment to the ability criterion, testing, guidance, and differentiated schooling has only been accentuated. While the character of work is changing, the school remains the primary labor training and selection mechanism.

[16]See Michael Katz, "The Emergence of Bureaucracy in Urban Education in the Boston Case, 1850–1884," *History of Education Quarterly,* VIII (Summer-Fall, 1968), 167–68.

4.7   *Corporate Liberalism and the Modern State*

The long-run forces—technological, economic, social and political—that have caused significant changes in business and labor under capitalism have clearly also affected the state. Within the past century the state has come to play an increasingly prominent role in capitalist economies. In the next reading James Weinstein discusses the historical origins and significance of the modern American "liberal" state. He traces the change in the meaning of liberalism from laissez-faire individualism in the nineteenth century to social control by the state in the twentieth century, and he argues that the modern liberal state had its origins in the Progressive Era at the beginning of this century.

Weinstein's account illustrates clearly how the changing role of the state evolved out of the changing needs of the dominant capitalist class, which in turn derived from the increasing complexity of production and economic organization in the growing American economy. Laissez-faire policies appropriate to an earlier era of open frontiers and simple technologies were found increasingly inadequate by the corporate leaders emerging at the turn of the century. Instead, new policies of centralized social engineering were required to maintain the capitalist system and to secure the hegemony of the corporate ruling class.

Source: The following is excerpted from the introduction to *The Corporate Ideal and the Liberal State* by JAMES WEINSTEIN. Copyright © 1968 by James Weinstein. Reprinted by permission of Beacon Press.

[My] two main theses . . . run counter to prevailing popular opinion and to the opinion of most historians. The first is that the political ideology now dominant in the United States, and the broad programmatic outlines of the liberal state (known by such names as the New Freedom, the New Deal, the New Frontier, and the Great Society) had been worked out and, in part, tried out by the end of the First World War. The second is that the ideal of a liberal corporate social order was formulated and developed under the aegis and supervision of those who then, as now, enjoyed ideological and political hegemony in the United States: the more sophisticated leaders of America's largest corporations and financial institutions.

This position is not based upon a conspiracy theory of history, but it does posit a conscious and successful effort to guide and control the economic and social policies of federal, state, and municipal governments by various business groupings in their own long-range interest as they perceived it. Businessmen were not always, or even normally, the first to advocate reforms or regulation in the common interest. The original impetus for many reforms came from those at or near the bottom of the American social structure, from those who benefited least from the rapid increase in the productivity of the industrial plant of the United States and from expansion at home and abroad. But in the current century, particularly on the federal level, few reforms were enacted without the tacit approval, if not the guidance, of the large corporate interests. And, much more important, businessmen were able to harness to their own ends the desire of intellectuals

and middle-class reformers to bring together "thoughtful men of all classes" in "a vanguard for the building of the good community."[1] These ends were the stabilization, rationalization, and continued expansion of the existing political economy, and, subsumed under that, the circumscription of the Socialist movement with its ill-formed, but nevertheless dangerous ideas for an alternative form of social organization.

There are two essential aspects of the liberal state as it developed in the Progressive Era, one tightly and sometimes indistinguishably intertwined with the other, but both clearly different. The first was the need of many of the largest corporations to have the government (usually the federal government) intervene in economic matters to protect against irresponsible business conduct and to assure stability in marketing and financial affairs. . . .

The second was the replacement of the ideological concepts of laissez faire, or the Darwinian survival of the fittest, by an ideal of a responsible social order in which all classes could look forward to some form of recognition and sharing in the benefits of an ever-expanding economy. Such a corporate order was, of course, to be based on what banker V. Everitt Macy called "the industrial and commercial structure which is the indispensable shelter of us all."[2]

[1] Sidney Kaplan, "Social Engineers as Saviours: Effects of World War I on Some American Liberals," *The Journal of the History of Ideas,* XVII (June, 1956), 347.

[2] Speech to the 17th Annual Meeting of the National Civic Federation, January 22, 1917, Box 187, National Civic Federation papers, New York Public Library.

The key word in the new corporate vision of society was responsibility, although the word meant different things to different groups of men. To most middle-class social reformers and social workers—men such as Frank P. Walsh of Kansas City, or Judge Ben B. Lindsey of Denver, or Walter Weyl of the *New Republic*, or Jane Addams of Hull House, responsibility meant, first of all, the responsibility of society to individual Americans or to underprivileged social classes. To the corporation executives it meant above all, the responsibility of all classes to maintain and increase the efficiency of the existing social order. Of course some middle-class reformers, like *New Republic* editor Herbert Croly, understood that progressive democracy was "designed" to serve as a counterpoise to the threat of working class revolution."[3] But even for them the promotion of reform was not an act of cynicism: they simply sought a way to be immediately effective, to have real influence. Their purpose was not only to serve as defenders of the social system, but also to improve the human condition. In the most profound sense they failed, and badly; yet they were a good deal more than simply lackeys of the capitalist class.

The confusion over what liberalism means and who liberals are is deep-seated in American society. In large part this is because of the change in the nature of liberalism from the individualism of laissez faire in the nineteenth century to the social control of corporate liberalism in the twentieth. Because the new liberalism of the Progressive Era put its emphasis on cooperation and social responsibility, as opposed to unrestrained "ruthless" competition, so long associated with businessmen in the age of the Robber Baron, many believed then, and more believe now, that liberalism was in its essence anti big business. Corporation leaders have encouraged this belief. False consciousness of the

nature of American liberalism has been one of the most powerful ideological weapons that American capitalism has had in maintaining its hegemony. An intellectual tradition has grown up among liberal ideologues that embodies this false consciousness. Arthur M. Schlesinger, Jr., intellectual in residence of the Kennedys, for example, writes that "Liberalism in America has been ordinarily the movement on the part of the other sections of society to restrain the power of the business community."[4] Consistent with this assertion is the popular image of movements for regulation and social reform —the Pure Food and Drug Act, the Federal Trade Commission, workmen's compensation, social security, unemployment insurance, the poverty program—as victories of "the people" over "the interests." In one sense this is true. Even so, Schlesinger's pronouncement is misleading. It is not only historically inaccurate, but serves the interests of the large corporations by masking the manner in which they have exercised control over American politics in this century.

Both in its nineteenth and twentieth century forms, liberalism has been the political ideology of the rising, and then dominant, business groups. Changes in articulated principles have been the result of changing needs of the most dynamic and rapidly growing forms of enterprise. Thus in the days of Andrew Jackson, liberalism's main thrust was against monopoly (and Arthur Schlesinger tells us this meant it was anti-business). But more recent scholarship has shown that it was the new business class, made up of individual small entrepreneurs (as well as threatened and declining farmers and artisans), that fought state chartered monopoly. Rising entrepreneurs struggled to free business enterprise of the outmoded restrictions of special incorporation and banking laws and to end what was then an overly central-

---

[3]Kaplan, "Social Engineers," pp. 354–55.

[4]Arthur M. Schlesinger, Jr., *The Age of Jackson* (Boston: Little, Brown, 1946), p. 505.

ized control of credit. Their laissez faire rhetoric in opposition to "unnatural" or artificial privilege was that of the common man, but their achievements—general incorporation and free banking laws, the spread of public education and popular suffrage—created the conditions for unfettered competition and rapid industrial growth. Half a century later that competition and industrial expansion had led to the development of new forms of monopoly, grown so powerful that a relative handful of merged corporations came to dominate the American political economy. Thereafter, liberalism became the movement for state intervention to supervise corporate activity, rather than a movement for the removal of state control over private enterprise.

To achieve conditions suitable for free competition during the Age of Jackson, the rising entrepreneurs and their political representatives had to believe in, and promote, ideals of equality of opportunity, class mobility, and noninterference by the government with individual initiative (although, even then, government subsidy of such necessary common services as railroads and canals was encouraged where private capital was inadequate to do the job). At the turn of the century the new trust magnates also pressed for reform in accordance with their new political, economic, and legal needs. The nature of the ideals and the needs in the two periods were different. In the first, the principles of competition and individual efficiency underlay many proposed reforms; in the second, cooperation and *social* efficiency were increasingly important. But in each case the rising businessmen—or, at least, many of them—helped promote reforms. In both instances, business leaders sponsored institutional adjustment to their needs, and supported political ideologies that appealed to large numbers of people of different social classes in order to gain, and retain, popular support for their entrepreneurial activity. In the Progressive Era, and ever since, corpora-

tion leaders did this by adapting to their own ends the ideals of middle-class social reformers, social workers, and socialists.

My main concern . . . is not with the social reformers, men and women who might be called ordinary liberals. Instead I . . . focus on those business leaders (and their various political and academic ideologues) who saw liberalism as a means of securing the existing social order. They succeeded because their ideology and their political economy alone was comprehensive. Radical critics of the new centralized and manipulated system of social control were disarmed and absorbed by the corporate liberals who allowed potential opponents to participate, even if not as equals, in a process of adjustment, concession, and amelioration that seemed to promise a gradual advance toward the good society for all citizens. In a formal democracy, success lay in evolving a social vision that could be shared by most articulate people outside the business community. Corporate liberalism evolved such a vision. More than that, it appealed to leaders of different social groupings and classes by granting them status and influence as spokesmen for their constituents on the condition only that they defend the framework of the existing social order.

As it developed, the new liberalism incorporated the concepts of social engineering and social efficiency that grew up alongside of industrial engineering and efficiency. The corollary was a disparagement of "irresponsible" individualism and localism. On the municipal level, as Samuel P. Hays has observed, the drama of business-led reform lay in competition between two systems of decision-making. One was based upon ward representation and traditional ideas of grassroots involvement in the political process; the other, growing out of the rationalization of social life made possible by scientific and technological developments, required expert analysis and worked more smoothly if decisions flowed from fewer and smaller centers outward toward the rest of society. The same competition went on at the federal level, although formal changes in the political structure were more difficult to make and, therefore, less extensive. In general, however, the Progressive Era witnessed rapid strides toward centralization and a decline in importance of those institutions which were based upon local representation, most obviously in the decline of Congress and the increasing importance of the executive branch in the shaping of policy and in the initiation of legislation. As Hays concludes, this development constituted an accommodation of forces outside the business community to political trends within business and professional life.[5] . . .

In short, . . . liberalism in the Progressive Era—and since—was the product, consciously created, of the leaders of the giant corporations and financial institutions that emerged astride American society in the last years of the nineteenth century and the early years of the twentieth.

[5]Samuel Hays, "The Politics of Reform in Municipal Government in the Progressive Era," *Pacific Northwest Quarterly*, LV, 4 (October, 1964), 168–69.

4.8   *The Expanding Role of the State*

The rise in significance of the large monopolistic corporation has led some observers to characterize modern capitalism as "monopoly capitalism."[1] The expanding role of the state has led James O'Connor in the following reading to use the term "state capitalism" as well. O'Connor identifies here many of the areas where the increasing socialization of labor in the productive process—i.e., the increasing degree of complexity and interdependence of the economy—has led to an increasing role for the state in the American capitalist economy.

In Chapter 3, the role of the state in preserving the basic institutions of the capitalist mode of production was given primary emphasis.[2] Under modern capitalism, the state must not only protect and enforce private property, but it must also intervene directly in an increasing variety of ways in the functioning of the economy in order that the privileges and hegemony of private capital not be eroded. Thus control over the state apparatus becomes increasingly important for the capitalist class, and the links between private business and the state become ever closer.

There is one important aspect of state intervention in a modern capitalist economy that we shall defer until Chapter 9: the role of the state in absorbing the surplus. Capitalist class interest calls not only for the many forms of specific government activity described by O'Connor, but also for general state action to protect the capitalist economy against catastrophic depressions of the kind that threatened the whole system in the

[1]This term has been most widely publicized by Paul Baran and Paul Sweezy, whose major recent work bears the title *Monopoly Capital* (New York: Monthly Review Press, 1966).

[2]See especially Sweezy, Section 3.8, p. 133 and Edwards and MacEwan, Section 3.9, p. 135.

1930's. We shall argue in Chapter 9 that government spending now plays a significant role in maintaining aggregate demand for goods and services at a level that approximately equals the corresponding aggregate supply, thereby contributing to the absorption of the aggregate economic surplus and preventing major crises of overproduction, underconsumption, and unemployment.[3]

After O'Connor's essay a statistical appendix is included to document the expansion of the public sector in the United States economy.

[3]For a detailed analysis of the problem of surplus absorption, see Weisskopf, Section 9.1, p. 364.

Source: The following is excerpted from "The Fiscal Crisis of the State" by JAMES O'CONNOR. From *Socialist Revolution* 1, Nos. 1 and 2 (Jan./Feb. and March/April 1970). Reprinted by permission of *Socialist Revolution*.

. . .   . . .

In general, the state budget continuously expands owing to the intensification of economic integration. Social production has advanced so rapidly and along so many fronts that it has pressed hard upon and finally spilled over the boundaries of immediate private property relations. In brief, state capitalism constitutes a higher and more general form of social integration rendered necessary by the advanced character of social production.

. . .

I

The first major category of [state] expenditures consists of facilities which are valuable to a specific industry, or group of related industries. These are projects which are useful to specific interests and whose financial needs are so large that they exceed the resources of the interests affected. They also consist of projects in which the financial outcome is subject to so much uncertainty that they exceed the risk-taking propensities of the interests involved. Finally, these are projects which realize external economies and economies of large-scale production for the particular industries.

The most important state investments serving the interests of specific industries are highway expenditures.[1] Domestic economic growth since World War II has been led by automobile production and suburban residential construction, which requires an enormous network of complementary highways, roads, and ancillary facilities. Rejecting public transportation, on the one hand, and toll highways, on the other, the state has "socialized intercity highway systems paid for by the taxpaper—not without great encouragement for the rubber, petroleum, and auto industries.[2] From 1944, when Congress passed the Federal Aid to Highways Act, to 1961, the Federal government expended its entire transportation budget on roads and highways. Today, approximately twenty percent of non-military government spending at all levels is destined for highways; inland waterway and airport expenditures total less than one billion yearly; and railroads and local rapid transit receive little or nothing. And in area redevelopment schemes, high-

[1]Weapon expenditures fall partly into this category, but since their ultimate determinant lies elsewhere, discussion of military spending is postponed until later.
[2]Payntz Taylor, *Outlook for the Railroads*, New York, 1960, p. 91.

ways receive the lion's share of the subsidies; more than eighty percent of the funds allocated by the Federal government to Appalachia for economic development, for example, have been destined for road construction. The reason was that the Federal planners needed the cooperation of the local governors, who together with electric power, steel and other companies combined to block other "solutions."[3]

. . .

II

The second major determinant of state expenditures stems from the immediate economic interests of corporate capital as a whole. The budgetary expression of these interests takes many forms—economic infrastructure investments, expenditures on education, general business subsidies, credit guarantees and insurance, social consumption, and so on. In the United States, most of these forms appeared or developed fully only in the twentieth century, although in Europe state capitalism emerged in an earlier period—in France, during the First Empire, generalized state promotion buoyed the private economy; in Germany, state economic policy received great impetus from political unification and war; in Italy, laissez-faire principles did not prevent the state from actively financing and promoting accumulation in the major spheres of heavy industry; and everywhere liberal notions of small, balanced budgets and indirect taxation came face to face with the fiscal realities of wartime economies.

In the United States, the budget remained small throughout the nineteenth century; transportation investments were chiefly private, and natural resource, conservation, public health, education and related outlays were insignificant. The state served the economic needs of capital as a whole mainly in non-fiscal ways—land tenure, monetary, im-

migration, tariff, and patent policies all "represented and strengthened the particular legal framework within which private business was organized."[4] State subsidies to capital as a whole were confined to the State government and local levels and were largely the product of mercantile, rather than industrial capital, impulses.[5]

In the twentieth century, however, corporate capital has combined with state capital to create a new organic whole. Corporate capital is not subordinated to state capital, or vice versa, but rather they are synthesized into a qualitatively new phenomenon, rooted in the development of the productive forces and the concentration and centralization of capital. More specifically, the rapid advance of technology has increased the pace of general economic change, the risk of capital investments, and the amount of uncontrollable overhead costs. Further, capital equipment is subject to more rapid obsolescence, and there exists a longer lead time before the typical investment is in full operation and thus is able to pay for itself. The development of the production relations has also compelled corporate capital to employ state power in its economic interests as a whole, and socialize production costs. . . .

The most expensive economic needs of corporate capital as a whole are the costs of research, development of new products, new production processes, and so on, and, above all, the costs of training and retraining the labor force, in particular, technical, administrative, and non-manual workers. Preliminary to an investigation of the process of the socialization of these costs, a brief review of the relationships between technology, on the one hand, and the production relations, on the other, is required.

[3]Wall Street Journal, June 28, 1965.

[4]Henry W. Broude, "The Role of the State in American Economic Development, 1820–1890," in Harry N. Scheiber, Ed., United States Economic History: Selected Readings, New York, 1964.

[5]Louis Hartz, Economic Policy and Democratic Thought: Pennsylvania, 1776–1860, Cambridge, Mass., 1948, pp. 290–91.

The forces of production include available land, constant capital, labor skills, methods of work organization, and last but not least, technology, which is a part of, but not totally identified with, the social productive forces. The advance of technology, the uses of technology, and its distribution between the various branches of the economy are all determined in the last analysis by the relations of production. The transformation from a labor-using to a labor-saving technology in mid-nineteenth century Europe was ultimately caused by the disappearance of opportunities for industrial capitalists to recruit labor "extensively" from the artisan and peasant classes at the given wage rate. During the last half of the nineteenth century, the established industrial proletariat faced less competition, their organizations were strengthened, and they were better able to win wage advances. Thus, it was the class struggle that compelled capital to introduce labor-saving innovations.

Despite the rapid advance of technology during the first half of the twentieth century, until World War II the industrial corporations trained the largest part of their labor force, excluding basic skills such as literacy. In the context of the further technological possibilities latent in the scientific discoveries of the nineteenth and twentieth centuries, this was a profoundly irrational mode of social organization.

The reason is that knowledge, unlike other forms of capital, cannot be monopolized by one or a few industrial-finance interests. Capital-as-knowledge resides in the skills and abilities of the working class itself. In the context of a free labor market—that is, in the absence of a feudal-like industrial state which prohibits labor mobility, a flat impossibility in the capitalist mode of production—no one industrial-finance interest can afford to train its own labor force or channel profits into the requisite amount of research and development. The reason is that, apart from the patent system, there is absolutely no guarantee that their "investments" will not seek employment in other corporations or industries. The cost of losing trained manpower is especially high in those industries which employ technical workers with skills which are specific to a particular industrial process.

World War II provided the opportunity to rationalize the entire organization of technology in the United States. As Dobb writes, "a modern war is of such a kind as to require all-out mobilization of economic resources, rapidly executed decisions about transfer of labor and productive equipment, and the growth of war industry, which ordinary market-mechanisms would be powerless to achieve. Consequently, it occasions a considerable growth of state capitalism. . . ."[6] The intervention of the state through government grants to finance research programs, develop new technical processes, and construct new facilities and the forced mobilization of resources converted production to a more social process. The division of labor and specialization of work functions intensified, industrial plants were diversified, the technical requirements of employment became more complex, and, in some cases, more advanced. The end result was a startling acceleration of technology.

At the end of the war, corporate capital was once again faced with the necessity of financing its own research and training its own technical work force. The continued rationalization of the work process required new forms of social integration which would enable social production to advance still further. The first step was the introduction of the GI Bill, which socialized the costs of training (including the living expenses of labor trainees) and eventually helped to create a labor force which could exploit the stockpile of technology created during the war. The second step was the creation of a vast system of lower and higher technical education at the local and state level, the transformation of private universities into Feder-

[6]Maurice Dobb, *Capitalism Yesterday and Today*, New York, 1962, p. 75.

al universities through research grants, and the creation of a system to exploit technology in a systematic, organized way which included not only the education system, but also the foundations, private research organizations, the Pentagon, and countless other Federal government agencies. This system required enormous capital outlays, a large expansion of teaching and administrative personnel, an upgrading of teachers at all levels, together with programs of specialized teaching training, scholarships, libraries—in short, vast new burdens on the state budget. In turn, this reorganization of the labor process, and, in particular, the free availability of masses of technical-scientific workers, made possible the rapid acceleration of technology. With the new, rationalized social organization of technology and the labor process completed, technical knowledge became the main form of labor power and capital. There occurred a decline in the relative importance of living labor, and an increase in the importance of dead labor in the production process. Thus, statistical studies, beginning in the mid-1950's and multiplying rapidly since then, indicate that the growth of aggregate production is caused increasingly less by an expansion in labor "inputs" and the stock of physical assets, and more by upgrading labor skills, improvements in the quality of physical assets, and better organization of work. One famous study demonstrated that increased education accounted for over three-fifths of the growth of output per man-hour in the United States from 1929–1957.[7]

. . .

The uncontrolled expansion of production by corporate capital as a whole creates still another fiscal burden on the state in the form of outlays required to meet the *social costs of private production* (as contrasted

[7]E. F. Denison, *The Sources of Economic Growth in the U.S. and the Alternatives Before Us*, New York, 1962, p. 148.

with the socialization of private costs of production, which we have discussed above). Motor transportation is an important source of social costs in the consumption of oxygen, the production of crop- and animal-destroying smog, the pollution of rivers and oceans by lead additives to gasoline, the construction of freeways that foul the land, and the generation of urban sprawl. These costs do not enter into the accounts of the automobile industry, which is compelled to minimize its own costs and maximize production and sales. Corporate capital is unwilling to treat toxic chemical waste or to develop substitute sources of energy for fossil-fuels that pollute the air. (There are exceptions to this general rule. In Pittsburgh, for example, the Mellon interests reduced air pollution produced by its steel mills in order to preserve the values of its downtown real estate.) And corporate farming—the production of agricultural commodities for exchange alone—generates still more social costs by minimizing crop losses (and thus costs) through the unlimited use of DDT and other chemicals that are harmful to crops, animals, water purity, and human life itself.

By and large, private capital refuses to bear the costs of reducing or eliminating air and water pollution, lowering highway and air accidents, easing traffic jams, preserving forests, wilderness areas, and wildlife sanctuaries, and conserving the soils. In the past these costs were largely ignored. Today, owing to the increasingly social character of production, these costs are damaging not only the ecological structure, but also profitable accumulation itself, particularly in real estate, recreation, agriculture, and other branches of the economy in which land, water, and air are valuable resources to capital. The portion of the state budget devoted to reducing social costs has therefore begun to mount. In the future, the automobile industry can be expected to receive large-scale subsidies to help finance the transition to the electric or fuel-cell car. Capital as a whole will receive more subsidies in the form of new public transportation systems. Subsidies to public utilities to finance the transition to solar, nuclear, or sea energy will expand. Corporate farmers will insist on being "compensated" for crop losses arising from bans on the use of DDT and other harmful chemicals. And more Federal funds will be poured into the states to help regulate outdoor advertising, alleviate conditions in recreational areas, finance the costs of land purchase or condemnation, and landscaping and roadside development, and otherwise meet the costs of "aesthetic pollution."

.   .   .

III

The third major category of state expenditures consists of the expenses of stabilizing the world capitalist social order: the costs of creating a safe political environment for profitable investment and trade. These expenditures include the costs of politically containing the proletariat at home and abroad, the costs of keeping small-scale, local, and regional capital at home, safely within the ruling corporate liberal consensus, and the costs of maintaining the comprador ruling classes abroad.

These political expenses take the form of income transfers and direct or indirect subsidies, and are attributable fundamentally to the unplanned and anarchic character of capitalist development. Unrestrained capital accumulation and technological change create three broad, related economic and social imbalances. First, capitalist development forces great stresses and strains on local and regional economies; second, capitalist growth generates imbalances between various industries and sectors of the economy; third, accumulation and technical change reproduce inequalities in the distribution of wealth and income and generate poverty. The imbalance

—described by Eric Hobsbawm as "the rhythm of social disruption"—not only are integral to capitalist development, but also are considered by the ruling class to be a sign of "healthy growth and change." What is more, the forces of the marketplace, far from ameliorating the imbalances, in fact magnify them by the multiplier effects of changes in demand on production. The decline of coal mining in Appalachia, for example, compelled other businesses and able-bodied workers to abandon the region, reinforcing tendencies toward economic stagnation and social impoverishment.

These imbalances are present in both the competitive and monopoly phases of capitalism. Both systems are unplanned and anarchic as a whole. But monopoly capitalism is different from competitive capitalism in two fundamental respects that explain why political subsidies are budgetary phenomena mainly associated with monopoly capitalism.

First, an economy dominated by giant corporations operating in oligopolistic industries tends to be more unstable and to generate more inequalities than a competitive economy. The source of both instability and inequality is oligopolistic price-fixing, since the interplay of supply and demand that clears specific commodity markets is no longer present. Shortages and surpluses of individual commodities now manifest themselves in the form of social imbalances. In addition, the national (and, increasingly, the international) character of markets means that economic and social instability and imbalances are no longer confined to a particular region, industry, or occupation, but rather tend to spread through the economy as a whole. Finally, Federal government policies for economic stability and growth soften the effects of economic recessions, lead to the survival of inefficient businesses, and hence, in the long-run to the need for more subsidies.

The second difference between competitive and monopoly capitalism concerns the way in which economic and social imbalances are perceived by capital and wage-labor. In a regime of competitive capitalism, businessmen exercise relatively little control over prices, production and distribution. Unemployment, regional underdevelopment, and industrial bankruptcy appear to be "natural" concomitants of "free markets." Moreover, the level and structure of wages are determined competitively, individual capitals are not able to develop and implement a wage policy, and, thus, the impact of wage changes on the volume and composition of production, the deployment of technology, and unemployment, appear to be the consequence of impersonal forces beyond human control. Because imbalances of all kinds are accepted by capital as natural and even desirable, and because the ideology of capital is the ruling ideology, the inevitability and permanence of imbalances and transitory crises tend to be accepted by society as a whole.

With the evolution of monopoly capitalism and the growth of the proletariat as a whole, this fatalistic attitude undergoes profound changes. Business enterprise gradually develops economic and political techniques of production and market control. Gradually, oligopolistic corporations adopt what Baran and Sweezy have termed a "live-and-let-live attitude" toward each other. In this setting, the imbalances generated by capitalist development begin to be attributed to the conscious policies of large corporations and big unions, rather than to the impersonal forces of the market. Corporate capital, small-scale capital, and the working class alike begin to fix responsibility for the specific policies on particular human agents. Only in this context can the proletariat, local and regional capital, and the comprador classes be contained and accommodated by corporate capital.

The politcial containment of the proletariat requires the expense of maintaining corporate liberal ideological hegemony, and, where that fails, the cost of physically repressing populations in revolt. In the first category are the expenses of medicare, unemployment, old age, and other social insurance, a portion of education expenditures, the welfare budget, the anti-poverty programs, non-military "foreign aid," and the administrative costs of maintaining corporate liberalism at home and the imperialist system abroad—the expenses incurred by the National Labor Relations Board, Office of Economic Opportunity, Agency for International Development, and similar organizations. The rising flow of these expenditures has two major tributaries.

In point of time, the first is the development of the corporate liberal political consensus between large-scale capital and organized labor. Through the 19th century, private charity remained the chief form of economic relief for unemployed, retired, and physically disabled workers, even though some state and local governments occasionally allocated funds for unemployed workers in times of severe crisis. It was not until the eve of the 20th century that state and local governments introduced regular relief and pension programs. Until the Great Depression, however, welfare programs organized by the corporations themselves were more significant than government programs. Economic prosperity and the extension of "welfare capitalism" throughout the 1920s made it unnecessary for the Federal government to make funds available (in the form of loans to the state) for economic relief until 1932.[8]

The onset of the Great Depression, the labor struggles that ensued, and the need to consolidate the corporate liberal consensus in order to contain these struggles, all led finally to state guarantees of high levels of employment, wage advances in line with productivity increases, and a standard of health, education, and welfare commensurate with the need to maintain labor's reproductive powers and the hegemony of the corporate

[8]James Weinstein, *The Corporate Ideal in the Liberal State* (Boston: Beacon Press, 1968), p. 22.

liberal labor unions over the masses of industrial workers.

· · ·

The second tributary runs parallel with, but runs faster and stronger than, the first, and flows from the same source—the development of modern technology. Corporate capital at home and abroad increasingly employs a capital-intensive technology, despite a surplus of unskilled labor, partly because of relative capital abundance in the advanced economies, and partly because of the ready supply of technical-administrative labor power. From the standpoint of large-scale capital, it is more rational to combine in production technical labor power with capital-intensive technology than to combine unskilled or semi-skilled labor power with labor-intensive technology. As we have seen, the fundamental reason is that many of the costs of training technical labor power are met by taxation falling on the working class as a whole.

Advanced capitalism thus creates a large and growing stratum of untrained, unskilled white, black and other Third-World workers that strictly speaking is not part of the industrial proletariat. The relative size of this stratum does not regulate the level of wages, because unskilled labor power does not compete with technical labor power in the context of capital-intensive technology. This stratum is not produced by economic recession and depression, but by prosperity; it does not constitute a reserve army of the unemployed for the economy as a whole. Unemployed, under-employed, and employed in menial jobs in declining sectors of the private economy (e.g., household servants), these workers increasingly depend on the state. "Make-work" state employment, health, welfare, and housing programs, and new agencies charged with the task of exercising social control (to substitute for the social discipline afforded by the wages system itself) proliferate. The expansion of the welfare rolls accompanies the expansion of employment. For the first time in history, the ruling class is beginning to recognize that welfare expenditures cannot be temporary expedients but rather must be permanent features of the political economy: that poverty is integral to the capitalist system.

· · ·

The second major cost of politically containing the proletariat at home and abroad (including the proletariat in the socialist world) consists of police and military expenditures required to suppress sections of the world proletariat in revolt. These expenditures place the single greatest drain on the state budget. A full analysis of these expenditures would require detailed development of the theory of imperialism, which cannot be undertaken here.[9]

· · ·

IV

In the preceding sections, we have attempted to analyze state expenditures in terms of the development of the forces and relations of production. We have seen that the increasingly social character of production requires the organization and distribution of production by the state. In effect, neo-capitalism fuses the "base" and "superstructure"—the economic and political systems—and thus places an enormous fiscal burden on the state budget.

· · ·

Statistical Appendix
(by the editors)

THE EXPANSION OF THE
PUBLIC SECTOR IN THE
UNITED STATES

The expansion of the public sector in the United States has been characterized by the growth of a great variety of government ac-

[9]See Chapter 10 (Editors' note).

tivities. This trend emerges from the following data, which relate to two quantifiable aspects of the public sector: expenditure and employment.

Table 4–O traces the growth of government purchases of goods and services in five-year intervals from 1929 to 1969. During this period, real GNP increased by 3½

TABLE 4–O THE GROWTH OF GOVERNMENT PURCHASES OF GOODS AND SERVICES IN THE U.S., 1929–1969

YEAR	(1)	(2)	(3)	(4)	(5)	(6)	(7)	(8)	(9)
	GNP	G	SLG	FG	D	G	SLG	FG	D
	billion dollars at constant 1958 prices					percentage of GNP			
1929	203.6	22.0	18.5	3.5	n.a.	10.8	9.1	1.7	n.a.
1934	154.3	26.6	18.6	8.0	n.a.	17.2	12.0	5.2	n.a.
1939	209.4	35.2	22.7	12.5	2.9	16.8	10.8	6.0	1.4
1944	361.3	181.7	16.3	165.4	162.3	50.3	4.5	45.8	45.0
1949	324.1	53.3	25.7	27.6	18.2	16.4	7.9	8.5	5.6
1954	407.0	88.9	32.1	56.8	49.5	21.8	7.9	13.9	12.2
1959	475.9	94.7	42.2	52.5	45.0	19.9	8.9	11.0	9.5
1964	581.1	111.2	53.2	58.1	44.6	19.1	9.1	10.0	7.7
1969	727.7	149.8	73.7	76.1	59.2	20.6	10.1	10.5	8.1

GNP = gross national product.
G = total government purchases of goods and services.
SLG = state and local government purchases of goods and services.
FG = federal government purchases of goods and services.
D = government defense expenditures.

SOURCES: (1)-(4): *Economic Report of the President*, 1970, Table C-2. (5): *Economic Report of the President*, 1970, Table C-1 (figures in current dollars converted into constant 1958 dollars using implicit price deflator for federal government purchases in Table C-3. (6)-(9): Calculated from (1)-(5).

TABLE 4–P THE GROWTH OF PUBLIC SECTOR EMPLOYMENT IN THE U.S., 1940–1969

	(1)	(2)	(3)	(4)	(5)	(6)	(7)	(8)	(9)	(10)
Year	Government Employment						Labor Force		Govt. Share of Labor Force	
	Federal '000	State '000	Local '000	Total Civilian '000	Armed Forces '000	Total '000	Civilian '000	Total '000	Civilian %	Total %
1940	1128	3346		4474	540	5014	55640	56180	8.0	8.9
1945	3375	3181		6556	11440	17996	53860	65300	12.2	27.5
1950	2117	1057	3228	6402	1650	8052	62208	63858	10.3	12.6
1955	2378	1250	3804	7432	3049	10481	65023	68072	11.4	15.4
1960	2421	1527	4860	8808	2514	11322	69628	72142	12.6	15.7
1965	2588	2028	5973	10589	2723	13312	74455	77178	14.2	17.3
1969	2975	2614	7102	12691	3506	16197	80733	84239	17.3	19.2

SOURCES: (1)-(4): U.S. Dept. of Commerce, Bureau of the Census, *Historical Statistics of the United States, Colonial Times to 1957*, Series Y 205-222, and *Statistical Abstract of the United States*, 1970, Table 631. (5), (7), (8): *Economic Report of the President*, 1970, Table C-22. (6) = (4) & (5) (9) = (4)/(7) (10) = (6)/(8)

times, but total government purchases increased by almost 7 times, to rise from 10.8 percent to 20.6 percent of GNP. The rise in state and local government expenditure was relatively modest, remaining not far from 10 percent of GNP throughout the period except when depressed by World War II. However, federal government expenditure multiplied by more than 20 times from 1929 to 1969, rising from less than 2 percent to more than 10 percent of GNP. The increase in federal government expenditure was almost entirely accounted for by the rise in military spending, which rose from negligible quantities in the 1930's to hover around 10 percent of GNP in the 1950's and 1960's.

Table 4-P documents the growth of public sector employment from 1940 to 1969. Both federal, and state and local civilian government employees have almost tripled in number in the past 30 years. Discounting the war year 1945, there has been a steady increase in the government share of the civilian labor force from 8 percent to 17.3 percent. Including the armed forces, some 16 million persons—almost 20 percent of the total labor force—are now employed in the public sector.

SELECTIVE BIBLIOGRAPHY

Further reading is recommended in Baran and Sweezy, *Monopoly Capital*, Chapter 2, in Weinstein, *The Corporate Ideal in the Liberal State*, and in O'Connor, "The Fiscal Crisis of the State," as cited in the source lines for Sections 4.3, 4.7, and 4.8. Heilbroner [5] is a very readable essay on the role of big business in America. Zeitlin [8] reprints a series of studies on the political economy of the contemporary United States; especially useful are the essays in Part 1 (Ownership and Control), Part 4 (Contemporary Capitalism), and Part 5 (The Structure of Power). Galbraith [4] illuminates many important features of American corporate capitalism in what he describes as "the new industrial state"; the reader need not accept the technological determinism that Galbraith attributes to industrial society. Mills [7] is a classic study of the changing structure of the American "middle classes"; Mills' figures are updated by Reich in Section 4.5. A thoroughly researched account of the changing role of education in the United States is provided by Cremin [2]. Kolko [6], in an historical study that parallels the work of Weinstein excerpted in Section 4.7, presents a persuasive reinterpretation of the so-called Progressive Era as one in which corporate business consolidated its control over American politics. Bottomore [1] provides a clear introduction to the concept of class and discusses the relevance of Marxian class analysis to contemporary capitalist societies. Finally, Domhoff [3] attempts to identify the membership and *modus operandi* of the American ruling class.

[1] Bottomore, T. B., *Classes in Modern Society*. New York: Pantheon, 1966.*

[2] Cremin, Lawrence A., *The Transformation of the School*. New York: Vintage, 1964.*

[3] Domhoff, G. William, *Who Rules America?* Englewood Cliffs, N.J.: Prentice-Hall, 1967.*

[4] Galbraith, John Kenneth, *The New Industrial State*. New York: Signet, 1968.*

[5] Heilbroner, Robert, "Capitalism in America," in his *The Limits of American Capitalism*. New York: Harper Torchbooks, 1967.*

[6] Kolko, Gabriel, *The Triumph of American Conservatism*. Chicago: Quadrangle Paperbacks, 1967.*

[7] Mills, C. Wright, *White Collar*. New York: Oxford U. P., 1956.*

[8] Zeitlin, Maurice, ed., *American Society Inc.* Chicago: Markham, 1970.*

*Available in paperback editions.

PART III

THE
FUNCTIONING
OF CAPITALISM
IN AMERICA

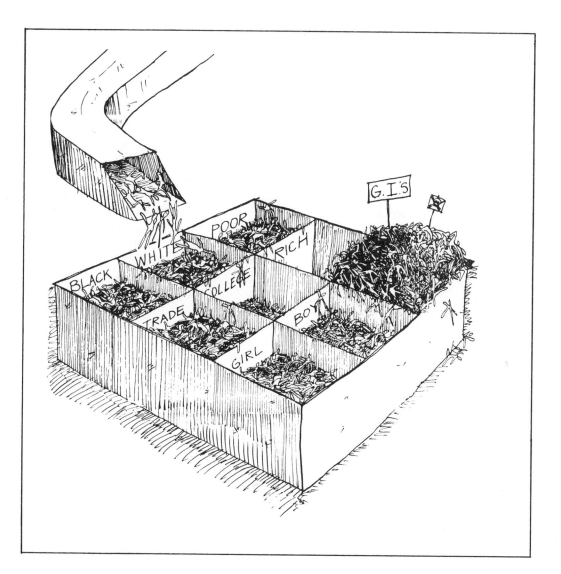

Inequality 5

CAPITALISM PRODUCES GREAT INEQUALITIES. Nowhere are these inequalities more manifest than in the unequal distribution of income and wealth in the United States. The top 5 percent of all families in the United States receive almost as much income as the bottom 40 percent; the top 1 percent of all adults own more than 60 percent of the nation's corporate wealth. And while inequalities in income and wealth reveal the primary dimension of inequality in a capitalist society, they also give rise to further inequalities —in power, political influence, occupational status, and privilege—which exist alongside and reinforce the inequality in income and wealth.

The generation of income inequality under capitalism can be traced directly to the operation of basic capitalist institutions.[1] People in capitalist societies receive income as payment for their labor-power or as a return to any capital which they may own. The basic requirements of production, labor-power, and capital, are called the "factors of production." How much income people receive depends both on the quantity of productive factors they own and on how highly their productive factors are valued in the relevant market. Workers' incomes depend on how much employers are willing to pay for their particular kind of labor. Capitalists' incomes depend on how much profit they can make with their capital, i.e., on how much more they can realize in revenues for the sale of their output than it costs them to produce the output. In each case the market plays a critical role in determining how much income each individual receives, for it is the market which establishes the value or "return" to different types of labor-power and productive property.

The distribution of income that results from the basic distributional process described above tends to be very unequal because different people have very unequal command over labor-power and productive property. Income inequalities resulting from existing inequalities in factor ownership are further exacerbated by the exercise of power by one group against others. The exercise of power can serve either to change the distribution of factor ownership, or to influence the market evaluation of existing factors in favor of the more powerful group.

Sometimes power may be exercised in direct political ways, as, for example, in a strike or the suppression of a strike. More frequently and more effectively, however, power is used to shape or "rig" the conditions surrounding institutions so that the normal operation of those institutions will ensure a favorable outcome. For example, a few large companies can jointly monopolize an industry and thereby effectively isolate themselves from some market competition and increase their profits. Once such a situation is established, no further exercise of power is needed: the continued functioning of the monopolized "free market" will yield the increased profits. Another example is provided by the medical profession. Doctors have carefully limited the number of new doctors trained every year, thereby ensuring a scarce supply. Once this has been done, the uninhibited operation of the market will necessarily produce high incomes for doctors.

Such exercise of power to affect the outcomes of institutions occurs in many forms. Several readings in Chapter 4 described the growth of monopoly, concentration, and the associated power to manipulate the market.[2] Discrimination against blacks and women, described in Chapters 7 and 8, serves to depress their income relative to whites and men. Another important use of power through institutions is the systematic maintenance of unequal access to schooling for children from different socioeconomic classes.

In this chapter we shall first examine the

[1]See Weisskopf, Section 3.7, p. 125, for a more thorough analysis of the fundamental aspects of income distribution under capitalism.

[2]See Means, Section 4.1, p. 145, and Baran and Sweezy, Section 4.3, p. 161.

extent of inequality in the United States, especially inequality in incomes and wealth. This inequality is created because people receive different incomes according to the market-determined return to their labor-power and productive property. Later in the chapter we examine why some important intermediary institutions, especially schools, have failed to ameliorate significantly the inequality which results from the basic capitalist institutions. Why, for example, have the public schools failed to provide the "equality of opportunity" which has long been claimed for them? It will be suggested that far from reducing inequality, the education system has become an important means for perpetuating inequality and passing it on from generation to generation.

Finally, we consider how the state affects the distribution of income. The increasing importance of the public sector in modern capitalist societies has led many people to look to the state to redistribute income so as to achieve greater equality. Progressive income taxes, programs such as the welfare system, the "War on Poverty," and other efforts have at various times been regarded as significant attacks on inequality in the United States. But the equalizing effects of these programs have in fact been almost negligible. Why has not the steeply progressive federal income tax contributed greatly to equality? Why have not the supposedly vast sums spent on the welfare system significantly increased the incomes of the poor?

Although we will concentrate here on inequality in the United States, it should be noted that the degree of inequality which characterizes the United States is not unique. As Table 10–H, p. 445 shows, there are some advanced capitalist countries with greater inequality and others with less inequality than the United States. What can be said of these countries, despite slight differences in degree, is that all of them are characterized by large and pervasive inequalities.

5.1   *The Extent of Income Inequality in the United States*

In the following reading Frank Ackerman, Howard Birnbaum, James Wetzler, and Andrew Zimbalist present detailed information about various aspects of inequality in the United States. The evidence clearly substantiates the assertion that the distribution of income is highly unequal and, moreover, is not becoming more equal over time.

The persistence of income inequality in America is well-known. Affluence in the suburbs contrasts starkly with the slums of any major city or the numerous "pockets" of rural poverty. This inequality is embarrassing in a democracy. Perhaps for this reason, income distribution is rarely an explicit political issue in the United States. The prevailing ideology seems to be that inequality is needed for economic growth and that soon the economy will be so prosperous that even the relatively poor will have a high standard of living. This argument gains some apparent plausibility from the history of Western Europe and North America: in these areas capitalism, with its great inequality, has been the agent of economic development.

For several reasons, we reject this neglect of distributional issues and its implicit toleration of existing inequality. First, it would require many decades of growth without redistribution to eliminate poverty, and there is no reason to assume that past rates of growth can be maintained this long. Economic growth is having increasingly intolerable ecological effects: either resources will be diverted to improve the environment or ecologically expensive production will be reduced. American growth, moreover, depends on consuming a disproportionate share of the world's natural resources: if currently underdeveloped countries ever begin to grow, America's share will be reduced.[1]

Second, the need for inequality to promote growth arises in our society because people are socialized to respond only to material incentives. Such responses are neither attractive nor unchangeable, and we can envision a society in which production takes place with little, if any, inequality.

Third, there are several human objections to inequality. Meaningful democracy is impossible in a society where political resources, such as wealth, are unequally distributed. Inequality is wasteful since, after elemental needs have been satisfied, people consume partly to emulate others; as a result, total social welfare (including our unhappiness over our rival's goods) increases more slowly than income. Finally, differ-

[1]In 1968, North America, with less than 9% of the world's population, had the following percentage of total world consumption of energy:

natural and imported gases	67.5%
liquid fuel	38.6%
total energy	37.5%

In the same year the United States, with approximately 6% of the world's population, had the following percentages of total world consumption of

steel	26%
rubber	42%
tin	35%
fertilizer (nitrogenous, potash, and phosphate)	26%

SOURCE: United Nations, *Statistical Yearbook*, 1969.

ences in material conditions tend to conceal more fundamental human qualities and pervert interpersonal relations.

Considerable confusion surrounds the concept and measurement of income. The Net National Income (NNI) is the sum of all of the income generated and received by anyone in a year. We divide NNI into three principal components: after-tax income received by persons (personal disposable income); after-tax income retained by corporations (undistributed corporate profits plus depreciation allowances); and income received by government, the net taxes (taxes minus net transfers from government to the private sector). Most of this essay deals with inequality within the first component of NNI, personal income. However, corporations and government are closely related to the personal income distribution: the individuals at the top of the personal income distribution also control substantial corporate incomes; and, contrary to popular belief, the government does not do much to alleviate personal income inequality.

The first section of this paper is an overview of inequality. We examine the distribution of income among people and its stability over time, the effect of taxes and government spending, the distribution of wealth, and the definition and extent of poverty. The second section focuses on income differences between particular categories of people. We consider inequalities by class, race, sex, education, and family background.

THE DISTRIBUTION OF INCOME

Personal Income Before Taxes

The best measure of ability to purchase goods and services is after-tax income. Appropriate data exist, however, only for the distribution of before-tax income, so we must look at that first and consider the tax structure separately. A good way to illustrate the income distribution is to rank the population by income and measure what percentage of total personal income accrues to the richest

TABLE 5—A   DISTRIBUTION OF BEFORE-TAX FAMILY INCOME

	1969	1964	1960	1956	1950	1947
Poorest fifth	5.6%	5.2%	4.9%	5.0%	4.5%	5.0%
Second fifth	12.3%	12.0%	12.0%	12.4%	12.0%	11.8%
Middle fifth	17.6%	17.7%	17.6%	17.8%	17.4%	17.0%
Fourth fifth	23.4%	24.0%	23.6%	23.7%	23.5%	23.1%
Richest fifth	41.0%	41.1%	42.0%	41.2%	42.6%	43.0%
Richest 5%	14.7%	15.7%	16.8%	16.3%	17.0%	17.2%

SOURCE: U.S. Census Bureau, *Current Population Reports*, Series P-60, No. 75, Table 11, p. 26.

20% of the population, the second richest 20%, and so forth (richest here meaning highest income). The more income going to the richest 20% and the less going to the poorest 20%, the more unequal is the distribution of income.

Table 5—A shows that in the U.S. during the postwar period, the poorest 20% of all families have consistently received less than 6% of total personal income, while the richest 20% have gotten over 40%. In 1969, the richest 5% of all families received over 14% of total family income, or over twice as much as the entire bottom 20%. Moreover, Table 5—A understates inequality since income received by people not in families (see Table 5—B) is much more unequally distributed than family income:[2]

The improvement in the relative position of the poorest fifth in 1969 is probably due to the reduction in unemployment during the Vietnam escalation (see the discussion of

black incomes and unemployment, below). The apparent decline in the share of the top income groups results entirely from the exclusion from Census Bureau income data of capital gains—that is, of the increase in value of assets such as corporate stocks. *If capital gains are included, the share of the top fifth has been constant over the past twenty years.*[3] We conclude that the entire

[3]See Edward C. Budd, *American Economic Review*, May, 1970; and John Gorman, "The Relationship Between Personal Income and Taxable Income," *Survey of Current Business*, May, 1970. Because fully one-half of capital gains and only a portion of dividends are tax-exempt, individual stockholders generally prefer capital gains to dividends; corporations now systematically retain earnings rather than pay them out in dividends, so capital gains are a customary, almost predictable source of income for many rich people. A complete picture of money income distribution should include capital gains.

The following table is a rough adjustment of the share of the top 20% to include estimated capital gains.

TABLE 5—B   THE DISTRIBUTION OF INCOME OF UNRELATED INDIVIDUALS, 1969

Poorest fifth	3.4%
Second fifth	7.7%
Middle fifth	13.7%
Fourth fifth	24.3%
Richest fifth	50.9%
Richest 5%	21.0%

SOURCE: U.S. Census Bureau, *Current Population Reports*, Series P-60, No. 75, Table 11, p. 26.

[2]For the family distribution in 1968, a family was in the top 5% if it had income exceeding approximately $23,000; in the top 20% with income over about $13,000; and in the bottom 20% with income under about $4,600.

Year	Share of Top Fifth Without Capital Gains (from Table 5—A)	Total Reported Capital Gains As a Percent of Total Personal Income	Share of Top Fifth With Capital Gains
1947	43.0%	2.2%	44.2%
1950	42.6%	2.6%	44.1%
1956	41.2%	2.8%	42.8%
1960	42.0%	2.6%	43.5%
1964	41.3%	3.2%	43.1%
1968	40.6%	5.2%	43.5%

Reported capital gains are two times taxable capital gains, since Federal income tax laws consider only half of long-term capital gains as taxable income. Data on taxable capital gains are in Gorman. We are assuming that all capital gains are long-term and go to the richest 20%, which is approximately true.

TABLE 5–C   INCOME DISTRIBUTION BEFORE AND AFTER THE FEDERAL INCOME TAX, 1962

	Poorest Fifth	Second Fifth	Middle Fifth	Fourth Fifth	Richest Fifth	Richest 5%
Before tax	4.6%	10.9%	16.3%	22.7%	45.5%	19.6%
After tax	4.9%	11.5%	16.8%	23.1%	43.7%	17.7%

SOURCE: Edward C. Budd, *Inequality and Poverty*, 1967, pp. xiii, xvi.

distribution has not really changed since World War II.

Taxes and Government Spending

In theory, Federal income taxes take a much higher percentage of income from the rich than from the poor. If this were true, the distribution of income after taxes would be much more equal than the distribution before the income tax. In reality, the effect of the income tax is rather modest, as is seen in Table 5–C.

In 1962, as in all years since World War II for which data are available, the share of the top 20% of the population is only about two percentage points lower after the income tax than before it. The Federal income tax laws have nominal tax rates that increase sharply with income, but they are vitiated by various deductions which reduce *taxable* incomes of the rich below their actual incomes. Thus, the rich gain the political advantages of high nominal rates and the economic advantages of low effective rates.[4]

But if the Federal income tax takes only

[4]See introduction to Section 5.4, p. 235.

a small step toward improving the income distribution, the overall tax structure takes a much smaller step. Less than 40% of all taxes are individual income taxes; an almost equal amount is collected in property and sales taxes (see Table 5–D). Most studies of property and sales taxes have concluded that they take a larger percentage of income from the poor than from the rich. There is an involved, and still unsettled, academic debate over how completely corporations shift their income taxes onto consumers by raising prices. If the corporation income tax is shifted, it could be considered similar to a sales tax. We might tentatively conclude that taxes other than individual income taxes do not reduce, and probably increase, income inequality.

It is sometimes argued that the government improves the income distribution through its spending policies. We believe that military spending, accounting for nearly one-third of government spending (federal, state, and local), disproportionately benefits the wealthy. Many other programs appear to be of little benefit to the poor: foreign aid,

TABLE 5–D   DISTRIBUTION OF TAX REVENUE BY TYPE OF TAX, FISCAL YEAR 1966–67

	All Levels of Government	Federal Government	State and Local Governments
All taxes	100.0%	100.0%	100.0%
Property and sales taxes	35.7	13.7	80.2
Individual income tax	38.2	53.4	9.6
Corporation income tax	20.6	29.5	3.7
Miscellaneous taxes	4.4	3.3	6.7

SOURCES: U.S. Bureau of the Census, *Census of Governments*, 1967, Vol. 4, No. 5; *Compendium of Government Finances*, Table 5. Motor vehicle license fees, 1.3% of all taxes, are combined with property and sales taxes.

TABLE 5–E DISTRIBUTION OF VARIOUS TYPES OF PERSONAL WEALTH, 1962

	Wealthiest 20 Percent	Top 5 Percent	Top 1 Percent
Total wealth	76%	50%	31%
Corporate stock	96%	83%	61%
Businesses & professions	89%	62%	39%
Homes	52%	19%	6%

SOURCES: Projector and Weiss, *Survey of Financial Characteristics of Consumers*, pp. 110–114, 151; and Irwin Friend, Jean Crockett and Marshall Blume, *Mutual Funds and Other Institutional Investors: A New Perspective*, p. 113.

space, police, interest on public debt (largely paying for past military spending), and highways which, combined with military spending, amounted to one-half of all government spending in 1966. By comparison, spending of the traditional welfare-state variety, on schools, parks and recreation, health and hospitals, and welfare, amounted to just over one-fourth of government spending, and it is by no means obvious that these programs are primarily beneficial to the poor.[5]

Wealth

Income distribution approximates the distribution of economic welfare because consumption is usually limited by income. By temporarily enabling some people to consume more than their income, personal wealth is a second source of economic well-being. More important, wealth is a principal source of power in our society, especially political power. It is their superior wealth that enables managements to outlast strikes. The wealthy control virtually all mass media and thus have a disproportionate influence over public opinion. They finance political campaigns and lobby in the legislature. Above all they own and control the giant corporations that make many important decisions about allocation of resources and distribution of income. For instance, corporations influence state and local govern-

ments (as well as foreign governments) by their ability to locate their businesses only in places where a favorable political environment exists. We must consider, then, the distribution of various types of wealth, particularly corporate stock.

The best recent data on distribution of personal wealth are in a government-sponsored survey of over 2,500 households.[6] Ranking households by wealth, Table 5–E shows the wealthiest 1% own 31% of total wealth and 61% of corporate stock.

Apologists for American capitalism often refer to the statistic that over 30 million people own corporate stock, implying that this form of wealth is widely distributed. This is clearly nonsense: many people do own a little stock, but the vast bulk of corporate stock is owned by a very few people. Ownership of unincorporated businesses and professions is only slightly more equally distributed than is corporate stock. The types of wealth that are relatively more equally distributed are such things as autos and homes, which are not sources of power as is ownership of businesses and corporations.

Personal wealth, of course, does not tell the whole story. Wealth is also held by pension funds and charitable foundations. The foundations are largely formed by the wealthy, but many pension funds exist for workers. In 1969, total pension fund assets

[5]See Edwards, Section 5.5, p. 244.

[6]Dorothy S. Projector and Gertrude Weiss, *Survey of Financial Characteristics of Consumers*, Federal Reserve System, 1966.

were $238 billion, less than 10% of national wealth.[7] In 1968, private non-insured pension funds held only 9.7% of the corporate stock held by domestic individuals, personal trusts, and private non-insured pension funds. So, including individuals' shares of pension fund assets probably raises slightly the share of the poorest 80% but does not alter the basic pattern of great inequality. The pension funds, moreover, are usually managed by either banks or the government, so their wealth is not a significant source of power to workers in the same sense that personal wealth is a source of power to capitalists.

A View From the Bottom

Extensive poverty accompanies the great concentrations of income and wealth. The most common figures on poverty, published by the Social Security Administration (SSA), define it as an income below $3,700 for a non-farm family of four (with different income cut-offs for different family sizes and residences). In 1969, 24.3 million people, or 12.2% of the population, were living in poverty by these criteria. The SSA allows food expenditures of 80¢ per person per day, and assumes that food makes up one-third of the total budget. We reject poverty lines in the neighborhood of $3,700, and thus most poverty figures published by government agencies, as implausibly low.

A more reasonable definition of poverty is the Bureau of Labor Statistics (BLS) subsistence budget for 1967.[8] It totals $5,900 for an urban family of four. The BLS calculates it on a much more detailed, and rea-

sonable, basis than the SSA budget. They assume that, of the $5,900, taxes and social security take $700, leaving $5,200 after tax. Food, assumed to cost less than $1.20 per person per day (this requires very careful shopping and cooking and no meals away from home), takes $1,650 for the year. They assume rent, heat and utilities for an inexpensive 5-room, one-bath apartment, to be under $90 per month, or $1,000 per year. House furnishings and household expenditures add another $300 per year. Clothing and personal care together total $700 for the family, or $175 per person. Transportation, assumed to be by an 8-year-old used car except in cities with good public transportation, costs $450. Medical care and medical insurance cost $475. Less than $700 remains for other expenses.

Most people would agree that a family of four living on the BLS subsistence budget would feel quite poor and be consistently concerned with making ends meet. By 1969, inflation had raised the cost of the BLS budget to $6,500. In that year, approximately 20% of all four-person families had incomes lower than $6,500.

Apologists for capitalism remind us that even though vast numbers of Americans are poor, poverty is declining. While it is gratifying to learn that 1.1 million fewer people were "officially" impoverished in 1969 than in 1968 and that fewer people are dying of starvation, the point is that a wealthy society should do much better.

INEQUALITIES BY CLASS, RACE, AND SEX

Class and Income

Most people with very high incomes are capitalists who own substantial assets, especially corporate stock, and receive income primarily from those assets.

---

[7]Securities and Exchange Commission, *Statistical Bulletin*, May, 1970.

[8]This is the lowest of the three budgets presented in Jean C. Brackett, "New BLS Budgets...," *Monthly Labor Review*, April, 1969. The more commonly quoted "modest, but adequate" budget is the middle of the three budgets, amounting to $9,800 for an urban family of four in 1967. For a discussion of the "modest, but adequate" budget and related problems of defining poverty, see

Donald Light, "Income Distribution: The First Stage in the Consideration of Poverty," URPE Occasional Paper #1.

TABLE 5–F   TYPES OF INCOME, 1966 (in billions of dollars)

Size of Taxable Income	Number of Tax Returns	All Types	Wage and Salary	Small Business	Capitalist
Total, all sizes	70,160,000	478.2	381.1	56.8	32.9
Under $20,000	68,230,000	401.1	349.1	35.1	12.3
$20,000–$50,000	1,644,000	48.0	24.7	14.8	7.0
$50,000–$100,000	218,000	15.4	5.3	5.0	4.4
Over $100,000	53,000	13.5	2.1	1.8	9.0

TYPES OF INCOME, 1966, AS PERCENT OF TOTAL INCOME

Size of Taxable Income	All Types	Wage and Salary	Small Business	Capitalist
Total, all sizes	100.0%	79.7%	11.9%	6.9%
Under $20,000	100.0%	87.0%	8.7%	3.1%
$20,000–$50,000	100.0%	51.4%	30.8%	14.5%
$50,000–$100,000	100.0%	34.3%	32.3%	28.4%
Over $100,000	100.0%	15.2%	13.3%	66.8%

SOURCE: Internal Revenue Service, *Statistics of Income, 1966: Individual Income Tax Returns*, Tables 7, 11, 19. See footnote 26 for a full description of these data. The lower table simply converts the data in the upper table to percentages.

The only source that describes capitalist income in any useful detail is the Internal Revenue Service.[9] In 1966 fewer than 2% of all taxpayers received 74% of all dividends and 76% of all capital gains. In the following discussion we define the capitalist class as this group of large shareowners.

Table 5–F shows the types of income of taxpayers at several income levels. We define "small business income" as interest, rent, and income of farmers, unincorporated businesses, proprietors, and self-employed professionals. "Capitalist income" is dividends and capital gains. Total small business income is almost twice as large as total capitalist income, but capitalist income is far more concentrated in the hands of the rich.

Taxpayers who reported under $20,000 in net taxable income, the vast majority, got 87% of their income from wages and salaries and only 3% from capitalist sources.

[9]See IRS, *Statistics of Income, 1966: Individual Income Tax Returns* (hereafter abbreviated Tax Returns).

At higher income levels, the share of wages and salaries falls steadily and that of capitalist income rises. The 53,000 taxpayers with net taxable incomes exceeding $100,000 received only 15% of their income from wages and salaries and 67% from dividends and capital gains.

Moreover, these IRS data are biased to minimize the relationship between class and income. About one-third of the capitalist income reported to the IRS was tax-exempt, and therefore excluded from net taxable income. So, many people who reported large capitalist incomes on their income tax returns were classified in Table 5–F as having small taxable income. A variety of tax loopholes also permit the wealthy to understate their taxable incomes. Interest on municipal bonds is completely tax-exempt. Exaggerated depreciation and depletion allowances are common. Tax-exempt charitable donations can be padded and overstated.

As a result of these and other loopholes, there were approximately 250 capitalists who reported zero taxable income, but over $100,000 each in capital gains or dividends. These individuals, all of whom are included in the lowest income class in Table 5–F, received at least $70 million in reported capitalist income, completely tax-free. Doubtless there were others who achieved somewhat less spectacular success in reporting their incomes as tax-exempt; no comprehensive statistics are available on the extent of such behavior.[10]

So those who receive profits (capitalists) earn much higher incomes than those who receive wages and salaries (workers).

It is no accident that incomes from ownership of corporations are so unjustly high. Many of America's most important social and political institutions act systematically to serve capitalist interests. Laws against larceny, for example, are enforced much more vigorously than laws (when they exist) against monopolistic combinations. The corporations are allowed to pollute the air and water, to create demands for such dangerous products as cigarettes, and to offset wage increases or corporate income taxes with price increases. Military spending by the government is an important source of profits, owing to the ambiguous relationship between the Pentagon and its military contractors. American foreign policies, supposedly designed to "contain communism," end up protecting profitable corporate foreign investments. Both mass media and government oppose ideas and behavior that discourage individuals from doing the meaningless work offered by big business. In sum, the economic power of corporate enterprise is reinforced by the other major institutions of our society.

Discrimination Against Blacks

A second pattern of inequality is discrimination against blacks. . . . This overlaps the class inequality discussed above because

[10]See Phillip M. Stern, *The Great Treasury Raid* (New York: Random House, 1964).

few blacks . . . are in the capitalist class; but it also accounts for substantial inequality within the working class. The labor market effectively preserves and aggravates inequality between groups of people. The inferior economic position of blacks . . . has survived more than a century after the abolition of slavery.

In 1969 the median income for all black males was $3,900, compared to $6,800 for white males. For workers who held year-round, full-time jobs, the median incomes were as shown in Table 5–G.

TABLE 5–G   MEDIAN INCOMES BY SEX AND RACE, 1969 WORKERS WITH YEAR-ROUND, FULL-TIME JOBS

	Male	Female
Black	$5,900	$4,100
White	$9,000	$5,200

SOURCE: *Current Population Reports*, Series P-60, No. 70, p. 5.

Thus even for workers with stable jobs, black male median income is only 67% of white male income and black female income only 80% of white female income.

While lack of schooling is one cause of the black-white income differential (a rather ambiguous cause, as we shall show below), discrimination persists when individuals with the same amount of schooling are compared (see Table 5–H).

Finishing high school is worth $1,300 per year in higher income to a white male, in the sense that if he completes high school, he can expect his income to be $1,300 higher every year than if he had not finished. By contrast, it is worth only $900 per year to a black male. A college degree is worth $2,500 per year to a black man and $3,800 to a white man. Black college graduates seem to face the most discrimination, but this may result from a higher proportion of whites attending graduate schools.

TABLE 5–H MEDIAN INCOME FOR ALL MALES (25 years old and over)
BY RACE AND EDUCATION, 1969

Years of Schooling		Black Male	White Male	Ratio
Elementary—less than 8		3,000	3,600	.82
	8	4,300	5,500	.79
High school	1–3	5,200	7,300	.71
	4	6,100	8,600	.71
College	1–3	7,100	9,600	.74
	4 or more	8,600	12,400	.69

SOURCE: *Current Population Reports*, Series P-60, No. 75, Table 47, p. 105.

TABLE 5–I MARITAL STATUS OF WOMEN IN THE LABOR FORCE, 1967

Status	Number of Women in the Labor Force	Percent of Women in the Labor Force
Total, all women in labor force	27.5 million	100.0%
Single	5.9	21.5%
Married, but husband absent	1.6	5.7%
Widowed	2.5	9.0%
Divorced	1.7	6.0%
Married, but husband earns less than $3,000 per year	2.5	9.2%
Total who must work	14.2	51.4%

SOURCE: *Current Population Reports*, Series P-60, No. 75, Table 47, p. 105.

Discrimination Against Women

The low status of women in the traditional family structure is translated into low pay and menial jobs for those women who work. Most working women are in the labor force not because they are bored with housework but because they must work to support themselves. 51.4% of all women in the 1967 labor force were either unmarried, separated from their husbands, or married to men earning less than $3,000 per year. The breakdown was as shown in Table 5–I.

Nevertheless, the job market is segmented so that men and women compete only among themselves for different jobs, with women eligible only for the lowest paying jobs. For workers with year-round, full-time jobs, female median income is 58% of male median income. This discrimination persists when we compare median incomes of men and women with the same education (see Table 5–J).

Restricting our comparison to workers with full-time, year-round jobs clearly understates discrimination against women because the female unemployment rate is much higher than the male rate. In 1969, the adult female unemployment rate was 4.7%, compared to an adult male rate of 2.8%. Moreover, a higher proportion of women withdraw from the labor force when they cannot find jobs or are forced to accept part-time or seasonal work and, in both cases, are not counted as unemployed.

Sex discrimination does not seem to be declining. The ratio of female to male median wage and salary income for full-time, year-round workers has declined from .63 in 1956 to .58 in 1968. Among the major occupational groups, the relative position of women seems to be improving (slowly) only

TABLE 5–J MEDIAN INCOME OF CIVILIANS (25 years and older) WITH
YEAR-ROUND, FULL-TIME JOBS, 1968

Years of Schooling		Male Income	Female Income	Ratio
Elementary—less than 8		$ 5,300	$3,300	.62
	8	$ 6,600	$3,600	.55
High School	1–3	$ 7,300	$3,900	.53
	4	$ 8,300	$4,800	.58
College	1–3	$ 9,300	$5,500	.59
	4	$11,800	$6,700	.57
	5 or more	$12,800	$8,300	.64
Total		$ 8,100	$4,700	.58

SOURCE: *Current Population Reports*, Series P-60, No. 66, Table 41, p. 98.

for professional and technical workers. In the past 10 years, the number of white female unrelated individuals and families headed by a woman below the poverty line has not changed, and the number of such nonwhite females and female-headed families has actually increased. All of the decline in poverty referred to above has affected families headed by men or male unrelated individuals.

Education and Social Mobility

The close relation of education and income distribution is obvious from Tables 5–H (p. 215) and 5–J. For men with full-time, year-round jobs, median incomes in 1968 were $11,800 with a college diploma, $8,300 with a high school diploma, and $6,600 for eight years of schooling. A simi-

lar relation is seen for both women and blacks.

The notion of social mobility through education is one of the most widespread beliefs about American society. Is your job terrible and poorly paid? Work hard, save money to put your kids through college, and they will escape into better jobs and comfortable lives. As much as any other idea, this has served to rationalize an alienated, impoverished existence for millions of Americans.

The belief that there is actual mobility through education, however, is a myth. It is true that better-educated people earn higher incomes. But it is also true that children of wealthier families become far better-educated. So the effect of education is to preserve and to legitimize existing inequalities in income distribution.

TABLE 5–K COLLEGE ATTENDANCE OF HIGH SCHOOL GRADUATES BY INCOME, 1966

Family Income in 1965	Percentage of 1966 High School Graduates Who Started College By February, 1967
Under $3,000	19.8
$3,000–$4,000	32.3
$4,000–$6,000	36.9
$6,000–$7,000	41.1
$7,500–$10,000	51.0
$10,000–$15,000	61.3
Over $15,000	86.7
Total, all incomes	46.9%

SOURCE: *Current Population Reports*, Series P-20, No. 185, Table 8.

Table 5–K shows that high school seniors are much more likely to enter college if they come from wealthy families. A high school senior from the top income group (family income over $15,000) is over four times as likely to enter college as a senior from the bottom income group (family income under $3,000).

It is not hard to understand why wealthier students stay in school longer. Even in states where public higher education is free, students still have significant living expenses which must be paid by their families. . . .

Family income affects education at all stages. Poor children are more likely to drop out of high school before the twelfth grade or to drop out of college before graduation. Rich children attend the better and more prestigious private universities. They also receive a disproportionate share of the benefits of public higher education.[11]

Public higher education is only one force tending to preserve inequality from one generation to the next. A direct (although rough) measure of intergenerational preservation of status can be seen in Table 5–L, taken from a Census Bureau study of occupations of men working in 1962.

71% of the sons of white-collar workers were themselves white-collar workers, while only 37% of the sons of blue-collar workers and 23% of the sons of farm workers (farm owners and employees combined) had white-collar jobs. In other words, the chances of ending up in a white-collar job were almost twice as high for a white-collar

TABLE 5–L OCCUPATIONS OF MEN WORKING IN 1962 (25-64 YEARS OLD) AND OF THEIR FATHERS

Father's Occupation When Son Was 16	Son's Occupation in March, 1962			
	Total	White Collar	Blue Collar	Farm
White-Collar	100.0%	71.0%	27.6%	1.5%
Blue-Collar	100.0%	36.9%	61.5%	1.6%
Farm	100.0%	23.2%	55.2%	21.6%
Total	100.0%	40.9%	51.4%	7.7%

SOURCE: Calculated from Blau and Duncan, *American Occupational Structure*, Table J2.1, p. 496. The data were obtained from a Census Bureau survey of 20,000 men.

[11]This was shown in a recent study of California higher education, one of the most extensive and progressive systems in the country. Median income for the entire state was $8,000, but it was $12,000 for families with children in the University of California, the top track of the educational system. The state subsidy, that is, the full cost of education less fees paid by the student, was considerably greater to families with children in the higher tracks, which were also the families with higher incomes. Moreover, public higher education is financed by state and local taxes, which take a higher percentage of income from the poor than from the rich.

DISTRIBUTION OF BENEFITS FROM PUBLIC HIGHER EDUCATION IN CALIFORNIA, 1964

	All Families	Families Without Children in Calif. Higher Education	Families With Children in		
			Junior College	State College	Univ. of Calif.
Median family income	$8,000	$7,900	$8,800	$10,000	$12,000
Average subsidy received	—	0	$1,700	$ 3,800	$ 4,900
Subsidy as % of median family income	—	0	12%	31%	41%

SOURCE: W. Lee Hansen and B. Weisbrod, "The Distribution of Costs and Direct Benefits of Public Education: The Case of California," *Journal of Human Resources*, Spring 1969, Tables 5 and 6.

worker's son as for a blue-collar worker's son, and three times as high for a white-collar worker's son as for a farmer's son. Of course there has been some movement from lower status jobs into white-collar jobs; there had to be, since the proportion of the labor force in white-collar jobs has been expanding rapidly.

To some extent Table 5–L reflects racial discrimination, since most nonwhites are in the blue-collar or farm categories. However, most of the men in each of the three major occupational categories are white; Table 5–L suggests the existence of a hierarchy of status, preserved across generations, even within the white male working class.

SUMMARY

We find, then, that American capitalism is characterized by considerable unjustifiable inequality of income and wealth, a state of affairs that is not improving over time. Causes of this inequality include social class distinctions between workers and capitalists and economic discrimination against women and minority groups. Legend has it that the United States is the land of equal opportunity; nevertheless, there is very little actual social mobility. Wealth, both personal and corporate, is perhaps the most important source of political power; and, in a vicious cycle, political power is used to preserve existing accumulations of wealth.

5.2   *Unequal Education and the Reproduction of the Hierarchical Division of Labor*

The first reading in this chapter documented in considerable detail the enormous inequalities that characterize the contemporary United States. The degree of inequality which emerges from the operation of the market insures huge accumulated fortunes for a few, and a great deal of poverty, disease, malnutrition, and inadequate facilities for others. Furthermore, the persistence of such great inequality exacerbates many further problems which we shall describe later: problems of environmental destruction, irrational production, waste, and a frantic desire to consume ever-increasing amounts of goods.[1]

Although almost everyone admits that the basic institutions of capitalism tend to generate immense inequality, it is often claimed that other institutions—progressive taxes which take more from the rich than from the poor, the educational system, welfare programs, etc.—significantly reduce inequality in the United States. The aggregate figures presented in the preceding reading refute such claims on a statistical basis. It was noted, for example, that the after-tax distribution of income hardly differed from the before-tax distribution.

In the next reading Samuel Bowles analyzes the relationship between the educational system and inequality in a capitalist society.

In modern America the school has replaced the frontier and the Horatio Alger type as the ultimate repository of that "equality of opportunity" which was promised to all. Yet the educational system does not and can-

[1]See the introduction to Chapter 9, p. 362, and the readings in that chapter.

not lead to much greater equality of opportunity or of income under capitalism. The American school system is in fact instrumental in the legitimation of inequality and its transmission from one generation to the next.

Source: The following is excerpted from "Unequal Education and the Reproduction of the Social Division of Labor" by SAMUEL BOWLES. Most references and a concluding section have been excerpted by the editors. From *Schooling in a Corporate Society: The Political Economy of Education in America and the Alternatives Before Us*, edited by Martin Carney (New York: David McKay Co., 1972). Copyright © 1971 by Samuel Bowles. Reprinted by permission of the author.

The ideological defense of modern capitalist society rests heavily on the assertion that the equalizing effects of education can counter the disequalizing forces inherent in the free market system. That educational systems in capitalist societies have been highly unequal is generally admitted and widely condemned. Yet educational inequalities are taken as passing phenomena, holdovers from an earlier, less enlightened era, which are rapidly being eliminated.

The record of educational history in the U.S., and scrutiny of the present state of our colleges and schools, lend little support to this comforting optimism. Rather, the available data suggest an alternative interpretation. In what follows I will argue (1) that schools have evolved in the U.S. not as part of a pursuit of equality, but rather to meet the needs of capitalist employers for a disciplined and skilled labor force, and to provide a mechanism for social control in the interests of political stability; (2) that as the economic importance of skilled and well educated labor has grown, inequalities in the school system have become increasingly important in reproducing the class structure from one generation to the next; (3) that the U.S. school system is pervaded by class inequalities, which have shown little sign of diminishing over the last half century; and (4) that the evidently unequal control over school boards and other decision-making bodies in education does not provide a suf-

ficient explanation of the persistence and pervasiveness of inequalities in the school system. Although the unequal distribution of political power serves to maintain inequalities in education, their origins are to be found outside the political sphere, in the class structure itself and in the class subcultures typical of capitalist societies. Thus unequal education has its roots in the very class structure which it serves to legitimize and reproduce. Inequalities in education are a part of the web of capitalist society, and likely to persist as long as capitalism survives.

THE EVOLUTION OF CAPITALISM AND THE RISE OF MASS EDUCATION

In colonial America, and in most precapitalist societies of the past, the basic productive unit was the family. For the vast majority of male adults, work was self-directed, and was performed without direct supervision. Though constrained by poverty, ill health, the low level of technological development, and occasional interferences by the political authorities, a man had considerable leeway in choosing his working hours, what to produce, and how to produce it. While great inequalities in wealth, political power, and other aspects of status normally existed, differences in the degree of autonomy in work were relatively minor, particularly when compared with what was to come.

Transmitting the necessary productive skills to the children as they grew up proved to be a simple task, not because the work was devoid of skill, but because the quite substantial skills required were virtually unchanging from generation to generation, and because the transition to the world of work did not require that the child adapt to a wholly new set of social relationships. The child learned the concrete skills and adapted to the social relations of production through learning by doing within the family. Preparation for life in the larger community was facilitated by the child's experience with the extended family, which shaded off without distinct boundaries, through uncles and fourth cousins, into the community. Children learned early how to deal with complex relationships among adults other than their parents, and children other than their brothers and sisters.[1]

It was not required that children learn a complex set of political principles or ideologies, as political participation was limited and political authority unchallenged, at least in normal times. The only major socializing institution outside the family was the church, which sought to inculcate the accepted spiritual values and attitudes. In addition, a small number of children learned craft skills outside the family, as apprentices. The role of schools tended to be narrowly vocational, restricted to preparation of children for a career in the church or the still inconsequential state bureaucracy. The curriculum of the few universities reflected the aristocratic penchant for conspicuous intellectual consumption.

The extension of capitalist production, and particularly the factory system, under-

mined the role of the family as the major unit of both socialization and production. Small peasant farmers were driven off the land or competed out of business. Cottage industry was destroyed. Ownership of the means of production became heavily concentrated in the hands of landlords and capitalists. Workers relinquished control over their labor in return for wages or salaries. Increasingly, production was carried on in large organizations in which a small management group directed the work activities of the entire labor force. The social relations of production—the authority structure, the prescribed types of behavior and response characteristic of the workplace—became increasingly distinct from those of the family.

The divorce of the worker from control over production—from control over his own labor—is particularly important in understanding the role of schooling in capitalist societies. The resulting hierarchical social division of labor—between controllers and controlled—is a crucial aspect of the class structure of capitalist societies, and will be seen to be an important barrier to the achievement of social class equality in schooling.

Rapid economic change in the capitalist period led to frequent shifts of the occupational distribution of the labor force, and constant changes in the skill requirements for jobs. The productive skills of the father were no longer adequate for the needs of the son during his lifetime. Skill training within the family became increasingly inappropriate.

And the family itself was changing. Increased geographic mobility of labor and the necessity for children to work outside the family spelled the demise of the extended family and greatly weakened even the nuclear family. Meanwhile, the authority of the church was questioned by the spread of secular rationalist thinking and the rise of powerful competing groups.

While undermining the main institutions of socialization, the rise of the capitalist sys-

---

[1] This account draws upon two important historical studies: P. Aries, *Centuries of Childhood* (New York: Random House, 1970); and B. Bailyn, *Education in the Forming of American Society* (New York: Random House, 1960).

tem was accompanied by urbanization, labor migration, the spread of democratic ideologies, and a host of other developments which created an environment—both social and intellectual—which would ultimately challenge the political order.

An institutional crisis was at hand. The outcome, in virtually all capitalist countries, was the rise of mass education. In the U.S., the many advantages of schooling as a socialization process were quickly perceived. The early proponents of the rapid expansion of schooling argued that education could perform many of the socialization functions which earlier had been centered in the family and to a lesser extent, in the church. An ideal preparation for factory work was found in the social relations of the school: specifically, in its emphasis on discipline, punctuality, acceptance of authority outside the family, and individual accountability for one's work. The social relations of the school would replicate the social relations of the workplace, and thus help young people adapt to the social division of labor. Schools would further lead people to accept the authority of the state and its agents—the teachers—at a young age, in part by fostering the illusion of the benevolence of the government in its relations with citizens. Moreover, because schooling would ostensibly be open to all, one's position in the social division of labor could be portrayed as the result not of birth, but of one's own efforts and talents. And if the children's everyday experiences with the structure of schooling were insufficient to inculcate the correct views and attitudes, the curriculum itself would be made to embody the bourgeois ideology. Where pre-capitalist social institutions—particularly the church—remained strong or threatened the capitalist hegemony, schools sometimes served as a modernizing counter-institution.

The movement for public elementary and secondary education in the U.S. originated in the 19th century in states dominated by the burgeoning industrial capitalist class, most notably in Massachusetts. It spread rapidly to all parts of the country except the South. The fact that some working people's movements had demanded free instruction should not obscure the basically coercive nature of the extension of schooling. In many parts of the country, schools were literally imposed upon the workers.

The evolution of the economy in the 19th century gave rise to new socialization needs and continued to spur the growth of education. Agriculture continued to lose ground to manufacturing; simple manufacturing gave way to production involving complex interrelated processes; an increasing fraction of the labor force was employed in producing services rather than goods. Employers in the most rapidly growing sectors of the economy began to require more than obedience and punctuality in their workers; a change in motivational outlook was required. The new structure of production provided little built-in motivation. There were fewer jobs like farming and piece-rate work in manufacturing in which material reward was tied directly to effort. As work roles became more complicated and interrelated, the evaluation of the individual worker's performance became increasingly difficult. Employers began to look for workers who had internalized the production-related values of the firms' managers.

The continued expansion of education was pressed by many who saw schooling as a means of producing these new forms of motivation and discipline. Others, frightened by the growing labor militancy after the Civil War, found new urgency in the social control arguments popular among the proponents of education in the antebellum period.

A system of class stratification developed within this rapidly expanding educational system. Children of the social elite normally attended private schools. Because working class children tended to leave school early, the class composition of the public high schools was distinctly more elite than the public primary schools. And university education, catering mostly to the children of upper-class families, ceased to be merely training for teaching or the divinity and became important in gaining access to the pinnacles of the business world.

Around the turn of the present century, large numbers of working class and particularly immigrant children began attending high schools. At the same time, a system of class stratification developed within secondary education. The older democratic ideology of the common school—that the same curriculum should be offered to all children —gave way to the "progressive" insistence that education should be tailored to the "needs of the child." In the interests of providing an education relevant to the later life of the students, vocational schools and tracks were developed for the children of working families. The academic curriculum was preserved for those who would later have the opportunity to make use of book learning, either in college or in white-collar employment. This and other educational reforms of the progressive education movement reflected an implicit assumption of the immutability of the class structure.[2]

The frankness with which students were channeled into curriculum tracks, on the basis of their social class background, raised serious doubts concerning the "openness" of the class structure. The relation between social class and a child's chances of promotion or tracking assignments was disguised— though not mitigated much—by another "progressive" reform: "objective" educational testing. Particularly after World War I, the capitulation of the schools to business values and concepts of efficiency led to the increased use of intelligence and scholastic achievement testing as an ostensibly unbiased means of measuring the product of schooling and classifying students. The com-

plementary growth of the guidance counseling profession allowed much of the channeling to proceed from the students' "own" well-counselled-choices, thus adding an apparent element of voluntarism to the system.

The class stratification of education during this period had proceeded hand in hand with the stratification of the labor force. As large bureaucratic corporations and public agencies employed an increasing fraction of all workers, a complicated segmentation of the labor force evolved, reflecting the hierarchical structure of the social relations of production.

The social division of labor had become a finely articulated system of work relations dominated at the top by a small group with control over work processes and a high degree of personal autonomy in their work activities, and proceeding by finely differentiated stages down the chain of bureaucratic command to workers who labored more as extensions of the machinery than as autonomous human beings.[3]

One's status, income, and personal autonomy came to depend in great measure on one's place in the hierarchy of work relations. And in turn, positions in the social division of labor came to be associated with educational credentials reflecting the number of years of schooling and the quality of education received. The increasing importance of schooling as a mechanism for allocating children to positions in the class structure, played a major part in legitimizing the structure itself.[4] But at the same time, it undermined the simple processes which in the past had preserved the position and privilege of the upper class families from generation to generation. In short, it undermined the processes serving to reproduce the social division of labor.

In pre-capitalist societies, direct inheritance of occupational position is common. Even in the early capitalist economy, prior

[2]See Cohen and Lazerson, Section 4.6, p. 183.

[3]See Reich, Section 4.5, p. 174.
[4]See Bowles, Section 11.5, p. 491.

to the segmentation of the labor force on the basis of differential skills and education, the class structure was reproduced generation after generation simply through the inheritance of physical capital by the offspring of the capitalist class. Now that the social division of labor is differentiated by types of competence and educational credentials as well as by the ownership of capital, the problem of inheritance is not nearly as simple. The crucial complication arises because education and skills are embedded in human beings, and—unlike physical capital—these assets cannot be passed on to one's children at death. In an advanced capitalist society in which education and skills play an important role in the hierarchy of production, then, laws guaranteeing inheritance are not enough to reproduce the social division of labor from generation to generation. Skills and educational credentials must somehow be passed on within the family. It is a fundamental theme of this paper that schools play an important part in reproducing and legitimizing this modern form of class structure.

CLASS INEQUALITIES IN U.S. SCHOOLS

Unequal schooling reproduces the hierarchical social division of labor. Children whose parents occupy positions at the top of the occupational hierarchy receive more years of schooling than working class children. Both the amount and the content of their education greatly facilitate their movement into positions similar to their parents'.

Because of the relative ease of measurement, inequalities in years of schooling are particularly evident. If we define social class standing by the income, occupation, and educational level of the parents, a child from the 90th percentile in the class distribution may expect on the average to achieve over four and a half more years of schooling than a child from the 10th percentile.[5] As can be seen in Table 5–M, social class inequali-

ties in the number of years of schooling received arise in part because a disproportionate number of children from poorer families do not complete high school. Table 5–N indicates that these inequalities are exacerbated by social class inequalities in college attendance among those children who did graduate from high school: even among those who had graduated from high school, children of families earning less than $3,000 per year were over six times as likely *not* to attend college as were the children of families earning over $15,000.[6]

Inequalities in schooling are not simply a matter of differences in years of schooling attained. Differences in the internal structure of schools themselves and in the content of schooling reflect the differences in the social class compositions of the student bodies. The social relations of the educational process ordinarily mirror the social relations of the work roles into which most students are likely to move. Differences in rules, expected modes of behavior, and opportunities for choice are most glaring when we compare levels of schooling. Note the wide range of choice over curriculum, life style, and allocation of time afforded to college students, compared with the obedience and respect for authority expected in high school. Differentiation occurs also within each level of schooling. One needs only to compare the social relations of a junior college with those of an elite four-year college, or those of a working class high school with those of a wealthy suburban high school, for verification of this point.

The differential socialization patterns in schools attended by students of different social classes do not arise by accident. Rather,

[5]The data for this calculation refer to white males who were in 1962 aged 25-34. See S. Bowles, "Schooling and Inequality from Generation to Generation," paper presented at the Far Eastern Meetings of the Econometric Society, Tokyo, 1970.

[6]For recent evidence on these points, see U.S. Bureau of the Census, *Current Population Reports*, Series P-20, Nos. 185 and 183.

TABLE 5–M PERCENTAGE OF MALE CHILDREN AGED 16-17 ENROLLED IN PUBLIC SCHOOL, AND PERCENTAGE AT LESS THAN THE MODAL GRADE LEVEL, BY PARENT'S EDUCATION AND INCOME, 1960[a]

	Percent of Male Children Aged 16-17 Enrolled in Public School	Percent of Those Enrolled Who Are Below the Modal Level
1. Parent's education less than 8 years Family income:		
less than $3,000	66.1	47.4
$3,000–4,999	71.3	35.7
$5,000–6,999	75.5	28.3
$7,000 and over	77.1	21.8
2. Parent's education 8-11 years Family income:		
less than $3,000	78.6	25.0
$3,000–4,999	82.9	20.9
$5,000–6,999	84.9	16.9
$7,000 and over	86.1	13.0
3. Parent's education 12 years or more Family income:		
less than $3,000	89.5	13.4
$3,000–4,999	90.7	12.4
$5,000–6,999	92.1	9.7
$7,000 and over	94.2	6.9

SOURCE: Bureau of the Census, Census of Population, 1960, Vol. PC-(2)5A, Table 5. a. According to Bureau of the Census definitions, for 16-year-olds 9th grade or less and for 17-year-olds 10th grade or less are below the modal level. Father's education is indicated if father is present; otherwise mother's education is indicated.

they stem from the fact that the educational objectives and expectations of both parents

TABLE 5–N COLLEGE ATTENDANCE IN 1967 AMONG HIGH SCHOOL GRADUATES, BY FAMILY INCOME*

Family Income†	Percent Who Did Not Attend College
Total	53.1
under $3,000	80.2
$3,000 to $3,999	67.7
$4,000 to $5,999	63.7
$6,000 to $7,499	58.9
$7,500 to $9,999	49.0
$10,000 to $14,999	38.7
$15,000 and over	13.3

*Refers to individuals who were high school seniors in October 1965 and who subsequently graduated from high school. Source: U.S. Department of Commerce, Bureau of the Census, *Current Population Report*, Series P-20, No. 185, July 11, 1969, p. 6. College attendance refers to both two- and four-year institutions.

†Family income for 12 months preceding October 1965.

and teachers, and the responsiveness of students to various patterns of teaching and control, differ for students of different social classes.[7] Further, class inequalities in school socialization patterns are reinforced by the inequalities in financial resources. The paucity of financial support for the education of children from working class families not only leaves more resources to be devoted to the children of those with commanding roles in the economy; it forces upon the teachers and school administrators in the working class schools a type of social relations which fairly closely mirrors that of the

[7]That working class parents seem to favor more authoritarian educational methods is perhaps a reflection of their own work experiences, which have demonstrated that submission to authority is an essential ingredient in one's ability to get and hold a steady, well-paying job.

factory. Thus financial considerations in poorly supported working class schools militate against small intimate classes, against a multiplicity of elective courses and specialized teachers (except disciplinary personnel), and preclude the amounts of free time for the teachers and free space required for a more open, flexible educational environment. The lack of financial support all but requires that students be treated as raw materials on a production line; it places a high premium on obedience and punctuality; there are few opportunities for independent, creative work or individualized attention by teachers. The well-financed schools attended by the children of the rich can offer much greater opportunities for the development of the capacity for sustained independent work and the other characteristics required for adequate job performance in the upper levels of the occupational hierarchy.

While much of the inequality in U.S. education exists between schools, even within a given school different children receive different educations. Class stratification within schools is achieved through tracking, differential participation in extracurricular activities, and in the attitudes of teachers and particularly guidance personnel who expect working class children to do poorly, to terminate schooling early, and to end up in jobs similar to their parents'.[8]

Not surprisingly, the results of schooling differ greatly for children of different social classes. The differing educational objectives implicit in the social relations of schools attended by children of different social classes has already been mentioned. Less important but more easily measured are differences in scholastic achievement. If we measure the output of schooling by scores on nationally standardized achievement tests, children whose parents were themselves highly educated outperform the children of parents with less education by a wide margin. A recent study revealed, for example, that among

[8]See Lauter and Howe, Section 5.3, p. 229.

white high school seniors, those students whose parents were in the top education decile were on the average well over three grade levels ahead of those whose parents were in the bottom decile.[9] While a good part of this discrepancy is the result of unequal treatment in school and unequal educational resources, it will be suggested below that much of it is related to differences in the early socialization and home environment of the children.

Given the great social class differences in scholastic achievement, class inequalities in college attendance are to be expected. Thus one might be tempted to argue that the data in Table 5–N are simply a reflection of un-

TABLE 5–O PROBABILITY OF COLLEGE ENTRY FOR A MALE WHO HAS REACHED GRADE 11*

		Socioeconomic Quartiles†			
		Low			High
		1	2	3	4
	Low 1	.06	.12	.13	.26
Ability	2	.13	.15	.29	.36
Quartiles†	3	.25	.34	.45	.65
	High 4	.48	.70	.73	.87

*Based on a large sample of U.S. high school students as reported in John C. Flannagan and William W. Cooley, *Project TALENT, One-Year Follow-Up Studies*, Cooperative Research Project No. 2333, School of Education, University of Pittsburgh, 1966.
†The socioeconomic index is a composite measure including family income, father's occupation and education, mother's education, etc. The ability scale is a composite of tests measuring general academic aptitude.

equal scholastic achievement in high school and do not reflect any *additional* social class inequalities peculiar to the process of college admission. This view is unsupported by the available data, some of which are presented in Table 5-O. Access to a college education is highly unequal, even for children of the same measured "academic ability."

The social class inequalities in our school

[9]Calculation based on data in James S. Coleman, *et al.*, *Equality of Educational Opportunity*, Vol. II (Washington: U.S. Dept. of Health, Education & Welfare, Office of Education, 1966), and methods described in S. Bowles, "Schooling and Inequality from Generation to Generation," mimeo, 1971.

TABLE 5–P AMONG SONS WHO HAD REACHED HIGH SCHOOL, PERCENTAGE WHO
GRADUATED FROM COLLEGE, BY SON'S AGE AND FATHER'S LEVEL OF EDUCATION

Son's Age in 1962	Likely Dates of College Graduation*	Less Than 8 Years	Father's Education					
			Some High School		High School Graduate		Some College or More	
			Percent Graduating	Ratio to <8	Percent Graduating	Ratio to <8	Percent Graduating	Ratio to <8
25–34	1950–1959	07.6	17.4	2.29	25.6	3.37	51.9	6.83
35–44	1940–1949	08.6	11.9	1.38	25.3	2.94	53.9	6.27
45–54	1930–1939	07.7	09.8	1.27	15.1	1.96	36.9	4.79
55–64	1920–1929	08.9	09.8	1.10	19.2	2.16	29.8	3.35

*Assuming college graduation at age 22.

SOURCE: Based on U.S. Census data as reported in William G. Spady, "Educational Mobility and Access: Growth and Paradoxes," *American Journal of Sociology*, Vol. 73, No. 3 (November 1967).

system and the role they play in the reproduction of the social division of labor are too evident to be denied. Defenders of the educational system are forced back on the assertion that things are getting better; the inequalities of the past were far worse. Yet the available historical evidence lends little support to the idea that our schools are on the road to equality of educational opportunity. For example, data from a recent U.S. Census survey reported in Table 5–P indicate that graduation from college has become increasingly dependent on one's class background. This is true despite the fact that the probability of high school graduation is becoming increasingly equal across social classes. On balance, the available data suggest that the number of years of schooling which the average child attains depends at least as much now upon the social class standing of his father as it did fifty years ago.[10]

[10]See P. M. Blau and O. D. Duncan, *The American Occupational Structure* (New York: Wiley, 1967). More recent data do not contradict the evidence of no trend towards equality. A 1967 Census survey, the most recent available, shows that among high school graduates in 1965, the probability of college attendance for those whose parents had attended college has continued to rise relative to the probability of college attendance for those whose parents had attended less than eight years of school. See U.S. Bureau of the Census, *Current Population Reports*, Series P-20, No. 185, July 11, 1969.

The argument that our "egalitarian" education compensates for inequalities generated elsewhere in the capitalist system is patently fallacious. But the discrepancy between the ideology and the reality of the U.S. school system is far greater than would appear from a passing glance at the above data. In the first place, if education is to compensate for the social class immobility due to the inheritance of wealth and privilege, education must be structured so that the poor child receives not less, not even the same, but *more* than equal benefits from education. The school must compensate for the other disadvantages which the lower-class child suffers. Thus the liberal assertion that education compensates for inequalities in inherited wealth and privilege is falsified not so much by the extent of the social class inequalities in the school system as by their very existence, or, more correctly, by the absence of compensatory inequalities.

Second, considering the problem of inequality of income at a given moment, a similar argument applies. In a capitalist economy, the increasing importance of schooling in the economy will increase income inequality even in the absence of social class inequalities in quality and quantity of schooling. This is so simply because the labor force becomes differentiated by type of skill or schooling, and inequalities in labor earnings therefore contribute to total income inequality, augmenting the inequalities due to the concentration of capital. The disequalizing tendency will of course be intensified if the owners of capital also acquire a disproportionate amount of those types of education and training which confer access to high-paying jobs.

CLASS CULTURE AND CLASS POWER

The pervasive and persistent inequalities in U.S. education would seem to refute an interpretation of education which asserts its egalitarian functions. But the facts of inequality do not by themselves suggest an alternate explanation. Indeed, they pose serious problems of interpretation. If the costs of education borne by students and their families were very high, or if nepotism were rampant, or if formal segregation of pupils by social class were practiced, or educational decisions were made by a select few whom we might call the power elite, it would not be difficult to explain the continued inequalities in U.S. education. The problem of interpretation, however, is to reconcile the above empirical findings with the facts of our society as we perceive them: public and virtually tuition-free education at all levels, few legal instruments for the direct implementation of class segregation, a limited role for "contacts" or nepotism in the achievement of high status or income, a commitment (at the rhetorical level at least) to equality of educational opportunity, and a system of control of education which if not particularly democratic, extends far beyond anything resembling a power elite. The attempt to reconcile these apparently discrepant facts leads us back to a consideration of the social division of labor, the associated class cultures, and the exercise of class power.

The social division of labor based on the hierarchical structure of production gives rise to distinct class subcultures. The values, personality traits, and expectations charac-

teristic of each subculture are transmitted from generation to generation through class differences in family socialization and complementary differences in the type and amount of schooling ordinarily attained by children of various class positions. These class differences in schooling are maintained in large measure through the capacity of the upper class to control the basic principles of school finance, pupil evaluation, and educational objectives.

The social relations of production characteristic of advanced capitalist societies (and many socialist societies) are most clearly illustrated in the bureaucracy and hierarchy of the modern corporation.[11] Occupational roles in the capitalist economy may be grouped according to the degree of independence and control exercised by the person holding the job. There is some evidence that the personality attributes associated with the adequate performance of jobs in occupational categories defined in this broad way differ considerably, some apparently requiring independence and internal discipline, and others emphasizing such traits as obedience, predictability, and willingness to subject oneself to external controls.

These personality attributes are developed primarily at a young age, both in the family and, to a lesser extent, in secondary socialization institutions such as schools. Because people tend to marry within their own class (in part because spouses often meet in our class segregated schools), both parents are likely to have a similar set of these fundamental personality traits. Thus children of parents occupying a given position in the occupational hierarchy grow up in homes where child-rearing methods and perhaps even the physical surroundings tend to develop personality characteristics appropriate to adequate job performance in the occupational roles of the parents. The children of

[11]See Edwards, Section 3.5, p. 115.

managers and professionals are taught self-reliance within a broad set of constraints; the children of production line workers are taught obedience.

While this relation between parents' class position and child's personality attributes operates primarily in the home, it is reinforced by schools and other social institutions. Thus, to take an example introduced earlier, the authoritarian social relations of working class high schools complement the discipline-oriented early socialization patterns experienced by working class children. The relatively greater freedom of wealthy suburban schools extends and formalizes the early independence training characteristic of upper-class families.

The operation of the labor market translates differences in class culture into income inequalities and occupational hierarchies. The personality traits, values, and expectations characteristic of different class cultures play a major role in determining an individual's success in gaining a high income or prestigious occupation. The apparent contribution of schooling to occupational success and higher income seems to be explained primarily by the personality characteristics of those who have higher educational attainments.[12] Although the rewards to intellectual capacities are quite limited in the labor market (except for a small number of high level jobs), mental abilities are important in getting ahead in school. Grades, the probability of continuing to higher levels of schooling, and a host of other school success variables, are positively correlated with "objective" measures of intellectual capacities. Partly for this reason, one's experience in school reinforces the belief that promotion and rewards are distributed fairly. The close relationship between the amount of education attained and later occupational suc-cess thus provides a meritocratic appearance to mask the mechanisms which reproduce the class system from generation to generation.

Positions of control in the productive hierarchy tend to be associated with positions of political influence. Given the disproportionate share of political power held by the upper class and their capacity to determine the accepted patterns of behavior and procedures, to define the national interest, and in general to control the ideological and institutional context in which educational decisions are made, it is not surprising to find that resources are allocated unequally among school tracks, between schools serving different classes, and between levels of schooling. The same configuration of power results in curricula, methods of instruction, and criteria of selection and promotion which confer benefits disproportionately on the children of the upper class.

The power of the upper class exists in its capacity to define and maintain a set of rules of operation or decision criteria—"rules of the game"—which, though often seemingly innocuous and sometimes even egalitarian in their ostensible intent, have the effect of maintaining the unequal system.

The operation of two prominent examples of these "rules of the game" will serve to illustrate the point. The first important principle is that excellence in schooling should be rewarded. Given the capacity of the upper class to define excellence in terms on which upper-class children tend to excel (for example, scholastic achievement), adherence to this principle yields inegalitarian outcomes (for example, unequal access to higher education) while maintaining the appearance of fair treatment.[13] Thus the prin-

---

[12]This view is elaborated in H. Gintis, "Education, Technology, and Worker Productivity," *American Economic Association Papers & Proceedings*, May 1971.

[13]Those who would defend the "reward excellence" principle on the grounds of efficient selection to ensure the most efficient use of educational resources might ask themselves this: Why should colleges admit those with the highest college entrance examination board scores? Why not the

ciple of rewarding excellence serves to legitimize the unequal consequences of schooling by associating success with competence. At the same time, the institution of objectively administered tests of performance serves to allow a limited amount of upward mobility among exceptional children of the lower class, thus providing further legitimation of the operations of the social system by giving some credence to the myth of widespread mobility.

The second example is the principle that elementary and secondary schooling should be financed in very large measure from local revenues. This principle is supported on the grounds that it is necessary to preserve political liberty. Given the degree of residential

---

lowest, or the middle? The rational social objective of the college is to render the greatest *increment* in individual capacities ("value added" to the economist), not to produce the most illustrious graduating class ("gross output"). Yet if incremental gain is the objective, it is far from obvious that choosing from the top is the best policy. And because no one has even attempted to construct a compelling argument that choosing from the top is the policy which maximizes the increment of learning for students, we can infer that the practice is supported by considerations other than that of efficient allocation of resources in education.

segregation by income level, the effect of this principle is to produce an unequal distribution of school resources among children of different classes. Towns with a large tax base can spend large sums for the education of their disproportionately upper-class children even without suffering a higher than average tax rate. Because the main resource inequalities in schooling thus exist between rather than within school districts, and because there is no effective mechanism for redistribution of school funds among school districts, poor families lack a viable political strategy for correcting the inequality.

The above rules of the game—rewarding "excellence" and financing schools locally— illustrate the complementarity between the political and economic power of the upper class. Thus it appears that the consequences of an unequal distribution of political power among classes complement the results of class culture in maintaining an educational system which has thus far been capable of transmitting status from generation to generation, and capable in addition of political survival in the formally democratic and egalitarian environment of the contemporary United States.

. . . .

5.3 *How the School System is Rigged for Failure*

The preceding essay described a variety of ways in which the school system is instrumental in transmitting inequality. Two important aspects of this process are (1) the fact that the children of the rich tend to stay longer in school than the children of the poor; and (2) the fact that the school system equips the children of the rich much more than the children of the poor with intellectual skills and personality characteristics appropriate to higher levels of the work hierarchy.

How exactly do schools operate so as to discriminate in favor of the more affluent children? After all, it is often argued that the educational system simply rewards those children who do well. According to this view, if the more affluent children perform better in school than others, they *deserve* to be rewarded; furthermore, *some* poor children do well and are rewarded for it. But even if schools did in fact work this way, the outcomes would remain highly unequal. And the reality of the American school system is far from this meritocratic "ideal."

The previous reading has suggested some ways in which—independently of "merit" or effort—upper-class children receive disproportionate benefits from public education. Schools in affluent communities tend to be better funded than schools in poorer districts—a consequence of the fact that American schools are largely financed through the local property tax. The structure and rules within the schools themselves differ according to the class character of the school neighborhood, so that children are prepared for the kind of jobs held by parents in the community. Even the definition of achievement itself is biased in such a way as to reward the kind of "learning" characteristic of middle- and upper-class families.

In the next reading Florence Howe and Paul Lauter describe one of the most blatant mechanisms whereby schools transmit inequality from generation to generation: the system of *tracking* (or "ability grouping" or "streaming"). The tracking system separates children by such categories as "college preparatory," "general," "vocational," and "basic"; a different curriculum for each track is then designed to best meet the "needs" of the children in the track. Such a system clearly favors those who manage at an early age to be placed in the higher tracks, and it is precisely children from the more affluent homes who have the initial advantages in placement. To determine how infrequently poor children "do well and are rewarded for it," one need only observe how disproportionately the children of the poor are placed in the lower tracks of public schools.

Source: The following is excerpted from "How the School System is Rigged for Failure" by FLORENCE HOWE and PAUL LAUTER. From *The New York Review of Books*, (June 18, 1970). This article, part of a longer chapter on the school system, is taken from Florence Howe and Paul Lauter, *The Conspiracy of the Young*, Copyright © 1970 by Florence Howe and Paul Lauter. Reprinted by permission of the authors.

.   .   .

There has hardly been a time during the last 150 years when Americans were not being told that the schools were at a "turning point," "confronted with a crucial challenge," "entering an era of new importance." At the same time, they have forever been at the edge of failure. Indeed, one major enterprise of educators in every generation has been to analyze that failure and propose new remedies.

.   .   .

But are the schools "failures"? If they do not accomplish the goals which educators have laid out for them, it may well be that all they need . . . is more money, more innovation, more machines, more specialization. It may also be, however, that the stated goals of American education are deceptive and irrelevant ones, that their grand rhetoric clouds the character and social objectives of the schools. A review of the alleged "failures" of the Selective Service System—the uncertainty it has engendered, its unfairness, its apparently arbitrary and harebrained procedures—reveals features that have been built in because they are necessary to its function of channeling young men into what are thought to be socially desirable activities. Looking at what the schools *do* rather than at what they should or might do may tell a similar story. What if the apparent "failures" of the American educational system have served necessary functions in American society? Perhaps the schools, like almost all other American institutions, have been very, indeed horrifyingly, successful.

. . .

In 1927 many Americans were troubled about their society. Morals seemed to be disintegrating, crime increasing. Indeed, some felt there was a "legal bias in favor of the criminal." He "is petted and pampered and protected to a degree which makes the punishment of crime relatively rare." Educators were quick to rise to this social crisis. They urged their fellow Americans to look to the schools to train citizens not to "set themselves against the state." After all, there was "no other organized force which aims primarily at citizenship and at the same time represents the state." Schools could, moreover, satisfy the demands of industry for "the type of help that knows something, that has social graces arising from extended social experience" of the sort provided by high schools.

There was one problem, however: how to keep the children *in* school. Many dropped out because their main experience in the classroom was one of frustration. A new way of organizing schools had to be found that would not forever be confronting those most in need of schooling with failure, that might more fully "individualize" their instruction in order to prepare children more efficiently for the kinds of jobs they would get. This way was "ability grouping."

Ability grouping in the junior high school is to be defined as the classification of the pupils of the school into groups which, within reasonable limits, are homogeneous

in ability to perform the kind of task which confronts those pupils in the classroom. It is not a social segregation. It is not a caste stratification. It is not an attempt to point out those who are worth while and those who are not. It is not a move to separate the leaders from the followers.[1]

Despite the best intentions of its promoters, ability grouping—or tracking, or streaming, as it is variously called—has unfortunately become all that they asserted it would not be. What it has *not* been is either a means of keeping children in school or of improving their performance while they attend.

In Washington, D.C., for example, where an elaborate track system reached far down into the elementary schools, 54 percent of the classes of 1965 and 1966 dropped out before graduation. The most extensive and careful study of ability grouping, moreover, concludes "that ability grouping, *per se*, produces no improvement in achievement for any ability level and, as an administrative device, has little merit."[2] The study indicates further that children may learn better in strongly heterogeneous groups. Arthur W. Foshay, who wrote the Foreword, suggests also that evidence from Sweden and England "raises the dark possibility that ability grouping functions . . . as selective deprivation." Tracking may actually *prevent* children from learning, the study indicates, because "teachers generally underestimate the capability of pupils in lower-track classes, expect less of them, and consequently the pupils learn less."[3] None of this is surprising, since teachers generally concentrate on students who respond. But why, then, if tracking has not succeeded in keeping most kids in school and has succeeded in creat-

[1]This quotation from Heber Hinds Ryan and Philpine Crecelius, *Ability Grouping in the Junior High School* (New York, 1927), pp. 1–10.
[2]Miriam L. Goldberg, *et al., The Effects of Ability Grouping* (New York, 1966), p. 163.
[3]Goldberg, *The Effects of Ability Grouping*, p. 165.

ing for those lower-tracked kids the "self-fulfilling prophecy" that they won't learn anything in school—why, then, has it persisted for more than forty years?

In the first place, tracking is to schools what channeling is to the draft. Its function is identical, namely, the control of manpower "in the National Interest." In democratic societies like that of the United States, individuals are encouraged to believe that opportunities for social advancement are unlimited; such beliefs are part of the national myth, and also necessary to encourage young people to achieve and get ahead. Yet opportunities are, in fact, limited. Not everyone with the talent can, for example, become a scientist, industrial manager, engineer, or even a college professor; the economy has greater need for technologists, technicians, salesmen, white-collar workers, not to speak of men on production lines. It has been estimated that industry demands five semi-professionals and technicians to enable every professional to function.

There must be "valves" which can help to control the flow of manpower into the economy. "Tracking" is one of those important valves; it helps to ensure that the American work force is not "overeducated" (as has been the case, for example, in India, where there are far too few jobs "suitable" for college graduates). It also helps to ensure that unpopular industries, like the Army, or less prestigious occupations, like sanitation work, are supplied with manpower.

.   .   .

Indeed, sociologist Theodore Caplow has argued that:

> . . . the principal device for the limitation of occupational choice is the education system. It does this in two ways: first, by forcing the student who embarks upon a long course of training to renounce other careers which also require extensive training; second, by excluding from training and eventually from the occupations themselves those students who lack either the intellectual qualities (such as intelligence, docility, aptitude) or the social characteristics (such as ethnic background, wealth, appropriate conduct, previous education) which happen to be required.[4]

Tracking is one of the educational system's major techniques for thrusting forward students with the necessary qualities of school-measured intelligence, docility, background, and the rest; and for channeling the others into "appropriate" slots. James Bryant Conant is explicit about this practice. "I submit," he writes in *Slums and Suburbs*, "that in a heavily urbanized and industrialized free society, the educational experiences of youth should fit their subsequent employment." Accomplishing this goal in cities is difficult, Conant continues, given the limitations of guidance personnel and parental indifference; therefore, "the system of rigid tracks may be the only workable solution to a mammoth guidance problem."[5]

.   .   .

Ability grouping has been operating effectively to limit competition with the children of white, middle-class parents who, on the whole, have controlled the schools.[6] In New York City in 1967, for example, nonwhites, the vast majority of them poor, made up 40 percent of the high school population; they constituted about 36 percent of students in the "academic" high schools and about 60 percent of those tracked into "vocational" high schools. In the Bronx High School of Science and in Brooklyn Tech, elite institutions for which students must qualify by examination, "nonwhites" totaled only 7 and 12 percent of the students respectively.

But the real effects of tracking can better

[4]*The Sociology of Work* (Minneapolis, 1954), p. 216.
[5]*Slums and Suburbs* (New York: McGraw-Hill, 1961), pp. 40, 66.
[6]See, for example, Patricia Cayo Sexton, *Education and Income* (New York, 1962), pp. 228, 234.

be seen in the statistics of students in the academic high schools. A majority of blacks and Puerto Ricans fill lower tracks, which lead them—if they stay at all—to "general" rather than "academic" diplomas. Only 18 percent of academic high school graduates were black or Puerto Rican (though they were, as we said, 36 percent of the academic student population); and only one-fifth of that 18 percent went on to college, as compared with 63 percent of whites who graduated. In other words, only 7 percent of the graduates of New York's academic high schools who went on to college were black or Puerto Rican. The rest, for the most part tracked into non-college-preparatory programs, left school with what amounted to a ticket into the Army.[7]

The statistics for Washington, D.C., are even more striking, in part because figures are available on the basis of income as well as race and ethnic background. In the nation's capital, where, in 1966, 91 percent of the students were black, 84 percent of those black children were in schools *without any honors track*. In areas with a median income of $3,872 a year, 85 percent of the children were in a basic or general track, neither of them college-bound; while in areas where the income was $10,374 or better, only 8 percent of the children were in the general track, and in such areas there was *no basic track at all*. Theoretically, tracking ranks students according to their ability to achieve. Yet Washington's statistics suggest that the children of the poor have less than one-tenth of the ability of the children of the well-to-do—an obvious absurdity. . . .

If one studies the means by which students are selected into tracks, one discovers a further layer of discrimination against the children of the poor. It is on the basis of

reading scores, IQ, and other standard achievement tests—as well as teachers' recommendations—that children are determined "slow" or "superior." Yet Herbert Kohl reports that he was able to help his students raise their reading scores from one to three years, within a period of months, simply by teaching them how to take tests. Middle-class children, Kohl points out, learn about tests early in their school careers; indeed, a "predominantly white school located less than a mile down Madison Avenue [from Kohl's Harlem school] even gave after-school voluntary classes in test preparation." But in the Harlem schools it was "against the rules" to provide copies of old tests so that teachers could help their pupils prepare for them; Kohl had to obtain such copies from friends who taught in white, middle-class schools, where back files were kept and made available.[8] Recent studies have suggested, moreover, that the content of "standardized" tests conforms to the experience and norms of white, middle-class children, thereby discriminating in still another manner against able children of poor or black parents.

. . .

But statistics and abstractions may obscure the lives of children trapped in what has been called "programmed retardation." A group of New York City parents, whose children have been tracked into the special "600" schools for allegedly "difficult" children, has begun to prepare a suit to challenge the compulsory-attendance law. While the state has the right to make laws for the health, welfare, or safety of children, they claim, it has no right to subject children to a system that deprives and injures them. Their point is that tracking is not simply a neutral "valve" to control manpower flow, as our initial image might at first have suggested. Rather, tracking harms some chil-

---

[7]These figures were obtained by Columbia University SDS from the records of the N.Y.C. Board of Education through the office of the Reverend Milton Galamison, then a member of the board.

[8]See Herbert Kohl, *36 Children* (New York, 1968), p. 178.

dren, depriving those we call "deprived," making them less competent, less able to reach, let alone to use, the instruments of power in U.S. society. In the light of tracking, schools become for such children not the means of democratization and liberation, but of oppression.

On the other hand, tracking is also one means of controlling middle-class students. The Selective Service's "channeling" system benefits the young man who can afford to go to college, and whose culture supports both higher education and avoiding the draft if he can. Channeling helps him, however, only so long as he lives up to the draft board's standards of behavior and work. Just as the threat of loss of deferment drives draft registrants into college or jobs in the "National Interest," so the threat of losing privileged status within the school system is used to drive students to fulfill upper-track, college-bound requirements. In a school in which students are tracked from, say, "12–1"—the twelfth-grade class for college-bound students—down to "12–34"—the class for alleged unteachables—demotion not only would threaten a student's social position, but his entire future life. Having a child placed in a lower track is a stigma for a college-oriented family, as every principal faced with angry parents pushing to have their children in the "best" classes will testify. Moreover, entry into prestige colleges, or even into college at all, normally depends upon track and other measures of school status. Thus though the threat, like that of channeling in the past, has been largely unspoken, it continues to push students to behaving and achieving as required by the system.

. . .

The track system provides a formal basis for translating class-based factors into academic criteria for separating students into different groups: those who will drop out;

those whose diplomas will not admit them to college; those who will be able to enter only two-year or junior colleges; and the lucky few in the honors classes who will go on to elite institutions and to graduate or professional schools. Thus while tracking may assure the "failure" of lower-class students, as a system it allows the schools to "succeed" in serving middle-class interests by preparing their children to fill the technological and professional needs of corporate society.

. . .

[Tracking also affects higher education.] Encouraged by U.S. society to believe that young people can rise to the top, whatever their race or class, blacks, Chicanos, Puerto Ricans, and some working-class white students are beginning to press into colleges. Higher education in the United States has had to manage an elaborate and delicate technique for diverting many of these students from goals toward which they have been taught to aspire, but which a stratified society cannot allow them all to reach. "Cooling" them "out," the term openly used in higher education and now beginning to become as familiar to students as "channeling," means that certain students are deliberately and secretively discouraged from aspirations middle-class youth take for granted. Working-class students are tracked into second-class or "junior" colleges, "cooled out" and counseled into substitute curricula (a medical technician's program rather than a premedical course), or if they get to a university, programmed for failure in large "required" courses.[9]

. . .

California's three-tiered system of higher education has provided a model for other

[9]See, for example, Burton R. Clark, "The 'Cooling-Out' Function in Higher Education," *American Journal of Sociology*, LXV (May, 1960).

states: the "top" eighth of high-school grad-uates may be admitted to the university sys-tem, the "top" third to the state colleges; the rest are relegated to what one writer has described as "those fancied-up super high schools, the local two-year 'community col-leges.' "[10] Factors closely related to race and economic class—students' high school track, grades, and College Board scores—determine placement into a particular level of higher education, though the fees students pay are relatively similar wherever they may go in the state. Like tracking in high schools, state-subsidized higher education channels students into distinctly inequitable systems. In Maryland, for example, the average per pupil expenditure during fiscal year 1966 was $802 in community colleges, $1,221 in the state colleges, and $1,724 (excluding re-search funds) in the University of Mary-land.[11]

. . .

The circular process is obvious: just as the economic class of a student's family largely determines his admission to a par-ticular college or university in the first place, so does his placement at that college deter-mine his future. Indeed, money is destiny! Given the process of "upgrading" jobs, one might find suitable the image of a squirrel in a circular cage: the faster he runs, the more firmly does he remain bound to his position. While the admission of working-class students to community colleges may seem to be serving their desire for upward mobility, in fact it may barely be keeping the lid on potentially explosive campuses.

[10]Kingsley Widmer, "Why Colleges Blew Up," *The Nation*, 208 (Feb. 24, 1969), p. 238.

[11]*Master Plan for Higher Education in Mary-land*, Section 2, p. 19.

5.4 *The Effect of Taxes and Government Spending on Inequality*

To complete our analysis of income inequality, one major consideration remains: the redistributive impact of the state. In the next two readings we turn to the direct impact of government tax and expenditure programs on the distribution of income. It must first be noted that the state is already importantly involved in our analysis of income distribution that has been presented up to this point. By defending the basic institutions of capital-ism, the state perpetuates the most fundamental source of inequality. Government also affects the distributional process by creating and sup-porting intermediary institutions such as schools which aid in the main-tenance and transmission of inequality.

But the state's impact on income inequality is not confined to such "system-maintenance" effects. In recent decades federal, state, and local governments have increasingly acted to redistribute income directly among different groups in the United States. In so doing, have they had a sig-nificant effect on the inequality which results from capitalist economic institutions?

In order to examine the distributional impact of government, we will look both at the revenue side of the budget (Who pays the taxes? Do the rich or the poor pay more?) and at the expenditure side (Who benefits from the expenditures on government programs?). This analysis must unfortunately ignore the more complicated but equally important distributive effects of nontax or nonexpenditure policies—e.g., Who benefits from the government's maintenance of high unemployment? What are the effects on capital earnings of the government's method of financing the public debt? What is the distributive impact of implicit subsidies such as the oil import quota or highway and airport programs?

Any discussion of government's role in redistributing income usually begins by considering the federal income tax. It is widely known that the nominal federal tax *rate* increases as one's income grows larger, so that an individual with a high taxable income must pay not only more taxes, but a higher *proportion* of his income in taxes. This should clearly result in greater equality in after-tax income. And since the tax rate increases to very high levels (70 percent for the highest income bracket), one would expect not only some movement toward greater equality, but *significantly* greater equality.

As Table 5–C (p. 236) shows, however, the actual equalizing impact of the federal income tax is considerably less than the rate structure would imply. The disparity is created by the divergence of *effective* tax rates (the rates people actually pay) from *nominal* rates (the rates established by the statute). Effective tax rates are much lower than nominal rates because of various tax loopholes which reduce taxable income.

Figure 5–A shows, for the federal income tax, the effective tax rates throughout the income scale after allowing successively for (1) personal exemptions; (2) personal deductions; (3) the capital gains provision; and (4) income splitting.[1] The overall impact of these various provisions is to make actual tax rates much less than the nominal rates; and the capital gains and deductions loopholes in particular greatly reduce the difference in tax rates for rich and poor. The relatively flat curve for effective rates explains why inequality is nearly identical between before-tax and after-tax incomes.

The federal income tax is not of course the only tax; in fact, other taxes account for roughly 60 percent of total taxes paid. These taxes— sales taxes, taxes on real estate, the corporate profits tax, excise taxes, etc. —generally fall much more heavily on the poor than on the rich. The sales and excise taxes, for example, take a fixed percentage of what people

---

[1]The personal exemptions provision allows one to subtract $600 of his income for himself and each dependent before computing taxes on the remainder. The deductions provision allows one to subtract certain expenses (e.g., medical, business expenses) from taxable income. Capital gains are the income received when assets (e.g., corporate stocks) are sold for a higher price than they were bought for; if the asset had been owned for at least six months before being sold, the capital gains tax provision permits this income to be taxed at a lower rate than income earned from other sources, e.g., from labor. The income splitting provision allows one to assign part of his income to children or other members of the family by transferring income-producing property to the other family member; thus it is possible to pay lower rates than if all income were attributed to one person.

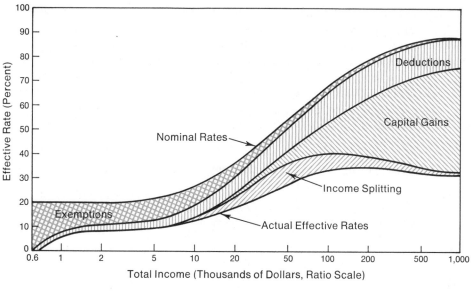

SOURCE: Richard Goode, *The Individual Income Tax* (Washington, D.C.: Brookings Institution, 1966), p. 236.

Figure 5–A Influence of Various Provisions on Effective Rates, Taxable Returns, 1960

spend; since poor people are forced to spend all of their incomes, while rich people save a good portion of their incomes, the poor wind up paying a higher proportion of their income in taxes. The corporate profits tax probably only raises the price at which the corporations sell their products, and therefore the cost of the tax is actually borne by the consumers; if so, the distributive impact would be similar to that of the sales tax.[2] Real estate taxes, where they refer to rental apartments, are probably passed on to the tenants in the form of higher rents.[3] It must be concluded that any tendency toward equality created by the federal income tax is wiped out by other taxes which take more from the poor than from the rich. The pre- and post-tax incomes given in Table 5–C refer only to the federal income tax. Taking all taxes together, it is likely that there would be no change at all.

Even if the tax system makes no contribution to equalizing incomes, it might still be true that government expenditures have an equalizing impact. If the government took as taxes the same proportion of income from rich and poor, the net impact of the government could still be in favor of the poor. This would happen if most of the money was spent on programs benefiting the poor. In this case, the poor would be better off as a consequence of government intervention, since the amount they re-

[2]The problem of determining whether consumers, corporate owners, the corporation's workers, or some combination of the three "really" pay the corporate income tax is still much debated.

[3]For a good discussion, see Gabriel Kolko, *Wealth and Power in America*, (New York: Frederick A. Praeger, Inc., 1962) Chapter 2.

ceived back in the form of services would be paid for not only by their own tax payments but also by those of the rich.

However, as James Bonnen demonstrates in the next reading, the reality is often the reverse. After failing to contribute to equality on the tax side, the government often *increases* inequality by undertaking programs which benefit the rich more than the poor. The following case study of government spending programs in the agricultural sector is an example of the unequal benefits that derive from government spending.

Source: The following is excerpted from "The Absence of Knowledge of Distributional Impacts: An Obstacle to Effective Public Program Analysis and Decisions" by JAMES T. BONNEN, from *The Analysis and Evaluation of Public Expenditures: The PPB System*, a compendium of papers prepared for the Subcommittee on Economy in Government of the Joint Economic Committee of the United States Congress, 91st Congress, 1st Session (Washington, D.C.: U.S. Government Printing Office, 1969). Reprinted by permission of the author.

. . . In a general way we have known for some time that [the farm] program has a concentrated distribution of benefits. Many agricultural economists, most prominently T. W. Schultz, have long drawn attention to this fact. However, there have not previously been any systematic quantitative measures of the degree of that concentration. Little has been known about distributional differences between commodities and between regions and States within commodities. Nor has there been any comparison of the differential distributional impacts of price supports and the direct payments that have entered into the program as a major factor since 1962.

In the United States in the middle of the Nineteenth Century, rural life meant farm life. There was little rural economic activity besides that generated by farming. The preponderance of U.S. population lived in rural areas and practically all of that was on farms. Today less than 30 percent of our population is rural, and less than 5 percent is on farms. While some of that rural population living in small rural communities are dependent on the economic activity generated in agriculture, it is a *prima facie* matter that farm programs in the nature of things simply cannot and do not serve all rural people today.

·   ·   ·

A 1967 study by the Department of Agriculture for the Senate Agricultural Committee provides a direct insight into the equity considerations that relate to the resource allocation argument.[1] Four different standards were used for computing a parity income or parity return to resources in farming. Farm programs enacted during the Kennedy and Johnson administration years had, by 1966, provided parity or higher income returns (by all four standards) for the 16 percent of all farmers who had gross sales of $20,000 or more. This group produced more than two-thirds of all agricultural products in 1966. The 16 percent of all farmers in the $10,000 to $20,000 gross sales category in 1966, who produced 18 percent of all output, earned 81 to 98 percent of a parity return depending upon the standard used. While there is a wide dispersion around these mean figures, these programs have not generated a parity return or

[1] *Parity Returns to Farmers*, Senate Document 44, 90th Congress, first session, August 10, 1967, p. 22.

better to the most efficient farmers who produce the bulk of our farm products.

The entire structure of the industry has been transformed from the traditional subsistence farming economy of the Nineteenth and early Twentieth Centuries into a highly specialized industrial enterprise in which command over resources, output, and income in agriculture have become far more highly concentrated. Today less than 10 percent of all farmers produce over half of all agricultural output; about half of the farmers produce 95 percent of all the U.S. agricultural output.[2] With few exceptions, farm programs, whether they are credit, conservation, or commodity programs, are designed today so that a farmer's access to them is directly related to the size of assets he controls, the amount of land he operates and his volume of output. Under these conditions it perhaps is not surprising that the farm programs are increasingly questioned with respect to the equity of their distributional consequences.

Recent work by the author throws considerable light on the distributional characteristics of farm commodity programs. For our purposes this presentation will be limited to a summary of the results and a sample of the statistical evidence for the reader's own inspection. The data presented are in the form of Lorenz curves and Gini concentration ratios. The Lorenz curve tells one what percentage of the farmers received what percentage of the benefits. The Gini concentration ratio measures the degree of concentration of the distribution of benefits —that is, it measures how far a given distribution departs from a completely equal distribution of benefits between all beneficiaries.

From Table 5–Q it can be seen that all of the commodity programs are fairly highly concentrated, some of them greatly so. Look-

[2]Economic Research Service, U.S. Department of Agriculture, Farm Income Situation (FIS-211), July 1968, pp. 64, 68–69.

ing down this table you will see that the 40 percent of the smallest farmers (allotment holders) receive much less than a proportionate share of the program benefits even in the case of the programs with the least concentrated distribution of benefits. In a typical program such as peanuts, Table 5–Q suggests that it would be necessary to generate about $10 of program benefits for every dollar going to the lowest 40 percent of smaller peanut farmers. Variation across all the commodity programs would range from about $6 to $34 of total benefits for every dollar going to the lowest 40 percent of the farmers. Looking at the very bottom of the distribution, this same table shows that it would be necessary to generate from $20 to $100 of benefits for each dollar going to the lowest 20 percent of farmers.

Even after considering all the qualifications that go with these numbers, the data suggest very clearly that the farm programs are not efficient means for affecting an income redistribution to the smaller low income farmers. Since it is clear from the parity income study that the more efficient farmers are already receiving near parity income or better, it seems an inescapable conclusion that any attempt to solve the low income small farmer problem via price supports would generate huge windfall profits to the more efficient larger scale operators.

The welfare impact of these distributions cannot actually be ascertained fully unless we have a measure of the current distribution of income and assets among beneficiaries for comparison with the distributions of program benefits. Ideally, one would desire to have this not only for the U.S. as a whole for all farmers but one should also have the income and asset distribution of cotton producers for comparison with cotton program benefits, and similarly for all the rest of the programs. Such estimates are not available. The best that is immediately available for this purpose is a measure of the Lorenz curve of the net money in-

TABLE 5–Q DISTRIBUTION OF FARM INCOME AND VARIOUS PROGRAM BENEFITS:
PROPORTION OF INCOME OR BENEFITS RECEIVED BY VARIOUS
PERCENTILES OF FARMER BENEFICIARIES[1]

	Percent of Benefits Received By the—						
	Lower 20 Percent of Farmers	Lower 40 Percent of Farmers	Lower 60 Percent of Farmers	Top 40 Percent of Farmers	Top 20 Percent of Farmers	Top 5 Percent of Farmers	Gini Concentration Ratio
Sugar Cane, 1965[2]	1.0	2.9	6.3	93.7	83.1	63.2	0.799
Cotton, 1964[2]	1.8	6.6	15.1	84.9	69.2	41.2	.653
Rice, 1963:	1.0	5.5	15.1	84.9	65.3	34.6	.632
Wheat, 1964:							
Price Supports	3.4	8.3	20.7	79.3	62.3	30.5	.566
Diversion Payments	6.9	14.2	26.4	73.6	57.3	27.9	.480
Total Benefits[4]	3.3	8.1	20.4	79.6	62.4	30.5	.569
Feed Grains, 1964:							
Price Supports	0.5	3.2	15.3	84.7	57.3	24.4	.588
Diversion Payments	4.4	16.1	31.8	68.2	46.8	20.7	.405
Total Benefits[4]	1.0	4.9	17.3	82.7	56.1	23.9	.565
Peanuts, 1964[2]	3.8	10.9	23.7	76.3	57.2	28.5	.522
Tobacco, 1965[3]	3.9	13.2	26.5	73.5	52.8	24.9	.476
Farmer and Farm Manager Total Money Income, 1963[5]	3.2	11.7	26.4	73.6	50.5	20.8	.468
Sugar Beets, 1965[2]	5.0	14.3	27.0	73.0	50.5	24.4	.456
Agriculture Conservation Program, 1964:[6]							
All Eligibles	7.9	15.8	34.7	65.3	39.2	(7)	.343
Recipients	10.5	22.8	40.3	59.7	36.6	13.8	.271

[1]This table presents portions of 2 Lorenz curves relating the cumulated percentage distribution of benefits to the cumulated percent of farmers receiving those benefits. Cols. 1 through 3 summarize this relationship cumulated up from the lower (benefit per farmer) end of the curve, and cols. 4 through 6 summarize the relationship cumulated down from the top (highest benefit per recipient) end of the curve.

[2]For price support benefits plus Government payments.

[3]For price support benefits.

[4]Includes price support payments and wheat certificate payments as well.

[5]David H. Boyne, "Changes in the Income Distribution in Agriculture," Journal of Farm Economics, Vol. 47, No. 5, December 1965, pp. 1221–22.

[6]For total program payments. Computed from data in "Frequency Distribution of Farms and Farmland, Agricultural Conservation Program, 1964," ASCS, U.S. Department of Agriculture, January 1966, Tables 3 and 8.

[7]Not available.

SOURCE: Except as noted all figures are from James T. Bonnen, "The Distribution of Benefits from Selected U.S. Farm Programs," *Rural Poverty in the United States: A Report of the President's National Advisory Commission on Rural Poverty*, Washington, D.C., G.P.O., 1968.

comes of farmers and farm managers estimated for 1963 by Boyne and for 1964 by Coffey.[3] Boyne's figures are arrayed in Table 5–Q where they can be compared with similar Lorenz distributions for the various programs. At the level of the lowest 40 percent

[3]David H. Boyne, "Changes in the Income Distribution in Agriculture," *Journal of Farm Economics*, Vol. 47, No. 5, December 1965, pp. 1213–24; and Joseph D. Coffey, "Personal Distribution of Farmers' Income by Source and Region," *American Journal of Farm Economics*, Vol. 50, No. 5, December 1968, pp. 1383–96.

of farmers only tobacco, sugar beet, and ACP programs have the effect of adding proportionately more program benefits to a farmer's income than he commands as a share of farm income. That is, this group of farmers receives 11.7 percent of farm income, but a higher percentage than this of tobacco, sugar beet, and ACP program benefits. The lowest 20 percent of farmers receives 3.2 percent of net farm money income. But they receive more than 3.2 percent of the benefits of the wheat, peanut, to-

TABLE 5-R DISTRIBUTION OF 1964 UPLAND COTTON PRICE SUPPORT BENEFITS: PROPORTION OF U.S., REGIONAL, AND STATE BENEFITS RECEIVED BY VARIOUS PERCENTILES OF FARMER BENEFICIARIES[1]

State	Lower 10 Percent of Farmers (1)	Lower 20 Percent of Farmers (2)	Lower 33 Percent of Farmers (3)	Lower 50 Percent of Farmers (4)	Top 50 Percent of Farmers (5)	Top 33 Percent of Farmers (6)	Top 20 Percent of Farmers (7)	Top 10 Percent of Farmers (8)	Top 1 Percent of Farmers (9)	Gini Concentration Ratio (10)
Alabama	2.1	4.3	8.0	17	83	73	60	45	15	.546
Florida	2.7	5.3	8.8	19	81	69	54	37	10	.483
Georgia	1.2	3.0	8.0	16	84	71	58	42	11	.531
North Carolina	2.5	4.9	8.2	13	87	76	64	47	15	.577
South Carolina	1.7	3.3	5.6	13	87	77	63	48	13	.594
Virginia	5.2	10.4	17.3	26	74	65	52	37	11	.401
Southeast	1.9	3.7	6.2	15	85	75	61	47	14	.571
Arkansas	0.8	2.6	5.2	11	89	80	70	56	20	.652
Illinois	1.2	2.4	4.9	11	89	83	71	53	12	.650
Kentucky	1.5	3.0	5.0	11	89	80	66	47	10	.613
Louisiana	1.0	2.8	6.4	12	88	79	69	54	16	.628
Mississippi	1.0	2.1	4.9	9	91	84	75	64	23	.701
Missouri	1.3	3.0	6.5	14	86	74	61	44	14	.565
Tennessee	2.4	4.8	9.0	18	82	72	58	42	13	.515
Delta	1.2	2.3	5.9	11	89	81	70	58	21	.657
Oklahoma	1.1	3.7	9.6	21	79	65	50	31	7	.446
Texas	.4	2.0	6.4	15	85	71	56	37	10	.530
Southwest	.5	2.0	6.3	14	86	73	56	39	11	.542
Arizona	.5	1.5	4.1	10	90	80	65	47	15	.628
California	.7	1.9	4.2	8	92	84	72	57	25	.686
New Mexico	.8	2.4	5.7	14	86	75	60	42	11	.565
West	.5	1.6	3.9	8	92	84	72	56	22	.682
United States	.9	1.8	4.9	10	90	80	69	53	21	.653

[1]This table presents portions of 2 Lorenz curves relating the cumulated percentage distribution of benefits to the cumulated percent of farmers receiving those benefits. Cols. 1 through 4 summarize this relationship cumulated up from the lower (benefit per farmer) end of the curve, and cols. 5 through 9 summarize the relationship cumulated down from the top (highest benefit per recipient) end of the curve.

SOURCES: (a) "1964 Upland Cotton: Final Planted Acres and Number of Farms Planting Cotton by Size of Effective Allotment," USDA, ASCS/Policy and Program Appraisal Division, mimeo, Nov. 6, 1964 (2 pages); (b) "Agricultural Statistics, 1966," USDA, 1966, p. 62. Prices from this source were used in computing State value of production figures for use as weights in combining the distributional data from source (a); (c) "Crop Production, 1965 Annual Summary," USDA, SRS, Dec. 20, 1965, p. 84. Yield and acreage data from this source were used in computing State value of production figures for use as weights in combining the distributional data from source (a).

bacco, sugar beet and ACP program. Rice, feed grains, cotton and sugar cane all provide to this lowest group of allotment holder less of a share of program benefits than they average as a share of farm income. One is tempted to say that these latter programs are regressive in their income impact in farming, but this is not proved by this crude though relevant comparison. Nor can we argue conclusively that the ACP, sugar beet and tobacco (and possibly peanuts and feed grains) programs have a progressive income impact—even though our data seem to suggest this.

There are too many logical difficulties to bridge. Cotton benefit distributions should be compared with cotton farmer income distributions—not all farm income. Also some regionalization of the farm income distribution is needed to allow for geographic and industry mix differences associated with differences in productivity. One cannot always assume that one is necessarily dealing with the same general set of low incomes, or indeed with low income at all, when one speaks of the lower end of the distribution of benefits from a program. While it may be fairly reasonable to assume that a small cotton allotment represents a small farmer, such an assumption is not necessarily reasonable in the case of wheat or feed grains. Farmers do grow more than one commodity typically, and a small allotment may sometimes represent a minor enterprise in a substantial operation. It also should be noted that farm income accounts for a relatively small part of the total income of quite a number of smaller producers. This partially accounts for the very low concentration of total income of farmers from all sources as compared to the high concentration of gross and net incomes from farming operations that can be seen in Table 5–S.

Thus, the net effect of these programs may be less regressive than the data suggest —or possibly more regressive—but the pattern is clear.

. . .

It is also worth remarking that the variation in concentration within a particular commodity program from state to state and region to region can be rather large. These reflect primarily great variations in productivity and yield, and rather substantial differences in the median allotments as well as the relative variation around those medians. See the example of cotton in Table 5–R.

. . .

Since the distribution of government payments are both very visible (unlike price support benefits) and highly concentrated, efforts have been made in Congress in recent years to place a limit on the size of the total payment that a single farmer may receive.

Recently available data on the distribution of total payments in 1967 make it possible to examine the concentration of total government payments and to test the distributional impact of a payment limitation.[4] A total of $3.1 billion in government payments were made in 1967. Eighty percent of this total went to three crops: $932 million to cotton, $865 million to feed grains and $731 million to wheat. The only other commodities with direct payments were sugar and wool which received $70 million and $29 million respectively. All the remaining $439 million went into conservation (ACP, $225 million) and land withdrawal.[5]

In Table 5–S it can be seen that the distribution of total payments in 1967 was highly concentrated, exhibiting a concentration ratio of 0.671. This exceeds the concentration in every commodity benefit distribution in Table 5–Q except sugar cane.

. . .

Changes in program design such as have occurred since 1961, shifting emphasis from price supports towards direct payments,

[4]Congressional Record, Vol. 114, No. 135, 90th Congress, Second Session (1968), p. H7928.
[5]See footnote 2.

TABLE 5-S DISTRIBUTION OF 1967 GOVERNMENT PAYMENTS AND FARM INCOME: PROPORTION RECEIVED BY VARIOUS PERCENTILES OF FARMERS[1]

1967	Percent of Income Received By the—						
	Lower 20 Percent of Farmers	Lower 40 Percent of Farmers	Lower 60 Percent of Farmers	Top 40 Percent of Farmers	Top 20 Percent of Farmers	Top 5 Percent of Farmers	Gini Concentration Ratio
1967 total government payments:							
With no limitation on size of total payment[2]	1.1	5.7	13.3	86.7	69.0	42.4	0.671
Assuming $25,000 limitation[3]	1.1	6.0	14.1	85.9	67.2	39.0	.652
Assuming $10,000 limitation[3]	1.2	6.5	15.3	84.7	64.4	33.8	.623
Various measures of farmer income in 1967:							
Gross receipts from farming[4]	1.6	3.3	10.1	89.9	72.3	40.4	.693
Realized net farm income[5]	4.5	9.0	19.3	80.7	50.0	26.2	.541
Nonfarm income of farmers	25.5	51.0	70.1	29.9	15.6	5.6	.125
Total income of farmers	14.9	29.8	44.5	55.5	37.0	16.0	.211

[1]This table presents portions of 2 Lorenz curves relating the cumulated percentage distribution of benefits to the cumulated percent of farmers receiving those benefits. Columns 1 through 3 summarize this relationship cumulated up from the lower (benefit per farmer) end of the curve, and columns 4 through 6 summarize the relationship cumulated down from the top (highest benefit per recipient) end of the curve.

[2]Government payments to farmers as actually distributed in 1967. Total payments were $3,100,000,000.

[3]Assumes all 1967 beneficiaries continue to participate in programs and are eligible for payments. Under the $25,000 limit payments would total $2,800,000,000 and under the $10,000 limit $2,600,000,000.

[4]Including Government payments and imputed nonmoney income from farm products consumed at home and from the rental value of the farm dwelling.

[5]Net of farm production expenses and changes in farm inventories of livestock and crops.

SOURCES: Computed from data in "Farm Income Situation," USDA, FIS-211, July 1968, pp. 68–69, except direct payment data which are from the Congressional Record, July 31, 1968.

have considerable effects upon the distribution of the costs of the program also. While no quantitative analysis is attempted here it is clear from the logic of the situation that the cost of the price support operation is borne through the taxes necessary to sustain the storage and control operation, and also through consumers who pay some of the cost through higher market prices. The shift toward direct payments shifts this relative burden away from the consumer and toward the taxpayer. One exception to this is the wheat program where direct payments are generated by a certificate system that is paid eventually by the consumer through the market. The price support approach, in which a higher proportion of the costs are borne by the consumer in the form of food costs, has a far greater impact on the low income consumer than would be the case of direct payments in which the cost is borne primarily by a progressive income tax. Thus, price support acreage diversion programs can be described as doubly regressive—that is, a major share of the cost is borne by consumers with below average incomes and a major share of the benefit is received by farm producers with above average incomes. The shift toward direct payments, while not significantly affecting the distribution of benefits among farmers, has reduced the regressiveness of the distribution costs.

5.5   *Who Fares Well in the Welfare State?*

The one government program which is supposed to be devoted exclusively to the poor is the welfare system. In fact, Richard C. Edwards in this essay *defines* the welfare system as all those programs which specifically benefit the poor. The welfare system has been expanding rapidly: expenditures are up, and the number of recipients keeps growing. According to the popular view, the welfare system must surely have had an equalizing impact. But a careful look at the facts suggests a different conclusion.

Source: The following essay was written by RICHARD C. EDWARDS for this book. Copyright © 1972 by Richard C. Edwards.

Official rhetoric aside, income inequality in the United States has diminished only slightly over the last several decades. Aggregate income data reveal that no significant progress toward more equality has been achieved since World War II, and in particular the poorest fifth of the population continues to receive the same small proportion of total income, less than 6 percent, which they received decades ago.[1]

These decades also witnessed the creation and growth of the manifold public assistance and other antipoverty programs. These programs—the "welfare system"—have often been perceived as a powerful force for greater equality; instead they have had a miniscule impact on the distribution of income in the United States.

The failure of the welfare system to attack inequality should not be surprising. Inequality is not only a consistent and normal by-product of capitalist development, it is also *necessary* for the functioning of capitalist institutions.[2] The welfare system in America must therefore operate within the constraints imposed by the need to maintain inequality. In the first part of this essay I describe the nature, size, and trends in welfare expenditures in the United States, in order to assess the impact of the welfare system. In the second part I investigate the theoretical reasons for the failure of the welfare

[1]See Table 5–A, p. 209.
[2]See Weisskopf, Section 3.7, p. 125.

system significantly to alter inequality in a capitalist society.

THE POVERTY OF WELFARE

Included in the "welfare system" as that term is used here are all those programs which grant either cash payments or goods and services exclusively or at least principally to poor people; eligiblity must be based at least in part on the beneficiary's lack of income.[3] Table 5–T lists the major programs which are included.

While the welfare system has provided gradually increasing absolute benefits to the

[3]For example, general education programs are not included, since they are undertaken on the part of the *general* population and not in particular for the benefit of poor people; on the other hand, some of Title I funds, which were designated as antipoverty monies, are included. The dividing line was generously applied, however, including for example the federally financed employment service, which with good justification could as well be considered as a subsidy to employers rather than part of the welfare system. One large program sometimes thought of as part of the welfare system which we have *not* included is the Social Security program, since it represents no (or very little) transfer to the poor from the rest of society but rather is mainly an insurance scheme in which poor recipients as a lifetime group have paid in as much as they receive back. It is true, of course, that the Social Security system redistributes income over people's lifetimes, returning income during that part of their lives when their incomes are low. This does not con-

TABLE 5–T EXPENDITURES UNDER THE WELFARE SYSTEM IN 1968. INCLUDING ALL FEDERAL, STATE, AND LOCAL PROGRAMS (billions of dollars)

Category	Amount Spent State and Local	Federal
Public aid	$ 4.6	$ 6.4
Unemployment insurance and employment service	2.1	.9
Workman's compensation	2.3	.1
Health and medical programs	3.9	1.1
Public housing	.1	.3
Education	—	1.0*
Other social welfare (O.E.O., school meals, etc.)	2.3	1.8
	$15.3	$11.6

Total: $26.9 billion

*Estimated for Title I, E.S.E.A.

SOURCE: *Statistical Abstract of the United States*: 1970, U.S. Bureau of the Census, Washington, D.C., 1970, p. 277.

poor, *it has never threatened the overall structure of inequality.* First, the total expenditures on welfare programs have never been great enough to affect the income distribution significantly; since the poor help finance the welfare system through their tax payments, the redistributive impact is even less than the total expenditures would indicate. Second, the level of welfare benefits as a percentage of median family income or average weekly wages has remained constant or declined, so one cannot argue that welfare programs have contributed much to greater equality over time. These facts, which I present below, explain why a rising amount of total benefits has been entirely consistent with a nearly constant degree of income inequality.

First let us look at the aggregate impact

stitute redistribution to the poor, however, since the beneficiaries have by and large paid for the benefits they receive. For a careful study which comes to this same conclusion, see Elizabeth Deran, "Income Redistribution Under Social Security," *National Tax Journal*, XIX, No. 3, p. 285. See also John Brittain, "The Real Rate of Interest on Lifetime Contributions Toward Retirement Under Social Security," in *Old-Age Income Assurance*, U.S. Congress, Joint Economic Committee, December, 1967, Part iii.

of the welfare system. Total welfare costs in 1968 were $26.9 billion. In order to grasp the impact of that magnitude, suppose that in 1968 (with no other changes in tax or welfare laws) the government had taxed an additional $26.9 billion from the richest fifth (20 percent) of the population. At the same time, imagine that this $26.9 billion had been transferred to the poorest fifth of the population, distributed evenly among them. What would have happened? The richest fifth would still be, by far, the richest; their "reduced" incomes would still be *more than one and one-half times greater* than the *next richest* fifth. Furthermore, the poorest fifth would still be the poorest; their "expanded" incomes would still be *less than three-quarters* of the income of the *next poorest* fifth of the population.[4]

This exercise, insignificant as it would be for income redistribution, *grossly overestimates* the impact of the welfare system. This is so for three reasons. First, only some benefits from the programs we have included go to poor people. For example, all federal

[4]This assumes that aggregate personal income, as it appears in Department of Commerce National Income Accounts, follows the income distribution which was calculated from CPS data and given in Ackerman, *et al.*, Section 5.1, p. 207.

health and medical spending, except that relating to defense and medical research, have been included, yet many of these programs are not at all directed toward the poor. Second, I have ignored all of the administrative costs, boondoggles, subterfuges, etc., which accompany welfare programs in this country. Certainly even with the best intentions, much of the $26.9 billion spent on welfare in 1968 never actually reached poor people; for example, the salaries of welfare workers, and the cost of most "poverty research" (including research support for this paper) are included in this figure. Third, I assumed that the entire tax burden required to finance the welfare program was paid for by the richest fifth. But the welfare system is in fact paid for out of general tax revenues to which the poor contribute, so the redistributive impact is overestimated to the extent that the poor pay for their own benefits.

That welfare expenditures have not been of sufficient magnitude to threaten the overall structure of inequality becomes even more evident if we relate the total cost of the programs we have included in the welfare system to other economic magnitudes. In 1938, while the United States was recovering from the Depression, welfare expenditures amounted to 6.78 percent of total personal income. But, as Table 5–U shows, since World War II the total amount spent on welfare programs by all federal, state, and local governments has remained a roughly constant—and lower—proportion of

total personal income. While welfare expenditures have been growing absolutely, they have not grown relative to other economic magnitudes: in comparison to personal income, welfare expenditures have barely maintained their position. Needless to say, the income-equalizing impact has likewise at best remained constant over time.

In order to determine the *overall* redistributive impact of the welfare system we must also consider who pays the taxes which finance welfare programs. Welfare expenditures redistribute income to the poor only to the extent that the poor do not themselves pay for those programs.

Welfare programs are financed slightly more from state and local tax revenues (57 percent) than from federal revenues (43 percent).[5] Since federal taxes are slightly redistributive toward the poor, and state taxes are considerably more biased against the poor, a *conservative* estimate of the poor's tax contribution toward financing the welfare system can be obtained by assuming that the $26.9 billion in 1968 was paid for by income groups in proportion to their incomes.[6] This assumption would mean that the poorest fifth would have contributed between $1.5 billion and $2.0 billion toward

[5]*Statistical Abstract*, 1970, p. 277.
[6]This assumption is used by Robert Lampman, "Transfer and Redistribution as Social Process," in Shirley Jenkins (ed.), *Social Security in International Perspective* (New York: Columbia University, 1969), p. 41. Remember that this figure includes only the *non*-Social Security taxes which the poor pay to finance welfare programs.

TABLE 5–U WELFARE EXPENDITURES AS A PERCENT OF TOTAL PERSONAL INCOME

Year	All Welfare Costs (billions of $)	Total Personal Income (billions of $)	Welfare as a Percent of Personal Income
1938	$ 4.7	$ 68.6	6.78%
1950	$ 8.8	$228.5	3.86%
1960	$13.3	$400.8	3.31%
1968	$26.9	$685.8	3.82%

SOURCE: Calculated from *Statistical Abstract*, 1940, pp. 366ff.; 1952, p. 219; 1960, p. 283; 1969, p. 275; and *The National Income and Product Accounts of the United States, 1929–1965* 1966, pp. 32–33.
(Supplement to the Survey of Current Business), Dept. of Commerce, G.P.O., Washington, D.C.,

TABLE 5–V GENERAL ASSISTANCE BENEFITS AS A PERCENT OF MEDIAN INCOME

	(1) Average Annual Money Payment Under General Assistance Program	(2) Median Income of Civilian Employed Males	(3) Average Payment As Percent of Median Income (1) / (2)
1950	$ 564	$2831	19.9%
1960	$ 804	$4822	16.7%
1968	$1128	$7080	15.9%

SOURCE: *Statistical Abstract, 1969*, p. 296, 327. *Current Population Reports*, U.S. Department of Commerce, Series P-60, No. 69, April 6, 1970, p. 82.

paying for welfare benefits, and the poorest two-fifths of the population (all of whose incomes were below $7,500) contributed between $5.5 billion and $6.0 billion. Hence any estimate of the *net* benefit to the poor from the welfare system would require our reducing welfare expenditures by between $1.5 and $6.0 billion.

The same point is made by examining the benefits from individual programs. Public assistance, one of the largest programs, is the program usually thought of when people mention "welfare." Suppose we express the average annual payment made to an individual under this program as a percentage of some comparable magnitude, say the median income of employed civilian males.[7] Then *each* of the five public assistance categories[8] had *lower* payments in 1968 than in 1950. The figures for the largest category, general assistance, are shown in Table 5–V. *Relative to the average income earner, the average welfare recipient suffered a decline in position.*

The same phenomenon—diminished or at best constant benefits relative to the median

[7] I chose median income of employed civilian males as our index only because the data are convenient. For example, since many welfare recipients are women, it might have been more appropriate to use median income of employed civilian females. The results, however, would have been the same since the ratio of median incomes of employed civilian males to females has remained nearly constant over the time period we are considering.

[8] Old age assistance, aid to dependent children, aid to the blind, aid to the disabled, and general assistance.

national income or to average wages—has occurred in other programs as well. For example, the unemployed worker, if he happened to be among the 63 percent of the civilian labor force who by 1968 were eligible for unemployment compensation, did little better: in 1950, average weekly benefits for a worker who was unemployed were 34.4 percent of the average weekly wage in manufacturing. In 1960, the average unemployment benefits had "increased" to 35.2 percent of the average manufacturing wage, but by 1968 benefits had fallen back to 34.7 percent. Thus there was no change in relative benefits.[9]

[9] *Statistical Abstract*, 1969, p. 292. The worker who was fully employed at the legal minimum wage did no better: as the following table shows, the minimum wage, while rising absolutely, has not increased sufficiently to keep pace with inflation and the general rise in wages. Thus a worker "protected" by the minimum wage has suffered a decline in position relative to the average worker.

The Minimum Wage as a Percent of Average Wages

	(1) Legal Minimum Wage†	(2) Average Hourly Wage in All Manufacturing	(3) Minimum Wage as Percent of Average Mfg. Wage: (1)/(2)
1940	$0.30	$0.66	45.9%
1950	$0.75	$1.44	52.1%
1955	$1.00	$1.86	53.8%
1960	$1.00	$2.26	44.2%
1965	$1.25	$2.61	47.9%
1968	$1.60	$3.01	38.2%

*Note: the minimum wage law in 1968 covered only 62% of the civilian labor force, some of whom were eligible only for a lower minimum wage than that given in (1); most of those not covered earn less than the minimum wage. See Marvin Kosters and Finis Welch, "The Effects of Minimum Wages on the Distribution of Changes in Aggregate Employment."

†According to a recent report to the Committee for Economic Development ("Who Are the Urban Poor?" by Anthony Downs), a job at the current Federal minimum

The same is true of the Social Security program. We do not include Social Security as part of the welfare system, since it is primarily an insurance scheme in which poor recipients as a lifetime group have paid in as much as they receive back. But popular illusion about Social Security's impact makes the case illustrative nonetheless. In the category of old-age retirement benefits, for example, the average annual stipend as a percentage of the average weekly wage in manufacturing industries fell from 17 percent in 1960 to 15.3 percent in 1967. Or again, taking together all categories for all Social Security programs, average annual benefits as a percentage of the average weekly wage in manufacturing fell from 21.1 percent in 1950 to 19.7 percent in 1960 to 18.8 percent in 1967.[10]

These trends are summarized in the following graph:

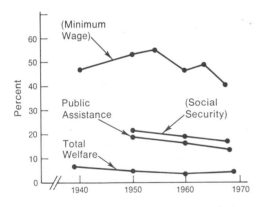

Total welfare is shown as percent of personal income.
Public assistance is shown as percent of median income of employed civilian male.
Socal security and minimum wage are shown as percent of average weekly wage in manufacturing industries.

Figure 5–B Welfare Benefits as Percent of Average Wages or Income

wage of $1.60 an hour brings in $225 a year less than enough for basic subsistence. See pages 7 and 40 of the report.
     SOURCE: *The Fair Standards Act, 1938–1968*, U.S. Department of Labor, Wage and Hour and Public Contracts Divisions. U.S. Government Printing Office, 1968; *Statistical Abstract*, 1969, p. 228.
     [10]*Statistical Abstract*, 1969, pp. 278 and 228.

None of the above is meant to deny that some poor people benefit from the welfare system or that in some absolute sense they were better provided for in 1968 or 1971 than in earlier years. Furthermore, struggles waged by groups such as the National Welfare Rights Organization to obtain rights for poor people directly improve the lives of those aided. Nonetheless, the conclusion to the previous analysis is clear: welfare programs have not been growing relative to the rest of the economy, and in many cases they have even suffered declines. The welfare system has never threatened the overall structure of inequality in the United States.

The evidence cited above *is* intended to show that the welfare system has operated within very narrow constraints. I suggested that those constraints are a consequence of capitalism. All the evidence, however, has been drawn from the U.S. context. In order to show that the constraints result from capitalism (rather than being something peculiar to the American political system, for example), it would be necessary to provide the same kind of evidence from other capitalist societies. While a thorough examination of other countries is beyond the scope of this paper, I can at least suggest some reasons why the U.S. evidence is particularly relevant.

First, the failure of the U.S. welfare system to generate greater equality must reflect something more fundamental than lack of political will, poor leadership, or "mistakes." Such *ad hoc* explanations would be acceptable for a short span of history. But starting at least as early as Franklin Roosevelt's New Deal, the liberals dominating national politics committed themselves to securing more income for America's poor. While we must doubt the depth of their commitment, *the immense political pressure apparently required in order to institute equalizing programs is itself testament to the strength of the underlying economic forces.* Even the public commitment mobilized by

Johnson's "War on Poverty" failed to produce any significant trend toward greater equality. Given this history, there is a *prima facie* presumption that the welfare system's failure to generate greater equality reflects a more basic characteristic of the economic system.

Second, evidence from abroad suggests remarkably similar conclusions. For example, a recent study of the celebrated "welfare state" in Denmark revealed that although the Danish welfare system is much larger and more comprehensive than its U.S. counterpart, it has had almost no impact on the distribution of income in Denmark.[11] Another study, by the Secretariat of the Economic Commission of Europe, considered the distributional impact of the entire system of taxes and benefits in Western European countries. After noting that there was some redistributive effect for the very poor and very rich, it concluded that "the general pattern of income distribution, by size of income, for the great majority of households, is only slightly affected by government action.[12]

WHY IS WELFARE SO INEFFECTIVE?

If we provisionally accept that the constraints within which the welfare system has worked over the past thirty years are imposed by the capitalist system, what can be

[11]The study, *Velstand Uden Velfaerd* (Wealth without Welfare) by the economist Bent Hansen, is discussed by Jacques Hersh in " 'Welfare State' and Social Conflict," *Monthly Review*, XXII, No. 6 (Nov. 1970), pp. 29–41. Hersh (p. 34) quotes Hansen as concluding: "Beneath the surface of a modern welfare society, social injustice and social barriers are still thriving. . . . In our time, the gap between the rich and the poor is growing deeper." The statement is all the more revealing since the author is a leading member of the Social Democrats, who until recently ruled the government almost uninterruptedly since World War II.

[12]Economic Commission of Europe, *Incomes in Postwar Europe: A Study of Policies, Growth, and Distinction*, Geneva, 1967, pp. 1–15.

said about the direct relation between those constraints and capitalism?

One of the consequences of the capitalist development process is that it destroys motivation for work other than that based on wages. In a society where individual material rewards—wages—are the main incentive to work, significant inequalities in labor earnings must exist in order to induce workers to work hard, to acquire and apply productive skills, to accept alienation at the workplace, and to acquiesce in their lack of control over productive activities.[13] Inequality is required so that "good workers" can be rewarded, "bad workers" can be punished; the incentives to "go along" and "work hard" are made clear to all. The need for inequality is most clearly manifest within bureaucratic offices, where both the incentive to rise and the *ex post* justification of hierarchical levels of authority are much strengthened by income differentials.

If the need for such inequality does not seem plausible, imagine the opposite: suppose all workers received the same wage. The standard response—"But then who would be willing to work hard?"—simply restates the case.

Inequality serves other functions as well. For example, the ideological rationale for accepting alienating work conditions—that alienating work makes possible higher consumption levels, and that higher consumption is the true path to personal fulfillment —also depends in part on the existence of inequality. An intense drive for higher consumption is more easily maintained, by advertising, for example, in an atmosphere of inequality, where a fundamental appeal can be made to the pleasure of consuming things which other people do not have.

An adequate welfare system would be even more tenuous in a capitalist society

[13]This abstracts from the most concentrated source of inequality in capitalist society, namely, concentration of capital ownership and capital income among a tiny portion of the population.

than equal wages. The welfare system provides income *without work*. The destructive impact on work incentives of an "adequate welfare income" would therefore be all the greater. The obstacle to an adequate welfare system is simply this: in a society which requires and depends on the wage incentive to force people to work, no one would work if an adequate income were available without work.

One important feature of the *current* welfare system is that it never in any fundamental way breaks the link between income and the necessity to work.[14] It avoids doing so in several ways. First, work is almost always more remunerative than welfare.[15] Second, few benefits are available to persons in the work force: 25 percent of the poor live in families headed by *fully* employed males who earn less than the poverty income;[16] yet these families are eligible for few benefits. Most benefits go to indigent children, old people, the blind, female heads of households with small children, etc., all of whom cannot participate in the labor market. The point is not that these persons are not deserving; clearly they are. However, the chief criterion for their benefit eligibility under the present system is not that they are poor, but rather that they cannot sell their labor-power on the market.

Third, benefits available to people potentially or actually in the labor force tend to be more like wage supplements than wage substitutes. Benefits provided in the form of services (health care, training, job counseling, etc.) cannot be used to purchase the family's food, shelter, and clothing. The food

stamp program is devised to insure that the stamps benefits a family only so long as the family has an alternative income with which to buy the stamps. Public housing requires people to pay rent. School meals, though subsidized, still require some money. Welfare benefits as wage supplements may marginally increase a family's standard of living, but they do not weaken the necessity to work.

A certain minimal level of welfare which does not undermine the work incentive is entirely consistent with the operation of capitalist institutions and the preservation of inequality. Unemployment compensation and employment services (counseling and referrals) help establish mobility in the labor market and therefore provide general benefits to employers as well as workers. Some expenditures for basic public health measures maintain the health and welfare of the national work force and increase its productivity. Public hospital expenditures divert the poor, when they are sick, to public hospitals, thereby freeing quality hospitals for their speciality, treating the rich.

Finally, some welfare programs are required just because extreme poverty poses a threat to the economic system. Those affected have no stake in maintaining the system and may make demands for change. The preservation of capitalism requires that poverty be alleviated, or at least that something be done about its appearance. In this sense, basic income support for persons *not* in the labor force stabilizes the system from two directions. It depoliticizes conflict and diverts poor people's demands around which they might otherwise organize to threaten the economic system. And by focusing exaggerated attention on welfare programs, it diverts the animosity and frustration of the lower-middle class downwards rather than upwards. Such expenditures therefore strengthen the stability of the system itself. In all of these ways, a minimal welfare system represents a good investment by capital-

[14]Even Nixon's proposed Family Assistance Plan would not do this, since the income payments would be so low that a family would still have to work to support itself.

[15]See Bradley R. Schiller, "The Permanent Poor: An Inquiry Into Opportunity Stratification," unpublished Ph.D. dissertation, Harvard University, 1969.

[16]Cited in Anthony Downs, "Who Are the Urban Poor" (CED Report).

ists in the preservation of the system and the increased productivity of its workers.

In conclusion, the welfare system cannot be viewed as a meaningful attack on inequality. Historically, it has never played that role. From the English Poor Laws of the sixteenth century to the Family Assistance Plan, welfare programs have simply kept the poor from becoming *too* poor, that is, from becoming *rebelliously* poor. And an adequate welfare system would directly and fundamentally conflict with the operation of the basic capitalist institutions. Under capitalism, we can never expect a welfare system which significantly reduces inequality.

SELECTIVE BIBLIOGRAPHY

Further reading is recommended in Lauter and Howe, "How the School System Is Rigged for Failure" as cited in the source line for Section 5.3. For more on the theory of income distribution, especially on the conflict between "efficiency" and "equity" and the great inequalities resulting from market-determined efficiency, see Meade [4], especially Chapters 1 and 4. Michelson [5] argues that actions of the state necessarily affect the market distribution process, so the state's distributive impact cannot be treated separately from and *ex post* to the market distribution. More data on income distribution, especially by categories of income recipients, is given in Miller [6]. Both Kolko [3] and Zeitlin [9], Parts 2 and 3, provide a broader view of inequality, including data on income and wealth inequality, stock ownership, particular data on the poorest and richest parts of the population, taxes, etc. Chapter 2 of Kolko [3] is a very readable description of the inability of the federal tax system to affect income distribution greatly; it also considers who pays state and local taxes, so it is an extremely useful discussion of the entire tax system. Gurley [1] is a good critique of the "conventional wisdom" on the distributional impact of tax policy. Hansen and Weisbrod [2] provide an excellent case study of the actual—as opposed to the alleged—equalizing benefits of public expenditures on education. Spady [8] investigates how educational attainments are related to age, race, and parents' social class, concluding not only that inequalities are great but that they are increasing. Sexton [7] describes inequalites within one school system (Detroit) and how they are systematically related to race and class.

[1] Gurley, John, "Federal Tax Policy," *National Tax Journal*, September, 1967.

[2] Hansen, W. Lee, and Burton A. Weisbrod, *Benefits, Costs, and Finance of Public Higher Education*. Chicago: Markham, 1969.

[3] Kolko, Gabriel, *Wealth and Power in America*. New York: Praeger, 1962.*

[4] Meade, James, *Efficiency, Equity, and the Ownership of Property*. Cambridge, Mass.: Harvard University Press, 1965.

[5] Michelson, Stephan, "The Economics of Real Income Distribution," *Review of Radical Political Economics*, II, No. 1, Spring, 1970.

[6] Miller, Herman P., *Rich Man Poor Man*. New York: New American Library, 1964.*

[7] Sexton, Patricia C., *Education and Income*. New York: Viking, 1961.*

[8] Spady, William, "Educational Mobility and Access: Growth and Paradoxes," *American Journal of Sociology*, November, 1967.

[9] Zeitlin, Maurice, *American Society, Inc.* Chicago: Markham, 1970.*

*Available in paperback editions.

Alienation

"ASKED IF HE LIKED HIS JOB, ONE OF John Updike's characters replied, 'Hell, it wouldn't be a job if I liked it.' "[1] After reading Elinor Langer's description of her job with the telephone company, that reply is understandable.[2] But why do most jobs seem so onerous? Must they necessarily be burdensome?

This chapter investigates the relationship between capitalist institutions and alienation —alienation not only at the job, but the alienation which characterizes many of every individual's most important social relations: relations in the family, in the community, in schools, at work. Hence, this chapter concerns a basic aspect of the *quality* of the relations among people under capitalism.

Alienation has come to have two meanings, closely related yet quite distinct. The term is most commonly used in its *psychological* or subjective sense, meaning "dislike of" or "separation of one's approval from." This is the alienation that individuals feel and experience. In this usage, for example, to be alienated from school means not to like school, for one's own values to be separated from the school's values and purposes. Seen as primarily a psychological problem and experienced individually, this alienation is typically categorized as a personal rather than a social problem. Yet most people feel alienated in some ways, and they usually can point to specific social sources of their alienation: workers point to their oppressive, meaningless jobs; students, to repressive schools; and so forth. All this suggests that psychological alienation, though it may be experienced individually, nonetheless has a *social basis*. One purpose of this chapter is to demonstrate that its social basis inheres in capitalist institutions.

Alienation also has a *social* or objective meaning, that used by Marx in his early writings:

> *The* alienation *of the worker in his product means not only that his labor becomes an object, assumes an* external *existence, but that it exists independently,* outside himself, *and alien to him, and* that it stands opposed to him as an autonomous power.[3]

In this usage, alienation from work means being *deprived of control over*, being separated from and uninvolved in the decision process determining the nature and purpose of work.

In the capitalist firm, both organization of work activities and disposition of the work product are determined by the owners of the firm rather than by those who perform the work; such work is therefore *alienated labor*. Likewise, one is (socially) alienated from his community if he is deprived of control over basic community decisions and hence plays no part in the process determining those decisions. Other and equally important forms of social alienation are the alienated family, where people, especially women, are bound by restrictive social traditions and are not free to determine the direction of their own lives; the alienated school, where students (and often teachers) do not participate in deciding what should be studied and how; and alienated consumption, where people follow consumption patterns which are socially approved but do not lead to individual satisfaction.

A person's social alienation—his exclusion from participation in decisions affecting his life—need not refer solely to things which the person actively dislikes. For example, a person can be alienated from meaningful community if he exists in a community where social contacts are superficial; yet, he may not recognize that alienation if he has never been a member of a

---

[1]Quoted in Paul Baran and Paul Sweezy, *Monopoly Capital* (New York: Monthly Review Press, 1966), p. 345.
[2]Elinor Langer, Section 1.2, p. 14.

[3]See Karl Marx, Section 3.3, p. 106 (last italics added).

closer community or if he has had no experience to know what community is. Objectively, he is alienated from community. A second purpose of this chapter is to illustrate the consequences of alienation in this second, social sense.

In general, people in capitalist society do not participate in making the basic decisions that affect their lives; instead, these decisions are made through capitalist institutions over which most individuals have little or no control. The actual decisions are likely, if not inevitably, independent of the interests of the persons involved, and the consequences of these decisions will be contrary to their needs. Hence, people's alienation from control over basic decisions ensures that their needs will not be met; that is, social alienation produces the material conditions for psychological alienation.

When people feel that they are powerless, this perception of their social alienation leads to psychological alienation. When people perceive that their needs are not being met through their work activities, their family life, or their community, the social basis of alienation creates its psychological manifestations. But experiencing alienation is different from recognizing its source, and for people to understand that their alienation derives fundamentally from social circumstances—rather than personal ones—is not automatic; neither does it follow inevitably that these social conditions are correctly identified with the (socially) alienated character of capitalist institutions.[4]

The first three readings in this chapter describe the personal experience and social roots of alienation in three distinct roles: the alienation of the worker, the alienation of the housewife, and the alienation of the consumer. The fourth reading links certain characteristics of alienation with the requirements of capitalist technology. The final reading provides a comprehensive analysis that relates the particular manifestations of alienation, as described in the preceding readings, to the operation of capitalist institutions.

Although we consider here some of the more direct consequences of alienation, the examples are illustrative and are not intended to describe all manifestations of alienation. The special and particularly oppressive alienation of blacks and Third-World Americans is only hinted at, and the alienation most widely commented upon, that of students and youth, is not dealt with at all.

[4]We return to this problem in Chapter 11, especially Sections 11.5 and 11.6.

6.1 *White-Collar Woes and Blue-Collar Blues*

In the following reading, Judson Gooding describes alienation at the job. Although his perspective is necessarily somewhat different from that of the actual workers, he nonetheless portrays well some aspects of what makes jobs alienating. In reading this description, it is important to keep in mind that about 35 percent of the labor force is occupied in blue-collar jobs, while an additional 50 percent of the workforce performs non-managerial white-collar and service jobs.[1]

Source: Part I of the following is excerpted from "The Fraying White Collar" by JUDSON GOODING, Associate Editor of *Fortune Magazine*.

[1]See Table 4-L, p. 178.

Part I: White-Collar Woes

There are many groups undergoing transitions in America today, but none more rapidly than the country's white-collar workers. The strong mutual loyalty that has traditionally bound white-collar workers and management is rapidly eroding. These workers—clerks, accountants, bookkeepers, secretaries—were once the elite at every plant, the educated people who worked alongside the bosses and were happily convinced that they made all the wheels go around. Now there are platoons of them instead of a privileged few, and instead of talking to the boss they generally communicate with a machine.

The jobs are sometimes broken down into fragmented components, either for the convenience of those machines or so that the poorly educated graduates of big-city high schools can perform them. Despite their air-conditioned, carpeted offices—certainly the most lavish working quarters ever provided employees in mass—the sense of distance and dissociation from management has increased sharply, and the younger white collars are swept by some of the same restlessness and cynicism that afflict their classmates who opted for manual labor. . . . All too often, the keypunch operator spends the workday feeling more like an automaton than a human being.

THE NEW MASSES

The white-collar worker is caught in the middle—and indeed is chief actor—in one of the most basic of the trends now sweeping the country. This is the trend toward a predominantly service economy. Already, the clerk rather than the man on the production line is the typical American worker. Under the broad definition of the white-collar category used by the Bureau of Labor Statistics—covering the whole sweep from professional and managerial through clerical and sales workers—the white collars outnumber blue-collar workers, by thirty-eight million to twenty-eight million. In this article, *Fortune* has excluded supervisors, proprietors, and degree-holding technicians and engineers—workers with authority over other employees or for committing company funds—and even by this narrower definition white-collar workers total about nineteen-million. Until the economy slowed down last winter, employment in these categories had been increasing by an average of 3 percent a year.

Now that they are needed by the millions, white-collar workers are also expendable. The lifetime sinecure is rapidly disappearing as management experts figure out yet another way to streamline the job, get in another machine, and cut down overhead. William Gomberg, a former union official and now a professor at the Wharton School of Finance, says, "White collars are where administrators look to save money, for places to fire. It's the law of supply and demand. Once you're in big supply, you're a bum." When an unprofitable division is closed or a big contract slips away to a competitor, layoffs are measured in thousands, and the workers usually hit the streets with no more severance benefits than management feels willing and able to provide.

Member firms of the New York Stock Exchange cut payrolls from 101,314 to 86,123 nonsales employees during the first seven months of 1970—a deep slash of 15,191 persons. In just one grim week in October,

Sylvania Electric Products, Inc., announced it was discontinuing semiconductor operations and the Celanese Corp. disclosed it was cutting 2,000 employees, most of them white-collar. Steel companies are reducing office staffs by the thousands. The unemployment rate for white-collar workers, "usually somewhat more impervious to a general rise in joblessness," according to the Bureau of Labor Statistics, rose a full percentage point during the first nine months of this year from 2.1 to 3.1 percent.

The pay advantage white-collar workers enjoyed when they were a select group has been eroded along with their job security. Until 1920, white-collar workers got between 50 and 100 percent more pay than blue-collar workers, but by 1952 they had fallen 4 percent behind. The pay gap has grown steadily since then. Raises for clerical workers came to 21.9 percent from 1964 to 1969, while factory workers, already ahead, got raises adding up to 26.2 percent. Production workers made an average of $130 a week last year and clerical workers only $105. A Penn Central station agent with twenty-four years of service complains: "New cleaning men make more than I do, counting overtime, although I'm in charge of running the station and handling the cash." Many white-collar workers feel their status has declined as well. A twenty-nine-year-old secretary in a government agency in Washington says, "We're lower people. Down at our level we're peons, that's what they think of you."

.   .   .

Enlightened managers already proclaim that a central concern in any enterprise must be to provide fulfilling, satisfying work for the people who spend so much of their lives inside company walls. More than economic needs must be met. The importance of this concept is reinforced by the fact that the job, dull as it may be, is the most active in-

volvement that many white-collar workers have with the world around them. Few of those interviewed by *Fortune* claimed much interest in reading, in music, in any cultural activity.

There is a terrible, striking contrast between the fun-filled, mobile existence of the young opulents of America as shown on television, and the narrow, constricting, un-fun existence that is the lot of most white-collar workers at the lower job levels. You can't buy much of what television is selling on the salaries these young workers earn; about all you do is stay at home watching those good things go by on the screen. The result is frustration, sometimes bitterness, even anger. Workers in this stratum cannot but notice that the federally defined poverty standard is climbing toward their level from below, while above them the salary needed to enjoy the glittery aspect of American life soars ever higher, further and further out of reach. For many, the office is the real world, not only a livelihood but a focus of existence. They expect it, somehow, to be more than it has yet become.

Part II: Blue-Collar Blues

I Spend 40 Hours a Week Here
—Am I Supposed to Work Too?
Sign in tavern near Ford Dearborn plant

Detroit knows a lot about building new cars, but there's a lot it doesn't know about the new young men building them. . . . Of the 740,000 hourly paid workers building cars today, 40 percent are under thirty-five. The automobile industry, justly proud of its extraordinary record of past accomplishments, is totally committed to the assembly line which comes down from that past, and its heroes are veteran production men who know how to "move the iron." At the plant level, managers are trying to build cars by the old methods with new workers they don't understand and often don't much like. While at headquarters top executives are beginning to worry about "who's down there" on those assembly lines, what "they" are like, what "they" want from their jobs, there is still a comprehension gap.

.   .   .

The central fact about the new workers is that they are young and bring into the plants with them the new perspectives of American youth in 1970. At the beginning of this year, roughly one-third of the hourly employees at Chrysler, General Motors, and Ford were under thirty. More than half of Chrysler's hourly workers had been there less than five years. The new workers have had more years in school, if not more of what a purist would call education: blue-collar workers between twenty-five and forty-four years old have completed twelve years of school, compared to ten years for those forty-five to sixty-four. It doesn't sound like much of a difference, but it means an increase of 20 percent. The new attitudes cut across racial lines. Both young blacks and young whites have higher expectations of the jobs they fill and the wages they receive, and for the lives they will lead. They are restless, changeable, mobile, demanding, all traits that make for impermanence—and for difficult adjustment to an assembly line. The deep dislike of the job and the desire to escape become terribly clear twice each day when shifts end and the men stampede out the plant gates to the parking lots, where they sometimes actually endanger lives in their desperate haste to be gone.

For management, the truly dismaying evidence about new worker attitudes is found in job performance. Absenteeism has risen sharply; in fact it has doubled over the past ten years at General Motors and at Ford, with the sharpest climb in the past year. It

has reached the point where an average of 5 percent of G.M.'s hourly workers are missing from work without explanation every day. Moreover, the companies have seen only a slight dip in absenteeism since car production started declining last spring and layoffs at the plants began. On some days, notably Fridays and Mondays, the figure goes as high as 10 percent. Tardiness has increased, making it even more difficult to start up the production lines promptly when a shift begins—after the foreman has scrambled around to replace missing workers. Complaints about quality are up sharply. There are more arguments with foremen, more complaints about discipline and overtime, more grievances. There is more turnover. The quit rate at Ford last year was 25.2 percent. . . . Some assembly-line workers are so turned off, managers report with astonishment, that they just walk away in mid-shift and don't even come back to get their pay for time they have worked. . . .

In some plants worker discontent has reached such a degree that there has been overt sabotage. Screws have been left in brake drums, tool handles welded into fender compartments (to cause mysterious, unfindable, and eternal rattles), paint scratched, and upholstery cut.

.   .   .

Absenteeism is notably higher on the less desirable late shifts, where there are more of the newer and younger employees. Lacking any precise knowledge of why the absentees stay away, beyond their often feeble excuses, the conclusion has to be that by staying out they are saying they don't like the job. . . . Automobile making is paced, in most of its production operations, by the inexorable demands of the assembly line, usually turning out about fifty-five cars per hour, leaving the men no flexibility of rhythm. At some plants there are sternly detailed work rules that would make a training sergeant at a

Marine boot camp smile with pleasure. The rules prohibit such offenses as catcalls, horseplay, making preparations to leave work before the signal sounds, littering, wasting time, or loitering in toilets. . . .

Working conditions in the plants, some of which are gloomy and old, do not match those in many other industries; the setting is often noisy, dirty, even smelly, and some jobs carry health hazards. The pace of the line and the separation of work stations limit the amount of morale-sustaining camaraderie that can develop. The fact that 100,000 of the 740,000 auto workers were laid off for varying periods this year has, of course, added to discontent. . . .

Walter Reuther [former United Automobile Workers Union President] pondered the industry's problem with youth in an educational-television interview a few weeks before his death. Young workers, he said, get three or four days' pay and figure, "Well, I can live on that. I'm not really interested in these material things anyhow. I'm interested in a sense of fulfillment as a human being." The prospect of tightening up bolts every two minutes for eight hours for thirty years, he said, "doesn't lift the human spirit." The young worker, said Reuther, feels "he's not master of his own destiny. He's going to run away from it every time he gets a chance. That is why there's an absentee problem."

The visual evidence of a new youthful individuality is abundant in the assembly plants. Along the main production line and in the subassembly areas there are beards, and shades, long hair here, a peace medallion there, occasionally some beads—above all, young faces, curious eyes. Those eyes have watched carefully as dissent has spread in the nation. These men are well aware that bishops, soldiers, diplomats, even Cabinet officers, question orders these days and dispute commands. They have observed that demonstrations and dissent have usually been rewarded. They do not look afraid,

and they don't look as though they would take much guff. They are creatures of their times.

Management has tended to assume that good pay with a good fringe is enough to command worker loyalty and performance. For some, it is. General Motors has issued to all its workers an elaborate brochure informing them that even its lowest-paid hourly employees are in the top third of the U.S. income spectrum. (The average weekly wage at G.M. is $184.60.) But absenteeism continues, and learned theoreticians take issue with the automobile executives about money as a reward, arguing that men work for more than pay and that their other psychological needs must be satisfied.

. . .

"I DON'T LIKE NOTHIN' BEST"

What the managers . . . hear is a rumbling of deep discontent and, particularly from younger production workers, hostility to and suspicion of management. A black worker, twenty-two years old, at Ford in Dearborn, says he dislikes "the confusion between the workers and the supervisor." By "confusion" he means arguments. He would like to set his own pace: "It's too fast at times." The job is "boring, monotonous," there is "no glory"; he feels he is "just a number." He would not want to go any faster, he says, "not even for incentive pay." A white repair man in the G.M. assembly plant in Baltimore, twenty-nine years old, says, "Management tries to get more than a man is capable of. It cares only about production."

A black assembly worker at Chrysler who shows up for work regularly and at twenty-four, after Army service, gets $7,400-a-year base pay, says, "I don't like nothin' best about that job. It really ain't much of a job. The bossman is always on our backs to keep busy."

Talks with dozens of workers produced few words of praise for management. There is cynicism about possibilities for advancement. "Promotion depends on politics in the plant," a twenty-seven-year-old trim worker for Ford said, and others expressed similar views. "They tell you to do the job the way it's wrote, even if you find a better way," says an assembly worker, thirty-two, at Cadillac.

Complaints about the lack of time for personal business recurred in different plants. "You're tied down. You do the same thing every day, day in, day out, hour after hour," says a union committeeman, thirty-one, who worked on the line twelve years. "You're like in a jail cell—except they have more time off in prison. You can't do personal things, get a haircut, get your license plates, make a phone call." With the increased complexity of life, including more administrative and reporting obligations, more license and permit requirements, more insurance and medical and school forms, workers tied to the production line have difficulty keeping up. Unable even to phone in many cases, as their white-collar brethren can, they feel frustrated, and one result is they sometimes take a whole absentee day off to accomplish a simple half-hour chore. The problem affects everyone similarly, but here as in other areas of discontent, the young workers are quicker to complain, and more vociferous.

A prominent and somewhat surprising complaint is that companies have required too much overtime. Workers, particularly the younger ones with fewer responsibilities, want more free time and want to be able to *count* on that time. . . . U.A.W. Vice-President Douglas A. Fraser says, "In some cases high absenteeism has been caused almost exclusively by high overtime. The young workers won't accept the same old kind of discipline their fathers did." They dispute the corporations' right to make them work overtime without their consent, he says, feeling this infringes on their individuality and freedom.

NOBODY LIKES THE FOREMAN

The foremen, as the most direct link between management and the workers, draw heavy criticism, most of it from the younger men. They are accused, variously and not always fairly, of too close supervision, of inattention or indifference, of riding and harassing men, of failing to show them their jobs adequately.

A young apprentice diemaker at Fisher Body says, "They could let you do the job your way. You work at it day after day. They don't." A General Motors worker in Baltimore, twenty-nine and black, says, "The foreman could show more respect for the workers—talk to them like men, not dogs. When something goes wrong, the foreman takes it out on the workers, who don't have nobody to take it out on."

.   .   .

"THEY HATE TO GO IN THERE"

The morale of the young workers is summed up grimly by Frank E. Runnels, the thirty-five-year-old president of U.A.W. Local 22 at Cadillac: "Every single unskilled young man in that plant wants out of there. They just don't like it." Runnels, who put in thirteen years on the assembly line, says there has been a sharp increase in the use of drugs and that heavy drinking is a continuing problem. "This whole generation has been taught by their fathers to avoid the production line, to go to college to escape, and now some of them are trapped. They can't face it; they hate to go in there."

.   .   .

Gene Brook, director of labor education at Wayne State University, blames the young auto workers' anger on "the guy's feeling that he is not a part of anything," that he is an interchangeable cog in the production process. "Workers who want a sense of self-development, and want to contribute," says management consultant Stanley Peterfreund, "instead are made to feel unimportant." Campus and factory ferment have similar origins, in the opinion of Fred K. Foulkes, an assistant professor at the Harvard Graduate School of Business Administration. "People want more control, more autonomy. They want to be the acting agent rather than acted upon." Foulkes, author of *Creating More Meaningful Work*, stresses that the discipline of the assembly line adds a special problem. "People *have* to be there," he says. "There's no relief until relief time comes around. The whole situation, therefore, is inconsistent with what seems to be going on in society— and it's too costly to change the technology. So the question remains: How do you permit men to be individuals?" [One suggested method] would have managers find ways to make the jobs varied and interesting through both motivation and technology. The industry is certainly looking. On the motivational

side, some G.M. plants have even tried rewarding regular attendance with Green Stamps, or initialed drinking glasses.

. . .

Whatever is done, says G.M.'s director of employee research, Delmar L. Landen Jr., it must be remembered that absenteeism and allied production problems are only symptoms of the trouble. For too long the automobile industry has "assumed economic man was served if the pay was okay," says Landen, who has a doctorate in industrial psychology and fourteen years experience with G.M. "It didn't matter if the job was fulfilling. Once the pay is good, though, higher values come into play." Other satisfactions are required. "One thing is sure: if they won't come in for $32.40 a day, they won't come in for a monogrammed glass."

. . .

Nobody disputes that these new workers are the brightest, best-educated labor force that ever came into the plants. If their potential were somehow fully released, they would be an asset instead of a problem.

6.2 *Women's Alienation: The Problem With No Name*

Women, to the extent that they perform alienated work or live in alienated communities, experience the consequences of alienation much as men do. But to leave matters there would be to ignore the critical special conditions that define women's alienation. In this reading, Betty Friedan describes some of those conditions.

> Source: The following is reprinted from Chapter 1 of *The Feminine Mystique* by BETTY FRIEDAN. By permission of W.W. Norton & Company, Inc., and Laurence Pollinger Ltd. Copyright © 1963 by Betty Friedan.

The problem lay buried, unspoken, for many years in the minds of American women. It was a strange stirring, a sense of dissatisfaction, a yearning that women suffered in

the middle of the twentieth century in the United States. Each suburban wife struggled with it alone. As she made the beds, shopped for groceries, matched slipcover material, ate peanut butter sandwiches with her children, chauffeured Cub Scouts and Brownies, lay beside her husband at night—she was afraid to ask even of herself the silent question—"Is this all?"

.   .   .

There was no word of this yearning in the millions of words written about women, for women, in all the columns, books and articles by experts telling women their role was to seek fulfillment as wives and mothers. Over and over women heard in voices of tradition and of Freudian sophistication that they could desire no greater destiny than to glory in their own femininity. Experts told them how to catch a man and keep him, how to breastfeed children and handle their toilet training, how to cope with sibling rivalry and adolescent rebellion; how to buy a dishwasher, bake bread, cook gourmet snails, and build a swimming pool with their own hands; how to dress, look, and act more feminine and make marriage more exciting; how to keep their husbands from dying young and their sons from growing into delinquents. They were taught to pity the neurotic, unfeminine, unhappy women who wanted to be poets or physicists or presidents. They learned that truly feminine women do not want careers, higher education, political rights—the independence and the opportunities that the old-fashioned feminists fought for. Some women, in their forties and fifties, still remembered painfully giving up those dreams, but most of the younger women no longer even thought about them. A thousand expert voices applauded their femininity, their adjustment, their new maturity. All they had to do was devote their lives from earliest girlhood to finding a husband and bearing children.

.   .   .

The suburban housewife—she was the dream image of the young American women and the envy, it was said, of women all over the world. The American housewife—freed by science and labor-saving appliances from the drudgery, the dangers of childbirth and the illnesses of her grandmother. She was healthy, beautiful, educated, concerned only about her husband, her children, her home. She had found true feminine fulfillment. As a housewife and mother, she was respected as a full and equal partner to man in his world. She was free to choose automobiles, clothes, appliances, supermarkets; she had everything that women ever dreamed of.

.   .   .

If a woman had a problem in the 1950s and 1960s, she knew that something must be wrong with her marriage, or with herself. Other women were satisfied with their lives, she thought. What kind of a woman was she if she did not feel this mysterious fulfillment waxing the kitchen floor? She was so ashamed to admit her dissatisfaction that she never knew how many other women shared it. If she tried to tell her husband, he didn't understand what she was talking about. She did not really understand it herself. . . . Women in America found it harder to talk about this problem than about sex. Even the psychoanalysts had no name for it. When a woman went to a psychiatrist for help, as many women did, she would say, "I'm so ashamed," or "I must be hopelessly neurotic." "I don't know what's wrong with women today," a suburban psychiatrist said uneasily. "I only know something is wrong because most of my patients happen to be women. And their problem isn't sexual." Most women with this problem did not go to see a psychoanalyst, however. "There's nothing wrong really," they kept telling themselves. "There isn't any problem." . . .

Just what was this problem that has no name? What were the words women used when they tried to express it? Sometimes a woman would say "I feel empty somehow . . . incomplete." Or she would say, "I feel as if I don't exist." Sometimes she blotted out the feeling with a tranquilizer. Sometimes she thought the problem was with her husband, or her children, or that what she really needed was to redecorate her house, or move to a better neighborhood, or have an affair, or another baby. Sometimes, she went to a doctor with symptoms she could hardly describe: "A tired feeling . . . I get so angry with the children it scares me . . . I feel like crying without any reason." (A Cleveland doctor called it "the housewife's syndrome.") A number of women told me about great bleeding blisters that break out on their hands and arms. "I call it the housewife's blight," said a family doctor in Pennsylvania. "I see it so often lately in these young women with four, five and six children who bury themselves in their dishpans. But it isn't caused by detergent and it isn't cured by cortisone."

Sometimes a woman would tell me that the feeling gets so strong she runs out of the house and walks through the streets. Or she stays inside her house and cries. Or her children tell her a joke, and she doesn't laugh because she doesn't hear it. I talked to women who had spent years on the analyst's couch, working out their "adjustment to the feminine role," their blocks to "fulfillment as a wife and mother." But the desperate tone in these women's voices, and the look in their eyes, was the same as the tone and the look of other women, who were sure they had no problem, even though they did have a strange feeling of desperation.

. . .

The actual unhappiness of the American housewife was . . . being reported . . . although almost everybody who talked about it found some superficial reason to dismiss it. It was attributed to incompetent appliance repairmen (*New York Times*), or the distances children must be chauffeured in the suburbs (*Time*), or too much PTA (*Redbook*). Some said it was the old problem —education: more and more women had education, which naturally made them un-

happy in their role as housewives. "The road from Freud to Frigidaire, from Sophocles to Spock, has turned out to be a bumpy one," reported the *New York Times* (June 28, 1960). "Many young women—certainly not all—whose education plunged them into a world of ideas feel stifled in their homes. They find their routine lives out of joint with their training. Like shut-ins, they feel left out. In the last year, the problem of the educated housewife has provided the meat of dozens of speeches made by troubled presidents of women's colleges who maintain, in the face of complaints, that sixteen years of academic training is realistic preparation for wifehood and motherhood."

There was much sympathy for the educated housewife. ("Like a two-headed schizophrenic . . . once she wrote a paper on the Graveyard poets; now she writes notes to the milkman. Once she determined the boiling point of sulphuric acid; now she determines her boiling point with the overdue repairman. . . . The housewife often is reduced to screams and tears. . . . No one, it seems, is appreciative, least of all herself, of the kind of person she becomes in the process of turning from poetess into shrew.")

Home economists suggested more realistic preparation for housewives, such as high-school workshops in home appliances. College educators suggested more discussion groups on home management and the family, to prepare women for the adjustment to domestic life. A spate of articles appeared in the mass magazines offering "Fifty-eight Ways to Make Your Marriage More Exciting." No month went by without a new book by a psychiatrist or sexologist offering technical advice on finding greater fulfillment through sex.

The problem was dismissed by telling the housewife she doesn't realize how lucky she is—her own boss, no time clock, no junior executive gunning for her job. What if she isn't happy—does she think men are happy in this world? Does she really, secretly, still want to be a man? Doesn't she know yet how lucky she is to be a woman?

The problem was also, and finally, dismissed by shrugging that there are no solutions: this is what being a woman means, and what is wrong with American women that they can't accept their role gracefully? As *Newsweek* put it (March 7, 1960):

> *She is dissatisfied with a lot that women of other lands can only dream of. Her discontent is deep, pervasive, and impervious to the superficial remedies which are offered at every hand.... An army of professional explorers have already charted the major sources of trouble.... From the beginning of time, the female cycle has defined and confined woman's role. As Freud was credited with saying: "Anatomy is destiny." Though no group of women has ever pushed these natural restrictions as far as the American wife, it seems that she still cannot accept them with good grace.... A young mother with a beautiful family, charm, talent and brains is apt to dismiss her role apologetically. "What do I do?" you hear her say. "Why nothing. I'm just a housewife." A good education, it seems, has given this paragon among women an understanding of the value of everything except her own worth....*

The alternative offered was a choice that few women would contemplate. In the sympathetic words of the *New York Times*: "All admit to being deeply frustrated at times by the lack of privacy, the physical burden, the routine of family life, the confinement of it. However, none would give up her home and family if she had the choice to make again." *Redbook* commented: "Few women would want to thumb their noses at husbands, children and community and go off on their own. Those who do may be talented individuals, but they rarely are successful women."

It is no longer possible . . . to dismiss the desperation of so many American women. This is not what being a woman means, no matter what the experts say. For human suffering there is a reason; perhaps the reason has not been found because the right questions have not been asked, or pressed far enough. I do not accept the answer that there is no problem because American women have luxuries that women in other times and lands never dreamed of; part of the strange newness of the problem is that it cannot be understood in terms of the age-old material problems of man: poverty, sickness, hunger, cold. The women who suffer this problem have a hunger that food cannot fill. It persists in women whose husbands are struggling internes and law clerks, or prosperous doctors and lawyers; in wives of workers and executives who make $5,000 a year or $50,000. It is not caused by lack of material advantages; it may not even be felt by women preoccupied with desperate problems of hunger, poverty or illness. And women who think it will be solved by more money, a bigger house, a second car, moving to a better suburb, often discover it gets worse.

It is no longer possible today to blame the problem on loss of femininity: to say that education and independence and equality with men have made American women unfeminine. I have heard so many women try to deny this dissatisfied voice within themselves because it does not fit the pretty picture of femininity the experts have given them. I think, in fact, that this is the first clue to the mystery. . . . Women who suffer this problem, in whom this voice is stirring, have lived their whole lives in the pursuit of feminine fulfillment. . . . These women are very "feminine" in the usual sense, and yet they still suffer the problem.

· · ·

If the secret of feminine fulfillment is having children, never have so many women, with the freedom to choose, had so many children, in so few years, so willingly. If the answer is love, never have women searched for love with such determination. And yet there is a growing suspicion that the problem may not be sexual, though it must somehow be related to sex.

Can the problem that has no name be somehow related to the domestic routine of the housewife? When a woman tries to put the problem into words, she often merely describes the daily life she leads. What is there in this recital of comfortable domestic detail that could possibly cause such a feeling of desperation? Is she trapped simply by the enormous demands of her role as modern housewife: wife, mistress, mother, nurse, consumer, cook, chauffeur; expert on interior decoration, child care, appliance repair, furniture refinishing, nutrition, and education? At the end of the day, she is so terribly tired that sometimes her husband has to take over and put the children to bed.

This terrible tiredness took so many women to doctors in the 1950s that one decided to investigate it. He found, surprisingly, that his patients suffering from "housewife's fatigue" slept more than an adult needed to sleep—as much as ten hours a day—and that the actual energy they expended on housework did not tax their capacity. The real problem must be something else, he decided—perhaps boredom.

I began to see in a strange new light the American return to early marriage and the large families that are causing the population explosion; the recent movement to natural childbirth and breastfeeding; suburban conformity, and the new neuroses, character pathologies and sexual problems being reported by the doctors. I began to see new dimensions to old problems that have long been taken for granted among women: menstrual difficulties, sexual frigidity, promiscuity, pregnancy fears, childbirth depression, the high incidence of emotional breakdown and suicide among women in their twenties and thirties, the menopause crises, the so-called passivity and immaturity of American men, the discrepancy between women's tested intellectual abilities in childhood and their adult achievement, the changing incidence of adult sexual orgasm in American women, and persistent problems in psychotherapy and in women's education.

If I am right, the problem that has no name stirring in the minds of so many American women today is not a matter of loss of femininity or too much education, or the demands of domesticity. It is far more important than any one recognizes. It is the key to these other new and old problems which have been torturing women and their husbands and children, and puzzling their doctors and educators for years. It may well be the key to our future as a nation and a culture. We can no longer ignore that voice within women that says: "I want something more than my husband and my children and my home."

6.3   *The Alienated Consumer*

Although alienation derives ultimately from capitalist relations of production, its repercussions are not confined to the workplace. The hegemony of economic institutions in a capitalist society insures that the effects of alienation will be felt throughout society. For example, in the political sphere alienation takes the form of voter apathy.

Alienation is also felt in the sphere of consumption and leisure. In our discussion of the basic institutions of capitalism,[1] we suggested that a central element of *homo economicus* was the assertion that the principal source of personal welfare and happiness is individual consumption. Successfully convincing people of this assertion legitimizes alienated labor and justifies the exploitative role of capitalists.

The dictates of *homo economicus* and the real needs of people diverge, however, and consumption in capitalist society becomes the source of alienation, not greater personal happiness. In the next reading, Erich Fromm points out some of the connections between capitalist institutions and alienation in consumption and leisure.

[1]Introduction to Chapter 3, p. 88.

Source: The following is excerpted from Chapter 5 of *The Sane Society* by ERICH FROMM. Copyright © 1955 by Erich Fromm. Reprinted by permission of Holt, Rinehart, and Winston, Inc., and Routledge & Kegan Paul Ltd.

The process of *consumption* is as alienated as the process of production. In the first place, we acquire things with money; we are accustomed to this and take it for granted. But actually, this is a most peculiar way of acquiring things. Money represents labor and effort in an abstract form; not necessarily *my* labor and *my* effort, since I can have acquired it by inheritance, by fraud, by luck, or any number of ways. But even if I have acquired it by *my* effort (forgetting for the moment that *my* effort might not have brought me the money were it not for the fact that I employed men), I have acquired it in a specific way, by a specific kind of effort, corresponding to my skills and capacities, while, in spending, the money is transformed into an abstract form of labor and can be exchanged against anything else. Provided I am in the possession of money, no effort or interest of mine is necessary to acquire something. If I have the money, I can acquire an exquisite painting, even though I may not have any appreciation for art; I can buy the best phonograph, even though I have no musical taste; I can buy a library, although I use it only for the purpose of ostentation. I can buy an education, even though I have no use for it except as an additional social asset. I can even destroy

the painting or the books I bought, and aside from a loss of money, I suffer no damage. Mere possession of money gives me the right to acquire and to do with my acquisition whatever I like. The *human* way of acquiring would be to make an effort qualitatively commensurate with what I acquire. The acquisition of bread and clothing would depend on no other premise than that of being alive; the acquisition of books and paintings, on my effort to understand them and my ability to use them. How this principle could be applied practically is not the point to be discussed here. What matters is that the way we acquire things is separated from the way in which we use them.

The alienating function of money in the process of acquisition and consumption has been beautifully described by Marx in the following words:

Money ... transforms the real human and natural powers into merely abstract ideas, and hence imperfections, and on the other hand it transforms the real imperfections and imaginings, the powers which only exist in the imagination of the individual into real powers. ... It transforms loyalty into vice, vices into virtue, the slave into the master, the master into the slave, ignorance into reason, and reason into ignorance. ... He who can buy valour is valiant although he be cowardly. . . . Assume man as man, and his relation to the world as a human one, and you can exchange love only for love, confidence for confidence, etc. If you wish to enjoy art, you must be an artistically trained person; if you wish to have influence on other people, you must be a person who has a really stimulating and furthering influence on other people. Every one of your relationships to man and to nature must be a definite expression of your real, individual life corresponding to the object of your will. If you love without calling forth love, that is, if your love as such does not produce love, if by means of an expression of life as a loving person you do not make of yourself a loved person, then your love is impotent, a misfortune.

But beyond the method of acquisition, how do we use things, once we have acquired them? With regard to many things, there is not even the pretense of use. We acquire them to *have* them. We are satisfied with useless possession. The expensive dining set or crystal vase which we never use for fear they might break, the mansion with many unused rooms, the unnecessary cars and servants, like the ugly bric-à-brac of the lower-middle-class family, are so many examples of pleasure in possession instead of in use. However, this satisfaction in possessing per se was more prominent in the nineteenth century; today most of the satisfaction is derived from possession of things-to-be-used rather than of things-to-be-kept. This does not alter the fact, however, that even in the pleasure of things-to-be-used the satisfaction of prestige is a paramount factor. The car, the refrigerator, the television set are for real, but also for conspicuous use. They confer status on the owner.

How do we use the things we acquire? Let us begin with food and drink. We eat a bread which is tasteless and not nourishing because it appeals to our phantasy of wealth and distinction—being so white and "fresh." Actually, we "eat" a phantasy and have lost contact with the real thing we eat. Our

palate, our body, are excluded from an act of consumption which primarily concerns them. We drink labels. With a bottle of Coca-Cola we drink the picture of the pretty boy and girl who drink it in the advertisement, we drink the slogan of "the pause that refreshes," we drink the great American habit; least of all do we drink with our palate. All this is even worse when it comes to consumption of things whose whole reality is mainly the fiction the advertising campaign has created, like the "healthy" soap or dental paste.

I could go on giving examples ad infinitum. But it is unnecessary to belabor the point, since everybody can think of as many illustrations as I could give. I only want to stress the principle involved: the act of consumption should be a concrete human act, in which our senses, bodily needs, our aesthetic taste—that is to say, in which *we* as concrete, sensing, feeling, judging human beings—are involved; the act of consumption should be a meaningful, human, productive experience. In our culture, there is little of that. Consuming is essentially the satisfaction of artificially stimulated phantasies, a phantasy performance alienated from our concrete, real selves.

.   .   .

Our way of consumption necessarily results in the fact that we are never satisfied, since it is not our real concrete person which consumes a real or concrete thing. We thus develop an ever-increasing need for more things, for more consumption. It is true that as long as the living standard of the population is below a dignified level of subsistence, there is a natural need for more consumption. It is also true that there is a legitimate need for more consumption as man develops culturally and has more refined needs for better food, objects of artistic pleasure, books, etc. But our craving for consumption has lost all connection with the real needs of man. Originally, the idea of consuming more and better things was meant to give man a happier, more satisfied life. Consumption was a means to an end, that of happiness. It now has become an aim in itself. The constant increase of needs forces us to an ever-increasing effort, it makes us dependent on these needs and on the people and institutions by whose help we attain them. "Each person speculates to create a new need in the other person, in order to force him into a new dependency, to a new form of pleasure, hence to his economic ruin. . . . With a multitude of commodities grows the realm of alien things which enslave man."[2]

Man today is fascinated by the possibility of buying more, better, and especially, new things. He is consumption-hungry. The act of buying and consuming has become a compulsive, irrational aim, because it is an end in itself, with little relation to the use of, or pleasure in the things bought and consumed. To buy the latest gadget, the latest model of anything that is on the market, is the dream of everybody, in comparison to which the real pleasure in use is quite secondary. Modern man, if he dared to be articulate about his concept of heaven, would describe a vision which would look like the biggest department store in the world, showing new things and gadgets, and himself having plenty of money with which to buy them. He would wander around open-mouthed in this heaven of gadgets and commodities, provided only that there were ever more and newer things to buy, and perhaps that his neighbors were just a little less privileged than he.

Significantly enough, one of the older traits of middle-class society, the attachment to possessions and property, has undergone a profound change. In the older attitude, a certain sense of loving possession existed between a man and his property. It grew on him. He was proud of it. He took good care

[2]Karl Marx, *Die Frühschriften*, Alfred Kröner Verlag, Stuttgart, 1953, p. 254 (my translation, E. F.).

of it, and it was painful when eventually he had to part from it because it could not be used any more. There is very little left of this sense of property today. One loves the newness of the thing bought, and is ready to betray it when something newer has appeared.

. . .

The alienated attitude toward consumption not only exists in our acquisition and consumption of commodities, but it determines far beyond this the employment of leisure time. What are we to expect? If a man works without genuine relatedness to what he is doing, if he buys and consumes commodities in an abstractified and alienated way, how can he make use of his leisure time in an active and meaningful way? He always remains the passive and alienated consumer. He "consumes" ball games, moving pictures, newspapers and magazines, books, lectures, natural scenery, social gatherings, in the same alienated and abstractified way in which he consumes the commodities he has bought. He does not participate actively, he wants to "take in" all there is to be had, and to have as much as possible of pleasure, culture and what not. Actually, he is not free to enjoy "his" leisure; his leisure-time consumption is determined by industry, as are the commodities he buys; his taste is manipulated, he wants to see and to hear what he is conditioned to want to see and to hear; entertainment is an industry like any other, the customer is made to buy fun as he is made to buy dresses and shoes. The value of the fun is determined by its success on the market, not by anything which could be measured in human terms.

In any productive and spontaneous activity, something happens within myself while I am reading, looking at scenery, talking to friends, etc. I am not the same after the experience as I was before. In the alienated form of pleasure nothing happens within me; I have consumed this or that; nothing is changed within myself, and all that is left are memories of what I have done. One of the most striking examples for this kind of pleasure consumption is the taking of snapshots, which has become one of the most significant leisure activities. The Kodak slogan, "You press the button, we do the rest," which since 1889 has helped so much to popularize photography all over the world, is symbolic. It is one of the earliest appeals to push-button power-feeling; you do nothing, you do not have to know anything, everything is done for you; all you have to do is to press the button. Indeed, the taking of snapshots has become one of the most significant expressions of alienated visual perception, of sheer consumption. The "tourist" with his camera is an outstanding symbol of an alienated relationship to the world. Being constantly occupied with taking pictures, actually *he* does not see anything at all, except through the intermediary of the camera. The camera sees for him, and the outcome of his "pleasure" trip is a collection of snapshots, which are the substitute for an experience which he could have had, but did not have.

6.4   *The Alienating Consequences of Capitalist Technology*

Work activities have a major impact on the way people develop psychologically. Work influences people directly, in the great amount of time and psychological effort expended during an adult's life on the job, and in the personal identification that is connected with one's vocation. Furthermore, socialization both at home and in schools is in part oriented toward preparing children for their future lives as workers.

In what specific ways do work activities affect people? If, as we have argued above, work activities in a capitalist society are not organized to satisfy the creative and self-developmental needs of workers, then we should be able to observe concrete conflicts between the needs of firms and the needs of workers in the actual organization of production. Earlier we suggested what form these conflicts might take.[1]

In the following reading, Kenneth Keniston describes how the organization of production, and especially the nature of capitalist technology, creates a "division of life" whereby the individual, in order to perform effectively on the job, is prevented from being an integrated person. He must "purge" part of himself in order to function as a worker; he must subordinate feelings and emotion to rationality and "cognition."

Notice that Keniston takes the nature of technology as already determined and proceeds to describe its impact on the worker. In the subsequent reading, Gintis raises the question of how technology develops and relates the contemporary characteristics of technology to the operation of capitalist institutions.

[1]See Edwards, Section 3.5, p. 115, and Bowles, Section 5.2, p. 218.

Source: The following is excerpted from Chapter 9 of *The Uncommitted: Alienated Youth in American Society* by KENNETH KENISTON. Copyright © 1962, 1965 by Kenneth Keniston. Reprinted by permission of Harcourt Brace Jovanovich, Inc.

. . .

We usually think of technology, like science, as "objective," uninterested in ultimate values, and uninvolved with basic philosophical assumptions. Thus, to speak of the "values" of technology may seem a contradiction, for among the chief characteristics of technology is that it *has* no final values, that it is little concerned with the ultimate ends of life, and deals hardly at all with the whys, whats, and wherefores of human existence. But though technology lacks final values, it does specify instrumental values, values about the procedures, techniques, processes and modes which should be followed, values about "how to do it."

The question "How to do it?" of course admits many possible answers. Some societies have given highest priority to those techniques we term intuition, sensibility, revelation, and insight. In such societies, inner vision, fantasy, and communication with the Divine are the most cherished aspects of human experience. "Realism," whether in art, literature, domestic life, or personal experience is almost unknown: superstition, magic, myth, and collective fantasies abound. The favored instruments of knowledge in these societies are those we consider "nonrational": prayer, mysticism, intuition, revelation, dreams, inspiration, "possession." But in a technological society, these human potentials take second place: we distrust intuition and consider revelation a token of mental illness; and in everyday language "sensitivity" connotes the quality of being too easily offended rather than the capacity to experience deeply.

The preferred techniques of technology involve two related principles: that we *give priority to cognition,* and that we *subordinate feeling.* By "cognition," I mean men's capacities for achieving accurate, objective, practically useful, and consensually verifiable knowledge and understanding of their world; and by "priority" I mean to suggest that

these capacities have increasingly become superordinate to other human potentials. Thus, feeling as a force of independent value —all of the passions, impulses, needs, drives, and idealisms which in some societies are the central rationales of existence—are increasingly minimized, suppressed, harnessed, controlled and dominated by the more cognitive parts of the psyche. Feeling does not, of course, cease to exist; but insofar as possible, it is subordinated to the cognitive demands of our society.

. . .

The characteristics of our technological values presuppose *empiricism,* a special view of reality that most Americans accept without question. In this metaphysic, what is "real" is external, sensory, and consensually validatable: "seeing is believing." Other cultures would of course have disagreed; for most men of the Middle Ages, Truth sprang not from the objective eye but from the divinely inspired soul. But for us, what is real and true is the visible, external, and scientifically verifiable; and the rest is "speculation," "mythical," "unverifiable," "merely a matter of opinion." Empiricism thus relegates the invisible world of poetry, art, feeling, and religion to a limbo of lesser reality, sometimes termed "fantasy gratifications" to permit men to repair the wounds incurred by their daily struggle in the "real world." American psychology sometimes reflects this empiricism by a discomfort at the invisible workings of the mind so extreme that it refers to thinking as "subverbal talking," or defines "reality factors" as those impinging on us from outside—as if fantasy, dream, and idealism were not "realities" as well. "Experience," a term which in principle includes everything that crosses consciousness, has come to mean "sensory experience"— "experience" of the "real world"—and we can suggest that human beings have other potentialities only by adding the awkward qualifier "inner." Those who have overwhelming self-evident inner experiences are relegated to our mental hospitals, though other societies would have honored them as saints, seers, and prophets. Our gods are accuracy, realism, verifiability, and objectivity; while intuition, fantasy, and private illumination are considered useful only insofar as they lead to "objective" achievements or help dissipate the tensions created by the "real" world.

The triumph of cognition in a technological society thus involves a subordination of feeling. The techniques of cognitive problem-solving—analysis, reduction, measurement, comparison, and empiricism—are all nonemotional: they stress objectivity, they demand dispassionateness, they purport to be universally applicable to all situations. Emotion must be "kept in its place"—and this place is ideally somewhere away from public life, work, politics, or the economy. From an early age we are taught that strong feelings on the job cause trouble—unless they are about doing an efficient job, in which case they are desirable. Ideally, the "good worker" is cool, impersonal, always friendly and ready to listen to others but never "personally involved." He does not panic, he is not jealous, he neither loves nor hates his fellow workers, he does not daydream at work. When all goes well, his work goes "by the book": it lives up to or exceeds the standards established in his field. Even the desire for personal advancement—one feeling our society does admit—must be controlled if it threatens to interfere with the worker's performance: one does not wreck General Motors in order to become its president.

Men and women of course inevitably continue to have strong feelings about their livelihoods, and the people involved in them. But we early learn that these feelings are usually a "problem" to be "dealt with" in other ways—in our families, in recreation— and not "acted out" on the job. The vocabulary of deprecation is filled with terms to describe those who disobey the imperative against emotion: "prima donnas," "unstable" or "impulsive" types, "daydreamers," people who "act out." Whatever we really feel, we must *behave* as if we only felt a reasonable eagerness to do a good job, and in reward are called "dispassionate," "objective," "self-controlled," "level-headed," "rational," and "stable."

Even the areas where these cognitive and antiemotional rules do not apply support the view that they take priority. For these other areas of life, family and leisure, are almost invariably relegated to a secondary role, termed outlets, recreation, havens, or exceptions to the basic rules of our social order. Implicitly or explicitly we view them as compensatory to the "real world"—they are the froth, frills, safety valves, and status-symbols a technological society must allow itself. We pay reluctant obeisance to the need to "work off steam" built up by the emotional suppressions required in work; we allow "unproductive" people like young married women with small children to occupy themselves with arts and antiques; we study emotions scientifically to learn how better to subordinate them; and we even approve if our pianists beat the Russians on the concerto front of the Cold War. A rich society can afford its clowns and dreamers; and a cognitive society may need them as "outlets." But let a young man announce his intention of becoming a poet, a visionary, or a dreamer, and the reactions of his family and friends will unmistakably illustrate the values most Americans consider central.

. . .

The meaning of work—In most traditional societies, young men and women have had little choice as to their work; they worked *because* they were men and women; their work was their life; and work, play, and social life flowed over into each other. Under such circumstances, men rarely think or speak in terms of "work" (which implies something else which is "not work"); they merely speak of the tasks to be done, the catching of fish, the tilling of crops, the saying of Mass. All things run together; distinctions between sectors of life are meaningless: "I work because I am a man."

For most Americans, in contrast, "work" has vaguely unpleasant connotations. It is most frequently paired with words like "hard," or used in phrases like "all work and no play." Work is implicitly felt as something to be gotten out of the way. If we ask the average American why he works, he will answer, "To earn a living"; and this expression says much about the relationship of work and life. The goal of work is to earn the money necessary for "living" when one is not working. The purpose of work is to make possible *other* things (a "living") which are only possible after work. Implicitly, work is seen as a necessary instrumental evil without inherent meaning. Just as for the Puritan, good work and good works were the way a man demonstrated his salvation—the pain of this life which guaranteed bliss in the next—so for most Americans, work remains a mildly painful ordeal.

The reasons for our implicitly negative attitudes toward work can be inferred from the characteristics of most jobs. The fragmentation of tasks means that the individual's relationship to the total product or the total task is highly attenuated. As specialization proceeds, each worker finds himself assigned a smaller and smaller corner of a task; the whole job, the finished product, the whole person as client or patient recedes into the far distance. A sense of connection with a tangible accomplishment and a sense of personal responsibility for what one does are inevitably vitiated in our highly organized society where the Ford Motor Company, the Community Hospital, or DeVitale Homes, Inc., is responsible for the task.

Even at upper levels of management, it takes considerable imagination for the executive to feel a personal relationship with, and to derive a sense of value from, his part in the production of iceboxes, soft drinks, insurance policies, or compact cars. Indeed, the reason high-level executives usually say they are relatively "satisfied" with their jobs may not be because these jobs are in fact more "meaningful," but merely because the executive's education, training, and conceptual ability give him greater capacity to understand his tenuous relationship to his work.

The rising demands for performance on the job further affect a man's feeling about his job. In some highly skilled jobs, growing demands for training and skill may permit a feeling of personal competence which compensates for a tenuous relationship to the total task. The skilled surgeon, the senior machinist, the executive trained in organizational theory, industrial management, and human relations—all may be able to enjoy the use of their highly developed skills. But for many men, more demanding job requirements simply mean more taxing and exacting work, greater demands to "keep up" in order to succed. Too few jobs challenge the heart, imagination, or spirit. On the contrary, most work enjoins a rigorous subordination of these feelings to the cognitive requirements of the job itself. It takes a very special kind of person to derive deep fulfillment from meeting the same exact specifications day after day, no matter how much skill these specifications require. The growing demands for precise and high-level skill, for a capacity to follow exact routines in an orderly way, to mesh without friction in large and highly organized firms, assembly lines, or sales offices often make work less rewarding to the individual despite his higher level of skill.

Nor do the cognitive demands of most jobs add to the meaningfulness of work. Most men and women cannot suppress emotion easily; they *do* have strong feelings about the work they do and the people they do it with, and the pressure to be cool, objective, and unemotional is a pressure to subordinate their deepest feelings. Inevitably, we find it hard to treat all our fellow workers the same way, since our feelings about them are never identical; and it is not easy to judge others only according to their "job-relevant" accomplishments, when in ordinary human relationships these are usually among the *least* determining factors in our feelings about them. Businessmen, like industrial workers, therefore traditionally arrive home tired from their work, full of pent-up feelings which their wives are exhorted to help them "release."

As a result, Americans mention "working for a living" a hundred times more often than they mention "living for their work." Even work that really does contribute to a socially useful product is often so organized that it yields little personal satisfaction. Most important of all, we have long since given up on work, long since stopped even expecting that work be "meaningful"; and if we enjoy our work, it is usually because of good working conditions, friends on the job, benevolent supervision, and above all because the "good living" we earn by working enables us to do other, really enjoyable things in our "spare" time. The phrases "meaningful work," "joy in work," "fulfillment through work" have an increasingly old-fashioned and quaint sound. Even our labor unions have given up any pressure for more meaningful work in favor of demands for less work and more fringe benefits and income to make "living" better instead. The loss of meaning in work goes far beyond the problems discussed by the youthful Marx, namely, the loss of worker's control over the means of production. It extends to the fragmentation of work roles, to the heavily cognitive demands made within work. Even when workers themselves own or control their

factories, work often remains meaningless.

The spirit of work and the human qualities demanded by work inevitably color the worker's conception of himself. In every society, men tend to identify themselves with what they exploit to earn their living: in our society, we often become identified with the machines we exploit to do our most onerous work. This identification is magnified by the parallel between the characteristics of a good worker and a good machine. Whether at high levels of management or on the most menial assembly-line tasks, the good worker is highly specialized, is expected to show few feelings, to operate "by the book," to be consistent, systematic, and precise, to treat all individuals impartially and unemotionally. A man operating under such a regime finds the most important parts of himself—his hopes, feelings, aspirations and dreams—systematically ignored. Like a brilliant child with less brilliant contemporaries, he is forced to suppress the major portion of himself on the job—to have it ignored by others and, most dangerous of all, to ignore it himself. To be treated as if one were only part of a man—and to have to act as if it were true—is perhaps the heaviest demand of all.

Work therefore assumes a new significance in technological society. It requires a dissociation of feeling, a subordination of passion, impulse, fantasy, and idealism before cognitive problems and tasks. As breadwinners, most Americans neither find nor even seek "fulfillment" in their jobs. Work, split away from "living" by convention and tradition, becomes instrumental, a dissociated part of life that makes possible, yet often vitiates, the rest of a "living." Yet to spend one's days at tasks whose only rationale is income and whose chief requirements are cognitive is another demand in our lives which makes our technological society less likely to inspire enthusiasm.

.   .   .

6.5   *Alienation in Capitalist Society*

The alienation that most people experience derives fundamentally from the quality of capitalist societies rather than from individual or personal characteristics. The previous readings in this chapter have illustrated a variety of ways in which alienation results from specific social circumstances: the meaningless experience of most jobs, the restrictive aspirations women are expected to embrace, the self-defeating alienation of seeking personal satisfaction through consumption. Finally, Keniston suggested some ways in which the nature of capitalist technology, requiring the repression of nonrational or "noncognitive" aspects of personality, leads to a fragmented and consequently alienated life.

But to leave matters there, as Herbert Gintis notes in the following reading, "fails to achieve the proper analytical depth," because the social roots of alienation must *themselves* be explained. The alienating organization of production is not simply given, but has developed historically in response to certain needs of capitalists. It is important to recognize that the technology embodied in capitalist production has emerged from a long process of capitalist choices about what innovations will be researched and careful selection of certain technologies from among the potential alternatives for actual application. Likewise, the place of women in the family, patterns of consumption, and other alienating institutions such as schools are products of a similarly conditioned development.

Thus, the final step in the analysis of alienation is to explain the social bases for the experience of alienation. In the following reading Gintis argues that, since capitalist institutions are characterized by the drive for profit, people's needs are considered only insofar as they coincide with the requirements of profit maximization. The resulting organization of production, distribution, and consumption will not therefore reflect or satisfy people's needs.

Source: The following essay was written by HERBERT GINTIS for this book. Copyright © 1972 by Herbert Gintis. Printed by permission of the author.

SOME SNAPSHOTS

A young ex-marine, perched atop a twenty-story University of Texas building with rifle and rangefinder, topples several dozen unknown passersby. He is alienated—alienated from his fellow men in the strongest sense of the word.

A car salesman spends his waking hours foisting on families automobiles more expensive than they can afford, less useful than he leads them to believe, and so constructed that the customer must return two and one-half years later for yet another sale. The salesman is alienated from his fellow men in that less dramatic manner familiar to us all.

A clot of people on a crowded rush-hour street see a man stagger and fall to the ground unconscious. They walk on by, unbothered, not wanting "to get involved." A young woman is threatened, then stabbed to death in full view of her Queens, N.Y. neigh-

mindful, conscious

bors. They do not intervene and they notify neither police nor ambulance. They are similarly alienated from their fellow man.

Showing her engagement ring to a friend, a girl said: "You know what did it? I prepared a home-cooked meal for him—in a bikini." She is alienated from her body, and the course of her life may consist in substituting her physical attributes for her true self—exchanging her body for affluence and security.

A man arrives home from a brutal day's work and sits before the television set watching football, hockey, boxing, baseball; he drinks beer and smokes cigarettes and never engages in sports or physical activity himself. He experiences the "humanity of his own body" only vicariously through a Hank Aaron, Joe Namath, or an Arnold Palmer, while he slowly kills himself. He is alienated from his body.

A teenager retreats to his room, liquifies twenty of his mother's diet pills, inserts the solution into a syringe, and finds a vein. He will be dead in three years. He is alienated from his body.

A junior sales and promotion executive has three Martinis for lunch at work—his wife does the same at her Bridge Club at home—and three more before dinner. Their common, nonworking life is diffused with Scotch and experienced in an alcoholic haze. They succeed in muting their anxieties and in staving off the brute realization of their personal loneliness and isolation at the cost of destroying themselves. They are also alienated from their bodies.

A throng of furious blacks in Watts (or Harlem or Detroit or Baltimore or Washington, D.C. or . . .) riot, loot, and burn, destroying square blocks of ghetto "property." They realize their lack of control over their communities and lives. They are alienated from their community in a most overt form.

An old couple sits in a dingy room with yellowed papers and magazines collecting in ragged and dusty piles, visited only on Christmas by their children living in other cities, inconscient of, unaided by, and cut off from their neighbors, waiting to die. They are alienated from their community.

A ghetto resident does not bother to vote in the municipal elections because, as he correctly perceives, "the people don't have any say anyway."

The suburbanite, who commutes thirty miles to work each day, does not know even his next door neighbors beyond their daily opinions on the weather prospects; he joins forces with them only in the face of such "external threats" as higher property taxes, a teachers' strike for better schools and working conditions, the threat of teaching sex education in the schools, or the imminent entrance of a black family down the street. These suburbanites are alienated from their community.

Similarly, people are alienated from their work: Monday is the start of a long, boring, anxious, unfulfilled week; Monday is a woman serving her bleary-eyed husband coffee, saying, "What do you mean 'Won't this day ever end?' This is Breakfast!"

THE EXPERIENCE OF ALIENATION

As Robert Blauner explains in his book *Alienation and Freedom*,[1] the worker experiences alienation from work in the form of powerlessness, meaninglessness, isolation, and self-estrangement. He or she is *powerless* because bureaucratic organization is ruled from the top, through lines of hierarchical authority treating the worker as just another piece of machinery, more or less delicate and subject to breakdown, to be directed and dominated.

Work seems *meaningless* because it is divided into numberless fragmented tasks, and the worker has some expertise over only one

[1] Robert Blauner, *Alienation and Freedom* (Chicago: University of Chicago Press, 1964), especially Chapter 1.

of these tasks; consequently, his contribution to the final product is minimal, impersonal, and standardized. Work also seems meaningless because most workers realize only too well the limited extent to which their activities contribute to perceived social welfare. If he produces steel, his factory pollutes atmosphere and streams. If he makes automobiles, his product congests, smogs, kills, and, finally, after thirty months of "service," falls apart. If he processes cost accounts or his secretary types the corporation's plan to avoid paying taxes, they know their work is unrelated to satisfying anyone's real needs. If he sells insurance, he understands that his success depends only on his relative cunning and talent in duping his customer.

Moreover, the worker is supremely and uniquely *isolated* in work: fragmentation of tasks precludes true solidarity and cooperation; hierarchical authority lines effectively pit workers on different "levels" against one another; and since workers do not come together to determine through their social interaction the important decisions governing production, no true work community develops. Lastly, the powerless, meaningless, and isolated position of the worker leads him to treat work merely as an *instrument*, as a *means* toward the end of material security, rather than an end in itself. But work is so important to a person's self-definition and self-concept, that he then comes to view *himself* as an instrument, as a means, to some ulterior end. Hence develops his *self-estrangement*.

That a person may be self-estranged— alienated from himself, his essence, and his psyche—has been characterized as the focal point of the industrial worker's self-concept, be he blue-collar or white-collar. As Erich Fromm notes:[2]

[2]Erich Fromm, *The Sane Society* (New York: Rinehart and Winston, Inc., 1955), p. 142.

[A man] does not experience himself as an active agent, as the bearer of human powers. He is alienated from these powers, his aim is to sell himself successfully on the market. His sense of self does not stem from his activity as a loving and thinking individual, but from his socio-economic role.... He experiences himself not as a man, with love, fear, convictions, doubts, but as that abstraction, alienated from his real nature, which fulfills a certain function in the social system. His sense of value depends on his success: on whether he can make more of himself than he started out with, whether he is a success. His body, his mind, and his soul are his capital, and his task in life is to invest it favorably, to make a profit of himself. Human qualities like friendliness, courtesy, kindness, are transformed into commodities, into assets of the "personality package" conducive to a higher price on the personality market.

A PROBLEM POSED

That capitalist society is alienating is a central element in the radical critique of capitalism, and the term has even attained general public acknowledgement—bemoaned by politicians everywhere, trotted out as a catch-all explanation of "youth unrest" by television commentators, and generally seen by youth themselves as characterizing their own condition. But exactly what alienation *is,* and the nature of its *causes,* remains shrouded in uncertainty and confusion.

The difficulty surrounding the concept of alienation arises from the fact that it comprises both subjective, psychological elements and objective, social elements. Before the rise of the New Left in the decade of the 1960s, alienation was treated as a purely subjective phenomenon, essentially independent of the structure of society. In the Silent Decades following World War II, alienation was proposed as a part of the "human condition" by noted French philosophers, among whom Sartre, Camus, and Beckett are the most widely read in the U.S. We personally encounter the phenomenon on this subjective level, and we respond most immediately to its manifestations in our own lives, in the Beatles' "Nowhere Man," Nichol's *The Graduate*, and Phillip Roth's *Portnoy's Complaint*. Yet the sources of alienation inhere in the social system itself. Alienation as a general phenomenon coincides with the rise of capitalism.

We now see the treatment of alienation as an element of human nature as merely symptomatic of the political quiescence of the Silent Decades. Indeed, the very *appearance* of the concept of alienation coincides with the breakdown of feudal society and the rise of capitalism, in the works of Hegel and Marx, and the literary works of Kafka and Doestoevsky.

Yet the growing awareness of the social basis of alienation—an awareness of quite recent vintage—still fails to achieve the proper analytical depth. This is due in part to the particular *form* in which this awareness is couched. Alienation is seen to arise directly from the nature of technology in "modern industrial society" and, hence, to remain independent of any particular set of economic institutions. This view is reinforced through our understanding of the historical development of capitalism's main competitor, state socialism in the Soviet Union and Eastern Europe. So-called "socialist man" seems to differ little from his capitalist counterpart, and so-called "socialist society" seems little better equipped to avoid the problems of Alienated Man and Alienated Woman than its avowed adversary.

This paper will try to show not only that alienation is a social rather than a psychological problem at its root but that it results from the structure of technology only in the most immediate and superficial sense, because the form that technological development takes is itself strongly influenced by the structure of economic institutions and their day-to-day operations. If capitalist and so-called socialist economies experience these same problems, it is due to some essential similarities of their basic economic institutions.

AN ANALYSIS

The root meaning of the verb "to alienate" is "to render alien" or, more concretely, "to separate from" (e.g., "She alienated my husband's affections" means "She separated my husband's affections from me"). We can use this root meaning to motivate a social definition of alienation: when your pocket is picked, you are "alienated" from your wallet; similarly, when the structure of society denies you access to life-giving and personally rewarding activities and relationships, you are alienated from your life. Alienation, on the subjective level, means that elements of personal and social life that should be meaningful and integral, become meaningless, fragmented, out of reach, and —if one has an existentialist bent—absurd. The alienated individual is powerless to control central aspects of his life, just as he cannot "control" the wallet snatched from him.

Alienation appears on many levels. Most of these can be explained in terms of *social roles*. A social role is a "slot" that people fit into, carrying with it characteristic duties and obligations, and defined by what other people expect of the person in that role. These expectations become institutionalized, so the same behavior is expected of any individual who occupies a particular role. For example, take the role of foreman. A foreman, no matter what particular individual happens to occupy the position, is expected to supervise his workers, remain somewhat aloof and above them, and in general be more responsive than are the workers to the company's interests in getting the work done. Butcher, baker, worker, soldier, capitalist, lover, husband, community member —all these are social roles.

The nature of these roles and their availability to the individual are quite as important as the distribution of material goods and power in assessing the value of a social system. Alienation occurs because the roles open to individuals do not satisfy their immediate needs in terms of their interpersonal activities in family, community, and work, and their requirements for healthy personal psychic development.[3] Thus, we center on the role concept to emphasize the inherently *social* nature of alienation. To be alienated is to be separated in concrete and specific ways from "things" important to well-being; however, these "things" are not physical objects or natural resources but are types of collaboration with others, with society, and with nature. These "things" are social roles.

The structure of roles at a point in time, and the way they change and develop over time, depends on criteria and priorities laid down by basic social and economic institutions. This is not an obvious assertion, and its truth can only be ascertained through specific examples, to be presented below. But its truth allows us a particularly simple *causal* explanation of alienation under capitalism: alienation arises when the social criteria determining the structure and development of important social roles are *essentially independent of individual needs*. These conditions are precisely what occur under capitalism: the social roles involving participation in work process and community (and to a lesser extent family life) develop in accordance with market criteria and are essentially independent of individual needs. The result is alienation.

[3]It is from this perspective that the other readings in this chapter can best be understood. That is, to what extent do the roles of white-collar or blue-collar worker, housewife, and consumer in capitalist society satisfy immediate interpersonal needs and are conducive to personal development? To what extent does capitalist technology further these goals? Other important roles (student; old person; participant in government) are equally alienated. [Eds.]

Decisions can be made either through institutions or, consciously, in a political manner. The bulk of decision mechanisms in capitalist society are institutionally organized. The distribution of income, the prices of factors of production, the historical development of technology, the organization of work activities, and the structure and development of communities are all basically directed through the impersonal operation of economic institutions and through the economic power they bestow on individuals.

The decisive nature of institutional decision making cannot be overemphasized, because it runs counter to our most immediate political experience. We *experience* the war in Vietnam—an inherently political decision—while the most important aspects of imperialism are effected through the normal operation of international commodity, factor, and financial markets. We *observe* the political battle over tax rates, minimum wage legislation, income redistribution, and welfare programs—all political decision mechanisms—while the fact that the income distribution is basically determined by supply and demand of privately owned factors of production, themselves derived from modes of productive organization, is so basic it remains unnoticed. We *observe* collective bargaining—again a political decision mechanism—when in fact the level of wages is determined by quite other forces, and the institutional context within which the wage bargain is fought sets the determining limits of its outcome. And so it is with the nature, development, and availability of social roles.

An institutional decision mechanism will be termed "alienated" when the criteria—implicit or explicit—that determine outcomes are substantially independent of the wills of individuals whom the outcome affects. Hence the *content* of these criteria are likely, if not inevitably, independent of the *needs* of affected individuals. In so far as this is true, we shall say that individuals are "alienated" from the social object (be it a physical object; a social role as worker, citizen, consumer, soldier, etc.; another individual; an element of culture; or himself) that is the outcome of the institutional decision.

ALIENATION OF WORK PROCESS

To illustrate the alienating consequences of capitalist institutions, consider the organization of work activities. An individual's work is of utmost importance for his personal life. Work directly engages nearly half of one's active life and is potentially the single major outlet for initiative, creativity, and craft. Moreover, work roles are basic and formative in individual personality development. But are these considerations reflected in the actual social decisions determining the structure of work roles? For instance, is the factory worker's welfare considered when the capitalist decides to produce automobiles by routine and monotonous assembly line operations? Are the secretary's needs considered when she is reduced to the full-time subservient role of typing, stenography, and stamp licking? The structure of work roles is essentially determined by a set of basic economic institutions that operate on quite different criteria. The market in labor means that the worker sells his services to the capitalist firm and essentially agrees to relinquish total control over his work activities, thus leaving the determination of work roles to those who control capital and technology. Both technology and work roles are essentially determined by the dictates of profit maximization or output maximization and maintenance of hierarchy.

Control of work activities through alienating institutions has implications on both subjective and objective levels. Subjectively, workers mostly experience their work activities as "alien"—as opposing rather than contributing to their personal well-being and psychic growth. This is understandable in that their own needs were peripheral in the decision process determining the nature of work roles—their work activities have been snatched from them.

Objectively, alienating control leads to predictable consequences. In the early stages of the Industrial Revolution, this control resulted in work activities that were brutal, unhealthy, boring and repetitive, and required long hours. More recently, it has taken the form of bureaucratic organization of production, where individual work roles are so fragmented and formalized that the worker finds his initiative and autonomy totally muffled by and subordinated to a mass of regulations and "operating procedures." Also, hierarchical stratification of workers along lines of status and authority subjugates some workers to the personal control of others, subjects all workers to the control of managers and capitalists, and precludes cooperation and equality as a condition of production. Hence, bureaucratic organization and hierarchical control are the concrete modern manifestations of the worker's alienation from his work activities.

Of course, there is a standard objection to the above analysis. Although we have attributed alienation from work activities to capitalist economic institutions, some argue that bureaucratic organization and hierarchical control are simply immutable aspects of "industrial technology"; that, in effect, any "advanced" society must experience alienated labor. There are major errors in this view. It is not true that bureaucratic organization is chosen by capitalists only because it is "efficient" and "modern." It is chosen as well (perhaps primarily) because it is the only means of maintaining and stabilizing control over the profit generated in production and of preventing workers from gaining enough general expertise and initiative to embark on cooperative production on their own. Technologies that potentially increase the breadth of collective and individual control of workers, however productive and efficient, must be avoided if the "stability" of the corporate enterprise is to be secured. The loss of control, even in minor areas, might get out of hand: workers collectives might voice "wild" and "unrealistic" demands in a sort of free-for-all; union and management alike might loose control over workers. I shall illustrate this through several empirical examples.

First, bureaucratized and routinized tasks do not flow from the nature of "technology" but from the needs of centralized control. As Vroom notes in his masterful survey of experimental literature in industrial social psychology:[4]

> [the evidence indicates that] decentralized structures have an advantage for tasks which are difficult, complex, or unusual, while centralized structures are more effective for those which are simple and routinized.

That is, given that the corporate unit is based on centralized control, the most efficient technologies will be those involving routinized, dull, and repetitive tasks. In a decentralized environment, the exact reverse would be true.

Second, workers do not like fragmented jobs. The experimental literature shows that job enlargement and decision-making control on the part of workers increase their satisfaction, while lowering absenteeism and turnover.[5] Nevertheless, managers have organized the normal bureaucratic diversion of tasks so that actual worker performance is *substantially independent of the worker's attitudes and satisfactions.* This startling, counterintuitive fact is one of the major results of fifty years of investigation by industrial psychologists.[6]

Third, this bureaucratic organization of production, while insuring managerial control and corporate security against the vagaries of worker morale, is by no means efficient in the wider sense. For even *moderate* worker participation in decisions and goal setting increases productivity.[7] The average quality of decisions made by a group is moreover greater than the average quality of individual decisions,[8] and the best results are obtained when individuals *think up* solutions individually and *evaluate and choose* among them as solidary team.[9]

Let us give some examples. The MIT-generated Scanlon Plan of "participatory management" has been tried in some ten U.S. plants. This plan gives workers unlimited power to organize and improve the work process and working conditions, and guarantees them a share in the proceeds of cost reduction. In these ten plants, the average yearly increase in productivity amounted to 23.1 percent, and in one company 408 out of the 513 innovative ideas were successfully implemented because they led to real improvements in the productive process. Clearly, a stable dialogue between workers, technicians, and planners would even increase this fertile activity.

These results are reproduced in many other individual studies. When workers are given control over decisions and goal setting, productivity rises dramatically.[10] As Blumberg concludes:

> There is scarcely a study in the entire literature which fails to demonstrate that satisfaction in work is enhanced or . . . productivity increases accrue from a genuine increase in worker's decision-making power. Findings of such consistency, I submit, are rare in social research . . . the participative worker is an involved worker, for his job becomes an extension of himself and by his

[4]Victor H. Vroom, "Industrial Social Psychology," *The Handbook of Social Psychology* V, 2nd ed., ed. Gardner Lindzey and Elliot Aronsen (Reading, Massachusetts: Addison-Wesley, 1969), p. 243.

[5]*Ibid.*, pp. 199–201.

[6]*Ibid.*, p. 199.

[7]*Ibid.*, p. 228.

[8]*Ibid.*, p. 230.

[9]*Ibid.*, p. 232–33.

[10]*Ibid.*, p. 234–36.

decisions he is creating his work, modifying and regulating it.[11]

But such instances of even moderate worker control are instituted only in marginal areas and in isolated firms fighting for survival. When the threat is over, there is a return to "normal operating procedure." The threat of worker escalation of demand for control is simply too great, and the usurpation of the prerogatives of hierarchical authority is quickly quashed. Hence, efficiency in the broader sense is subordinated to the needs of bureaucratic control.

Moreover, it is wrong to think of technology as a single unidimensional force of which an economy can only have "more" or "less," but whose substance and form are essentially independent of social decision. What technology is at a point in time is the sum total of the past decisions made as to what *forms of research* are undertaken and which *results of research* are embodied in actual production in factory and office. Technology is "alienating" in capitalist society (and its state-socialist imitators) in the first instance because it is developed and diffused on the sole criterion of profit, and it is locked into bureaucratic organization only because capitalist and managerial representatives will introduce no new technology that is incompatible with their maintenance of power. So liberated, integrated, and anti-hierarchical technologies will develop only when we replace capitalist economic institutions by a system of direct worker and community control. Workers are alienated from their work activities because they are powerless to determine, or even significantly affect, the nature of work roles that hold sway over their lives. Work is for the most part "meaningless," not because of the nature of technology and the division of labor, but because the institutions determining them are not tailored to workers' needs.

[11]Paul Blumberg, *Industrial Democracy* (New York: Schocken Books, 1969).

ALIENATION FROM COMMUNITY

The institutional basis of alienation from work activities is mirrored in other alienating forms. Individuals are also alienated from their community in capitalist society. The roles open to the individual allowing him to relate to his social community are among the most central to his welfare and personal development, and they define his contact with social life. Aside from his work and his basic living and consumption unit—be it nuclear family or more extended commune—social community is the most important potential contribution to his well-being. Yet when his community is ugly, vast, and impersonal and through its fragmented and impotent role structure it fails to provide adequate personal outlets, the individual becomes estranged from his community.

The community in capitalist society is molded by its economic institutions. Because land is controlled individually rather than communally, its use conforms to private as opposed to social interests. If this individual control were distributed equally throughout the population, possibly commonness of interest would lead owners to cooperate in the interests of all. But land and property are very unequally apportioned.

How do powerful owners of land and capital decide its use? Clearly the motive is to maximize their own benefit—that is, their profit. Here a basic economic institution enters in, the "free market in land," whereby each parcel of community property is allocated to the highest bidder for its most remunerative personal use. Traditional economic theory shows that free markets in factors of production and commodities insure, as did Adam Smith's famous "invisible hand," the amassing of labor and the allocation of land according to their most "efficient" use in individual commodity production. This maximal remuneration leads to gargantuan accumulation of individuals in "urban environments" and "sleeping suburbs" whose only purpose is to supply the labor needs of monolithic bureaucratic enterprise. Commercial land use conforms to profit criteria independent of community needs.

Since the community as an autonomous entity, aside from minor zoning and tax regulations, has no control over economic activity and patterns of land use, the basis of stable and solidary community relations withers and disappears. An architecturally and socially integrated community cannot thrive when the only power the community holds over the autonomous activities of profit-maximizing capitalists takes the form of crude constraints on their creative, synthesizing enterprises and activities.

Rather, a true community must be *itself* a creative, initiating, and synthesizing agent, with the power to determine the architectural unity of its living and working spaces and their coordination, the power to allocate community property to social uses such as participatory child-care and community recreation centers, and the power to insure the preservation and development of its natural ecological environment. It is not surprising that capitalist "communities" evince so little and such apathetic support from their members. The individual estranged from his community is realistic in understanding his lack of control over major community decisions. Clearly, alienation from community corresponds to our general proposition: the institutions determining the role structure, the power structure, and the physical structure of a community operate apart from the needs of individuals.

ALIENATION EXTENDED: PRODUCT AND SELF

Alienation from work activities and community are the basis of the individual's estrangement from all aspects of social life.

They lie, for one, at the root of his alienation from the product of his labor. When the individual feels that the good or service he helps produce neither reflects his personal contribution through its properties and attributes nor contributes to his welfare either personally or through those with whom he has bonds of community, the *goal* of his work activities becomes meaningless and absurd; he is alienated from his product. In an integrated society, workers control their activities and, hence, the attributes of their product, as true skilled craftsmen. The worker's attachment to his product results not only from his pride in the object of his labor, but also in the personal value he holds for the community it serves. But in capitalist society, both disappear. Since the free market in labor and capitalist control of production eliminate worker control, and since the free market in land and private control of resources fragment and impersonalize community, his product becomes impersonal and external.

According to this explanation, alienation is a form of deprivation—deprivation from important social roles. But this deprivation holds deep subjective implications because individual psychic development is controlled by social experience. Just as "individuals develop through their social relations of production" and become incomplete individuals when alienated from their work activities, so individuals develop through their roles relating to community, product, and other individuals. When deprived of these formative influences in healthy forms, they become "self-alienated." To continue a metaphor, society may alienate a man's psyche as much as a pickpocket his wallet. We are alienated from ourselves when we are not what we really could be—when we cannot love, play, run, work, spiritualize, relate, create, empathize, or aid as much as our potential allows.

Self-alienation in this sense is often seen

as a personal rather than social problem, and the "afflicted" troop to counselors and psychiatrists (and drugs) in search of themselves. But the social base of even this most intimate form of alienation lies in the deprivation of social environments and relationships conducive to personal growth, and its cure is accordingly *social*. When one grows up alienated from others, he cannot love or relate; alienated from work, he cannot create; from community, he cannot mature as a social being. Capitalist economic institutions, by which decisions are made on the basis of profit rather than human need provide unrewarding social roles. So psychic growth is thwarted, much as vitamin deprivation inhibits physical development.

Individuals become alienated from themselves for yet another reason. To produce workers with the proper ideologies, values, and personalities to participate effectively in alienated social roles requires special attention on the part of those institutions that regulate the development of youth. Communications media, especially advertising, instill materialist values that hold meaningful work and community of no importance in comparison with individual consumption. They depersonalize and objectivize interpersonal, intersexual, interracial, and international relations, reducing them to brute power, competition, and ruse by equating the individual's success as lover, worker, or community member with what he possesses in the form of goods or status.

Similarly, by mirroring the impersonal and competitive relations of community and the bureaucratic-authoritarian aspects of alienated work, schools thwart the development of true initiative, independence, and creativity in their charges. As a result they tend to produce docile, unimaginative workers fitting the needs of hierarchical commodity production. The media and the schools are alienating but are not the true culprits, they merely serve an economic mechanism that shapes community and work in patterns alien to human needs.

ALIENATION AND SOCIAL CHANGE

The virtue of capitalism is its level of economic growth in individual—as opposed to social—commodities, and the system accomplishes this at the expense of destruction in other social realms. Capitalism "delivers the goods" at the expense of destroying society, and this cannot be cured by merely altering the forms of political control.

Capitalism's virtue in delivering the goods would be acceptable to workers and community members only under one condition: that the goods the system delivers be valued as the ultimate source of individual welfare. The submission of the individual to his personal alienation is thus based on the ideological belief—capitalism's assertion—that material goods are the path to personal salvation; this belief is instilled and reinforced through media and schools. Yet it is doubtless false.

An individual's welfare and happiness is determined not by what he *has* in the form of individual commodities but by what he *is* and what he *does*, by his ability to undertake self-fulfilling *activities*. Commodities cannot do for you what you cannot do for yourself; they can act only as *instruments* in the process of human activity. The possibility of self-realizing activity depends as much on the *social contexts* open to the individual as on the means available to their performance. Thus the quality of community, work, and environment appear alongside of individual commodities as sources of individual welfare. An increase in the mass of goods available to the individual will enhance his well-being only in so far as they *expand the sphere of his activities* and only if the social roles involved in individual activity—roles defined by community, work, and environment—are themselves maintained or expanded. Economic growth cannot overcome the individual's alienation from these social spheres.

The individual's ability to undertake self-fulfilling activities depends on his own *level of personal psychic development*, in terms of physical, emotional, cognitive, aesthetic, and spiritual capacities. The individual alienated from himself, being alienated from growth-conducive social roles through his forced reduction to a purely efficient worker or child-raiser, is incapable of true fulfillment, and for him or her, commodities become a substitute for, rather than a complement to, personal activities. The individual discovers his alienation only by realizing this basic fact.

But the consciousness of alienation occurs not through the moral exhortations of the "converted" but the day-to-day experiences of people themselves, and a major force in this realization is the *process of economic growth*. Capitalist ideology holds that increasing personal income is the main path to happiness, that all we are not our money and status can be for us. Yet even taking account of inflation, incomes double every twenty-five or thirty years in the U.S., and we are not happier. On the contrary, social life continues to disintegrate and fragment. Economic growth itself gives the lie to the ethic of individual consumption as the sole social source of personal well-being. We cannot buy decent environment with increased income, the total supply of ecological bal-

ance is limited and declines through the normal operation of economic institutions, and the rich bid away this dwindling supply. We cannot buy decent community and decent work activities when their very destruction is the basis of capitalist growth.

So economic growth, the "virtue" of capitalism, the force in terms of which the system is justified and stabilized, is itself subject to a self-negating dialectic. If capitalist society justifies itself by delivering the goods, its very deliverance undercuts its justification; for once satisfied in this direction, individuals will make other demands on their social system, and such demands cannot be satisfied by a society wherein "all social value is reduced to exchange value."

A basic contradiction that capitalism faces, then, is the following: economic growth is a prerequisite to social stability; yet people have essentially satisfiable material needs, satisfiable in the sense that any further increase in material goods and services plays a minor part in securing their welfare regardless of whether they think it will or not; economic growth leads to the capacity for satisfying these material needs but cannot satisfy their other basic needs; and further economic growth will render the truth of this argument ever more manifest, ever closer to the daily experience of the worker. Therefore, economic growth, the prerequisite for stability, leads to instability.[12]

12This theme is elaborated more fully in Chapter 11.

SELECTIVE BIBLIOGRAPHY

Further reading is recommended in Friedan, *The Feminine Mystique*, in Fromm, *The Sane Society*, and in Keniston, *The Uncommitted*, as cited in the source lines for Sections 6.2, 6.3, and 6.4. Good descriptions of work alienation are Josephson [5], especially the essays by Alan Harrington, "Life in the Crystal Palace," and Harvey Swados, "The Myth of the Happy Worker"; and Rappaport [7]. Blauner [1] provides an analytic framework for describing work alienation, centering on the worker's powerlessness, his work's meaninglessness, his isolation, and his self-estrangement. Nisbet [7] discusses the destruction of traditional communities and the consequent alienation from and search for community. Weaver [8] describes how the need to turn students into (future) disciplined workers creates alienation among students. Friedenberg [3], especially Chapter 2, relates the oppressiveness of high schools to their structure, rules, and teacher attitudes toward the students. Dreeben [2] provides the most sophisticated, though not easily readable, argument that the structure of schools (for example, teacher-authority, punctuality, etc.) is more important for what is learned than the subject content. Henry [4] investigates schools, the media, advertising, and popular culture in general in showing the pervasiveness of capitalist values as a source of alienation.

[1] Blauner, Robert. *Alienation and Freedom.* Chicago: University of Chicago Press, 1964.

[2] Dreeben, Robert. *On What Is Learned in School.* Reading, Mass.: Addison-Wesley Publishing Co., 1968.*

[3] Friedenberg, Edgar Z. *Coming of Age in America.* New York: Random House, 1965.*

[4] Henry, Jules. *Culture Against Man.* New York: Vintage Books, 1963.*

[5] Josephson, Eric, and Josephson, Mary, eds. *Man Alone.* New York: Dell Publishing Co., Inc., 1962.*

[6] Nisbet, Robert A. *Community and Power.* New York: Oxford University Press, 1953.*

[7] Rappaport, Roger. "Life on the Line." In *Labor in an Affluent Society.* Published as a pamphlet. Boston, Mass.: New England Free Press, 1968. Available from the New England Free Press, 791 Tremont St., Boston, Mass. 02118.

[8] Weaver, James. "The Student as Worker." In Gary R. Weaver and James H. Weaver, *The University and Revolution.* Englewood Cliffs, N.J.: Prentice-Hall, Inc., 1969.

*Available in paperback editions.

Racism 7

IN CHAPTER 2 EUGENE GENOVESE ARGUED that the ante-bellum North, a society based on the capitalist mode of production, could not coexist with the Old South, a society based on the slave mode of production.[1] However, although the outcome of the Civil War was an important triumph for the Northern industrial bourgeoisie, the destruction of the slave system and the extension of the capitalist mode of production into the South did not result in true freedom or equality for blacks. On the contrary, as the history of the more than one hundred years since 1865 demonstrates, capitalism has had no apparent difficulty coexisting with and perpetuating racism.

Racism can be defined as the "predication of decisions and policies on considerations of race for the purpose of subordinating a racial group and maintaining control over that group," or "the systematized oppression of one race by another."[2] Modern racism differs from the casual prejudices and ethnocentrism that Europeans held against Africans in the fifteenth and sixteenth centuries. It differs also from the slavery systems of ancient Greece and Rome, which were not based on racial differences. In the United States, racism has permeated every sphere of social life; the systematic oppression of blacks has cultural, psychological, sexual, and political as well as economic dimensions.

Racism can take two different forms: *individual racism*, the attitudes and practices of individual whites against blacks; and *institutional racism*, the normal functioning of institutions in ways that result, often without conscious or deliberate intent, in the subordination of blacks.

A substantial degree of both individual and institutional racism is evident in the United States. Blacks continue to face discrimination in employment, housing, education, and just about everywhere else, as several of the readings in this chapter describe. And racial stereotypes, cultural deprivation, police harassment, and so on still abound. However, in recent decades the overt individual form of racism has been superseded to some extent by the more subtle institutional form of racism as the principal means of subordinating blacks. For example, the situation of urban ghettoes is in large part a result of institutional racism; the natural functioning of urban markets in land, labor, and commodities automatically leads to the deterioration of black ghettoes within the rest of the urban economy. The urban ghetto is an internal, racial "colony," doomed just as are the poor capitalist nations of Asia, Africa, and Latin America to a state of underdevelopment because of its subordinate economic relationship to the dominant metropolis.[3]

The effects of racism in the United States include continued differentials in income, occupational status, infant mortality rates, and many other measures. For example, blacks continue to lag far behind whites in income. Data on the relative incomes of black males and white males (see Table 7–A) show that between 1945 and 1969 median black incomes have been fluctuating above and below an average level of 55 percent of white incomes. Black incomes rise relative to white incomes only during years of economic boom when labor shortages reduce black unemployment and open new employment areas for blacks. But the gains are all but eliminated during recessions; little permanent improvement in the *relative* income position of blacks has occurred since World War II. Table 7–A suggests that, even after accounting for inflation, the *absolute* black-

---

[1] See Genovese, Section 2.6, p. 72.

[2] These definitions are presented in Sections 7.1 and 7.3 below.

[3] For a detailed exposition of the debilitating effects of subordination to the metropolis in the international context, see Weisskopf, Section 10.4, p. 442.

TABLE 7–A   MEDIAN INCOME OF WHITE AND NONWHITE MALES

Year	Median Income*		W-N†	N/W
	White (1)	Nonwhite (2)	Gap (1)-(2)	Ratio (2) / (1)
1948	2510	1363	1147	.54
1949	2471	1196	1275	.48
1950	2709	1471	1238	.55
1951	3101	1708	1393	.55
1952	3255	1784	1471	.55
1953	3396	1870	1526	.55
1954	3359	1678	1681	.50
1955	3542	1868	1674	.53
1956	3827	2000	1827	.52
1957	3910	2075	1835	.53
1958	3976	1981	1995	.50
1959	4208	1977	2231	.47
1960	4297	2258	2039	.53
1961	4432	2292	2140	.52
1962	4660	2291	2369	.49
1963	4816	2507	2209	.52
1964	4936	2797	2139	.57
1965	5290	2847	2443	.54
1966	5592	3097	2495	.55
1967	5862	3448	2414	.59
1968	6267	3827	2440	.61
1969	6765	3992	2773	.59

SOURCES: *U.S. Bureau of the Census, *Current Population Reports—Consumer Income,* Series P-60, "Income of Families and Persons in the United States," annual issues; figures are in current dollars.

†The gap in incomes is in current dollars of the year indicated. Because the money income overstates the changes in real income due to inflation, the increase in the gap in real incomes is slightly overstated.

white income gap has more than doubled since 1947.

Furthermore, occupational statistics indicate that whites have maintained their relative advantage in occupational status over blacks since at least 1919. A comparison of U.S. census data from 1910 to 1960 showed that although the overall occupational distribution changed markedly during the fifty-year period, the relative concentration of black males in the lowest-paid occupations changed very little.[4] Noneconomic indices display the same pattern. For example, in 1966 the infant mortality rate was 20.6 per

1,000 white births compared to 38.8 per 1,000 nonwhite births.[5]

Despite these gloomy statistics, it has often been argued that racism is an aberration in the United States, a legacy from the past that must gradually disappear in a democratic, capitalist society. Proponents of this view argue as follows: the capitalistic drive to rationalize production and expand profits is itself a strong force against racial discrimination. Employers are profit-seekers, and in organizing their workforce they will be interested in a worker's productivity and potential contribution to profits and not in his

[4]Dale L. Hiestand, *Economic Growth and Employment Opportunities for Minorities* (New York: Columbia University Press, 1964), p. 53.

[5]U.S. Bureau of the Census, *Statistical Abstract of the United States: 1970* (Washington, D.C.: Government Printing Office, 1970), p. 55.

or her skin color. The pressures of economic competition from other firms can and will overcome the resistance of racist employers who persist in discriminating. Similarly, purchasers of goods and services will be interested only in the product's price and its quality and not in the race of the workers who produce it. Thus, market forces, by allocating labor to its most efficient use, are themselves a strong stimulus for ending discrimination. And if market forces do not operate with sufficient speed or effectiveness, the government can pass and implement antidiscrimination legislation, create job-training and compensatory education programs, provide aid for ghetto economic development, and so on for the purpose of hastening the eradication of racism. There has, in fact, been much governmental activity along these lines in recent decades.

Why then has racism proven so difficult to eradicate in the United States? We argue in this chapter that the conventional analysis in the above paragraph is inadequate. Racism is not an aberration; it has persisted in the United States precisely because the oppression of blacks is consistent with the logic of class divisions under capitalism and reinforces the interests of the capitalist class as a whole. By contributing to divisions and antagonisms among the population, thereby weakening hostility to the capitalist class, and by providing to whites a convenient scapegoat for social oppression that is generated by capitalism itself, racism plays an important role in *stabilizing* a capitalist society. Whatever its origins—and we should keep in mind the historical importance for Northern capitalism of the westward expansion against Indian opposition and the profits from black slavery—racism is likely to take firm root in a capitalist society. Racism is useful to capitalism; moreover, the hierarchical, materialistic, competitive, and individualistic environment of capitalism is not conducive to the elimination of racism. It is therefore unlikely that racism can be eradicated within the framework of a capitalist society.

.   .   .

7.1   *Institutional Racism and the Colonial Status of Blacks*

Many of us are accustomed to think of racism as consisting primarily of overt discriminatory attitudes and acts by individual whites against individual blacks. But as Stokely Carmichael and Charles Hamilton point out in the following reading, racism is also to a great extent subtly embedded in the normal operation of established social institutions. Often an institution's operating rules appear fair and unbiased on the surface, but have the effect of penalizing blacks anyway. Carmichael and Hamilton analyze such *institutional* racism in terms of a colonial model and examine the operation of black colonial status in its political, economic, and social dimensions.

What is racism? The word has represented daily reality to millions of black people for centuries, yet it is rarely defined—perhaps just because that reality has been such a commonplace. By "racism" we mean the predication of decisions and policies on considerations of race for the purpose of *subordinating* a racial group and maintaining control over that group. That has been the practice of this country toward the black man; we shall see why and how.

Racism is both overt and covert. It takes two, closely related forms: individual whites acting against individual blacks, and acts by the total white community against the black community. We call these individual racism and institutional racism. The first consists of overt acts by individuals, which cause death, injury or the violent destruction of property. This type can be recorded by television cameras; it can frequently be observed in the process of commission. The second type is less overt, far more subtle, less identifiable in terms of *specific* individuals committing the acts. But it is no less destructive of human life. The second type originates in the operation of established and respected forces in the society, and thus receives far less public condemnation than the first type.

When white terrorists bomb a black church and kill five black children, that is an act of individual racism, widely deplored by most segments of the society. But when in that same city—Birmingham, Alabama—five hundred black babies die each year because of the lack of proper food, shelter and medical facilities, and thousands more are destroyed and maimed physically, emotionally and intellectually because of conditions of poverty and discrimination in the black community, that is a function of institutional racism. When a black family moves into a home in a white neighborhood and is stoned, burned or routed out, they are victims of an overt act of individual racism which many people will condemn—at least

in words. But it is institutional racism that keeps black people locked in dilapidated slum tenements, subject to the daily prey of exploitative slumlords, merchants, loan sharks and discriminatory real estate agents. The society either pretends it does not know of this latter situation, or is in fact incapable of doing anything meaningful about it. We shall examine the reasons for this in a moment.

Institutional racism relies on the active and pervasive operation of anti-black attitudes and practices. A sense of superior group position prevails: whites are "better" than blacks; therefore blacks should be subordinated to whites. This is a racist attitude and it permeates the society, on both the individual and institutional level, covertly and overtly.

"Respectable" individuals can absolve themselves from individual blame: *they* would never plant a bomb in a church; *they* would never stone a black family. But they continue to support political officials and institutions that would and do perpetuate institutionally racist policies. Thus *acts* of overt, individual racism, may not typify the society, but institutional racism does—with the support of covert, individual *attitudes* of racism.

.   .   .

To put it another way, there is no "American dilemma" because black people in this country form a colony, and it is not in the interest of the colonial power to liberate them. Black people are legal citizens of the United States with, for the most part, the same *legal* rights as other citizens. Yet they stand as colonial subjects in relation to the white society. Thus institutional racism has another name: colonialism.

Obviously, the analogy is not perfect. One normally associates a colony with a land and people subjected to, and physically separated from, the "Mother Country." This is not always the case, however; in South Africa and Rhodesia, black and white inhabit the same land—with blacks subordinated to whites just as in the English, French, Italian, Portuguese and Spanish colonies. It is the objective relationship which counts, not rhetoric (such as constitutions *articulating* equal rights) or geography.

The analogy is not perfect in another respect. Under classic colonialism, the colony is a source of cheaply produced raw materials (usually agricultural or mineral) which the "Mother Country" then processes into finished goods and sells at high profit—sometimes back to the colony itself. The black communities of the United States do not export anything except human labor. But is the differentiation more than a technicality? Essentially, the African colony is selling its labor; the product itself does not belong to the "subjects" because the land is not theirs. At the same time, let us look at the black people of the South: cultivating cotton at $3.00 for a ten-hour day and from that buying cotton dresses (and food and other goods) from white manufacturers. Economists might wish to argue this point endlessly; the objective relationship stands. Black people in the United States have a colonial relationship to the larger society, a relationship characterized by institutional racism. That colonial status operates in three areas —political, economic, social—which we shall discuss one by one.

POLITICAL COLONIALISM

Colonial subjects have their political decisions made for them by the colonial masters, and those decisions are handed down directly or through a process of "indirect rule." Politically, decisions which affect black lives have always been made by white people—the "white power structure."

· · ·

The black community perceives the "white power structure" in very concrete terms. The man in the ghetto sees his white landlord come only to collect exorbitant rents and fail to make necessary repairs, while both know that the white-dominated city building inspection department will wink at violations or impose only slight fines. The man in the ghetto sees the white policeman on the corner brutally manhandle a black drunkard in a doorway, and at the same time accept a payoff from one of the agents of the white-controlled rackets. He sees the streets in the ghetto lined with uncollected garbage, and he knows that the powers which could send trucks in to collect that garbage are white. When they don't he knows the reason: the low political esteem in which the black community is held. He looks at the absence of a meaningful curriculum in the ghetto schools—for example, the history books that woefully overlook the historical achievements of black people—and he knows that the school board is controlled by whites.[1] He is not about to listen to intellectual discourses on the pluralistic and fragmented nature of political power. He is faced with a "white power structure" as monolithic as Europe's colonial offices have been to African and Asian colonies.

There is another aspect of colonial politics frequently found in colonial Africa and in the United States: the process of indirect rule . . . in other words, the white power structure rules the black community through local blacks who are responsive to the white leaders, the downtown, white machine, not to the black populace. These black politi-

[1] Studies have shown the heavy preponderance of business and professional men on school boards throughout the country. One survey showed that such people, although only 15 percent of the population, constituted 76 percent of school board members in a national sample. The percentage of laborers on the boards was only 3 percent. William C. Mitchell, *The American Polity: A Social and Cultural Interpretation* (Glencoe, Illinois: Free Press, 1962).

cians do not exercise effective power. They cannot be relied upon to make forceful demands in behalf of their black constituents, and they become no more than puppets. They put loyalty to a political party before loyalty to their constituents and thus nullify any bargaining power the black community might develop. Colonial politics causes the subject to muffle his voice while participating in the councils of the white power structure. The black man forfeits his opportunity to speak forcefully and clearly for his race, and he justifies this in terms of expediency. Thus, when one talks of a "Negro Establishment" in most places in this country, one is talking of an Establishment resting on a white power base, of handpicked blacks whom that base projects as showpieces out front. These black "leaders" are, then, only as powerful as their white kingmakers will permit them to be. This is no less true of the North than the South.

. . .

ECONOMIC COLONIALISM

The economic relationship of America's black communities to the large society also reflects their colonial status. The political power exercised over those communities goes hand in glove with the economic deprivation experienced by the black citizens.

Historically, colonies have existed for the sole purpose of enriching, in one form or another, the "colonizer"; the consequence is to maintain the economic dependency of the "colonized." All too frequently we hear of the missionary motive behind colonization: to "civilize," to "Christianize" the underdeveloped, backward peoples. But read these words of a French Colonial Secretary of State in 1923:

What is the use of painting the truth? At the start, colonization was not an act of civilization, nor was it a desire to civilize.

It was an act of force motivated by interests. An episode in the vital competition which, from man to man, from group to group, has gone on ever increasing; the people who set out to seize colonies in the distant lands were thinking primarily of themselves, and were working for their own profits, and conquering for their own power.[2]

One is immediately reminded of the bitter maxim voiced by many black Africans today: the missionaries came for our goods, not for our good. Indeed, the missionaries turned the Africans' eyes toward heaven, and then robbed them blind in the process. The colonies were sources from which raw materials were taken and markets to which finished products were sold. Manufacture and production were prohibited if this meant—as it usually did—competition with the "mother country." Rich in natural resources, Africa did not reap the benefit of these resources herself. In the Gold Coast (now Ghana), where the cocoa crop was the largest in the world, there was not one chocolate factory.

This same economic status has been perpetrated on the black community in this country. Exploiters come into the ghetto from outside, bleed it dry, and leave it economically dependent on the larger society. As with the missionaries, these exploiters frequently come as the "friend of the Negro," pretending to offer worthwhile goods and services, when their basic motivation is personal profit and their basic impact is the maintenance of racism. Many of the social welfare agencies—public and private—frequently pretend to offer "uplift" services; in reality, they end up creating a system which dehumanizes the individual and perpetuates his dependency. Conscious or unconscious, the paternalistic attitude of many of these

[2]Albert Sarraut, French Colonial Secretary of State, speaking at the Ecole Coloniale in Paris. As quoted in Kwame Nkrumah's *Africa Must Unite* (London: Heinemann Educational Books, Ltd., 1963), p. 40.

agencies is no different from that of many missionaries going into Africa.

.   .   .

Again, as in the African colonies, the black community is sapped senseless of what economic resources it does have. Through the exploitative system of credit, people pay "a dollar down, a dollar a week" literally for years. Interest rates are astronomical, and the merchandise—of relatively poor quality in the first place—is long since worn out before the final payment. Professor David Caplovitz of Columbia University has commented in his book, *The Poor Pay More*, "The high markup on low-quality goods is thus a major device used by merchants to protect themselves against the risks of their credit business" (p. 18). Many of the ghetto citizens, because of unsteady employment and low incomes, cannot obtain credit from more legitimate businesses; thus they must do without important items or end up being exploited. They are lured into the stores by attractive advertising displays hawking, for example, three rooms of furniture for "only $199." Once inside, the unsuspecting customer is persuaded to buy lesser furniture at a more expensive price, or he is told that the advertised items are temporarily out of stock and is shown other goods. More frequently than not, of course, all the items are overpriced.

The exploitative merchant relies as much on threats as he does on legal action to guarantee payment. Garnishment of wages is not particularly beneficial to the merchant—although certainly used—because the employer will frequently fire an employee rather than be subjected to the bother of extra bookkeeping. And once the buyer is fired, all payments stop. But the merchant can hold the threat of garnishment over the customer's head. Repossession is another threat; again, not particularly beneficial to the merchant. He knows the poor quality of his goods in the first place, and there is little

resale value in such goods which have probably already received substantial use. In addition, both the methods of garnishment and repossession give the merchant a bad business image in the community. It is better business practice to raise the prices 200 to 300 percent, get what he can—dogging the customer for that weekly payment—and still realize a sizable profit. At the same time the merchant can protect his image as a "considerate, understanding fellow."

The merchant has special ways of victimizing public welfare recipients. They are not supposed to buy on credit; installment payments are not provided for in the budget. Thus a merchant can threaten to tell the caseworker if a recipient who isn't meeting his payments does not "come in and put down something, if only a couple of dollars." Another example: in November, 1966, M.E.N.D. (Massive Economic Neighborhood Development), a community action, antipoverty agency in New York City, documented the fact that some merchants raise their prices on the days that welfare recipients receive their checks. Canned goods and other items were priced as much as ten cents more on those specific days.

Out of a substandard income, the black man pays exorbitant prices for cheap goods; he must then pay more for his housing than whites. Whitney Young, Jr. of the Urban League writes in his book, *To Be Equal*: "most of Chicago's 838,000 Negroes live in a ghetto and pay about $20 more per month for housing than their white counterparts in the city" (pp. 144–45). Black people also have a much more difficult time securing a mortgage. They must resort to real estate speculators who charge interest rates up to 10 percent, whereas a FHA loan would carry only a 6 percent interest rate. As for loans to go into business, we find the same pattern as among Africans, who were prohibited or discouraged from starting commercial enterprises. "The white power structure," says Dr. Clark in *Dark Ghetto*, "has collaborated in the economic serfdom of Negroes by its reluctance to give loans and insurance to Negro business" (pp. 27–28). The Small Business Administration, for example, in the ten-year period prior to 1964, made only *seven* loans to black people.

This is why the society does nothing meaningful about institutional racism: because the black community has been the creation of, and dominated by, a combination of oppressive forces and special interests in the white community. The groups which have access to the necessary resources and the ability to effect change benefit politically and economically from the continued subordinate status of the black community. This is not to say that every single white American consciously oppresses black people. He does not need to. Institutional racism has been maintained deliberately by the power structure and through indifference, inertia and lack of courage on the part of white masses as well as petty officials. Whenever black demands for change become loud and strong, indifference is replaced by active opposition based on fear and self-interest. The line between purposeful suppression and indifference blurs. One way or another, most whites participate in economic colonialism.

Indeed, the colonial white power structure has been a most formidable foe. It has perpetuated a vicious circle—the poverty cycle—in which the black communities are denied good jobs, and therefore stuck with a low income and therefore unable to obtain a good education with which to obtain good jobs. They cannot qualify for credit at most respectable places; they then resort to unethical merchants who take advantage of them by charging higher prices for inferior goods. They end up having less funds to buy in bulk, thus unable to reduce overall costs. They remain trapped.

In the face of such realities, it becomes ludicrous to condemn black people for "not showing more initiative." Black people are not in a depressed condition because of some defect in their character. The colonial power structure clamped a boot of oppression on the neck of the black people and then, ironically, said "they are not ready for freedom." Left solely to the good will of the oppressor, the oppressed would never be ready.

SOCIAL COLONIALISM

The operation of political and economic colonialism in this country has had social repercussions which date back to slavery but did not by any means end with the Emancipation Proclamation. Perhaps the most vicious result of colonialism—in Africa and this country—was that it purposefully, maliciously and with reckless abandon relegated the black man to a subordinated, inferior status in the society. The individual was considered and treated as a lowly animal, not to be housed properly, or given adequate medical services, and by no means a decent education.

. . .

The fact of slavery had to have profound impact on the subsequent attitudes of the larger society toward the black man. The fact of slavery helped to fix the sense of superior group position. Chief Justice Taney, in the Dred Scott decision of 1857, stated ". . . that they (black people) had no rights which the white man was bound to respect; and that the negro might justly and lawfully be reduced to slavery for his benefit." The emancipation of the slaves by legal act could certainly not erase such notions from the minds of racists. They believed in their superior status, not in paper documents. And that belief has persisted. When some people compare the black American to "other immigrant" groups in this country, they overlook the fact that slavery was peculiar to the blacks. No other minority group in this country was ever treated as legal property.

. . .

The social and psychological effects on black people of all their degrading experiences are . . . very clear. From the time black people were introduced into this country, their condition has fostered human indignity and the denial of respect. Born into this society today, black people begin to doubt themselves, their worth as human beings. Self-respect becomes almost impossible. Kenneth Clark describes the process in *Dark Ghetto*:

> *Human beings who are forced to live under ghetto conditions and whose daily experience tells them that almost nowhere in society are they respected and granted the ordinary dignity and courtesy accorded to others will, as a matter of course, begin to doubt their own worth. Since every human being depends upon his cumulative experiences with others for clues as to how he should view and value himself, children who are consistently rejected understandably begin to question and doubt whether they, their family, and their group really deserve no more respect from the larger society than they receive. These doubts become the seeds of a pernicious self- and group-hatred, the Negro's complex and debilitating prejudice against himself.*
>
> *The preoccupation of many Negroes with hair straighteners, skin bleachers, and the like illustrates this tragic aspect of American racial prejudice—Negroes have come to believe in their own inferiority* [pp. 63–64].

There was the same result in Africa. And some European colonial powers—notably France and Portugal—provided the black man "a way out" of the degrading status: to become "white," or assimilated. France pursued a colonial policy aimed at producing a black French elite class, a group exposed and acculturated to French "civilization."

In a manner similar to that of the colonial powers in Africa, American society indicates avenues of escape from the ghetto for those individuals who adapt to the "mainstream." This adaptation means to disassociate oneself from the black race, its culture, community and heritage, and become immersed (dispersed is another term) in the white world. What actually happens, as Professor E. Franklin Frazier pointed out in his book, *Black Bourgeoisie*, is that the black person ceases to identify himself with black people yet is obviously unable to assimilate with whites. He becomes a "marginal man," living on the fringes of both societies in a world largely of "make believe." This black person is urged to adopt American middle-class standards and values. As with the black African who had to become a "Frenchman" in order to be accepted, so to be an American, the black man must strive to become "white." To the extent that he does, he is considered "well adjusted"—one who has "risen above the race question." These people are frequently held up by the white Establishment as living examples of the progress being made by the society in solving the race problem. Suffice it to say that precisely because they are required to denounce—overtly or covertly—their black race, *they are reinforcing racism in this country*.

In the United States, as in Africa, their "adaptation" operated to deprive the black community of its potential skills and brain power. All too frequently, these "integrated" people are used to blunt the true feelings and goals of the black masses. They are picked as "Negro leaders," and the white power structure proceeds to talk to and deal only with them. Needless to say, no fruitful, meaningful dialogue can take place under such circumstances. Those handpicked "leaders" have no viable constituency for which they can speak and act. All this is a classic formula of colonial cooptation.

At all times, then, the social effects of colonialism are to degrade and to dehumanize the subjected black man. White America's School of Slavery and Segregation, like the School of Colonialism, has taught the subject to hate himself and to deny his own humanity. The white society maintains an attitude of superiority and the black community has too often succumbed to it, thereby permitting the whites to believe in the correctness of their position. Racist assumptions of white superiority have been so deeply engrained into the fiber of the society that they infuse the entire functioning of the national subconscious. They are taken for granted and frequently not even recognized. . . .

The time is long overdue for the black community to redefine itself, set forth new values and goals, and organize around them.

. . .

7.2 *Institutional Racism in Urban Labor Markets*

The labor market is one of the most important institutions in which racism is structurally embedded. In the next reading, based on a detailed study of Chicago, Harold Baron and Bennett Hymer describe how institutional racism in the labor market operates to keep blacks at the bottom of the economic hierarchy. The division of the labor market along racial lines, supplemented by *de facto* segregation in housing and education and reinforced by both the ideology of racism and black political powerlessness, perpetuate the second-class economic status of blacks in cities.

> Source: The following is excerpted from "The Negro Worker in the Chicago Labor Market" by HAROLD BARON and BENNETT HYMER. From *The Negro and the American Labor Movement*, edited by Julius Jacobsen. Copyright © 1968 by Julius Jacobsen. Reprinted by permission of Doubleday & Company, Inc.

. . .

Modern-day racial institutions in Northern labor markets were forged in the early twenties when Negroes entered the labor force in large numbers. The ideology developed to defend contemporary Northern racial institutions was expressed in psychological and individualistic terms, in contrast to the Southern experience where racism was based upon an entire way of life. Racial attitudes of Northern whites were attributed to factors like prejudice, stereotypes, and discrimination. These attitudes were rationalized by relating the economic plight of the Negro to his specific handicaps and circumstances— lack of education and training, ill-health, weak motivation, and the instability of Negro family life. The gaps in income, occupation, and education, resulting from discrimination and segregation, were interpreted as being the factors that produced the discrimination and segregation.

The emerging pattern of Northern racial differences that was becoming institutionalized was explained by social scientists in terms of the individual preferences of whites to exclude Negroes and the failure of the Negro worker to bring certain acquired attributes to the labor market—education, incentive, skills, and middle-class habits and appearances. The North refused to admit that its own racial practices, like those in the South, formed a well-institutionalized socioeconomic structure of subjugation. Negroes and whites were seen only as an aggregate of separate entities relating to each other within a *laissez-faire* market.

The racial folklore of the Negro worker's experience in the Northern labor market can now be replaced with a more sophisticated analysis. By utilizing recent findings in the study of Northern race relations and urban labor markets, the disparities between white and Negro workers can be related to institutional factors within the large urban labor market—the existence of barriers that divide the labor market into distinct compartments based upon race.

For expository purposes a blueprint of the typical Northern labor market will be drawn. Although the main point of reference is Chicago, the model is highly applicable to other urban labor markets having a sizable Negro labor force. Basically, the blueprint consists of three generalizations describing the way in which the Chicago labor market generates differences based upon race. These generalizations are:

1. The labor market is divided into two racial components—a sector for the deployment of white labor and a sector for the deployment of Negro labor. Each sector has its own separate institutions and mechanisms for the recruitment, training, and allocation of jobs and workers. Firms are cognizant of this division and have different perceptions of the two labor forces when they shop for labor.

2. The Negro labor force has served as a pool of surplus labor used to fill shortages of white labor that occur during war years or periods of rapid economic growth. A large segment of the Negro labor force has been frozen into positions that are regarded as traditionally Negro jobs. These jobs are usually marginal and low paying; they require little skill or formal training; they often involve physical hazards; they frequently offer only seasonal or cyclical employment; and they are frequently in stagnant or declining industries.

3. Northern *de facto* segregation, in general, is maintained by a complex of interrelated and mutually supportive institutions whose combined effect is greater than the sum of the effects of each institution considered singularly. The racial distinctions and differentiations created in any one institutional area operate as effective barriers supporting the segregation and status differentiation that occurs in other institutions. The

division of the labor market into a Negro sector and a white sector is made more effective by the existence of the barriers in non-labor-market institutions. These barriers feed back to limit the Negro worker's access in many areas of the labor market.

RACIAL DUALISM IN THE URBAN LABOR MARKET

The racially dual labor markets found in Northern cities have their origins in the earlier system of Southern slavery and rural peonage. However, if the Negro's subordinate position in the North were merely a historical atavism from his Southern past, it would be expected that race would lose its significance as a social and economic category with the passage of time. Instead, we find that the Negro's second-class status has been effectively institutionalized in the Northern city—far removed from Southern rural conditions.

The marked and systematic disparities that exist between whites and Negroes in regard to income, employment, occupation, and labor-force participation offer *prima facie* evidence that a dual racial labor market exists. The two distinct and enduring patterns of employment characteristics that have been described cannot be explained in terms of a single homogeneous market. The description of these disparities, however, documents the dualism at only a general level of observation.

In more specific terms, a racially dual labor market means that there exists a primary metropolitan labor market in which firms recruit white workers and in which white workers look for jobs; side by side with the major market, there exists a smaller labor sector in which Negroes are recruited and in which Negroes look for employment.[1] For

---

[1] In the Chicago area Negro workers comprise one-seventh of the total labor force.

each sector there are separate demand and supply forces determining the allocation of jobs to workers and workers to jobs. Over time, this dualism is characterized by a transfer of jobs from the white sector to the Negro sector as the economy develops and as the Negro labor force expands in absolute and relative numbers.[2]

To understand the perpetuation of the Negro's second-class status, it is necessary to examine the mechanisms by which the labor market and in a broader sense the general socioeconomic structure have distributed jobs between whites and Negroes. The conception of a division of the labor market along racial lines in a city such as Chicago is an important factor in understanding how racial differences have been systematically maintained.

The racial divisions in the Chicago labor market are visible in many dimensions—by industry, by occupation, by geographic area, by firms, and by departments within firms. In general, Negro workers tend to be hired by certain industries and by particular firms within those industries. Some firms have absolute racial barriers in hiring, with Negroes being completely excluded. Within all industries and even in government employment there is unmistakable evidence of occupational ceilings for Negroes. Within single establishments that hire both white and nonwhites, Negro workers are usually placed in particular job classifications and production units. A good rule of thumb is that the lower the pay or the more disagreeable and dirty the job, the greater the chance of finding a high proportion of Negroes.

Racial concentration by industry in Chicago is shown in the fact that 20 percent of employed Negro males work for federal,

[2]It should be noted that the generalization concerning the dual labor market is made at a high level of abstraction and that there are obvious exceptions at the level of particulars. The need here is to comprehend the process, and comprehension requires some degree of abstraction.

state, or local government as compared to only 6 percent of employed white males. Six percent of Negro males are in the primary metal industry as compared to 3 percent of white males. At the other extreme, 1.5 percent of white males are in the banking and finance industry as compared to only 0.2 percent of Negro males. The existence of limited entry for Negroes can also be found in manufacturing—for example, 6 percent of all white men are employed in the nonelectrical machinery industry while only 2 percent of all Negro men are in that field.

While an examination of broad industrial classifications indicates certain tendencies toward racial dualism in the labor market, the pattern becomes much more distinct when individual firms and occupations within an industry are considered. A recent survey based on a sample of firms from the membership of the Chicago Association of Commerce and Industry makes this point strongly by showing the percentage of firms in the Chicago labor market that do not employ nonwhites. Seven out of every ten small firms, one out of every five medium-sized firms, and one out of every thirteen large firms do not hire nonwhites. Construction, transportation and utilities, and finance and insurance are the *most segregated* industries. Those small firms that employ any nonwhites tend to have labor forces with a very high proportion of nonwhite workers. While nonwhites account for 10.4 percent of total employment by small firms, they are confined to 30.9 percent of the universe of small firms.

Employment of some nonwhites by a firm does not necessarily mean that it has an integrated work force. Within a firm, racial segregation can take place on the basis of production units, branch operation, or occupational classification. Table 7–B offers conclusive proof of this point. For each major occupation it shows the percentage of employees working for firms that have no nonwhites in that particular occupational

TABLE 7–B PROPORTION OF EMPLOYMENT
SEGREGATION BY OCCUPATIONAL GROUPS
AND COLOR

Occupation	Percent Segregated (nonwhite)
Professional	43.3%
Managers	75.1
Clerical Workers	27.3
Sales Workers	54.7
Craftsmen, Skilled	66.2
Semiskilled	11.5
Service Workers	8.0
Laborers	11.0

SOURCE: Chicago Association of Commerce and Industry, *Manpower Survey, 1964*, p. 16, Table 11.

classification. It stands out clearly that within individual firms, four occupations—professional, managerial, sales, and craftsmen—tend to exclude nonwhites. In the case of professionals and managers Table 7–B understates the segregation of Negroes, as a high proportion of the nonwhites in these classifications are Orientals.

In some firms that are integrated by occupation, departments within that occupational group may be divided along racial lines. Negroes are especially segregated into hot, dirty departments like foundries and heat-treating shops. Sometimes within the same operation there will be occupational segregation in which the laborers are Negro and the machine operators are white, or in other cases the machine operators are Negro and the higher paid mechanics are white. A plant might have an integrated semiskilled work force, but it will almost invariably have segregation of its craftsmen and lower-level supervisory employees, even though most of these jobs are filled by within plant recruitment. In general, the lower the position on the occupational scale, the greater the chance that there will be integration for a particular job classification.
. . .

In response to this segregated job pattern in the total labor market, Negroes and whites have developed separate patterns of job seeking. Whites do not seek employment with firms that they identify as being totally in the Negro labor market, nor do they seek jobs that they identify as being Negro jobs. In firms which have integration among their unskilled or semiskilled workers, it is the whites in these categories who operate with the expectation that they will be chosen for on-the-job training or considered for promotion.

Negroes, on the other hand, shop in what they consider to be the Negro labor market. Firms are identified as employing Negroes, e.g. in Chicago certain mail-order houses and the Post Office; or jobs, such as laborer or foundry work, are identified as being Negro jobs. The Negro job seeker expects automatic rebuff outside the identified Negro labor market, and he accordingly limits his shopping to the places where he feels that he has some chance of success. Not surprisingly, most jobs in the white labor market are never sought by Negroes.

These segregated job-seeking patterns are reinforced by several practices. Many firms fill vacancies by word of mouth to friends and relatives of employees, thus recruiting from the same racial groups as their present labor force. Labor-market intermediaries—the Illinois State Employment Service, some five hundred private employment agencies, and vocational counselors—tend to operate on the basis of the dual labor market. Negro youngsters in school are encouraged to seek careers in occupations that are traditionally Negro jobs. Nonwhite job seekers are counseled to apply for positions within the Negro labor market. Both public and private employment services, in spite of legal prohibitions, tend to respect the racial lines of the labor market in their referrals.

SURPLUS LABOR SUPPLY

The concept of dualism is a convenient way of describing a major feature of Northern race relations in the area of employment—the segregation and division of the white and Negro labor forces. To understand further the operation of urban labor markets where there is a sizable Negro labor force, it is necessary to describe the processes of how Negroes advance occupationally and how certain jobs are either kept from or allocated only to the Negro labor force.

Our second generalization, i.e. the surplus labor pool, shows that the Negro labor force has served as an excess supply of labor utilized for jobs that whites have recently vacated, or for jobs where there are shortages of white labor, or for jobs that have become traditionally Negro jobs. According to this generalization, the Negro labor force can be broken down into three distinct groups:

1. A Negro *service sector* selling goods and services to the Negro community;
2. A *standard sector* regularly employed by major white-controlled firms or institutions, including government;
3. A *surplus labor factor* that is without work or tenuously employed in low-paying, marginal jobs.

By the Negro service sector we refer to Negroes self-employed or employed by firms, either white or Negro owned, which service the Negro community. In the case of professional services, such as medical or legal, the persons within this sector are usually well paid. At the other extreme are small neighborhood retail establishments providing only a subsistence income to their proprietors. In general, the size of the service sector is dependent upon the amount of money that Negroes have available for consumption expenditures.

By the standard sector of the Negro labor force we refer to workers regularly employed in firms and institutions that supply goods and services to the total economy. Annual earnings in this sector are well above the subsistence level and in many cases are comparable to those for whites. Jobs in this sector are either with major employers or with firms that are competitive with the major companies. Within this standard sector Negro workers are often segregated by firm and within firms by job classification or production unit. The size of this sector is generally determined by the extent to which past or present labor shortages have allowed the entry of Negro workers into areas where previously just whites were hired. Currently, approximately half the Negro labor force is in this category.

The surplus sector of the Negro labor jobs consists of workers occupied in traditional Negro jobs outside the standard sector and workers who are unemployed or are out of labor force, or are in marginal jobs. Workers in the surplus sector who have jobs occupy positions that are at the very bottom of the occupational ladder. These jobs are low paying, involve dirty and unsafe work, are often of short duration, and have little advancement potential. Many of these jobs are assigned to the Negro labor force only as the white labor force advances into higher occupations. Traditional Negro jobs like bootblacks, car washers, busboys, washroom attendants, porters, and servants are positions that through custom have gradually formed an area of employment exclusively for Negroes, or other minority groups, regardless of employment conditions elsewhere in the labor market.

. . .

DE FACTO BARRIERS

Racial dualism in the labor market is only one of the several major forms in which the system of Northern segregation perpetuates the second-class status of Negro workers in the Northern city. Housing segregation and school segregation restrict them in the acquisition of both skills and jobs. At the same time, the ideology of racism and the lack of Negro political power reinforce these major institutional patterns. Within the labor market these practices together with employment discrimination act as the barriers that produce and maintain the dualism.

The overall effect of Northern racial institutions—housing segregation, school segregation, employment discrimination—operating concurrently is not confined just to the labor market. There is an overriding system of race relation characterized by the social and economic subjugation of the Negro via the whole constellation of institutions. In examining the components of this system we find a number of similarities. Discrimination and segregation in the labor market operates in much the same way as residential segregation and de facto school segregation. In each case there are no modern laws either regulating or maintaining the practice, yet the institutions operate almost as though they were ordained by a body of statute. Second, none of these particular racial practices could persist by itself if there were not an array of reinforcing social, economic, psychological, and geographical elements supporting it. The various types of de facto segregation in housing, education, and employment each make the other types that much more effective and absolute. Consequently a reduction in one barrier—say, employment discrimination—will have only a limited effect unless the other institutions also change. Third, each of these racial barriers considered by itself has fuzzy edges and exceptions. However, when they are examined as a group, they produce an overall pattern of sharp racial differences and little interracial contact.

The total network of de facto segregation in Chicago is so pervasive that the second-class status of Negro workers is passed on from generation to generation. Urban segregation in the Northern city cannot be explained merely in terms of the problems of rural Southern migrants learning to cope with city life—this is only one of many factors.

The system of de facto segregation breeds its own children within its confines and keeps many at the lowest possible level of income. For example, in 1960, 25 percent of the Negro mothers on ADC[3] Public Assistance had been born in Chicago—Northern-born women had almost as high a representation on the welfare roles as did women born in the South.

EMPLOYMENT DISCRIMINATION

Firms seeking to discriminate can exclude Negroes in a number of different ways. They can directly turn down Negroes because of race, or screen them out by criteria that appear to be color-blind. Certain job requirements—residence near the job, a stable work record, a high school diploma, and no arrest—will tend to exclude a greater proportion of Negroes than of white applicants. Some of these criteria serve as cutoff points and job-rationing devices, rather than actually being related to job performance.

Individual decision makers involved in the recruitment and hiring process—personnel men and foremen—will exert their own conscious or unconscious preferences by applying ambiguous and discriminatory hiring criteria—looks, dress, speech patterns—rigidly for Negroes and loosely for whites. Many of the tests used by firms to select workers will contain cultural biases that handicap applicants from low-income nonmiddle-class homes. Finally, a firm may discriminate by shopping only in the white labor market, not advertising in Negro newspapers or informing Negro placement agencies of vacancies.

Employment discrimination is seldom an all or nothing proposition (as we have noted in our section dealing with dualism). In

[3]Greenleigh Associates, *Facts, Fallacies and Future: A Study of the Aid-to-Dependent Children Program of Cook County, Illinois* (New York: Greenleigh Associates, 1960), p. 9.

practice there is a wide range of hiring policies that may be in operation. Although some firms completely exclude Negroes, most big firms will recruit Negro workers for certain occupations or for certain departments and certain job classifications, while still excluding them from others. Often firms that hire Negroes establish job ceilings through on-the-job discrimination in promotion. In general, the hiring and promotion policies of most firms depend upon their immediate manpower requirements and the extent to which the government and civil rights groups are exerting pressure.

An individual firm may discriminate from the irrational motive of prejudice. In other cases firms may discriminate to placate customers or employees. The discrimination may be secondary, as in cases where union membership is a requirement for employment and the unions exclude Negroes from membership. A firm may also discriminate unintentionally because it is well within the area regarded by Negro job seekers as being part of the white labor market. Some firms may also use racial divisions as a means of weakening unions in organizing and in collective-bargaining negotiations.

In the past some firms may have been able to benefit from the dual labor market by paying Negro workers less than whites for similar work. This point is indirectly suggested by a national study which showed that in 1959 there was a 13 percent difference in hourly earnings between Negroes and whites having the same individual attributes.[4]

Employment discrimination is not totally regulated by the employers. For certain occupations trade unions have an important voice in hiring procedures. In the skilled trades, especially those with apprenticeships, unions—either solely or in joint councils with employers—determine who can enter

[4]James M. Morgan et al., *Income and Welfare in the United States* (New York: McGraw-Hill, 1963), p. 56.

the craft. The result has been the widespread exclusion of Negroes from these skilled jobs. After four years of strong criticism by civil rights groups and governmental bodies the Washburne Trade School, which provides the training for most of the apprenticeship opportunities in the Chicago area, has only reached the stage where 2 percent of its enrollment is Negro.

Even when Negroes have managed to enter the building trades, they have frequently been shunted into Jim Crow locals. These segregated locals and discrimination in hiring-hall procedures in the integrated locals serve as a rationing device in passing out the jobs. Negro bricklayers have difficulty finding employment except in the peak season; in the slack season the available work is shared among the white bricklayers and the Negroes are excluded. In other cases, such as the painters, Negroes are generally confined to working in the ghetto areas while whites can work anywhere.

The industrial-type unions, on balance, have had a positive influence in breaking down racial discrimination. This influence has not been of particular importance in the initial hiring procedure. It has been felt primarily through the operation and the strict enforcement of seniority provisions. Seniority rules have given Negro workers job security and greater access to promotion to better paying jobs that are included in the bargaining unit. Nevertheless, even in industrial union shops Negroes are still grossly underrepresented in the higher paying skilled jobs.

HOUSING SEGREGATION

The persistence of housing segregation in Chicago has recently been documented in the Chicago Urban League's *Map of Negro Areas of Residence: 1950, 1960 and 1964*. The map shows that the large Negro ghettos on the South and West Side are expanding in accordance with the long-established Chicago pattern of segregated housing on a block-by-block basis. Residential segregation in Chicago is not on the decline, despite the changes in attitudes of whites concerning the acceptability of integrated housing and despite changes in public and private policies. Professor Karl Taeuber of the University of Wisconsin has demonstrated that the intensity of residential segregation actually increased in Chicago between 1950 and 1960.[5] Housing segregation has resulted from the practices and policies of members of the Chicago real estate industry, the Chicago Board of Education's adherence to a narrow type of neighborhood school policy, and the influence of the ideology of racism on individuals.

The effect of housing segregation is to confine the Negro labor force to certain geographical areas of the labor market. The access of Negro workers to many jobs is limited as they can seek employment only within reasonable traveling distances. Even when workers are willing to travel long distances, proximity to the job is often used as a hiring criterion.

Most new jobs in the Chicago labor market are located in areas remote from the Negro ghetto and generally out of reach for Negro workers. Since 1957 there has been a continual movement of plants and offices away from the inner city near the ghetto to the outlying, lily-white areas of the metropolitan region. Between 1957 and 1963 the number of jobs near the Negro ghetto declined by almost 93,000 while the number of jobs in outlying and suburban areas increased by 72,000—generally in the northwestern suburbs farthest away from any sizable Negro population. The residential remoteness of Negroes from new jobs in growing industries reinforces the pattern of hiring Negroes in declining industries.

[5]Karl and Alma E. Taeuber, *Negroes in Cities* (Chicago: Aldine, 1965).

SCHOOL SEGREGATION

Racial segregation in Chicago schools creates extreme differentials between whites and Negroes in the skills and training which they bring to the labor market. The system of segregation is highly efficient—in 1964, 85.6 percent of all Negro pupils were in Negro-segregated schools (90 percent or more Negro) and 78 percent of all white pupils were in white-segregated schools (90 percent or more white). The segregation is more extreme at the grade school level than at the high school level. During the school year 1964–65 there was a decline both in the number of integrated schools and in the number of pupils attending them.

Chicago's Negro schools are definitely of inferior quality. Less money is spent per pupil in them; they have more pupils per classroom and a higher concentration of inexperienced teachers. It is more often the rule than the exception that substitute teachers are not provided in Negro schools when the regular teachers are absent. In economic terms the segregated school system has served as a device for rationing insufficient educational resources to whites on a preferred basis.

The school system has low expectations for Negro pupils, and it graduates them with far less demanding standards. The Negro child tends to incorporate within himself the low estimate that the educational establishment has of Negroes. Accordingly, the segregated school system tends to dampen his motivation and to instill low career expectations in him. Test scores show that formal skills imparted to the Negro child are drastically lower than those given the white child.

The effect of inferior segregated education on the Negro student is obvious. He is less likely to obtain a high school diploma, less likely to score well on a placement test, and less prepared to acquire further skills on the job. The situation was recently summed up in a quip by Professor Kenneth Clark, the distinguished social psychologist: "Personnel managers need no longer exercise prejudicial decisions in job placement; the educational system in Chicago screens Negroes for them."

. . .

CONCLUSION

Segregation in the Northern labor market has been as efficient a mechanism for subjugating Negroes to second-class status as segregation in housing and education. In Chicago the process of allocating jobs to white workers is so effectively separated from the process of allocating jobs to Negro workers that year after year the differentials between white and Negro workers are maintained. At the same time, a large segment of the Negro labor force is relegated to the role of an urban peasantry destined to live off welfare payments and white paternalism. The Negro labor force, unlike those of other large ethnic groups, has not been allowed to assimilate into the metropolitan labor market. One hundred years after emancipation and forty-five years after urbanization, Negroes in Chicago are still systematically restricted in both the skills they may acquire and the extent to which they can utilize any given level of skills.

Racial dualism in the urban labor market is a structural phenomenon. While this does not necessarily mean that the social and economic order depends on segregation, it does tell us that our basic social and economic institutions have to be revamped in order to achieve equality. A dual structure based upon race is not merely a slight deviation from some acceptable norm as to how the labor market should function, but an essential feature of urban labor markets and American race relations.

. . .

7.3 The Rise of Capitalism and the Rise of Racism

The previous two readings have described a number of facets of the operation of racism in the contemporary United States. We turn next to examine the historical development of racism in the United States and its relationship to the capitalist mode of production.

Numerous instances of color prejudice and ethnocentricity can be found in the histories of pre-capitalist societies, for example, in Ancient Egypt. Why, then, do we suggest that there is an historical link between racism and capitalism? In the following reading, James and Grace Boggs associate the development of *systematic* oppression of one race by another with the rise of capitalism. The enslavement of Africans played a crucial role in the early accumulation of capital; after slavery became entrenched, casual racial prejudices were transformed into a systematized and codified ideology and practice of racial subordination. Moreover, the continued development of capitalism has been and still is accelerated by the systematic underdevelopment of the black community. The origins of racism are thus related to the development of the capitalist mode of production itself.

Source: The following is excerpted from Chapter 12 of *Racism and the Class Struggle* by JAMES and GRACE BOGGS. Copyright © 1970 by James Boggs. Reprinted by permission of Monthly Review Press.

. . .

The first thing we have to understand is that racism is not a "mental quirk" or a "psychological flaw" on an individual's part.[1] Racism is the systematized oppression by one race of another. In other words, the various forms of oppression within every sphere of social relations—economic exploitation, military subjugation, political subordination, cultural devaluation, psychological violation, sexual degradation, verbal abuse, etc.—together make up a whole of interacting and developing processes which operate so normally and naturally and are so much a part of the existing institutions of the society that the individuals involved are barely conscious of their operation. As Fanon says, "The racist in a culture with racism is therefore normal."

This kind of systematic oppression of one race by another was unknown to mankind in the thousands of years of recorded history before the emergence of capitalism four hundred years ago—although racial prejudice was not unknown. For example, some Chinese in the third century B.C. considered yellow-haired, green-eyed people in a distant province barbarians. In Ancient Egypt the ruling group, which at different times was red or yellow or black or white, usually regarded the others as inferior.

Slave oppression had also existed in earlier times, but this was usually on the basis of military conquest and the conquerors—the ancient Greeks and Romans— did not develop a theory of racial superiority to rationalize their right to exploit their slaves.

Just as mankind, prior to the rise of capitalism, had not previously experienced an economic system which naturally and normally pursues the expansion of material productive forces at the expense of human forces, so it had never known a society which

[1] See Frantz Fanon, "Racism and Culture," in *Toward the African Revolution* (New York and London: Monthly Review Press, 1967).

naturally and normally pursues the systematic exploitation and dehumanization of one race of people by another. An organic link between capitalism and racism is therefore certainly suggested.

The parallel between the rise of capitalism and the rise of racism has been traced by a number of scholars. The Portuguese, who were the first Europeans to come into contact with Africans at the end of the fifteenth and beginning of the sixteenth centuries, treated them as natural friends and allies. They found African customs strange and exotic but also found much to admire in their social and political organization, craftsmanship, architecture, and so on. At this point the chief technological advantages enjoyed by the Europeans were their navigation skills and firepower (both, by the way, originally learned from the Chinese). In the next four centuries these two advantages would be used to plunder four continents of their wealth in minerals and people and thereby to increase the technological superiority of Europeans by leaps and bounds.

Africa was turned into a hunting ground for slaves to work the land of the West Indies and the Southern colonies that had been stolen from the Indians. As the slave trade expanded, its enormous profits concentrated capital in Europe and America for the expansion of commerce, industry, and invention, while in Africa the social fabric was torn apart. In the Americas the blood and sweat of African slaves produced the sugar, tobacco, and later cotton to feed the refineries, distilleries, and textile mills, first of Western Europe and then of the Northern United States.

The more instrumental the slave trade in destroying African culture, the more those involved directly and indirectly in the slave traffic tried to convince themselves and others that there had never been any African culture in the first place. The more brutal the methods needed to enforce slavery against rebellious blacks, the more the brutalizers insisted that the submissiveness of slavery was the natural state of black people. The more valuable the labor of blacks to Southern agriculture, precisely because of the relatively advanced stage of agriculture in their African homeland, the more white Americans began to insist that they had done the African savage a favor by bringing him to a land where he could be civilized by agricultural labor. Thus, step by step, in order to justify their mutually reinforcing economic exploitation and forceful subjugation of blacks, living, breathing white Americans created a scientifically cloaked theory of white superiority and black inferiority.

In order to understand the ease with which racism entrenched itself in Europe and North America, it is important to emphasize that not only the big merchants, manufacturers, and shipowners benefited from the slave trade and slavery. All kinds of little people on both sides of the Atlantic drew blood money directly from the slave traffic. Thus, "though a large part of the Liverpool slave traffic was monopolized by about ten large firms, many of the small vessels in the trade were fitted out by attorneys, drapers, grocers, barbers, and tailors. The shares in the ventures were subdivided, one having one-eighth, another one-fifteenth, a third one-thirty-second part of a share and so on. . . . 'almost every order of people is interested in a Guinea cargo.' "[2]

The middle classes benefited indirectly from the general economic prosperity created by the slave trade. "Every port to which the slave ships returned saw the rise of manufactures in the eighteenth century—refineries, cottons, dyeworks, sweetmaking—in increasing numbers which testified to the advance of business and industry."[3] In the expanding economy the shopkeeper found a growing number of customers for his goods,

the farmer for his produce, the doctor and lawyer for their skills.

To white workers at the very bottom of white society, African slavery also brought substantial benefits. First, the expanding industry made possible by the profits of slave trafficking created jobs at an expanding rate. Second, in the Americas particularly, white indentured servants were able to escape from the dehumanization of plantation servitude only because of the seemingly inexhaustible supply of constantly imported African slaves to take their place.

. . .

In the late nineteenth century . . . monopoly capitalism began to export "surplus capital" to what we today call the Third World. . . . The capital invested in the colonies could be used to extract surplus values from a work force prevented by the military power of a colonial administration from organizing for better working conditions, shorter hours, higher wages. Finally, the surplus profits thus extracted from the colonial work force were not reinvested in the colonies but were sent home to add to the total social capital available for modernization in the oppressing country. In this way the colonial countries were systematically kept in a state of undevelopment in order to accelerate economic development at home.

An analogous process has taken place within the borders of the United States, where the black work force has been used as a colonial work force to preserve the value of existing capital.

The role which blacks were to play in this process was fixed after Reconstruction when blacks were kept on the cotton plantations not only by the brute force of Southern planters and sheriffs but by the violent hostility of white workers to their entry into the advancing industries of the North and South. Between 1880 and 1890 alone there were fifty strikes in the North against the em-

[2]Eric Williams, *Capitalism and Slavery* (New York: G. P. Putnam & Sons, 1966).

[3]Ernest Mandel, *Marxist Economic Theory* (New York: Monthly Review Press, 1969), p. 444.

ployment of black workers in industry. The result was that in 1910 the number of blacks in industries other than cotton production was less than 0.5 percent, while as late as 1930, 68.75 percent of gainfully employed blacks were still in agriculture and domestic service.

As blacks began to move into the cities in this country, white workers acted as the principal human agent assisting American capitalism to counteract the fundamental contradiction between constantly advancing technology and the need to maintain the value of existing plants. They have done so by collectively and often forcibly restricting blacks to technologically less advanced industries or to what is known as "common labor" inside the modern plant or in construction. A perfect example of the system in operation on the job has been in the building industry. "The black man digs a ditch. Then the white man steps in and lays the pipes and the black man covers the ditch. The black man cleans the tank and then the white boilermaker comes on and makes the repairs."[4]

This is the scavenger role in production which white workers, acting *consciously* on behalf of their own social mobility and *unconsciously* on behalf of constantly advancing capitalism, have assigned to blacks and other colored peoples, such as the Chinese and Japanese on the West Coast, and the Mexicans and Puerto Ricans.

But the scavenger role has not been restricted to jobs. In the same way that blacks have been forced to take on the old substandard jobs, disdained and discarded by socially mobile whites, they have been confined to used homes, used schools, used churches, and used stores. (Only in the matter of the most ephemeral consumer goods —cars, deodorants, hair spray, clothing, etc. —are they able and in fact encouraged to buy the latest models.) For the used homes

and churches they make excessive payments which add to the total capital available to the entire economy for new buildings, new plants, new churches, new homes. As in the days of primitive accumulation, the entire white community benefits, not only from the direct receipt of interest and principal on these homes and churches but in terms of new industries with their streamlined buildings and their increasingly skilled jobs.

The situation has reached its climax in the role assigned by the military-industrial state to young blacks on the frontlines of Vietnam. The disproportionate number of black youth fighting and dying to preserve the system in Asia makes it possible for an increasing number of white youth to attend college and be prepared for the new industries of the future. The systematic undevelopment of the black community is thus the foundation for the systematic development of the white community.

The economic advantages to the United States of having a colony inside its own borders have been tremendous. By using the colonial force of blacks, U.S. capitalism has been able to moderate the general contradiction of capitalist accumulation. That is to say, it has been able to accelerate technological expansion and at the same time keep profits coming in from continuing exploitation of its obsolescent, "used" factories, homes, schools, stores, etc. As a result, the United States has developed into the technologically most advanced country in the world.

But the human costs of this counteracting of internal economic contradictions have been equally tremendous. On the one hand, for the sake of American economic development, twenty to thirty million blacks and thousands of black communities across the country have paid the high cost of economic backwardness. As I noted earlier, "Their present stage of decay, decline, and dilapidation—their present stage of undevelopment —is a product of capitalist exploitation. They have been used and reused to produce

---

[4]Sterling D. Spero and Abram L. Harris, *The Black Worker* (New York: Atheneum, 1968).

profit by every form of capitalist: landlords, construction industries, merchants, insurance brokers, bankers, finance companies, racketeers, and manufacturers of cars, appliances, steel, and every kind of industrial commodity."

Less obvious but increasingly dangerous has been the human price paid by the entire country for advancing capitalism by all means necessary. In the course of making America a unique land of opportunity in which whites climb up the social and economic ladder on the backs of blacks, the American people have become the most materialistic, the most opportunistic, the most individualistic—in sum, the most politically and socially irresponsible people in the world. Step by step, choice by choice, year after year, decade after decade, they have become the political victims of the system they themselves created, unable to make political decisions on the basis of principle no matter how crucial the issue.

. . .

7.4 Monopoly Capital and Race Relations

In the past several decades blacks have moved in enormous numbers out of the rural, agricultural South and into the urban, industrial North. Although this migration has brought them some gains in money income, blacks are still concentrated at the bottom of the overall income distribution.[1] Earlier in this chapter, Harold Baron and Bennett Hymer showed *how* the mechanisms of institutional racism have prevented blacks from rising in the urban economy.[2] In the following reading, Paul Baran and Paul Sweezy argue *why* racial inequality will tend to persist in a monopoly capitalist society. They examine (a) the benefits derived by capitalist employers from a divided working class; (b) the sociopsychological needs of capitalism for a lowest status scapegoat group; and (c) the long-run decline in the demand for unskilled labor.

It should be noted that Baran and Sweezy overstate the significance of (c), the decline in unskilled jobs. As the entire occupational structure has moved toward more skilled jobs, the number of black workers in basic industrial and transportation sectors of the economy has grown rapidly; for example, blacks now comprise a large majority in many automobile plants. Although blacks continue to occupy the lowest-paid and most onerous jobs that are available, they have become more central to economic production, not more marginal, as Baran and Sweezy suggest.

[1] See Ackerman et al., Section 5.1, p. 207.
[2] Baron and Hymer, Section 7.2, p. 297.

Source: The following is excerpted from Chapter 9 of *Monopoly Capital* by PAUL BARAN and PAUL SWEEZY. Copyright © 1966 by Paul Sweezy. Reprinted by permission of Monthly Review Press.

. . .

. . . The conclusion seems inescapable that since moving to the cities, Negroes have been prevented from improving their socioeconomic position: they have not been able to follow earlier immigrant groups up the occupational ladder and out of the ghetto. . . . What social forces and institutional mechanisms have forced Negroes to play the part of permanent immigrants, entering the urban economy at the bottom and remaining there decade after decade?

There are, it seems to us, three major sets of factors involved in the answer to this crucially important question. First, a formidable array of private interests benefit, in the most direct and immediate sense, from the continued existence of a segregated subproletariat. Second, the sociopsychological pressures generated by monopoly capitalist society intensify rather than alleviate existing racial prejudices, hence also discrimination and segregation. And third, as monopoly capitalism develops, the demand for unskilled and semiskilled labor declines both relatively and absolutely, a trend which affects Negroes more than any other group and accentuates their economic and social inferiority. All of these factors mutually interact, tending to push Negroes ever further down in the social structure and locking them into the ghetto.

Consider first the private interests which benefit from the existence of a Negro subproletariat. (a) Employers benefit from divisions in the labor force which enable them to play one group off against another, thus weakening all. Historically, for example, no small amount of Negro migration was in direct response to the recruiting of strikebreakers. (b) Owners of ghetto real estate are able to overcrowd and overcharge. (c) Middle- and upper-income groups benefit from having at their disposal a large supply of cheap domestic labor. (d) Many small marginal businesses, especially in the service trades, can operate profitably only if cheap labor is available to them. (e) White workers benefit by being protected from Negro competition for the more desirable and higher paying jobs. Hence the customary distinction, especially in the South, between "white" and "Negro" jobs, the exclusion of Negroes from apprentice programs, the refusal of many unions to admit Negroes, and so on. In all these groups—and taken together they constitute a vast majority of the white population—what Marx called "the most violent, mean, and malignant passions of the human breast, the Furies of private interest," are summoned into action to keep the Negro "in his place."

With regard to race prejudice, it has already been pointed out that this characteristic white attitude was deliberately created and cultivated as a rationalization and justification for the enslavement and exploitation of colored labor. But in time, race prejudice and the discriminatory behavior patterns which go with it came to serve other purposes as well. As capitalism developed, particularly in its monopoly phase, the social structure became more complex and differentiated. Within the basic class framework, which remained in essentials unchanged, there took place a proliferation of social strata and status groups, largely determined by occupation and income. These groupings, as the terms "stratum" and "stratus" imply, relate to each other as higher or lower, with the whole constituting an irregular and unstable hierarchy. In such a social structure, individuals tend to see and define themselves in terms of the "status hierarchy" and to be motivated by ambitions to move up and fears of moving down. These ambitions and fears are of course exaggerated, intensified, played upon by the corporate sales apparatus which finds in them the principal means of manipulating the "utility functions" of the consuming public.

The net result of all this is that each status group has a deep-rooted psychological need to compensate for feelings of inferiority and envy toward those above by feelings of superiority and contempt for those below. It thus happens that a special pariah group at the bottom acts as a kind of lightning rod for the frustrations and hostilities of all the higher groups, the more so the nearer they are to the bottom. It may even be said that the very existence of the pariah group is a kind of harmonizer and stabilizer of the social structure—so long as the pariahs play their role passively and resignedly. Such a society becomes in time so thoroughly saturated with race prejudice that it sinks below the level of consciousness and becomes a part of the "human nature" of its members. The gratification which whites derive from their socioeconomic superiority to Negroes has its counterpart in alarm, anger, and even panic at the prospect of Negroes attaining equality. Status being a relative matter, whites inevitably interpret upward movement by Negroes as downward movement for themselves. This complex of attitudes, product of stratification and status consciousness in monopoly capitalist society, provides an important part of the explanation why whites not only refuse to help Negroes to rise but bitterly resist their efforts to do so. (When we speak of whites and their prejudices and attitudes in this unqualified way, we naturally do not mean all whites. Ever since John Brown, and indeed long before John Brown, there have been whites who have freed themselves of the disease of racial prejudice, have fought along with Negro militants for an end to the rotten system of exploitation and inequality, and have looked forward to the creation of a society in which relations of solidarity and brotherhood will take the place of relations of superiority and inferiority. Moreover, we are confident that the number of such whites will steadily increase in the years ahead. But their number is not great today, and in a survey which aims only at depicting the broadest contours of the current social scene it would be wholly misleading to assign them a decisive role.)

The third set of factors adversely affecting the relative position of Negroes is connected with technological trends and their impact on the demand for different kinds and grades of labor. Appearing before a Congressional committee in 1955, the then Secretary of Labor, James P. Mitchell, testified that unskilled workers as a proportion of the labor force had declined from 36 percent in 1910 to 20 percent in 1950. A later Secretary of Labor, Willard Wirtz, told the Clark Committee in 1963 that the percentage of unskilled was down to 5 percent by 1962. Translated into absolute figures, this means that the number of unskilled workers declined slightly, from somewhat over to somewhat under 13 million between 1910 and 1950, and then plummeted to fewer than 4 million only twelve years later. These figures throw a sharp light on the rapid deterioration of the Negro employment situation since the Second World War. What happened is that until roughly a decade and a half ago, with the number of unskilled jobs remaining stable, Negroes were able to hold their own in the total employment picture by replacing white workers who were moving up the occupational ladder. This explains why . . . the Negro unemployment rate was only a little higher than the white rate at the end of the Great Depression. Since 1950, on the other hand, with unskilled jobs disappearing at a fantastic rate, Negroes not qualified for other kinds of work found themselves increasingly excluded from employment altogether. Hence the rise of the Negro unemployment rate to more than double the white rate by the early 1960s. Negroes, in other words, being the least qualified workers are disproportionately hard hit as unskilled jobs (and, to an increasing extent, semi-skilled jobs) are eliminated by mechanization, automation, and cybernation. Since this technological revolution has not yet run its course—indeed many authorities think that it is still in its early stages—the job situation of Negroes is likely to go on deteriorating. To be sure, technological trends are not, as many believe, the *cause* of unemployment: that role . . . is played by the specific mechanisms of monopoly capitalism. But within the framework of this society technological trends, because of their differential impact on job opportunities, can rightly be considered a cause, and undoubtedly the most important cause, of the relative growth of Negro unemployment.

All the forces we have been discussing—vested economic interests, sociopsychological needs, technological trends—are deeply rooted in monopoly capitalism and together are strong enough to account for the fact that Negroes have been unable to rise out of the lower depths of American society. Indeed so pervasive and powerful are these forces that the wonder is only that the position of Negroes has not drastically worsened. That it has not, that in absolute terms their real income and consuming power have risen more or less in step with the rest of the population's, can only be explained by the existence of counteracting forces.

One of these counteracting forces we already commented upon: the shift out of Southern agriculture and into the urban economy. Some schooling was better than none; even a rat-infested tenement provided more shelter than a broken-down shack on Tobacco Road; being on the relief rolls of a big city meant more income, both money and real, than subsistence farming. And as the nation's per capita income rose, so also did that of the lowest income group, even that of unemployables on permanent relief. As we have seen, it has been this shift from countryside to city which has caused so many observers to believe in the reality of a large-scale Negro breakthrough in the last two decades. Actually, it was an aspect of a structural change in the economy rather than a change in the position of Negroes within the economy.

But in one particular area, that of government employment, Negroes have indeed scored a breakthrough, and this has unquestionably been the decisive factor in preventing a catastrophic decline in their relative position in the economy as a whole. . . .

Between 1940 and 1962, total government employment somewhat more than doubled, while nonwhite (as already noted, more than 90 percent Negro) employment in government expanded nearly five times. As a result nonwhite employment grew from 5.6 percent of the total to 12.1 percent. Since nonwhites constituted 11.5 percent of the labor force at mid-1961, it is a safe inference that Negroes are now more than proportionately represented in government employment.

Two closely interrelated forces have been responsible for this relative improvement of the position of Negroes in government employment. The first, and beyond doubt the most important, has been the increasing scope and militancy of the Negro liberation movement itself. The second has been the need of the American oligarchy, bent on consolidating a global empire including people of all colors, to avoid as much as possible the stigma of racism. If American Negroes had passively accepted the continuation of their degraded position, history teaches us that the oligarchy would have made no concessions. But once seriously challenged by militant Negro struggle, it was forced by the logic of its domestic and international situation to make concessions, with the twin objectives of pacifying Negroes at home and projecting abroad an image of the United States as a liberal society seeking to overcome an evil inheritance from the past.

The oligarchy, acting through the federal government and in the North and West through state and local governments, has also made other concessions to the Negro struggle. The armed forces have been desegregated, and a large body of civil rights legislation forbidding discrimination in public accommodations, housing, education, and employment, has been enacted. Apart from the desegregation of the armed forces, however, these concessions have had little effect.

Critics often attribute this failure to bad faith: there was never any intention, it is said, to concede to Negroes any of the real substance of their demand for equality. This is a serious misreading of the situation. No doubt there are many white legislators and administrators to whom such strictures apply with full force, but this is not true of the top economic and political leadership of the oligarchy—the managers of the giant corporations and their partners at the highest government levels. These men are governed in their political attitudes and behavior not by personal prejudices but by their conception of class interests. And while they may at times be confused by their own ideology or mistake short-run for long-run interests, it seems clear that with respect to the race problem in the United States they have come, perhaps belatedly but none the less surely, to understand that the very existence of their system is at stake. Either a solution will be found which insures the loyalty, or at least the neutrality, of the Negro people, or else the world revolution will sooner or later acquire a ready-made and potentially powerful Trojan horse within the ramparts of monopoly capitalism's mightiest fortress.

When men like Kennedy and Johnson and Warren champion such measures as the Civil Rights Act of 1964, it is clearly superficial to accuse them of perpetrating a cheap political maneuver. They know that they are in trouble, and they are looking for a way out.

Why then such meager results? The answer is simply that the oligarchy does not have the power to shape and control race relations any more than it has the power to plan the development of the economy. In matters which are within the administrative jurisdiction of government, policies can be effectively implemented. Thus it was possible to desegregate the armed forces and greatly to increase the number of Negroes in government employment. But when it comes to housing, education, and private employment, all the deeply rooted economic and socio-psychological forces analyzed above come into play. It was capitalism, with its enthronement of greed and privilege, which created the race problem and made of it the ugly thing it is today. It is the very same system which resists and thwarts every effort at a solution.

7.5   *The Economics of Racism*

In the introduction to this chapter we pointed out that racism is often seen as an aberration in the United States. According to conventional analyses of racial discrimination, employers hurt themselves financially by discriminating against blacks since the labor supply that employers draw upon is thereby restricted. On the other hand, white workers are said to benefit since discrimination reduces the competition from blacks for the jobs and wages of white workers.

In the following reading Michael Reich draws upon the perspective of earlier readings in this chapter[1] to undertake a statistical test of the effects of racism in the United States. Reich criticizes the conventional explanation of racism and concludes from his analysis that racism benefits white employers and other rich whites while it hurts poor whites and white em-

[1]See especially Baran and Sweezy, Section 7.4, p. 309.

ployees. Thus racism is seen as a phenomenon of *capitalist* society. Racism is useful to capitalism because it obfuscates class interests and provides a convenient psychological outlet for worker frustration, thereby reinforcing the existing class structure.

It should be stressed that Reich argues not that racism is necessary to capitalism but that capitalism nurtures racist ideologies and practices which help to stabilize the capitalist system. Racism is likely to take firm root in a capitalist society and to last as long as do capitalist institutions themselves.

Source: The following is a revised version of "The Economics of Racism" by MICHAEL REICH. From *Problems in Political Economy: An Urban Perspective*, edited by David M. Gordon. Copyright © 1970 by Michael Reich. Reprinted by permission of D.C. Heath & Co.

In the early 1960s it seemed to many that the elimination of racism in the U.S. was proceeding without requiring a radical restructuring of the entire society. There was a growing civil rights movement, and hundreds of thousands of blacks were moving to Northern cities where discrimination was supposedly less severe than in the South. Government reports pointed to the rapid improvement in the levels of black schooling as blacks moved out of the South: in 1966 the gap between the median years of schooling of black males aged twenty-five to twenty-nine and white males in the same age group had shrunk to one-quarter the size of the gap that had existed in 1960.[1]

By 1970, however, the optimism of earlier decades had vanished. Despite new civil rights laws, elaborate White House conferences, special ghetto manpower programs, the War on Poverty, and stepped-up tokenist hiring, racism and the economic exploitation of blacks has not lessened. During the past twenty-five years there has been virtually no permanent improvement in the relative economic position of blacks in America. Median black incomes have been fluctuating at a level between 47 percent and 60 percent of

median white incomes, the ratio rising during economic expansions and falling to previous low levels during recessions.[2] Segregation in schools and neighborhoods has been steadily increasing in almost all cities, and the atmosphere of distrust between blacks and whites has been intensifying. Racism, instead of disappearing, seems to be on the increase.

Besides systematically subjugating blacks so that their median income is 55 percent that of whites, racism is of profound importance for the distribution of income among white landowners, capitalists, and workers. For example, racism clearly benefits owners of housing in the ghetto where blacks have no choice but to pay higher rents there than is charged to whites for comparable housing elsewhere in the city. But more importantly, racism is a key mechanism for the stabilization of capitalism and the legitimization of inequality. We shall return to the question of who benefits from racism later, but first we shall review some of the economic means used to subjugate blacks.

THE PERVASIVENESS OF RACISM

Beginning in the first grade, blacks go to schools of inferior quality and obtain little

[1] U.S. Department of Labor, Bureau of Labor Statistics, Report No. 375, "The Social and Economic Status of Negroes in the United States, 1969," p. 50.

[2] The data refer to male incomes: see Table 7–A, p. 289.

of the basic training and skills needed in the labor market. Finding schools of little relevance, more in need of immediate income, and less able anyway to finance their way through school, the average black student still drops out at a lower grade than his white counterpart. In 1965 only 7.4 percent of black males aged twenty-five to thirty-four were college graduates, compared to 17.9 percent of whites in the same age bracket.[3]

Exploitation really begins in earnest when the black youth enters the labor market. A black worker with the same number of years of schooling and the same scores on achievement tests as a white worker receives much less income. The black worker cannot get as good a job because the better paying jobs are located too far from the ghetto or because he or she was turned down by racist personnel agencies and employers or because a union denied admittance or maybe because of an arrest record. Going to school after a certain point doesn't seem to increase a black person's income possibilities very much. The more educated a black person is, the greater is the disparity between his income and that of a white with the same schooling. The result: *in 1966 black college graduates earned less than white high school dropouts.*[4] And the higher the average wage or salary of an occupation, the lower the percentage of workers in that occupation who are black.

The rate of unemployment among blacks is generally twice as high as among whites.[5] Layoffs and recessions hit blacks with twice the impact they hit whites, since blacks are the "last hired, first fired." The ratio of average black to white incomes follows the business cycle closely, buffering white workers

[3]U.S. Bureau of the Census, Series P–60, "Educational Attainment."

[4]U.S. Bureau of the Census, Series P–60, "Income in 1966 of Families and Persons in the United States."

[5]See, for example, U.S. Department of Labor, *Manpower Report of the President*, various years.

from some of the impact of the recession.

Blacks pay higher rents for inferior housing, higher prices in ghetto stores, higher insurance premiums, higher interest rates in banks and lending companies, travel longer distances at greater expense to their jobs, suffer from inferior garbage collection and less access to public recreational facilities, and are assessed at higher property tax rates when they own housing. Beyond this, blacks are further harassed by police, the courts, and the prisons.

When conventional economists attempt to analyze racism they usually begin by trying to separate various forms of racial discrimination. For example, they define "pure wage discrimination" as the racial differential in wages paid to equivalent workers, that is, those with similar years and quality of schooling, skill training, previous employment experience and seniority, age, health, job attitudes, and a host of other factors. They presume that they can analyze the sources of "pure wage discrimination" without simultaneously analyzing the extent to which discrimination also affects the factors they hold constant.

But such a technique distorts reality. The various forms of discrimination are not separable in real life. Employers' hiring and promotion practices; resource allocation in city schools; the structure of transportation systems; residential segregation and housing quality; availability of decent health care; behavior of policemen and judges; foremen's prejudices; images of blacks presented in the media and the schools; price gouging in ghetto stores—these and the other forms of social and economic discrimination interact strongly with each other in determining the occupational status and annual income, and welfare, of black people. The processes are not simply additive but are mutually reinforcing. Often, a decrease in one narrow form of discrimination is accompanied by an increase in another form. Since all aspects of racism interact, an analysis of racism should incorporate all its aspects in a unified manner.

No single quantitative index could adequately measure racism in all its social, cultural, psychological, and economic dimensions. But while racism is far more than a narrow economic phenomenon, it does have very definite economic consequences: blacks have far lower incomes than whites. The ratio of median black to median white incomes thus provides a rough, but useful, quantitative index of the economic consequences of racism for blacks. We shall use this index statistically to analyze the causes of racism's persistence in the United States. While this approach overemphasizes the economic aspects of racism, it is nevertheless an improvement over the narrower approach taken by conventional economists.

COMPETING EXPLANATIONS OF RACISM

How is the historical persistence of racism in the United States to be explained? The most prominent analysis of discrimination among economists was formulated in 1957 by Gary Becker in his book, *The Economics of Discrimination.*[6] Racism, according to Becker, is fundamentally a problem of tastes and attitudes. Whites are defined to have a "taste for discrimination" if they are willing to forfeit income in order to be associated with other whites instead of blacks. Since white employers and employees prefer not to associate with blacks, they require a monetary compensation for the psychic cost of such association. In Becker's principal model, white employers have a taste for discrimination; marginal productivity analysis is invoked to show that white employers lose while white workers gain (in monetary terms) from discrimination against blacks.

Becker does not try to explain the source

[6]Gary Becker, *The Economics of Discrimination* (Chicago: University of Chicago Press, 1957).

of white tastes for discrimination. For him, these attitudes are determined outside of the economic system. (Racism could presumably be ended simply by changing these attitudes, perhaps by appeal to whites on moral grounds.) According to Becker's analysis, employers would find the ending of racism to be in their economic self-interest, but white workers would not. The persistence of racism is thus implicitly laid at the door of white workers. Becker suggests that long-run market forces will lead to the end of discrimination anyway: less discriminatory employers, with no "psychic costs" to enter in their accounts, will be able to operate at lower costs by hiring equivalent black workers at lower wages, thus bidding up the black wage rate and/or driving the more discriminatory employers out of business.

The approach to racism argued here is entirely different. Racism is viewed as rooted in the economic system and not in "exogenously determined" attitudes. Historically, the American Empire was founded on the racist extermination of American Indians, was financed in large part by profits from slavery, and was extended by a string of interventions, beginning with the Mexican War of the 1840s, which have been at least partly justified by white supremacist ideology.

Today, by transferring white resentment toward blacks and away from capitalism, racism continues to serve the needs of the capitalist system. Although individual employers might gain by refusing to discriminate and hiring more blacks, thus raising the black wage rate, it is not true that the capitalist class as a whole would benefit if racism were eliminated and labor were more efficiently allocated without regard to skin color. We will show below that the divisiveness of racism weakens workers' strength when bargaining with employers; the economic consequences of racism are not only lower incomes for blacks but also higher incomes for the capitalist class and lower incomes for white workers. Although capitalists may not have conspired consciously to create racism, and although capitalists may not be its principal perpetuators, nevertheless racism does support the continued viability of the American capitalist system.

We have, then, two alternative approaches to the analysis of racism. The first suggests that capitalists lose and white workers gain from racism. The second predicts the opposite—capitalists gain while workers lose. The first says that racist "tastes for discrimination" are formed independently of the economic system; the second argues that racism interacts symbiotically with capitalistic economic institutions.

The very persistence of racism in the United States lends support to the second approach. So do repeated instances of employers using blacks as strikebreakers, as in the massive steel strike of 1919, and employer-instigated exacerbation of racial antagonisms during that strike and many others.[7] However, the particular virulence of racism among many blue- and white-collar workers and their families seems to refute our approach and support Becker.

SOME EMPIRICAL EVIDENCE

Which of the two models better explains reality? We have already mentioned that our approach predicts that capitalists gain and workers lose from racism, whereas the conventional Beckerian approach predicts precisely the opposite. In the latter approach racism has an equalizing effect on the white income distribution, whereas in the former racism has a disequalizing effect. The statistical relationship between the extent of rac-

ism and the degree of inequality among whites provides a simple yet clear test of the two approaches. This section describes that test and its results.

First, we need a measure of racism. The index we use, for reasons already mentioned, is the ratio of black median family income to white median family income (abbreviated as B/W). A low numerical value for this ratio indicates a high degree of racism. We have calculated values of this racism index, using data from the 1960 Census, for each of the largest forty-eight metropolitan areas (boundaries are defined by the U.S. Census Bureau, who use the term standard metropolitan statistical areas—SMSA's). There is a great deal of variation from SMSA to SMSA in the B/W index of racism, even within the North; Southern SMSA's generally demonstrated a greater degree of racism. The statistical techniques used are based on this variation.

We also need measures of inequality among whites. Two convenient measures are: (1) the percentage share of all white income that is received by the top 1 percent of white families; and (2) the Gini coefficient of white incomes, a measure which captures inequality within as well as between social classes.[8]

Both of these inequality measures vary considerably among the SMSA's; there is also a substantial amount of variation in these within the subsample of Northern SMSA's. Therefore, it is very interesting to examine whether the pattern of variation of the inequality and racism variables can be explained by causal hypotheses. This is our first source of empirical evidence.

A systematic relationship across SMSA's between our measure of racism and either

---

[7]See, for example, David Brody, *Steelworkers in America: the Nonunion Era* (Cambridge: Harvard University Press, 1966); Herbert Gutman, "The Negro and the United Mineworkers," in *The Negro and the American Labor Movement,* ed. J. Jacobson (New York: Anchor, 1968); S. Spero and H. Harris, *The Black Worker* (New York: Atheneum, 1968), *passim.*

[8]The Gini coefficient varies between 0 and 1, with 0 indicating perfect equality and 1 indicating perfect inequality. For a more complete exposition, see H. Miller, *Income Distribution in the United States* (Washington, D.C.: Government Printing Office, 1966).

measure of white inequality does exist and is highly significant: where racism is greater, income inequality *among whites* is also greater.[9] This result is consistent with our model and is inconsistent with the predictions of Becker's model.

This evidence, however, should not be accepted too quickly. The correlations reported may not reflect actual causality since other independent forces may be simultaneously influencing both variables in the same way. As is the case with many other statistical analyses, the model must be expanded to control for such other factors. We know from previous inter-SMSA income distribution studies that the most important additional factors that should be introduced into our model are: (1) the industrial and occupational structure of the SMSA's; (2) the region in which the SMSA's are located; (3) the average income of the SMSA's; and (4) the proportion of the SMSA population that is black. These factors were introduced into the model by the technique of multiple regression analysis. Separate equations were estimated with the Gini index and the top 1 percent share as measures of white inequality.

All the equations showed strikingly uniform statistical results: racism as we have measured it was a significantly disequalizing force on the white income distribution, even when other factors were held constant. A 1 percent increase in the ratio of black to white median incomes (that is, a 1 percent decrease in racism) was associated with a .2 percent decrease in white inequality, as measured by the Gini coefficient. The corresponding effect on top 1 percent share of white income was two and a half times as large, indicating that most of the inequality among whites

generated by racism was associated with increased income for the richest 1 percent of white families. Further statistical investigation reveals that increases in the racism variable had an insignificant effect on the share received by the poorest whites and resulted in a decrease in the income share of the whites in the middle income brackets.[10] This is true even when the Southern SMSA's are excluded.

Within our model, we can specify a number of mechanisms that further explain the statistical finding that racism increases inequality among whites. We shall consider two mechanisms here: (1) total wages of white labor are reduced by racial antagonisms, in part because union growth and labor militancy are inhibited; (2) the supply of public services, especially in education, available to low- and middle-income whites is reduced as a result of racial antagonisms.

Wages of white labor are lessened by racism because the fear of a cheaper and underemployed black labor supply in the area is invoked by employers when labor presents its wage demands. Racial antagonisms on the shop floor deflect attention from labor grievances related to working conditions, permitting employers to cut costs. Racial divisions among labor prevent the development of united worker organizations both within the workplace and in the labor movement as a whole. As a result, union strength and union militancy will be less the greater the extent of racism. A historical example of this process is the already mentioned use of racial and ethnic divisions to destroy the solidarity of the 1919 steel strikers. By contrast, during the 1890s, black-white class solidarity greatly aided mine-

---

[9] For example, the correlation coefficient between the B/W measure of racism and the Gini coefficient of white incomes is $r = -.47$. A similar calculation by S. Bowles, across states instead of SMSA's, resulted in an $r = -.58$.

[10] A more rigorous presentation of these and other variables and the statistical results is available in Michael Reich, "Racial Discrimination and the White Income Distribution" (Unpublished Ph.D. diss., Harvard University, 1971).

workers in building militant unions among workers in Alabama, West Virginia, and other coalfield areas.[11]

The above argument and examples contradict the common belief that an exclusionary racial policy will strengthen rather than weaken the bargaining power of unions. Racial exclusion increases bargaining power only when entry into an occupation or industry can be effectively limited. Industrial-type unions are much less able to restrict entry than craft unions or organizations such as the American Medical Association. This is not to deny that much of organized labor is egregiously racist or that some skilled craft workers benefit from racism.[12] But it is important to distinguish actual discriminatory practice from the objective economic self-interest of most union members.

The second mechanism we shall consider concerns the allocation of expenditures for public services. The most important of these services is education. Racial antagonisms dilute both the desire and the ability of poor white parents to improve educational opportunities for their children. Antagonisms between blacks and poor whites drive wedges between the two groups and reduce their ability to join in a united political movement pressing for improved and more equal education. Moreover, many poor whites recognize that however inferior their own schools, black schools are even worse. This provides some degree of satisfaction and identification with the status quo, reducing the desire of poor whites to press politically for better schools in their neighborhoods. Ghettos tend to be located near poor white neighborhoods more often than near rich white neighborhoods; racism thus reduces

the potential tax base of school districts containing poor whites. Also, pressure by teachers' groups to improve all poor schools is reduced by racial antagonisms between predominantly white teaching staffs and black children and parents.[13]

The statistical validity of the above mechanisms can be tested in a causal model. The effect of racism on unionism is tested by estimating an equation in which the percentage of the SMSA labor force that is unionized is the dependent variable, with racism and the structural variables (such as the SMSA industrial structure) as the independent variables. The schooling mechanism is tested by estimating a similar equation in which the dependent variable is inequality in years of schooling completed among white males aged twenty-five to twenty-nine years old.

Once again, the results of this statistical test strongly confirm the hypothesis of our model. The racism variable is statistically significant in all the equations and has the predicted sign: a greater degree of racism results in lower unionization rates and greater degree of schooling inequality among whites. This empirical evidence again suggests that racism is in the economic interests of capitalists and other rich whites and against the economic interests of poor whites and white workers.

However, a full assessment of the importance of racism for capitalism would probably conclude that the primary significance of racism is not strictly economic. The simple economics of racism does not explain why many workers seem to be so vehemently racist, when racism is not in their economic

[11]See footnote 7 above.

[12]See, for example, H. Hill, "The Racial Practices of Organized Labor: the Contemporary Record," in *The Negro and the American Labor Movement*, ed. J. Jacobson (New York: Anchor, 1968).

[13]In a similar fashion, racial antagonisms reduce the political pressure on governmental agencies to provide other public services that would have a pro-poor distributional impact. The two principal items in this category are public health services and welfare payments in the Aid to Families with Dependent Children program.

self-interest. In noneconomic ways, racism helps to legitimize inequality, alienation, and powerlessness—legitimization that is necessary for the stability of the capitalist system as a whole. For example, many whites believe that welfare payments to blacks are a far more important factor in their taxes than is military spending. Through racism, poor whites come to believe that their poverty is caused by blacks who are willing to take away their jobs, and at lower wages, thus concealing the fact that a substantial amount of income inequality is inevitable in a capitalist society. Racism thus transfers the locus of whites' resentment towards blacks and away from capitalism.

Racism also provides some psychological benefits to poor and working-class whites. For example, the opportunity to participate in another's oppression compensates for one's own misery. There is a parallel here to the subjugation of women in the family: after a day of alienating labor, the tired husband can compensate by oppressing his wife. Furthermore, not being at the bottom of the heap is some solace for an unsatisfying life; this argument was successfully used by the Southern oligarchy against poor whites allied with blacks in the interracial Populist movement of the late nineteenth century.

Thus, racism is likely to take firm root in a society which breeds an individualistic and competitive ethos. In general, blacks provide a convenient and visible scapegoat for problems that actually derive from the institutions of capitalism. As long as building a real alternative to capitalism does not seem feasible to most whites, we can expect that identifiable and vulnerable scapegoats will prove functional to the status quo. These noneconomic factors thus neatly dovetail with the economic aspects of racism discussed earlier in their mutual service to the perpetuation of capitalism.

SELECTIVE BIBLIOGRAPHY

Further reading is recommended in Baron and Hymer, "The Negro Worker in the Chicago Labor Market," in Boggs, *Racism and the Class Struggle*, and in Baran and Sweezy, *Monopoly Capital*, Chapter 9, as cited in the source lines for Sections 7.2, 7.3, and 7.4. Williams [8] analyzes the role of slavery in the early development of capitalism. Spero and Harris [7] trace the relationship between black workers and the labor movement from 1865 to 1930; their account is complemented and brought up to date in both Jacobson [3] and Baron [1], although the latter's primary emphasis is on the effects of capitalist development on black labor. The contemporary persistence of racial inequality is amply documented in statistical terms in the essays in Parsons and Clark [5]. A more graphic account of racism is presented by Malcolm X [4]. The psychological aspects of racism, as well as its historical roots, are the subject of much attention in Schwartz and Disch [6]. Finally, Fusfeld [2] analyzes the economic roots of the urban and racial crises and examines the anatomy of the ghetto economy.

[1] Baron, Harold M. "The Demand for Black Labor: Historical Notes on the Political Economy of Racism." *Radical America* (March-April 1971): pp. 1–46.

[2] Fusfeld, Daniel R. "The Basic Economics of the Urban and Racial Crisis." In *Conference Papers of the Union for Radical Political Economics December 1968*. Available as Reprint No. 1 from the Union for Radical Political Economics, 2503 Student Activities Building, University of Michigan, Ann Arbor, Michigan 48104.

[3] Jacobson, Julius, ed. *The Negro and the American Labor Movement*. New York:

Doubleday & Co., Inc., 1968. See especially Herbert Gutman: "The Negro and the United Mineworkers."*

[4] Malcolm X, with the assistance of Alex Haley, *The Autobiography of Malcolm X*. New York: Grove Press, Inc., 1966.*

[5] Parsons, Talcott, and Clark, Kenneth B., eds. *The Negro American*. Boston: Beacon Press, 1967. See especially St. Clair Drake, "The Social and Economic Status of the Negro in the United States"; and Rashi Fein: "An Economic and Social Profile of the Negro American."*

[6] Schwartz, Barry N., and Disch, Robert, eds. *White Racism: Its History, Pathology and Practice*. New York: Dell Publishing Co., Inc., 1970.*

[7] Spero, Sterling D., and Harris, Abram L. *The Black Worker*. New York: Atheneum, 1970.*

[8] Williams, Eric. *Capitalism and Slavery*. New York: Capricorn Books, 1966.*

*Available in paperback editions.

Sexism  8

A PROFILE OF THE SUBORDINATE STATUS OF women in the United States should begin with women's relationship to work in this, the most "economic" of societies. The work that dominates women's image—child bearing and rearing, and maintenance of the family (cooking, housekeeping, shopping)—is not paid by wages, is not a commodity on a market, and is done in the home for private consumption. Since in a capitalist society status and power derive from one's wealth, income, or occupation, attributes which denote one's importance in the production of commodities that are sold on a market, it follows naturally that women are subordinated.

In fact, many women do participate in the labor market; in 1969 nearly two-fifths of the labor force were women and nearly half of all women between eighteen and sixty-four were wage or salary workers. But this aspect of women's work is often not recognized. Moreover, women are generally confined to subordinate roles in the occupational hierarchy of the capitalist economy; as Table 8–A indicates, the wages and salaries of full-time female workers average three-fifths of full-time male workers' earnings.

Although it may have both economic causes and manifestations, the subordinate status of women is more than an economic phenomenon. Women are everywhere subordinated and degraded as sexual objects by men—in the media, in literature, in fashion, in advertising, in the very definition of "femininity." Women are taught that they are inferior and that they are expected to nurture and sustain the men above them. Women are denied access to power and are prevented by social patterns and custom from pursuing a whole range of activities which are considered "unfeminine" or for which women are alleged to be biologically or temperamentally unfit. In short, women's subjugation is not confined to the economic sphere but extends into all aspects of life. We shall use the term sexism or, alternately, male supremacy, to denote this systematic oppression of women.

From the perspective of what human relationships *could* be, the system of male supremacy can be viewed as a structure of expected sex roles that distorts and warps *all* interpersonal relationships, creating barriers

TABLE 8–A   MEDIAN TOTAL MONEY INCOME OF MALES AND FEMALES*

Year	All Income Recipients			% Full-time†		Full-Time Workers		
	Male	Female	F/M	M	F	Male	Female	F/M
1956	3608	1146	.32	62.4	29.3	$4462	$2828	.63
1957	3684	1199	.32	60.8	29.6	4720	3006	.64
1958	3742	1176	.31	57.4	28.4	4948	3101	.63
1959	3996	1222	.31	58.5	27.4	5242	3205	.61
1960	4081	1262	.31	58.3	28.3	5435	3296	.60
1961	4189	1279	.31	57.5	27.5	5663	3342	.59
1962	4372	1342	.31					
1963	4511	1372	.30	59.1	28.4	6070	3557	.59
1964	4647	1449	.31	59.5	28.2	6283	3710	.59
1965	4824	1564	.32	59.8	29.3	6479	3883	.60
1966	5306	1638	.31	60.2	30.0	6955	4026	.58
1967	5571	1819	.33	60.7	31.7	7302	4253	.58
1968	5980	2019	.34	60.3	31.0	7814	4568	.58
1969	6429	2132	.33	59.0	30.7	8668	5077	.58

*Income in current prices of civilians 14 years or older.
†Year-round full-time workers.
SOURCES: U.S. Dept. of Commerce, Bureau of the Census, *Current Population Reports,* Series P-60, annual issues.

between men and women as well as among men and among women and preventing the full and free development of all human beings. For example, men's relationships with women are often artificial and objectified. The cult of *machismo* pressures men not only to abuse women, but also to appear strong and hard and not to express their internal emotions; thus, men close many social roles to themselves. However, women and men are obviously not equally oppressed by sexism. All men derive some privileges and power from it, and men are in many ways the actual agents of the oppression of women. Men are clearly less likely to see all the ways in which women are oppressed, and they are not likely to give up their privileges willingly.

How can we account for the present situation of women, and what are its connections with capitalism? Contrary to common belief, the subordinate role of women is not biologically inevitable, but it is, as Juliet Mitchell points out in this chapter, a product of social coercion.[1] Male supremacy was probably the first form of oppression of one group in society by another; men were dominant over women in most precapitalist societies. Certainly by the time the capitalist mode of production had emerged, male supremacy had already become a deep-rooted and fully developed social phenomenon.

It is not surprising, therefore, that male supremacy influenced the lines along which capitalism developed. In particular, as a market in wage-labor was created, it became necessary for men to discriminate against women in the labor market in order to preserve the basis of male supremacy in the family. As a result, women became a vulnerable and easily manipulatable segment of the labor force: as such, they were used extensively in the early factories. Sexism in this way assisted capitalism.

Capitalist development in turn reinforced sexism. Whereas in the precapitalist family-economy women and men worked together as a single productive unit, the transfer of production from the home to factories and the creation of a wage-labor market reduced the economic interdependence between men and women and enabled men to work separately from women. Women were increasingly excluded from productive areas in which they had once participated; the consequent loss of sources of income made them more economically dependent upon men. Moreover, as Peggy Morton argued in Chapter 3, the patriarchal nuclear family both supports capitalism—by maintaining and reproducing labor power—and has been modified in different stages of capitalism to meet the changing requirements for the maintenance and reproduction of labor power.[2] It is largely in the family and in schools that the personality and character structures needed for alienated labor are molded.

The subordination of women within the conventional nuclear family, the subordination of women in the labor market, and the needs of capitalism are thus intimately linked. On the one hand, capitalism's limitless drive to expand has in recent decades brought more women into the job market, undermining somewhat the economic dominance of males within the family. While there are many areas of mutual reinforcement between capitalism and male supremacy, there are also areas of conflict.

This chapter explores the relationship between sexism and capitalism, the ways in which capitalism has used, enlarged, and transformed male supremacy, and the obstacles that capitalism poses to the liberation of women and the end of deleterious sex role constraints. Some of the readings examine the situation of women in relation to production, reproduction, sexuality, and the socialization of children. Others analyze the family as an economic unit under capitalism and consider how capitalist development has in

[1]See Mitchell, Section 8.1, p. 326.

[2]See Morton and Gintis, Section 3.6, p. 119.

some respects been undermining the nuclear family at the same time that it makes good use of it. As we shall see, the relationship between capitalism and sexism is in many ways symbiotic. Nonetheless, the sole elimination of capitalism need not spell the doom of male supremacy. Since the *ultimate* basis of sexism lies in the power of men, the elimi-

nation of capitalism is necessary but not sufficient to eradicate sexism. On the other hand, sexism is an important prop of capitalism, and it is unlikely that capitalist relations of production can be overthrown in the United States without the simultaneous eradication of sexism.

8.1   *The Situation of Women*

It is often argued that the inferior position of women in society is the natural and inevitable consequence of their biological differences from men. How significant are the *biological* differences of men and women in determining social roles? In the following reading, Juliet Mitchell analyzes female roles in the four areas of production, reproduction, sex, and the socialization of children. Mitchell argues that female roles in each area are in large part the product of *social* coercion; her conclusion is that the social subordination of women is not an insurmountable biohistorical fact.

An analysis of female roles must examine the whole situation of women, since the four areas distinguished by Mitchell are inextricably linked to one another. For example, the partial exclusion of women from production is related directly to their confinement to and role in the family. Mitchell goes on to analyze the uneven development of each area today and the interrelationships among them.

Source: The following is excerpted from "Women: The Longest Revolution" by JULIET MITCHELL. From the *New Left Review*, No. 40 (Nov.-Dec. 1966). Reprinted by permission of the *New Left Review*.

.   .   .

The unity of women's condition at any one time is the product of several structures . . .: Production, Reproduction, Sex and Socialization of children. The concrete combination of these produces the "complex unity" of her position; but each separate structure may have reached a different "moment" at any given historical time. Each then must be examined separately in order to see what the present unit is and how it might be changed. The discussion that follows does not pretend to give a historical account of each sector. It is only concerned with some general re-

flections on the different roles of women and some of their interconnections.

PRODUCTION

The biological differentiation of the sexes and the division of labour have, throughout history, seemed an interlocked necessity. Anatomically smaller and weaker, woman's physiology and her psycho-biological metabolism appear to render her a less useful member of a work force. It is always stressed how, particularly in the early stages of social development, man's physical superiority gave him the means of conquest over nature which was denied to women. Once woman was accorded the menial tasks involved in maintenance whilst man undertook conquest and creation, she became an aspect of the things preserved: private property and children. All socialist writers on the subject . . . link the confirmation and continuation of woman's oppression after the establishment of her physical inferiority for hard manual work with the advent of private property. But woman's physical weakness has never prevented her from performing work as such (quite apart from bringing up children)— only specific types of work, in specific societies. In Primitive, Ancient, Oriental, Medieval and Capitalist societies, the *volume* of work performed by women has always been considerable (it has usually been much more than this). It is only its form that is in question. Domestic labour, even today, is enormous if quantified in terms of productive labour.[1] In any case women's physique has never permanently or even predominantly relegated them to menial domestic chores. In many peasant societies, women have worked in the fields as much as, or more than men.

Physique and Coercion

The assumption behind most classical discussion is that the crucial factor starting the

[1] Apologists who make out that housework, though time-consuming, is light and relatively enjoyable, are refusing to acknowledge the null and degrading routine it entails. Lenin commented crisply: "You all know that even when women have full rights, they still remain factually down-trodden because all housework is left to them. In most cases housework is the most unproductive, the most barbarous and the most arduous work a woman can do. It is exceptionally petty and does not include anything that would in any way promote the development of the woman." (Collected Works XXX. 43). Today it has been calculated in Sweden, that 2,340 million hours a year are spent by women in housework compared with 1,290 million hours in industry. The Chase Manhattan Bank estimated a woman's overall working hours as averaging 99.6 per week.

whole development of feminine subordination was women's lesser capacity for demanding physical work. But, in fact, this is a major oversimplification. Even within these terms, in history it has been woman's lesser capacity for violence as well as for work that has determined her subordination. In most societies woman has not only been less able than man to perform arduous kinds of work, she has also been less able to fight. Man not only has the strength to assert himself against nature, but also against his fellows. *Social coercion* has interplayed with the straightforward division of labour, based on biological capacity, to a much greater extent than generally admitted. Of course, it may not be actualized as direct aggression. In primitive societies women's physical unsuitability for the hunt is evident. In agricultural societies where women's inferiority is socially instituted they are given the arduous task of tilling and cultivation. For this coercion is necessary. In developed civilizations and more complex societies woman's physical deficiencies again become relevant. Women are no use either for war or in the construction of cities. But with early industrialization coercion once more becomes important. As Marx wrote: "Insofar as machinery dispenses with muscular power, it becomes a means of employing labourers of slight muscular strength, and those whose bodily development is incomplete, but whose limbs are all the more supple. The labour of women and children was, therefore, the first thing sought for by capitalists who used machinery."[2]

René Dumont points out that in many zones of tropical Africa today men are often idle, while women are forced to work all day. This exploitation has no "natural" source whatever. Women may perform their "heavy" duties in contemporary African peasant societies not for fear of physical reprisal by their men, but because these duties

[2] Karl Marx: *Capital* I, 394.

are "customary" and built into the role structures of the society. A further point is that coercion implies a different relationship from coercer to coerced than exploitation does. It is political rather than economic. . . . For far from woman's physical weakness removing her from productive work, her social weakness has in these cases evidently made her the major slave of it.

This truth, elementary though it may seem, has nevertheless been constantly ignored by writers on the subject, with the result that an illegitimate optimism creeps into their predictions of the future. For if it is just the biological incapacity for the hardest physical work which has determined the subordination of women, then the prospect of an advanced machine technology, abolishing the need for strenuous physical exertion would seem to promise, therefore, the liberation of women. For a moment industrialization itself thus seems to herald women's liberation. . . . Industrial labour and automated technology both promise the preconditions for woman's liberation alongside man's—but no more than the preconditions. It is only too obvious that the advent of industrialization has not so far freed women in this sense, either in the West or in the East. In the West it is true that there was a great influx of women into jobs in the expanding industrial economy, but this soon leveled out, and there has been relatively little increase in recent decades. De Beauvoir hoped that automation would make a decisive, qualitative difference by abolishing altogether the physical differential between the sexes. But any reliance on this in itself accords an independent role to technique which history does not justify. Under capitalism, automation could possibly lead to an evergrowing structural unemployment which would expel women—the latest and least integrated recruits to the labour force and ideologically the most expendable for a bourgeois society—from production after only a brief interlude in it. Technology is mediated

by the total social structure and it is this which will determine woman's future in work relations. Physical deficiency is not now, any more than in the past, a sufficient explanation of woman's relegation to inferior status. . . .

REPRODUCTION

Women's absence from the critical sector of production historically, of course, has been caused not just by their physical weakness in a context of coercion—but also by their role in reproduction. Maternity necessitates periodic withdrawals from work, but this is not a decisive phenomenon. It is rather women's role in reproduction which has become, in capitalist society at least, the spiritual "complement" of men's role in production.[3] Bearing children, bringing them up, and maintaining the home—these form the core of woman's natural vocation, in this ideology. This belief has attained great force because of the seeming universality of the family as a human institution. There is little doubt that Marxist analyses have underplayed the fundamental problems posed here. . . .

The biological function of maternity is a universal, atemporal fact, and as such has seemed to escape the categories of Marxist historical analysis. From it follows—apparently—the stability and omnipresence of the family, if in very different forms.[4] Once this is accepted, women's social subordination—however emphasized as an honourable, but different role (cf. the equal but "separate" ideologies of Southern racists)—can be seen

[3]Maternity is the distinctive feature on which both sexes base their hopes: for oppression or liberation.

[4]Philippe Ariès in *Centuries of Childhood* (1962) shows that though the family may in some form always have existed it was often submerged under more forceful structures. In fact according to Ariès it has only acquired its present significance with the advent of industrialization.

to follow inevitably as an *insurmountable* bio-historical fact. The causal chain then goes: Maternity, Family, Absence from Production and Public Life, Sexual Inequality.

The lynch-pin in this line of argument is the idea of the family. The notion that "family" and "society" are virtually coextensive terms, or that an advanced society not founded on the nuclear family is now inconceivable, is widespread. It can only be seriously discussed by asking just what the family is—or rather what women's role in the family is. Once this is done, the problem appears in quite a new light. For it is obvious that woman's role in the family—primitive, feudal or bourgeois—partakes of three quite different structures: reproduction, sexuality, and the socialization of children. These are historically, not intrinsically, related to each other in the present modern family. Biological parentage is not necessarily identical with social parentage (adoption). It is thus essential to discuss: not the family as an unanalysed entity, but the separate *structures* which today compose it, but which may tomorrow be decomposed into a new pattern.

Reproduction, it has been stressed, is a seemingly constant atemporal phenomenon—part of biology rather than history. In fact this is an illusion. What is true is that the "mode of reproduction" does not vary with the "mode of production"; it can remain effectively the same through a number of different modes of production. For it has been defined till now, by its uncontrollable, natural character. To this extent, it has been an unmodified biological fact. As long as reproduction remained a natural phenomenon, of course, women were effectively doomed to social exploitation. In any sense, they were not masters of a large part of their lives. They had no choice as to whether or how often they gave birth to children (apart from repeated abortion), their existence was essentially subject to biological processes outside their control.

Contraception

Contraception which was invented as a rational technique only in the nineteenth century was thus an innovation of world-historic importance. It is only now just beginning to show what immense consequences it could have, in the form of the pill. For what it means is that at last the mode of reproduction could potentially be transformed. Once child-bearing becomes totally voluntary (how much so is it in the West, even today?) its significance is fundamentally different. It need no longer be the sole or ultimate vocation of woman; it becomes one option among others.

. . .

The fact of overwhelming importance is that easily available contraception threatens to dissociate sexual from reproductive experience—which all contemporary bourgeois ideology tries to make inseparable, as the *raison d'être* of the family.

Reproduction and Production

At present, reproduction in our society is often a kind of sad mimicry of production. Work in a capitalist society is an alienation of labour in the making of a social product which is confiscated by capital. But it can still sometimes be a real act of creation, purposive and responsible, even in conditions of the worst exploitation. Maternity is often a caricature of this. The biological product—the child—is treated as if it were a solid product. Parenthood becomes a kind of substitute for work, an activity in which the child is seen as an object created by the mother, in the same way as a commodity is created by a worker. Naturally, the child does not literally escape, but the mother's alienation can be much worse than that of the worker whose product is appropriated by the boss. No human being can create another human being. A person's biological origin is an abstraction. The child as an autonomous person inevitably threatens the activity which claims to create it continually merely as a *possession* of the parent. Possessions are felt as extensions of the self. The child as a possession is supremely this. Anything the child does is therefore a threat to the mother herself who has renounced her autonomy through this misconception of her reproductive role. There are few more precarious ventures on which to base a life.

Furthermore even if the woman has emotional control over her child, legally and economically both she and it are subject to the father. The social cult of maternity is matched by the real socioeconomic powerlessness of the mother. The psychological and practical benefits men receive from this are obvious. . . .

Unlike her nonproductive status, her capacity for maternity *is* a definition of woman. But it is only a physiological definition. So long as it is allowed to remain a substitute for action and creativity, and the home an area of relaxation for men, women will remain confined to the species, to her universal and natural condition. . . .

SEXUALITY

Sexuality has traditionally been the most tabooed dimension of women's situation. The meaning of sexual freedom and its connexion with women's freedom is a particularly difficult subject which few socialist writers have cared to broach. . . . Yet it is obvious that throughout history women have been appropriated as sexual objects, as much as progenitors or producers. Indeed, the sexual relation can be assimilated to the statute of possession much more easily and completely than the productive or reproductive relationship. Contemporary sexual vocabulary bears eloquent witness to this. . . .

Some historical considerations are in order here. . . . What is necessary, . . . is some account of the co-variation between the degrees of sexual liberty and openness and the position and dignity of women in different societies. Some points are immediately obvious. The actual history is much more dialectical than any liberal account presents it. Unlimited juridical polygamy—whatever the sexualization of the culture which accompanies it—is clearly a total derogation of woman's autonomy, and constitutes an extreme form of oppression. Ancient China is a perfect illustration of this. Wittfogel describes the extraordinary despotism of the Chinese *paterfamilias*—"a liturgical (semi-official) policeman of his kin group."[5] In the West, however, the advent of monogamy was in no sense an *absolute* improvement. It certainly did not create a one-to-one equality —far from it. Engels commented accurately: "Monogamy does not by any means make its appearance in history as the reconciliation of man and woman, still less as the highest form of such a reconciliation. On the contrary, it appears as the subjugation of one sex by the other, as the proclamation of a conflict between the sexes entirely unknown hitherto in prehistoric times."[6] But in the Christian era, monogamy took on a very specific form in the West. It was allied with an unprecedented régime of general sexual repression. In its Pauline version, this had a markedly antifeminine bias, inherited from Judaism. With time this became diluted —feudal society, despite its subsequent reputation for asceticism, practised formal monogamy with considerable actual acceptance of polygamous behaviour, at least within the ruling class. But here again the extent of sexual freedom was only an index of masculine domination. In England, the truly major change occurred in the sixteenth century with the rise of militant puritanism and the increase of market relations in the economy. . . .

[5] Karl Wittfogel: *Oriental Despotism* (1957) p. 116.
[6] Friedrich Engels: *The Origin of the Family, Private Property and the State* (1884), in Marx-Engels: *Selected Works* (1962) II 224.

Capitalism and the attendant demands of the newly emergent bourgeoisie accorded women a new status as wife and mother. Her legal rights improved; there was vigorous controversy over her social position; wife-beating was condemned. The patriarchal system was retained and maintained by the economic mode of production. The transition to complete effective monogamy accompanied the transition to modern bourgeois society as we know it today. Like the market system itself, it represented a historic advance, at great historic cost. The formal, juridical equality of capitalist society and capitalist rationality now applied as much to the marital as to the labour contract. In both cases, nominal parity masks real exploitation and inequality. But in both cases the formal equality is itself a certain progress, which can help to make possible a further advance.

For the situation today is defined by a new contradiction. Once formal conjugal equality (monogamy) is established, sexual freedom as such—which under polygamous conditions was usually a form of exploitation—becomes, conversely, a possible force for liberation. It then means, simply, the freedom for both sexes to transcend the limits of present sexual institutions.

Historically, then, there has been a dialectical movement, in which sexual expression was "sacrificed" in an epoch of more-or-less puritan repression, which nevertheless produced a greater parity of sexual roles, which in turn creates the precondition for a genuine sexual liberation, in the dual sense of equality *and* freedom—whose unity defines socialism.

. . .

Obviously, the main breach in the traditional value-pattern has so far been the increase in premarital sexual experience. This is now virtually legitimized in contemporary bourgeois society. But its implications are explosive for the ideological conception of marriage that dominates this society: that of an exclusive and permanent bond.

The current wave of sexual liberalization, in the present context, could become conducive to the greater general freedom of women. Equally it could presage new forms of oppression. The puritan-bourgeois creation of woman as "counterpart" has produced the *precondition* for emancipation. But it gave statutory legal equality to the sexes at the cost of greatly intensified repression. Subsequently—like private property itself—it has become a brake on the further development of a free sexuality. Capitalist market relations have historically been a precondition of socialism; bourgeois marital relations (contrary to the denunciation of the *Communist Manifesto*) may equally be a precondition of women's liberation.

SOCIALIZATION

Woman's biological destiny as mother becomes a cultural vocation in her role as socializer of children. In bringing up children, woman achieves her main social definition. Her suitability for socialization springs from her physiological condition; her ability to lactate and occasionally relative inability to undertake strenuous work loads. It should be said at the outset that suitability is not inevitability.

. . . Anthropologist, Margaret Mead, comments on the element of wish-fulfillment in the assumption of a *natural* correlation of femininity and nurturance: "We have assumed that because it is convenient for a mother to wish to care for her child, this is a trait with which women have been more generously endowed by a careful teleological process of evolution. We have assumed that because men have hunted, an activity requiring enterprise, bravery, and initiative, they have been endowed with these useful aptitudes as part of their sex-temperament."[7] However,

[7]Margaret Mead: *Sex and Temperament*, in *The Family and the Sexual Revolution*, ed. E. M. Schur (1964) pp. 207–8.

the cultural allocation of roles in bringing up children—and the limits of its variability—is not the essential problem for consideration. What is much more important is to analyse the nature of the socialization process itself and its requirements.

Parsons in his detailed analysis claims that it is essential for the child to have two "parents," one who plays an "expressive" role, and one who plays an "instrumental" role.[8] The nuclear family revolves around the two axes of generational hierarchy and of these two roles. . . . In all groups, he and his colleagues assert, even in those primitive tribes discussed by Pritchard and Mead, the male plays the instrumental role *in relation* to the wife-mother. At one stage the mother plays an instrumental and expressive role *vis-a-vis* her infant: this is preoedipally when she is the source of approval and disapproval as well as of love and care. However, after this, the father, or male substitute (in matrilineal societies the mother's brother) takes over. In a modern industrial society two types of role are clearly important: the adult familial roles in the family of procreation, and the adult occupational role. The function of the family as such reflects the function of the women within it; it is primarily expressive. The person playing the integrated-adaptive-expressive role cannot be off all the time on instrumental-occupational errands—hence there is a built-in inhibition of the woman's work outside the home. Parsons' analysis makes clear the exact role of the maternal socializer in contemporary American society. It fails to go on to state that other aspects and modes of socialization are conceivable.

.   .   .

Infancy and Familial Patterns

. . . One of the great revolutions of modern psychology has been the discovery of the decisive specific weight of infancy in the

[8]Talcott Parsons and Robert F. Bales: *Family, Socialization and Interaction Process* (1956), p. 313.

course of an individual life—a psychic time disproportionately greater than the chronological time. . . . These undoubted advances in the scientific understanding of childhood have been widely used as an argument to reassert women's quintessential maternal function, at a time when the traditional family has seemed increasingly eroded. . . .

This ideology corresponds in dislocated form to a real change in the pattern of the family. As the family has become smaller, each child has become more important; the actual *act* of reproduction occupies less and less time and the socializing and nurturance process increase commensurately in significance. Bourgeois society is obsessed by the physical, moral and sexual problems of childhood and adolescence. Ultimate responsibility for these is placed on the mother. Thus the mother's "maternal" role has retreated as her socializing role has increased. In the 1890s in England a mother spent fifteen years in a state of pregnancy and lactation; in the 1960s she spends an average of four years. Compulsory schooling from the age of five, of course, reduces the maternal function very greatly after the initial vulnerable years.

The present situation is then one in which the qualitative importance of socialization during the early years of the child's life has acquired a much greater significance than in the past—while the quantitative amount of a mother's life spent either in gestation or child-rearing has greatly diminished. It follows that socialization cannot simply be elevated to the woman's new maternal vocation. Used as a mystique, it becomes an instrument of oppression. Moreover, there is no inherent reason why the biological and social mother should coincide. The process of socialization is invariable—but the person of the socializer can vary.

.   .   .

CONCLUSION

The lesson of these reflections is that the liberation of women can only be achieved if *all four* structures in which they are integrated are transformed. A modification of any one of them can be offset by a reinforcement of another, so that mere permutation of the form of exploitation is achieved. The history of the last sixty years provides ample evidence of this. In the early twentieth century, militant feminism in England or the U.S. surpassed the labour movement in the violence of its assault on bourgeois society, in pursuit of suffrage. This political right was eventually won. Nonetheless, though a simple completion of the formal legal equality of bourgeois society, it left the socio-economic situation of women virtually unchanged. The wider legacy of the suffrage was nil: the suffragettes proved quite unable to move beyond their own initial demands, and many of their leading figures later became extreme reactionaries. The Russian Revolution produced a quite different experience. In the Soviet Union in the 1920s, advanced social legislation aimed at liberating women above all in the field of sexuality: divorce was made free and automatic for either partner, thus effectively liquidating marriage; illegitimacy was abolished, abortion was free, etc. The social and demographic effects of these laws in a backward, semiliterate society bent on rapid industrialization (needing, therefore, a high birth-rate) were—predictably—catastrophic. Stalinism soon produced a restoration of iron traditional norms. Inheritance was reinstated, divorce inaccessible, abortion illegal, etc. "The State cannot exist without the family. Marriage is a positive value for the Socialist Soviet State only if the partners see in it a lifelong union. So-called free love is a bourgeois invention and has nothing in common with the principles of conduct of a Soviet citizen. Moreover, marriage receives its full value for the State only if there is progeny, and the consorts experience the highest happiness of parenthood," wrote the official journal of the Commissariat of Justice in 1939. Women still retained the right and obligation to work, but because these gains had not been integrated into the earlier attempts to abolish the family and free sexuality no general liberation has occurred. In China, still another experience is being played out today. At a comparable stage of the revolution, all the emphasis is being placed on liberating women in *production*. This has produced an impressive social promotion of women. But it has been accompanied by a tremendous repression of sexuality and a rigorous puritanism (currently rampant in civic life). This corresponds not only to the need to mobilize women massively in economic life, but to a deep cultural reaction against the corruption and prostitution prevalent in Imperial and Kuo Ming Tang China (a phenomenon unlike anything in Czarist Russia). Because the exploitation of women was so great in the *ancien régime* women's participation at village level in the Chinese Revolution, was uniquely high. As for reproduction, the Russian cult of maternity in the 1930s and 1940s has not been repeated for demographic reasons: indeed, China may be one of the first countries in the world to provide free State authorized contraception on a universal scale to the population. Again, however, given the low level of industrialization and fear produced by imperialist encirclement, no all-round advance could be expected.

It is only in the highly developed societies of the West that an authentic liberation of women can be envisaged today. But for this to occur, there must be a transformation of all the structures into which they are integrated, and an *"unité de rupture."* A revolutionary movement must base its analysis on the uneven development of each, and attack the weakest link in the combination. This may then become the point of departure for a general transformation. What is the situation of the different structures today?

1. *Production*: The long-term development of the forces of production must command any socialist perspective. The hopes which the advent of machine technology

raised as early as the nineteenth century have already been discussed. They proved illusory. Today, automation promises the *technical* possibility of abolishing completely the physical differential between man and woman in production, but under capitalist relations of production, the *social* possibility of this abolition is permanently threatened, and can easily be turned into its opposite, the actual diminution of woman's role in production as the labour force contracts.

This concerns the future, for the present the main fact to register is that woman's role in production is virtually stationary, and has been so for a long time now. In England in 1911 30 percent of the work force were women; in the 1960s 34 percent. The composition of these jobs has not changed decisively either. The jobs are very rarely "careers." When they are not in the lowest positions on the factory-floor they are normally white-collar auxiliary positions (such as secretaries)—supportive to masculine roles. They are often jobs with a high "expressive" content, such as "service" tasks. Parsons says bluntly: "Within the occupational organization they are analogous to the wife-mother role in the family."[9] The educational system underpins this role structure. Seventy-five percent of eighteen-year-old girls in England are receiving neither training nor education today. The pattern of "instrumental" father and "expressive" mother is not substantially changed when the woman is gainfully employed, as her job tends to be inferior to that of the man's, to which the family then adapts.

Thus, in all essentials, work as such—of the amount and type effectively available today—has not proved a salvation for women.

2. *Reproduction*: Scientific advance in contraception could, as we have seen, make involuntary reproduction—which accounts for the vast majority of births in the world today, and for a major proportion even in the West—a phenomenon of the past. But oral contraception—which has so far been developed in a form which exactly repeats

[9]Talcott Parsons and Robert F. Bales: *Family, Socialization and Interaction Process* (1956), p. 15.

the sexual inequality of Western society—is only at its beginnings. It is inadequately distributed across classes and countries and awaits further technical improvements. Its main initial impact is, in the advanced countries, likely to be psychological—it will certainly free women's sexual experience from many of the anxieties and inhibitions which have always afflicted it. It will definitely divorce sexuality from procreation, as necessary complements. . . .

3. *Socialization*: The changes in the composition of the work force, the size of the family, the structure of education, etc.—however limited from an ideal standpoint—have undoubtedly diminished the societal function and importance of the family. As an organization it is not a significant unit in the political power system, it plays little part in economic production and it is rarely the sole agency of integration into the larger society; thus at the macroscopic level it serves very little purpose.

The result has been a major displacement of emphasis on to the family's psycho-social function, for the infant and for the couple. . . . The vital nucleus of truth in the emphasis on socialization of the child has been discussed. It is essential that socialists should acknowledge it and integrate it entirely into any programme for the liberation of women.

. . . However, there is no doubt that the need for permanent, intelligent care of children in the initial three or four years of their lives can (and has been) exploited ideologically to perpetuate the family as a total unit, when its other functions have been visibly declining. Indeed, the attempt to focus women's existence exclusively on bringing up children, is manifestly harmful to children. Socialization as an exceptionally delicate process requires a serene and mature socializer—a type which the frustrations of a *purely* familial role are not liable to produce. Exclusive maternity is often in this sense "counter-productive." The mother discharges her own frustrations and anxieties in a fixation on the child. An increased awareness of the critical importance of socialization, far from leading to a restitution of classical maternal roles, should lead to a reconsideration of them—of what makes a good socializing agent, who can genuinely provide security and stability for the child.

The same arguments apply, *a fortiori*, to the psycho-social role of the family for the couple. The beliefs that the family provides an impregnable enclave of intimacy and security in an atomized and chaotic cosmos assumes the absurd—that the family can be isolated from the community, and that its internal relationships will not reproduce in their own terms the external relationships which dominate the society. The family as refuge in a bourgeois society inevitably becomes a reflection of it.

4. *Sexuality*: It is difficult not to conclude that the major structure which at present is in rapid evolution is sexuality. Production, reproduction, and socialization are all more or less stationary in the West today, in the sense that they have not changed for three or more decades. There is moreover, no widespread *demand* for changes in them on the part of women themselves—the governing ideology has effectively prevented critical consciousness. By contrast, the dominant sexual ideology is proving less and less successful in regulating spontaneous behaviour. Marriage in its classical form is increasingly threatened by the liberalization of relationships before and after it which affects all classes today. In this sense, it is evidently the weak link in the chain—the particular structure that is the site of the most contradictions. The progressive potential of these contradictions has already been emphasized. In a context of juridical equality, the liberation of sexual experience from relations which are extraneous to it—whether procreation or property—could lead to true intersexual freedom. But it could also lead simply to new forms of neocapitalist ideology and practice. For one of the forces behind the current acceleration of sexual freedom has undoubtedly been the conversion of contemporary capitalism from a production-and-work ethos to a consumption-and-fun ethos. . . . In a society bored by work, sex is the only activity, the only reminder of one's energies, the only competitive act; the

last defense against *vis inertiae*. This same insight can be found, with greater theoretical depth, in Marcuse's notion of "repressive desublimation"—the freeing of sexuality for its own frustration in the service of a totally coordinated and drugged social machine. Bourgeois society at present can well afford a play area of premarital *non*-procreative sexuality. Even marriage can save itself by increasing divorce and remarriage rates, signifying the importance of the institution itself. These considerations make it clear that sexuality, while it presently may contain the greatest potential for liberation—can equally well be organized against any increase of its human possibilities. New forms of reification are emerging which may void sexual freedom of any meaning. This is a reminder that while one structure may be the *weak link* in a unity like that of woman's condition, there can never be a solution through it alone.

.   .   .

What, then, is the responsible revolutionary attitude? It must include both immediate and fundamental demands, in a single critique of the *whole* of women's situation, that does not fetishize any dimension of it. Modern industrial development, as has been seen, tends towards the separating out of the originally unified function of the family—procreation, socialization, sexuality, economic subsistence, etc.—even if this "structural differentiation" (to use a term of Parsons') has been checked and disguised by the maintenance of a powerful family ideology. This differentiation provides the real historical basis for the ideal demands which should be posed: structural differentiation is precisely what distinguishes an advanced from a primitive society (in which all social functions are fused *en bloc*).

In practical terms this means a coherent system of demands. The four elements of women's condition cannot merely be considered each in isolation; they form a structure of specific interrelations. The contemporary bourgeois family can be seen as a triptych of sexual, reproductive and social-izatory functions (the woman's world) embraced by production (the man's world)— precisely a structure which in the final instance is determined by the economy. The exclusion of women from production—social human activity—and their confinement to a monolithic condensation of functions in a unity—the family—which is precisely unified in the *natural part* of each function, is the root cause of the contemporary *social* definition of women as *natural* beings. Hence the main thrust of any emancipation movement must still concentrate on the economic element—the entry of women fully into public industry. The error of the old socialists was to see the other elements as reducible to the economic; hence the call for the entry of women into production was accompanied by the purely abstract slogan of the abolition of the family. Economic demands are still primary, but must be accompanied by coherent policies for the other three elements, policies which at particular junctures may take over the primary role in immediate action.

Economically, the most elementary demand is not the right to work or receive equal pay for work—the two traditional reformist demands—but *the right to equal work itself.*

. . .

Only if it is founded on equality can production be truly differentiated from reproduction and the family. But this in turn requires a whole set of noneconomic demands as a complement. Reproduction, sexuality, and socialization also need to be free from coercive forms of unification. Traditionally, the socialist movement has called for the "abolition of the bourgeois family." This slogan must be rejected as incorrect today. It is maximalist in the bad sense, posing a demand which is merely a negation without any coherent construction subsequent to it. Its weakness can be seen by comparing it

to the call for the abolition of the private ownership of the means of production, whose solution—social ownership—is contained in the negation itself. . . . The reasons for the historic weakness of the notion is that the family was never analysed structurally—in terms of its different functions. It was a hypostasized entity; the abstraction of its abolition corresponds to the abstraction of its conception. The strategic concern for socialists should be for the equality of the sexes, not the abolition of the family. The consequences of this demand are no less radical, but they are concrete and positive, and can be integrated into the real course of history. The family as it exists at present is, in fact, incompatible with the equality of the sexes. But this equality will not come from its administrative abolition, but from the historical differentiation of its functions. The revolutionary demand should be for the liberation of these functions from a monolithic fusion which oppresses each. Thus dissociation of reproduction from sexuality frees sexuality from alienation in unwanted reproduction (and fear of it), and reproduction from subjugation to chance and uncontrollable causality. It is thus an elementary demand to press for free State provision of oral contraception. The legalization of homosexuality—which is one of the forms of nonreproductive sexuality—should be supported for just the same reason, and regressive campaigns against it in Cuba or elsewhere should be unhesitatingly criticized. The straightforward abolition of illegitimacy as a legal notion as in Sweden and Russia has a similar implication; it would separate marriage civically from parenthood.

From Nature to Culture

The problem of socialization poses more difficult questions, as has been seen. But the need for intensive maternal care in the early years of a child's life does not mean that the present single sanctioned form of socialization—marriage and family—is inevitable. Far from it. The fundamental characteristic of the present system of marriage and family is in our society its *monolithism*: there is only one institutionalized form of intersexual or intergenerational relationship possible. It is that or nothing. This is why it is essentially a denial of life. For all human experience shows that intersexual and intergenerational relationships are infinitely various—indeed, much of our creative literature is a celebration of the fact—while the institutionalized expression of them in our capitalist society is utterly simple and rigid. It is the poverty and simplicity of the institutions in this area of life which are such an oppression. Any society will require some institutionalized and social recognition of personal relationships. But there is absolutely no reason why there should be only one legitimized form—and a multitude of unlegitimized experience. Socialism should properly mean not the abolition of the family, but the diversification of the socially acknowledged relationships which are today forcibly and rigidly compressed into it. This would mean a plural range of institutions—where the family is only one, and its abolition implies none. Couples living together or not living together, long-term unions with children, single parents bringing up children, children socialized by conventional rather than biological parents, extended kin groups, etc.—all these could be encompassed in a range of institutions which matched the free invention and variety of men and women. . . .

8.2   *Families and the Oppression of Women*

The structure of the contemporary patriarchal nuclear family is basically defined by the social division of labor within it: the husband is primarily responsible for the family's financial support, while the wife is primarily responsible for housework and child-rearing. This division of labor and its attendant division of power limits the full creative development of every family member, placing the greatest burdens on women and children. In the following reading, Linda Gordon examines the structure of the modern family as it is generally constituted and, in particular, its male supremacist nature. In her assessment, Gordon points out that the family system is not the sole source of the oppression of women and that the family does serve some human needs. However, the family will have to be radically reformed or restructured if real human needs for warm and intimate groups are to be fulfilled in a nonexploitative, nonhierarchical manner.

Source: The following is excerpted from "Families" by LINDA GORDON, published as a pamphlet by The New England Free Press. Reprinted by permission of the author.

. . . The family serves to reinforce the economic system and maximize profits only at a tremendous human cost—the crushing of human potential in some areas and the limiting of it in many more. The family system is bad for men but worse for women and children.[1]

For example, families create an oppressive situation for many men, placing on them the near certainty of having to be responsible all their lives not just for their own livelihood but for that of one or more others. (In the law of many states of the U.S., for example, no marriage "contract" that envisages the women to be the chief provider is permissible.) A preference for nonlucrative activity, such as painting or writing or philosophizing, endangers a man's family or deprives him of the possibility of having a woman and children to live with. Even prior to this, and destructive not just to the individual man but to the whole society, the constant social expectation that each man must become a life-long wage-earner deprives men of even the possibility of forming a preference for nonprofit activity in the first place. Perhaps I should point out that this is not inevitable: that if groups of people larger than the nuclear family lived together fewer people could work full-time or many people could work part-time to provide for the community. This way more people could have more free time to do useful things that are nonprofit—study, teach, grow up, sculpt, play. Lacking such arrangements, the family in capitalist society helps to deprive us of cultural activity that cannot be made to produce a profit; or worse, it distorts cultural activity to make it produce a profit.

Any benefits housewives might reap from being exempt from money-making responsibilities are usually undercut by housework and child-raising responsibilities. But even should she have leisure time to spend on voluntary activity, the social value of that activity is diminished by her own low social status. There is a vicious circle here: in capitalist society a person's social importance tends to be related to his capacity to earn money, whether or not the person is exercising that capacity. Since most women are not seen as having that capacity, nothing they produce is likely to be treated with the respect that a man's work might engender. The low social esteem of women's work is, naturally, internalized by many women: the results are that most women who try to express themselves in writing, painting, or politics tend to suffer from their low, prior self-esteem; and for most women, that self-esteem is *so* low that they never try at all.

In terms of the devaluation of women, families are both cause and effect—this is another vicious circle. The division of labor in the nuclear family is a result of women's low status and also helps to perpetuate it. It is reasonable, in capitalist society, that the family who earns the money should assume the largest share of decision-making power. Thus in many young families, beginning with high resolutions about equality between husband and wife, the fact that the husband is the sole or chief breadwinner makes that equality difficult or impossible to realize. This is particularly true since many of the key decisions within families are taken without knowing it. The family moves where the man's job takes it, for example. As the wife becomes increasingly bogged down in administering details of cooking, cleaning, diapers, and children's squabbles, she becomes *in fact* less interesting and important in the eyes of her husband. A typical middle-class example is that of a brilliant college student passionately involved in philosophy, math, or medieval history—and who ten years later believes herself, and is believed by others, to be incapable of any serious intellectual endeavor. It is everywhere the story of tough, spirited women who are broken and become terrified but infinitely forgiving when their selfish and chauvinist husbands desert

---

[1] It is probably worst of all for children, and we will try to point out how and where when possible, but to discuss the effects of the family on children properly would require an entire separate study.

them time after time for other women, "the boys," drunkenness, fishing, golf, the office.

As women's minds and spirits can be destroyed by life on the inside of a nuclear family, our sexuality is almost universally repressed and distorted by the nuclear family, whether or not we choose to enter into one. Historically, families help to repress and control sexuality so that it would interfere as little as possible with production while allowing for continued reproduction. For most of history, in most of the world, this was accomplished by imposing strict sexual fidelity on women.[2] With the birth of capitalism, when harder work for the accumulation of capital was valued, a special ethic—Puritanism—strengthened the sexual repression still further and made monogamy the mutual obligation of husband and wife.

Despite the weakening of that ethic today, women still carry its burden. Women in families are trained to see themselves primarily as mothers and reproducers, not as enjoyers of sex, while women outside families are pressured to see themselves primarily as sex objects—in order to catch a man and enter a family and "relax" into motherhood. Thus the family structure limits the alternatives of most women even before they marry. The fear of not finding a mate, translated as the necessity of being always desirable, conditions a woman's whole world from the age of puberty and sometimes earlier: the need to be always beautiful and sweet-smelling; to avoid competing with, or outstripping men, or just being too skilled at anything not specifically considered the feminine province; above all, the fear of appearing too aggres-

sive. Women who have attempted to fight the family's sexual repression individually, by becoming "promiscuous," or even by remaining celibate, suffer both from social castigation and from the inner necessity of adopting the social definition as their own identity—by *becoming* the "loose woman," the "tease," or the prudish spinster. The fact is that there is no acceptable way for a woman to have a sex life after age twenty-five except in marriage and that to choose therefore not to have a sex life is to condemn oneself to not having a satisfying social life.

Within marriage, the family system in the past has tended to chain women to their reproductive function by implying, first, that sex is inevitably connected with reproduction and, second, that biological motherhood is inevitably connected with the responsibility for raising the child. The first connection is now rapidly being broken down with birth control and an accelerating nationwide attack on restrictive abortion laws. Breaking down the second connection is still far away. It is interesting that we already have a rhetoric about collective responsibility for children: politicians are always telling us that youth are the future of our society. The women's liberation movement is beginning to call them on that rhetoric now, and it seems likely that the state, big businesses, schools, and all public institutions will increasingly be called upon to provide free child-care facilities. If women are really to be freed from the special burdens of child-raising, we will have to see to it that *no* woman is denied any opportunity open to anyone else in the society because of special responsibilities to children. This will mean, for example, that instead of demanding of employers special provisions to make women's jobs compatible with their child-care responsibilities, we need to start thinking of demanding that men's jobs be made compatible with their assuming a full half of all responsibilities for children.

[2]Sexual fidelity was probably originally imposed upon women by men when the system of private property made the ruling sex anxious to ensure that inherited property remained in his family. Earlier sexual fidelity was unnecessary because succession and inheritance was probably matrilineal, and it was always evident who the mother of the child was; since it is not always certain who the father is, patrilineal succession made necessary the strict enforcement of monogamy for women.

But a child-raising system based on the nuclear family supplemented by child-care centers, no matter how equal the distribution of labor, is not good enough because it is not good for children. Children need much more than babysitting. They need a great deal of love and attention from a small number of people who are *especially* devoted to and committed to just a few children. The nuclear family provides this, but it is damaging to children in other ways. To put it most bluntly, families have oppressed children by making private property of them. Most children today are raised in an atmosphere of possessiveness, rivalry with siblings for the love of two parents, and the sense that they must earn that love by behaving and achieving well. To insist that children should not be the property of their parents is not to deny what we have just argued—that children benefit from the special love of some adults who cherish those children above others. Indeed, the fact that parental love is often confused with parental proprietorship demonstrates how much love itself has become a commodity—something to be owned or possessed exclusively. Love is not ownership. Property in human beings is slavery.

In early industrial and agricultural societies, children are valuable because they can be put to work to help provide for the family; in these societies children are property in a sense close to our conventional understanding of property, like cars and women in harems. In affluent bourgeois society the services that children perform for their masters are often psychological: they are to be what the parents always dreamed of being, or they are to maintain the family name and tradition; frustrated parents, especially mothers, must pour their creative energy into hopes and nagging directed at the child.

R. D. Laing's analysis of how schizophrenia is induced in children (particularly girls in his case studies, incidentally) by parents who are not capable of accepting the child as a separate being, as a subject, is exactly relevant here. To make children the property of a commune, or of the state, would be no improvement. Thus it seems that the liberation of children could not occur until the liberation of adults made them no longer need to use children as the carriers of their own aspirations.

·   ·   ·

CONCLUSION

The nuclear family is one among many . . . institutions and ideologies which help to keep women down. We are not claiming that the family is alone in playing this role. Especially important, we are not asserting that the destruction of the family would automatically bring down the whole system and allow women to be liberated. There are many alternative structures that could contain, mold, and channel people along sexist lines equally well. Consider the society of ancient Sparta, based on slavery, in which men lived only with men, and women lived with women, old people, and children—controlled by the community in general rather than by fathers or husbands. In contemporary society one could imagine all sorts of substitutes for the family's various functions that would be more, rather than less, oppressive. Men organized in monkish business clubs could be induced to pour more sublimated energy than ever into production for U.S. imperialism. Child care could be given over to large nurseries and schools, providing huge profits for U.S. corporations, and which could serve as efficiently as families to the task of brainwashing children. Without marriage, that is, without possessive arrangements between mates, this society might well organize its women into a system of harems, that is, a system of collective possession of women by men, because women would still be seen as commodities that could be possessed.

Some of these nightmares may not be so fantastic. In certain places and strata of our society families are already breaking down. Divorces, birth control pills, youth rebellion, and unemployment are splintering families, and this movement is an objectively revolutionary force. This is not to say that it is an entirely desirable movement, nor do we think its outcome predetermined. We do not cheer the way the hip capitalists are exploiting the hippies and their "chicks" as a market for tie-dyed shirts, fancy marijuana pipes, incense, and black light. We find the cycles of divorces, remarriages, and divorces painful and sometimes stupid. But we must not hide from the knowledge that the old society must disintegrate before a new one can be born. The women's liberation movement is tending something to strengthen that movement towards disintegration, and it ought to consider itself especially to supporting women who are outside of families and to provide alternative supportive communities.

But it would be foolish to make the destruction of the family a *program*. That would be like making the abolition of capitalism a program; an ideal is not a program.

Similarly a frontal propaganda assault on the family would be of limited usefulness, for families are not like a vice to be cast off. Even if their functions are on balance oppressive, they are only successful at performing those functions because they serve certain needs. Families can only cease to exist when those needs can be met in other ways, we hope, in a socialist society where individuals can have the freedom to develop their potential without the exploitation of others. And even now, the family in itself is not the ultimate or the only enemy. It is one time-worn social structure adapted to the purpose of exploitation through a basic form of the division of labor. The women's liberation movement has discovered and rediscovered that everywhere, in every aspect of the society, the division of labor supports antiwoman, chauvinist ideologies that in turn support continued exploitation. The radical thrust of the women's liberation movement is precisely that it challenges all aspects of the division of labor, all at once. *Venceremos*!

8.3 *The Economic Exploitation of Women*

Male supremacy and capitalism reinforce each other in many ways. For example, the oppression of women in the family facilitates their exploitation by capitalists in vital but menial jobs and provides capitalism with a convenient reserve army of labor that can be drawn upon as needed when shortages of male labor develop.

In the first part of the next reading, Marilyn Power Goldberg focuses on the exploitation of women by capitalists in the labor market. In the second part, Goldberg explores the role of sexism in stimulating wasteful consumption and in perpetuating both possessive individualism and authoritarianism. Such practices and values are functionally important for the viability of a capitalist society.

Source: The following is reproduced from "The Economic Exploitation of Women" by MARILYN POWER GOLDBERG. From *The Review of Radical Political Economics* II, No. 1 (Spring 1970). Reprinted by permission of the author.

There are many ways in which capitalism endeavors to keep the pressure on it from becoming too great. One of the most important is by creating divisions in the work force in order to keep wages low and otherwise limit the power of labor. It does this by creating a labor hierarchy, through differences in working conditions and through perpetuating, reinforcing ideology, so that skilled workers will feel superior to unskilled, white to black, and male to female. At the same time capitalism repeatedly tells all workers that they have never before had it so good, that they are better off than workers (blacks, women) have ever been before. The division of the labor force is of further importance to capitalism because it allows certain groups, namely minorities and women, to be superexploited, used as a marginal work force in order to smooth over cycles in the economy, and to perform vital but menial and poorly paid jobs. Ideology is very important in perpetuating these superexploited groups, as it affects not only society's assumptions about them but also their expectations about themselves.

Capitalism did not invent the nuclear family or the concept that the role of women is to mind the home and the children. These institutions go back thousands of years, to the origins of private property, when man the hunter began to acquire land and desired heirs to pass it on to. But capitalism actively promotes the isolated family unit and the woman's role in it, through such propaganda devices as the glorification of motherhood, in order to facilitate its economic exploitation both of men and women.

SOCIALIZATION TO BE SECONDARY

Women are taught from the time they are children to play a serving role, to be docile and submissive, get what they want by being coy instead of aggressive. They are socialized to expect that they will spend their lives as housewives and mothers—for toys they are given the tools of their trade: dolls, tea sets, frilly dresses, and so on. They are never encouraged to think in terms of a career, unless it be one which is an extension of the serving, subordinate role in the family, such as nursing or being a secretary. As they grow they learn that it is unfeminine and therefore abhorrent to be self-assertive or to compete with men. Thus most women mature with the understanding that their primary role is that of housewife and mother and that, while they may per chance work, their contribution will be merely supplemental and temporary; they will not have a career. This is true despite the fact that most women who work are essential to support themselves and their families: 70 percent of women who worked in March 1964 supported themselves or others or had husbands who earned less than $5,000 in 1963.[1] In a survey of women who graduated from college in 1957, while most were working or planned to work at some point in their lives, only 18 percent planned to have a career.[2] Another survey taken in 1964 found much the same result, although of Negro women college graduates, 40 percent planned a career, and many women who do work feel guilt pangs about being outside the home (although most of them face their traditional household tasks unaided at the end of the work day).[3] In a study of working wives in the Detroit area in 1956, nine out of ten often felt that a job makes personal relations in the home more difficult, hurts the husband's pride, or disrupts the home.[4]

These attitudes which women have learned about themselves and their work make them a convenient, cheap marginal labor force for capitalism. Because they con-

[1] Women's Bureau, U.S. Department of Labor, *Fact Sheet on the Relative Position of Women and Men Workers in the Economy.*
[2] Valerie Oppenheimer, "The Sex-Labeling of Jobs," *Industrial Relations* (May 1968), p. 231.
[3] *Ibid.*
[4] Harold Wilensky, "Women's Work," *Industrial Relations* (May 1968), p. 234.

sider their economic contribution supplementary even when it is necessary to maintain a decent standard of living for their families, they are more willing than men to accept low pay and poor working conditions. Because they have been socialized to be docile and accept subordinate positions, they are far less likely than men to organize or create trouble for the employer. As they feel responsible to continue their role as housewives and mothers while working (and there are no facilities to relieve them of this burden), they are forced to accept a very low economic position and, even if skilled, to be exploited as a cheap labor force. They are bound to search for work near their homes and very often for only part of the day or the year. Thus, they are in a poor bargaining position vis-a-vis their employers. This situation is further exacerbated by the tendency of many women to work until their children are born, drop out of the work force for ten, fifteen, even twenty years, then return to work after their children are grown. Thus they never acquire seniority or qualify for retirement and other benefits—employers, who are reluctant to promote women to prestigious or high paying jobs, have an excuse not to do so. Besides these considerations of the detrimental effects the traditional roles of women have on their economic position, there is also plain discrimination on the part of employers, who are reluctant to hire women to positions of importance or where they will have authority over male workers and who, given the opportunity, prefer to promote men and to lay off women. Many labor unions also discriminate and not only show no interest in organizing women but frequently negotiate preferential treatment or pay for male workers.

PART-TIME WORKERS—
A MARGINAL WORK FORCE

Women constitute a significant proportion of the supply of part-time workers. While 66 percent of all men in the labor force worked full-time, full-year in 1965, only 39 percent of the 33.8 million women who worked, or 13.1 million, did so. Of the rest, 10 million worked full-time less than a full year, and 10.6 million worked part-time for all or part of the year.[5] By 1967, 42.1 percent of women who worked, worked full-time, full-year, an increase probably due in large part to the drafting of men to fight the Vietnam War.

Thus, women form a marginal work force, important for several reasons. First, as indicated above, part-time or temporary workers never achieve seniority or become eligible for fringe benefits. Thus an employer might well find it more economical and convenient to hire two such workers to perform basic or menial chores, rather than invest in one full-time, full-year worker. Temporary workers can be taken on or let go according to fluctuations in business, taking the brunt of cycles and uncertainties that otherwise might spread to the rest of the economy. They are the last to be hired and the first to be fired. Business offices in particular feel this need, as they have no product that can be stockpiled in case of waning demand. If they have overhired, their employees simply go idle. This has been institutionalized in the flourishing temporary worker agencies—the Kelly Girl and so on—allowing an employer to hire extra help by the week or the month. Women form a significant portion of this temporary office work force. Ninety-seven percent of all stenographers and typists are women, and one-third of all women workers were in clerical work—the most in any job category.[6] The importance of temporary workers as a marginal work force is indicated by the rapid growth in this job cate-

[5]Eli Ginzberg, "Paycheck and Apron-Revolution in Woman Power," (sic), *Industrial Relations* (May 1968), p. 194.

[6]Gertrude Bancroft McNally, "Patterns of Female Labor Force Activity," *Industrial Relations* (May 1968), p. 195.

gory. In the years 1950–1965, the average annual increase of part-time jobs for women was 300,000, or just below the average increase in full-time male workers.[7] Women workers' role concept facilitates their acceptance of part-time or temporary work. Thus, of the 17.6 million women who worked less than full-time throughout the year—while 22 percent did so because they were going to school and 26 percent either could not find full-time work or were kept from working by illness, disability, or other reasons— a full 52 percent chose to work in order to take care of their homes.[8]

UNEMPLOYMENT

One of the important aspects of temporary workers, as mentioned above, is precisely their "temporary-ness." That is, they can be taken on in time of need and let go when the need is finished. Women are ideally suited to this purpose, both because they consider their income of supplementary, and therefore secondary, importance to the family and are therefore less likely to put up a fight; and because they tend not to enter the unemployment roles but rather to disappear back into their homes. They are not "unemployed," they are housewives. Further, labor unions tend to be male supremacist and are unlikely to fight the laying off of women workers. The unemployment rate for women is still higher than for men—5.3 percent in 1965, as compared with 3.2 percent for men. If the number of women who return to their homes could be included, the figure would undoubtedly be much higher.

First, their tendency to divide their career between work and home means they have a higher turnover in labor force participation. Thus, since many of them are occasional and seasonal workers, they are more exposed to the risks of unemployment. Second, the

lack of maternity leave means that pregnancy results in loss of job. Third, in industry they tend to have less seniority than men, and custom and sentiment favor laying off women in preference to men, since women's work is considered secondary and even an aberration, taking employment away from men (once again, women bear the brunt of economic fluctuations). Fourth, since women have a more narrow range of job opportunities, stemming from a reluctance to hire them in many occupations, and their frequent concomitant lack of training in these fields, they do not have as many potential employment opportunities. And finally, there is an element of discrimination that means that many employers will not hire a woman for a job she is qualified for, especially if there are also male applicants for the position. For nonwhite women the problem is even more serious; they tend to have an unemployment rate twice that of white women at 7.8 percent in 1968, as compared with 3.9 percent for white women.[9]

WORK CYCLE OF WOMEN

The tendency of women to drop in and out of the labor force in their life cycle further leaves them open to economic exploitation. Two-thirds of women in the age group eighteen to twenty-five worked at some time in 1965. However, in the age group twenty-five to thirty-four, this figure dropped to one-third.[10] This drop is sufficient to give employers an excuse to pay their young women employees less and not to promote them to positions of importance, since there is a danger that the women will work for a short time and then quit to marry or have children. This danger is increased by the fact that their hubands' careers are not yet set-

[7]*Ibid.*, p. 197.
[8]*Ibid.*, p. 194.

[9]Women's Bureau, U.S. Department of Labor, *Report of the Task Force on Labor Standards,* 1968.
[10]McNally, *op. cit.,* p. 197.

tled, and the women's work being secondary, if he wants to leave the area, she must quit. When women return to the labor force after their children have grown, they have not worked for a long time, so that employers discount their previous experience and whatever skills they might have had are considerably rusty. Currently, 58 percent of women aged forty-five–fifty-four work, more than any other group except aged eighteen–twenty-five.[11]

JOB DISCRIMINATION— SEX-TYPING

Whether working full-time or part-time, women tend to be employed in the less remunerative occupations, frequently in work that is an extension of their role in the family—that is, secondary, serving work; traditional housewives' tasks of cooking, cleaning, etc.; tasks requiring patience, waiting; work requiring an attractive appearance; and work dealing with children. They are rarely placed in positions requiring individual initiative or decision-making and almost never in a position of supervising or giving orders to men. A survey shows that 74 percent of employers in New Haven and 53 percent of employers in Charlotte preferred men for administrative and executive positions.[12] It was felt that men should deal with other men, such as most clients, other management people, suppliers, and so on, and that it was not appropriate for a woman to do so. Also, male supervisors were felt to command more respect, even from women workers. Men, after all, are accustomed to giving orders to women, not receiving them, in the home as well as on the job; and women are used to taking orders from men and, looking at other women as rivals and competitors, would resent taking orders from them.

The sex-typing of jobs available to

women is evident from the great concentration of women in certain occupations. Ninety-seven percent of all stenographers, typists, and private household workers are women, as are two-thirds of all health service workers, teachers (except college), waitresses and clerks, and other clerical workers.[13] Many of these jobs remain female-dominated at least in part because they combine a need for a fairly high level of training and education with very low pay (stenography, nursing, teaching).

DIFFERENCE IN INCOME

The economic exploitation of women is indicated by their low median income in comparison with men. In 1965, women received a median of $2,098, or 40 percent of the male median of $5,194.[14] This inequality can be explained in part by the tendency discussed above for women to be relegated to part-time and/or part-year work, but even women who work full-time, full-year make only around three-fifths of the male median for the same work load. This relative earning position, moreover, has not improved in the last twenty-five years, except for nonwhite women. White men have the highest median income, then nonwhite men, then white women, and finally nonwhite women. Table 8–B shows the median income for full-time, full-year male and female workers.

Calculating from this table, white women had an income which was 90.1 percent of that of nonwhite men, and nonwhite women had 41.0 percent of white men. It may be noted that white women and nonwhite men have exchanged relative economic positions since 1939.

In the category of full-time, full-year jobs, the discrepancy between the median incomes of men and women exists not only in general but also within every occupational field.

[11]*Ibid.*, p. 194.
[12]Oppenheimer, *op. cit.*, p. 199.

[13]McNally, *op. cit.*, p. 195.
[14]*Ibid.*

TABLE 8–B   MEDIAN INCOME BY SEX AND RACE, 1939 AND 1964

| | 1964 Median Income | | | 1939 Median Income | | |
	Men	Women	W as % of M	Men	Women	W as % of M
White	$6,497	$3,859	59.4	$1,419	$863	60.8
Nonwhite	4,285	2,674	52.4	639	327	51.2

SOURCE: U.S. Department of Labor, Women's Bureau, *Fact Sheet on the Relative Position of Women and Men Workers in the Economy.*

For example, in 1965, for sales workers, the median income for women was $3,000 and for men $7,000; for managers and officials, $4,500 for women and $8,600 for men; and for professionals, $5,500 for women and $8,200 for men.[15] From these figures, we can see that the lower pay for women is not simply due to their being employed in the less remunerative occupations, although this is an important factor; they are also paid less than men for doing the same or similar work. Indeed, among full-time, full-year workers, the median income of women as a proportion of the median income of men has fallen from 1939 to 1964 in every major industrial group in which the number of women employed is significant.[16]

WASTEFUL CONSUMPTION BY NUCLEAR FAMILY

The other aspect of the economic exploitation of women which this paper will discuss is less readily apparent, not easily quantifiable, and inextricably involved with the exploitation of men as well. This involves the concept of the nuclear family as an economic, consumptive, and psychic unit unto itself. On the most obvious level, the nuclear family unit helps keep demand at an artificially high level, as it leads to wasteful consumption of indivisible goods, often of a

[15]*Ibid.,* p. 196.
[16]See Women's Bureau, *Fact sheet on the Relative Position of Women and Men Workers in the Economy, op. cit.*

high cost, durable nature. Thus, each family unit must have its own washer, dryer, automobiles, camera, and so on, even though they may sit idle much of the time. Further, the isolation of family units from their neighbors may result in competitive, conspicuous consumption among them. One has only to fly over Los Angeles and look at the row upon row of individual backyard swimming pools to comprehend the extent of the waste, and profit, thus generated.

CONSUMPTION AND THE HOUSEWIFE

The role of housewife, one whose primary concern is with the house, stimulates more expenditure on it. This is especially true as prepackaged foods, smaller homes, fewer children, and so on, make the basics of housewivery much less time-consuming than in the past. A modern housewife has time to concern herself with buying new gadgets for her profession, expressing herself through redoing the living room. Advertising encourages her to attempt to assuage her feelings of inadequacy through consuming—providing she is indeed fulfilling her role well by buying for her home, her children, and her husband.

Housewives also spend a good deal of money on themselves. They share with other women's professions such as prostitution, modeling, receptionists, the circumstance that their continuing in their job is dependent on their remaining sexually and personally desirable to their employer, in this case the husband. Therefore, housewives spend a good deal of money making themselves attractive objects. After all, as the song says, "Day after day there are girls in the office, and men will always be men. Don't send him off with your hair up in curlers, you may not see him again."

PERPETUATION OF IDEOLOGY

The home perpetuates the authoritarian structures required in capitalist society. In any relationship, even the most intimate, there is always a dominant member. Thus in a *Chronicle* in June (long since relegated to the garbage, unfortunately), the Questionman asked young men and women who were about to be married, "Who will be the boss in your marriage?" All replied that the man would be although some qualified it somewhat. None questioned that a relationship between two people required a boss or that the male naturally fills that role.

The nuclear family allows the man to get rid of his feelings of frustration and humiliation about his job by dominating his family: "The petty dictatorship which most men exercise over their wives and families enables them to vent their anger and frustration in a way which poses no challenge to the system. The role of the man in the family reinforces aggressive individualism, authoritarianism, and a hierarchical view of social relations—values which are fundamental to the perpetuation of capitalism."[17]

The housewife, in her role as preserver of the family, is a profoundly conservative force, promoting stability, and discouraging any activity that would rock the boat. "A woman is judged as a wife and mother—the only role she is allowed—according to her ability to maintain stability in her family and to help her family 'adjust' to harsh realities. She therefore transmits the values of hard work and conformity to each generation of workers. It is she who forces her children to stay in school and 'behave' or who urges her husband not to risk his job by standing up to the boss or going on strike."[18]

Finally, the separation of workers into isolated family units, which are thought of as complete unto themselves, so that the entrance of an outsider into them is always more or less an invasion, inhibits the workers from feeling community among themselves or organizing against their common oppression. The housewife, who creates and maintains the home, becomes the symbol of its isolated nature and may feel competitive with the homes around hers. Further, the husband comes to see his wife and children as his possessions, which he must defend jealously against interlopers. Thus, workers are kept separate from each other, competing instead of cooperating.

What, then, is the solution—the program to end the exploitation of women in the economy? It is not in merely demanding equal job opportunities with men; few men in this society have creative or satisfying work, and they are also exploited—the difference between the exploitation of men and women is largely a question of degree and of technique. Nor is the solution in a demand that women no longer be socialized to be docile and subservient but be socialized in the same manner as men. The competitive, individualistic values which our society encourages in men are not a desirable alternative. We must struggle, rather, for an unoppressive, nonexploitative society, where individuals are encouraged to lead creative lives within a communal context. This must include a communal alternative to the isolated nuclear family, which has been shown to play an active role in facilitating economic exploitation.

---

[17]Kathy McAfee and Myrna Wood, "Bread and Roses," *Leviathan* (June 1969), p. 9.

[18]*Ibid.*

IMPORTANCE OF WOMEN'S STRUGGLE

The role women play in the modern American economy is a vital one. If women refused to accept their economic position, American capitalism would experience severe difficulties. In the work force, women, in their jobs as secretaries, teachers, and so on, set the context in which capitalist activity can take place. If production cannot continue without production workers, neither can it long carry on if its paper work is not done. As part-time and temporary workers, women provide a mobile semi-skilled (sometimes skilled) labor force which helps prevent labor bottlenecks and assures business of a docile work force at low wages. This position women share with minority groups. This is a very important factor in encouraging new investments. The fact that employers can pay women less for the same work as their male employees, often in collaboration with labor unions, keeps the workers divided against each other and severely limits their effectiveness.

Women cannot successfully defeat their exploitation within the context of the present economic system; it is inherently exploitative (there is simply no merit to demanding an end to superexploitation, equal exploitation with men). We must recognize that we are fighting for a common goal with our exploited black and white brothers. But we must also recognize that women have a crucial position in fighting their economic exploitation, because they are so important in shoring up the economic system. Without the guarantee of a docile, low paid marginal work force, investors might well hesitate to risk their money. If women begin to seek communal, nonauthoritarian alternatives to the nuclear family housing and living unit, the expectations of the work force, and its concomitant docility might be changed. Also, as the vast majority of elementary school teachers are women, they could break down the socializing functions of school. Finally, in developing a consciousness of common oppression and uniting around common struggles, women may provide the impetus for the consciousness of a collective struggle in the working class as a whole.

8.4   On the Relationship Between Sexism and Capitalism

As we have seen, male supremacy and capitalism are not unrelated. In several important ways, capitalism and male supremacy reinforce each other, and in some ways they conflict. The following reading by Margery Davies and Michael Reich examines several aspects of this complex relationship. The intention is to suggest some significant connections, rather than present a definitive statement on the topic.

Davies and Reich begin with a short addendum to Goldberg's discussion of the obstacles facing women in the labor market,[1] and they go on to discuss briefly how the subordinate position of women in the labor market leaves them economically with few alternatives to marriage. Finally, they examine the emerging contradiction between sexism and capitalism: while the dynamics of capitalism seem to be undermining even the nuclear

[1]See Goldberg, Section 8.3, p. 341.

family, at the same time capitalism and male supremacy benefit from the maintenance of sexist institutions and therefore attempt to preserve the nuclear family in its sexist form.

I

In the previous reading, Marilyn Power Goldberg analyzed a number of ways in which the subordinate role of women in the family, as well as the socialization of women, result in their economic exploitation in the labor market. To the many obstacles facing women in the labor market that Goldberg describes, we would emphasize in addition:

1. Married women who work in the market economy actually hold down two jobs. In addition to their job in the labor market, they are also expected to perform the functions of housewife. It is unusual to find a family in which both husband and wife work and the household and child-raising chores are shared equally. A woman with no children may manage both a job and housework, but many women with small children withdraw from the labor market entirely, since satisfactory social arrangements for their children's care are generally unavailable.

2. Educational institutions deny women preparation for jobs that are considered the unquestioned prerogative of men. Sexual tracking in school systems explicitly channels girls into home economics and typing and away from shop and drafting. Girls are socialized to believe that they have neither an interest in nor a talent for science and mathematics, and therefore they tend to avoid these subjects in school. But even girls who are interested in such "masculine" subjects will often not bother to take these courses, since they know that their chances of successfully pursuing a career in such fields are slim. Furthermore, admissions policies for many professional schools discriminate against women, making it more difficult for women to enter medical, law, or graduate school than it is for men. Educational institutions, by denying to women the training they need to break down sexual discrimination in the labor market, reinforce the subordinate position of women in the labor market.

3. Employers often treat women solely as sexual objects. For example, corporations hiring secretaries and receptionists who deal with the public or with male executives are often more interested in attractive window-dressing than competent workers. Consequently, women are often judged by prospective employers in terms of their physical appearance and not their skills.

4. All women are not equally limited in the job market; some have access to more schooling and training, and many see careers in the job market as primary and child-raising or housework as secondary. Although all women are far from identical, employers and schools nonetheless tend to treat women as a homogeneous group and to *discriminate against them as a group*. Even those educational institutions and firms that claim not to discriminate against women *per se* argue that it would be too costly to determine whether or not each individual woman is seriously committed to a career. Cost minimization by business depends on the calculation of probabilities and, given the social context of male supremacy, the probability that any individual woman will advance in her career is small relative to the probability for a man. Thus, women who have no intention of ever marrying or raising children are still considered bad risks by firms and educational institutions.

This discrimination against women as a group brings particular hardship to those women who must support themselves. One third of all women who worked year-round and full-time in 1967 were single, separated, divorced, or widowed women holding a job out of economic necessity. But few of the jobs open to them paid well enough to provide adequate support for themselves, let alone their children: the median income of such women in 1967 was about $4500.[1]

II

This brings us to our next point: the subordinate position of women in the market economy locks them into a dependent position with the nuclear family. In 1969, the median money income of all women fourteen years or older in the civilian labor force was $2,132, compared to a median income for men of $6,429. For women who worked year-round and full-time in 1969, median income was $5,077: this represented 58 percent of the corresponding income for men, having declined from a figure of 63 percent in 1956.[2] Since the opportunities for supporting themselves are so meager, many women must view marriage as a matter of economic survival. Although the motives for marriage are generally love, desire for psychological security, or escape from competition with men for jobs, it is nonetheless true that women are forced into marriage for a reason similar to that which forces workers to sell their labor to a capitalist for a wage —namely, economic necessity. This economic dependency of the wife on the husband confers, at least implicitly, a certain amount of power to the husband over the wife.

The economic factors operate to strengthen the many social pressures forcing women into marriage. On the one hand, women are made to feel inadequate as women if they do not prove themselves capable of attracting a man and bearing "his" children. On the other hand, women often turn to marriage as the means to an economic security which the labor market generally prevents them from attaining themselves. Economic forces place women in an inferior position in the labor market, and cultural and social forces lead women to believe that they have failed their destiny in life if they do not marry; the two sets of forces reinforce one another and operate symbiotically.

III

The subordinate position of women in the family and in society as a whole has been analyzed from a different perspective by Margaret Benston in a recent essay entitled "The Political Economy of Women's Liberation."[3] Benston emphasizes the importance of examining the *precapitalist* nature of women's relation to production in the home. Unlike workers under capitalism, women in the home are not paid for their work and do not produce commodities that are bought and sold on a market. Women produce services in return for which husbands are expected to provide financial support. The subordinate position of women is thus explained in structural terms:

> *The material basis for the inferior status of women is to be found in just this definition of work. In a society in which money determines value, women are a group who work outside the money economy. Their work is not worth money, is therefore valueless, is therefore not even real work. And women themselves, who do this valueless work, can hardly be expected to be worth as much as men, who work for money. In structural terms, the closest thing to the condition of women is the condition of others who are or were also outside of commodity production, i.e., serfs and peasants.*

However, capitalist development has, in spite of itself, been breaking down the "feudalis-

[1]U.S. Bureau of the Census, *Current Population Reports*, Series P–60, No. 64, "Supplementary Report on Income in 1967 of Families and Persons in the United States."

[2]See Table 8–A, p. 324.

[3]Margaret Benston, "The Political Economy of Women's Liberation," *Monthly Review* (September 1969), pp. 13–27.

tic" relationship that characterizes the nuclear family. We now turn to this point.

IV

To see how the spread of capitalist market relations has been undermining the nuclear family, it is instructive to review how the spread of markets in land, labor, and commodities disrupted traditional community life and reintegrated culture around commodities.[4] The spread of a market in land determined that the sole criterion for land use was profitability. The need for architectural integration and planning was ignored, and the dictates of profit uprooted communities and tore them apart. Meanwhile, the geographical and occupational mobility required by a smoothly-operating market in labor undermined both neighborhood ties and ties to the traditional extended family.[5] As the location of jobs and industry shifted, young people and individual nuclear families broke away from neighborhoods and relatives to pursue economic opportunities. Communities and extended families were fundamentally incompatible with the needs of a capitalist market in labor, since immobility impeded the allocation of labor to its most profitable use.

At the same time, much of the precapitalist production of commodities and provision of social services that took place within the community and the extended family was superseded by the purchase of mass-produced commodities on the market. Today, the decline in home production for use has extended to more than the necessities of food, clothing, and shelter. Services such as entertainment and leisure recreation activi-

ties, care of the aged and the sick, and psychological counseling that once were provided through the community and the extended family are today increasingly purchased as commodities on a market. The extension of markets in commodities, by undermining production for internal use, removed one of the prime forces binding communities and extended families together.

Of course, the hegemony of these economic mechanisms is not total. Neighborhood communities and extended families are still present in many areas of the United States, particularly where ethnic and religious ties have been strong. But in general, such social institutions are breaking down. To a large degree the extended family has disappeared and the family has become nuclear—one husband and wife together with children form the basic living unit; the husband primarily responsible for supporting the family financially, the wife primarily responsible for housework and both sharing responsibility for rearing the children (although the wife must often bear the heaviest part of this load).

But just as capitalist development undermined the community and the extended family, the extension of markets in labor and commodities has put the nuclear family under attack as well: an increasing proportion of married women work in the market economy, while the penetration of commodities into the home has reduced the necessary amount of housework. This undermining of the nuclear family creates a contradiction in capitalist development, for the family performs functions that are themselves important for the maintenance of the capitalist system. We shall argue below that the apparent resiliency of the family in the face of undermining forces is due, in large part, to the combined dynamics of male supremacy and capitalism. In recent years, the tension created by this contradiction has become apparent in the development of a women's liberation movement.

[4]See Polanyi, Section 3.1, p. 92, and Gintis, Section 6.5, p. 274, for a more thorough discussion of these issues.

[5]An extended family is one that includes not only parents and children but also grandparents, aunts, uncles, cousins, in-laws, etc.

The Undermining of the Nuclear Family

Women were important in the wage labor force in the early days of capitalism. Together with children they constituted an overwhelming majority of factory workers at the time of the emergence of the capitalist mode of production in both England and the United States. For example, women comprised a large proportion of the work force in textiles, one of the first large-scale manufacturing industries in the United States. Female labor has always been important in the labor-intensive, low-wage industries and for use as a convenient labor reserve to be drawn upon during upswings in the business cycle and released during recessions. But dramatic changes have occurred in the number, marital status, age and length of working life of women participating in the capitalist labor market. These changes have potentially important implications for the material basis of male supremacy and the nuclear family.

In 1890, only 18 percent of adult women in the United States worked at jobs outside the home; most of these women were single, under twenty-five, and tended to leave employment never to return as soon as they were married. Most older women were married and worked primarily at home. Today, however, a large and increasing number of women are wage and salary workers for a large proportion of their adult lives. In an average month in 1967, 49 percent of women between the ages of sixteen and sixty-four were in the labor force; nearly three out of five of these working women were married, and over half were between the ages of thirty-five and sixty-four. One-fourth of married women with children under six years and nearly half of all married women with children six to seventeen years are in the labor force. Women are also in the labor force on a more permanent basis: if past trends continue, women born in 1960 will spend an average of twenty years in the labor force. Between 1946 and 1968 the number of women in the labor force increased by 75 percent, while the number of men in the labor force rose only 16 percent. By 1969 women comprised nearly two-fifths of the total civilian labor force.

What factors have produced these changes? First, the logic of capitalism demands that it constantly expand.[7] The consequent need for an ever expanding labor force has steadily increased the demand for female wage labor and brought married and single women into the labor market in large numbers. The importance of female labor grew especially as the reserve supplies of male immigrants, farmers and blacks were progressively exhausted. A substantial proportion of economic growth in the United States is attributable to the increased direct participation of women in production and distribution of goods and services in the market economy. Furthermore, the character of work in factories has been changing with advances in technology. The shift from heavy physical and manual labor to lighter work in modern industry has facilitated the expansion of demand for female labor.

Second, in advanced capitalism, employment in service and white-collar occupations has grown more rapidly than the labor force as a whole. The growth of employment in these occupations, for example, secretarial work, retail sales, teaching, nursing, social work, and so on—occupations that women have traditionally numerically dominated precisely because of their "service" character—brought more women into the market economy. Indeed, one third of women in the labor force are employed in seven occupations—secretaries-stenographers, saleswomen, cleaning women, elementary school

[6]Data cited here is from U.S. Department of Labor, Women's Bureau, *Handbook of Women Workers 1969*, Ch. 1.
[7]See Edwards, Section 3.2, p. 98.

teachers, bookkeepers, waitresses and nurses.[8]

Third, since children now attend more years of school, they have fewer opportunities to work at jobs that would supplement their family's income. As a result, many more married women must work, since the additional income is still needed. In 1967, the income of husbands of 35 percent of working wives was $5,000 or less.[9]

Fourth, women now spend a smaller proportion of their lives bearing and raising children. The long-term trend has been for women to marry at a younger age, have fewer babies, and have their last child at an earlier age. Today, the average woman has her last child before she is thirty, so that about the time she is thirty-six her children are all either in school or on their own. Furthermore, life expectancy has risen from forty-eight years for women born in 1900 to seventy-four years for women born in 1966.[10] Thus the potential work-life of married women has grown dramatically.[11]

Finally, the decline of production within the home and the introduction of labor-saving devices has reduced the amount of time women need to spend on housework. The materials for food and clothing go through several stages of processing before being purchased. Women once spent long hours tending vegetable gardens, churning butter and cheese, washing clothes by hand, and even spinning and weaving the cloth necessary to make those clothes. Today, these commodities are mass-produced and purchased in the market. Frozen foods, "TV" dinners, and cake mixes are only the most recent manifestation of the trend towards preprocessing and production in the

market replacing home production for use.

Similarly, labor-saving devices such as vacuum cleaners, washing machines, and dishwashers reduce the necessary labor time needed in housework. Women, of course, still spend a great amount of time in cleaning and cooking. This results largely from the socially induced elevation of "standards" of cleanliness and cooking to absurd heights. The job of housewife is probably more frustrating now than it was in the past, since much housekeeping is not really necessary; and women, at least subconsciously aware of this fact, find it less and less intrinsically rewarding. Furthermore, preprocessed commodities and labor-saving devices undermine whatever potential creativity some homemaking tasks once had. So women increasingly turn to the labor market in search of rewarding work.

It is instructive to note that labor-saving home appliances have only *facilitated* the entry of women into the labor market. A recent study examined the factors influencing the varying degrees of participation of married women in the labor market in different metropolitan areas. The study concluded that, apart from the need to supplement family income, the principal factor explaining the extent of female employment in a metropolitan area was the quantity of *employer demand* for labor in occupations in which females predominate.[12]

The Perpetuation of the Nuclear Family

The above changes in female labor force participation rates ought to have had repercussions on marriage and the patriarchal nuclear family. The increased number of women who work and receive a wage or salary should have shifted power relation-

[8]U.S. Department of Labor, Women's Bureau, *Handbook of Women Workers 1969*, Ch. 1.

[9]*Ibid.*, p. 34.

[10]*Ibid.*, p. 7.

[11]Alternative child-care arrangements could, of course, result in further increases.

[12]William Bowen and T. Aldrich Finnegan, *The Economics of Labor Force Participation* (Princeton: Princeton University Press, 1969).

ships within the family, since it is now possible for more women to live outside the nuclear family, if they are willing to survive on a fairly low income. In this context, the resiliency of the family seems quite astonishing. In 1969, 82.8 percent of all women eighteen and over and more than 90 percent of women over thirty were married or widowed, whereas 78.7 percent of women twenty years and over were married or widowed in 1900.[13] The perpetuation of the nuclear family, we shall argue, can be explained as a result of the collective interests, ideologies and actions of males as a caste and capitalists as a class. But though male supremacy and the nuclear family have been retained, the contradictions created by the changing role of women in production have not been resolved.

The Family and Male Chauvinism. Males as a caste enjoy privileges within the family as it is now constituted and they have supported its perpetuation. Women generally perform most of the menial household chores and service men's physical and emotional needs. The unequal power relationship between husband and wife is at root based on the general unavailability for most women of adequate alternative sources of income and on the social conditioning of children in the family to a patriarchal society. Men, individually and as a group, are loathe to see destroyed the material basis of their power. So they attempt, both on an individual basis with women and through male-dominated social institutions, to maintain their power and preserve the nuclear family in its present form. For example, many husbands discourage their wives from taking a job, arguing that a woman's duty is to care for her house, children, and husband. Similarly, the media promote the image of the successful woman as one who finds fulfillment in pleasing and

caring for a man and "his" children. Most important, and as we have already indicated, women are actively discriminated against when they do participate in the labor market.

The Family and Capitalism. The functions the patriarchal nuclear family serves for capitalism also help explain the family's perpetuation. Goldberg points out how the maintenance of a sexually segmented labor market is important in obfuscating class interests among male and female workers and providing a convenient reserve labor supply.[14] In addition, male supremacy lessens hostility to the capitalist system by providing a source of psychological gratification for male workers who, although without control over their work, can at least exercise power within their families.

Here we would like to suggest two additional crucial functions which the contemporary family serves for capitalism. First, the family, along with the schooling system, is the primary institution that reproduces and maintains the labor force. As Morton has argued, the maintenance and reproduction of the labor force has become increasingly important and also increasingly complex in modern capitalism.[15] It is in the family, as presently structured, that much of the socialization of children into the hierarchical roles necessary in a capitalist society takes place. Whether a child will become one of the few who control or one of the majority who are controlled, all children must be trained for such a hierarchical system and to accept it as the natural order. One of the major sources of this education is the manner in which parents treat their children and what children observe, copy, and internalize from the hierarchical relationship between their parents.

Parents who force their children to obey them without question condition them to

---

[13]U.S. Bureau of the Census, *Statistical Abstract of the United States*, 1970, p. 32, and *Twelfth Census of the United States* (1900).

[14]See Goldberg, Section 8.3, p. 341.
[15]See Morton, Section 3.6, p. 119 and Bowles, Section 5.2, p. 218 for elaboration of these points.

accept and cooperate with arbitrary orders. Children obey parents, generally not because of the logic or justice of an order, but because their parents are authority figures with a relatively great amount of power. Children have often been beaten or humiliated, not because their misdeeds have been very serious, but because they must learn to obey. Children also come to believe that an authority figure (parent) is more capable than they of making decisions. Such attitudes carry over into adult life, as in the common assumption that decisions of the boss or the President are not to be questioned by virtue of their august position—"They must know what is best." Children who have internalized hierarchical social relations will make good workers under capitalism where the social relations of production are themselves hierarchical.[16]

It is also crucial to capitalism that the existing labor force be maintained. The wife labors every day so that her husband will produce efficiently at the workplace. Women feed their husbands, wash their clothes, support them psychologically, soothe their nerves when they come home, and reinforce their competitiveness in the job market.

Second, the family is important to the maintenance of the ethos of possessive individualism—a value highly congenial to capitalism. People tend to see themselves as owing primary allegiance to a very small group whose interests are opposed to other such small groups. For example, families compete with each other for the best manicured lawn on the block. And children are treated as pieces of property, subject to parental whim.

Families, of course, serve some positive functions: they are often based on love and provide an important refuge from a society

---

[16]Notice that here we are abstracting from differences in family structure by social class and race, differences which are important for any detailed analysis of families.

that judges people according to what they do or own. With the disintegration of intermediary units of social organization, such as clubs, neighborhood bars, the church, and small communities, the family becomes increasingly important in providing individuals with small close-knit groups based on warm and personal relations. People cling to the family because it is one of the few small and intimate groups that they have.

A good society would provide people with such groups. But many different kinds of groups could exist, and the opportunity for choice among them is itself important. Part of the repressiveness of contemporary society is that only one choice is available. Furthermore, it is neither necessary nor desirable that women play a subordinate role within these groups. Both men and women could share responsibility for raising children as well as housework. And these small communities need not be governed by the authoritarian relationships that exist in the contemporary nuclear family, nor need they be as small and as atomized as are nuclear families.

V

To summarize, the development of capitalism has resulted both in an expanded role for women in the labor force and the reduction of necessary household work, thus undermining the institution of the nuclear family which performs important functions for capitalism. Capitalism attempts to deal with the tensions thus created as follows:

At the same time that women enter the labor force bourgeois society continues to sanctify the family and attempts to convince women that their basic social role consists of maintaining a happy, comfortable home. Women learn to be "high need achievers" and to adapt themselves to the male bourgeois ethic of personal ambition and competitiveness but simultaneously learn that they must subordinate their own aspirations to their primary role as homemaker. The mass media, the women's magazines, the government, and business propaganda promise "productive careers" and "creative homemaking" through commodities, and simultaneously drum away at the theme of women as submissive to men and as the mainstay of the home. This theme repeats itself in the entreaties and demands of the husband, who wants to escape alienated labor in leisure, to be taken care of, but who also believes that he needs a passive, dependent mate.

Women thus experience life as a series of conflicting demands. . . .[17]

[17]"The Making of Socialist Consciousness," editorial statement, *Socialist Revolution* 1, no. 2 (1970). Excerpts are reprinted in Section 11.6, p. 503.

The role that women customarily play in the family is often unfulfilling. Yet, when women seek liberation in work, they find only alienation. Most work in capitalist society is alienating, and the jobs open to most women are particularly unsatisfying. Nonetheless, more women are able to survive economically outside the male-dominated nuclear family and so can challenge the traditional power relationships in the family. But when they seek to improve their lot, redefine their social relationships with men, and eliminate the harmful dominant-submissive sex role dichotomies, women find the path blocked not only by individual men but also by the institutions of a capitalist and male supremacist society. It is out of such tensions that a women's movement develops.

8.5   Goals of the Women's Movement: A Clarification

The transformation of the sexual division of labor involves much more than women approaching the present position of men. As Elizabeth Katz and Janice Weiss point out in the following reading, the liberation of women (and of men) requires a fundamental *redefinition* of the sex roles, "masculine" and "feminine." Many aspects of "femininity" are desirable and should be fostered for all in a good society.

Source: The following essay was written by ELIZABETH KATZ and JANICE WEISS for this book. Copyright © 1972 by Elizabeth Katz and Janice Weiss. Printed by permission of the authors.

The women's liberation movement is sometimes viewed as an effort to "raise" women to the positions men presently occupy. In this view, what women want is a piece of the pie—of the power, status, and income—that men currently have. One would infer from this view that a solution to women's problems lies in somehow getting parents and schools to train girls in the "toughness" and competitive spirit now reserved for boys and in somehow convincing or forcing

employers to consider women equal to men when hiring people for high-level jobs.

To us, this interpretation is based on a distorted concept of liberation, a definition of liberation as access to power and to well-paying but nonetheless alienating jobs in the man's world. As such, it represents neither our analysis of the present situation nor our aspirations for change.

Generally, women are expected, encouraged, and forced to have two qualities: unassertiveness and supportiveness (being prepared to serve others, to consider other people's needs before one's own). This is so in the personal relationships a woman has (especially with men) in her work life and within her marriage. Basically, women are expected to practice various forms of self-denial; in fact, they are virtually required to be this way if they are not to be widely ostracized as "unpleasant" and even "unnatural." The result is, very often and not surprisingly, a feeling of frustration and resentment in women. Yet to end an analysis at this point can lead and often has led to distortions: that women want to be able to compete with men for the "top" jobs, that the "feminine" inability to consider things purely "objectively" is a weakness to be overcome, that being supportive means being submissive and is therefore a quality that would not be needed or desired in a good society.

Rather than stopping at this point, we carry the analysis further. Women are expected, encouraged, and forced to be supportive to others—boyfriends, bosses, husbands, children—which means that women are expected to be sensitive to others' feelings and needs and to be of help to others in various ways. To us, these seem *desirable* qualities, humane qualities which a good society would foster and *on which a good society would be based*. Women's apparently heightened sensitivity to human needs and suffering has meant that women are considered "naturals" for such jobs as nursing, social work, teaching (except at the higher levels), and child care. Yet these jobs, in the current male-dominant, capitalist ideology, are considered low-status, and so very few men take them. And again, in the current male-supremacist ideology, the sensitivity of women to human needs and suffering is viewed as a weakness when women find it difficult to be "objective" when human concerns are involved or to be competitive and self-aggrandizing when seeking and performing a job.

It is of course true that some aspects of men's roles are desirable, and the fact that men have a near monopoly on them arouses resentment and envy in women. Simply by virtue of being of the masculine sex in a male-dominant society, men are awarded more social respect than women (for their talents, intellect, "strength,") and are thus freer to express themselves and be listened to seriously, initiate social relations, support themselves financially, and walk down the street without continual fear. Thus women envy men's status not for the power, but for the freedom and dignity that status alone now confers.

For us, freedom and dignity mean not having to bear most of the burden of drudgery-work—housework, typing and clerical work, diaper washing. They mean not being assigned, on the basis of sex alone, the entire burden of the delicate and demanding task of child care and rearing. They mean control of our bodies, preconditions of which are easily available and safe contraceptives and abortion. They also mean not being viewed as mere sexual prey, fair game for continual harassment, molestation, and all too often, rape. Far from having dignity and self-respect, women now often feel scorn for themselves, which comes from viewing themselves through men's eyes. They tend not only to judge themselves on the basis of their sexual attractiveness to men but, still more demeaning and debilitating, to feel that they are simply not very important and that what they do has little worth. The logical consequence of these attitudes is that women tend to scorn each other, judging each other on men's terms. This, in combination with other factors (women's oppressive work, lack of financial security, and genuine need of intimacy and affection), leads women into competition with each other for the favors (attention, money) of men. Freedom and dignity require access to enough money so that we can live decently and are not forced to prostitute ourselves (in the form of marrying only for "security" or in other forms) out of desperation. The pseudo-respect we are now offered, as when men hold doors open for us and let us step off the elevator first, hardly qualifies as respect, which seems to be available only to men.

Yet to be a male in our society requires certain characteristics that we do *not* want: we do not want to program ourselves to be "objective" and competitive from nine to five and then to "unwind" the rest of the time. We do *not* want to hide our feelings or to try to project images of self-confidence and decisiveness if we don't feel that way. We regret that men are expected to do this, not only because we are often made to suffer as a direct result of it but because we consider these inhuman and inhumane modes of behavior.

In sum, our aim is a radical shift to a society in which roles are not imposed upon people by virtue of their sex (or any other "given" they are born with, such as race or socio-economic background); in which people's work has social value, nonmanagers are respected and participate in decision-making, and the innately unpleasant tasks are shared by all; in which people can relate to each other not as objects or competitors but as fellow members of the human family. We seek a humane society in which the needs of all are weighed equally, not as secondary concerns to be taken care of, if possible, after considerations of "efficiency," "output," and "profit" have been dealt with, but as the primary concern.

Thus we do not aspire to men's roles, but to a completely different framework of things for women *and* men. Women have a crucial part to play in a struggle for such a change, for they have had more experience in dealing with human concerns on a human level. Further, men are not likely to give up their privileges through acts of good will. We have seen socialist revolutions—in Russia, China, Cuba—that professed similar goals to ours and yet have not eradicated the subordination of women to men. As long as sexual oppression exists, half the society— at a low estimate—is not free.

SELECTIVE BIBLIOGRAPHY

Graphic accounts of the subordination of women and the emergence of the present-day women's movement are contained in Morgan [5]. The New England Free Press [7] has an excellent packet of pamphlets as well as periodicals covering all aspects of the women's movement. The most comprehensive statistical source on the position of women is [8]. Engels [3] is a classic Marxist statement, attempting to relate the origin of the family and women's subordination to the rise of private property. Recent anthropological evidence and a mid-twentieth-century perspective have led to some criticisms of Engels' thesis. Two such works, highly important in their own right, are de Beauvoir

[1] and Millet [4]. Millett, for example, stresses the historical continuity of patriarchy and the importance of power, that is, politics, in all interpersonal relationships between men and women. Benston [2] is a recent attempt to reformulate the analysis of women's oppression from a Marxist perspective by analyzing the common relationship of women to production. This task is continued and extended by Morton [6], excerpts of which are reprinted in Section 3.6.

[1] de Beauvoir, Simone. *The Second Sex.* New York: Bantam Books, 1970.*

[2] Benston, Margaret. "The Political Economy of Women's Liberation." *Monthly Review* 21 (September 1969): pp. 13–27.

[3] Engels, Friedrich. *The Origin of the Family, Private Property and the State.* First published 1884. New York: International Publishers, 1962.*

[4] Millett, Kate. *Sexual Politics.* New York: Doubleday & Co., 1970.*

[5] Morgan, Robin, ed. *Sisterhood is Powerful.* New York: Random House, 1970.*

[6] Morton, Peggy. "A Woman's Work is Never Done." *Leviathan* (March 1970): pp. 32–37.

*Available in paperback editions.

[7] Literature Packet on Female Liberation and the Sexual Caste System. See especially Laurel Limpus. "Liberation of Women: Sexual Repression and the Family," and Meredith Tax. "Women and Their Minds." Boston, Mass.: New England Free Press, 1970. Available from the New England Free Press, 791 Tremont Street, Boston, Mass. 02118

[8] U.S. Department of Labor, Women's Bureau, *Handbook of Women Workers 1969.* Washington, D.C.: U.S. Government Printing Office, 1970.*

Irrationality 9

THE AVERAGE AMERICAN IS RICHER THAN the average citizen of any other nation in the world. Yet is he or she any happier? Every year the productive capacity of the United States economy grows larger. Yet does it increase the capacity of the society to meet the real needs of its people? The answers to these questions are not at all obvious.

In a rationally organized society, one would expect that the productive capacity of the economy would be used to contribute as far as possible to human well-being and to the growth of human potentialities. Yet in our society, we observe countless examples of productive capacity and individual effort devoted to activities that add nothing to human well-being and often impede the growth of human potentialities.

The United States economy turns out every year more new cars, more new television sets, more cigarettes, more cosmetics, and more of an infinite variety of consumer goods per person than any other economy in the world. The energies and the resources of millions of people are devoted to the invention and the promotion of new products for popular consumption. In 1969, American firms spent almost twenty billion dollars on advertising alone.[1] Yet at the same time it is widely recognized that the United States faces an acute housing crisis.[2] Recreational and transportation facilities in urban areas are deteriorating, and it is becoming increasingly difficult to obtain adequate medical care.

The United States government channels billions of dollars into the production of modern weapons, the maintenance of powerful armed forces, and the construction of ever more sophisticated defense systems. In 1969, the federal government spent roughly eighty billion dollars on "national defense"

while many important social services were starved for funds.[3] Expenditures by federal, state, and local governments on health, welfare, natural resources, public transportation, urban renewal, and public housing totalled less than forty billion dollars. Even without considering the waste and the unequal distribution of benefits that characterize many of these expenditures, their absolute size is far too small to meet adequately the social needs they are intended to satisfy.

Not only are useless activities undertaken both in the private and the public sectors, but the organization of economic activity and the choice of production techniques often lead to unnecessary waste in the form of environmental disruption. No one needs to be reminded of the pollution of air and water, the ravaging of forests and wild life, and the threat to ecological balance posed by productive activity in the modern United States economy. And daily life in both cities and suburbs has become increasingly difficult as urban agglomerations have sprawled mindlessly outward, swallowing up more and more of the surrounding land.

All the phenomena described above—consumerism, militarism, inadequate social services, and environmental disruption—are manifestations of the fundamental *irrationality* of the capitalist system. The extent and seriousness of these problems vary from one capitalist nation to another. Some of them also arise in contemporary state socialist nations. Yet there are powerful forces arising directly from the basic institutions of capitalism that serve to exacerbate these forms of irrationality and to inhibit their eradication in capitalist societies. It is perhaps no accident that the problems seem to be most serious in the United States, the leading capitalist power and the center of the capitalist world.

[1] U.S. Dept. of Commerce, *Statistical Abstract* (1970), Table 1197.

[2] See the *Report of the President's Committee on Urban Housing* (Washington, D.C.: Government Printing Office, 1968).

[3] The data cited in this paragraph were obtained from the U.S. Dept. of Commerce, *Survey of Current Business* (July, 1970), National Income and Product Accounts, Tables 1.1 and 3.10.

In this chapter we examine some of the basic forces that affect production decisions under capitalism. How does a capitalist society decide what to produce and what not to produce, how much to produce and how to produce it? We shall argue that the process whereby such production decisions are made under capitalism is one that cannot take into account the real needs of the people and therefore is irrational in the most fundamental sense of the word.

Several basic characteristics of capitalism underlie the irrationality of the process whereby production priorities are determined. First of all, there is the *logic of expansion* which is inherent in the capitalist system. The pursuit of profits and the desire to accumulate lead to more and more production for the sake of production and an ever expanding productive capacity.[4] But why must an economy always expand? The more productive an economy becomes, the more seriously does the desirability of increasing production come into question.

On the one hand, continual expansion exacerbates the problem of maintaining an ecological balance between human beings and their environment. The higher the rate of production, the higher the rate at which natural resources are used up or destroyed and the higher the rate at which waste products are dumped back onto the land and into the water. We have reached a point in the rich nations where a good society may require not only an end to population growth but also an end to industrial growth. Yet continuous growth in productive capacity is inherent in capitalist institutions and could not be restrained without a fundamental change in the mode of production.

On the other hand, apart from its damaging ecological consequences, continual expansion under capitalism gives rise to the problem of "surplus absorption": how to dispose of the continually increasing surplus

of total productive capacity over the essential consumption requirements of the society. In order that this surplus be absorbed, it is necessary that the *demand* for goods and services keep pace with the expanding *supply* that a capitalist economy is capable of producing. It will be argued in several of the readings to follow that a capitalist society must resort to wasteful military expenditures and/or artificially contrived consumption expenditures in order to absorb the surplus. The overall preoccupation with the production and consumption of material goods and services contributes to an increasing imbalance between the satisfaction of material and nonmaterial human needs. Nothing could be more illustrative of the fundamental irrationality of the capitalist system than the intensity with which it seeks to create and satisfy new material wants at the same time as basic human needs for community, for stability, and for creative self-expression are ignored.

A second fundamental characteristic of capitalism that contributes to irrationality is its reliance on *individual profit incentives*. The relatively unrestricted pursuit of private profit that fuels the capitalist economy results in an exclusive concern on the part of decision makers with *private* benefits and costs, that is, those gains and losses which show up on the balance sheet of the firm. But in a modern industrial society, many of the effects of social and economic activity do not get translated into private gains or losses. For example, the benefits that accrue to a whole community from a well-designed neighborhood, a good public health system, accessible outdoor recreational facilities, and so on, could not easily and fully be realized in the form of money receipts by any private firm that tried to sell such "goods." And the costs imposed on a community by polluted waters, smog-filled air, or noisy highways and airports are rarely paid for by the principal offenders.

Economists use the terms "external econ-

---

[4] See Edwards, Section 3.2, p. 98.

omy" and "external diseconomy" to refer to those benefits and costs resulting from a private action that do not result in corresponding monetary gains or losses for the person who took the action. Economic theory shows clearly that such externalities invalidate the claim of a free market economy to optimal resource allocation, but most economists dismiss external effects as relatively insignificant. It is becoming increasingly clear, however, that external effects are less the exception than the rule in modern industrial societies. External economies characterize the provision of almost all collective social services; the inadequacy of such services under capitalism can be attributed in part to the inability of private enterprise to realize private monetary gains corresponding to the social benefits provided. External diseconomies abound in the form of the environmental disruption that results from the private cost-cutting behavior of capitalist enterprise.

Finally, a third basic fact of life under capitalism—which is partly the result of the first two—is the *unequal distribution of income and power*. To the extent that private enterprise responds to needs felt and expressed by the consuming public, it responds to "dollar votes." That is, it provides goods and services where the existence of significant purchasing power promises a profitable return. Needless to say, such a response is biased in favor of those whose incomes afford them the greatest purchasing power and whose political power can influence the state to intervene where the response of private decision makers is not deemed adequate. Apart from its obviously inequitable implications, the distribution of income and power under capitalism helps to perpetuate the inadequacy of public collective services by depriving such governmental programs of a strong political and economic base. So long as the rich can fill privately their own needs for health, education, transportation, and so on, it remains difficult to provide for everyone's welfare in a collective manner that would not only bring greater benefits to the poor but also provide all the services in a more effective and less costly manner.

The readings in this section elaborate on the way in which the drive for expansion, the private basis of decision making, and the inequality in the distribution of income and power that characterize a capitalist society interact to produce the rampant irrationality that one observes in the United States today. The first reading is designed to examine in greater detail the nature and consequences of the problem of surplus absorption. The remaining readings deal selectively with various forms of irrationality as they have arisen out of the logic of capitalism.

9.1   *The Problem of Surplus Absorption in a Capitalist Society*

In the following reading Thomas E. Weisskopf defines the concept of the surplus and describes the problem of surplus absorption. The essay is intended to provide an overall theoretical framework for analyzing how the problem of surplus absorption gives rise to various forms of irrationality in a capitalist society. Many of the points raised here in general terms are pursued in much greater detail in subsequent readings in this chapter.

The concept of the surplus was developed initially by Karl Marx[1] and

[1] Karl Marx, *Capital*, first published in 1867.

has been elaborated in a modern context by Paul Baran and Paul Sweezy.[2] In this essay the Marxist concept of the surplus is integrated with some basic elements of the macroeconomic theory of income determination originated by John Maynard Keynes.[3] The result is an analysis of the problem of surplus absorption that is broadly similar to—but in some respects different from—the analysis of Baran and Sweezy.

A brief appendix to the essay documents the role of military spending in absorbing the surplus of the United States economy.

[2]See Paul Baran, *The Political Economy of Growth* (New York: Monthly Review Press, 1956), especially Chapters 2–4, and Paul Baran and Paul Sweezy, *Monopoly Capital* (New York: Monthly Review Press, 1966) for the most comprehensive modern Marxist analyses of the problem of surplus absorption.

[3]John Maynard Keynes, *The General Theory of Employment, Interest and Money* (New York: Harcourt Brace & Co., 1936).

Source: The following essay was written by THOMAS E. WEISSKOPF for this book. Copyright © 1972 by the author.

INTRODUCTION

In the last century, the advanced capitalist economies of the world have witnessed a tremendous expansion of productive capacity. There can be little doubt that—whatever its implications for the quality of life —the capitalist system has enabled the richest countries of the world to multiply steadily their riches. Even the periodic crises of output and employment that afflicted capitalist economies in earlier times, culminating in the Great Depression of the 1930s, seem to have yielded to the control of Keynesian macroeconomic policy measures since the Second World War. The evidence is that rates of growth in developed capitalist countries have increased substantially in the postwar period. (See Table 9–A.)

Yet the expansion of productive capacity, which has become both more regular and more rapid in recent years, is not an unmixed blessing for the capitalist system. Behind the superficially impressive rates of growth lies a major problem which poses a continual threat to the stability of a capital-

TABLE 9–A LONG-TERM GROWTH RATES IN DEVELOPED CAPITALIST COUNTRIES (AVERAGE ANNUAL % RATES OF GROWTH)

	1865–1950*		1950–1967	
	Total Output	Per Capita Output	Total Output	Per Capita Output
1. United States	3.5	2.0	3.9	2.2
2. Canada	3.5	1.9	4.1	2.3
3. United Kingdom	2.1	1.2	2.9	2.3
4. France	1.5	1.3	4.2	3.1
5. Germany	2.5	1.4	6.2	5.1
6. Italy	1.7	1.0	5.2	4.6
7. Sweden	3.0	2.5	4.0	3.4
8. Japan	3.7	2.4	9.2	8.0
Unweighted Average	2.9	1.9	5.0	3.9

*The initial and terminal periods vary slightly from one country to another; see the original source.

SOURCES: Data for 1865–1950: Kuznets, *Six Lectures on Economic Growth* (New York: Free Press, 1961), Table 1.

Data for 1950–1967: United Nations, *Statistical Yearbook*, 1968, Table 187.

ist economy: the problem of "surplus absorption." In order to understand the nature of this problem, it is necessary first to define the concept of the surplus and then to discuss the process of its absorption in a capitalist society.

THE CONCEPT OF THE SURPLUS

The surplus of an economy in any given year represents the excess of potential total production over socially essential production in that year. Potential total production is a measure of the maximum that the economy could produce, given its natural and technological environment and its employable productive resources. Socially essential production is the minimum amount of production required to maintain the (growing) population at a standard of living necessary to its survival. It includes both production contributing directly to the essential consumption of the population and production required to replace whatever capital stock and/or natural resources are used up in the process of that production.

The key to the definition of the surplus is the concept of socially essential production. Socially essential production will vary not only with the population of a society but also with such factors as the climate, the degree of urbanization, the nature of conventional social customs, and so on. More clothing and stronger shelter is required to survive in a cold than in a hot climate; more elaborate health, sanitation, and transportation facilities are required in urban than in rural areas. Although socially essential production is extremely difficult to measure precisely, it is not difficult to conceptualize. What basically distinguishes socially essential production from the surplus is that the former represents a first and largely unavoidable charge on the output of a society —without which it would begin to decay—

whereas the latter is that part of its productive capacity that a society has some potential freedom to allocate among competing alternatives.

In a very significant sense, the nature of a society is revealed by the manner in which it disposes of its surplus. Societies are different to the extent that they make different choices about how to use the natural and human resources they have available. But there is little choice to make about the provision of essential consumption such as food, clothing, and shelter; these are necessary for the subsistence of the people and the survival of the society. There is a real choice to make only about the use of the surplus. The surplus could be used to provide additional (nonessential) consumption for some or all the people; it could be used to invest in expanding the productive capacity of the economy; it could be used in fighting wars, in building palaces or churches; it could go unused if leisure were substituted voluntarily or involuntarily for the full use of productive capacity. In various parts of the world, and in various historical periods, different societies have been characterized by the different ways in which they have used their surplus.

It is characteristic of a capitalist society to devote a significant part of its surplus to investment that expands the productive capacity of the economy. Increases in productive capacity can be generated both by increasing the supply of resource inputs into the production process (labor power and capital) and by increasing the productivity of the production process through improved organization and technology. The economic growth of the advanced capitalist countries has been due in considerable part to the increases in the quantity and the quality of both labor power and capital made possible by investment in education and new plant and equipment.

As is evident from Table 9–A, the growth

of total output in the advanced capitalist countries has been sufficiently rapid to allow for a substantial growth of per capita output in spite of unprecedented increases in population. Even allowing for occasional shortfalls of total output below productive capacity, it is clear that potential output per person has been increasing steadily and is likely to continue doing so. At the same time, to be sure, the increasing urbanization and the mounting complexity of industrial life under capitalism are causing a gradual increase in socially essential production per person. Yet it can hardly be doubted that the rate of growth of potential output per person in advanced capitalist societies is faster than that of socially essential production. As a result, the surplus tends to rise more or less steadily both as an absolute amount and as a proportion of potential output. It is this steady rise of the surplus that raises the problem of surplus absorption: how can a capitalist society absorb (utilize) the surplus that it causes to rise continuously?

THE ABSORPTION OF THE SURPLUS

The problem of absorbing the surplus can be viewed as the problem of finding enough buyers to purchase all the goods and services that the capitalist economy can produce. In economic terms, the problem is to maintain a sufficiently high level of total or "aggregate" demand so as to provide a market for the potential output of the economy. To the extent that aggregate demand falls short of potential output, producers will not be able to sell all that they can produce, and they will fail to realize maximum profits from their productive activity. If aggregate demand remains below potential output, either goods and services will go unsold or producers will have to curtail their output. Since producers only have an interest in

producing what they can sell, the capitalist economy as a whole will tend toward an equilibrium at which actual output is equal to aggregate demand.[1]

The consequences of a failure to maintain sufficient aggregate demand to absorb the surplus are several. First, the shortfall in actual output below potential output results in a corresponding loss of goods and services and a decline in the profits realized by producers. Second—and far more important from a human point of view—it also results in a loss of employment opportunities and a rise in unemployment. In a society in which both one's income and one's self-respect depend on regular full-time employment, the loss of one's job is catastrophic. High levels of unemployment due to a failure to absorb the surplus can prove to be very unstabilizing for a capitalist society.

The problem of surplus absorption in a capitalist society is not insoluble. In recent decades the surplus has in fact largely been absorbed in most of the advanced capitalist nations: there has been varying degrees of unemployment, but not on a scale approaching that of the 1930s.[2] Yet it remains critical to examine *how* the surplus is absorbed, for this has profound implications for the nature of a society. It will be argued below that the capitalist system sets important constraints on the manner in which aggregate demand is maintained sufficiently high to absorb the surplus.

There are three principal sources of aggregate demand in a capitalist economy: private consumption, private investment. and

[1]For a more thorough presentation of this (Keynesian) theory of the determination of actual output in a capitalist economy, see the chapters on macroeconomic theory in any elementary economics textbook.

[2]In the United States, the overall rate of unemployment has fluctuated between 2 percent and 7 percent during the postwar period; at the height of the Great Depression in 1933 it was close to 25 percent (see Figure 9–B).

government expenditure.[3] In the following sections of this paper, the private and public sources of demand are considered in turn.

THE PRIVATE SECTOR

The pronounced inequality of income distribution under capitalism implies that while people with low incomes will have to spend most or all their income on essential consumption, people with high incomes will have much more than they need to spend to maintain even a high standard of living. Thus, there will always be more total income than total private consumption demand; and the more unequal the distribution of income, the greater the gap is likely to be. Since total income in an economy is necessarily equal to the total value of actual production from which the income derives,[4] private consumption demand will remain well below actual output and *a fortiori* below potential output.

A second principal source of private demand in a capitalist economy that can help to raise the level of aggregate demand is investment demand. Businesses desiring to expand their productive capacity will devote part of their profits to increasing the capital stock of the enterprise, and they may also borrow some of the income saved by private consumers in order to undertake further investment. The rate at which businesses want to expand through investment clearly depends on their expectations about the prospects of selling additional output in the future. Whether or not such investment demand will be sufficient to make up for the deficit between total consumption demand and potential output remains a key question.

In dealing with this question, it should first be observed that, to the extent that investment demand fills the gap in any given year, it exacerbates the problem in the following year. For the more output that goes into investment this year, the greater will be the increase in capital stock, and the greater will therefore be the potential output and the potential surplus of the economy in the following year.

There is no general agreement as to whether private demand can remain sufficiently buoyant in the long run to absorb the surplus in a capitalist economy. The early orthodox Keynesian economists were very pessimistic on this score and believed that stagnation was inevitable—that the growth of private consumption and investment demand would be insufficient to match the growing productive capacity of the capitalist economy.[5] More recently, bourgeois economists have tended to assume optimistically that the appetites of consumers and investors will be continuously and sufficiently stimulated by new products and new techniques of production. However, in an increasingly affluent as well as unequal society, it is no trivial matter to ensure the steady growth of private demand.

---

[3]A fourth source of demand is net foreign demand: the excess of the demand for exports over the supply of imports. In most countries, net foreign demand constitutes an insignificant proportion of total aggregate demand, and for the purposes of this paper it can be ignored. For further details, refer to any elementary economics textbook.

[4]The equality of total income and the total value of output produced in an economy follows from the definition of the two terms. The total value of the output of an economy is the sum of the "value added" in every productive activity. Value added is the difference between the value of the output produced in the activity and the value of the materials used up as inputs into the production process. This difference represents the income of the activity: part of it is paid in wages or salaries to the workers, and the remainder accrues as profit, interest, or rent to the owners of the capital and natural resources applied in production. Total (national) income is the sum of the wages and salaries, profits, interest, and rent received by all persons in the economy: it is necessarily equal to the sum of the value added in all productive activities, that is, total (national) output.

[5]See, for example, Alvin Hansen, "Economic Progress and Declining Population Growth," *American Economic Review* 29, no. 1 (March 1939).

One would ordinarily expect the urgency of consumption for an individual to diminish as his level of consumption increased beyond the minimum necessary for survival. It is true that even in a country as rich as the United States there are many people who have less to spend on consumption than what would be considered a socially essential minimum, for example, all those families whose income is below the "poverty line."[6] Yet the majority of the population clearly have more to spend, and the rich have very much more. What is to induce the more affluent to raise their demand for goods and services continually over time?

The answer lies in one of the most deeply rooted characteristics of capitalist society—the ethos of consumerism. Consumerism derives from a fundamental tenet of capitalist ideology: the assertion that the primary requirement for individual self-fulfillment and happiness is the possession and consumption of material goods. Like all aspects of capitalist ideology, this consumerist assertion is grounded in the basic capitalist relations of production. A society based on alienated labor allows most people little opportunity for individual expression in production; the main outlet for expression is in one's life as a consumer. Relations among people in capitalist production assume the form of relations among commodities. The resulting commodity fetishism reinforces consumerism, for it emphasizes the importance of material goods—rather than social relations—as the primary source of individual welfare.[7]

Within this ideological framework, there are also more direct mechanisms that operate to stimulate consumption. No person in the United States, nor in other advanced capitalist nations, can escape the effort of producers to induce consumers to buy their wares. Massive advertising is only the most obvious manifestation of the pervasive sales effort that characterizes the capitalist system. Frequent model changes, fancy packaging, planned obsolescence, contrived fads, and so on, all serve to increase private consumption demand at a considerable cost in wasted sources.[8] Irrational as it is, such stimulation of private expenditure plays a functional role in helping to absorb the surplus of a capitalist economy.

THE PUBLIC SECTOR

Yet even the widespread propagation of the consumptionist ethic has not enabled the growth of private demand to keep pace with the growth of productive capacity under capitalism. The historical evidence for most advanced capitalist countries—and notably so for the United States—is that, in order for aggregate demand to match potential output, it has become increasingly necessary to rely on *government* expenditure, the third major component of demand. The share of government expenditure (G) in total output (GNP) has been rising over time in almost every capitalist country.[9] In the

[6]In 1969, 24.3 million Americans (12.2 percent of the total population) were living below the official poverty line of the Social Security Administration. For a nonfarm family of four, the line was drawn at a money income of $3,743. See the U.S. Dept. of Commerce, Bureau of the Census, *Current Population Reports*, Series P–60, No. 76.

[7]For a more thorough analysis of the ethos of consumerism, see the introduction to Section 9.2, p. 374, and the references cited therein.

[8]The best-documented example of waste in consumer goods is discussed in an innovative study by Fisher, Griliches, and Kaysen, "The Costs of Automobile Model Changes Since 1949," *Journal of Political Economy* 70, no. 4 (October 1962). The authors estimate conservatively that the cost of model changes amounted to five billion dollars a year over the 1956–60 period, plus a total of seven billion dollars in future gasoline costs. See also Paul Baran and Paul Sweezy, *Monopoly Capital* (New York: Monthly Review Press, 1966), pp. 131–38.

[9]For evidence from the period 1950–1967, see the United Nations, *Statistical Yearbook*, 1968, Table 185. Of the advanced capitalist countries, only Japan, Luxemburg, and Switzerland failed to show an increase in G/GNP during this period.

United States, the ratio of G to GNP has risen from 10.8 percent in 1929 to 16.4 percent in 1949 and to 20.6 percent in 1969. (see Table 4–O on page 200).

Increases in government expenditure do not necessarily imply equal increases in aggregate demand. To the extent that the government finances its expenditure by taxing the private sector, private consumers and businesses sacrifice income and presumably cut back on private consumption and investment. But economists are in general agreement that the net effect of raising government expenditure and taxation by an equal amount is to raise aggregate demand. This is because private individuals would have used only *part* of their taxed income for consumption purposes, saving the rest of it, while the government typically spends *all* the money it receives.

Thus higher levels of government expenditure do lead to higher levels of aggregate demand. Had the share of government expenditure not been increasing in most of the advanced capitalist countries, they might well have had much greater difficulty absorbing the surplus. In fact, it is precisely because the governments of these countries have learned to use their budgets to bolster aggregate demand that the production and employment crises of earlier years have been more successfully avoided in the postwar period.[10]

The mere fact of a rise in government expenditure does not carry any negative implications for the quality of life in a capitalist society. In order to evaluate the social consequences of the growth of government expenditure, it is clearly necessary to examine its nature as well as its size.

To some extent, the increasing importance of government expenditure in advanced capitalist countries reflects a growing supply of essential public services that meet genuine social needs. This is certainly true of at least part of the public provision of health care, educational facilities, housing, and so on. Yet many of the activities undertaken or supported by the capitalist state serve primarily to socialize the costs of private production. Public programs of highway construction, vocational schooling, job training, and pollution control, often have the effect of shifting some of the costs of private production on to the taxpaying public.[11] Finally, an important share of government expenditure serves neither of the above two functions but represents simply a wasteful way of absorbing the surplus. Such waste is most evident in military spending, but it permeates other government programs as well.

There are significant constraints on the ability of any capitalist government to undertake public programs that serve genuine social needs.[12] As a result, growing levels of government expenditure are likely to involve increasing socialization of private production costs and/or increasing waste. In the United States, the historical record suggests that for the past forty years the government has had to rely largely on military spending to absorb the surplus (see the appendix to this paper). In general, the growth of government expenditure in a capitalist society is likely to be no more rational than the growth of private consumption.

THE EXCLUDED ALTERNATIVES

The irrationality of the process of surplus absorption under capitalism can be fully appreciated only when one considers the more rational alternatives excluded by the capi-

---

[10]An elaborate econometric study of the postwar American economy by Bert Hickman, *Investment Demand and U.S. Economic Growth* (Washington, D.C.: Brookings Institution, 1965), concluded that without the stimulus of government spending the level and rate of growth of output in the U.S. would have been substantially lower.

[11]See also O'Connor, Section 4.8, p. 192.
[12]For a thorough analysis of these constraints, see Reich and Finkelhor, Section 9.6, p. 392.

talist mode of production. In a rational society, productive capacity would be expanded and utilized only insofar as it contributes to the satisfaction of genuine individual and social needs. Rather than attempt to create new wants among those people who have more income than is required to satisfy their existing wants, a rational society would use its productive capacity to meet the needs of people whose current income does not allow them to satisfy even their most basic needs. Rather than spend enormous sums of money on military weapons, space exploration, and other expensive pursuits of dubious social value, a rational state would devote itself to the provision of adequate health care, cultural and recreational facilities, and many other essential collective services.

Such a reorientation of production priorities would require major changes in basic capitalist institutions. In effect, it would require that claims to the output of the economy be distributed according to need rather than according to productive "ability." The distribution of real income, as well as the distribution of power to influence the state, would have to be greatly equalized. But inequalities of income, wealth, and power are inherent in the capitalist mode of production.[13]

A rational society would not only reorient its production priorities; it would also determine the overall scale of production in a rational manner. If actual output falls below potential output in a capitalist society, many people lose their jobs while others remain fully employed. To avoid the inequalities of a high rate of unemployment, it is therefore essential to maintain a level of actual output close to potential output. Since the logic of capitalist expansion[14] leads to continual growth in potential output, it calls for continual growth in actual output as well.

But ever increasing levels of actual output

may not be necessary and may in fact be undesirable in an affluent society. The uninhibited growth of material production leads to a growing ecological imbalance between people and their environment and to a growing psychological imbalance within people themselves.[15] Thus it becomes increasingly rational for a wealthy society to limit the growth of production and for individuals to substitute leisure for work.

To do this equitably, it would be necessary to reduce working hours across the board rather than to lay off a fraction of the labor force. Individual workers would need to have the option of reducing their working hours rather than being forced to choose between full-time work or no work at all. Yet in a society in which private firms compete with one another to maximize their profits, and in which capitalists and their managers retain firm control of workers and the work process, a general reduction of working hours is bound to proceed very slowly, and individual options on working hours are unlikely to be granted at all.

In conclusion, the surplus generated by a capitalist society is necessarily absorbed—if indeed it is successfully absorbed—in a very irrational manner. The rational alternatives of limiting the scale of production and devoting all productive activity to socially useful ends are excluded by the capitalist mode of production.

Appendix: Military Spending and the American Economy

Over the past forty years, from 1929 to 1969, the prosperity of the American economy has been closely linked to government military expenditure. This brief appendix documents the link by presenting some relevant aggregate data on the historical experience of the United States. To facilitate their

---

[13]For substantiation of this point, see Weisskopf, Section 3.7, p. 125.
[14]See Edwards, Section 3.2, p. 98.

[15]See Bookchin, Section 9.5, p. 388, and W. Weisskopf, Section 9.3, p. 379.

interpretation, the data are depicted in two graphs.[1]

Figure 9–A traces the growth of potential and actual output,[2] as well as several major

[1]All the data used in preparing the graphs were drawn from the *Economic Report of the President* transmitted to the Congress in February 1970. Figures for actual output, as well as private consumption expenditure, (gross) private (domestic) investment expenditure, government expenditure and net foreign demand (exports minus imports) in constant dollars at 1958 prices, were obtained from Table C–2 of the report. Potential output figures were estimated as described in footnote 2, below. Military expenditure figures were obtained in current prices from Table C–1 and converted to constant 1958 prices using the implicit price deflators for government expenditure given in Table C–3. The unemployment figures were drawn from Table C–22.

[2]There is no precise way to estimate the potential output of an economy, since total productive capacity depends in part upon the intensity with which the available productive resources are used. The estimation procedure used here was

expenditure categories, from 1929 to 1969. When actual output falls below potential output, the difference is a measure of the idle productive capacity of the economy. When actual output exceeds potential output, the difference is a measure of the (temporary) overutilization of productive capacity. In the short run, it is possible to raise actual output

designed to reflect the level of output that the U.S. economy could achieve with reasonably full employment of the regular labor force and reasonably full utilization of plant and equipment. By these criteria, potential output was set equal to actual output in 1929. For subsequent years, potential output was assumed to increase by an annual rate of 2½ percent from 1929 to 1939, 3 percent from 1939 to 1946, 3½ percent from 1946 to 1961, and 4 percent from 1961 to 1969. While these figures are necessarily somewhat arbitrary, they do provide an acceptable order of magnitude for potential output with which to compare the actual output achieved by the economy.

Figure 9–A Potential Output and its Utilization in the U.S., 1929–1969

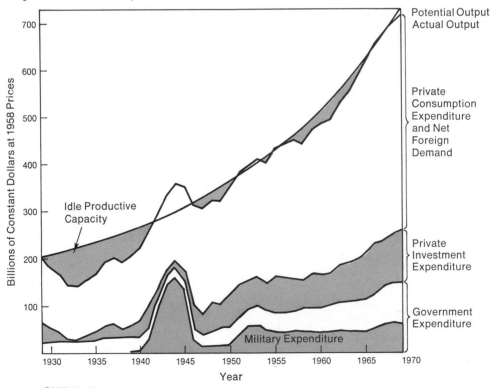

SOURCE: See footnote 1, p. 372.

above potential output by bringing into the labor force people who would not ordinarily be economically active and by increasing the number of work shifts per week above its normal level. This is clearly what happened during World War II and—to a lesser extent—during the Korean War.

It is readily apparent from Figure 9–A that, for much of the forty-year period, actual output in the United States was less than potential output. The Great Depression of the 1930s, and the smaller recessions of the late 1940s, late 1950s and early 1960s, arose from the failure of the economy fully to absorb the surplus. Only during World War II, the Korean War, and the Vietnam War did actual output reach and even exceed potential output. The changing pattern of actual output is also clearly reflected in the changing pattern of employment in the United States. The percentage rate of unemployment from 1929 to 1969 is plotted in Figure 9–B. From its peak level of almost 25 percent in the middle of the Great Depression, unemployment fell to its minimal level of less than 2 percent during World War II and tended to rise again thereafter except during the periods of the Korean and Vietnam Wars.

Figure 9–A shows also the division of actual output into the three major categories[3] of aggregate demand—private consumption, private investment, and government expenditure—and military expenditure is shown separately as part of government expendi-

[3]The fourth minor category—net foreign demand—is included with private consumption. (See footnote 3 on p. 368).

Figure 9–B   Government Expenditure, Military Expenditure, and Unemployment in the U.S. 1929–1969

SOURCE: See footnote 1, p. 372.

ture. Figure 9–B plots total government expenditure and military expenditure as a proportion of potential output (to measure their surplus absorbing impact). Close examination of the figures reveals a remarkable correlation between economic prosperity, government expenditure in general, and military expenditure in particular.

Military spending was negligible, and government purchases were relatively low during the depression years of the 1930s. The massive military mobilization for World War II put an end to unemployment and idle productive capacity where New Deal programs had failed. The postwar cutback in military and government expenditure was followed by several years of minor recession that would no doubt have been far more serious were it not for the special conditions that obtained after the war. Because consumers had been unable to spend freely during the war years, a tremendous backlog of pent-up demand was released after the war to buoy up both private consumption and investment and temporarily avert the need for the government to absorb the surplus.

The renewed arms buildup for the Korean War once again heated up the economy and reduced unemployment rates in the early 1950s. But the subsequent reduction of military spending led to a measure of recession during the late 1950s that continued into the 1960s as military spending fell gradually as a proportion of potential (and actual) output. Only in the second half of the 1960s, when expenditures on the Vietnam War begain to accelerate, did actual output again reach potential output. Unemployment rates declined slowly during the 1960s but never reached the levels that had been attained during the Second World War and the Korean War.

In sum, the historical record suggests that the prosperity of the United States economy has been closely linked to military expenditure for the past forty years. To the extent that the government has been successful in getting the surplus absorbed, it has had to rely largely on military spending to do so.

9.2 On the Creation of Consumer Wants

The "dollar votes" of buyers in the market represent the principal force determining production priorities in a capitalist society. The market system for deciding what goods are produced leads to many forms of irrationality: for example, the whims of the wealthy take precedence over the needs of the poor (since the rich have many times the "dollar votes" of the poor), and consumers can express only private, individual consumption wants. Furthermore, even the conscious consumption decisions of the individual consumer do not necessarily reflect his or her real needs.

In this section we will explore the reasons why the consumer cannot be regarded as the final arbiter of production priorities in a capitalist system.

We begin by noting that consumers' wants in our society are not god-given nor simply "human nature" but are instead the product of a specific historical context. As Richard Lichtman put it,

> Every society, in order merely to survive, must satisfy the basic subsistence needs of its members for food, shelter, clothing and human recognition.

> *There is a level of productivity that must be achieved by any social group; for human beings have fundamental needs whose violation brings social disorganization or death. That is one half of the truth. The other is that human needs are satisfied through specific means of production that shape and alter the original needs and give rise to new needs whose satisfaction depends upon new technical instruments and new forms of social organization. Every society, therefore, in struggling to satisfy fundamental human needs, shapes these needs in distinctive ways and produces new needs which were not part of any original human nature.[1]*

The capitalist mode of production conditions the needs and wants of consumers: the extreme emphasis placed on consumption, variously referred to as "consumerism," "consumptionism," or the "ethic of consumption," pervades both the consumption patterns and the production priorities of capitalist society.

Consumerism derives first of all from the alienated nature of work under capitalist relations of production. Work is eliminated as a potential arena for the worker's expression and self-fulfillment; that the principal incentive to work is wages—external to the work process and useful only during the non-work part of the day or week—testifies to the depersonalizing content of work and the reasons for people's consequent "escape" into consumerism.[2]

The alienation of the worker from production thus leaves only the sphere of consumption as an arena for expressing one's individuality, asserting one's humanity, and simply escaping the debilitating effects of one's job. Ellen Willis points out that:

> *As it is, the profusion of commodities . . . is a bribe, but like all bribes, it offers concrete benefits—in the average American's case, a degree of physical comfort unparalelled in history. Under present conditions, people are preoccupied with consumer goods not because they are brainwashed, but because buying is the one pleasurable activity not only permitted but actively encouraged by the power structure. The pleasure of eating an ice cream cone may be minor compared to the pleasure of meaningful, autonomous work, but the former is easily available and the latter is not. A poor family would undoubtedly rather have a decent apartment than a new TV, but since they are unlikely to get the apartment, what is to be gained by not getting the TV?[3]*

Furthermore, the commodity fetishism inherent in capitalist production relations reinforces this emphasis on consumption; for commodity consumption is seen not as a means but as an end in itself.[4] Capitalism asserts that the best and indeed the only proper means for achieving greater happiness or a better life is by increased consumption. To solve one's problems, to

[1]Richard Lichtman, "Capitalism and Consumption," *Socialist Revolution* 1, no. 3 (May/June 1970): 83.
[2]See Keniston, Section 6.4, p. 269; and Gintis, Section 6.5, p. 274.
[3]Ellen Willis, "Consumerism and Women," *Socialist Revolution* 1, no. 3 (May/June 1970): 70.
[4]See Fromm, Section 6.3, p. 265.

find happiness, to "lead the good life," one need only have the money to buy the right things or to go to the right places.[5] Thus, increased consumption, a higher "standard of living" (that is, more goods), and economic growth become goals of society and unquestioned ends in and of themselves.

Capitalist firms take an active role in stimulating consumption demand. Many commodities are purposely designed and constructed in order to wear out or fall apart very quickly, insuring that consumers will periodically have to buy a new model of the product. Automobiles are one of the most blatant examples of such planned obsolescence, but they are by no means atypical. Unnecessary frills are often attached to products such as automobiles and forced upon the consumer in need of the basic good. Needless to say, the embodiment of superfluous accessories onto basic goods is a convenient way to stimulate consumption demand.

Firms also stimulate consumption demand by undertaking a tremendous sales effort, exemplified by massive advertising. This advertising attempts to convince people that the acquisition of commodities, for which they otherwise would not have any use, will result in greater happiness. In a society based on alienated labor, the effect of so much propaganda for consumption is bound to be significant.

For all of the above reasons, it is simply false to assert that production priorities in a capitalist society follow the dictates of consumers. John Kenneth Galbraith helps to destroy the myth of "consumer sovereignty" in the next reading.

[5]Recall the discussion of this point in the introduction to Chapter 3, p. 88.

Source: The following is excerpted from Chapter 11 of *The Affluent Society* by JOHN KENNETH GALBRAITH (Second Edition, Revised). Copyright © 1958, 1969 by John Kenneth Galbraith. Reprinted by permission of Houghton Mifflin Co. and Hamish Hamilton Ltd.

I

The notion that wants do not become less urgent the more amply the individual is supplied is broadly repugnant to common sense. It is something to be believed only by those who wish to believe. Yet the conventional wisdom must be tackled on its own terrain. Intertemporal comparisons of an individual's state of mind do rest on technically vulnerable ground. Who can say for sure that the deprivation which afflicts him with hunger is more painful than the deprivation which afflicts him with envy of his neighbor's new car? In the time that has passed since he was poor, his soul may have become subject to a new and deeper searing. And where a society is concerned, comparisons between marginal satisfactions when it is poor and those when it is affluent will involve not only the same individual at different times but different individuals at different times. The scholar who wishes to believe that with increasing affluence there is no reduction in the urgency of desires and goods is not without points for debate. However plausible the case against him, it cannot be proven. In the defense of the conventional wisdom, this amounts almost to invulnerability.

However, there is a flaw in the case. If the

individual's wants are to be urgent, they must be original with himself. They cannot be urgent if they must be contrived for him. And above all, they must be contrived by the process of production by which they are satisfied. For this means that the whole case for the urgency of production, based on the urgency of wants, falls to the ground. One cannot defend production as satisfying wants if that production creates the wants.

Were it so that a man on arising each morning was assailed by demons which instilled in him a passion sometimes for silk shirts, sometimes for kitchenware, sometimes for chamber pots, and sometimes for orange squash, there would be every reason to applaud the effort to find the goods, however odd, that quenched this flame. But should it be that his passion was the result of his first having cultivated the demons, and should it also be that his effort to allay it stirred the demons to ever greater and greater effort, there would be question as to how rational was his solution. Unless restrained by conventional attitudes, he might wonder if the solution lay with more goods or fewer demons.

So it is that if production creates the wants it seeks to satisfy, or if the wants emerge *pari passu* with the production, then the urgency of the wants can no longer be used to defend the urgency of the production. Production only fills a void that it has itself created.

II

The point is so central that it must be pressed. Consumer wants can have bizarre, frivolous, or even immoral origins, and an admirable case can still be made for a society that seeks to satisfy them. But the case cannot stand if it is the process of satisfying wants that creates the wants. For then the individual who urges the importance of production to satisfy these wants is precisely in the position of the onlooker who applauds the efforts of the squirrel to keep abreast of the wheel that is propelled by his own efforts.

That wants are, in fact, the fruit of production will now be denied by few serious scholars. And a considerable number of economists, though not always in full knowledge of the implications, have conceded the point. . . . [John Maynard] Keynes [has] noted that needs of "the second class," i.e. those that are the result of efforts to keep abreast or ahead of one's fellow being "may indeed be insatiable; for the higher the general level, the higher still are they."[1] And emulation has always played a considerable role in the views of other economists of want creation. One man's consumption becomes his neighbor's wish. This already means that the process by which wants are satisfied is also the process by which wants are created. The more wants that are satisfied, the more new ones are born.

However, the argument has been carried farther. A leading modern theorist of consumer behavior, Professor Duesenberry, has stated explicitly that "ours is a society in which one of the principal social goals is a higher standard of living. . . . [This] has great significance for the theory of consumption . . . the desire to get superior goods takes on a life of its own. It provides a drive to higher expenditure which may even be stronger than that arising out of the needs which are supposed to be satisfied by that expenditure."[2] The implications of this view are impressive. The notion of independently established need now sinks into the background. Because the society sets great store by ability to produce a high living standard, it evaluates people by the products they pos-

[1] J. M. Keynes, *Essays in Persuasion,* "Economic Possibilities for Our Grandchildren" (London: Macmillan, 1931), p. 365.

[2] James S. Duesenberry, *Income, Saving and the Theory of Consumer Behavior* (Cambridge, Mass.: Harvard University Press, 1949), p. 28.

sess. The urge to consume is fathered by the value system which emphasizes the ability of the society to produce. The more that is produced, the more that must be owned in order to maintain the appropriate prestige. The latter is an important point, for, without going as far as Duesenberry in reducing goods to the role of symbols of prestige in the affluent society, it is plain that his argument fully implies that the production of goods creates the wants that the goods are presumed to satisfy.

III

The even more direct link between production and wants is provided by the institutions of modern advertising and salesmanship. These cannot be reconciled with the notion of independently determined desires, for their central function is to create desires —to bring into being wants that previously did not exist. This is accomplished by the producer of the goods or at his behest. A broad empirical relationship exists between what is spent on production of consumer goods and what is spent in synthesizing the desires for that production. A new consumer product must be introduced with a suitable advertising campaign to arouse an interest in it. The path for an expansion of output must be paved by a suitable expansion in the advertising budget. Outlays for the manufacturing of a product are not more important in the strategy of modern business enterprise than outlays for the manufacturing of demand for the product. None of this is novel. All would be regarded as elementary by the most retarded student in the nation's most primitive school of business administration. The cost of this want formation is formidable. In 1956, total advertising expenditure—though, as noted, not all of it may be assigned to the synthesis of wants —amounted to about ten billion dollars. For some years, it had been increasing at a rate

in excess of a billion a year.[3] Obviously, such outlays must be integrated with the theory of consumer demand. They are too big to be ignored.

But such integration means recognizing that wants are dependent on production. It accords to the producer the function both of making the goods and of making the desires for them. It recognizes that production, not only passively through emulation, but actively through advertising and related activities, creates the wants it seeks to satisfy.

The businessman and the lay reader will be puzzled over the emphasis which I give to a seemingly obvious point. The point is indeed obvious. But it is one which, to a singular degree, economists have resisted. They have sensed, as the layman does not, the damage to established ideas which lurks in these relationships. As a result, incredibly, they have closed their eyes (and ears) to the most obtrusive of all economic phenomena, namely, modern want creation.

. . .

In unraveling the complex, we should always be careful not to overlook the obvious. The fact that wants can be synthesized by advertising, catalyzed by salesmanship, and shaped by the discreet manipulations of the persuaders shows that they are not very urgent. A man who is hungry need never be told of his need for food. If he is inspired by his appetite, he is immune to the influence of Messrs. Batten, Barton, Durstine & Osborn. The latter are effective only with those who are so far removed from physical want that they do not already know what they want. In this state alone, men are open to persuasion.

IV

The general conclusion of these pages . . . had perhaps best be put with some formality.

[3]In 1969 advertising expenditures amounted to almost 20 billion dollars. [Editors' note.]

As a society becomes increasingly affluent, wants are increasingly created by the process by which they are satisfied. This may operate passively. Increases in consumption, the counterpart of increases in production, act by suggestion or emulation to create wants. Or producers may proceed actively to create wants through advertising and salesmanship. Wants thus come to depend on output. In technical terms, it can no longer be assumed that welfare is greater at an all-around higher level of production than at a lower one. It may be the same. The higher level of production has, merely, a higher level of want creation necessitating a higher level of want satisfaction.

. . .

Among the many models of the good society, no one has urged the squirrel wheel. . . . [Yet] now we find [that] our concern for goods . . . does not arise in spontaneous consumer need. Rather, [the fact that wants depend on the process by which they are satisfied] . . . means that [our concern for goods] . . . grows out of the process of production itself. If production is to increase, the wants must be effectively contrived. In the absence of the contrivance, the increase would not occur. This is not true of all goods, but that it is true of a substantial part is sufficient. It means that since the demand for this part could not exist, were it not contrived, its utility or urgency, *ex* contrivance, is zero. If we regard this production as marginal, we may say that the marginal utility of present aggregate output, *ex* advertising and salesmanship, is zero. Clearly the attitudes and values which make production the central achievement of our society have some exceptionally twisted roots.

9.3   *Economic Growth Versus Psychological Balance*

The drive to expand is a fundamental characteristic of capitalist production. The maintenance and expansion of profits requires the expansion of output, whether or not such expansion is socially rational.

In the previous section we suggested that consumerism derives from alienated labor and that consumer wants are shaped and intensified by advertising and the sales effort. Thus the emphasis on economic growth, and especially the stress on its efficacy for increasing individual well-being, is misplaced. In this reading, Walter Weisskopf evaluates the consequences of continuous growth for the satisfaction of human needs.

Source: The following is excerpted from "Economic Growth Versus Existential Balance" by WALTER WEISSKOPF. From *Ethics* LXXV, No. 2 (January 1965). Copyright © 1965 by the University of Chicago. Reprinted by permission of the author and the University of Chicago Press.

This paper is concerned with a reexamination of the concept of economic growth not as a short-run goal of economic policy but as a basic orientation and a mode of life. Such reexamination may put in doubt some of the values which underlie our scientific, technological, and business activities and institutions. Such an inquiry will have to transgress the traditional limits of economic thought. It will require criticism of economic values from the point of view of psychology and philosophy. The main guidepost for this

inquiry is the effect which economic concepts, values, and activities have on the individual and how they affect his existence. I
would like to advance the hypothesis . . . that
there is a conflict between the idea of continuous economic growth on the one hand
and certain prerequisites of human existence
on the other.

There is hardly any disagreement among
economists, businessmen, and politicians
about the desirability of aggregate growth of
the economy defined as an ever increasing
national income or product. There are differences about the details of national-income
accounting and serious differences about the
means of accomplishing economic growth.
The desirability of overall growth for the
individual and for society is hardly questioned. A gross national product (GNP)
growing, if possible, at an increasing rate
has become a dogma of economic reasoning
and an object of economic worship. There is
an obsessive preoccupation with the growth
and the rate of growth of the GNP which
one could call *GNP fetishism*. GNP figures,
conjectural and tentative at best, are watched
by businessmen and politicians alike. Their
decline, or allegedly insufficient growth, is
considered a national calamity. The comparison of growth rates of Eastern and Western nations has become a part of the cold
war and a matter of international competition.

· · ·

The concept of growth reflects the value-
attitude system of early capitalism before
and during the Industrial Revolution. The
terms "acquisitive society" (Tawney) or the
"civilisation de toujours plus" (the civilization of more and more [Bertrand de Jouve-
nel]) characterize this attitude. Max Weber
has called it the "spirit of capitalism" and
described it as a value system which elevates
the acquisition of riches pursued systematically through hard work, frugality, and
thrift to the dignity of a way of life and of

an ultimate goal.[1] In distinction from previous societies where the pursuit of wealth
and hard work were considered as inferior
activities and as a curse, left to slaves,
women, and inferior social groups, industrial society made the acquisition of wealth
morally acceptable and considered it as a
moral obligation. Economic thought justified
this attitude by assuming that acquisitiveness
and the propensity to truck, barter, and exchange in order to increase one's wealth is
a basic human propensity.[2] Here, a unique
historical phenomenon, the acquisitive attitude, was interpreted as a universal human
inclination. Thus it made acceptable an ideal
which ran counter to the traditional Christian ethics. . . . Thus the ideas of economic
growth on the individual and on the social
levels are conceptualizations of the ethics
of acquisition. In present discussions this
origin has been forgotten because growth
and acquisition have become accepted
values. Growth is discussed not from the
ethical psychological but from the functional
point of view. The pursuit of economic
growth has been rationalized by arguments
that it is necessary for full employment, for
defense, for the increase in population, for
the maintenance of the current economic
institutions; whether it should be accepted as
a basic economic value is hardly ever questioned.

· · ·

. . . [The basic equilibrium of a con-
sumer] is a physiological one and, as such,
is a temporary stage of saturation. It is
modeled according to the pattern of physiological needs and their satisfaction. There is
the "pain" of tension which is relieved by
the "pleasure" of need satisfaction. There is
a general trend in economics as well as in
psychology to interpret all needs according
to this pattern. "The needs that are taken

[1] *The Protestant Ethic and the Spirit of Capitalism* (New York: 1958).
[2] Smith, *op. cit.*, p. 13.

as the starting point for motivation theory are the so-called physiological drives."[3] The physiological needs are appetites caused by an actual physical need or lack in the body; the drives "aim" at procuring what is lacking and thereby move toward a state of saturation, equilibrium, and homeostasis. Such states of equilibrium are temporary; tension arises again and again in the life of the individual organism to be eliminated by need satisfaction leading to homeostatic equilibrium.

Economic growth and acquisition can lead only to such a temporary, homeostatic equilibrium. No lasting satisfaction or equilibrium can be reached on the physiological level. The "pleasure" of such need satisfaction presupposes a state of tension which is relieved by satisfaction. Without the emergence of tension no pleasure can be received from physiological need satisfaction. Without hunger the intake of food is not pleasurable.

This statement is so trite that one hesitates to make it. However, this obvious truth is overlooked when it comes to an evaluation of economic acquisition and growth. . . . The industrial economy has immensely enlarged the field of need satisfaction and raised the standards of living to a peak never reached before. We have come such a long way that many social scientists and philosophers talk about an imminent state of affairs in which men will be freed of economic necessity altogether.[4] They predict that, in the foreseeable future, man in the advanced industrial economy may be able to take the "leap from the realm of necessity into the realm of freedom." However that may be, even at the present time the advanced Western economies have reached a level of production which has reduced immensely the

[additional] utility of additional goods and services. This is not a situation of which people are conscious. The ideology of "more and more" is still so strong that people are not aware of the fact that they are forced into more work and more acquisition by the socioeconomic system rather than by their free inclination.[5] However, the intensive advertising and the pervasive fact of artificial obsolescence are clear and present symptoms of this unconscious situation. Artificial obsolescence is the man-made correlate to physiological needs. *Nolens volens,* people get hungry several times a day. Planned obsolescence replaces the emergence of physiological tension where no automatic tension arises. What firms and advertisers are doing is to create a hunger where nature has not provided for it. By changing styles of such articles as cars and clothes and by exploiting the desire for conformity and for avoidance of being different from the "other," they "force" people to develop a "need" for change. The same purpose is accomplished by the continuous development of new products. Once the new product is marketed, the pressure of conformity creates a need for it.

Therefore, a relatively permanent balance and equilibrium is impossible as long as all needs are experienced and interpreted as physiological ones. On this level pleasure requires preceding pain and tension. In order to have pleasure, pain and tension have to be artificially created. This was age-old wisdom of mankind until Western civilization buried it under its empirical, naturalistic approach. That sensual satisfaction requires ever more excitation, titillation, tension, and pain was known not only to the Hindus and Buddhists but also to the Greek philosophers. It was of course known to Christian thought from the fathers of the church to the Middle Ages. Only modern civilization has elevated physiological satisfaction to the

[3] A. H. Maslow, *Motivation and Personality* (New York: 1954), p. 80.
[4] J. K. Galbraith, *The Affluent Society* (Boston: 1958); R. Theobald, *Free Men and Free Markets* (New York: 1963); H. Marcuse, *Eros and Civilization* (Boston: 1955).

[5] H. Marcuse, *One-Dimensional Man* (Boston: 1964).

dignity of an ultimate goal. Economic growth as an individual and social ideal is a reflection of this attitude which has pulled modern man into a vortex of continuous change and expansion without peace and without end.

. . .

All this is quite in line with some findings of modern psychology. A. H. Maslow[6] suggested that there is a hierarchy of needs. Proceeding from the lower and progressing to the higher needs he classifies them as follows: physiological needs, such as hunger; safety needs, such as the need for physical *and mental* security, including the need for a comprehensive "philosophy that organizes the universe and the men in it into a sort of satisfactorily coherent meaningful whole"; the needs for belongingness and love; the need for esteem; and the need for self-actualization. What matters is not whether this classification is correct and exhaustive, but that there is a hierarchy of needs. "It is quite true that man lives by bread alone—when there is no bread. But what happens to man's desires when there *is* plenty of bread and when his belly is chronically filled? At once, other (and higher) needs emerge." Various needs related to different dimensions of existence have to be brought into balance although certain physiological and quasiphysiological needs are prevalent if they are not satisfied. "Basic human needs are organized into a hierarchy of relative prepotency."[7] Consequently, *need satisfaction which continuously increases the supply of means along one level and neglects needs on a different level is contrary to human well-being.* What is required is a *balanced system of need satisfaction* on various levels.

. . .

The dimensions that are neglected in industrial society are those which transcend the dimension of physiological and creature comforts because all goals of life are reduced to a quasi-physiological level. Neglected are thus all the "higher needs" in Maslow's terms, the needs for mental safety in the form of a unifying world philosophy, the needs for love and belongingness, the need for self-actualization in work. In Hannah Arendt's[8] hierarchy of values the neglected dimensions are the field of creative work where a durable whole is created that forms a part of our stable environment; the opportunity for meaningful political action by individuals; and the dimension of contemplation in the broadest sense: where man opens his mind and soul receptively to truth, beauty, justice, and the good (the Platonic *agathon*).

Our overemphasis on economic growth and on acquisition leads to a disturbance of the balance of our existence. Too much time and energy used for the procurement of goods and services for the market must, by necessity, lead to a neglect of all those faculties and modes of life for which not enough time and energy is left. Our excessively economic orientation develops only those faculties which are necessary for economic growth. We are sacrificing those alternative faculties and attitudes which cannot contribute to an increase in wealth. Too much economic growth tends to destroy the balance between activistic effort and receptivity, doing and being, grasping and receiving, between conscious intentional effort and passive inner experience, between intellect and feeling. This destructive effect is wrought by excessive individual striving for acquisition as well as by the exclusive emphasis on national economic growth. Unless an increase in the national income is counterbalanced by some gains in these neglected dimensions, such an increase may actually cause a decline in human well-being.

. . .

[6]Maslow, *op. cit.*, p. 83.

[7]G. Vickers, *The Undirected Society* (Toronto: 1959), pp. 73, 114.

[8]H. Arendt, *The Human Condition* (Chicago: 1958).

9.4 *Private Priorities and Collective Needs*

We have already noted how the unequal distribution of income biases production priorities in favor of the rich, which results in inadequate food, homes, health care, and other necessities for the poorest segment of the population.

Capitalist production is also biased against collective needs. In the following reading, André Gorz describes the limitations that the capitalist system of production imposes upon the possibility of satisfying the fundamental collective needs of a society. Gorz argues that the criterion of private profitability, dependent as it is on existing market demands, will inevitably bias investment in favor of individually salable commodities and against socially valuable services. He cites the predominance of the private automobile rather than public transportation as a means of urban transportation to illustate the bias imposed by the private profit incentive.

Gorz argues that many collective services by their very nature cannot be profitably marketed by private capitalist firms, even if the distribution of income were far more equitable than it is. Such services must necessarily be operated and financed by a government authority that is willing to limit the range of private investment in the interests of social needs. Yet increasing government control of this kind runs counter to the natural logic of the capitalist system and hence cannot be expected to prevail.

SOURCE: The following is excerpted from Chapter 4 of *Strategy for Labor* by ANDRE GORZ. Copyright © 1964 by Les Editions de Seuil; English translation copyright © 1967 by Beacon Press. Reprinted by permission of Beacon Press and Allen Lane The Penguin Press.

· · ·

The effects of capitalist production on the environment and on society are a . . . source of waste and of distortion. . . . The most profitable production for each entrepreneur is not necessarily the most advantageous one for the consumers; the pursuit of maximum profit and the pursuit of optimum use value do not coincide when each product is considered separately. But if instead of considering the action of each entrepreneur (in fact of each oligopoly) separately, we consider the resulting total of all such actions and their repercussions on society, then we note an even sharper contradiction between this overall result and the social and economic optimum.

This contradiction results essentially from the limits which the criteria of profitability impose on capitalist initiative. According to the logic of this initiative, the most profitable activities are the most important ones, and activities whose product or result cannot be measured according to the criteria of profitability and return are neglected or abandoned to decay. These nonprofitable activities, whose desirability cannot even be understood in capitalist terms, consist of all those investments which cannot result in production for the market under the given social and political circumstances, that is to say, which do not result in a commercial exchange comprising the profitable sale of goods and services. In fact this category includes all investments and services which answer to human needs that cannot be expressed in market terms as demands for salable commodities: the need for education, city planning, cultural and recreational facilities, works of art, research, public health, public transportation (and also economic planning, reforestation, elimination of water and air pollution, noise control, etc.)—in short, all economic activities which belong to the "public domain" and cannot arise or survive except as public services, regardless of their profitability.

The demand for the satisfaction of these needs, which cannot be expressed in market terms, necessarily takes on political and collective forms; and the satisfaction of these collective needs, precisely because it cannot be procured except by public services belonging to the collectivity, constitutes a permanent challenge to the laws and the spirit of the capitalist system. In other words, there is a whole sphere of fundamental, priority needs which constitute an objective challenge to capitalist logic.

The acuteness of this antagonism—and the sharpness of the contradiction between capitalist initiative and collective needs—necessarily grows. It grows principally as a result of the fact that collective needs and the cost of their satisfaction are not in principle included in the cost of capitalist decisions and initiatives. There is a disjunction between the direct cost of the productive investment for the private investor, and the indirect, social cost which this investment creates to cover the resulting collective needs, such as housing, roads, the supply of energy and water; in short, the infrastructure. There is also a disjunction between the computation of direct production costs by the private investor and the social cost which his investment will bring with it: for example, expenses for education, housing, transportation, various services; in short, the entrepreneur's criteria of profitability, which measure the desirability of the investment, and the criteria of human and collective desirability, are not identical. As a conse-

quence, the collective needs engendered by capitalist investment are covered haphazardly or not at all; the satisfaction of these needs is neglected or subordinated to more profitable "priorities" because these needs were not foreseen and included in advance in the total cost of the project.

Thus, when a capitalist group decides to invest in a given project and a given locality, it need not bother to ask itself what degree of priority its project has in the scale of needs, what social costs it will entail, what social needs it will engender, what long term public investments it will make necessary later on, or what alternatives its private decision will render impossible. The decision of the capitalist group will be guided rather by the existing market demand, the available facilities and equipment, and the proximity of the market and the sources of raw materials.

The first result of this situation is that the decision of a private trust to invest does not in most cases have any but an accidental relationship to the real but nonmarketable needs of the local, regional, or national unit: the model of development which monopoly capitalism imposes on insufficiently developed regions is as a general rule a colonial model. The balanced development of Brittany or Southern Italy, for example, if it were to answer real needs would in the first place demand investments to revive agricultural productivity, to assure local processing of raw materials, and to occupy the underemployed population in industries having local outlets. Priority thus would have to be given to educational and cultural services, to food and agricultural industries, to light industry, chemical and pharmaceutical manufacturing, to communication and transportation. If these priorities were chosen, the local communities could develop toward a diversification of their activities, toward a relative economic, cultural, and social autonomy, toward a fuller development of social relations and exchanges, and thus toward a fuller development of human relations and abilities.

Capitalist initiative functions only in terms of the existing *market* demand. If there is no such demand in the underdeveloped regions for the products capable of bringing about balanced development, then capitalist initiative will consist of setting up export industries in these regions. The resulting type of development, besides being very limited, will reverse the real priorities: the underemployed local manpower will be drained toward assembly workshops (although not to the extent of providing full employment), toward satellite factories which are subcontractors of distant trusts, and toward the production or extraction of raw materials or of individual components which will be transformed or assembled elsewhere.

The local community, instead of being raised toward a new, richer internal equilibrium, will thus be practically destroyed by having a new element of imbalance grafted onto its already out-of-date structures: agriculture, instead of being made healthier and richer, will be ruined by the exodus of manpower and the land will be abandoned; the local industries, instead of being diversified in terms of local needs, will undergo specialization and impoverishment; local or regional autonomy, instead of being reinforced, will be diminished even more, since the centers of decision making for the local activities are in Paris or Milan and the new local industries are the first to suffer the shock of economic fluctuations: the quality of the local community's social relations, instead of being improved, will be impoverished; local manpower will get the dirtiest and the most monotonous jobs; the ancient towns (*bourgs*) will become dormitory cities with new cafés and juke boxes in place of cultural facilities; the former civilization will be destroyed and replaced by nothing; those of the new workers who do not travel one, two, or even three hours daily by bus to go to and from their work will be penned up in concrete cages or in shanty towns: in the mother country as well as in the colonies there is a process of "slummification" ("*clochardisation*"). The colonies, at least, can free themselves of foreign colonialism; the underdeveloped regions in the mother country, however, are often irreversibly colonized and deprived of independent livelihood by monopoly capitalism, or even emptied of their population and turned into a wasteland.

The drift of industry toward the underdeveloped regions, in the conditions which have just been described, cannot really be compared to an industrialization of these areas. It tends rather to destroy all possibility of balance between the city and the countryside by the creation of new, giant agglomerations which empty the back country. The small peasants will not be able to rationalize their methods (that would require a policy of credit and equipment favoring cooperative or collective modes of farming); instead they will sell their holdings to the benefit of the agrarian capitalists. The former peasants will install themselves as shop keepers, café owners, or unskilled laborers in the new big city or in the capital. The drift of certain industries toward less developed regions is therefore not at all comparable to decentralization. On the contrary, it is only a marginal phenomenon of industry's tendency to concentrate geographically. Industry is attracted by industry, money by money. Both go by preference where markets and conditions of profitability already exist, not where these must first be created. Thus regional disparities tend to grow.

The principal cause of geographic concentration of industry has been the public prefinancing, during the past decades, of the social bases of industrial expansion in the highly dense zones: housing, transportation, trained manpower, infrastructure. Now, the savings realized by individual industries due to geographic concentration are an extra burden for the collectivity. After a certain point has been reached the operating costs of the large cities grow dizzily (long traveling time, air pollution, noise, lack of space, etc.). The overpopulation of the urban centers has as a counterpart the depopulation of nondeveloped areas below the threshold of economic and social viability, their economic and human impoverishment, and the obliteration of their potential; and the cost of the social reproduction of labor power is multiplied. . . .

This double process of congestion and decline has one and the same root: the concentration of economic power in a small number of monopolistic groups which drain off a large part of the economic surplus realized in production and distribution and which reinvest that surplus where conditions of immediate profitability are already present. Therefore the resources available for a regional and social policy consonant with real needs are always insufficient, especially because monopoly competition engenders new consumer needs and new collective expenses which are incompatible with a government policy aimed at balanced development.

The costs of infrastructure (roads, transportation, city maintenance and planning, provision of energy and water) which monopoly expansion imposes on the collectivity as it spreads (namely in the congested zones), in practice make it impossible to provide such services in the areas where the need is greatest: the billions swallowed up by the great cities are in the last analysis diverted from economically and humanly more advantageous uses.

Furthermore, the cost of the infrastructure, which the orientation given by monopoly capitalism to consumption demands, represents an obstacle to the satisfaction of priority needs. The most striking example in this regard is that of the automobile industry. For the production of a means of evasion and escape, this industry has diverted productive resources, labor, and capi-

tal from priority tasks such as housing, education, public transportation, public health, city planning, and rural services. The priority given by monopoly capitalism to the automobile gets stronger and stronger: city planning must be subordinated to the requirements of the automobile, roads are built instead of houses (this is very clear in Italy, for example), and public transportation is sacrificed.

And finally the private automobile becomes a social necessity: urban space is organized in terms of private transportation; public transportation lags farther and farther behind the spread of the suburbs and the increasing distance required to travel to work; the pedestrian or the cyclist becomes a danger to others and himself; athletic and cultural facilities are removed from the city, beyond the reach of the nonmotorized suburbanite and often even of the city dweller. The possession of an automobile becomes a basic necessity because the universe is organized in terms of private transportation. This process is halted only with difficulty in the advanced capitalist countries. To the extent that the indispensability of private automobiles has made life unbearable in the large, overpopulated cities where air, light, and space are lacking, motorized escape will continue to be an important—although decreasing—element in the reproduction of labor power, even when priority has returned to city planning, to collective services, and to public transportation.

. . .

On the level of collective needs, and only on this level, the theory of impoverishment thus continues to be valid. The social cost of the reproduction of labor power . . . tends to rise as fast as or faster than individual purchasing power; the workers' social standard of living tends to stagnate, to worsen, even if their individual standard of living (expressed in terms of monetary purchasing power) rises. And it is extremely difficult, if not impossible, for urban workers to obtain a qualitative improvement in their living standard as a result of a raise in their direct wages within the framework of capitalist structures. It is this quasi-impossibility which gives demands in the name of collective needs a revolutionary significance.

The nature of collective needs, in effect, is that they often cannot be expressed in terms of monetary demands. They involve a set of collective resources, services, and facilities which escape the law of the market, capitalist initiative, and all criteria of profitability. These needs, inexpressible in economic terms, are at least virtually in permanent contradiction to capitalism and mark the limit of its effectiveness. These are the needs which capitalism tends to neglect or to suppress, insofar as capitalism knows only the *homo economicus*—defined by the consumption of merchandise and its production —and not the human man, the consumer, producer, and user of goods which cannot be sold, bought, or reproduced. It is these needs which, although they are basically biological, all have a necessarily cultural and at least potentially creative dimension, due to the destruction by industry of a natural environment for which human praxis must substitute a new social environment and civilization.

Among these needs are:

—Housing and city planning, not only in quantitative but in qualitative terms as well. An urban esthetic and an urban landscape, an environment which furthers the development of human faculties instead of debasing them, must be recreated. Now it is obvious that it is not profitable to provide 200 square feet of green area per inhabitant, to plan parks, roads, and squares. The application of the law of the market leads, on the contrary, to reserve the best living conditions for the privileged, who need them least, and to deny them to the workers who, because they do the most difficult and the lowest-paid work, need them profoundly. The workings of this law also push the workers farther and

farther from their place of work, and impose on them additional expense and fatigue.

—Collective services, such as public transportation, laundries and cleaners, child day-care centers and nursery schools. These are nonprofitable in essence: for in terms of profit, it is necessarily more advantageous to sell individual vehicles, washing machines and magical soap powders. And since these services are most needed by those who have the lowest incomes, their expansion on a commercial basis presents no interest at all for capital. Only public services can fill the need.

—Collective cultural, athletic, and health facilities: schools, theatres, libraries, concert halls, swimming pools, stadiums, hospitals, in short, all the facilities necessary for the reestablishment of physical and intellectual balance for the development of human faculties. The nonprofitability of these facilities is evident, as is their extreme scarcity (and usually great cost) in almost all of the capitalist countries.

—Balanced regional development in terms of optimum economic and human criteria, which we have already contrasted to neo-colonialist "slummification."

—Information, communication, active group leisure. Capitalism not only does not have any interest in these needs, it tends even to suppress them. The commercial dictatorship of the monopolies cannot in fact function without a mass of passive consumers, separated by place and style of living, incapable of getting together and communicating directly, incapable of defining together their specific needs (relative to their work and life situation), their preoccupations, their outlook on society and the world —in short, their common project. Mass pseudo-culture, while producing passive and stupefying entertainments, amusements, and pastimes, does not and cannot satisfy the needs arising out of dispersion, solitude, and boredom. This pseudo-culture is less a consequence than a cause of the passivity and the impotence of the individual in a mass society. It is a device invented by monopoly capital to facilitate its dictatorship over a mystified, docile, debased humanity, whose impulses of real violence must be redirected into imaginary channels.

Collective needs are thus objectively in contradiction to the logic of capitalist development. This development is by nature in-capable of giving them the degree of priority which they warrant. This is why demands in the name of collective needs imply a radical challenge of the capitalist system, on the economic, political, and cultural levels.

.   .   .

9.5   *The Crisis Of Our Environment*

The pollution and destruction of the natural environment reflect one particular way in which the collective needs of society are ignored in capitalist production. The society at large has an immense stake in protecting the natural environment, but this interest is not mirrored in the determination of capitalist priorities. The focus on gross national product and on consumption ignores the environmental costs of producing goods and the environmental costs of disposing of goods. Such a focus might have made sense in an earlier age characterized by open frontiers and an apparently limitless natural environment. In the present age, however, it is all too clear that we live within a closed system of limited natural and environmental resources. As a result, we must devote much greater attention to the *quality* of the world environment and restrain the unlimited exploitation of resources for increases in the *quantity* of goods and services. The implications of this necessary change in orientation are profound.

In the next reading, Murray Bookchin argues that environmental disruption cannot be considered simply as a combination of various pollution problems, but rather it must be considered as a fundamental ecological crisis of mankind. This perspective illustrates the fundamental nature of the conflict between social needs and capitalist institutions.

> Source: The following is excerpted from "Towards an Ecological Solution" by MURRAY BOOKCHIN. From *Ramparts Magazine* 8, No. 11 (May 1970). Copyright © 1970 by *Ramparts Magazine*, Inc. Reprinted by Permission of the Editors.

Popular alarm over environmental decay and pollution did not emerge for the first time merely in the late 60s, nor for that matter is it the unique response of the present century. Air pollution, water pollution, food adulteration and other environmental problems were public issues as far back as ancient times, when notions of environmental diseases were far more prevalent than they are today. All of these issues came to the surface again with the Industrial Revolution—a period which was marked by burgeoning cities, the growth of the factory system, and an unprecedented befouling and polluting of air and waterways.

Today the situation is changing drastically and at a tempo that portends a catastrophe for the entire world of life. What is not clearly understood in many popular discussions of the present ecological crisis is that the very nature of the issues has changed, that the decay of the environment is directly tied to the decay of the existing social structure. It is not simply certain malpractices or a given spectrum of poisonous agents that is at stake, but rather the very structure of modern agriculture, industry and the city. Consequently, environmental decay and ecological catastrophe cannot be averted merely by increased programs like "pollution control" which deal with sources rather than systems. To be commensurable to the problem, the solution must entail far-reaching revolutionary changes in society and in man's relation to man.

I

To understand the enormity of the ecological crisis and the sweeping transformation it requires, let us briefly revisit the "pollution problem" as it existed a few decades ago. During the 1930s, pollution was primarily a muckraking issue, a problem of expose journalism typified by Kallet and Schlink's "100 Million Guinea Pigs."

This kind of muckraking literature still exists in abundance and finds an eager market among "consumers," that is to say, a public that seeks personal and legislative solutions to pollution problems. Its supreme pontiff is Ralph Nader, an energetic young man who has shrewdly combined traditional muckraking with a safe form of "New Left" activism. In reality, Nader's emphasis belongs to another historical era, for the magnitude of the pollution problem has expanded beyond the most exaggerated accounts of the 1930s. The new pollutants are no longer "poisons" in the popular sense of the term; rather they belong to the problems of ecology, not merely pharmacology, and these do not lend themselves to legislative redress.

What now confronts us is not the predominantly specific, rapidly degradable poisons that alarmed an earlier generation, but long-lived carcinogenic and mutagenic agents, such as radioactive isotopes and chlorinated hydrocarbons. These agents become part of the very anatomy of the individual by entering his bone structure, tissues and fat deposits. Their disperson is so global that they become part of the anatomy of the environment itself. They will be within us and around us for years to come, in many cases for generations to come. Their toxic effects are usually chronic rather than acute; the deadly and mutational effects they produce in the individual will not be seen until many years have passed. They are harmful not only in large quantities, but in trace amounts; as such, they are not detectable by human senses or even, in many cases, by conventional methods of analysis. They damage not only specific individuals but the human species as a whole and virtually all other forms of life.

No less alarming is the fact that we must drastically revise our traditional notions of what constitutes an environmental "pollutant." A few decades ago it would have been absurd to describe carbon dioxide and heat as "pollutants" in the customary sense of the term. Yet in both cases they may well rank among the most serious sources of future ecological imbalance and pose major threats to the viability of the planet. As a result of industrial and domestic combustion activities, the quantity of carbon dioxide in the atmosphere has increased by roughly 25 percent in the past one hundred years, a figure that may well double again by the end of the century. The famous "greenhouse effect," which increasing quantities of the gas is expected to produce, has already been widely discussed: eventually, it is supposed, the gas will inhibit the dissipation of the earth's heat into space, causing a rise in overall temperatures which will melt the polar ice caps and result in an inundation of vast coastal areas. Thermal pollution, the result mainly of warm water discharged by nuclear and conventional power plants, has disastrous effects on the ecology of lakes, rivers and estuaries. Increases in water temperature not only damage the physiological and reproductive activities of fish; they also promote the great blooms of algae that have become such formidable problems in waterways.

What is at stake in the ecological crisis we face today is the very capacity of the earth to sustain advanced forms of life. The crisis is being drawn together by massive increases in "typical" forms of air and water pollution; by a mounting accumulation of nondegradable wastes, lead residues, pesticide residues and toxic additives in food; by the expansion of cities into vast urban belts; by increasing stresses due to congestion, noise and mass living; by the wanton scarring of the earth as a result of mining operations, lumbering, and real estate speculation. The result of all this is that the earth within a few decades has been despoiled on a scale that it unprecedented in the entire history of human habitation on the planet.

Finally, the complexity and diversity of life which marked biological evolution over many millions of years is being replaced by a simpler, more synthetic and increasingly homogenized environment. Aside from any esthetic considerations, the elimination of this complexity and diversity may prove to be the most serious loss of all. Modern society is literally undoing the work of organic evolution. If this process continues unabated, the earth may be reduced to a level of biotic simplicity where humanity—whose welfare depends profoundly upon the complex food chains in the soil, on the land surface and in the oceans—will no longer be able to sustain itself as a viable animal species.

II

In recent years a type of biological "cold warrior" has emerged who tends to locate the ecological crisis in technology and population growth, thereby divesting it of its explosive social content. Out of this focus has emerged a new version of "original sin" in which tools and machines, reinforced by sexually irresponsible humans, ravage the earth in concert. Both technology and sexual irresponsibility, so the argument goes, must be curbed—if not voluntarily, then by the divine institution called the state.

The naivete of this approach would be risible were it not for its sinister implications. History has known of many different forms of tools and machines, some of which are patently harmful to human welfare and the natural world, others of which have clearly improved the condition of man and the ecology of an area. It would be absurd to place plows and mutagenic defoliants, weaving machines and automobiles, computers and moon rockets, under a common rubric. Worse, it would be grossly misleading to deal with these technologies in a social vacuum.

Technologies consist not only of the devices humans employ to mediate their relationship with the natural world, but also the attitudes associated with these devices. These attitudes are distinctly social products, the results of the social relationships humans establish with each other. What is clearly needed is not a mindless deprecation of technology as such, but rather a reordering and redevelopment of technologies according to ecologically sound principles. We need an ecotechnology that will help harmonize society with the natural world.

The same oversimplification is evident in the neo-Malthusian alarm over population growth. The reduction of population growth to a mere ratio between birth rates and death rates obscures the many complex social factors that enter into both statistics. A rising or declining birth rate is not a simple biological datum, any more than is a rising or declining death rate. Both are subject to the influences of the economic status of the individual, the nature of family structure, the values of society, the status of women, the attitude toward children, the culture of the community, and so forth. A change in any single factor interacts with the remainder to produce the statistical data called "birth rate" and "death rate." Culled from such abstract ratios, population growth rates can easily be used to foster authoritarian controls and finally a totalitarian society, especially if neo-Malthusian propaganda and the failure of voluntary birth control are used as an excuse. In arguing that forcible measures of birth control and a calculated policy of indifference to hunger may eventually be necessary to stabilize world populations, the neo-Malthusians are already creating a climate of opinion that will make genocidal policies and authoritarian institutions socially acceptable.

It is supremely ironic that coercion, so clearly implicit in the neo-Malthusian outlook, has acquired a respected place in the public debate on ecology—for the roots of the ecological crisis lie precisely in the coercive basis of modern society. The notion that man must dominate nature emerges directly from the domination of man by man. The patriarchal family may have planted the seed of domination in the nuclear relations of humanity; the classical split between spirit and reality—indeed, mind and labor—may have nourished it; the antinaturalistic bias of Christianity may have tended to its growth; but it was not until organic community relations, be they tribal, feudal or peasant in form, dissolved into market relationships that the planet itself was reduced to a resource for exploitation.

This centuries-long tendency finds its most exacerbating development in modern capitalism: a social order that is orchestrated entirely by the maxim "Production for the sake of production." Owing to its inherently competitive nature, bourgeois society not only pits humans against each other, but the mass of humanity against the natural world. Just as men are converted into commodities,

so every aspect of nature is converted into a commodity, a resource to be manufactured and merchandised wantonly. Entire continental areas in turn are converted into factories, and cities into marketplaces. The liberal euphemisms for these unadorned terms are "growth," "industrial society" and "urban blight." By whatever language they are described, the phenomena have their roots in the domination of man by man.

As technology develops, the maxim "Production for the sake of production" finds its complement in "Consumption for the sake of consumption." The phrase "consumer society" completes the description of the present social order as an "industrial society." Needs are tailored by the mass media to create a public demand for utterly useless commodities, each carefully engineered to deteriorate after a predetermined period of time. The plundering of the human spirit by the marketplace is paralleled by the plundering of the earth by capital. The tendency of the liberal to identify the marketplace with human needs, and capital with technology, represents a calculated error that neutralizes the social thrust of the ecological crisis.

The strategic ratios in the ecological crisis are not the population rates of India but the production rates of the United States, a country that produces more than 50 percent of the world's goods. Here, too, liberal euphemisms like "affluence" conceal the critical thrust of a blunt word like "waste." With a vast section of its industrial capacity committed to war production, the U.S. is literally trampling upon the earth and shredding ecological links that are vital to human survival. If current industrial projections prove to be accurate, the remaining thirty years of the century will witness a five-fold increase in electric power production, based mostly on nuclear fuels and coal. The colossal burden in radioactive wastes and other effluents that this increase will place on the natural ecology of the earth hardly needs description.

In shorter perspective, the problem is no less disquieting. Within the next five years, lumber production may increase an overall 20 percent; the output of paper, 5 percent annually; folding boxes, 3 percent annually; metal cans, 4 to 5 percent annually; plastics (which currently form 1 to 2 percent of municipal wastes), 7 percent annually. Collectively, these industries account for the most serious pollutants in the environment. The utterly senseless nature of modern industrial activity is perhaps best illustrated by the decline in returnable (and reusable) beer bottles from fifty-four billion bottles in 1960 to twenty-six billion today. Their place has been taken over by "one-way bottles" (a rise from eight to twenty-one billion in the same period) and cans (an increase from thirty-eight to fifty-three billion). The "one-way bottles" and cans, of course, pose tremendous problems in solid waste disposal, but they do sell better.

It may be that the planet, conceived as a lump of minerals, can support these mindless increases in the output of trash. The earth, conceived as a complex web of life, certainly cannot. The only question is, can the earth survive its looting long enough for man to replace the current destructive social system with a humanistic, ecologically oriented society.

The apocalyptic tone that marks so many ecological works over the past decade should not be taken lightly. We are witnessing the end of a world, although whether this world is a long-established social order or the earth is a living organism still remains in question. The ecological crisis, with its threat of human extinction, has developed appositely to the advance of technology, with its promise of abundance, leisure and material security. Both are converging toward a single focus: At a point where the very survival of man is being threatened, the possibility of removing him from the trammels of domination, material scarcity and toil has never been more promising. The very technology that has been used to plunder the planet can now be deployed, artfully and rationally, to make it flourish.

It is necessary to overcome not only bourgeois society but also the long legacy of propertied society: the patriarchal family, the city, the state—indeed, the historic splits that separated mind from sensuousness, individual from society, town from country, work from play, man from nature. The spirit of spontaneity and diversity that permeates the ecological outlook toward the natural world must now be directed toward revolutionary change and utopian reconstruction in the social world. Propertied society, domination, hierarchy and the state, in all their forms, are utterly incompatible with the survival of the biosphere. Either ecology action is revolutionary action or it is nothing at all. Any attempt to reform a social order that by its very nature pits humanity against all the forces of life is a gross deception and serves merely as a safety valve for established institutions.

.   .   .

9.6   Capitalism and the Military-Industrial Complex

The immense military expenditures by the U.S. government—some eighty billion dollars in 1970—constitute the most blatant and dangerous irrationality of capitalism. The armaments stockpiled (or used in Vietnam or elsewhere) represent not only resources wasted, but more importantly they threaten to annihilate rebellious peoples around the world and ultimately mankind itself.

Yet military expenditures, because they are *government* expenditures, are often thought to result from particular *political* circumstances rather than from the institutional structure of capitalism. The high level of military expenditures is sometimes explained in terms of external forces (for example, the threat to national security) or in terms of unfortunate but atypical events (perhaps a few powerful Southern Congressmen in alliance with the Pentagon).

In response to these arguments, three points should be made. First, the threat to national security used to justify a high level of military expenditure is not entirely autonomous but is, in part, a direct consequence of the American capitalist system. In Chapter 10 we will argue that imperialism abroad is a natural consequence of capitalism at home, and that keeping the world open for capitalist penetration requires a substantial commitment of military strength.[1]

Second, military expenditures maintain effective demand and therefore act as a significant outlet for surplus absorption. The close correlation between military expenditures and national prosperity testifies to the importance of "defense" spending.[2] While expenditures to maintain effective demand need not necessarily take the form of military expenditures, there are, as Michael Reich and David Finkelhor show in the following reading, powerful forces in a capitalist system making these expenditures most acceptable.

Finally, military expenditures benefit the largest and most powerful corporations (contrary to the "enclave" view which holds that only a few special corporations benefit), and their impact extends to many smaller companies as well. Thus, the role of "defense" spending is not to line the pockets of a few unscrupulous profiteers; instead, as Reich and Finkelhor demonstrate, "the military sector comprises the very heart of Capitalist America."

[1]See especially MacEwan, Section 10.1, p. 409, and Magdoff, Section 10.2, p. 420.

[2]See appendix to Weisskopf, Section 9.1, p. 371.

Source: The following is excerpted from "The Military Industrial Complex: No Way Out" by MICHAEL REICH and DAVID FINKELHOR. From *Up Against the American Myth*, edited by Tom Christoffel, David Finkelhor and Dan Gilbarg. Copyright © 1970 by Michael Reich and David Finkelhor. Reprinted by permission of the authors and Holt, Rinehart and Winston, Inc.

THE IMPACT OF MILITARY SPENDING ON THE ECONOMY[1]

Before World War II, military spending never exceeded 1 percent of the Gross National Product. Over a trillion dollars have been spent on the military since 1951, consuming on the average about 10 percent of the GNP. In 1967, 4.08 million civilian employees worked on defense-related jobs;[2] add to this the 3.5 million soldiers in uniform,

[1]Our debts to Paul Sweezy and Paul Baran throughout this essay will be obvious to readers familiar with *Monopoly Capital* (New York: 1966).

[2]Richard Oliver, "The Employment Impact of Defense Expenditures," *Monthly Labor Review* 90, no. 9 (Sept. 1967), pp. 9–11.

and we have well over 10 percent of the entire labor force engaged in military-related employment.

The military sector of the economy is huge. Yet the image of the weapons industry often projected by liberals is of a small, albeit powerful, coterie of contractors, many of whom owe their existence solely to defense work. Producing exotic military hardware, these corporations form an economic *enclave* somehow separated from the remainder of the economy.[3]

According to the enclave view, most corporations in the country are not affected one way or another by the military budget (except, of course, insofar as aggregate incomes and demands are stimulated). There is some superficial evidence for this image. After all, only one hundred corporations receive over two-thirds of all prime contract awards each year and fifty corporations receive 60 percent, and the list of the top one hundred contractors has exhibited very little turnover in the last twenty years.[4] Prime contract awards are concentrated among just four industries: aircraft (43%), electronics and telecommunications (19.3%), shipbuilding and repairing (10.3%), and ammunition (5%).[5] Moreover, subcontracts appear to be just as concentrated among the big firms.[6]

But this enclave image is highly misleading. First, a list of the top military contractors is virtually a list of all the largest and most powerful industrial corporations in America (see Table 9-B). Nathanson esti-

[3]Emile Benoit, "The Economic Impact of Disarmament in the United States," in *Disarmament: Its Politics and Economics*, ed. S. Melman (Boston: 1962).

[4]W. Baldwin, *The Structure of the Defense Market, 1955–64* (Durham: 1967), p. 9.

[5]U.S. Congress, Senate, Joint Economic Committee, "Economic Impact Analysis," *Economic Effect of Vietnam Spending*, vol. II 1967, Research Analysis Corporation (Washington, D.C.: Govt. Printing Office) p. 827.

[6]M. Peck and F. Scherer, *The Weapons Acquisition Process* (Boston: 1962), pp. 150–52, and M. Weidenbaum, *The Modern Public Sector*, (New York: 1969), p. 40.

mates that of the 500 largest manufacturing corporations in 1964, *at least* 205 were significantly involved in military contracts, either in production or in research and development.[7] Among the top 100 firms, 65 are significantly involved in the military market. As Table 9-B shows, all but 5 of the largest 25 industrial corporations in 1968 were among the 100 largest contractors for the Defense Department. Of these 5, one— Union Carbide—is the largest Atomic Energy Commission contractor, two are oil companies indirectly involved in military sales, and one is a steel company also indirectly involved. It is difficult to think of these top corporations as constituting an "enclave."

Second, there are no self-contained enclaves in the American economy. As the study of input-output economics has revealed, the structure of American industry is highly interdependent. Focusing only on the prime contractors is like looking at only the visible part of an iceberg. This is only the direct impact of the military budget; the indirect impact on subcontractors, on producers of intermediate goods and parts, and on suppliers of raw materials ties military spending into the heart of the economy. For evidence, look at Table 9-C, which indicates the wide range of industries over which direct and indirect effects of military spending were distributed in 1967. With the exception of the aircraft and electrical equipment industries, no one industry accounted for more than 7 percent of total private military-related employment. Aircraft and parts accounted for 15 percent, and electrical equipment and supplies accounted for 13 percent. This industrial profile shows that despite the enclave image, a broad spectrum of the domestic corporate economy is involved in military production.

[7]C. Nathanson, "The Militarization of the American Economy," in *Corporations and the Cold War*, ed. D. Horowitz (New York: 1969), p. 231.

TABLE 9–B MILITARY CONTRACTORS IN THE AMERICAN ECONOMY

Pentagon[1]	Largest Defense Contractors — A.E.C.[2]	Largest Defense Contractors — NASA[3]	Largest Industrial Corporations[4]
1 General Dynamics	1 Union Carbide	1 North American Rockwell	1 General Motors (10)[5]
2 Lockheed	2 Sandia Corp.	2 Grumman	2 Standard Oil (N.J.) (25)
3 General Electric	3 General Electric	3 Boeing	3 Ford (19)
4 United Aircraft	4 DuPont	4 McDonnell-Douglas	4 General Electric (3)
5 McDonnell-Douglas	5 Reynolds Electrical	5 General Electric	5 Chrysler (43)
6 A.T.&T.	6 Westinghouse	6 I.B.M.	6 Mobil (51)
7 Boeing	7 Bendix	7 Bendix	7 I.B.M. (30)
8 Ling Temco Vought	8 Holmes & Narver	8 Aerojet-General	8 Texaco (46)
9 North American Rockwell	9 Douglas United Aircraft	9 RCA	9 Gulf Oil (78)
10 General Motors	10 Dow Chemical	10 Chrysler	10 U.S. Steel (60)
11 Grumman	11 Goodyear Atomic	11 General Dynamics	11 A.T.&T. (6)
12 AVCO	12 Idaho Nuclear	12 TRW	12 Standard Oil (Calif.) (49)
13 Textron	13 Aerojet-General	13 General Motors	13 DuPont (38)
14 Litton	14 Atlantic Richfield	14 Ling Temco Vought	14 Shell Oil
15 Raytheon	15 E.G.&G.	15 Lockheed	15 RCA (26)
16 Sperry-Rand	16 Gulf General Atomic	16 Philco-Ford	16 McDonnell-Douglas (5)
17 Martin Marietta	17 Monsanto	17 Sperry Rand	17 Standard Oil (Ind.) (27)
18 Kaiser Industries	18 Kerr-McGee	18 Martin Marietta	18 Westinghouse (7)
19 Ford	19 National Lead	19 T.W.A.	19 Boeing
20 Honeywell	20 Mason & Hanger	20 Federal Electric	20 Swift
21 Olin Mathieson	21 North American Rockwell	21 Catalytic-Dow (joint venture)	21 I.T.&T. (29)
22 Northrop	22 Homestake-Sapin	22 United Aircraft	22 Goodyear Tire & Rubber (48)
23 Ryan Aeronautical	23 United Nuclear	23 Brown Engineering	23 General Telephone and Electronics (41)
24 Hughes	24 Pan American	24 Honeywell	24 Bethlehem Steel
25 Standard Oil (N.J.)	25 Phillips Petroleum	25 Control Data	25 Union Carbide

[1]100 Companies and Their Subsidiary Corporations Listed According to Net Value of Military Prime Contract Awards (Fiscal Year 1968), Department of Defense.
[2]Annual Report for 1968, Atomic Energy Commission.
[3]Annual Procurement Report, NASA (Fiscal Year 1968).
[4]500 Largest U.S. Industrial Corporations, Fortune Directory (1968).
[5]Number in parentheses indicates rank among one hundred largest Defense Department contractors.
SOURCE: Richard F. Kaufman, "We Must Guard Against Unwarranted Influence by the Military-Industrial Complex," New York Times Magazine, 22 June 1969.

TABLE 9–C SECTORAL DISTRIBUTION OF PRIVATE EMPLOYMENT ATTRIBUTABLE
TO MILITARY EXPENDITURES IN 1967

Sector	Percent of Total Military-Related Employment in Sector
1. Agriculture, forestry, and fisheries	2.5
2. Mining	1.3
3. Construction	2.3
4. Ordnance and accessories	6.2
5. Textile and apparel products	3.4
6. Chemicals and allied products	2.1
7. Petroleum and refining	0.5
8. Rubber and plastic products	1.1
9. Other nondurable goods manufacturing*	3.5
10. Primary metals	4.5
11. Fabricated metals	2.9
12. Machinery, not electrical	5.9
13. Electrical equipment and supplies	13.3
14. Aircraft and parts	16.0
15. Other transportation equipment	3.2
16. Instruments	1.9
17. Other durable goods manufacturing†	2.6
18. Miscellaneous manufacturing	0.3
19. Transportation and warehousing	6.9
20. Communications and public utilities	2.1
21. Wholesale and retail trade	5.6
22. Finance, insurance and real estate	2.1
23. Business services	4.3
24. Medical, educational services and nonprofit organizations	3.2
25. Other services	1.7
Total, manufacturing	68.0
Total, all private employment	100.0

*Food and kindred products, tobacco, paper and related products, printing and publishing, leather and leather products.
†Lumber and wood products, furniture and fixtures, stone, clay, and glass products.
SOURCE: R. Oliver, "The Employment Effect of Defense Expenditures," *Monthly Labor Review* (September 1967), Table I, pp. 10–11.

Third, corporations in the civilian market have been racing to get a piece of the military action. Between 1959 and 1962, years for which a study was done, "manufacturing firms outside the defense sector purchased 137 companies in the defense sector (i.e., aircraft and parts, ships and boats, ordnance, electrical machinery, scientific instruments and computers)." By 1966, ninety-three of the top five hundred manufacturing firms had diversified into the defense sector from a traditional nondefense base.[8]

[8]*Ibid.*, pp. 215–16.

Military spending is very important for a large number of industries within manufacturing. As Table 9-D shows, about 11.5 percent of all manufacturing output as early as 1958 is attributable to military-related expenditures; the corresponding figure is 20 percent for the metal-working production sector, comprised of metals and metal products, nonelectrical machinery, electrical equipment and supplies, transportation equipment, ordnance, and instruments. The percentage of profits attributable to military spending are probably even higher, given that profits rates are higher on military contracts—as is shown below.

. . .

HOW GREAT A STAKE
IN THE MILITARY

Having seen that the military sector comprises the very heart of Capitalist America, we can now ask what stake the economy has in the existence of this Leviathan.

First, we shall point out the stake of the most privileged and powerful segments of the economy. Military spending is in large part responsible for the increasing concentration of economic power in the hands of a small group. It plays a role in the perpetuation of substantial inequality among the population as a whole. And it is a key factor behind the profitability of many of America's largest corporations.

But we shall go further and argue that the entire capitalist economy has a stake in militarism. For military spending is responsible for much of the economic growth the country has experienced in the postwar period. Without militarism, the whole economy would return to the state of collapse from which it was rescued by the Second World War.

Military spending has been a key force behind the trend toward increasing concentration of economic power. We have already observed that prime contract awards are concentrated among a small number of corporations; fifty firms in an average year get 60 percent of the procurement contract dollar, about 94 percent of the research, development and testing contract dollar.[9] This makes the war industry much more concentrated

[9] A.D. Little Co., "How Sick is the Defense Industry," (1963).

TABLE 9–D DIRECT AND INDIRECT DEPENDENCE OF INDUSTRIAL SECTORS ON MILITARY EXPENDITURES, 1958

Sector	Percent of Total Output Attributable to Military
1. Food and kindred products	1.6
2. Apparel and textile mill products	1.9
3. Leather products	3.1
4. Paper and allied products	7.0
5. Chemicals and allied products	5.3
6. Fuel and power	7.3
7. Rubber and rubber products	5.6
8. Lumber and wood products	3.9
9. Nonmetallic minerals and products	4.7
10. Primary metals	13.4
11. Fabricated metal products	8.0
12. Machinery, except electrical	5.2
13. Electrical equipment and supplies	20.8
14. Transportation equipment and ordnance	38.4
15. Instruments and allied products	20.0
16. Misc. manufacturing industries	2.8
17. Transportation	5.9
18. Construction	2.1
Average, metalworking industries (Sectors 10–15)	19.9
Average, all manufacturing (Sectors 1–16)	11.5
Average, sectors 1–18	9.6

SOURCE: Computed from Leontief and Hoffenberg, "The Economic Impact of Disarmament," *Scientific American* (April 1961).

than the economy as a whole, where the top one hundred firms usually account for only 35 percent of the manufacturing sales. The business of the war industry goes to the biggest firms and is used by them as a base from which to expand their area of control. So it is not surprising that between 1947 and 1963 the top two hundred industrial corporations, boosted by defense business, increased their share of total value added in the economy from 30 percent to 41 percent.[10]

Let's look at the increasing concentration produced by military spending on an industry level. Almost all of military spending goes to the most concentrated industries in the economy. The standard measure of concentration in an industry is the percentage of sales accounted for by the top four firms. Industries in which four firms monopolized over 50 percent of the sales accounted for about one-quarter of all sales by manufacturing industries in 1958.[11] But 90 percent of all military contracts go to these most concentrated industries.[12] The most powerful elements in the economy have a large stake in the military production because of the opportunities it provides them to increase the concentration of their economic control. Military expenditures have a political base far stronger than the magnitudes involved would suggest.

Military spending has also created privileged interest groups within the occupational structure; it is an important factor tying many professionals, universities, and labor union leaders to government policy. A large number of the most highly trained people in the economy owe their jobs to defense spending. For example, nearly half of all engineers and scientists employed in private

industry are at work on military or space-related projects. Many of the scientists and engineers pursuing research in the universities receive money from the Pentagon.

The military industries generally employ a highly skilled work force. A 1962 Department of Labor study of the electronics industry showed that at military- and space-oriented plants 59.2 percent of employees were highly paid engineers, executives, or skilled blue-collar craftsmen. In the consumer-oriented plants of the same electronics industry, in contrast, 70.2 percent of the employees were semiskilled and unskilled blue- and white-collar workers.[13] Professional and managerial workers comprise 22 percent of all private defense-related employment, but only 15 percent of all U.S. manufacturing employment.[14] Thus, a large proportion of the people in the most educated strata, many still university-based, are tied by military spending to a vested interest in existing national priorities. A large number of blue-collar workers are engaged in military-related work. The carrot the government can dangle in front of major union leaders has been a factor in their growing conservatism and endorsement of Cold War policies.

Military spending has a regressive impact on the distribution of income within the U.S., that is, benefits the rich and hurts the poor. This is suggested by the higher proportion of professional and skilled workers in defense-related work. Computations by economist Wassily Leontief show that one dollar of military spending generates half as many jobs, but 20 percent more in salaries, then does one dollar of civilian spending.[15] This

[10]U.S. Census of Manufacturers, *Concentration Ratios in Manufacturing*, 1963.

[11]J. Bain, *Industrial Organization* (New York: 1968), p. 158.

[12]U.S. Congress, Senate, "Economic Impact Analysis," *op. cit.* These industries, as we have already mentioned, are highly interdependent with the rest of the economy.

[13]Bureau of Labor Statistics, *Bulletin, 1963,* (October 1963), p. 37.

[14]Joseph F. Fulton, "Employment Impact of Changing Defense Programs," *Monthly Labor Review* 87, no. 5 (May 1964), p. 514.

[15]From W. Leontief and M. Hoffenberg, "The Economic Impact of Disarmament," *Scientific American* (April 1961): 9, and W. Leontief et al., "The Economic Effect—Industrial and Regional—of an Arms Cut," *Review of Economics and Statistics* 47, no. 3 (August 1965), pp. 217–41.

means that tax money extracted from the whole population is paid out in such a way as to benefit high earners much more than low earners. Perhaps by accident, or perhaps by design, military spending is one of the mechanisms by which higher income groups use the government to prevent redistribution of income from taking place.

Last, but not least, the military sector is a source of enormous profits for the corporate elite. It is an organized system of governmental subsidy for corporate coffers, or as C. Wright Mills called it, "socialism for the rich." We can see how deeply wedded the corporate giants are to this arrangement by examining the opportunities the military sector presents to them.

ATTRACTIVENESS OF THE MILITARY MARKET

The attractiveness of the military market to big corporations—the opportunities for growth and fantastic profits—has been described by a number of journalists and muckrakers.[16] In recent years, the hearings conducted by the Senate Subcommittee on Economy in Government (chaired by Senator William Proxmire) have provided further glimpses into the shadowy world of the military contractor. The mass media have reported horror stories from these hearings and tales of corporate greediness and bureaucratic favoritism gleaned from the Proxmire investigations have been retold in excellent analyses by Henry Nieburg, Walter Adams, Richard Kaufman, and by the Proxmire Committee itself (in its pamphlet, *The Economics of Military Procurement*).[17] The

reader is strongly urged to examine one or more of these documentations of the waste and profiteering endemic to the military sector of the economy. These studies reveal that the excesses and horror stories presented in the mass media about the military contracting business are far from isolated or atypical examples. Where these studies fall short, however, is in failing to emphasize that the waste and profiteering have a systematic basis in the structure of the military "market." This market differs in several important respects from markets in the civilian economy.

Unlike other industries, military contract work is not determined in a "market" at all, in any usually understood sense of the word. Contracts are arrived at through negotiations between a company and Pentagon contracting officers. The arrangement is rife with opportunities for the companies. Government as purchaser is alleged to have the same interest as a private consumer in cutting costs and buying only what is needed. In fact, this is not the case. First of all, procurement officers—who represent the government in these affairs—have an interest as military men in expanding the arsenal of weapons and thus the power and prestige of their branch of service. And so long as there is slack in the economy, higher-ups don't pressure them to hold down costs. Second, if they are on the lookout for their future in the business world, and they are, they have the most appealing reasons for currying the favor of the corporations with whom they are supposed to "bargain." When they retire, many military men involved in procurement regulation go directly to jobs in one of the defense companies. In 1967, 2,072 retired regular military officers were employed by

[16]For example, F. Cook, *The Warfare State* (New York: 1961); V. Perlo, *Militarism and Industry* (New York: 1963); and B. Nossiter, *The Mythmakers* (Boston: 1964), Ch. 6.

[17]H. Nieburg, *In the Name of Science* (Chicago: 1966); W. Adams, "The Military-Industrial Complex and the New Industrial State," *American Economic Review* (May 1968); R. Kaufman, "We

Must Guard Against Unwarranted Influence by the Military-Industrial Complex," *New York Times Magazine*, 22 June 1969; U.S. Congress, Senate, Joint Economic Committee, *The Economics of Military Procurement* (Washington, D.C.: Govt. Printing Office, 1969).

the ninety-five top contractors. The top ten contractors had an average of 106 former officers a piece on their payrolls.[18]

Contracting is supposed to take place competitively. In fact, it almost never does. Any one of a catalogue full of excuses can be reason for by-passing the competitive bidding procedure, for example, if the item is critical, if delivery is urgent, if security considerations preclude it, etc.; 90 percent of the Pentagon's contract dollars are negotiated under such "exceptions."[19]

The exotic technologies involved in weapons provide a perfect opportunity for boondoggles. Only specialists understand what is a superfluous and what is a necessary expenditure. This allows for enormous padding and excessive costs, as a number of Senate investigations have charged. A contractor may sell the Pentagon a two billion dollar missile when a one billion dollar one would have worked equally well. Subcontracting creates the opportunity for pyramiding profits on multiple tiers of subcontracts. Moreover, once a contractor has done some work on a weapons system—whether in another contract or in a research and development study—he obtains a virtual monopoly over the area. Since he is the only one with relevant experts and the relevant experience, the government is stuck with giving him the business. It is practically impossible to oversee and account for the operations in these areas. Both the complex technology and security considerations bar most outsiders.

So there is no bad blood created when costs of production far overrun those that were written into the contract. Final costs average 320 percent of the original cost estimates.[20] That is, the average contractor ends up charging the government over three times the cost estimate he initially submitted to "win" the contract. Since most contracts are on a cost-plus basis, his profits go up three times also.

Companies do not lose their privileged status if their weapons do not meet up to specifications or perform properly. A recent study of thirteen major aircraft and missile programs since 1955, which cost in total forty billion, revealed that only four of these (costing five billion) performed at as much as 75 percent of the design specifications. Yet the companies with the poorest performance records reported the highest profits.[21]

What this all amounts to, of course, is that profits for defense work are higher than those in every industry except pharmaceuticals. This is obscured by the Defense Department, which sometimes releases profits computed as a percentage of sales or costs. But, in the normal business world, profits are figured as a percentage of *investment*. Defense contractors invest very little of their own money because in most cases the government provides most of the investment and working capital needed by contractors to set up plants and machinery and to buy the necessary materials and parts. The profits when measured against investment are often huge.

A study by Murray Weidenbaum, formerly an economist for the Boeing Company and now Assistant Secretary of the Treasury, of a sample of large defense contractors showed that between 1962 and 1965 they earned 17.5 percent on investment, compared to average civilian market earnings of 10.6 percent.[22] And this probably understates the case. Many military contractors also sell in the civilian market. The machinery provided free by the Pentagon, the allocation of all overhead costs to military contracts, and the technological edge gained in cost-plus military contracts can be of enormous importance in increasing profits on *civilian* sales for firms doing some business with the

[18]R. Kaufman, *op. cit.*, p. 70.

[19]*The Economics of Military Procurement, op. cit.*, p. 4.

[20]Peck and Scherer, *op. cit.*

[21]*The Economics of Military Procurement, op. cit.*, p. 1.

[22]Weidenbaum, *op. cit.*, p. 56.

Pentagon. In one of the most outrageous cases that has come to light, a tax count showed in 1962 that North American Aviation Company had realized profits of 612 percent and 802 percent on its investment on "military" contracts in two successive years.[23]

Everyone—except the Pentagon, of course—agrees that laxity and profiteering are part and parcel of military procurement. Liberals take this to be indicative of the way in which the military complex has escaped the normal checks and balances of the political process. To radicals, this seems a gross understatement of reality. Politicians, bureaucrats, and businessmen all know that these "excesses" exist. These "excesses" are not a subversion of normal government procedure—they are the normal government procedure.

The waste and profiteering—the enormous amount of military spending—are not aberrations or mistakes. Waste is winked at because the entire economy has a stake in it.

Of course, military men dabble in corrupt practices. Of course, large corporations use strong-arm pressures to obtain favors. But waste of this magnitude is neither simple profiteering nor economic gangsterism. Massive, wasteful military spending is allowed to exist because it fulfills a need of the system as a whole. The waste is what helps military spending fulfill its function: providing a cushion to ward off stagnation and economic crisis.

MILITARY SPENDING AND STAGNATION

Among liberal optimists, one used to be able to find those who argued that government spending of any kind could be cut with no ill effects on long-run economic growth. The money freed from spending could be

[23]R. Kaufman, op. cit.

returned to taxpayers and corporations in the form of tax cuts. This would quickly be ploughed back into the economy in the form of increased consumption and increased investment—no slowdown necessary. There are few proponents of this view left.

Most everybody understands today that high levels of government spending are necessary for economic stability and growth. The depression of the 1930s illustrated the incredible levels of unemployment and business lethargy the system would generate if left alone. Only World War II showed how to cope with the problem. Massive levels of government spending in defense were necessary to create demand and alleviate unemployment. In the post-war period too, military spending has been responsible for a large part of the economic growth that has taken place. The fluctuation of military spending has virtually determined the cyclical pattern of the economy. Declines in military spending have been followed by declines in overall economic growth.

Not all advanced capitalist countries have leaned on military spending to the extent the United States has. In part this is because the United States, as the most industrialized country in the world, has the greatest problem of inadequate aggregate demand. But there is more to American militarism than this. After World War II, the United States emerged as by far the dominant leader of the worldwide capitalist system. It took on the task of defending the "Free World." This required a large military establishment, and the United States, the only country with its industrial economy intact after World War II, was the only country capable of taking on this role. Furthermore, the necessity of rebuilding in Western Europe and Japan postponed aggregate demand problems in these countries for almost two decades—the destruction of antiquated machinery also removed some of the fetters on production. Hence, the United States was far more in need of a stimulus for demand than other advanced capitalist countries. Finally, the tradition of "étatisme" is much stronger in Western Europe, where most governmental functions are highly centralized. The decentralized and multilevel nature of government in the United States provides an additional fetter on civilian government spending.

Liberals do not deny that arms spending has served the necessary function of averting stagnation. But they argue that other forms of public sector spending are equally feasible. Instead of weapons, the Federal government could sponsor vast projects to improve health, education, housing, transportation, etc., etc.—some even envisage a "domestic Marshall plan."

But in order to provide an equivalent aggregate economic stimulus, social welfare spending like that called for by liberals would have to be roughly the same magnitude as the present level of military spending. It would have to be just as expandable to keep pace with the growth of the economy. Can social welfare spending do this? The historical answer seems to be no.

Massive civilian government spending was tried as a stimulus in the 1930s and failed. In the depths of the depression, one of the impulses of the New Deal had been to increase social spending to stimulate the economy back to life. Between 1929 and 1939 government expenditures on nondefense purchases and transfer payments nearly doubled from 9.1 billion dollars in 1929 to 17.8 billion dollars in 1939.[24] But this stimulus was not enough—the economy hardly budged. The GNP in the same period slumped from 104.4 billion to 91.1 billion and unemployment rose from 3.2 to 17.2 percent. Enough stimulus was just not generated by social spending. But government spending on arms, once the war mobilization had begun, was enough—exactly what the disease called for. Between 1939 and 1944,

[24]Baran and Sweezy, *op. cit.*, p. 159.

military spending increased from 1 billion to 77 billion; GNP shot up in the same years to 211.4 billion.

Spending on arms succeeded where social services spending had failed, because only government spending on arms can be enormous and expandable almost without limit. Why is this so? For one, only military spending is so amenable to waste that can be made publicly and politically acceptable. Second, only military spending can expand so freely without damaging the basic framework of the economy. Massive social spending would compete with the private sector; it would damage the labor market; it would clash head on with hundreds of powerful vested interests at every level of the economy. Given such opposition, social spending could never expand adequately to fill the economic gap. Consider the factors that allow the enormous size, rapid expandability, and wastefulness of the military budget.

First, a convenient rationalization of the need for massive armaments expenditures exists. The ideology of anticommunism and the Cold War has been drummed into politicians and public alike for over twenty years. This is a powerful force behind defense spending as well as a general legitimizer of capitalism.

Second, armaments are rapidly consumed or become obsolete very quickly. Bombers get shot down over Vietnam, ammunition gets used up or captured, and so on. More important, the technology of advanced weapons systems becomes obsolete as fast as defense experts can think of "improvements" over existing weapons systems (or as soon as Soviet experts do). Thus, many weapons systems have proved obsolete even before production on them was completed. The demand for weaponry is a bottomless pit.

Third, the kind of machinery required for armament production is highly specific to particular armaments. So each time a new weapon is needed or a new process created, all existing production machinery must be scrapped. Extensive retooling at very great new outlays is required.

Fourth, there is no generally agreed upon yardstick for measuring how much defense we have. How do we know when an adequate level of military security is achieved? National Security Managers can always claim that by some criteria what we have is not enough. Terms like nuclear parity and superiority are easily juggled. Military men always have access to new "secret intelligence reports" not available to the general public. Since few people are willing to gamble with national defense, the expertise of the managers is readily accepted. Politicians and the general public have little way of adequately questioning their judgment.

These factors combine so that defense expenditures can be enormous and expandable probably without limit. But the same is not the case for social services spending. The above factors are all highly specific to the military sector.

No readily available rationalization yet exists behind massive social service spending. Of course, everyone has to admit health care, hospitals, and schools are good, but that does not mean they are prepared to see masses of federal tax dollars funneled into these areas.

Investments in social facilities are usually durable—they do not become obsolete very quickly and are not rapidly consumed. Right now, of course, there are plenty of unmet needs in these areas. But once everyone is provided with a decent house, once there are new schools and health clinics stocked with materials, then what? They cannot be immediately torn down and built all over again.

The technology of social welfare facilities is not particularly exotic. Very conventional standards exist to tell us how much a house should cost and how much a hospital should cost. There is no possibility for enormous padding here to absorb funds.

Furthermore, there are generally accessible yardsticks to ascertain how well social needs have been met. The public knows when adequate and convenient public transportation is available. No one would want to extend it out to a suburb that did not exist.

In general, social spending beyond a certain point cannot be rapidly and wastefully expanded. The difference here is that investment in social services deals with people, not objects like weapons. People are much more resistant to allowing their lives to be dominated by the priorities of waste—even if it does help to keep the economy running.

For example, what would happen if a housing project were built in the same way as a new missile? If a missile doesn't work, the company is excused and the planners go back to their drawing boards armed with another huge contract. Since it already has the expertise, the same company is more than likely to get a new missile contract. Imagine the political repercussions of a lousy, but expensive, housing project? The tenants complain, a public scandal is declared, and all contracts are canceled. The housing bill has a rough going the next time it comes up in the legislature.

So social spending can never provide the opportunities for waste that are provided by military spending. But this is not the most important reason why social spending is impossible. For massive social spending inevitably interferes with the basic operations of a capitalist system. How does this occur?

First, many kinds of social spending put the government in direct competition with particular industries and with the private sector as a whole. This is taboo in a capitalist economy. For example, if the government built low-cost housing in large amounts, it would cut heavily into profits of private builders and landlords who own the existing housing stock. It would add to the supply of housing and take land away from private developers who want to use it for commercial purposes. Similarly, building *effective* public transportation would compete with the automobile interests.

Any one of these interests taken by itself might not be sufficient to put insurmountable obstacles in the way of social spending. Most social service programs affect only one particular set of interests in the private economy. But there are so many forms of potential interference. Each of the vested interests are aware of this and so work to help one another out. They fuel a general ideology that says that too much social spending is dangerous. They refer to creeping socialism, the dangers of bureaucracy, the faith in individualism and self-help, and the unpleasant image of giving handouts to those who don't deserve it. The spectre of interference haunts all those in the private sector. So they engage in the practice of "log-rolling." You oppose interference with me, and I'll oppose interference with you. Massive political opposition to rather minor increases in social spending is thus forged. Furthermore, the capitalist system as a whole is threatened by massive governmental social spending because the very necessity of private ownership and control over production is thereby called into question. The basic assumption in any capitalist society that goods and services should be produced by private enterprise according to criteria of market profitability also fuels the general ideology limiting social spending.

Second, social spending upsets the labor market, one of the essential institutions of a capitalist economy. Public expenditures on an adequate welfare program would make it difficult for employers to get workers. If the government provided adequate nonwage income without social stigma to recipients, many workers would drop out of the labor force rather than take low paying and unpleasant jobs. Those who stayed at jobs would be less likely to put up with demeaning working conditions. The whole basis of the capitalist labor market is that workers have no income source other than the sale of their labor power. Capitalist ideology has long made a cardinal rule that government must not interfere with this incentive to work. Powerful political forces thus operate to insure that direct income subsidization at adequate levels can never come into being.

Third, social service spending is opposed because it threatens the class structure. Education, for example, is a crucial stratification mechanism that determines who gets to the top and legitimizing their position there. Good universal education, extending through college, would put the whole system of inequality into question. Moreover, having the possibility to get an advanced education would undermine the labor market as well. Few workers would settle so willingly for the miserable, low paying jobs they now do.

Finally, good social services, since they give people security, comfort, and satisfaction, that is, fulfill real needs, interfere with the market in consumer goods. Corporations can only sell people goods in an economy of abundance by playing on their unsatisfied needs and yearnings. In an era when most basic necessities have been provided, these new needs are mostly artificially created; the need for status, sex appeal, etc. They are based on fears and anxieties and dissatisfactions that people have and that are continually pandered to by the commercial world. But if people's needs were being fulfilled by the public sector, that is, if they had access to adequate housing, effective transportation, good schools, and good health care, they would be much less prey to the appeals of the commercial hucksters. These forms of collective consumption would have interfered with the demand for consumer products in the private market.

In addition, massive social services spending runs up against the obstacles of the existing vested interests in the social services sector itself. The AMA opposes the extension of federal aid to medical education and is thereby able—in part with corporate assistance from the drug companies—to limit the supply of doctors produced each year. Entrenched civil service bureaucracies find grave threats in extensive Federal intervention in local programs. The list could be prolonged indefinitely.

The opposition of vested interests, the constraints of capitalist institutions and a much lower potential for expandability—these are the most important factors distinguishing the social service sector from the military weapons sector. Military spending is acceptable to all corporate interests. It does not compete with already existing industries, it does not undermine the labor market, it does not challenge the class structure. Social spending does all these things and, thus, faces insurmountable obstacles for its own expansion. Liberals have not been able to overcome these obstacles to obtain even small increases in social services. How can they expect to overcome these obstacles on the massive scale that would be needed if the defense outlet were cut off?

The facile liberal response to this argument—one that views the problem in an abstract fashion—is that "anything can be made appealing" to corporations just by making the incentive sufficiently large. With enough promised profit, defense corporations can be lured away from defense to just about anything. Even assuming that a total giveaway to corporations could be somehow made politically palatable—a dubious assumption—this view lacks plausibility.

Corporations do not make large scale investment decisions just in terms of short-term profit from a particular project. Their minimum horizon is much greater, and a substantial element of inertia operates. First, what is to convince corporations that there are long-term growth opportunities in the social services sector? Corporate executives are well aware that social service spending has in the past been very capricious. Since the impetus behind a conversion program might well dry up after a few years, corporations are reluctant to make large long-term commitments for fear of becoming shipwrecked. The risk of navigating uncharted waters is large. No convincing proof will ever be offered that conversion is profitable like defense has been profitable.

There have been attempts by major defense contractors in the last twenty-five years to initiate large-scale conversion. But almost without exception, these have been failures. Murray Weidenbaum, the expert on military economics cited earlier, has reviewed the history of these efforts from the end of World War II to the late 1960s.[25] He concludes his survey of early diversification efforts as follows:

Most of the diversification activities by the major, specialized defense contractors which were begun at the end of World War II were abandoned as unsuccessful or marginal or sold to firms traditionally oriented to industrial or consumer markets. The expansion of the military budget brought on by the Korean War soon turned the primary attention of these firms back to the military market. When faced with the alternative, few aircraft companies preferred to manufacture powered wheelbarrows or busses rather than bomber or fighter airplanes.

Efforts at diversification after the Korean War were equally unsuccessful:

Most of these industrial diversification efforts outside of aerospace fields have since been abandoned. The surviving diversification programs continue generally at marginal levels—either actually losing money, barely breaking even, or at best showing profit results below typical military business returns.

[25]See Weidenbaum, *op. cit.*, Ch. 3. More recent expression of corporate sentiment on conversion can be found in a series of articles by Bernard Nossiter in the *Washington Post*, December 1968.

The explanation of these failures is offered by Weidenbaum; many top corporate executives were convinced that military spending would continue to expand, perhaps a self-fulfilling prophecy:

> ...the belief of the top managements (is) that there are adequate sales opportunities in government work and that the profit rates are, if anything, higher than on risky commercial ventures. Interviews with chief executives of the defense industry repeatedly brought out their firm belief in the long-term nature and rising trend of the military market. Also, their many prior unsuccessful diversification attempts have engendered a strong conviction that inadequate commercial opportunities exist for companies which have become oriented primarily to government work. [Italics added.]

The corporate elite is not going to sponsor a move away from military expenditures on its own. If they continue to oppose conversion, and we have every reason to believe they will, there is little reason to believe their opposition can be overcome within the existing political and economic framework. The conclusion which emerges: the military sector is just too crucial to capitalist stability and to capitalist profits.

SELECTIVE BIBLIOGRAPHY

Further reading is recommended in Gorz, *Strategy for Labor*, especially Chapter 4, as cited in the source line for section 9.4. A classic statement and analysis of the problem of surplus absorption in a modern capitalist society is provided in Baran [1], Chapters 1–4. This analysis is applied more thoroughly and more specifically to the United States in Baran and Sweezy [2]; Chapters 4–8 are especially relevant and most useful. Lichtman [6] examines the role of consumerism in the stabilization of capitalist society, while Willis [8] criticizes much radical theory on consumerism as elitist and basically reactionary. In a rather dry but useful exposition, Kapp [4] analyzes the various ways in which a private enterprise system leads to significant social problems. Gordon [3] reprints a great variety of essays on the problems of the contemporary United States; Parts VI–IX contain numerous illustrations of the irrationality associated with the fields of health, housing, transportation, and the environment. *Ramparts* [7] has devoted a full issue to a set of stimulating essays on the ecological crisis of modern capitalism, including the Bookchin essay excerpted in Section 9.5. One of several excellent studies on the American military-industrial complex is Lens [5]; others are cited in the footnotes to the essay by Reich and Finkelhor in Section 9.6.

[1] Baran, Paul A. *The Political Economy of Growth.* 2nd ed. New York: Monthly Review Press, 1962.*

[2] Baran, Paul A., and Sweezy, Paul M. *Monopoly Capital.* New York: Monthly Review Press, 1966.*

[3] Gordon, David M., ed. *Problems in Political Economy: An Urban Perspective.* Lexington, Mass.: D.C. Heath & Co., 1971.*

[4] Kapp, K. William. *Social Costs of Business Enterprise.* 2nd ed. New York: Asia Publishing House, 1963.

[5] Lens, Sidney. *The Military-Industrial Complex.* Philadelphia: The Philadelphia Pilgrim Press, 1970.

[6] Lichtman, Richard. "Capitalism and Consumption," *Socialist Revolution* no. 3 (May-June 1970): 83–95.

[7] *Ramparts* 8, no. 11, (May 1970) Ecology Special.

[8] Willis, Ellen. "Consumerism and Women." *Socialist Revolution* 1, no. 3 (May-June 1970): 76–82.

*Available in paperback editions.

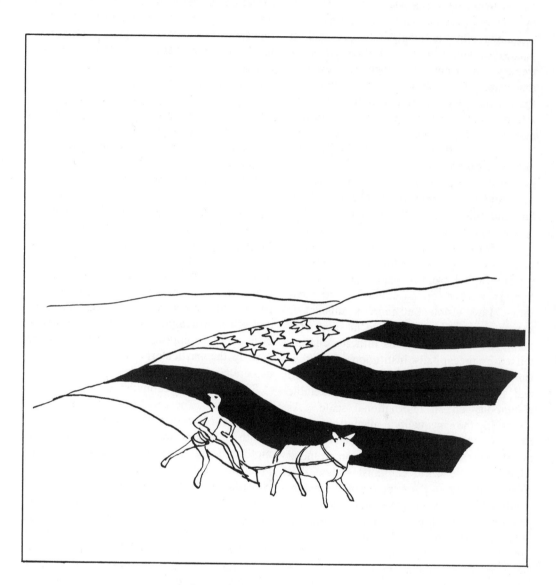

Imperialism

UP TO NOW, WE HAVE DISCUSSED THE CAPI-
talist system as if it were more or less self-
contained within national boundaries and, in
particular, within the United States. It is extremely important to recognize, however,
that capitalism cannot be so contained—
that, in its very essence, it is bound to be
international. Since *expansion* is fundamental to the capitalist mode of production,[1]
it is inevitable that sooner or later—barring
major disruptions of the world economy—
capitalist firms should cross national boundaries and link distant areas together within
one and the same economic system.

We will define imperialism very simply
as the internationalization of capitalism. It
manifests itself most visibly in the flow of
private capital from stronger capitalist nations to weaker foreign countries and territories. Less visible but more significant is
the extension of capitalist social and economic institutions to areas hitherto characterized by precapitalist institutions. Imperialism is the process whereby labor is alienated
and (with land) turned into a marketable
commodity on an international scale.[2] As
a result, the inequality, alienation, irrationality, and so on, that characterize national capitalist systems are compounded
within a single world capitalist system that
benefits the few at the expense of the many.

In order to facilitate the international expansion of capitalist firms and the international extension of capitalist institutions, the
capitalist state must play an active role. The
development of capitalism within the rich
capitalist nations required that power be
exercised by the rising capitalist class in
order to overcome the many obstacles to its
hegemony.[3] Similarly, the internationalization of capitalism requires that power be

exercised on behalf of the capitalist class in
order to overcome nationalist and other
types of resistance to capitalist expansion.
In the modern world of nation-states, this
power is most often exercised through political control and—when necessary—military
intervention. Thus imperialism necessarily
involves the extension of *control* by the
stronger capitalist powers over the weaker
countries and territories within the world
capitalist system as a whole.

Expansion, control, and intervention are,
of course, not unique to capitalism. A reading of world history suggests that empire-
building has been the rule rather than the
exception for human societies. The point of
this chapter is not to argue that expansionist
drives arise only out of a capitalist society
but to examine the particular form that expansionism takes under capitalism. This
concern is warranted both by the dominant
position of capitalism in the modern world
and by the particularly tenacious character
of capitalist expansion, that is, imperialism.

The process of capitalist expansion has a
long history. The early explorations of European explorers in the fifteenth and sixteenth centuries were largely precapitalist,
motivated by a spirit of acquisition and
plunder rather than capital accumulation.
Nonetheless, they did serve as an important
source of primitive capital accumulation:
the profits from foreign ventures returned
home and ultimately helped to stimulate the
rise of the new capitalist class. With the rise
of capitalism in England and later in other
European countries, the race to buildup
overseas empires as a basis for economic expansion was on, and it reached its peak in
the late nineteenth and early twentieth centuries as competing European powers fought
to carve up the world. In the nineteenth and
early twentieth centuries, vast amounts of
capital flowed out of Europe and into the
lesser developed regions of the world, helping to establish the political and economic
predominance of the major capitalist powers

[1]See Edwards, Section 3.2, p. 98.
[2]See the introduction to Chapter 3, p. 88, and
Polanyi Section 3.1, for an analysis of the fundamental significance of alienated labor and marketable land and labor for capitalism.
[3]See, for example, Marx, Section 2.4, p. 61.

and providing a base for lucrative economic gains for the rich at the expense of the poor.[4]

The competitive imperialism of the early twentieth century—based largely but not entirely on direct colonial control of overseas territories—was shaken by the disruptive events of the first half of the twentieth century. Two world wars, a major worldwide depression, and a series of revolutions that took one third of the population of the world out of the capitalist orbit, altered completely the shape of the world economy.

Since the end of World War II, a new imperialist system has been rising to take the place of the old one. Once again, the logic of capitalism has dictated the expansion of capitalist firms into the world arena. In contrast to the earlier period of competitive imperialism, however, the postwar internationalization of capitalism has been dominated by the single major capitalist power that emerged with overwhelming economic strength after World War II: the United States. In the wake of the world wars and the dismantling of the old European colonial empires that ensued, United States business has increasingly penetrated not only the economies of the underdeveloped capitalist countries but also those of the other advanced capitalist countries. As a result,

modern imperialism is characterized by the progressive welding of national capitalist economies into a single world capitalist system dominated by the United States. Just as the nature of capitalism has evolved over time, so the competitive imperialism of the nineteenth century has become the "monopoly imperialism" of the twentieth century.

In Chapter 4 we examined the way in which the unit of business enterprise under capitalism has evolved from the small family firm to the multinational corporation.[5] Based most often in the United States, its operations extend over all that part of the world which is "safe for free enterprise." The multinational corporation, in spearheading the international integration of the capitalist system, is clearly the exemplary institution of modern imperialism.

The readings in this section are intended to demonstrate the importance of international expansion to the capitalist system and some of its major damaging consequences. These consequences include *militarism* at the center of the world capitalist system and *underdevelopment* in the periphery. For, on the one hand, the maintenance of the worldwide capitalist system in the face of opposition not only from the socialist world but also—increasingly—from within the capitalist system itself (among the many victims of capitalist expansion) requires an increasingly powerful military force. On the other hand, the very logic of capitalist expansion involves uneven development: development in one part of the world capitalist system implies underdevelopment elsewhere.

[4]The benefits of the capital investment made in the lesser developed regions accrued primarily to the owners of the capital in the form of profit remittances and debt payments. Much of the investment was geared to the export of raw materials for the home market and had little favorable impact on the local economy. See Hans Singer, "The Distribution of Gains Between Investing and Borrowing Counties," *American Economic Review* 40, no. 2 (May 1950): 473–85.

[5]See Hymer, Section 4.2, p. 156.

10.1   *Capitalist Expansion, Ideology, and Intervention*

In the first chapter of this book, Ngo Vinh Long described in chilling detail some aspects of the American impact on Vietnam.[1] There

[1]See Long, Section 1.6, p. 30.

is clearly no more blatant and destructive example of modern imperialism than the Vietnam War. Yet the very magnitude and horror of the United States involvement in Vietnam has suggested to many observers that this is a unique phenomenon, an aberration rather than a natural consequence of American capitalist society.

In the following essay Arthur MacEwan argues to the contrary that the Vietnam War is only the most obvious example of a consistently imperialist American foreign policy and that imperialism necessarily arises from a capitalist system. MacEwan's essay develops further and in much greater detail some of the points raised initially in the introduction to this chapter. He shows first that the logic of capitalist expansion leads inevitably to the flow of capital across national boundaries and that large monopolistic firms tend to dominate the expansionary process. He then goes on to discuss the role of the state in the expansion of capitalism, and he illustrates this role with a brief look at the history of United States foreign policy since the turn of the century. Finally, MacEwan examines the critical role of capitalist ideology in supporting an imperialist foreign policy.

Source: The following essay was written by ARTHUR MACEWAN for this book. Another version of this essay was published in *Upstart*, No. 2 (May 1971). Copyright © 1972 by Arthur MacEwan. Printed by permission of the author.

The war in Vietnam has forced us all to ask questions about the foreign policy of the United States. Such an inquiry reveals that the United States has a long history of intervening—militarily, politically, economically—in the affairs of other nations. The intervention in Vietnam is unusual only in that it has developed into a full scale war that the U.S. is unable to win.

In order to understand the origins of the Vietnam War, it would thus be an error to confine oneself to the history and immediate bases of that particular *military* intervention. The Vietnam War should be examined in the context of the entire history of U.S. foreign involvement. This history reveals the extent to which the United States has extended its control over other nations. It is this extension of control, in all of its aspects, that I shall describe by the term "imperialism."

While United States imperialism operates in many spheres—political, economic, cultural—it is in its most fundamental sense an economic phenomenon. That is, this international extension of control has its basis in the economic organization of American society. Within a capitalist economic system—and the U.S. is the most advanced capitalist system in history—there are basic forces which push that system toward expansion. This expansion carries with it an extension of control; hence, a capitalist system necessarily develops into an imperialist system.

THE EXPANSION OF CAPITAL

The fundamental principle of operation for the capitalist firm is the search for profits. This principle has its origins in purely competitive conditions, where a failure to continually find new ways to expand the profit margin will lead to the failure of the firm. In the modern capitalist economy of the United States, where monopolistic market conditions dominate, it is certainly not the case that at every moment the survival of the large firm is in danger if it slackens its search for profits. Nonetheless, foreign firms, smaller domestic firms, and firms producing substitutable products present a challenge that cannot be ignored. Moreover, in order to protect their profits, large firms must be attuned to shifts in demand and changes in labor and resource supply conditions. These pressures translate into the general operating rule: continually pursue the search for profits.[1]

The search for profits is a process which takes on many forms. One form is the introduction of new techniques of production and organization which allow cost reductions. The introduction of new techniques is often associated with a dependence upon expansion in the size of the enterprise's operation. For example, an extension of the division of labor—that hallmark of capitalist efficiency —is almost always dependent upon an expansion of sales. In this manner, technical change in the production process is often intricately bound up with another form of the search for profits, namely, the search for new markets. Whether or not cost-cutting innovations are introduced, the opening of new markets allows an expansion of sales without a corresponding decline in price. In the absence of increasing costs, new markets thus provide a basis for expanding profits.

Particularly important for the purposes of this essay is that the search for markets will often involve an expansion of the geographic sphere of operations. Geographic expansion has many advantages. For a firm operating in a competitive industry, geographic expansion allows the exploitation of markets where the downward pressure on prices is not so severe. For firms selling a relatively new product, the size of the local market may not be sufficient to take advantage of economies of scale, and international sales are necessary if production is to be profitable. In each case profitability is, of course, the criterion of geographic expansion, but profitability is often limited by uncertainty, lack of information, and political or economic instability. These factors can be significant barriers to the geographic expansion of the small firm.

For the large monopolistic firm, such matters of information, uncertainty, and instability are of less importance. In confronting each of these problems, the large firm has a natural advantage. It has the facilities to gain knowledge and gauge the possibility for profits, and it can help insure its investments against instability. There are additional reasons why the monopolistic firm is apt to place particular importance upon international expansion of its markets. First, simply in order to maintain its monopolistic position, it must control markets outside its original sphere of operation. Otherwise new firms may develop in those areas and eventually threaten the original base of operation. The consequences of a failure to control new markets is clear from the development of the European and Japanese automobile industries and their subsequent inroads on U.S. markets. While U.S. firms did attempt to control through the purchase of some European firms (e.g., Opel) they were unable to halt the European competition.[2]

Second, in the same manner that it will search for new products rather than expand its own product line, the monopolistic firm will seek to expand in new markets rather than expand and cut profits (through a lowering of the price) in its basic market. This is exemplified by the pharmaceuticals industry,

[1]For a more thorough discussion of the profit-making orientation of the capitalist firm, see Edwards, Section 3.2, p. 98, and Baran and Sweezy, Section 4.3, p. 161.

[2]Ernest Mandel, *Europe vs. America* (New York: Monthly Review Press, 1970), provides much information and an analysis of the competition for markets among enterprises from advanced capitalist nations.

which is notorious for its monopolistic practices in the U.S. and which has become a leader in the development of international markets.[3]

In addition to the search for new markets, there are other forms of the international search for profits. The availability of raw materials has always drawn capitalist enterprises throughout the world. While a firm of any size may be attracted by the profitability of obtaining raw materials, it is the large monopolistic firm that is particularly active and successful. In the first place, the exploitation of raw materials often requires large capital resources. Second, the large firm which is vertically integrated (e.g., the bauxite-aluminum-aluminum products companies) and thus uses the raw materials and sells the final product often has a special advantage. Third, and perhaps most important, the monopolistic firm is concerned about control. Whatever the narrow profitability of obtaining particular raw materials, controlling their supply is often important to the large firm which must continue to insure that other firms do not make inroads on its realm. The petroleum industry is the most prominent example of an international exploiter of raw materials, and it exhibits each of these advantages of monopolistic operation. Aluminum, copper, and other mineral industries also provide good examples.[4]

Another form which the internationalization of business takes is the extension to new areas of the production process itself. On the one hand, the establishment of produc-

tion operations in new areas is a means to exploit the markets of those areas. Sometimes the nature of the product is such that it is necessary or desirable to undertake production, or at least the final stages of production, close to the market in which it is sold. The refining of oil, the processing or packaging of food products (Coca-Cola!), the provision of a service, and construction projects all provide examples. Sometimes legal restrictions of the host country—tariffs, for example—require that a product be produced in the area where it is to be sold. This is true of the automobile industry in Mexico and in several other Latin American countries. Insofar as the establishment of production operations in a new area is based on such motives, it often involves not a complete operation but only the final assembly of a product.

On the other hand, production activities are frequently established in a new area in order to exploit the relatively low-cost labor in that area. The assembly of electronic components in Taiwan, punching IBM cards in Hong Kong, making shoes in Italy, and hand typesetting in several countries have all been developed by U.S. industries to avoid the relatively high labor costs at home. As with other types of international expansion, we can expect the monopolistic enterprise to take the lead in the international exploitation of labor. In terms of its ability to control and to transfer technology, its ability to secure sufficient demand for the new production enterprise, and its political ability to cope with the local population as a work force, the large firm has marked advantages.

In summary, the basic method of operation of the capitalist firm leads to international expansion in several ways. While the overall motivation is always profit, the particular medium through which the profits are gained can be the extension of markets, the obtaining of raw materials, or the exploitation of new sources of labor. In gen-

[3]Michael Kidron, *Foreign Investments in India* (New York: Oxford University Press, 1965), Ch. 4, Section 5, provides a particularly interesting description of the inroads of Western pharmaceutical firms into the Indian market.

[4]For accounts of the operations of the petroleum industry that develop these points see: M. Tanzer, *The Political Economy of International Oil and the Underdeveloped Countries* (Boston: Beacon Press, 1969), R. Engler, *The Politics of Oil* (New York: Macmillan & Co., Inc., 1961), H. O. Connor, *World Crisis in Oil* (New York: Monthly Review Press, 1962).

eral, monopolistic enterprises can be expected to take the leading role in the internationalization of capital.

The internationalization of capital is a process which does not take place in a political vacuum. Capital requires direct protection and the institutions through which it operates must be protected. Thus the expansion of the area of operation of capital is always associated with an expansion of the political influence of the state with which that capital is associated. In the following section I shall examine the historical operation of state and capital in the expansionary process.

STATE AND CAPITAL IN THE PROCESS OF EXPANSION

In the history of capitalist development, we may distinguish three broad stages of expansionary activity. These stages, while they do not conform in a precise way to historical eras, are useful analytical tools for examining the internationalization of capital. First is the stage of creating *national economies* in which the locus of economic activity moves from cities or small regions toward a national framework. Second is the stage of *colonialism and spheres of influence* in which the business interests of advanced nations extend their control beyond their own boundaries but with each nation operating in separate geographic areas. Third is the stage of *international capitalist integration*, or *modern imperialism*, in which barriers to economic activity among capitalist countries tend to be eliminated and domination of the international economy becomes centralized in one nation. In each of these stages the state can be seen providing the essential framework for expansion.

The First Stage: The Development of National Economies

The early development of capitalism required the expansion of the size of the capitalist economic unit. In this expansion the state played a crucial role.

The key aspect of capitalist production is that the worker must be separated from the control of any productive factors other than his or her own labor and that the production process must be controlled by the owner of capital.[5] The process of separating workers from their means of production, and thus forcing them into the labor market and into capitalist production relationships, was facilitated by the power of the state. The state was instrumental in the development of capitalism in England, for example, through promotion of the enclosure movement in the eighteenth century and through legislation forcing the poor to enter the work force in the nineteenth century. It played a similar role in other parts of Western Europe and in Japan (after the Meiji Restoration in 1868), where the persistence of feudal institutions threatened to impede the growth of capitalism.

The profitable use of a developing labor force by the capitalist firm depends upon an expansion in the size of the unit of production. The division of labor which provides the basis for capitalist efficiency could not take place in a small craft shop of the precapitalist era. However, an enterprise could be profitably expanded only to the extent that there was a market for increased output. (This was true, for example, of the development of textile mills in England: a national market was necessary to support these harbingers of the factory system.) Thus it was necessary for capitalist development that local restrictions on trade be broken down, that means of transportation and communication be developed, that a uniform system of law and order be established over a wide area—in short, it was necessary that national economic units be developed and strengthened.

[5]See the introduction to Chapter 3, p. 88, for a more detailed discussion of the capitalist mode of production.

The Second Stage:
Colonies and Spheres

The stage in capitalist development which followed the political and economic development of the nation was characterized by colonial expansion and the creation of spheres of influence. As in the preceding stage, the economic integration of a larger geographic area was the key to the expansion process. However, while the need for markets and labor played some role, the effort to develop sources of supply for important foodstuffs and raw materials became particularly important in the second stage. The role of the state remained as before: to break down local restrictions on economic activity; to create a labor force; to create means of transportation and communication; to insure stability through the imposition of law and order.

Britain, for example, united the regional economies of India and opened the whole subcontinent to penetration by British capital. Each colonial power established its own currency as the medium of exchange throughout its realm. The European colonial powers in Africa imposed monetary taxes on the local population, forcing them to leave the traditional economy and enter the capitalist labor force to earn cash incomes to pay the taxes. Throughout the colonial world, railways directed toward import-export activity were given priority. Britain, France, Germany, and all of the colonial powers backed up their economic decisions in the most direct manner—with armed force.

In organizing trade within its particular sphere, each nation reserved for its own capitalist class special economic privileges—both with respect to the subordinate areas in its control, as well as with regard to other leading capitalist powers. Thus, for example, Portugal prohibited the development of manufacturing in Brazil, reserving the market for goods produced in the parent country, and England restricted the trade of its North American colonies with other European powers.

The Third Stage:
United States Hegemony

It is not surprising that the United States was a latecomer in building spheres of influence and establishing colonies. First, the United States itself had been under the control of Britain and became a nation only when many European nations were well-established as international powers. Second, as long as the United States was able to expand westward within the North American continent, there was little pressure for the more typical overseas expansion.[6]

As continental boundaries were reached, the United States began to enter seriously the competition among the big powers for new areas of exploitation. Around the turn of the last century, the U.S. and Britain were instrumental in ushering in a new era of capitalist international relations. The policies of the new era were typified by the U.S. demand for an "open door" in the Far East. With several European powers scrambling to establish control in China, the U.S. in 1899 demanded that all countries be allowed commercial access to this area—that the door be left open to all. This policy signified a movement away from national spheres of influence toward a single integrated international capitalist economy. Two world wars were to be fought, however, before this final stage would be firmly established.

Part of the reason that the U.S. government took a diplomatic lead in altering the relations of international capitalism was that U.S. business interests were latecomers to international activity. Thus, short of all-out war with other imperialist powers, the government had no way other than diplomatic initiative to gain access to many areas for

[6]See Magdoff, Section 10.2, p. 420.

U.S. business. More important, the government's demand for open access and equal terms was natural since the nation was rapidly becoming the world's greatest economic power. Under conditions of open access, the emerging political and economic strength of the U.S. would insure that its interests would prevail more often than not.

Coincidentally with the rising international power of U.S. business, the U.S. government engaged in numerous military interventions around the beginning of the century. The Spanish-American War led to the establishment of formal U.S. colonies in Puerto Rico and in the Philippines (an important stepping stone for establishing influence in China) and virtual colonial control over Cuba (only nominally independent). In each of these areas, the extension of U.S. political control was followed by a rapid increase of U.S. economic interests.[7]

In 1912 the U.S. intervened militarily in Nicaragua in order to assure that the interests of U.S. banks financing a railway were not interfered with. In 1915 the U.S. occupied Haiti in order to insure that the Haitian government "honor" its obligations to U.S. bankers. In 1916, the U.S. Marines were sent to Santo Domingo and seized control of the customs and treasury of that nation in order to insure that obligations to American companies would be fulfilled. And again in 1916, when U.S. oil interests were threatened in Mexico, the Marines were sent to the scene. While the majority of U.S. military interventions in this period were in the Caribbean, they were by no means limited exclusively to that area. In 1911 and 1912, and later in 1924 and 1926, U.S. armed forces made their presence felt in China in order to protect U.S. private property during civil disturbances there; these military actions provided the backdrop for the growth

[7] See S. Nearing and J. Freeman, *Dollar Diplomacy* (New York: Monthly Review Press, 1966), for the details of the early period of U.S. military interventions.

of U.S. trade and financial interests in China.[8]

Military interventions, however, should not necessarily be taken as typical of the operation of U.S. imperialism. More often than not, control has been exercised through economic power or through nonmilitary political pressure.

IDEOLOGY AND INTERVENTION

The ideology of capitalist expansion—the set of ideas that justify and support the system —has developed out of the needs of the expansionary process. In providing support for the system, one of its most important functions is to establish criteria for judging political activities. Thus, growing out of economic process, the capitalist ideology pro-

[8] This era is summed up in the following statement by a retired Marine commander:

I spent thirty-three years and four months in active service as a member of our country's most agile military force—the Marine Corps. I served in all commissioned ranks from a second lieutenant to major-general. And during that period I spent most of my time being a high-class muscle man for Big Business, for Wall Street, and for the bankers. In short, I was a racketeer for capitalism....

Thus I helped make Mexico and especially Tampico safe for American oil interests in 1914. I helped make Haiti and Cuba a decent place for the National City Bank boys to collect revenues in.... I helped purify Nicaragua for the international banking house of Brown Brothers in 1909–1912. I brought light to the Dominican Republic for American sugar interests in 1916. I helped make Honduras "right" for American fruit companies in 1903. In China in 1927 I helped see to it that Standard Oil went its way unmolested.

During those years I had, as the boys in the back room would say, a swell racket. I was rewarded with honors, medals, promotion. Looking back on it, I feel I might have given Al Capone a few hints. The best he could do was operate his racket in three city districts. We Marines operated on three continents.

Major-General Smedley D. Butler, *Common Sense* (November 1935), as quoted by L. Huberman and P. Sweezy in *Cuba: Anatomy of a Revolution* (New York: Monthly Review Press, 1960).

vides a basis for unifying the economic and political realms of the system and for facilitating their joint operation.

The expansionist ideology is based on the functioning of the capitalist enterprise, and its primary element is simply the belief that the function of economic enterprise is the pursuit of profit. As was argued in section 1 of this article, acceptance of the pursuit of profit as a guiding principle means that the behavior of capitalist firms will be expansionary. In order for capitalist expansion to be successful, it is necessary that basic capitalist institutions be created and maintained: the labor market and other basic factor and commodity markets; private property; legal sanction for economic contracts; control of the work process by the owners of capital. According to the ideology of capitalism, these institutions promote "economic freedom." Actions taken by the state that preserve this "freedom" or that facilitate its operation become synonymous with actions that preserve a decent society.

Translated into the realm of foreign policy, the task of the capitalist state then becomes that of facilitating and protecting the international business activities of its nationals. On the level of particular interests, for example: the U.S. diplomatic mission in India sees to it that U.S. pharmaceutical companies are allowed to produce and sell under "reasonable" conditions; in Bolivia and Peru, when U.S. owned oil companies are nationalized, it is the business of the U.S. government; when Brazilian coffee producers begin to sell instant coffee below the price at which U.S. companies can produce, the U.S. government "encourages" the Brazilian government to impose an export duty.[9] On a broader level, the government provides

[9]The Indian example is discussed by Kidron in the book cited above in footnote 3. The Brazilian example is from *The Economist*, Feb. 24, 1968, and is cited by Harry Magdoff in *The Age of Imperialism* (New York: Monthly Review Press, 1969), p. 163. The Bolivian and Peruvian cases are well-known.

mechanisms for the general expansion of U.S. interests abroad: the U.S. government encourages foreign governments to lower tariffs for U.S. goods and to enter reciprocity arrangements with the U.S.; the U.S. government provides insurances against nationalization or other political "disasters" in unstable areas; the international sections of various government departments—e.g., commerce, labor—devote themselves to providing U.S. business with investment and trade information on countries throughout the world. Finally, on the broadest level, the role of the government in protecting the international business interests of its citizens is the protection of the system that allows those interests to operate, i.e., the protection of international capitalism.

The need to preserve the system of international capitalism has extremely broad implications. For example, to explain the government's actions, from aid-giving to military intervention, we need not point to any particular interests or set of interests that are being served. It need only be argued that the system is being threatened, that the rules of international capitalist operation are in jeopardy.

Such is the case with Vietnam. U.S. business has had relatively few direct economic interests in Vietnam or even in Indochina as a whole. While one can point to its economic potential or argue that Indochina is the key to a much larger economic realm, an argument that reasons directly from particular interests to military intervention is clearly inadequate. In terms of particular interests, there is simply not very much at stake for U.S. business in Vietnam. However, in terms of the general interest of maintaining South Vietnam as part of the international capitalist system, there is very much at stake. A military defeat for the U.S. or a withdrawal would mean a government and social system for South Vietnam that would break all the rules of international capitalism.

To argue that even such an entire loss of

South Vietnam is not important would be to miss the point. *What is at stake in Vietnam is not just a geographic area but a set of rules, a system.* A capitalist government will and must go all out to protect that set of rules. In part, this is a tactical issue: failure to protect the system in Vietnam would lead to further and more effective threats against the system elsewhere. The "domino" argument is a very real one. One need only look at the impact of the Cuban Revolution in Latin America or the impact of the Russian and Chinese Revolutions throughout the world to perceive the implications of a victory for the socialist forces in Vietnam.

In addition, and more fundamentally, a violation of the system is a serious offense in and of itself. In order to function effectively, a social system must be supported by a set of beliefs regarding its legitimacy and even its sanctity. These beliefs constitute the ideological support for the system. If violation or destruction of the system in various areas is allowed on a pragmatic basis, then those beliefs are called into question and the whole system is in danger.[10]

Imperialist Control

Economic power provides the basis for control in a modern imperialist system. Imperialism is simply the internationalization

of capitalist economic relations, and this includes the internationalization of capitalist power relations. In the first place, the rationale of commodity markets is that those who can sell products the cheapest will hold the dominant position. Thus, important sectors of the economies of secondary capitalist countries are dominated by the more advanced enterprises of the primary imperialist nations. While such domination has an impact at all levels of the international system, it takes on its most overt form in the poor countries. Their indigenous industrial development is severely limited, and they tend to remain dependent upon the export of agricultural products and raw materials to the rich countries and upon the import of manufactures and technology from the rich.[11]

Second, international capitalism tends to develop or reinforce a class structure in poor countries that serves its interests. Classes in subservience to and alliance with international capital tend to control the political apparatus; their power derives directly from their association with international capital. Both directly through the market and indirectly through the class structure, the economic power of the capitalist elite in the advanced capitalist nations enables them to dominate the economies of the poor countries.

The rapid growth in recent years of multinational corporations has greatly enhanced this economic power. The multinational corporations have a great deal of bargaining power in setting the terms on which their capital will be deployed in host countries simply because they have numerous options. They control technology and can regulate its dissemination according to their own priorities. They have the power, through internal pricing and bookkeeping adjustments, to artificially adjust the international loca-

[10]An analogy may be useful. Suppose that the Baltimore Orioles are playing the Washington Senators in the last game of the regular season. Baltimore has already secured the pennant by twenty-five games and the Senators are in last place by an equal margin. Baltimore is ahead by a score of 31 to 2; there are two outs and no men on in the last of the ninth. The Senator at bat who is batting .208 for the season, has two strikes. He swings and misses a third pitch. But instead of walking off, the batter turns to the umpire and says, "How about a fourth strike?" He alludes to the above mentioned facts, and he points out that no one's interests can possibly be seriously jeopardized by giving him a fourth strike. No immediate interests are at stake, but is it conceivable that such a violation of the rules of the game, a violation of the system, would be allowed?

[11]For an analysis of the impact of international capitalism on the poor countries, see Weisskopf, Section 10.5, p. 442.

tion of their revenues and outlays and thereby affect the finances and balance of payments of host countries. The international capitalist market is like any national capitalist market: those who dominate the control of the means of production dominate the economy.

Imperialist control operates through political as well as economic channels. First, day-to-day control operates through normal diplomatic channels. The role of U.S. diplomatic missions throughout the world is defined as looking after the interests of its nationals, and this means in practice looking after the interests of U.S. business. Second, long-run control operates through the determination of the institutions of the international capitalist economy. Good examples are the negotiation of trade agreements favorable to U.S. capital and the establishment of an international monetary system in which the dollar is key. Such operations serve to maintain the long-run international hegemony of U.S. capital.[12]

Finally, the dominance of the world capitalist economy by the United States is backed up by tremendous military strength. Modern imperialist operations depend on the actual deployment of the military only when problems arise which economic power and quiet political dealings cannot handle. But today imperialism is being presented with serious challenges, and as these challenges become a threat to the entire system, military responses become increasingly necessary.

The Challenge to the System

With the Russian Revolution in 1917—but more clearly following World War II when the Soviet Union emerged as a major world power, socialism "spread" to Eastern Europe, and successful socialist revolutions occurred in China, Korea, Vietnam—the

[12]For elaboration and substantiation of the assertions of this paragraph see Harry Magdoff, *The Age of Imperialism* (New York: Monthly Review Press, 1969), Chaps. 3 and 4.

political position of international capitalism has been severely altered. The system has been forced to move from a purely offensive political strategy toward a defensive posture.

In the early part of this century the state functioned to establish and to assure the operation of capitalist relationships in areas where those relationships had not been fully established or were unstable. This was true of the numerous Caribbean military interventions cited above. Failures by foreign governments to honor contractual commitments with U.S. businesses, an elementary condition of capitalism, brought on the U.S. military. In the post-World War II era, however, the dominant concern of foreign policy has been the prevention of moves toward socialism by countries within the capitalist system. Thus, the interventions in Iran in 1953, in Guatemala in 1954, in Cuba in 1961, and in the Dominican Republic in 1965 should be seen primarily as defensive efforts against the threat—real or perceived—that the nations in question would opt out of the international capitalist system.

As capitalism has moved to a final stage in its international development, it is challenged by a system that is threatening to displace capitalism entirely and inaugurate a new historical epoch. Indeed, the development of socialism has in some degree been a direct outgrowth of and response to the international expansion of capitalism. The progress of the socialist response, however, cannot be viewed as an automatic historical phenomenon. Its development will depend at least in part on the nature of the capitalist counter-response. It is the purpose of the following section to examine mechanisms of that counter-response.

Spreading the Ideology

The preservation of international capitalism by the U.S. government is a goal in which not everyone has an equal interest. On a direct and material level, income returned to the U.S. from foreign activity amounts to less than 1 percent of gross national income.[13] Taken as the direct contribution to overall employment or as an average contribution to individual income, this figure would indicate that the international involvement of the U.S. economy is not very important. However, this income from international activity goes predominantly to those who obtain their income from profits. As a percentage of after-tax corporate profits, earnings from foreign investment have risen to almost 20 percent of the total in recent years (see Table 10-B). If one examines the very large corporations, the importance of the international economy becomes even more apparent. In 1965, for example, thirteen firms from among Fortune's top twenty-five industrial corporations received more than 40 percent of the total foreign earnings of all industrial corporations; these foreign profits accounted for close to 30 percent of the total profits of those firms (see Table 10-E).

These data support two points. First, that U.S. business in general, and large firms in particular, have a very real interest in international operations taken as a whole. They clearly benefit from the foreign policy described above. Second, people who earn their income from sources other than capital, and even a good deal of the business community, do not significantly depend directly on the preservation of international capitalism. This mass of the population should not find such great appeal in a foreign policy explicitly based on the concept that the government must protect and facilitate the search for profits overseas.

Where economic interest is lacking, however, a popular form of the ideology of capitalist expansion provides the domestic sup-

[13]In 1969, direct investment income returned to the United States was $5.6 billion (see Table 10–A), while gross national product was $932.3 billion (see U.S. Dept. of Commerce, *Statistical Abstract of the United States*, 1970, p. 311).

port for the U.S. government's foreign policy. The keystone of the ideology during the post-World War II period has been anticommunism. Communism has been presented to the American people as an international conspiracy which has as its design the enslavement of all the peoples of the world and the consequent destruction of everything that they are taught to hold dear, from the private family and religion to freedom of speech and the two-party system. Such a threat must be fought at every step of the way, partly to protect those immediately in danger, but ultimately to protect the American people themselves. The fact that communism presents a systematic threat to the uninhibited operation of international capital is not emphasized in the popular form of the ideology.

Anticommunism is not the only form in which the ideology of expansionist policy has been popularized. At an earlier time, Christianity, Manifest Destiny, and the White Man's Burden have all done service to imperialist strategy. Indeed, today, as the force of anticommunism has begun to wane, a new set of popular justifications for U.S. interventions is taking form under the heading of "modern liberalism." At its base lies the sentiment that it is the task of the rich, powerful United States to help the poor, backward countries of the world in their quest for development. Economic advisory missions, foreign investment, the Peace Corps, and ultimately military involvement can all be justified on this basis.

In any society, over time the dominant class molds ideology in terms of its own interests. We need only mention various ways in which the business community shapes ideas about foreign affairs to indicate how all-pervasive is its influence. First, the individuals who hold foreign policy positions in the government are drawn heavily from the business community. The point here is not the importance of these individuals in making particular decisions but rather their role over a long period in shaping the institutions and developing the criteria by which decisions are made.[14] Second, by its control over resources, directly or through foundations, the business community sponsors in conjunction with the government virtually all of the writing, research, and teaching that is done in the area of foreign affairs. Here, the concept of "a market place of ideas" is truly apt. As in any commodity market, the goods demanded by those who control resources and who have purchasing power are the ones that continue to be produced. By this process, not only are the dominant ideas reinforced and strategy and apologia developed for actions, but the growth of any ideological counterforce is severely limited. Other means by which the business community can shape concepts of foreign policy include its control over the media, its sponsorship of the Council on Foreign Relations and lesser organizations of policy consideration, and its extensive lobbying practices. In each case, power rests not on any formal arrangements but on the control over resources and on a common objective interest in the general design sign of policy.

Having established the conceptual framework for foreign policy, the business community can expect relatively little difficulty in having its way in particular cases. More-

over, the development of particular policies need not involve any immediate action at all by business. A powerful ideology provides the guide for action, the link between economic interests and political policy.

I have argued that ideology provides the link between economic interests and political action, but I do not wish to imply that the link is in any way weak or malleable. It might be thought, for example, that the problem I have described is simply a problem of "ideas" and that it can be dealt with by changing the ideas and thus breaking the ideological link.

The essence of my argument supports a very different position. The ideology of capitalist expansion is an expression of the basic nature of capitalist enterprise: it reflects the needs and supports the operations of the system. While the form of that ideology may vary, its basic elements have a long and consistent development in the history of capitalism. It would be futile to talk of seriously altering the ideology without changing the social forces which generate and sustain that ideology.

Thus, while the system remains intact, the U.S. government might be forced to abandon its aggression in Vietnam, but it will not abandon the policies which led to that aggression. As long as those policies and the socioeconomic organizations which produce them are maintained, continued U.S. intervention around the world can be expected.

[14]See G. William Domhoff, "Who Made American Foreign Policy 1945–1963," in *Corporation and the Cold War*, ed. David Horowitz (New York: Monthly Review Press, 1969).

10.2   *Militarism and Imperialism*

In the following reading Harry Magdoff documents the extent to which the growth of the United States since its independence has been intertwined with economic expansion and—as a consequence—military spending. It becomes clear that militarism is an inevitable consequence of imperialism, especially at the center of the world capitalist system.

Source: The following is excerpted from "Militarism and Imperialism" by HARRY MAGDOFF. From the *Monthly Review* 21, No. 9 (February 1970). Copyright © 1970 by Monthly Review, Inc. Reprinted by permission of Monthly Review, Inc.

Peace reigns supreme in the realm of neoclassical economics. War, militarism, and the pacification of natives are treated as merely elements which disturb the harmonious equilibrium models which are to supply us with the universal truths about the allocation of scarce resources.

One of the distinguishing features of Marxist thought, on the other hand, is the conviction that economic processes must be understood as part of a social organism in which political force plays a leading role and in which war is at least as typical as peace. In this context, militarism and imperialism are seen as major determinants of the form and direction of technological change, of the allocation of resources within a country, and of the allocation of resources between countries (notably, between rich and poor countries). Accordingly, price and income relations, treated as the ultimate yardsticks of economic efficiency and social justice in neoclassical economics, are viewed, in the Marxist context, as evolutionary products of capitalist institutions in which political force and "pure" economics are intertwined. Rosa Luxemburg put the Marxist case this way:

Bourgeois liberal theory takes into account only [one aspect of economic development]: the realm of "peaceful competition," the marvels of technology and pure commodity exchange; it separates it strictly from the other aspect: the realm of capital's blustering violence which is regarded as more or less incidental to foreign policy and quite independent of the economic sphere of capital.

In reality, political power is nothing but a vehicle for the economic process. The conditions for the reproduction of capital provide the organic link between these two aspects of the accumulation of capital. The historical career of capitalism can be appreciated only by taking them together.[1]

The facts of U.S. history provide eloquent testimony to the accuracy of this diagnosis. Thus, Professor Quincy Wright, who directed a major study of war under the auspices of Chicago University, observed in 1942: "The United States, which has, perhaps somewhat unjustifiably, prided itself on its peacefulness, has had only twenty years during its entire history when its army or navy has not been in active operation some days, somewhere."[2]

Professor Wright identifies years of peace as those in which no action of any sort occurred. A more revealing picture is obtained if we measure months of war against months of peace and bring the information up to the present. Adding up the months during which U.S. military forces were engaged in action —starting from the Revolutionary War and including wars against the Indians, punitive expeditions to Latin America and Asia, as well as major wars—we find that the United States was engaged in warlike activity during three-fourth of its history, in 1,782 of the last 2,340 months.[3] In other words, on the average, there have been three full years in

[1] Rosa Luxemburg, *The Accumulation of Capital* (New York: 1964), pp. 452–53.
[2] Quincy Wright, *A Study of War*, vol. I (Chicago: 1942), p. 236.
[3] Calculated from list in Lawrence Dennis, *Operational Thinking for Survival* (Colorado Springs: 1969), appendix II.

which our armed forces have been engaged in action for every full year of peace. This comparison does not indicate the full extent of the use of military power by the United States to enforce its will. For example, it does not include activities such as those formerly conducted by U.S. gunboats in a "constant patrol in the Yangtze River . . . from the mouth of the river up nearly 2,000 miles into the very heart of China."[4]

It should therefore come as no surprise to discover that war-related expenditures have constituted the dominant sector of the federal budget throughout our history. Omitting the years of the Second World War and the postwar period, where the record is so well-known, a tabulation of federal expenditures by decade, from 1800 to 1939, for army, navy, veterans' compensation and pensions, and interest on the debt—prior to the New Deal federal debt incurred was primarily a result of war spending—shows that except for one decade, at least 54 percent of federal expenditures were for military activities or preparations during the decade or to meet obligations arising from previous military activity.[5] The one exception was the decade of the great depression (1930–1939) when the percentage dropped to somewhat below 40 percent. In seven of the fourteen decades the war-related share of the federal budget was 70 percent or more.

This almost continuous preoccupation with military affairs was clearly not inspired by fears of invading barbarians. Of course, the competing colonial and commercial interests of France, England, Spain, and Russia were part of the reality in which the infant and adolescent United States had to operate. At times, self-defense had to be considered. Moreover, resolution of internal tensions, as in the Civil War, exercised a major influence on military aspects of U.S. life. All of this, however, occurred within a context of empire-building. For there has been a continuous thread in U.S. history, beginning with colonial and revolutionary days, of economic, political, and military expansionism directed towards the creation and growth of an American empire. The original expansionism, for which military investment was needed, concentrated on three main thrusts: (1) consolidation of a transcontinental nation, (2) obtaining control of the Caribbean area, and (3) achieving a major position in the Pacific Ocean.[6] It should be noted that this expansionism was not confined to what is now considered the continental territory of the United States: striving for control of the seas, as a shield and promoter of international commerce, has been an ingredient of U.S. policy from its earliest days. In fact, the struggle to incorporate the West Coast into the United States was, among other things, prompted by the desire to control Pacific Ocean ports for the Asian trade.[7]

The experience thus gained in the early stages of empire-building turned out to be most useful when the leading nations of the world entered the stage of imperialism. Several decisive and coinciding developments in the late nineteenth and early twentieth centuries mark off this new stage:

(1) The onset of significant concentration of economic power in the hands of a relatively small number of industrial and financial giants in advanced nations. Competing interest groups continued to exist, but now the success or failure of the advanced economies became closely identified with the prosperity of the new giant corporations whose *modus operandi* required control over

[4]Office of Naval Intelligence, *The United States Navy as an Industrial Asset* (Washington, D.C.: 1923), p. 4.

[5]Calculated from data in *Historical Statistics of the United States, Colonial Times to 1957* (Washington, D.C.: 1961), pp. 718–19.

[6]Richard W. Van Alstyne, *The Rising American Empire* (Chicago, 1965).

[7]*Ibid.*, Chap. 5, "Manifest Destiny and Empire, 1820–1870."

international sources of supply and markets.

(2) The decline of Great Britain's monopoly position as world trader and world banker. The burgeoning competitive industrial powers—notably, Germany, France, the United States, and Japan—pressed for a reshuffle of established trade relations and a redistribution of world markets.

(3) Industrialization and new naval technology enabled competitive nations to build up their own naval strength to the point where Great Britain could no longer maintain unilateral control over the major sea lanes. As Quincy Wright put it in the study already referred to, "Naval inventions and the spread of industrialization had ended the *pax Britannica.*"[8] Control over sea routes also involved establishing military bases where naval units could be refueled and repaired. The availability of decisive mobile military power on the one hand required acquisition of strategic foreign territory to support bases and on the other hand provided the means for aggressive pursuit of colonial possessions.

(4) The earliest stage of the new imperialism engendered a race by the major powers for control of available foreign real estate. According to Theodore Ropp, after 1880 "every great power except Austria-Hungary . . . became involved in . . . active, conscious colonial expansionism . . . ."[9] Of the traditional colonial powers—the Netherlands, Portugal, Spain, Britain, France, and Russia—the last four continued to add to their holdings. (Spain, after losing Cuba and the Philippines, proceeded to conquer Spanish Morocco.) And at the same time five new powers entered the race for colonial territory: Germany, Italy, Belgium, Japan, and the United States. As for the United States, it was the Spanish-American War, of course, that placed it with both feet in the imperialist camp. And it was success in this war, plus the subsequent pacification of the Cuban and Philippine "natives," which satisfied two long-term U.S. expansionist ambitions: a leading position in the Caribbean,

broadening the highway to the rest of Latin America, and a solid base in the Pacific for a greater stake in Asian business.

As far as the United States is concerned, there have been three distinct stages in the drive to empire: (1) the period when the United States was the supplier of food and raw materials to the rest of the world, when it was an importer of capital, and when maritime commercial interests were relatively very strong; (2) the period when the United States began to compete with other industrialized nations as an exporter of manufactured goods and an exporter of capital —a time when a small number of industrial and financial giants began to dominate the economic scene; and (3) the period when the United States becomes the major, dominant capitalist economy, the largest manufacturer, foreign investor, trader, the world's banker, and the dollar becomes the key international currency.

The energy and determination with which the expansionist strategy is pursued change from time to time. In the transition from one period to another, and because of internal as well as external conditions, it appears at times as if the United States is "isolationist" and uninterested in further extension of its influence and control.[10] Yet it is especially noteworthy that the drive for business opportunities on a world scale is ever present. Even when, as in New Deal days, domestic solutions were sought for crises, the development of foreign business was high on the agenda of government and private enterprise. Given the structure of the economy, the major operating levers work in such a way as to repeatedly reassert expansionism as the dominant strategy. In this perspective, the history of the years since the end of the Second World War are far from a new departure; instead, they are a culmination of

[8]Wright, *op cit.*, vol. I, p. 299.

[9]Theodore Ropp, *War in the Modern World* (New York: 1962), p. 206.

[10]The isolationism was usually more apparent than real. See William Appleman Williams, *The Tragedy of American Diplomacy* (New York: 1952), chap. 4, "The Legend of Isolationism."

long-term tendencies which profited by and matured most readily in the environment created by the course of the last major war.

The postwar leap forward in empire-building and the transition of U.S. society to rampant militarism are associated with two phenomena: (1) the desire to resist and repress socialist nations and to defeat national liberation movements designed to release underdeveloped countries from dependence on the imperialist network, and (2) the extension of U.S. power to fill "vacuums" created by the decline of Western European and Japanese influence in Asia, Africa, and Latin America.

Combating the rise of socialism is of course not a new objective. The destruction of the Russian Revolution was a top priority of the imperialist powers beginning in 1917. In this connection, Thorstein Veblen's observations on the Versailles Treaty in his 1920 review of Keynes' *The Economic Consequences of the Peace* are most pertinent:

> *The events of the past months go to show that the central and most binding provision of the Treaty (and of the League) is an unrecorded clause by which the governments of the Great Powers are banded together for the suppression of Soviet Russia—unrecorded unless record of it is to be found somewhere among the secret archives of the League or of the Great Powers. Apart from this unacknowledged compact there appears to be nothing in the Treaty that has any character of stability or binding force. Of course, this compact for the reduction of Soviet Russia was not written into the text of the Treaty; it may rather be said to have been the parchment upon which the text was written.*[11]

The failure of the United States to join the League of Nations reflected no slackness in its efforts to contain antiimperialist revo-

lutions: in Russia, these efforts took the form of armed intervention and support of anti-Bolshevik forces with food and other economic supplies; in Hungary, the manipulation of food supplies to help defeat the Bela Kun government. Surely the issue at that time was not fear of aggressive Russion or Hungarian militarism. Nor can much credit be given to political or religious idealism. The relevant motive, clearly, was recovery of territory lost to free enterprise and prevention of the spread of the contagious revolutionary disease to Western Europe and the colonies. Any such spread, it was recognized, would severely affect the stability and prosperity of the remaining capitalist nations.

Capitalism as an economic system was never confined to one nation. It was born, developed, and prospered as part of a world system. Karl Marx went so far as to claim, "The specific task of bourgeois society is the establishment of a world market, at least in outline, and of production based upon this world market."[12] One might add that it has been the specific task of imperialism to fill out this outline and establish a complex international network of trade, finance, and investment. Given this network, it follows that limitation of opportunity to trade and invest in one part of the world restricts to a greater or lesser extent the freedom of action of private enterprise in other parts of the world. The dimensions of the defense of free enterprise therefore become worldwide.

The United States had long ago accepted its destiny to open and keep open the door for trade and investment in other parts of the world. The obstacles were not only the heathens who wanted to be left alone, but the preference systems established in the colonies of the older nations. The decline

---

[11]Thorstein Veblen, "The Economic Consequences of the Peace," in *Essays in Our Changing Order* (New York: 1934), p. 464.

[12]In a letter from Marx to Engels, October 8, 1858, in Karl Marx and Friedrich Engels, *Correspondence 1846–1895* (New York: 1934), p. 117.

of political colonialism and the weakness of the other great powers thus placed upon the United States a primary responsibility for the defense of the capitalist system and at the same time afforded golden opportunities to obtain special beachheads and open doors for U.S. enterprise.

With a task of this magnitude, it is little wonder that the United States now has a larger "peacetime" war machine, covering a greater part of the globe, than has any other nation in all of past history. Imperialism necessarily involves militarism. Indeed, they are twins that have fed on each other in the past, as they do now. Yet not even at the peak of the struggle for colonies did any of the imperialist powers, or combination of powers, maintain a war machine of such size and such dispersion as does the United States today. In 1937, when the arms race in preparation for the Second World War was already under way, the per capita military expenditures of all the great powers combined —the United States, the British Empire, France, Japan, Germany, Italy, and the Soviet Union—was $25. (Germany's per capita of $58.82 was then the largest.)[13] In 1968, the per capita military expenditures of the United States alone, in 1937 prices, was $132. This was only in part due to the Vietnam War: in 1964, our most recent "peace" year, the per capita military expenditures in 1937 prices was $103.[14]

One of the reasons for this huge increase in military outlays is no doubt the greater sophistication of weaponry. (By the same token, it is the advanced airplane and missile

technology which makes feasible the U.S. globe-straddling military posture.) An additional reason, of course, is the military strength of the socialist camp. I would like to suggest a third reason: that a substantial portion of the huge military machine, including that of the Western European nations, is the price being paid to maintain the imperialist network of trade and investment *in the absence of colonialism*. The achievement of political independence by former colonies has stimulated internal class struggles in the new states for economic as well as political independence. Continuing the economic dependence of these nations on the metropolitan centers within the framework of political independence calls for, among other things, the worldwide dispersion of U.S. military forces and the direct military support of the local ruling classes.

Precise information on the dispersion of U.S. forces is kept an official secret. However, retired General David M. Shoup, former head of the Marine Corps, who should be in a position to make a realistic estimate, stated in a recent article in *The Atlantic*: "We maintain more than 1,517,-000 Americans in uniform overseas in 119 countries. We have 8 treaties to help defend 48 nations if they ask us to or if we choose to intervene in their affairs."[15] The main substance of U.S. overseas power, aside from its present application in Vietnam, is spread out over 429 major and 2,972 minor military bases. These bases cover 4,000 square miles in 30 foreign countries, as well as Hawaii and Alaska.[16] Backing this up, and acting as a coordinator of the lesser imperialist powers and the Third World incorpo-

[13]Wright, *op. cit.*, pp. 670–71.

[14]The data on military expenditures are the purchases of goods and services for "national defense" and "space research and technology" as used in computing Gross National Product. The 1964 and 1968 data are reported in the *Survey of Current Business*, July 1968 and July 1969. The adjustment for price changes was made by using the implicit price deflators for federal purchases of goods and services, as given in the *Economic Report of the President*, January 1969.

[15]General David M. Shoup, "The New American Militarism," *The Atlantic*, April 1969. The figure of 119 countries seems too large. General Shoup was probably including bases on island locations, which he counted as separate countries. Our guess is that U.S. armed forces to man bases, administer military assistance, and train foreign officers are located in 70 to 80 countries.

[16]*New York Times*, April 9, 1969.

rated in the imperialist network, is a massive program of military assistance. According to a recent study:

> U.S. military aid ... since 1945 has averaged $2 billion per year. It rose to as much as $5 billion in fiscal year (FY) 1952 and fell to as low as $831 million in FY 1956. The number of recipient countries rose from 14 in 1950 to a peak so far of 69 in 1963. In all, some 80 countries have received a total of $50 billion in American military aid since World War II. Except for 11 hard-core communist countries and certain nations tied closely to either Britain or France, very few nations have never received military aid of one kind or another from the United States.[17]

The above factual recital by no means exhausts the international functions of U.S. militarism. Space considerations permit no more than passing reference to (a) the active promotion of commercial armament sales abroad (contributing a sizable portion of the merchandise export surplus in recent years), (b) the extensive training of foreign military personnel, and (c) the use of economic-aid funds to train local police forces for "handling mob demonstrations and counterintelligence work."[18] These are, in the main, additional instruments for maintaining adherence and loyalty of the nonsocialist world to the free-enterprise system in general, and to the United States in particular.

.   .   .

[17]George Thayer, *The War Business, The International Trade in Armaments* (New York: 1969), pp. 37–38. This is a summary of data presented in *Military Assistance Facts*, May 1, 1966, brought up-to-date through Fiscal Year 1968.

[18]For (a), see *ibid.* (b), see John Dunn, *Military Aid and Military Elites: The Political Potential of American Training and Technical Assistance Programs* unpublished Ph.D. dissertation (Princeton University: 1961). (c), see Edwin Lieuwen, *The United States and the Challenge to Security in Latin America* (Ohio: 1966), p. 16.

10.3   *United States Foreign Private Investment: An Empirical Survey*

The previous two readings have analyzed the origins and nature of imperialism and emphasized the extension of political control and the growth of militarism that result directly from capitalist expansion. In the next reading we turn to the most visible economic manifestation of imperialism: foreign private investment from the advanced capitalist nations.

The United States has accounted for the lion's share of the direct foreign private investment undertaken in the postwar period.[1] Investment by American private enterprise in foreign countries has grown rapidly since 1950 and has been a major force in bringing about an increasingly integrated world capitalist system in which the United States predominates. In this brief reading Thomas E. Weisskopf presents some pertinent data to

[1]The United States' share of the outflow of direct private investment from the advanced capitalist countries averaged approximately 70 percent during the period 1957–1964. See S. Hymer and R. Rowthorn, "Multinational Corporations and International Oligopoly: The Non-American Challenge," in *The International Corporation*, ed. C. P. Kindleberger (Cambridge, Mass.: M.I.T. Press, 1970), Table 9, p. 78.

document the growth and significance of United States foreign private investment.

Source: The following essay was written by THOMAS E. WEISSKOPF for this book. Copyright © 1972 by Thomas E. Weisskopf.

The value of American private investment assets held in foreign countries grew rapidly from 1950 to 1969; annual data are presented in Table 10-A. Long-term assets account for the bulk of the total value of U.S. private investment abroad; and among long-term assets, equity capital (in the form of direct private investment) is far more important than loan capital (in the form of commercial bonds). Total assets, long-term assets and direct private investment abroad, have all multiplied by more than five times within the nineteen-year period, growing at an average annual rate of almost 10 percent.[1]

Table 10-A also lists the annual value of capital outflow and capital inflow associ-

[1]All the data presented in this reading are based on dollar values at current prices. Thus real rates of growth are overstated by the amount of price inflation that took place in the period under consideration. From 1950 to 1969, the price level of exports and of imports (presumably most relevant to international transactions) rose by little more than 1 percent per year. (See *The Economic Report of the President*, 1970, Table C-3.)

TABLE 10-A   THE GROWTH OF U.S. FOREIGN PRIVATE INVESTMENT, 1950–1969

Year	Value of Assets			Direct Capital Outflow	Direct Investment Income
	Total	Long-Term	Direct		
	(Billions of dollars at year-end)			(Billions of dollars during year)	
1950	19.0	17.5	11.8	0.6	1.3
1951	20.5	19.0	13.0	0.5	1.5
1952	22.1	20.6	14.7	0.9	1.4
1953	23.8	22.2	16.3	0.7	1.4
1954	26.6	24.4	17.6	0.8	1.7
1955	29.1	26.8	19.4	0.8	1.9
1956	33.0	30.1	22.5	1.8	2.2
1957	36.8	33.6	25.4	2.1	2.3
1958	40.8	37.3	27.4	1.1	2.2
1959	44.8	41.2	29.7	1.4	2.2
1960	49.4	44.4	31.9	1.7	2.4
1961	55.5	49.0	34.7	1.6	2.8
1962	60.0	52.7	37.3	1.7	3.0
1963	66.5	58.3	40.7	2.0	3.1
1964	75.8	64.9	44.5	2.3	3.7
1965	81.5	71.4	49.5	3.5	4.0
1966	86.3	75.7	54.8	3.7	4.0
1967	93.6	81.7	59.5	3.1	4.5
1968	102.5	89.5	65.0	3.2	5.0
1969	110.2	96.0	70.8	3.1	5.6

SOURCE: U.S. Dept. of Commerce, *Survey of Current Business* (monthly), annual articles on the international investment position of the U.S.

ated with U.S. direct private investment. A major share of this investment is financed abroad, both from local sources and from the reinvested earnings of foreign enterprises. Thus the annual outflow of capital is much less than the corresponding annual increase in the value of direct investment assets. The return flow of capital from abroad represents that part of the income from existing foreign investment that is repatriated back to the United States. As Table 10-A clearly shows, both the inflow of investment income and outflow of new investment capital have increased rapidly from 1950 to 1969, but the former has been consistently higher than the latter. Thus there has been a continuous net capital inflow associated with U.S. direct private investment abroad.[2]

During the period from 1950 to 1969, the value of U.S. direct private investment abroad grew steadily as a proportion of the value of total corporate investment (at home and abroad). This is hardly surprising, for the average rate of profit on foreign capital was substantially higher than on domestic capital throughout this period.

Table 10-B presents annual data that document the increasing importance and relatively high profitability of foreign investment. After-tax profits, invested capital, and the corresponding rate of profit are listed first for all corporate activity and then for foreign private investment.[3] The foreign per-

centage of total profits and of total capital in each year is also shown. The figures indicate that the value of direct investment abroad rose from 5 percent of the invested capital of all corporations in 1950 to almost 10 percent in 1969. The share of foreign profits in total after-tax corporate profits was consistently higher than the share of invested capital, rising from about 7 percent in 1950 to almost 18 percent in 1969. This higher share of foreign profits reflects the greater profitability of foreign investment; the foreign profit rate averaged between 13–14 percent during the whole period as compared to an overall rate of about 7–8 percent.

The geographical and sectoral distribution

---

[2]This net capital inflow belies the notion that private capital from the United States adds directly to the capital resources available to the rest of the world. In fact the return flow of profits exceeds the outflow of new capital. But foreign private investment has indirect as well as direct effects on the availability of capital in foreign countries. An estimate of the overall impact of United States private investment abroad would have to take account of its net contribution to domestic income, the extent to which it displaces or inhibits domestic capital formation and other such variables which affect the availability of capital in foreign countries.

[3]To obtain comparable figures on profits from foreign private investment, it is necessary to make some adjustments on the reported data on foreign earnings. The data available from the Department of Commerce show foreign earnings after foreign taxes but before U.S. taxes. Because U.S. tax laws allow firms to deduct from their U.S. taxes an amount equal to foreign taxes paid on repatriated income (provided foreign tax rates do not exceed the U.S. tax rates), the effective U.S. tax rate on foreign earnings is much lower than the rate (about 50 percent) which applies to domestic profits. Evidence for recent years from the Internal Revenue Service (see *Statistics of Income— 1962, Supplemental Report on Foreign Income and Taxes Reported in Corporation Income Tax Returns,* Table 10) suggests that the average rate of U.S. tax on foreign earnings—after deductions —was approximately 10 percent. In addition to subtracting U.S. taxes, it is also desirable to add to reported foreign earnings the reported value of royalties, management charges, and other fees which are levied by U.S. corporations on their overseas affiliates and which constitute in effect a significant transfer of profits. The figures for total after-tax foreign profits thus calculated are shown in Table 10-B.

It should be noted that even these adjusted figures tend to understate the profitability of foreign investment. On the one hand, profits made by overseas affiliates can be disguised by artificially high prices charged for the supply of inputs imported from the parent company. Such over-invoicing has the effect of transferring the profits from the accounts of the overseas affiliate to the accounts of the parent company in the U.S. On the other hand, the reported value of foreign assets may well overstate the true value of the invested capital because of overpricing of the capital equipment and/or capitalization of costless assets such as brand names, etc.

TABLE 10-B THE RELATIVE SIZE AND PROFITABILITY OF U.S. DIRECT FOREIGN PRIVATE INVESTMENT 1950–1969

Year	Corporate Totals			Foreign Private Investment			Foreign Total Ratios	
	After-Tax Profits (Billions of dollars)	Invested Capital[1] (Billions of dollars)	Profit Rate %	After-Tax Profits[2] (Billions of dollars)	Invested Capital[3] (Billions of dollars)	Profit Rate %	After-Tax Profits %	Invested Capital %
1950	24.9	223.6	11.1	1.70	11.2	15.2	6.8	5.0
1951	21.6	239.0	9.0	2.14	12.4	17.3	9.9	5.2
1952	19.6	254.0	7.7	2.24	13.8	16.2	11.4	5.4
1953	20.4	265.2	7.7	2.19	15.5	14.1	10.7	5.8
1954	20.6	279.8	7.4	2.33	16.9	13.8	11.3	6.0
1955	27.0	305.5	8.8	2.78	18.5	15.0	10.3	6.1
1956	27.2	327.7	8.2	3.18	20.9	15.2	11.7	6.4
1957	26.0	344.4	7.5	3.44	23.9	14.4	13.2	6.9
1958	22.3	369.2	6.0	2.99	26.4	11.3	13.3	7.1
1959	28.5	389.0	7.4	3.25	28.5	11.4	11.8	7.3
1960	26.7	409.0	6.5	3.60	30.8	12.0	13.5	7.5
1961	27.2	434.2	6.3	3.89	33.3	11.7	14.3	7.7
1962	31.2	(456.0)	6.8	4.37	36.0	12.1	14.0	7.9
1963	33.1	476.6	6.9	4.79	39.0	12.3	14.5	8.2
1964	38.4	503.4	7.6	5.32	42.6	12.5	13.9	8.5
1965	46.5	536.0	8.7	5.83	47.0	12.4	12.5	8.8
1966	49.9	567.1	8.2	6.16	52.1	12.0	12.4	9.2
1967	46.6	613.0	7.6	6.57	57.1	11.5	14.1	9.3
1968	48.2	(660.0)	7.3	7.57	62.2	12.2	15.7	9.4
1969	48.5	(710.0)	6.8	8.53	68.4	12.5	17.6	9.6

[1]Data in brackets represent rough estimates extrapolated where precise data were unavailable.
[2]Calculated as 90 percent of reported earnings, plus royalties, fees, etc. (See footnote 3.)
[3]Figures for each year represent the average of the year-end book value of assets for the preceding and the given year.
SOURCES: a. Corporate after-tax profits: U.S. Dept. of Commerce, National Income and Product Accounts, Table 6.15.
b. Corporate invested capital: U.S. Internal Revenue Service, Statistics of Income: Corporate Income Tax Returns (annually), data on net worth of corporations.
c. Reported earnings; royalties, fees, etc.; invested capital of foreign private investment: U.S. Dept. of Commerce, Survey of Current Business (monthly), annual articles on the international investment position of the United States.
d. After-tax profits on foreign private investment calculated as indicated in footnote 2.
e. Percent rates calculated directly from data in table.

of U.S. direct private investment abroad is tabulated in Table 10-C for the years 1929, 1950, 1959, and 1969. Although the absolute value of foreign investment has increased dramatically in all areas and all sectors during this period, there have been significant shifts in its distribution. The share of the underdeveloped countries has dropped from about 50 percent of the total in 1929 and 1950 to slightly less than 30 percent in 1969. The major area for U.S. investment has shifted from Latin America in 1929 and 1950 to Canada in 1959 and to Western Europe in 1969.

These geographical shifts reflect the increasing emphasis on the manufacturing sector that has characterized foreign investment in recent decades. From 24 percent of total foreign investment in 1929, the share of the manufacturing sector rose to 42 percent by 1969. Because of much higher standards of living, the developed countries offer a more lucrative market for manufacturers than do the underdeveloped countries; almost half of U.S. direct private investment in the developed countries is in manufacturing.

In the underdeveloped countries, the extraction of raw materials remains the most significant activity of foreign investors: more

TABLE 10–C   VALUE OF U.S. DIRECT FOREIGN PRIVATE INVESTMENT BY AREA AND SECTOR, 1929–1969 (all figures in millions of dollars)

	1929	1950	1959	1969
All Countries	7,528	11,788	29,735	70,763
Latin America	3,519	4,576	8,990	13,811
Africa[1]	25	147	520	2,215
Asia[2]	334	982	2,026	3,974
Canada	2,010	3,579	10,171	21,075
Europe	1,353	1,733	5,300	21,554
Other areas[3]	287	771	2,728	8,133
Mining and Smelting	1,185	1,129	2,858	5,635
Petroleum	1,117	3,390	10,423	19,985
Manufacturing	1,813	3,831	9,692	29,450
Other Sectors	3,413	3,438	6,762	15,693
Underdeveloped Countries[4]	3,878	5,705	11,536	20,000
Mining and Smelting	751	718	1,604	2,321
Petroleum	721	2,139	5,127	7,830
Manufacturing	297	847	1,614	5,167
Other Sectors	2,109	2,001	3,191	4,682
Developed Countries[5]	3,650	6,083	18,199	50,763
Mining and Smelting	434	411	1,254	3,314
Petroleum	396	1,251	5,296	12,155
Manufacturing	1,516	2,984	8,078	24,283
Other Sectors	1,304	1,437	3,571	11,011

[1]excluding South Africa.
[2]excluding Japan.
[3]including international.
[4]includes the first three areas listed above.
[5]includes the last three areas listed above.
SOURCES: 1929 and 1950 data: S. Pizer and F. Cutler, *U.S. Business Investment in Foreign Countries.* 1959 and 1969 data: U.S. Dept. of Commerce, *Survey of Current Business* (Sept. 1960 and Oct. 1970).

than half of U.S. direct private investment is in petroleum and mining and smelting. But even in the underdeveloped countries, the share of the manufacturing sector in total U.S. investment has been growing, and it is likely to surpass the share of the raw material extracting sector within the next decade.

The increasing significance of foreign investment in manufacturing has important implications for the (nonsocialist) underdeveloped countries. Where foreign investors in an earlier era were primarily concerned with extracting and exporting valuable raw materials, they are now becoming more and more directly involved in the local economy. This leads on the one hand to a greater degree of influence and control over domestic economic affairs. It leads also to a new kind of relationship with the host government. Rather than simply requiring a minimum of interference with their activities, foreign investors now seek the active cooperation of the host government in measures

designed to promote capitalist social and economic relations within the country. The desire to create a "favorable investment climate" results in a continued spread of capitalism and an increasingly integrated world capitalist system.

Although the *value* of U.S. direct private investment is now much higher in the developed than in the underdeveloped countries, there is much less of a difference in the level of *income* from that investment. Table 10-D presents data on the reported earnings (after foreign taxes but before U.S. taxes), the value of investment, and the corresponding rate of earnings by area and by sector in 1959 and 1969.[4] While the share of total foreign investment located in underdeveloped countries was only 39 percent in 1959 and 28 percent in 1969, the

[4] The data in Table 10-D are intended to illustrate geographical and sectoral differences in foreign investment activity. They have not been adjusted so as to be made comparable with the figures in Table 10-B. (On the adjustments in Table 10-B, see footnote 3, p. 428.)

TABLE 10-D   EARNINGS ON U.S. DIRECT FOREIGN PRIVATE INVESTMENT BY AREA AND SECTOR, 1959 and 1969

	Reported Earnings (millions of dollars during year)	Value of Investment (Millions of dollars at year-end)	Rate of Earnings (%)
1959			
Total investment	3,255	29,735	11.0
Underdeveloped countries	1,615	11,536	14.0
Developed countries	1,640	18,199	9.0
Mining and smelting	315	2,858	11.0
Petroleum	1,185	10,423	11.4
Manufacturing	1,129	9,692	11.6
Other sectors	626	6,762	
1969			
Total investment	7,955	70,763	11.3
Underdeveloped countries	3,747	20,000	18.7
Developed countries	4,208	50,763	8.3
Mining and smelting	844	5,635	15.0
Petroleum	2,494	19,985	12.5
Manufacturing	3,185	29,450	10.8
Other sectors	1,432	15,693	9.2

SOURCE: U.S. Dept. of Commerce, *Survey of Current Business* (Sept. 1960 and Oct. 1970).

data indicate that the corresponding share of earnings was 50 percent in 1959 and 47 percent in 1969. These differences reflect a much higher average rate of earnings in underdeveloped than in developed countries: 14 percent as against 9 percent in 1959, and 18.7 percent as against 8.3 percent in 1969 (the gap is apparently widening). The differential rates of earnings do not arise merely from differences in the sectoral mix of investment, for the earnings rates shown in Table 10-D do not differ as greatly among sectors as among areas. The evidence clearly suggests that within each sector the average rate of earnings is higher in underdeveloped than in developed countries.

The significance of foreign investment for the United States economy is much greater than is suggested by aggregate comparisons of foreign and domestic activity. For direct private investment abroad is highly concentrated in the large industrial corporations that dominate private enterprise.[5] Table 10-E presents data on the foreign operations of the top twenty-five U.S. industrial corporations (ranked by sales volume) in 1965, the latest year for which extensive data were available. The value of foreign sales, assets and earnings—and the foreign percentage of the total—are listed for each corporation insofar as the data were available. At the bottom of the table the figures are summed for reporting corporations among the top twenty-five they are also compared with the corresponding total values for all industrial corporations.

Table 10-E suggests that foreign operations on the average account for between 25 percent and 30 percent of the total sales, assets and earnings of the top twenty-five industrial corporations: most of these can hence truly be labeled multinational firms. The sixteen firms for which data on assets

[5]For an examination of business concentration within the United States economy, see Means, Section 4.1, p. 145, and Tables 4–A, 4–B, 4–C, 4–D in the statistical appendix, p. 153.

were available account for more than 40 percent of total foreign earnings. These figures indicate that the overseas activity is even more highly concentrated than the domestic activity of American private enterprise.

The power of multinational firms within the world capitalist system is brought out vividly by the data in Table 10-F, where nonsocialist nations and firms are ranked together by two indices of economic strength. First of all, the volume of sales of the top industrial corporations is compared with the gross domestic product of the leading nations. These figures measure the value of the gross output that is produced within the firm and within the nation. Second, the level of after-tax profits of the top corporations is compared with the revenues that are raised by the central governments of the leading nations. These figures measure the share of gross output that actually accrues to the firm and to the national government in the form of net income.

Table 10-F indicates that in 1965 the top twelve industrial corporations, each with sales in excess of three billion dollars, ranked among the top thirty-eight nations whose gross domestic product exceeded three billion dollars. The majority of these thirty-eight represent developed capitalist economies. Each of the top twelve corporations ranked ahead of the hundred-odd countries and territories (not listed in the table) whose gross domestic product was less than three billion dollars. The ranking of nations and firms by net income is similar to the ranking by gross output, although slightly less favorable to the multinational corporations. Among the top forty-seven with net income in excess of 400 million dollars, forty are nations and seven are firms.

In sum, the major multinational firms are comparable in economic power to the smaller developed capitalist nations and to all but the very largest of the underdeveloped nations.

TABLE 10–E   FOREIGN OPERATIONS OF TOP 25 INDUSTRIAL CORPORATIONS IN THE U.S., 1965

Rank Corporation	% Foreign			Value of Foreign (million dollars)		
	Sales	Assets	Earnings	Sales	Assets	Earnings
1 General Motors	18	12	10	3,730	988	213
2 Ford Motor	22[2]	27	12[2]	2,540	1,211	84[2]
3 Standard Oil (N.J.)	68	52	60	7,800	4,510	622
4 General Electric	18			1,119		
5 Chrysler	25	26		1,325	412	
6 Mobil Oil	49	43	52	2,405	1,500	166
7 U.S. Steel						
8 Texaco	35[1]		25[1]	1,540		159
9 IBM	30	32	30	1,133	824	143
10 Gulf Oil		33	29		1,260	124
11 Western Electric						
12 DuPont	17	17		514	372	
13 Swift						
14 Bethlehem Steel	2			52		
15 Shell Oil						
16 Standard Oil (Indiana)		16			433	
17 Standard Oil (Calif.)	35[1]	9[1]	43[1]	855	295	168[1]
18 Westinghouse Electric						
19 International Harvester	28	26	19	650	290	19
20 Goodyear		40	34		360	37
21 Union Carbide	29	17	22	599	231	50
22 Armour		11			132	
23 Procter and Gamble		16	18		147	24
24 RCA	6	6	5	123	36	5
25 General Telephone & Electronics	11			224		
A No. of firms with data available:	15	16	13	15	16	13
B Total for these corporations:	29%	28%	27%	24,609	13,001	1,814
C Total for all industrial corporations	—	—	—	—	38,394	4,415
D B as % of C:	—	—	—	—	33.9	41.2

[1]Excludes Western hemisphere
[2]Excludes Canada
SOURCES: a. Rank of top twenty-five industrial corporations: *Fortune* (June 1966) Directory of the Top 500 Industrial Corporations.

b. Percent foreign sales, assets, and earnings: Bruck and Lees, "Foreign Investment, Capital Controls, and the Balance of Payments," *The Bulletin*, the Institute of Finance, New York University (April 1968), Appendix, Table II.

c. Value of foreign sales, assets, earnings: calculated by multiplying percentage figures by total value as given in *Fortune* (June 1966) Directory of the Top 500 Industrial Corporations.

d. Total foreign assets and earnings for all industrial corporations: U.S. Dept. of Commerce, *Survey of Current Business* (Sept. 1966), figures for mining and smelting, petroleum and manufacturing.

TABLE 10–F COMPARATIVE ECONOMIC POWER: NATIONS AND FIRMS (Figures for 1965 in millions of dollars)

Nation/Firm	(1) Rank	(2) GDP	(3) Sales	(4) Rank	(5) Central Gov't Revenues	(6) After-Tax Profits
United States	1	688,000		1	117,000	
West Germany	2	116,713		4	16,100	
United Kingdom	3	97,720		2	29,000	
France	4	94,044		3	19,500	
Japan	5	85,207		5	11,300	
Italy	6	56,742		6	10,200	
India	7	49,623		8	5,150	
Canada	8	49,104		7	8,400	
Australia	9	23,113		10	4,510	
Brazil	10	22,173		15	2,330	
Spain	11	21,420		13	3,080	
General Motors	12		20,733	16		2,126
Mexico	13	19,705		19	1,770	
Sweden	14	19,223		9	4,660	
Netherlands	15	18,829		11	4,250	
Belgium	16	16,660		12	3,420	
Argentina	17	14,982		22	1,480	
Switzerland	18	13,668		26	1,150	
Ford Motor	19		11,537	34		703
Standard Oil (N.J.)	20		11,472	28		1,036
South Africa	21	10,550		21	1,490	
Denmark	22	10,040		17	1,870	
Pakistan	23	10,028		33	800	
Austria	24	9,341		14	2,580	
Turkey	25	8,745		23	1,460	
Venezuela	26	8,466		20	1,640	
Finland	27	8,054		18	1,790	
Indonesia	28	7,371		45	420	
Norway	29	7,093		24	1,420	
Iran	30	6,323		32	865	
General Electric	31		6,214			355
Greece	32	5,751		29	925	
Colombia	33	5,427		37	625	
New Zealand	34	5,345		25	1,350	
Chrysler	35		5,300			233
Phillipines	36	5,209		46	420	
Chile	37	4,936		31	895	
Mobil Oil	38		4,908			320
U.A.R.	39	4,701		27	1,110	
Texaco	40		4,400	36		637
U.S. Steel	41	4,400				275
Peru	42	4,345		38	585	
Nigeria	43	4,040			205	
Thailand	44	3,931		40	535	
IBM	45		3,779	43		477
Portugal	46	3,689		41	525	
Israel	47	3,602		30	895	
Gulf Oil	48		3,385	44		427

TABLE 10–F, continued

Nation/Firm	(1) Rank	(2) GDP	(3) Sales	(4) Rank	(5) Central Gov't Revenues	(6) After-Tax Profits
Western Electric	49		3,362			168
DuPont	50		3,021	47		407
Malaysia			2,939	42	490	
Ireland			2,719	35	665	
Iraq			2,268	39	545	

SOURCES: a. Sales and after-tax profits of industrial corporations: *Fortune*, (May 1970) Directory of Top 500 industrial corporations.

b. GDP of nations: Hagen and Hawlyryshyn, "Analysis of World Income and Growth, 1955–1965," *Economic Development and Cultural Change* 18, No. 1 (October 1969), Part II.

c. Central government revenues: United Nations, *Statistical Yearbook*, 1968, Table 199; data converted into dollars using exchange rates given in Hagen and Hawlyryshyn, *op. cit.*

10.4 The Multinational Corporation and Modern Imperialism

The importance of the multinational corporation emerges clearly from the data presented in Tables 10–E and 10–F. No study of imperialism can begin without an understanding of the nature of the multinational corporation: its goals, its interests, and its methods of operation.

In Chapter 4, Stephen Hymer traced the growth of the capitalist unit of enterprise from the small family firm to the giant multinational corporation and examined the internal structure of the latter.[1] In the following reading, Paul Baran and Paul Sweezy focus upon the international operations of the multinational corporation. The case of Standard Oil of New Jersey is used for illustrative purposes; as Baran and Sweezy point out, Standard Oil is typical of the many giant corporations that now dominate the United States and the world economy.

[1]Hymer, Section 4.2, p. 156.

Source: The following is excerpted from "Notes on the Theory of Imperialism" by PAUL BARAN and PAUL SWEEZY. From the *Monthly Review* 17, No. 10 (March 1966). Copyright © 1966 by Monthly Review, Inc. Reprinted by permission of Monthly Review, Inc.

I

One can no longer today speak of either industrialists or bankers as the leading echelon of the dominant capitalist classes. The big monopolistic corporations, which were formed and in their early years controlled by bankers, proved to be enormously profitable and in due course, through paying off their debts and plowing back their earnings, achieved financial independence and indeed in many cases acquired substantial control over banks and other financial institutions. These giant corporations are the basic units of monopoly capitalism in its present stage; their (big) owners and functionaries constitute the leading echelon of the ruling class. It is through analyzing these corporate giants and their interests that we can best comprehend the functioning of imperialism today.

In size, complexity of structure, and multiplicity of interests the corporate giant of today differs markedly from the industrialist or the banker of an earlier period. This can be most graphically illustrated by an actual case, and for this purpose we can hardly do better than select Standard Oil of New Jersey (hereafter referred to as Standard or Jersey). This corporation was the earliest of its kind anywhere in the world; it is today the second largest industrial corporation in the world (second only to General Motors); and its international ramifications are at least as complicated and far reaching as those of any other corporation. It shows in clearest and most developed form the "ideal type" to which hundreds of other giant corporations, both in the United States and in the other advanced capitalist countries, are more or less close approximations.

Here, in brief summary form, are some of the most important data about the size, structure, and operations of Jersey.[1]

Size

As of December 31, 1962, Jersey had total assets of $11,488 million. Its aggregate revenues for the year 1962 came to $10,567 million, and its net income to $841 million (*Form* 10–K).

Geographical Distribution of Assets and Earnings

As of the end of 1958, the percentage distribution of earnings and assets by various regions was as follows (*Notice*):

[1]The sources are the company's *1962 Annual Report*, its *Notice of Special Stockholders' Meeting* (October 7, 1959), and its *Form 10-K for the Fiscal Year Ended December 31, 1962*, filed with the Securities and Exchange Commission pursuant to Section 13 of the Securities Act of 1934. These sources are identified as *Annual Report, Notice,* and *Form 10-K*, respectively.

	Assets	Earnings
U.S. and Canada	67	34
Latin America	20	39
Eastern Hemisphere	13	27
Total	100	100

Rate of Return on Stockholders' Equity

During 1962 the percentage rates of return on stockholders' equity in different regions were as follows (*Annual Report*):

United States	7.4
Other Western Hemisphere	17.6
Eastern Hemisphere	15.0

Number of Subsidiaries

As of the end of 1962, Jersey owned 50 percent or more of the stock in 275 subsidiaries in 52 countries. The following is a list of the number of such subsidiaries by country of organization (*Form* 10–K):

U.S.A.	77	Morocco	2
Canada	37	Switzerland	2
Great Britain	24	Uruguay	2
Panama	17	Venezuela	2
France	12	Algeria	1
Bahamas	8	Dominican Republic	1
Italy	6	Egypt	1
Sweden	6	El Salvador	1
Colombia	5	Finland	1
Netherlands	5	Hungary	1
Australia	4	India	1
Brazil	4	Indonesia	1
Chile	4	Kenya	1
Germany	4	Luxemburg	1
Philippines	4	Madagascar	1
Argentina	3	Mexico	1
Denmark	3	New Zealand	1
Ireland	3	Paraguay	1
Japan	3	Peru	1
Neth. Antilles	3	Republic of Congo	1
Norway	3	Singapore	1
Austria	2	South Africa	1
Belgium	2	Spain	1
Bermuda	2	Surinam	1
Iraq	2	Tunisia	1
Malaya	2		

Recapitulating by regions, we find that Jersey had 114 subsidiaries in the United States and Canada, 43 in Latin America, 77 in Europe, 14 in Asia, 9 in Africa, and 18 in other regions.

Countries Marketed in

According to the *Annual Report*, Jersey sold to "more than 100" countries in 1962.

It would obviously be wrong to expect a corporation like this to behave like a British cotton mill owner interested in getting his raw cotton from abroad at the lowest possible price and in exporting his products to a duty-free India, or like a Rothschild or a Morgan disposing over great amounts of liquid capital and interested in investing it abroad at the highest attainable rate of profit. Standard's interests are much more complicated. Take, for example, the question of exports and imports. Though Standard, through its principal U.S. affiliate, Humble Oil and Refining Company, is one of the biggest producers in the country, the company is definitely not interested in protectionist measures. Quite to the contrary, it is a strong opponent of the present system of controls which limit the importation of fuel oil. "In the interests of consumers, the national economy, and the international relations of our country," states the *1962 Annual Report*, "we hope that these unnecessary controls not only will be relaxed . . . but will be completely removed." Behind this public spiritedness, of course, lies Standard's interest in having its relatively low-cost Venezuelan subsidiary, Creole Petroleum, sell freely in the lucrative East Coast fuel-oil market.

Or take the question of capital exports. On the face of it, one might be tempted to conclude from the tremendous magnitude and variety of Standard's foreign operations that over the years the corporation has been a large and consistent exporter of capital. The conclusion, however, would not be justified. From the data presented above, it appears clearly that foreign operations are much more profitable than domestic, and this has been the case since the early days of the corporation. Under these conditions, a small initial export of capital could, and undoubtedly did, expand rapidly through the reinvestment of its own earnings. Not only that. So great have been the profits of foreign operations that in most years even after the needs of expansion have been covered, large sums have been available for remittance to the parent corporation in the United States. The year 1962 may be taken as an example: Standard paid out dividends to its shareholders, the vast majority of whom are resident in the United States, a total of $538 million. In the same year, however, operations in the United States produced a net income of only $309 million. It follows that some 40 percent of dividends plus whatever net investment may have been made in the United States during the year were financed from the profits of foreign operations. Far from being an exporter of capital, the corporation is a large and consistent *importer* of capital into the United States.

The foregoing gives hardly more than a hint of the complexity of Standard's interests. It takes no account of the fact that the oil industry as organized by the giant international corporations is in reality a congeries of businesses: extraction of the raw material from the subsoil, transportation by pipe-line and tanker, processing in some of the most technologically advanced plants in the world, and finally selling a variety of products in markets all over the world. Nor is Standard confined to the oil industry even in this comprehensive sense. It is a large and growing supplier of natural gas to the gas pipe-line companies; it is a major producer of artificial rubber, plastics, resins and other petrochemical products; and it recently entered the fertilizer business with plans which, according to the *1962 Annual Report*, "will make Jersey an important factor in the world fertilizer industry." Finally, Jersey, like other giant corporations, maintains a large research and development program the purpose of which is not only to lower costs and hence increase profits from existing operations but also to invent new products and open up new lines of business. As an illustration of the latter, we may cite the following from the *1962 Annual Report*: "Food from oil through biological fermentation is an intriguing possibility. Esso Research, in a small pilot plant, has produced a white powder that resembles powdered milk or yeast. It is odorless, has a bland taste, and is high in protein and B vitamins. The first goal is to develop food supplements for animals, but it is hoped that the technique may one day help to improve the diet and health of the world's growing population." Quite a promising market, one must admit.

This is, of course, not the place for a detailed examination of the structure and interests of Standard Oil or any other corporation. But enough has been said, we hope, to carry the conviction that such a huge and complicated institutional "capitalist" can hardly be assumed to have exactly the same attitudes and behavior patterns as the industrial or finance capitalists of classical Marxian theory. But before we explore this subject further, we must ask whether Standard Oil is indeed an ideal type which helps us to distil the essence of capitalist reality, or whether on the contrary it may not be an exceptional case which we should rather ignore than put at the center of the analytical stage.

II

Up to the Second World War, it would have been correct to treat Standard Oil as a sort of exception—a very important one, to be sure, exercising tremendous, and at times even decisive, influence on United States world policy. Nevertheless, in the worldwide scope and ramifications of its operations not only was it far ahead of all others; there were only a handful that could be said

to be developing along the same lines. Many U.S. corporations of course had large interests in exports or imports, and quite a few had foreign branches or subsidiaries. In neither respect, however, was the situation much different from what it had been in 1929. Direct investments of U.S. corporations indeed declined slightly between 1929 and 1946.[2] Most of the giant corporations which dominated the U.S. economy were, in the words of *Business Week*, "domestically oriented enterprises with international operations" and not, like Standard Oil, "truly world oriented corporations."[3]

A big change took place during the next decade and a half. To quote *Business Week* again: "In industry after industry, U.S. companies found that their overseas earnings were soaring, and that their return on investment abroad was frequently much higher than in the U.S. As earnings abroad began to rise, profit margins from domestic operations started to shrink. . . . This is the combination that forced development of the multinational company."[4] The foreign direct investments of U.S. corporations increased sharply—from the already cited figure of $7.2 billion in 1946 to $34.7 billion in 1961.[5] While this tremendous jump of course involved actual capital exports by many individual companies, it cannot be overemphasized that for the United States as a whole the amount of income transferred to the United States on direct investment account far exceeded the direct capital outflow.[6]

[2]The figure was $7.5 billion in 1929 and $7.2 billion in 1946, U.S. Department of Commerce, Office of Business Economics, *U.S. Business Investments in Foreign Countries: A Supplement to the Survey of Current Business*, 1960, p. 1.

[3]"*Multinational Companies*," A Special Report, *Business Week* (April 20, 1963).

[4]*Ibid.*

[5]U.S. Department of Commerce, *Survey of Current Business* (August 1962), p. 22. [Editors' note: By 1969 the value of U.S. direct private investment abroad had surpassed $70 billion; see Table 10–A, p. 427.]

[6][Editors' note: See Table 10–A, p. 427.]

. . .

But this is not the aspect of the matter which primarily concerns us at the moment. The point is that in the course of expanding their foreign assets and operations in this spectacular way, most of the corporate giants which dominate the U.S. economy have taken the road long since pioneered by Standard Oil. They have become, in *Business Week's* terminology, multinational corporations. It is not enough that a multinational corporation should have a base of operations abroad; its true *differentia specifica* is that "its management makes fundamental decision on marketing, production, and research in terms of the alternatives that are available to it anywhere in the world."[7] This, of course, is what Standard Oil has been doing since roughly the beginning of the century. The difference is that what was then the exception has today become the rule.

III

One cannot say of the giant multinational company of today that it is primarily interested, like the industrialist of the nineteenth century, in the export of commodities; or, like the banker of the early twentieth century, in the export of capital. General Motors, for example, produces automobiles for the rapidly expanding European market not in Detroit but in Britain and West Germany; and it probably exports many more from its European subsidiaries to the underdeveloped countries than it does from the United States. In many cases, indeed, the foreign subsidiaries of U.S. companies are large-scale exporters to the U.S. market. In 1957, for example, the aggregate sales (excluding intercorporate petroleum sales) of direct-investment enterprises abroad was $32 billion. Of this amount, more than $3.5 billion (11 percent) was exported to the

United States.[8] Considering that aggregate merchandise imports into the United States in 1957 came to $13.2 billion, it is a most striking fact that more than a quarter of this total was supplied by the foreign subsidiaries of U.S. companies. And as for capital export, we have already seen that U.S. multinational companies are on balance massive importers, not exporters, of capital.

What all this means is that one must beware of easy generalizations about the specifically economic interests of the leading actors on the imperialist stage. Their interests are in fact variegated and complex, often contradictory rather than complementary. Subsidiaries of a U.S. company in two foreign countries may both be in a good position to export to a third country. If one gets the business, the interests of the other will be damaged. Which should be favored? Or a certain company produces raw materials through a subsidiary in one country, processes the materials through another subsidiary in a second country, and sells the finished product through yet another subsidiary in the United States. Intercorporate prices can be so fixed as to allocate revenues and profits in any number of ways among the subsidiaries and countries. Which set of prices should actually be selected? These examples illustrate the kind of problem which the top managements of the multinational corporations have to solve every day; and about the only valid generalization one can make is that in every case they will seek a solution which maximizes the (long-run) profits of the enterprise as a whole. And this of course means that whenever necessary to the furtherance of this goal, the interests of particular subsidiaries and countries will be ruthlessly sacrificed. This is admitted with refreshing candor by the authors of the *Business Week* report already cited: "The goal, in the multinational corporation, is the greatest good for the whole unit, even if the in-

---

[7] *"Multinational Companies," op. cit.*

[8] U.S. Department of Commerce, *U.S. Business Investments in Foreign Countries*, p. 3.

terests of a single part of the unit must suffer. One large U.S. manufacturer, for example, concedes that it penalizes some of its overseas subsidiaries for the good of the total corporation by forcing them to pay more than necessary for parts they import from the parent and from other subsidiaries. Says one of the company's executives: 'We do this in countries where we either anticipate or already face restrictions on profit repatriation. We want some way to get our money out.' "

A whole treatise could—and should—be written about the way the national interests of the subordinate countries fare under the regime of multinational corporations. Here we will have to be content with one illustration—a case which is less well-known than it deserves to be but which we believe to be fully typical. One of the most important natural resources of the Caribbean area is bauxite. Jamaica, Surinam, British Guiana, and the Dominican Republic are all important producers, with operations being organized and controlled by a few U.S. and one Canadian corporate giants. Separate figures on the operations of these subsidiaries are not published. However, the U.S. Department of Commerce does report the profits accruing to U.S. mining companies on their operations in Western Hemisphere dependencies of European countries, at least 90 percent of which must be attributable to bauxite production in Jamaica, Surinam, and British Guiana. Adding a conservatively estimated figure for profits of the Canadian company, profits from operations in these three countries in 1961 were between $70 and $75 million on an investment estimated at between $220 and $270 million.[9] This profit rate of between 26 and 34 percent suggests, in the opinion of Philip Reno, that

[9]All figures are from an article "*Aluminum Profits and Caribbean People,*" by Philip Reno, *Monthly Review* (October 1963). Mr. Reno spent several months in British Guiana studying the operations of the aluminum companies.

"this could well be among the most profitable U.S. investment structures in the world." However, this is only part of the story. Commerce Department figures give current costs of U.S. aluminum company operations in the three countries for 1957. Of the total of $81 million, no less than $31 million, or almost 40 percent, are classified under the heading of "Materials and Services." Since it is simply incomprehensible how materials and services could constitute so large a share of the costs of an extractive operation of this kind (more than 50 percent greater than wages and salaries), one can only conclude that this item is artificially padded to cover excessive payments to U.S. shipping, insurance, and other interests. In this manner, profits (and hence taxes) can be kept down and funds can be remitted from the colony to the metropolis.

Nor is even this all. The price of bauxite produced in the United States doubled in the two decades from 1939 to 1959, while the price of bauxite imported from Surinam and British Guiana remained almost the same throughout the whole period. This means that profits which should have been realized by the subsidiary companies and been taxed by the Surinam and British Guiana governments were in fact realized in the United States. At length, however, the parent aluminum companies, with one exception, began to alter this price structure, and here we get a revealing glimpse of the kind of considerations that determine the policy decision of the multinational corporations. In Philip Reno's words: "The prices set on bauxite from all the Caribbean countries except British Guiana did finally begin to rise a few years ago. The explanation lies with the law granting tax concessions to U.S. companies operating in other countries of this Hemisphere through what are called Western Hemisphere Trade Corporations. Instead of a 52 percent corporate income tax, Western Hemisphere Trade Corporations pay the U.S. only 25 percent.

By raising the price of bauxite, U.S. companies could now reduce their total income taxes. The price of bauxite began to rise for the first time in twenty years, except for British Guiana bauxite mined by Altd, Canada-based and unaffected by Western Hemisphere Trade Corporation maneuvers."

If this is a fair sample of how the underdeveloped countries are treated by the multinational companies, it does not follow that these giant enterprises are any more concerned to promote the national interests of the advanced countries, including even the one in which their headquarters are situated. Quite apart from particular actions—like the Ford Motor Company's remittance abroad of several hundred million dollars to buy out the minority interest in Ford of Britain at a time when the U.S. government was expressing serious concern about the state of the country's balance of payments—a plausible argument could be made that in the last fifteen years U.S. corporations have developed their foreign operations at the expense of, and often in direct competition with, their domestic operations and that these policies have constituted one of the causes of the lagging growth rate of the U.S. economy and hence of the rising trend of unemployment which is now perhaps the nation's number one domestic problem. Whether or not this is really the case—and it would probably be impossible to *prove* either that it is or isn't—it remains true that the decisions and actions of the multinational companies are taken solely with a view to promoting the interests of the companies themselves and that whatever effects, beneficial or injurious, they may have on the various countries in which they operate are strictly incidental.

IV

Does this mean that the giant multinational companies have no interests in common on which they can unite? Are there no *general* policies which they expect their governments—and the governments of the dominant imperialist states are indeed theirs—to follow? The answer is that there are common interests and desired general policies, but that for the most part they are not narrowly economic in nature. The multinational companies often have conflicting interests when it comes to tariffs, export subsidies, foreign investment, etc. But they are absolutely united on two things: First, they want the world of nations in which they can operate to be as large as possible. And second, they want its laws and institutions to be favorable to the ūnfettered development of private capitalist enterprise. Or to put the point in another way, their ideal would be a world of nations in every one of which they could operate uninhibited by local obstacles to their making and freely disposing of maximum attainable profits. This means not only that they are opposed to revolutions which threaten to exclude them altogether from certain areas—as, for example, the Cuban Revolution excluded all U.S. corporations from Cuba—but also that they are adamantly opposed to all forms of state capitalism (using the term in its broadest sense) which might tend to hamper their own operations or to reserve potentially profitable areas of economic activity for the nationals of the countries in question.[10] Their attitude is well expressed in the *1962 Annual Report* of Standard Oil on which we have already drawn for illustrative material: "Both at home and abroad, a greater awareness is needed of the importance of private investment to economic progress. Some countries have shown a trend toward state enterprise both through government participation in new commercial ventures and through

[10]This does not mean, of course, that they oppose foreign governments' undertaking public works—roads, harbors, public health and education programs, etc., etc.—of a kind that will benefit their own operations. For such beneficent activities they even favor generous "foreign aid" from their own government.

nationalization of established private businesses. The interest of these nations will best be served, however, by fostering societies that are based on those principles of free enterprise which have produced the outstanding economic development of many other nations. It is reassuring to see steps taken—such as the Hickenlooper Amendment to the Foreign Assistance Act of 1961 —to ensure that economic assistance funds from the United States encourage a climate of progress by emphasizing the importance and protection of private investment in nations receiving aid from the United States." It would be wrong to think that the management of Standard Oil opposes government enterprise in the subordinate countries because of a naive belief that state action is identical with socialism. The explanation is much more rational: government enterprise and state action in these countries generally represent attempts on the part of the native bourgeoisies to appropriate for themselves a larger share of locally produced surplus at the expense of the multinational companies. It is only natural that such attempts should be resolutely opposed by the multinational companies.

The general policy which the multinational companies require of their government can thus be summed up in a simple formula: to make a world safe for Standard Oil. In more ideological terms, this means to protect the "free world" and to extend its boundaries wherever and whenever possible, which of course has been the proclaimed aim of U.S. policy ever since the promulgation of the "Truman Doctrine" in 1947. The negative side of the coin is antiCommunism. The necessary complement is the building up and maintenance of a tremendous global military machine.

All the major struggles going on in the world today can be traced to this hunger of the multinational corporations for maximum *Lebensraum*. And the connection usually has a direct, immediate, and visible aspect. We cite just two facts relative to Cuba and Vietnam where the essence of present-day imperialist policy can be seen in its clearest form. Under the heading "Standard Oil Co. (New Jersey)," in Standard and Poor's *Standard Corporate Descriptions*, dated July 24, 1961, we learn that "loss of $62,269,000 resulting from expropriation of Cuban properties in 1960 was charged to earned surplus." And from the same company's *1962 Annual Report* we learn that "Jersey continues to look for attractive opportunities both in areas where we now operate and in those where we do not," and that the following are among the measures being taken to implement this policy: "A refinery in which the company will have majority interest is under construction in Malaya, and affiliates have part interests in a refinery under construction in Australia and one that is being planned for Vietnam."

Losses in Cuba, plans for South Vietnam: what more eloquent commentary could there be on the struggles now going on in and around those two little countries on opposite sides of the globe?

10.5 *Capitalism and Underdevelopment in the Modern World*

The postwar period has been characterized by the growth and spread of capitalism in most of the poor countries of Asia, Africa, and Latin America. On the one hand, foreign private investment in these areas has multiplied rapidly[1] with the rise of a newly integrated world capitalist system in the wake of the disruption caused by two world wars and a major worldwide depression. On the other hand, capitalist forms of production and organization have grown in scope and significance within most of the poor countries—partly in response to the growth of international capitalism. While the degree of penetration of capitalist institutions into the poor countries varies from one country to another, the overall trend is unmistakably clear.

Most observers of modern capitalism would agree that it has become increasingly international, but they reject the word "imperialism" because of its negative connotations, and they argue that capitalist expansion is a *good thing* because it spreads economic progress throughout the world. It is a matter of great importance in evaluating modern capitalism, then, to ascertain what impact it really has on the poor countries. In the following reading Thomas E. Weisskopf argues that the expansion of world capitalism from the rich to the poor countries is likely to perpetuate rather than to alleviate their underdevelopment. The historical experience of capitalist growth in the rich countries in an earlier era is irrelevant to the poor countries today, for the latter have been and remain the victims rather than the agents of imperialism.

[1]United States' direct private investment in the poor countries of Latin America, Asia, and Africa increased from $5.7 billion to $20.0 billion in the period 1950–1969, at an average annual rate of close to 7 percent (see Table 10–C). About one-half of the total private investment of the rich capitalist countries comes from the United States (see The Commission on International Development, *Partners in Development*, Annex II, Table 2).

Source: The following is an excerpted and revised version of "Capitalism, Underdevelopment and the Future of the Poor Countries" by THOMAS E. WEISSKOPF. From *Economics and World Order*, edited by Jagdish Bhagwati. Copyright © 1972 by the Macmillan Company, Inc. Reprinted by permission of the Macmillan Company, Inc.

I shall argue in this paper that capitalism in the poor countries of the modern world is likely to *perpetuate* underdevelopment in several important respects. First, the increasing integration of the world capitalist system will tend to heighten the economic, political, and cultural subordination of the poor countries to the rich. Second, capitalist institutions within the poor countries will tend to aggravate rather than to diminish inequalities in the distribution of income and power. And third, capitalism will be unable to promote in most poor countries a long-run rate of economic growth suffi-ciently rapid to provide benefits to the whole population or to reduce the income gap between the poor and the rich countries.

THE PRESENT SITUATION

To analyze the role of capitalism in the poor countries, it is useful first to consider some economic characteristics of contemporary underdevelopment. These characteristics are to a significant degree the result of the colonial history of the poor countries—a long history of subjugation that has transformed their social, political, and economic structure.

First of all, and most obviously, there is an enormous gap between standards of living in the poor and the rich countries. The average per capita income of the poor countries of Asia, Africa, and Latin America is less than one-tenth of its value for the rich capitalist countries (see Table 10-G). Second, the distribution of income and wealth tends to be even more unequal in the poor than in the rich countries. The available evidence suggests that the top 5 percent of the population receive on the average about 30 percent of the income in the nonsocialist poor countries and about 20 percent in the nonsocialist rich countries (see Table 10-H).

Third, the poor countries today are in various respects economically dependent upon the rich.[1] Exports from the poor countries consist chiefly of primary products (agricultural produce and raw materials) and flow mainly to markets in the rich countries, whereas the imports of the poor countries consist chiefly of manufactures that are obtained mainly from the rich countries. Export earnings in most poor countries are highly concentrated in a few commodities: on the average, the principal export commodity accounts for almost one-half, and the top three commodities almost three-quarters, of total earnings from merchandise exports. This concentration makes the poor countries extremely vulnerable to changes in a few commodity prices

[1]For statistical documentation of the economic dependence of the poor countries on the rich, see Tables 3 and 4 of the original essay (cited in source line) from which this reading was drawn.

TABLE 10–G   WORLD DISTRIBUTION OF AVERAGE PER CAPITA INCOME, 1965

	Average Per Capita Income (U.S. $)	Population (millions)	Total Income (billion U.S. $)
Nonsocialist Countries			
South and East Asia (exc. Japan)	106	908.2	96.4
Africa (exc. South Africa)	126	279.9	35.2
Oceania (exc. Australia, New Zealand)	176	3.4	0.6
Middle East (exc. Israel)	287	82.8	23.8
Latin America (exc. Cuba)	407	235.5	96.0
Poor Countries	167	1,509.8	252.0
Southern Europe	630	49.5	31.0
Japan, Israel, South Africa	840	118.4	99.4
Western Europe	1,730	273.5	472.3
Australia, New Zealand	2,030	14.0	28.5
North America	3,440	214.2	737.1
Rich Countries	2,040	669.6	1,368.3
Socialist Countries			
Asia	99	732.1	72.6
Cuba	540	7.6	4.1
Poor Countries	104	739.7	76.7
Eastern Europe	820	121.3	99.8
USSR	1,150	230.6	265.2
Rich Countries	1,040	351.9	365.0

SOURCE: Hagen and Hawlyryshyn, "Analysis of World Income and Growth, 1955–1965," *Economic Development and Cultural Change* XVIII, No. 1 (Oct. 1969), Part II, Tables 3–8.

TABLE 10–H SIZE DISTRIBUTION OF INCOME: SELECTED COUNTRIES

	Percentage of Total Income Received by							
Poor Countries	Bottom Fifth	2nd Fifth	3rd Fifth	4th Fifth	Top Fifth	Top Tenth	Top 5%	Gini Ratio*
1. India[1] (1951–60)	3.7	6.8	10.1	14.7	64.7	(44.0)	(32.0)	0.57
2. Mexico[2] (1963)	3.5	6.6	10.8	19.6	59.5	42.1	28.8	0.53
3. Ceylon[3] (1952–53)	4.3	8.4	12.2	18.5	56.6	42.5	32.4	0.50
4. Colombia[3] (1953)	(5.0)	(10.0)	(16.4)	12.2	56.4	48.4	41.6	0.50
5. Guatemala[3] (1948)	(5.0)	(9.0)	(14.8)	15.8	55.4	43.8	34.5	0.48
6. Argentina[2] (1959)	6.6	9.7	12.3	16.8	54.6	41.9	31.8	0.45
7. Barbados[3] (1951–52)	3.6	9.3	14.2	21.3	51.6	34.2	22.3	0.45
8. El Salvador[3] (1946)	(5.0)	(10.0)	(17.2)	15.7	52.1	43.6	35.5	0.45
9. Puerto Rico[2] (1963)	4.5	9.2	14.2	21.5	50.6	(34.0)	22.0	0.44
Rich Countries								
1. W. Germany[3] (1950)	4.0	8.5	16.5	23.0	48.0	34.0	23.6	0.44
2. Netherlands[3] (1950)	4.2	9.6	15.7	21.5	49.0	35.0	24.6	0.43
3. Denmark[3] (1952)	3.4	10.3	15.8	23.5	47.0	30.7	20.1	0.42
4. Sweden[3] (1948)	3.2	9.6	16.3	24.3	46.6	30.3	20.1	0.42
5. U.S.A.[4] (1962)	4.6	10.9	16.3	22.7	45.5	(30.0)	19.6	0.40
6. Italy[3] (1948)	6.1	10.5	14.6	20.4	48.5	34.1	24.1	0.40
7. Norway[3] (1950)	5.5	10.4	15.4	23.7	45.0	29.0	18.2	0.39
8. United Kingdom[3] (1951–1952)	5.4	11.3	16.6	22.2	44.5	30.2	20.9	0.38
9. Australia[3] (1954–1955)	5.6	12.5	17.8	22.4	41.7	27.9	18.9	0.35

SOURCES: [1]Subramanian Swamy, "Structural Changes and the Distribution of Income by Size: the Case of India," *The Review of Income and Wealth* (June 1967), Series 13, No. 2, pp. 155–74. [2]Richard Weisskoff, *Income Distribution and Economic Growth: An International Comparison*, unpublished Ph.D. thesis, Harvard University, 1969. [3]Simon Kuznets, "Quantitative Aspects of the Economic Growth of Nations (VIII): Distribution of Income by Size," *Economic Development and Cultural Change* (Jan. 1963). [4]Edward C. Budd, ed., *Inequality and Poverty* (New York: W.W. Norton and Co., Inc., 1967), Table 1, p. xiii.

*Gini ratios were computed directly from the figures given in the table, including the bracketed figures which were estimated by rough interpolation to make up for missing data.

and results in periodic balance of payments crises for which external assistance is required. Most areas of the underdeveloped world show a marked deficit in their balance of trade that must be met by an inflow of foreign capital. Furthermore, there remains in most poor countries a substantial degree of foreign ownership and/or control of domestic resources.

Finally, most of the poor countries are characterized by a pronounced economic dualism. A modern, foreign-oriented, largely capitalist sector can be found in a few major urban centers and around important sources of raw materials, while the rest of the country remains dominated by a more traditional, wholly indigenous, largely pre-capitalist sector. The significance of the modern sector varies greatly among poor countries, depending upon their colonial history and the more recent impact of the postwar expansion of world capitalism.

Related to these economic characteristics are several important sociopolitical features of contemporary poor countries that affect the growth and operation of capitalist institutions. First of all, the poor countries are typically characterized by a class structure in which power is highly concentrated among a small set of elites. These include on the one hand classes whose power is associated with the traditional sector and who constitute an aristocracy of long standing: large holders of land, wealthy traders, and other precapitalist elites whose dominance in the countryside was accepted and often strengthened by colonial rule. The elites also include several newer classes whose prominence is associated with the growth of the modern sector and the achievement of political independence: the big bourgeoisie, including established foreigners and emerging nationals, and the highly educated and westernized national professionals, bureaucrats, and military officers who have displaced their colonial predecessors. While the relative strength of these elite classes varies from country to country, depending on the local conditions and the extent of social and economic change, their combined membership is almost everywhere very small in comparison to the mass of small cultivators, landless agricultural laborers, unskilled workers, and unemployed or underemployed persons of all kinds who make up the bulk of the population. Between the elite classes at the top and the masses at the bottom there is usually only a very small middle class of petty businessmen, semiskilled blue- and white-collar workers and small property owners.

Such a class structure in turn results in a state apparatus that is largely controlled by and responsive to the interests of the elites— no matter what the formal nature of the political system. Because of their overwhelming power and prestige, the elites form a relatively cohesive ruling class: internal conflicts are minimized by a strong common interest in maintaining overall ruling class hegemony. Thus there are rarely decisive struggles between older and newer elites; the society remains in some degree both precapitalist and capitalist, and the non-ruling classes are rarely able to turn ruling class divisions to their own advantage.

A final important characteristic of contemporary poor countries is their dependent relationship with the centers of capitalist enterprise. This dependence arises partly out of the colonial legacy. Many economic activities in the modern capitalist sector depend either directly on foreign ownership and control or indirectly on foreign technological or managerial aid. Under such circumstances, it is only natural that a considerable fraction of the emerging domestic capitalist class finds itself in a subordinate and dependent position vis-à-vis the foreign capitalist class. For similar reasons, many governments in the poor countries are dependent upon the advanced capitalist powers for political and military support. Thus, capitalism in the poor countries today is not the relatively independent capitalism of old which stimulated the economic growth of England, the United States, Japan, and other rich capitalist countries. Rather, the capitalism which is spreading in today's poor countries is far better described as a dependent form of capitalism, embedded within the world capitalist system as a whole.

INCREASING SUBORDINATION

There are several factors at work within the world capitalist system to reinforce the subordination of the poor to the rich countries. These can briefly be described as the demonstration effect, the monopoly effect, the brain-drain effect, and the technology effect. Each of these effects serves to intensify the demand of the poor countries for resources and skills available mainly in the rich, thereby contributing directly to economic dependence and indirectly also to political and cultural subordination.

First of all, the increasingly close ties between the poor and the rich countries that accompany the integration of world capitalism give rise to a "demonstration effect" whereby the consumption patterns of the rich countries are to some extent emulated by those citizens in the poor countries who are in a position to afford it. Of course, the majority of the population of a poor country cannot afford to consume like the majority of the population in a rich country; however, the elite classes in the poor countries (and, to some extent, the middle classes) can orient their consumption patterns toward those of their counterparts in the rich countries. To the extent that they do so, their consumption tends to rise and to be oriented toward characteristically foreign types of goods. This in turn leads to a relatively high demand for foreign exchange, either because the goods must be directly imported from a foreign country, or because their production in the underdeveloped countries requires the import of foreign raw materials, technology, or expertise.

The second important factor that tends to perpetuate the economic dependence of the poor on the rich countries—the "monopoly effect"—arises from the relationship between domestic and foreign private enterprise. Foreign enterprise has a distinct advantage over domestic enterprise in the poor countries with respect to technology, know-how, markets, finance, etc.; often their monopolistic control of some or all of these factors accounts for their interest in investing in the poor countries. Even when the poor country does not rely directly on foreign enterprise to produce goods and services, it is often the case that it must rely on collaboration with foreign firms or on some kind of indirect affiliation with foreign private enterprise. While such collaboration and affiliation may serve to increase the productive capacity of the economy, at the same time it carries with it an unavoidable relationship of dependence.

Furthermore, it is typically within the interest of foreign private enterprise to maintain the conditions in which its activities or its aid are essential, for considerable monetary rewards accrue to its monopoly of productive techniques and expertise. Thus the incentives are structured in such a way that it is usually not in the interest of a foreign firm to impart to a domestic counterpart the knowledge or the skills or the advantages upon which its commercial success is based. Under such circumstances, domestic enterprise remains in a subordinate position and an important part of the indigenous capitalist class remain dependent upon foreign capitalists. The interest of this part of the indigenous capitalist class becomes associated with that of their foreign collaborators or benefactors, and the impetus as well as the means for them to develop into an autonomous national bourgeoisie is dulled.

The technical and managerial dependence of poor on rich countries is often exacerbated by a substantial "brain drain": the emigration of scientists, engineers, business managers, and other highly educated professionals from the poor to the rich countries where they can expect better-paying jobs and a more stimulating work environment. This outward flow of skilled labor, small in absolute size but very great in potential value because of its scarcity in the poor countries, is both facilitated and promoted by the increasing integration of world capitalism. Where people are encouraged to respond to individual monetary rewards, rather than collective social goals, and where strong forces are operating to attract valuable resources from backward to advanced areas, disparities tend to become cumulatively greater over time.

The last general factor that tends to reinforce the economic dependence of the poor on the rich countries within the world capitalist system results from the choice of production techniques adopted in the poor countries. The technology that is used both by foreign and domestic firms in the modern sectors of the economy is typically very much influenced by production techniques that are used in the rich countries. Such techniques, arising as they do from an economic environment in which labor is scarce and capital is relatively abundant, tend to use more capital and less labor than would be desirable in poor countries. Since the required capital goods—and often also the patents and other rights associated with the production and marketing of the output—must usually be imported from abroad, these techniques tend also to generate a relatively high demand for foreign exchange. This effect is most pronounced when a foreign firm establishes itself directly in a poor country because that enterprise will have an interest in using equipment and services from its own country. But the same effect comes about indirectly when domestic firms collaborate with foreign firms or even if they simply borrow technology from a rich country.

Continued economic dependence implies also continued political subordination. So long as governments of poor countries must seek short- and long-term economic aid from the advanced capitalist countries and the international organizations that are primarily funded by those same countries (the International Bank for Reconstruction and Development, the International Monetary Fund, etc.), their political autonomy will be severely restricted. Furthermore, it follows from the nature of the links between domestic and foreign capital described above that a significant part of the domestic capitalist class is likely to be relatively uninterested in national autonomy insofar as it conflicts with the interests of its foreign capitalist partners or benefactors. Thus the state is likely to be under considerable domestic pressure to curtail whatever nationalist instincts it might otherwise have.

Finally, the continuation of economic and political dependence is likely to limit the development of cultural autonomy as well. The more dependent the country is on foreign help of one kind of another, the greater will be the foreign presence in the country, and the greater the impact on indigenous social and cultural life. International capitalism is especially threatening to the cultural autonomy of poor countries because of the strong interest that capitalist firms have in transmitting the kind of consumerist mentality that stimulates the market for their products. The same kind of demonstration effect that biases demand in the poor countries in favor of foreign goods and services also serves to favor the import of foreign styles and fashions at the expense of domestic cultural autonomy. Just as a concentration of purchasing power in the hands of the elite classes accentuates the demand bias, so the dominance by the foreign-oriented elite—and often foreigners themselves—of educational institutions, communications media, and cultural resources tends to amplify the threat to indigenous cultural development.

INCREASING INEQUALITY

The nonsocialist poor countries are already characterized by great inequality in income, wealth, and power—greater even than in most of the nonsocialist rich countries (see Table 10-H). Yet there are forces at work in the poor countries that are likely to increase further the degree of inequality over time. Some of these forces are common to all capitalist societies; others are operative only in poor countries within the contemporary world capitalist system. The tendency toward increasing inequality in the poor countries means that the benefits of any economic growth will accrue primarily—if not wholly —to a privileged minority, and very little will trickle down to the masses.

In analyzing the distribution of income in the poor countries, it is useful to distinguish not only between the two basic factors of production—labor power and capital[2]—but also between "pure" labor power and labor "skills." Pure labor power represents the natural productive ability that every able-bodied person has; it is by definition very equally distributed in any so-

[2]Labor power is defined to include all of the productive attributes of an individual; capital includes all of the physical means of production, e.g., land, machinery, etc. For an analysis of income distribution in a capitalist society, see also Weisskopf, Section 3.7, p. 125.

ciety. Labor skills represent additional productive attributes that can be acquired by an individual through a process of formal or informal education and training. Like capital, labor skills can be very unequally distributed.

The vast majority of the people in the poor countries depend wholly or primarily on their own pure labor power for their sustenance. The ownership of most of the capital and labor skills is confined to a small minority of the population, including often foreigners as well as domestic elite groups. In a society in which income is distributed roughly according to the market value of the factors of production owned by each individual such equal factor ownership necessarily results in a very unequal distribution of income. In order for income inequality to be reduced in the non-socialist poor countries, there would have to be either: (a) a more equitable distribution of ownership of capital and labor skills; or (b) an increase in the share of national income representing the returns to the most equally distributed factor —pure labor power.

A redistribution of existing claims to capital is not likely to get very far. In the first place, the respect for private property that is fundamental to capitalism precludes any large-scale dispossession of the rich in favor of the poor. The requirement of compensation and the political strength of the rich vis-à-vis the poor will work to limit the comprehensiveness and the effectiveness of any measures of redistribution. And the labor skills acquired by the educated elites cannot by definition be redistributed among the population.

Increases in the supply of capital and labor skills are unlikely to be any more equitably distributed. Capitalist growth has always been characterized by a tendency toward increasing concentration of capital.[3]

Even the distribution of new skills through the expansion of the educational system tends to provide disproportionately great benefits to those classes already most favored.[4] To expect intervention by the state to counter effectively these tendencies is to attribute to the lower classes a degree of political power and influence that could only result from a fundamental transformation of the social structure of the society.

The prospects for any improvement in the distribution of income thus appear to hinge on the possibility of an increase in the share of national income due to pure labor power. The amount of income due to pure labor power is equal to the product of the number of fully employed workers (or their equivalent) and the basic annual wage paid for pure labor. In order for this amount to increase as a share of national income, either the level of employment or the basic wage rate (or some combination of the two) would have to rise more rapidly than the total income of the economy.

In most of the poor countries in recent times the rate of growth of population has not been as rapid as the rate of growth of total income (see Table 10-J), and we can infer that the growth of the labor force has also lagged behind the growth of income. Under such circumstances, it would take a continuous and substantial reduction in the rate of unemployment merely to enable the level of employment to keep pace with the growth of income. A long-run increase in the share of total income due to pure labor power would most likely depend upon a rise in the basic wage rate more rapid than the growth of income. In fact, however, there are several forces which restrain the growth of demand for pure labor in a nonsocialist poor country and thereby limit reduction of unemployment and increases of the basic

---

[3]See Means, Section 4.1 (with appendix), p. 145; and Hymer, Section 4.2, p. 156.

[4]The disequalizing effects of education in a capitalist system are analyzed in Bowles, Section 5.2, p. 218.

wage rate. As a result, the share of total income due to pure labor power is unlikely to increase over time.

First of all, the adoption of techniques of production in both industry and agriculture that have been developed in the rich countries tends to limit the demand for pure labor power. This is because the technology developed in the rich countries, where capital and labor skills are relatively less expensive, is designed to economize on the use of the relatively more expensive pure labor power. But foreign firms naturally tend to import techniques of production from their home country. And domestic firms that collaborate or enter into licensing agreements with foreign concerns are also likely to be influenced by foreign technology. In general, the more closely the poor country is integrated into the world capitalist system, the stronger will be the tendency to adopt excessively labor-saving techniques of production.

A second factor influencing the choice of techniques by capitalist enterprise in the poor countries relates to the problem of labor discipline. Because of the difficulty of organizing large numbers of untrained workers, the individual capitalist employer often has an incentive to keep down the size of his work force and to pay a small number of more skilled workers relatively high wages rather than pay a large number of untrained workers low wages. And the capitalist class as a whole has an interest in cultivating a labor aristocracy whose interests will be tied to those of the ruling elites rather than to the masses; this serves to fragment the labor force and thus to inhibit the development of a revolutionary working class consciousness. To the extent that such forces operate, the benefits of employment are limited to only a part of the working classes, and labor skills are substituted for pure labor power.

The tendency to underutilize pure labor power is further reinforced by the distorted prices that often characterize markets in the nonsocialist poor countries. Money wage rates in urban areas of poor countries are usually higher than the rate at which employers would be willing to hire all the available labor. This results *inter alia* from concessions made by the state to organized labor in response to union pressures; it favors the minority of organized workers at the expense of the majority who are unorganized. At the same time, the price of capital to private enterprise is often understated because of the various types of government programs, subsidies, and other benefits which aid the investor. The result is that firms tend to use more capital and less labor than would be desirable from the point of view either of greater efficiency or of a more equitable distribution of income.

All these effects serve to restrain the growth of demand for pure labor power in the poor nonsocialist countries. As a result, the share of pure labor power in national income is likely to decrease over time, and growing inequalities in the ownership of the other factors—capital and labor skills—will contribute to growing inequality in the overall distribution of income. Corresponding to this increasing economic inequality—and continually reinforcing it—will be an increasing inequality in the distribution of political power as well.

INADEQUATE GROWTH

Increasing subordination and increasing inequality are not necessarily inconsistent with a positive rate of economic growth. Yet capitalist institutions—both domestic and international—impose serious constraints upon the ability of poor countries to sustain a long-run rate of growth adequate to provide material gains for everyone. Economic growth depends in large measure upon the accumulation of physical capital, the spread of labor skills and education, and the adoption of improved methods of economic organization and production. These, in turn, require that the economic resources of a society be mobilized on a substantial scale and channeled into productive investment and other growth-oriented activities. In the following pages, the constraints imposed by capitalism on resource mobilization and resource utilization in the poor countries will be discussed in turn.

Resources can be mobilized either from internal sources, principally in the form of domestic savings, or from external sources, in the form of foreign aid or private capital inflow. The highly unequal distribution of income that characterizes the nonsocialist poor countries would at first appear to favor relatively high rates of domestic saving, for it restrains the consumption of the majority of the population while placing very high incomes in the hands of the few. These high income recipients might be expected to save a larger share of their excess income than would be saved by the poor if the income were redistributed to them.

Yet there are also important forces working in the other direction. The demonstration effect of consumption patterns of the rich countries on the upper and even middle classes in the poor countries tends to stimulate luxury consumption rather than saving. This effect is likely to increase with the increasing integration of the world capitalist system and, therefore, to constitute an increasingly serious obstacle to private domestic saving in the poor countries. As for public domestic saving, the high concentration of political power that follows from the inequality of income distribution in nonsocialist poor countries seriously limits the ability—if not the desire—of governmental authorities to raise revenues from the excess income of the upper classes. Furthermore, the demonstration effect often operates just as strongly on government officials to increase public consumption as it does on private individuals to increase private consumption.

Even where a substantial amount of domestic savings can potentially be mobilized in a poor country, these savings may not in fact be transformed into productive investment because of a shortage of critical imported materials required for investment. It has been noted earlier that world capitalist integration tends to generate an excessive demand for imported products in the poor countries. The result is often serious balance of payments difficulties which limit the availability of foreign exchange for investment projects.

Finally, one potentially very important source of domestic resource mobilization in the poor countries is largely ruled out by a capitalist system of social organization. In many poor countries—especially in densely populated areas—there is much labor power that remains idle because of widespread unemployment or underemployment. In principle, this labor power could be usefully applied to public development projects. Yet it has proven very difficult in the nonsocialist poor countries to mobilize this labor for productive purposes, because the workers potentially involved have little reason to believe that the benefits of their endeavors would be distributed any more equally than income is generally distributed in their society. Furthermore, an important element in mobilizing a large and previously idle labor force to useful activity is a psychological sense of solidarity and commitment to a common, worthwhile cause. With its emphasis on individual achievement and competition, capitalism fails to provide an ideological basis for rallying large numbers of inexperienced and previously idle laborers to a constructive, collective effort.

Because of the difficulties of domestic resource mobilization, many of the governments of poor countries have looked to the richer countries for much needed resources. Unfortunately, for those countries that are inclined to rely on foreign help, the prospects for increasing net inflows of foreign capital from the rich countries to the poor do not appear very bright. As far as foreign aid is concerned, the overall level of net aid provided by the rich capitalist countries to the poor fluctuated between six and seven billion dollars in the 1960s and now shows every sign of decreasing rather than increasing. At its peak, the flow of net aid was only equal to approximately 15 percent of gross investment in the nonsocialist poor countries.[5]

Even though the prospects for high levels of foreign aid appear rather bleak, it remains conceivable that the flow of private capital could take up the slack. Such is in fact the exhortation often made in the rich capitalist countries.[6] Yet foreign private capital does not flow to the poor countries out of a sense of service; it flows in the expectation of generating profits which will ultimately be remitted at home. Whether these profits are repatriated directly in the form of investment income or indirectly in the form of artificially high prices of inputs exported from the home base, they constitute a return flow of capital that sooner or later offsets the original flow to the poor country. In every year since

World War II, the reported income repatriated from U.S. foreign private investment has in fact exceeded the outward flow of private investment funds (see Table 10-A). Unless foreign investment rises continuously and rapidly in a poor country, it is unlikely to make a net contribution to the mobilization of resources.

In sum, only these countries whose small size makes it possible for limited amounts of foreign capital to go a long way can expect to rely largely on external sources of funds. The only nonsocialist poor countries that are likely to escape any problems of resource mobilization are those which are fortunate enough to be well-endowed with scarce natural resources (such as oil) that yield both high profits to the firms exploiting them and high tax revenues to the state. In such countries, the question is simply whether the available resources will in fact be utilized productively by the existing government authorities.

There are several forces at work in nonsocialist poor countries which tend to limit the effectiveness of resource utilization. In the first place, a substantial amount of private investment resources is drawn into activities which are relatively unproductive from the point of view of long-run growth. Such fields as trade, commerce, and real estate are attractive to private investors because they often promise quicker and surer returns than agricultural or industrial investment. For similar reasons, private—and especially foreign—investors typically prefer to invest in consumer goods industries rather than in capital goods industries. Consumer goods cater to well-established markets and involve limited risks, while capital goods often require a larger and longer commitment of resources and generally face less predictable demand conditions. This preference for consumer goods on the supply side serves to reinforce the consumption-oriented structure of demand that limits the mobilization of resources for growth. The failure to

[5]Data on the net flow of aid from the rich capitalist countries to the poor are tabulated for the years 1956–68 in the Commission on International Development, *Partners in Development* (New York: Praeger Publishers, Inc., 1969), Annex II, Table 15. The real value of the aid disbursed is in fact greatly overstated by the money value because of the practice of tying aid to purchases in the donor country and because of the overvaluation of U.S. surplus agricultural commodities; see, for example, Harry Johnson, *Economic Policies Towards Less Developed Countries* (New York: Praeger Publishers, Inc., 1967), esp. pp. 80–84. A complete evaluation of the role of foreign aid in economic development must of course go beyond the issue of resource mobilization to consider the political impact of aid, e.g. in buttressing the reactionary role of privileged elites and thereby perpetuating economic dependence.

[6]See, for example, the report to President Richard Nixon by the White House task force on foreign aid headed by Rudolph A. Peterson, March 1970.

develop domestic capital goods industries in a poor country also hinders long-run growth because it confines the available technological options to productive techniques associated with the use of foreign capital equipment.

Just as capitalist market institutions in poor countries tend to turn the sectoral allocation of investment against growth-oriented activities, they also have an unfavorable impact on the choice of techniques within any given activity. For reasons described in sections 2 and 3 of this article, there tends to be insufficient employment of unskilled labor and excessive use of skilled labor, capital, and foreign exchange in nonsocialist poor countries. Quite apart from its impact on subordination and inequality, this represents a form of resource utilization that is inefficient from the point of view of increasing output and growth. Skilled labor, capital, and foreign exchange are scarce resources in the poor countries and should be carefully economized rather than lavished on a limited number of activities. And unskilled labor is an abundant resource that could make a much greater contribution to output if given adequate employment opportunity.

The inefficiencies inherent in the use of the free market criterion of private profit maximization to allocate resources have been widely recognized and much discussed in the literature on economic development.[7] There are many good theoretical and institutional reasons to expect that the unconstrained operation of the free market would not maximize economic growth, much less any more broadly defined social goal. For these reasons, the state is usually called upon to intervene directly or indirectly into the operation of a capitalist economy in order to steer it

[7]For a concise discussion of the problem of market failure and the need for government planning, see Keith Griffin and John Enos, *Planning Development* (London: Addison-Wesley Publishing Co., 1970), Chapter 3.

toward desired objectives. In many nonsocialist poor countries, the government does in fact affect significantly the allocation of resources. However, the critical question is not *whether* the state intervenes, but *how* it affects the operation of the economy.

To answer this question, one must recognize that the capitalist state does not function in a political vacuum; it responds to the dominant political forces in the society. Thus the government of a nonsocialist poor country will intervene to promote economic growth only insofar as this does not significantly conflict with the interests of the more privileged and influential classes. Unless the interests of the latter coincide with a growth-maximizing strategy, government policy cannot be expected to lead to maximum growth.

In fact, in many important respects a growth-oriented policy does conflict with powerful class interests. The disinclination or inability of government authorities to raise substantial revenues by direct taxation of upper-class incomes has already been cited as an obstacle to resource mobilization in nonsocialist poor countries. As far as resource utilization is concerned, government policy can and does in many ways serve limited interests at the expense of overall economic growth. High import tariffs to protect domestic industries often permit indigenous and foreign firms to make lavish profits while producing in a costly and inefficient manner. Government rationing of capital and foreign exchange often allows the most influential firms to obtain these factors at a relatively low price and thereby permits high profits while encouraging low priority use of scarce factors. As noted in section 3 of this article, minimum wage legislation can serve the interests of organized labor at the cost of overpricing and hence underutilizing unskilled labor.

The allocation of government expenditure is also subject to many points of conflict between a growth-maximizing strategy and the interests of elite minorities. For example, the power of the urban upper classes operates to influence the educational expenditures of the state in favor of urban and higher education at the expense of rural and lower education. Yet there is evidence that the economic returns to primary education are much greater than to higher education in most poor countries.[8] Government expenditures on public sector activities that might compete with private enterprise—domestic or foreign—tend to be discouraged in favor of investment in infrastructural facilities that lower the cost of essential inputs to private firms. All this is not to deny that—within the limits imposed by its ability to raise resources—the state in a nonsocialist poor country can and does undertake programs to stimulate growth. The essential point, however, is that the extent and the effectiveness of these programs are invariably compromised by the class interests that constrain the functioning of the state apparatus.

In sum, capitalist institutions in the poor countries—linked to and strengthened by the expanding world capitalist system—place important constraints upon the mobilization and the utilization of resources for economic growth. As a result, it would appear likely that only a few of the most favored nonsocialist poor countries could achieve a satisfactory long-run rate of growth.

RECENT EVIDENCE

As the world capitalist system has gained strength in recent decades, and as capitalist institutions have developed on a wider scale within most poor countries, one should be able to observe and document the tendencies toward increasing subordination, increasing inequality, and inadequate growth as de-

scribed above. Unfortunately, the available data do not permit a thorough test of the hypotheses advanced in the preceding three sections—especially with respect to subordination and inequality. Yet there is a limited amount of evidence from the postwar experience of the nonsocialist poor countries that can be used to throw light on some general trends.

Table 10-I presents data on the postwar growth of the nonsocialist poor countries, the nonsocialist rich countries, and the socialist countries of Eastern Europe. The rate of growth of per capita income in the nonsocialist poor countries was on the average slightly over 2 percent per year, as compared with more than 3 percent in the nonsocialist rich countries and almost 7 percent in the socialist countries. Obviously the gap between the poor and the rich countries is widening. Furthermore, a substantial part of the population of the poor countries is unlikely to have gained anything at all from the growth that has taken place. If the overall rate of growth of per capita income in a country is 2 percent per year, and if the 10–15 percent of the population that gets half of the total income manages to increase its per capita income by 4 percent per year, then there is no incremental income left for the other 85–90 percent of the population.

Comprehensive data on the distribution of income by families or individuals are seldom available in a poor country for one point in time, much less for different years. To generalize about trends in income distribution, one must therefore turn to indirect evidence. Some insight can be obtained from published data on the relative rates of growth of different sectors within an economy. Table 10-J presents data relating to the significance and the growth of the industrial sector in nonsocialist countries. The first two columns show the share of industrial output in total output and the share of persons occupied in the industrial sector in the total economically active population. To the ex-

[8]See Samuel Bowles, "Class Power and Mass Education: The Beginnings of a Study of Social Structure and Educational Policy," mimeo, Department of Economics, Harvard University, March 1970.

TABLE 10–I AGGREGATE ECONOMIC GROWTH IN THE POSTWAR PERIOD

	Average Annual % Rates of Growth, 1950–1967		
	Per Capita Income[4]	Population	Total Income[4]
Non-Socialist Countries			
South and East Asia[1]	2.0	2.2	4.2
Latin America	2.1	2.7	4.9
Poor Countries[2]	2.2	2.4	4.6
North America	2.2	1.8	4.0
Western Europe	3.4	1.1	4.6
Rich Countries[3]	3.0	1.3	4.4
Socialist Countries			
USSR and Eastern Europe	6.7	1.4	8.3

[1]Excludes Japan.
[2]Includes also Africa (minus South Africa) and the Middle East.
[3]Includes also Japan, South Africa, Australia, and New Zealand.
[4]Gross domestic product at constant prices for nonsocialist countries. Net material product at constant prices for socialist countries.
SOURCE: Growth rates calculated from growth indices in United Nations, *Statistical Year-book*, 1968, Tables 3, 4.

TABLE 10–J INDUSTRIAL GROWTH IN THE POSTWAR PERIOD

	Share of Industry[1]		Annual % Rates of Growth[2]			
	In Gross Domestic Product (ca. 1965)	In Eco-nomically Active Population (ca. 1965)	Industrial Output	Industrial Employment	Industrial Output Per Person	Gross Domestic Product Per Capita
	%	%		1948–1966		1950–1967
Area	(1)	(2)	(3)	(4)	(5)	(6)
Nonsocialist Countries						
Asia[3]	18	10	8.3	3.9	4.3	2.0
Latin America	29	15	5.8	2.0	3.7	2.1
Poor countries[4]	22	11	7.1	3.5	3.5	2.2
North America	32	28	4.7	1.0	3.7	2.2
Western Europe	37	33	6.3	1.6	4.6	3.5
Rich countries[5]	34	30	5.6	1.9	3.6	3.1

[1]Includes mining, manufacturing, electricity, gas, and water.
[2]All growth rates based on constant prices.
[3]Excludes Japan and Israel (and entire Middle East for growth of product per capita)
[4]Includes also Africa (minus South Africa)
[5]Includes also Australia, New Zealand, Japan, South Africa, and Israel.

SOURCES: (1) Calculated by aggregating country data (by gross domestic product) in United Nations, *Statistical Yearbook*, 1968, Table 186.
(2) Calculated by aggregating country data (by population) in International Labor Office, *Yearbook of Labor Statistics*, 1969, Table 2.
(3) Calculated from growth indices in United Nations, *ibid.*, Table 9.
(4) Calculated from growth indices in United Nations, *ibid.*, Table 10.
(5) Calculated from (3) and (4).
(6) Calculated from growth indices in United Nations, *ibid.*, Table 4.

tent that the former share exceeds the latter, the output per person in the industrial sector is greater than in the rest of the economy. The data in Table 10-J indicate that this is true in all areas but especially so in the poor countries where on the average 11 percent of the active population generates 22 percent of the total output.

The last two columns in Table 10-J show further that the rate of growth of output per person in the industrial sector is considerably more rapid than in the economy as a whole—especially in the poor countries. Thus the sector which is already characterized by a relatively high per capita output is increasing its per capita output more rapidly than the rest of the economy, thereby accentuating the differential. Barring major intervention by the state to redistribute income (highly unlikely in any capitalist country), the increasing sectoral inequality in per capita output will be matched by increasing sectoral inequality in per capita income. To the extent that income is also more unequally distributed *within* the industrial sector over time, the increasing sectoral inequality understates the increase in the inequality of income distribution among families or individuals.

Inequalities can at least in principle—if not in practice—be quantified. Subordination, especially in its political, cultural, and psychological manifestations, is almost impossible to measure statistically. To measure economic subordination, it would be desirable to have extensive data on foreign ownership and control of domestic resources and on the dependence of domestic enterprise on foreign assistance of one kind or another. In the absence of comprehensive published information on these subjects, one can only draw inferences from the limited data available.

The overall pattern of merchandise trade between the poor and the rich nonsocialist countries has not significantly changed in the postwar period: it is still dominated by

a flow of primary products from the poor to the rich countries and a flow of manufactured products in the reverse direction. Furthermore, in most areas of the underdeveloped world the deficit in the balance of trade increased as a proportion of domestic output during this period, giving rise to greater inflows of foreign capital and correspondingly higher levels of foreign debt.[9] The cumulative external debt of the poor countries more than doubled in the 1960s alone; by 1968, the sum of total debt payments and profit remittances from the poor to the rich nonsocialist countries exceeded 25 percent of export earnings in seven poor countries and exceeded 10 percent of export earnings in twenty-nine countries.[10] The increasing significance of foreign private investment in the poor countries can be gauged by the rapid growth of the foreign assets of the major capitalist investing country, the United States, form $5.7 billion in 1950 to $20 billion in 1969 (see Table 10-C).

It is quite clear from such data that there has been no major break in the postwar period with the pattern of economic subordination established in the poor countries in colonial times. The continuing economic subordination of most poor countries is reflected in the political sphere by a plethora of political and military alliances with the major capitalist powers.[11] These alliances

[9]For statistical documentation of the points made in the first two sentences of this paragraph, see Tables 7 and 8 of the original essay (cited in source line) from which this reading was drawn.

[10]These data are given in The Commission on International Development, *Partners in Development* (New York: Praeger Publishers, Inc., 1969), Annex II, Tables 9 and 11.

[11]As of 1969, the United States alone had "mutual defense" treaties with forty-five nations—most of them poor—and operated approximately four hundred major military bases in thirty-two overseas countries and territories. The U.S. provided military aid to fifty-eight foreign countries and trained military personnel from sixty-four countries. See *Global Defense: U.S. Military Commitments Abroad*, published by the Congressional Quarterly Service, September 1969.

not only directly limit the political autonomy of the weaker poor countries; they also strengthen the domestic classes most oriented to foreign interests and thereby indirectly further hamper the development of national autonomy.

CONCLUSION

Both the theoretical analysis and the empirical evidence presented above point to the likelihood of increasing subordination, increasing inequality and inadequate growth in poor countries that are integrated into the world capitalist system. These fundamental problems of underdevelopment are unlikely to be soluble without a complete break with capitalist institutions, both domestic and international.

SELECTIVE BIBLIOGRAPHY

The single most useful book on modern American imperialism is Magdoff [5], who focuses on the economic basis and structure of the new imperialism. Williams [8] provides an excellent historical account of the persistence of imperialist tendencies in the United States since the late nineteenth century; the shaping of an imperialist foreign policy is examined in a set of stimulating essays contained in Horowitz [3]. Turner [7] is a good and up-to-date source on the nature and functioning of the multinational corporation. Alternative theories of imperialism are considered and evaluated by Alavi [1], who stresses the changes in the nature of imperialism over time. Rhodes [6] reprints a valuable collection of essays dealing with various aspects of imperialism but particularly its impact on underdeveloped countries; the essays by Arrighi, Baran, and Frank are especially stimulating. A more thorough analysis of the predicament of the underdeveloped countries within the world capitalist system is presented by Baran [2], Chapters 5–7, and Jalee [4] provides much useful data on the uneven economic relations between the rich and the poor countries.

[1] Alavi, Hamza. "Imperialism: Old and New." In *The Socialist Register 1964.* Edited by Ralph Miliband and John Saville. New York: Monthly Rievew Press, 1964.

[2] Baran, Paul. *The Political Economy of Growth.* 2nd ed. New York: Monthly Review Press, 1962.*

[3] Horowitz, David, ed. *Corporations and the Cold War.* New York. Monthly Review Press, 1969.

[4] Jalee, Pierre. *Pillage of the Third World.* New York: Monthly Review Press, 1968.*

[5] Magdoff, Harry. *The Age of Imperialism.* New York: Monthly Review Press, 1969.*

[6] Rhodes, Robert, ed. *Imperialism and Underdevelopment.* New York: Monthly Review Press, 1970.*

[7] Turner, Louis. *Invisible Empires.* New York: Harcourt Brace & Jovanovich, Inc., 1971.

[8] Williams, William A. *The Tragedy of American Diplomacy.* New York: Dell Publishing Co., Inc., 1962.*

*Available in paperback editions.

PART **IV**

TOWARD
AN ALTERNATIVE
TO THE
CAPITALIST SYSTEM

Contradictions
of Advanced
Capitalism 11

AT THE PRESENT TIME THE CAPITALIST system is under severe attack from many quarters. Victims of inequality, alienation, racism, sexism, irrationality, and imperialism are engaged in simultaneous struggles to overcome their oppression, and they are finding that capitalism is one of their principal enemies. The very existence of such challenges suggests that capitalism is neither a smoothly operating system in which little protest is heard nor a system unsusceptible to any change. On the contrary, the entire history of the capitalist era has been marked by resistance from those whom capitalism has sought to subordinate. Often this resistance has been overcome only through the use of violent force and coercion by the state.

The social oppression which capitalism perpetuates and generates, and the protests and challenges that arise in response, lead us to the question: Is it ultimately possible to bring about a radical social transformation of capitalism, one that would result in a more humane society? We already know that to achieve a better society, a *radical* transformation of capitalism is necessary; we have seen in Part III that each of the forms of oppression that gave us titles to Chapters 5 to 10 are *functional* to the capitalist mode of production and will persist unless capitalism itself is fundamentally transformed.

Social systems do not fall simply because they are oppressive or considered by some to be unjust. Dynamic forces within capitalist society insure that *some* social change will take place; but this social change will not necessarily nor inevitably take the form of a fundamental transformation of the capitalist mode of production into a better society. Capitalism can be radically transformed only if it produces dysfunctional social forces that have the potential for fundamental change. Equally important, a radical transformation of capitalism can occur only if men and women understand the historical social forces at work in a capitalist society and intervene actively and collectively in a conscious attempt to direct and control those forces and turn them to desired human ends. In short, a strategy for radical social change must be based on an understanding of the *contradictions* at work in a capitalist society. The purpose of this chapter is to elucidate the principal contradictions of advanced capitalism.

What is meant by the term contradiction? By contradiction we mean more than simply a flaw in the logic of an argument or a conflict of interests. A contradiction of capitalism results when the very process of capitalist development produces simultaneously the conditions needed to transform it fundamentally; that is, when the successes of capitalist development create situations which are fundamentally antagonistic to capitalism itself. Contradictions tend to intensify with time and cannot be resolved within the existing social framework. In the following paragraphs we shall outline some of the domestic and international contradictions of advanced capitalism.

We have already noted that capitalism is not a static society. The production process itself is constantly being revolutionized and capital continually attempts to extend its area of influence and domination. But these developments contain major contradictions: They produce changes that ultimately call into question the social desirability of the capitalist drive for profits and the necessity of capitalist production relations. Capitalism has reached a stage where it is incompatible with and holds back the further development of human potentials and capacities.

On the one hand, capitalism promises to meet basic human needs but is increasingly unable to deliver on that promise. Throughout the underdeveloped world, and among the oppressed minorities in the developed countries—such as Blacks and Chicanos in the United States, Quebecois (French-Canadians) in Canada, and Catholics in Northern Ireland—it is apparent that real economic and social development is impossible within the confines of the international capitalist system. Capitalism by its very nature creates unequal development and is unable to institute economic reforms that would co-opt burgeoning anti-imperialist struggles for national liberation. Yet it is capitalism itself which, in attempting to extend its area of domination, promised economic development in these areas and created an awareness of the possibility of development. Capitalism thus becomes caught in a web of international contradictions.

In the developed world, where modern capitalism has delivered a wealth of material goods, it has sought to define well-being in terms of individual commodity consumption. But with continued economic growth, the desirability of more individual material consumption fades in comparison to other dimensions of well-being, such as the availability of creative and socially useful work, meaningful community, and liberating education for individual development. Yet, because capitalism must constantly expand, the realization of these needs is incompatible with capitalist relations of production. Instead, capitalist economic growth deepens the alienation of work and community, and poisons the environment, and commercializes all social relationships. People increasingly recognize that well-being consists of more than the individual acquisition and consumption of commodities, and that capitalism cannot meet their felt needs.

Moreover, capitalist economic growth itself becomes increasingly predicated on irrationality and production of waste (e.g., military and space expenditures and planned obsolescence in consumer goods) as production for profit increasingly subordinates production for use. Continued economic growth threatens the ecological balance of the earth, and the expanding role of the state in direct production and maintenance of economic growth both undermines the ideological legitimacy of private ownership of capital and politicizes the issue of economic priorities.

Equally important, the expansion of capitalist production draws an ever-increasing share of the population into alienating wage and salary work. Modern capitalist production has become incredibly complex and interdependent, requiring the drawing together and cooperation of labor from all over the globe. An enormous expansion in the size of the proletariat occurs within the United States as blacks and women increasingly join the ranks of wage and salary workers, and small entrepreneurial businessmen and professional white-collar workers are subordinated to large capital. The proletarianization of these groups produces an awareness of the constraints of capitalist production relations; the oppression of women and blacks becomes linked to their oppression as workers.

At the same time, the internationalization of capital, accelerated by developments in high-speed communications and transportation, creates a worldwide proletariat and necessarily heightens the awareness within the United States of social interdependence with the Third World. The interrelationships between the logic of capitalism at home and abroad become clearer. Thus, the war in Vietnam exposes the destructive effect of U.S. foreign policy on poor nations and reveals the linkages between poverty, racism, and sexism at home and imperialism abroad.

Finally, as production has grown in complexity, capitalism requires a more skilled work force—workers with more developed capabilities. The simple rote tasks of the past are replaced by work which involves a certain degree of initiative and autonomy, some ability to conceptualize, analyze, and synthesize, and a more active involvement of workers in the production process; but by educating workers capitalism provides them both with a greater awareness of their material and emotional needs and the capacity to grasp the system's essential irrationality. This leads very quickly to questioning the present hierarchical social division of labor and distribution of power.

In these ways capitalism becomes increasingly caught in its own contradictions. Capitalist development generates expectations that it cannot fulfill. As the impoverishment of daily life deepens, the gap between people's felt needs and what capitalism can deliver grows wider, and both the necessity for and feasibility of radical social change become widely recognized. As the capitalist class appears more and more parasitic and the capitalistic system less and less instrumental to the welfare of society as a whole, each of the oppressive social problems discussed in Chapters 5 to 10 become a locus around which opposition to capitalist society can develop. It is not surprising that the revolts from the Third World, blacks, women, students, and factory and office workers against inequality, alienation, racism, sexism, irrationality, and imperialism have grown in frequency and intensity in recent years.

However, the emergence of contradictions in advanced capitalism is not sufficient by itself to insure the fundamental transformation of capitalism. Indeed, there are countless examples of spontaneous individual protests and rebellions that are either self-destructive, because they strike at wrong targets, or strike in a purely symbolic and ineffectual way, or become coopted and commercialized as part of the capitalist system itself. Fundamental social change will occur only if a self-conscious class emerges and engages in organized political struggle around the contradictions of capitalism in such a way as to challenge the basic capitalist relations of production, for capitalism will not "evolve" or "develop naturally" into the transformed society we desire.

The capitalist class is a privileged and exploiting class, and it is not about to give up its special place without resistance. In the absence of a conscious political movement, the capitalist class will always be able to obfuscate and mystify discontent, offer sham concessions, co-opt leaders and causes, divide the movement, and suppress movement organizations. What it cannot do, however, is to resolve the contradictions of advanced capitalism. Only a change in the mode of production can do that.

One final implication of our analysis should be noted. Precisely because advanced capitalism has sought to reorganize and commercialize every aspect of daily life, the transformation of capitalism cannot be separated from the overthrow of all forms of oppression with which capitalism has associated itself. Purely economic exploitation, as we have argued, is significantly intertwined by capitalist development with dehumanization in psychological, cultural, racial, sexual, and other dimensions. All oppressed groups share a certain solidarity in that each is struggling for self-determination. At any one time the contradictions around particular forms of oppression may be sharper than around others. But the revolutionary process is not reducible to struggle against economic exploitation or the alienation of labor; it must incorporate simultaneous struggles against dehumanization in *all* its forms. That is, it must articulate and struggle for a vision of a liberated society, in which all social relations are transformed and all hierarchical divisions of labor are abolished.

11.1 *The Development of a Revolutionary Proletariat*

During most of its lifetime, capitalism has been extensively challenged by its industrial workers. We begin this chapter with a second reading from the *Communist Manifesto*[1] in which Karl Marx and Friedrich Engels described the social forces in nineteenth-century capitalism that they expected would weld the developing industrial proletariat into a revolutionary force. Although the industrial proletariat did not rise to break its chains in the revolutionary manner foreseen by Marx and Engels in 1848, this account is important and instructive in illustrating Marx's *method* of analysis. This method remains useful in exploring the contradictions of contemporary capitalism, and it will be applied to that end in the succeeding readings in this chapter.

It is important to note that the *Communist Manifesto* was not just a detached scientific inquiry. In another place, Marx once said that "the philosophers have only interpreted the world, in various ways; the point, however, is to change it."[2] In this same spirit the *Manifesto* was intended to help bring about the very changes that it "predicted" on the basis of scientific reasoning.

[1] An earlier part of the *Manifesto* is reprinted in Marx and Engels, Section 2.5, p. 66.
[2] *Theses on Feuerbach*, XI.

Source: The following is excerpted from *The Communist Manifesto* by KARL MARX and FRIEDRICH ENGELS (first published in 1848).

With the development of industry the proletariat not only increases in numbers; it becomes concentrated in greater masses, its strength grows, and it feels its strength more. The various interests and conditions of life within the ranks of the proletariat are more and more equalized, in proportion as machinery obliterates all distinctions of labor and nearly everywhere reduces wages to the same low level. The growing competition among the bourgeois, and the resulting commercial crises, make the wages of the workers ever more fluctuating. The unceasing improvement of machinery, ever more rapidly developing, makes their livelihood more and more precarious; the collisions between individual workmen and individual bourgeois take more and more the character of collisions between two classes. Thereupon the workers begin to form combinations (trade unions) against the bourgeoisie; they club together in order to keep up the rate of wages; they found permanent associations in order to make provision beforehand for these occasional revolts. Here and there the contest breaks out into riots.

Now and then the workers are victorious, but only for a time. The real fruit of their battles lies, not in the immediate result, but in the ever expanding union of the workers. This union is furthered by the improved means of communication which are created by modern industry, and which place the workers of different localities in contact with one another. It was just this contact that was needed to centralize the numerous local struggles, all of the same character, into one national struggle between classes. But every class struggle is a political struggle. And that union, to attain which the burghers of the Middle Ages, with their miserable highways, required centuries, the modern proletarians, thanks to railways, achieve in a few years.

This organization of the proletarians into a class, and consequently into a political party, is continually being upset again by the competition between the workers themselves. But it ever rises up again, stronger, firmer, mightier. It compels legislative recognition of particular interests of the workers, by taking advantage of the divisions among the bourgeoisie itself. Thus the ten-hour bill in England was carried.

Altogether, collisions between the classes of the old society further the course of development of the proletariat in many ways. The bourgeoisie finds itself involved in a constant battle. At first with the aristocracy; later on, with those portions of the bourgeoisie itself whose interests have become antagonistic to the progress of industry; at all times with the bourgeoisie of foreign countries. In all these battles it sees itself compelled to appeal to the proletariat, to ask for its help, and thus, to drag it into the political arena. The bourgeoise itself, therefore, supplies the proletariat with its own elements of political and general education, in other words, it furnishes the proletariat with weapons for fighting the bourgeoisie.

Further, as we have already seen, entire sections of the ruling classes are, by the advance of industry, precipitated into the proletariat, or are at least threatened in their conditions of existence. These also supply the proletariat with fresh elements of enlightenment and progress.

Finally, in times when the class struggle nears the decisive hour, the process of dissolution going on within the ruling class, in fact within the whole range of old society, assumes such a violent, glaring character, that a small section of the ruling class cuts itself adrift, and joins the revolutionary class, the class that holds the future in its hands. Just as, therefore, at an earlier period, a section of the nobility went over to the bourgeoisie, so now a portion of the bourgeoisie goes over to the proletariat, and in particular, a portion of the bourgeois ideologists, who have raised themselves to the level of comprehending theoretically the historical movement as a whole.

Of all the classes that stand face to face with the bourgeoisie today, the proletariat alone is a really revolutionary class. The other classes decay and finally disappear in the face of modern industry; the proletariat is its special and essential product.

The lower middle class, the small manufacturer, the shopkeeper, the artisan, the peasant, all these fight against the bourgeoisie, to save from extinction their existence as fractions of the middle class. They are therefore not revolutionary, but conservative. Nay more, they are reactionary, for they try to roll back the wheel of history. If by chance they are revolutionary, they are so only in view of their impending transfer into the proletariat; they thus defend not their present, but their future interests; they desert their own standpoint to adopt that of the proletariat.

The "dangerous class," the social scum (*Lumpenproletariat),* that passively rotting mass thrown off by the lowest layers of old society, may, here and there, be swept into the movement by a proletarian revolution; its conditions of life, however, prepare it far more for the part of a bribed tool of reactionary intrigue.

The social conditions of the old society no longer exist for the proletariat. The proletarian is without property; his relation to his wife and children has no longer anything in common with bourgeois family relations; modern industrial labor, modern subjection to capital, the same in England as in France, in America as in Germany, has stripped him of every trace of national character. Law, morality, religion, are to him so many bourgeois prejudices, behind which lurk in ambush just as many bourgeois interests.

All the preceding classes that got the upper hand, sought to fortify their already acquired status by subjecting society at large to their conditions of appropriation. The proletarians cannot become masters of the productive forces of society, except by abolishing their own previous mode of appropriation, and thereby also every other previous mode of appropriation. They have nothing of their own to secure and to fortify; their mission is to destroy all previous securities for, and insurances of, individual property.

All previous historical movements were movements of minorities, or in the interest of minorities. The proletarian movement is the self-conscious, independent movement of the immense majority, in the interest of the immense majority. The proletariat, the lowest stratum of our present society, cannot stir, cannot raise itself up, without the whole superincumbent strata of official society being sprung into the air.

Though not in substance, yet in form, the struggle of the proletariat with the bourgeoisie is at first a national struggle. The proletariat of each country must, of course, first of all settle matters with its own bourgeoisie.

In depicting the most general phases of the development of the proletariat, we traced the more or less veiled civil war, raging within existing society, up to the point where that war breaks out into open revolution, and where the violent overthrow of the bourgeoisie lays the foundation for the sway of the proletariat.

Hitherto, every form of society has been based, as we have already seen, on the antagonism of oppressing and oppressed classes. But in order to oppress a class, certain conditions must be assured to it under which it can, at least, continue its slavish existence. The serf, in the period of serfdom, raised himself to membership in the commune, just as the petty bourgeois, under the yoke of feudal absolutism, managed to de-

velop into a bourgeois. The modern laborer, on the contrary, instead of rising with the progress of industry, sinks deeper and deeper below the conditions of existence of his own class. He becomes a pauper, and pauperism develops more rapidly than population and wealth. And here it becomes evident, that the bourgeoisie is unfit any longer to be the ruling class in society, and to impose its conditions of existence upon society as an overriding law. It is unfit to rule because it is incompetent to assure an existence to its slave within his slavery, because it cannot help letting him sink into such a state, that it has to feed him, instead of being fed by him. Society can no longer live under this bourgeoisie, in other words, its existence is no longer compatible with society.

The essential condition for the existence and sway of the bourgeois class, is the formation and augmentation of capital; the condition for capital is wage-labor. Wage-labor rests exclusively on competition between the laborers. The advance of industry, whose involuntary promoter is the bourgeoisie, replaces the isolation of the laborers, due to competition, by their revolutionary combination, due to association. The development of modern industry, therefore, cuts from under its feet the very foundation on which the bourgeoisie produces and appropriates products. What the bourgeoisie therefore produces, above all, are its own grave-diggers. Its fall and the victory of the proletariat are equally inevitable.

.   .   .

11.2 International Contradictions of Advanced Capitalism

The evolution of modern capitalism has created a worldwide international system dominated economically by a few giant, multinational corporations and dominated politically by the United States. This evolution has produced new tensions for capitalism. The following reading combines ex-

cerpts from two separate sources to present an exposition of the significance of international contradictions to the capitalist system. In Part I,
Paul Sweezy argues that the decline of revolutionary consciousness among
the industrial proletariat in advanced capitalist countries has resulted from
the development of modern methods of production. As documented in an
earlier reading,[1] the modern capitalist labor force has become increasingly
stratified and differentiated with the growth of hierarchy in production,
the growth of white-collar occupations, and the relative decline in importance of the blue-collar workforce. Nonetheless, according to Sweezy,
the basic Marxian analysis of the contradictions and ultimate overthrow
of capitalism remains valid. For capitalism must be recognized and analyzed as a global system within which revolutionary class conflict is very
much alive—although its primary locus has shifted from the advanced
to the underdeveloped countries.

In part II of this reading, drawn from the closing pages of their book
Monopoly Capital, Paul Baran and Paul Sweezy argue that anti-imperialist
movements in the underdeveloped countries do indeed present revolutionary challenges to the world capitalist system dominated by the United
States. They find the capitalist system incapable of containing revolutionary
struggles with adequate reforms, and they contend that this failure will
help to reveal the irrationality of the present system to people within the
United States.

[1]See Reich, Section 4.5, p. 174.

Source: Part I of the following is excerpted from "Marx and the Pro-
letariat" by PAUL SWEEZY. From the *Monthly Review* 19, No. 7
(December 1967). Copyright © 1967 by Monthly Review, Inc. Reprinted
by permission of Monthly Review, Inc. Part II is excerpted from
Chapter 11 of *Monopoly Capital* by PAUL BARAN and PAUL SWEEZY.
Copyright © 1966 by Paul Sweezy. Reprinted by permission of Monthly
Review Press.

Part I

Marx's theory of capitalism, which was
sketched with broad and sweeping strokes in
the *Communist Manifesto* and achieved its
most comprehensive and polished form in
the first volume of Capital . . . holds that
capitalism is a self-contradictory system
which generates increasingly severe difficulties and crises as it develops. But this is only
half the story: equally characteristic of capitalism is that it generates not only difficulties and crises but also its own grave-diggers
in the shape of the modern proletariat. A
social system can be ever so self-contradictory and still be without a revolutionary

potential: the outcome can be, and in fact
history shows many examples where it has
been, stagnation, misery, starvation, subjugation by a stronger and more vigorous society.
In Marx's view capitalism was not such a
society; it was headed not for slow death or
subjugation but for a thorough-going revolutionary transformation. And the reason was
precisely because by its very nature it had
to produce the agent which would revolu-
tionize it. This is the crucially important role
which the proletariat plays in the Marxian
theoretical schema.

In the eyes of many people, including not
a few who consider themselves to be essentially Marxists, this theory of the revolu-

tionary agency of the proletariat is the weakest point of the whole system. They point to the fact that the English and other Western European proletariats, which Marx considered to be the vanguard of the international revolutionary movement, have actually developed into reformist forces which, by accepting the basic assumptions of capitalism, in fact strengthen it. And they note that the proletariat of what has become the most advanced and powerful capitalist country, the United States of America, has never developed a significant revolutionary leadership or movement, and shows fewer signs of doing so today than at any time in its history.

I do not believe that the empirical observations which support this type of criticism of Marx's theory can be seriously challenged. And yet it certainly will not do to jump from there to the conclusion that Marx's theory is "refuted" and must be abandoned.

. . .

I will restrict myself to indicating in a very general way why the advance of modern technology tends to shape a proletariat which is less rather than more revolutionary than that which emerged from the industrial revolution in the middle of the nineteenth century.

I would not put the main emphasis on the consequences of technological change for the workers who actually mind the machines and do functionally similar work, much of it virtually unknown in Marx's time, such as manning assembly lines. These are still for the most part dehumanizing jobs requiring little skill; and speed-up of machinery and increasing work loads certainly do not make them more bearable, not to say attractive. A proletariat dominated by operatives of this general description might well have as great a revolutionary potential as its mid-nineteenth-century predecessor. The point is that relative to the total work force there are so many fewer jobs of this kind than there used to be. Progressive mechanization of

particular processes, and more recently the perfection of generally applicable methods of partial or full automation, have reduced this traditional blue-collar segment of the proletariat from what was once a large majority to what is today in the most industrialized societies a small minority. Since the output of this minority has at the same time enormously increased, it is clear that modern technology has multiplied the productivity of labor many times over and put within society's grasp a potential surplus of vast proportions.

The obverse of this development is that a great variety of new categories of jobs has been created. Some of these are integrally related to the new technology—scientists, researchers, engineers, technicians, highly skilled maintenance and repair men, etc.—but many more (both absolutely and relatively) are concerned in one way or another with the manipulation and absorption of the surplus made possible by the increased productivity of the underlying production workers. Under this heading one could list government workers of all kinds, including teachers; those employed in the many branches of the sales apparatus, including most of the personnel of the mass communication media; workers and salaried personnel in finance, insurance, and real estate; and the providers of many different kinds of personal services from beauty treatment to sports spectacles. In the United States today these job categories, taken all together, probably account for close to three quarters of the employed nonagricultural labor force.

In terms of the occupational composition of the labor force, then, the two chief consequences of modern industry's revolutionary technology have been (1) a drastic (and continuing) reduction in the production-worker component, and (2) a vast proliferation of job categories in the distribution and service sectors of the economy. At the same time there has taken place a slow but cumulatively substantial increase in the real wages

of both production and nonproduction workers. In part this reflects an increase in the
cost of production of labor power as the educational and training requirements of the
new employment categories have risen. And
in part it reflects the fact that the workers—
and here we mean primarily production
workers—have been able through nonrevolutionary class struggle to wrest from the
capitalists a part of the fruits of increasing
productivity.

To sum up: The revolutionary technology
of modern industry, correctly described and
analyzed by Marx, has had the effect of multiplying by many times the productivity of
basic production workers. This in turn has
resulted in a sharp reduction in their relative
importance in the labor force, in the proliferation of new job categories, and in a
gradually rising standard of living for employed workers. In short, the first effects of
the introduction of machinery—expansion
and homogenization of the labor force and
reduction in the costs of production (value)
or labor power—have been largely reversed.
Once again, as in the period of manufacture,
the proletariat is highly differentiated; and
once again occupational and status consciousness has tended to submerge class consciousness.

It might be thought that despite these
changes the blue-collar proletariat would remain a revolutionary element within the
working class as a whole. No doubt there is
a tendency for this to happen, and it would
be short-sighted in the extreme to overlook
the revolutionary potential still remaining in
this large body of workers. But one must not
go too far in isolating them from the rest of
the labor force. As James Boggs says: "Today most workers in the plant [i.e. blue-
collar workers] have been to high school and
quite a few have even been to college. All
either plan or wish to send their sons and
daughters to college—their sons so they
won't have to work in the factory on what
they call a dull and automated job; their

daughters . . . so they won't have to marry
some bum but can make their own living
and be free to decide whether they want to
marry or not marry. . . ." (*The American
Revolution*, p. 14.) In other words, blue-
collar workers, being a diminishing minority
of the whole working class, do not think of
their families as permanently stuck in the
stratum which they occupy. As long as this
is so, their attitudes and ideology are not
likely to be radically different from those of
the nonrevolutionary majority of the working class which surrounds them.

. . .

The belief that the *industrial* proletariat is
the only possible revolutionary agent under
capitalism stems from focusing attention too
exclusively on the advanced capitalist countries where modern industry got its start
and where the new technology has had a
chance to develop under favorable conditions. But capitalism as a social order has
never consisted only of industrialized countries. In fact, as Marx explicitly recognized,
the industrialization of some countries had
as its counterpart from the outset the non-
industrialization of others, with the two sets
of countries being integrally tied together in
a single-system.

> So soon . . . as the general conditions re-
> quisite for production by the modern in-
> dustrial system have been established, this
> mode of production acquires an elasticity,
> a capacity for sudden extension by leaps
> and bounds that finds no hindrance except
> in the supply of raw material and in the
> disposal of the produce. On the one hand,
> the immediate effect of machinery is to in-
> crease the supply of raw material in the
> same way, for example, as the cotton gin
> augmented the production of cotton. On the
> other hand, the cheapness of the articles
> produced by machinery, and the improved
> means of transport and communications
> furnish the weapons for conquering foreign
> markets. By ruining handicraft production
> in other countries, machinery forcibly con-
> verts them into fields for the supply of its
> raw material. In this way East India was

compelled to produce cotton, wool, hemp, jute, and indigo for Great Britain. . . . A new and international division of labor, a division suited to the requirements of the chief centers of modern industry springs up, and converts one part of the globe into a chiefly agricultural field of production for supplying the other part which remains a chiefly industrial field. (Capital, *Vol. I,* pp. 492–93.)

Once it is recognized that capitalism is not and never has been confined to one or more industrializing countries but is rather a global system embracing both the (relatively few) industrializing countries and their (relatively numerous) satellites and dependencies, it becomes quite clear that the future of the system cannot be adequately analyzed in terms of the forces at work in any part of the system but must take full account of the *modus operandi* of the system as a whole.

Lenin was the first Marxist to see this and to begin work on the theoretical extensions and reformulations which it made necessary. His major contribution was his little book *Imperialism: the Highest Stage of Capitalism* which, having been published in 1917, is exactly half as old as the first volume of *Capital.* There he argued that "Capitalism has grown into a world system of colonial oppression and of the financial strangulation of the overwhelming majority of the people of the world by a handful of 'advanced' countries. And this 'booty' is shared between two or three powerful world pirates armed to the teeth. . . ." He also argued that the capitalists of the imperialist countries could and do use a part of their "booty" to bribe and win over to their side an aristocracy of labor. As far as the logic of the argument is concerned, it could be extended to a majority or even all the workers in the industrialized countries. In any case it is clear that taking account of the global character of the capitalist system provides strong additional reasons for believing that the tendency in this stage of capitalist development

will be to generate a less rather than a more revolutionary proletariat.

But once again the coin has two sides. If imperialist exploitation brings wealth to the industrialized countries and enables them to raise further the standard of living of their working classes, it brings poverty and misery to the great mass of the working people —agricultural as well as industrial—in the dependencies. These masses now become an agent of revolutionary change in precisely the sense that Marx believed the industrial proletariat of the mid-nineteenth century to be. . . . And does not the pattern of successful socialist revolutions since the Second World War—highlighted by Vietnam, China, and Cuba—demonstrate beyond any doubt that these masses do indeed constitute a revolutionary agent capable of challenging and defeating capitalism?

.   .   .

Part II

The United States dominates and exploits to one extent or another all the countries and territories of the so-called "free world" and correspondingly meets with varying degrees of resistance. The highest form of resistance is revolutionary war aimed at withdrawal from the world capitalist system and the initiation of social and economic reconstruction on a socialist basis. Such warfare has never been absent since the Second World War, and the revolutionary peoples have achieved a series of historic victories in Vietnam, China, Korea, Cuba, and Algeria. These victories, taken together with the increasingly obvious inability of the underdeveloped countries to solve their problems within the framework of the world capitalist system, have sown the seeds of revolution throughout the continents of Asia, Africa, and Latin America. Some of these seeds will sprout and ripen rapidly, others slowly, still others perhaps not until after a long period of germination. What seems in any case clear is that they are now implanted beyond any prospect of extirpation. It is no longer mere rhetoric to speak of the world revolution: the term describes what is already a reality and is certain to become increasingly the dominant characteristic of the historical epoch in which we live.

The implications of this fact for the future of monopoly capitalism are only beginning to become apparent. The ruling class of the United States understands, instinctively and through experience, that every advance of the world revolution is a defeat —economic, political, and moral—for itself. It is determined to resist such advances wherever they may threaten, by whatever means may be available; and it counts on its enormous superiority in the technology of warfare to bring it victory. But the truth is that in this struggle there can be no real victories for the counter-revolutionary side. Underlying the revolutionary upsurge are real economic, social, and demographic problems; and it is the very nature of counter-revolution to prevent these problems from being rationally attacked, let alone solved. Counter-revolution may win, indeed already has won, many battles, but the war goes on and inexorably spreads to new peoples and new regions. And as it spreads so does the involvement of the United States.

No one can now foresee all the consequences for the United States of this increasing commitment to the cause of world counter-revolution, but equally no one can doubt that it will profoundly affect the inner as well as the outer course of events. In the long run its main impact may well be on the youth of the nation. The need for military manpower seems certain to rise sharply; it may soon be normal for young Americans to spend several years of their lives, if they are lucky enough to survive, fighting in the jungles and mountains of Asia, Africa, and Latin America. The psychic stress and physical suffering experienced by them and their families will add a new

dimension to the agony inflicted by an anti-human social order. Will the effect be merely to hasten the process of decay already so far advanced? Will the shock perhaps awaken more and more people to the urgent need for basic change? Or will, as some believe, the increasingly evident hopelessness of its cause lead the American ruling class to the ultimate irrationality of unleashing nuclear holocaust?

That no one can now answer these questions means that all the options are not foreclosed, that action aimed at altering the course of events has a chance to succeed. There are even indications, especially in the Negro freedom movement in the South, in the uprisings of the urban ghettos, and in the academic community's mounting protest against the war in Vietnam, that significant segments of the American people are ready to join an active struggle against what is being cumulatively revealed as an intolerable social order. If this is so, who can set limits to the numbers who may join them in the future?

But even if the present protest movements should suffer defeat or prove abortive, that would be no reason to write off permanently the possibility of a real revolutionary movement in the United States. As the world revolution spreads and as the socialist countries show by their example that it is possible to use man's mastery over the forces of nature to build a rational society satisfying the human needs of human beings, more and more Americans are bound to question the necessity of what they now take for granted. And once that happens on a mass scale, the most powerful supports of the present irrational system will crumble and the problem of creating anew will impose itself as a sheer necessity. This will not happen in five years or ten, perhaps not in the present century: few great historical dramas run their course in so short a time. But perhaps even fewer, once they are fairly started, change their nature or reverse their direction until all their potentialities have been revealed. The drama of our time is the world revolution; it can never come to an end until it has encompassed the whole world.

In the meantime, what we in the United States need is historical perspective, courage to face the facts, and faith in mankind and its future. Having these, we can recognize our moral obligation to devote ourselves to fighting against an evil and destructive system which maims, oppresses, and dishonors those who live under it, and which threatens devastation and death to millions of others around the globe.

11.3   *From Petrograd to Saigon*

In the past two decades, the most damaging and significant challenges to the hegemony of the capitalist system have come from the people of Vietnam. The struggles and victories of the Vietnamese have produced repercussions that undermine capitalism not only in the underdeveloped world but also in the developed countries.

In the following reading Goran Therborn analyzes the meaning and consequences of the Vietnam War, now the Second War of Indochina, in these terms. Whereas the Cold War *blocked* the contradictions within capitalism, the Indochina War has *reactivated* the internal contradictions within the United States. The international military operations of the world's foremost capitalist democracy increasingly reveal themselves as logical outcomes and not aberrations of the capitalist mode of production. In this way they cast a searchlight upon the domestic inadequacies of Western society, and the profound crisis of the international capitalist system penetrates the United States itself.

Source: The following is excerpted from "From Petrograd to Saigon" by GORAN THERBORN. From the *New Left Review*, No. 48, (March-April 1968). Reprinted by permission of the *New Left Review*.

The staggering blows that the National Liberation Front has now dealt the American military expedition in Vietnam have changed history. When some half a million American troops with enormous technological superiority are no longer capable of keeping even the U.S. Embassy in Saigon safe, the most rabid spokesmen of imperialism have temporarily lapsed into a stunned silence. The incredible heroism of the Vietnamese militants has awed the world. They have proved, once and for all, that revolutionary peoples, not imperialism, are invincible. Socialists everywhere owe them an immense homage.

. . .

To understand the meaning and consequences of the Vietnamese War today, a comparison of it and the classical phase of the Cold War, above all in Europe, is essential. This is the fundamental context in which it emerges with all its explosive force. For American imperialism is fighting the Vietnamese Revolution today with the identical ideological banner—Anticommunism—under which it trampled on the Greek Revolution twenty years ago. Yet the outcome and impact of the conflict has been totally different. Why?

THE STRUCTURE OF THE COLD WAR

No properly constituted theory of the Cold War exists. But its essential political character is clear. *The Cold War was a fundamentally unequal conflict, that was presented and experienced on both sides as being equal.* The Soviet Union was put forward as a direct alternative model of society to that of the Western capitalist countries. The conflict was seen, both within the Communist movement and within capitalism, as a struggle as to which was the better society, compared at a single moment of time. Posed like this, the conflict was inevitably detrimental to the advance of socialism everywhere. For Russia in no way represented an equivalent economic base to that of Western Europe or the United States. It was still a society marked by poverty and scarcity, aggravated by the tremendous losses and devastations of the Second World War, and engaged in the inhuman imperatives of isolated primitive accumulation. (This condition naturally determined its relationship to the countries of Eastern Europe.) The affluent and advanced West was never deeply challenged from within by this social model. Russia was manifestly authoritarian and violent, whereas Western capitalist societies had in most cases a long bourgeois-democratic tradition. But politically, violence and bureaucracy was pitted, without historical mediations, against the bland parliamentarianism of the West, in a world where socialism was an encircled enclave within the world imperialist economy. This was the meaning and genesis of the Cold War. The specific form taken by the contradiction between socialism and capitalism thus determined an internal neutralization of the contradictions within capitalism. The working class was by and large mobilized in the anticommunist crusade, because of its fear of the Soviet model, symbolized by a regime of shortages and repression. Both economic and political "competition" between the blocs was, under these circumstances, to the advantage of the West.

Neither, in the form they took, threatened bourgeois rationality. While the U.S.S.R., anyway a vastly poorer society, was shattered by the German invasion, the USA—already much the wealthiest society in the world—emerged not merely unscathed but actually economically assisted by the war. It was thus able to pour a profusion of dollars into Western Europe (while the U.S.S.R. was securing reparations from Eastern Europe), and get it on the path of a successful capitalist restoration and reconstruction, greatly strengthened by the armaments boom of the fifties. Saturated with Cold War ideology, the working class in the West was by and large enlisted in the cause of the Truman Doctrine and Nato, the defenders of both freedom (parliament) and prosperity (free enterprise) from the evils of international Communism. The Communists in Italy, France, Finland and elsewhere retrenched themselves in isolated enclaves, and waited for the international situation to change. The nonCommunist Left was crushed or compromised. The Cold War, fought out as a competitive conflict between the USSR and the USA in Europe, resulted in the massive political and ideological consolidation of capitalism in the West. *An unequal conflict fought as equal redoubles the inequality.* The Cold War was a long penalization of socialism.

THE STRUCTURE OF THE WAR
OF NATIONAL LIBERATION: VIETNAM

The contemporary conflict between imperialism and national liberation, of which the war in Vietnam is the principal aspect today, is totally different in structure. *It is a conflict between unequal forces presented and lived as unequal.* There is no question of any comparison between the desperately deprived and rebellious workers and peasants of Asia, Africa and Latin America and the wealthy capitalist societies of the West which sends its praetorians to obliterate

them. The very essence of the struggle between them is their incommensurability.
This, indeed, is the meaning of the military
form of the conflict. The Cold War was a
struggle on the same plane between two
forces at different levels. The protracted war
of a guerrilla army against an imperialist
military expedition is the armed expression
of a conflict where the inequality of the parties is matched by a struggle on disparate
planes—each party fighting on different terrain. All of Mao's writings on guerrilla warfare are concerned with this fundamental
strategic asymmetry. The rule is, of course,
that normally there is only a one-way connection between the two planes. Successfully
fought and led, the guerrilla army can erode
and eventually disintegrate the social, political and military position of its cumber-
some conventional enemy, while the latter
unavailingly unleashes its technological fury
on the population—before being decisively
defeated.

But this strategic asymmetry reflects a
deeper historical relationship. The struggle
in Vietnam today and Cuba yesterday is for
liberation from imperialist exploitation and
oppression. Given the global structure of
capitalism, this means not merely secession
from, but a frontal attack on, capitalism as
a system and the bourgeois rationality that
integrates it. Two social models are now in
a quite new relationship with each other.
Socialist liberation in Vietnam does not
compete with U.S. capitalism, it focuses a
diamond light on the internal structure of
the rich capitalist societies which compels
their negation of the freedom and development of other societies. Thus whereas the
"competitive" contradiction between socialism and capitalism during the Cold War
blocked the contradictions within capitalism,
the Vietnamese conflict has *detonated* the
contradictions with U.S. capitalism itself.
For there is now no question of comparing
a scarcity political model with the affluent
societies of the West—the ideological device which successfully mystified a genera-

tion of the Western proletariat.[1] On the contrary, the ideologies of imperialism and
racism with which the U.S.A. is fighting the
war in Vietnam have recoiled on it. The
war in Asia has triggered a war in the ghettoes. For the young in the West, the examples of dedication and heroism are now
drawn from the movements of liberation in
Asia, Africa and Latin America.

Socialism here is no longer a dull, harsh
austerity threatening the consumers of the
West, but a heroic fight by exploited and
starving peoples for a human existence, denied them by imperialism and its lackeys. It
is no longer an alien social mode, but an
immediate ideological inspiration—a source
of emulation. The Vietnamese Revolution
has thus done what no other economic or
political force in the world has achieved for
thirty years—it has shattered the cemented
unity of American society and at last *reactivated* its internal contradictions. The potential shift in the international class struggle
that this represents is enormous, and may
still not be perceived by those whose political horizons have become habituated to a
world in which the citadel of imperialism
was itself an undivided monolith. The emergence of a militant, revolutionary Left in the
U.S.A.—no matter how quantitatively limited as yet—is a tremendous change in
world politics. The most lucid spokesmen of
imperialism are aware of this today, and
they fear more than anything else the impact of the Vietnamese War at home.

The Vietnamese War, then, shows that
*an unequal struggle waged as unequal equal-
izes the inequality*. All the political and
ideological consequences in the world at

---

[1] It might be added that the abandonment of
the comparison of socialist accumulation with
capitalist affluence has been accompanied, in
China, Cuba, and North Vietnam, by a new
theoretical and political insistence on economic
egalitarianism (criticized in the U.S.S.R. during
the thirties). The Cultural Revolution, the "simultaneous construction of socialism and communism" in Cuba, and the war-time practice of
the DRV share this preoccupation.

large are reversed. Imperialism today is on the defensive. The social peace installed by the Cold War is disintegrating in the vortex of the Vietnamese War. The tranquil conscience of 1949 has become the brutalized demoralization of 1968. The mass defection of hithero conventionally anticommunist American intelligentsia from the Johnson administration and its war is the most evident sign today of this extraordinary transformation.

.   .   .

THE NATURE OF THE RESISTANCE: NLF AND DRV

The crimes committed in Vietnam today are not committed by a Nazi Germany or a colonial France. They are committed by the "Land of the Free," the world's premier bourgeois democracy. They thus lead, without any confusion or side issue, straight to the political core of the system that perpetrates them: capitalism. The Vietnamese War has produced a parallel unprecedented focusing of the essential conflicts on the other side. The Cold War did not pass uninterruptedly into the Vietnamese conflict, of course. There was a considerable intermediary phase, during which détente developed in Europe. Destalinization and polycentrism greatly modified the communist world. Abroad, "neutralism" had become the official doctrine of many ex-colonial countries within the capitalist system, while sentimentalism about underdevelopment often replaced aggressive Cold War liberalism. In the West, some important internal anomalies began to be rediscovered by the Left. The myths of social equality and the abolition of poverty were exploded; structural unemployment and urban neglect reemerged as major political issues. In this context, identification with the cause of the oppressed peoples of the three continents became increasingly frequent among the young on the Left—but often still in the form of a well-meaning anticolonialism dissociated from any understanding of the concrete dynamics of class

struggle, in the age of imperialism. An important example of this new phenomenon was the antinuclear movement (CND) in Britain. We know that CND never theoretically and strategically assumed the challenge it constituted to the "whole contemporary teleology of British society." It rebelled against the ideological positions of both East and West, but it never developed any other articulated theory and ideology at all. It was quite natural that the antinuclear and neutralist movements should never have done so, because such a theory would have undermined the whole ideological rationale of the movements, showing the inevitability of the Cold War, given the irreconcilability of capitalism and socialism and the current structures of that conflict. But in the absence of such a theory, the movements soon collapsed, leaving a very modest inheritance indeed. The Cuban Revolution, with its decisive option for Marxism and Leninism, had already rendered this tendency obsolete.

Today, the Vietnamese Revolution has radically changed the coordinates of the situation. For just as it is the world's major bourgeois democracy which is waging an imperialist war in Vietnam, so the Vietnamese Revolution is organized and led—superbly—by communist revolutionaries. The Vietnamese Revolution is not inspired by any cloudy "Third World" doctrines, but by the ideas of Marx and Lenin. There is thus no room for any ambiguity on the central issue. Opposition to the American War in Vietnam sooner or later logically implies support for a socialist revolution led by Marxists and supported by a communist State. Increasingly, even one-time Cold War liberals in the U.S.A. have admitted this logic and publicly affirmed their support for the NLF.

The political lesson, of course, is that only such a Marxist-Leninist ideology and organization today can prevail over the juggernaut of American imperialism: resistance movements all over the world will remember this from now on. But within the West, the lesson is no less salutary. The most sacred beliefs of the Cold War are being widely rejected by the young. The antinuclear movement was an opposition against a conflictual relationship between the capitalist and socialist Big Powers, stressing what united them, the threat of nuclear annihilation. The Vietnam movement, on the other hand, is based on opposition against an imperialist war waged by the leading capitalist state against a socialist country and a movement sustained by Communists. It necessarily produces solidarity with the latter. The rupture with bourgeois society is much sharper and deeper than with the antinuclear movement, no longer just drop-out but active support of the enemy. It is an index of the changed situation that the Vietnam movement has to fight, not so much systematic ideologies (as did the antinuclear movement), as antiscientific and *ad hoc* "explanations" of the war in terms of the ignorance, errors and misjudgments of the Johnson administration. Against this, there is no reason why a theory of imperialism and a theory of advanced capitalism should not at last emerge on the Left. It is evident that it can only come from within Marxism. The dialectic of the war has transferred the ideology of the guerrillas into the culture of the metropolis.

THE NEW DIALECTIC: FROM PETROGRAD TO SAIGON

The international contradiction between socialism and capitalism has thus been radically redefined by the Vietnamese Revolution. After a long and inescapable detour, it has been restored to a direct and unequivocal confrontation. This is the decisive meaning of this unequal war. Its reverberations have already shaken the world. A generation is now being formed in the homelands of imperialism which has experienced the truth of their own "democratic" and "affluent" societies. It is no accident that all

over the advanced capitalist world—in the U.S.A., Japan, Germany, Sweden, France, Italy and England—the new social force which has been the vanguard of the struggle against American imperialism is the student, high-school and youth population. For it is precisely their age which divides them from the myths of the bygone era of the Cold War. They no longer constitute a selected elite with a secure future status in the ruling class, but a young generation massed together in crowded and bureaucratic institutions adapted to the needs of private industry and the politico-military apparatus. For traditional cultural reasons, they are the social group that is most influenced by international issues, and they have been most affected by the de-Westernization of their conception of the world. In all capitalist countries, their numbers have grown enormously in the last decade. Set apart from the established society, in conflict with bourgeois morality and bureaucratic routines, deriving—and rapidly departing—from the spirit and methods of left-wing liberalism (the antinuclear campaign, the campaign against apartheid and, in the U.S.A., the Civil Rights movement) the students have constituted the vanguard of the Vietnam movement.

In doing so, they have opened a new phase in international socialist solidarity. For many decades, this essential duty was conceived as an unconditional support for the "workers' fatherland"—a constituted socialist state, which commanded the loyalty, and often the actions, of revolutionaries abroad. The adverse effects of this form of solidarity are now indisputable. During Stalin's life, the relationship of socialist state to socialist opposition (abroad) was paramount—one of complete loyalty of the latter to the former. During Khrushchev's tenure in office, the stress of peaceful coexistence was a state relationship between socialist and capitalist powers—one of economic competition and diplomatic negotiation. Today, however, the Vietnamese have not imposed or requested any determinate form of solidarity whatever. They have welcomed the solidarity movements but have not organized or guided them. The Vietnam movements in the West have often spontaneously developed from below, without any *a priori* directions. In the process, they have—especially in the U.S.A., Japan and Germany, the "vanguard" countries—discovered the violence and coercion of Western societies behind the veils of consumer affluence and parliamentary institutions. Imperialism is not a peripheral phenomenon: it is inseparable from contemporary capitalism. The Vietnamese War has sent a searchlight to the core of the West. The result has been a *simultaneous* multiplication and radicalization of the resistance to it. The cause of Republican Spain and the Popular Fronts rallied even liberals to antifascism; but it did not often make socialists of them. The Vietnamese have welcomed any form of opposition to the American aggression, no matter what its political character. But the course of the war itself, the example of the Vietnamese struggle, has shifted the whole axis of the Vietnam movements in the West towards revolutionary socialism, among its main driving force—students and young people. There has been no incompatibility between this and the broadening of opposition to the war, as the great U.S. mobilizations in Washington and New York have shown. On the contrary, the one has had a crucial impact on the other, by radicalizing a whole spectrum of intermediate opinion. The fundamental job of mobilizing the working class of the U.S.A., England, Germany and other countries—only marginally affected outside Japan—has, of course, yet to be done. It is obviously the strategic priority of the Vietnam movement. But the longer the war goes on, the more difficult it will be for anachronistic Cold War anticommunism to mystify the Western working class. Already, large sectors of the Negro population of the U.S.A. have thrown off this degrading opiate. The future is now once again open, as the whole moral and ideological bases of Western imperialist society are increasingly widely questioned. The deepest fear of American capitalism is not of the Vietnamese peasants but of the drugged and gagged American population. Its morale has never been lower than today, for the war is raging on its own territory.

The crisis of the worldwide capitalist system, which first matured in backward and peripheral Russia, is now penetrating the United States. The Vietnamese War will probably become its first serious, direct military and political defeat. This will mean peace and independence to the Vietnamese, at least. But the general political crisis of a starving world fettered by capitalist relations of production will not disappear. The internal contradictions and conflicts of the rich capitalist countries will doubtless be aggravated. Other revolutions will follow. The end of the Vietnamese War will not be the end of imperialism, but it may herald the beginning of the end. For something unprecedented has happened. The socialist revolution in a poor Asian country has liberated the dialectic in its oppressor. Internationalism has passed into the facts.

11.4   *Domestic Contradictions of Advanced Capitalism*

The attainment of higher wages for workers, it is commonly thought, has precluded the possibility of fundamental worker-capitalist conflict within the developed capitalist countries. In Part I of the following reading

("Workers' Control: Some Recent Experiences"), Andre Gorz differs sharply with this view. Gorz argues that the gap between the needs and the actual lives of industrial workers is as great as ever. The trade union bureaucracies have coopted much discontent, but this cannot last because unions necessarily become progressively more distant from their rank and file once they accept the constraints of capitalist institutions. They avoid qualitative issues relating to oppressive working conditions and the social division of labor, even though such issues take on greater importance because of the widening discrepancy between the fragmentation and regimentation of work and the creative abilities and skills of workers.[1] As a result, waves of wildcat strikes have occurred, particularly in some of the European countries, and the revolutionary implications of the demand for workers' control in the factories and offices have emerged.

In Part II ("Capitalist Relations of Production and the Socially Necessary Labor Force"), Gorz examines some of the contradictions created by advances in capitalist production. Modern capitalism requires workers with augmented skills and ability to reason in order that they can carry out complex tasks; but intellectual independence is dangerous, since it might lead to challenges by workers to the present division of social labor and the distribution of power. Furthermore, the increasingly autonomous and cooperative character of production within plants and offices undermines the rational basis for industrial hierarchy and challenges the necessity of capitalist relations of production. Such contradictions can easily explode.

[1]See also Gintis, Section 6.5, p. 274.

Source: Part I of the following is excerpted from "Workers' Control: Some European Experiences" by ANDRE GORZ, an address given on November 12, 1970, as a Political Economy Lecture at Harvard University and published in *Upstart*, No. 1 (January 1971). Reprinted by permission of the author. Part II is excerpted from "Capitalist Relations and the Socially Necessary Labor Force" by Andre Gorz. From *International Socialist Journal*, No. 10 (August 1965). Reprinted by permission of the *International Socialist Journal*.

Part I: Workers' Control: Some Recent Experiences

. . .

Workers everywhere are not reconciled with, but only resigned to, being workers, and they secretly dream of escaping from their condition. This yearning for some unlikely individual escape keeps them alive and makes for low class consciousness. Class consciousness will develop only if workers become aware, first, that there is no hope for individual escape and, second, that by acting all together they can actually change or hope to change the oppressiveness of their working conditions and of their lives. Both these points have been illustrated by striking examples such as these:

In the early 1960s, a British professor of sociology by the name of Goldthorpe made an extensive investigation of the Vauxhall workers at Luton. He wanted to find out what class consciousness was left with them, how they felt about their work, about wages, about life generally and what chances there were that acute conflicts should break out in a well-managed and advanced big factory. Professor Goldthorpe had about 80 percent of the Vauxhall workers interviewed individually. His investigation lasted two years. His conclusions were very optimistic: he found the Vauxhall workers to be completely integrated into the system. They had, so he said, no deeply felt grudges. They were rather satisfied with their wages. They neither liked nor disliked their work. They looked at it as a rather boring but inevitable part of life. They didn't want to give it too much thought. Their general attitude toward work, according to Professor Goldthorpe, was to perform it so as to get rid of it; they wanted to forget about it at the end of the working day, to go home, to watch television, to grow vegetables in their gardens, to fiddle around in their homes. Their working lives were rather marginal to them, and what really mattered to them were their lives at home, which were their real lives.

Therefore, Professor Goldthorpe concluded that class consciousness was practically nonexistent at the Vauxhall plant, that the workers were behaving according to middle-class patterns, and that class struggle belonged to the past.

The Goldthorpe report was still at the printer's when a few militants got hold of a resumé of Professor Goldthorpe's conclusions. They had the resumé mimeographed and handed out a few hundred copies at the plant. A week or so later, the *Daily Mail* printed a report about the profits that had been made by Vauxhall. The net profit for that year amounted to about nine hundred pounds on each worker, and this net profit had been sent back to General Motors in the United States. This piece of news also was circulated among the workers. The next day something happened which the *Times* reported as follows:

Wild rioting has broken out at the Vauxhall car factories in Luton. Thousands of workers streamed out of the shops and gathered on the factory yard. They besieged the management offices, calling for the managers to come out, singing the "Red Flag" and shouting "string them up." Groups attempted to storm the offices and battled the police which had been called to protect them.

The rioting lasted for two days.

Professor Goldthorpe had made a major mistake: he interviewed each worker separately and found each worker to be individually *resigned to*, if not *reconciled with*, his condition. And then he concluded that all these thousands of individual resignations made for a collective apathy. But then something happened which he had not thought of: all these workers who had said individually "that's how life is, there is nothing much that can be done about it," all these workers started to discuss things among themselves. They started to discuss them because Mr. Goldthorpe's conclusions were circulated in the factory. And as they discussed things, they found out that they all felt alike: they felt apathetic but frustrated; they *were* apathetic because, as individuals, in their individual isolation, they could do nothing but dream of escape. But when people start discussing their loneliness, their frustration, their powerlessness, they cease to be isolated and powerless. They find that there is no hope for individual escape, and they start melting into a group which holds immeasurably greater power than the added-up power of all those who compose it.

The experience at Vauxhall is by no means an isolated example. As a matter of fact, wherever extensive interviews and investigations have been made in factories and fed back to the workers, these investigations have been followed within a very short time by violent outbreaks and spontaneous strikes. What happened at the Vauxhall works in Luton also happened at the Firestone plant in Oslo. It also happened at the

Ford plant near Cologne, where the head of the local union had complained for years that wages, working conditions and labor relations were so good that there was nothing much that the union could do in the factory. It so happened that the head of the Ford union died and was replaced by an inquisitive young militant. This new man decided to have a more thorough look at things. He handed out questionnaires, inviting the workers to say freely how they felt about a variety of issues: about working conditions, about working speeds, about piece work, about the foremen, etc. The replies were devastating. The immense majority of workers complained bitterly about the working speeds, monotony, nervous exhaustion; about the lack of breaks; about the despotic behavior of foremen, etc. A summary of the replies was circulated. And a week later, when management announced that the assembly lines would have to be sped up provisionally, just for two days, the whole factory broke out into strike for the first time in fifteen years.

The same kind of story could be told about the Alfa Romeo car factory at Milan, about the shipyards at Genoa, about the Pirelli tire factory at Turin, about the steelworkers at Dunkerque, and so on. What does it all mean? First of all, it shows that when workers are given a chance to discuss and decide among themselves in open gatherings, the grudges and the claims that they want to voice, their demands and their methods always prove more radical than what top union leadership had expected. Free discussion and exchange within the rank and file about factory life almost inevitably lead up to violent outbursts of protest and to unforeseen strike action.

The Limiting Role of Unions

We may then draw the lesson, I suggest, that a potential of frustration and of revolt permanently lies dormant within the work-ing class and that, in so-called *normal* periods, no one knows how deeply the working class feels oppressed, exploited, frustrated. No one knows, neither the union leadership nor the workers themselves. Their feelings and awareness about their conditions are normally repressed because they have no opportunity and no words to express them, to speak about them, to make themselves heard. It is because of this repression that expression of discontent always comes as a surprise and always takes the form of violent outbreaks, of so-called spontaneous wildcat strikes.

The recurrence and growing number of wildcat strikes all over the advanced capitalist world presently demonstrate that the basic assumption on which modern trade unionism was built no longer holds true: this assumption was that improved wages could compensate the workers for the changes which technological innovation was making in their lives. In other words, unions as well as management took to considering workers as commodities that could be bought into submission if the price offered for their labor was high enough. Workers were held by union and management alike to care for their wages only, and all the union's bargaining power was concentrated on quantitative demands. Potential qualitative demands were left aside.

There are various reasons for this purely quantitative approach. One of the more fundamental reasons is the unions' inability or reluctance to question the basic criterion of capitalist decision making. This criterion is maximizing output, efficiency and profits. The quality of life, the physical and mental health of the people, the personal development of production or white-collar workers, the social costs and nuisances of corporate growth are not normally the concern of corporate management. Needs are considered legitimate only in so far as they are functional to the concern with increased production, efficiency, and commodity consumption. The needs for meaningful, enjoyable, enriching, healthy work and working conditions are fundamentally considered illegitimate or even subversive since they basically challenge the quantitative criteria on which managerial decisions rest. Unions therefore thought it wiser and more productive to voice quantitative demands only, that is, demands that do not challenge the prerogatives of management, and that in fact appear negotiable to management.

There is another important reason for the quantitative approach: only quantitative demands can be dealt with centrally by the union in institutionalized nationwide negotiations. Qualitative demands, on the contrary, are held to be too specific, subjective, and diverse to be handled by the union apparatus in central bargaining. Moreover, qualitative demands, were their legitimacy recognized, might get out of hand: workers' collectives might voice wild and unrealistic demands in a sort of free-for-all; the union might thus lose control over the workers, and this loss of control would jeopardize the bargaining power of top union leadership.

This fear by union leaders of loss of control has not always existed. Originally, unions were nothing else but organs for the workers' self-organization and self-defense. As such they tended to be quite radical: they did not care about the legitimacy and acceptability of their demands since they held no legal and legally codified existence. The turning point came when unions were officially recognized or coopted as permanent institutions holding legal rights and responsibilities. Their recognition by management and by the state was made dependent on two conditions:

1. First, that unions must voice demands only that are realistic, and that do not call capitalism into question—demands that are *negotiable*.

2. Second, that once an agreement has been bargained out, unions must stick to it and prevent the workers from breaking it.

Wherever these two conditions have been accepted, labor unions have become permanently structured and therefore hierarchical and bureaucratic organizations; they hold tremendous bargaining power, but they also hold the power to discipline and to police reluctant workers. As institutions holding institutionalized power within the capitalist state, union bureaucracies of course showed less and less inclination to jeopardize their self-interest by stimulating demands and aspirations that are incompatible with the logic and the power structure of the capitalist system. Demands that cannot be won by bargaining and by juridically defined forms of action were considered pointless. Demands that have no chance of being accepted by capitalist managers were thus discarded from the outset. They were eliminated because top union leadership would not engage in risky and losing battles. Realism thus led union leaders to translate all demands that sprang up from the rank and file into propositions that would prove acceptable and negotiable to the representatives of capital. The objective function of labor unions has thus become a function of ideological and political mediation. Union leadership has become a conservative force.

It was inevitable from there on that a divorce should appear between the union bureaucracy and the feelings and aspirations of the rank and file. This divorce grew sharper as management learned to defend the corporations ever more rigid financial planning against the inroads which rising wages threatened to make on corporate profit rates. There are, as you know, several ways by which management can take away with one hand what it grants to workers with the other. Namely:

1. Raising prices will reduce real wages;

2. Work will be intensified and sped up and some of the workers laid off;

3. The work process will not only be sped up, it will be "rationalized," which means new equipment will be installed, skilled work will be replaced by unskilled work, the evaluation of skills and of jobs will be made according to new criteria.

In one word, workers can be made to pay dearly and heavily for their increased wages.

So whatever the national agreement negotiated centrally by top union leaders, workers will remain at the complete mercy of unilateral management decisions unless they win sufficient power on the factory floor to refuse new work rules, new work speeds, new definitions of skills and of rates, etc.— unless, in other words, they win direct power over the work process. This is what workers' control is mostly about, at first sight. It aims to prevent management from taking away with one hand what it grants with the other hand. It aims at limiting or at blocking the discretionary power which the management holds over the organization of the work process.[1]

The demand for control, of course, immediately raises two questions. First, is

[1]There is a distinct difference between workers' *control* and workers' *management*. Control aims at holding power on the shop floor so as to compel management to take the physical and psychic needs of workers into account. Management remains a separate entity with which workers entertain an antagonistic relation of class struggle. So-called participatory management, on the contrary, aims at negating class struggle by giving workers a stake in successful *capitalist* management.

As regards workers' self-management (as in Yugoslavia), this should be considered an accomplished formula of *collective capitalism*, not of socialism: it perpetuates market relations and capitalist relations of production since each factory is still managed as a *separate unit* pursuing maximum valorization of its capital, i.e., maximum profit. To break with the logic of maximum profit would require *economic* units that are larger than production units and that can plan economic growth according to economic calculations in which all socially useful effects of production on the one hand, harmful effects (nuisances, environmental destruction, etc.) on the other hand, can be taken account of so as to *optimize* (and not to *maximize*) meaningful balanced growth.

workers' control something that capitalist management can accept? And second, is the demand for workers' control compatible with the centralized and bureaucratic structure of trade unions? The answer to these questions of course depends on the way in which control is exercised and on the nature of control. Shall this control really be exercised collectively by the workers' assembly of any shop or plant? Or shall there be token control only *on behalf* of the workers by appointed delegates and spokesmen? That is the issue.

Up to now, only the second formula has been accepted in any country by capitalist management, namely in Sweden. And it works quite ineffectively. Swedish management retains undisputed power over the organization of the production process. It may introduce whatever technical changes it deems best for increasing productivity. All union-appointed shop delegates may do is to bargain out certain technicalities of work speed, wage rates, and bonuses. This token control, which does not differ much from what nominally [exists in the United States] in fact amounts to union control over the workers: once the union has made a bargain as to working conditions, speeds, and wage rates, it becomes responsible for the workers' submission and for their discipline. Tensions and dissatisfactions with the union are as great in Sweden as anywhere else, and wildcat strikes have developed there in a spectacular manner in the last two years.

The Italian approach to workers' control is totally different and, to my view, much more real than anywhere else. Union activists in Italy are well-aware that capitalist management will never take into account the material, physical and psychic needs of the workers, unless forced to do so. No medical or psychiatric report on health-damaging work conditions has ever moved any corporation to do away with such conditions. In this as in other countries, the tendency has been rather to suppress such reports or to prevent medical experts from entering factories.

In Italy, as in France, union activists therefore think it pointless to demand improvements: improvements must be forced upon management, they must, wherever possible, be enacted by the workers themselves; they must take control of the work process; they will be given rights of control only after they have taken control already. In other words, workers' control is held to be inseparable from the collective and antagonistic struggle of the workers to break the power of management.

The Italian workers' struggle for control began ten years ago. In its first stage, in 1960–62, the union wanted to build up militancy in the factories by raising issues that were of more immediately direct concern to the workers than nationally agreed wage rates. The union would strike a central bargain over wages and fringe benefits but refuse to make this bargain binding for each factory: the implementation of national agreements would have to be renegotiated in each factory and take local conditions into account. In particular, all aspects of the work situation, including the organization of the work process, could be challenged permanently by the local union at any moment. The union thus hoped to achieve two things: first, to win the loyalty and to stimulate the militancy of the workers; second, to hold effective veto power over management decisions and to keep issues open and struggles on-going all the time. There would be no truce any longer between national bargaining rounds.

These formal rights of permanent union control were forced upon Italian industry in 1962, after a nine-month struggle that culminated in a general strike. But the union never had the power to enforce the rights it had won. Italian industrialists reacted fiercely to the working class's formal victory. One million workers were laid off. There

was a sharp recession; most activists were fired from the plants. Unemployment was such that wages remained beneath the agreed minimum rate and that industrialists had the power to speed up the work process ferociously.

It took the union five years to gather strength for a new offensive. To make sure that they would not be defeated again, the unions this time decided that the workers themselves should determine what they wanted. Strikes had been declared spontaneously in many places for demands that union leadership had hardly thought of itself. By giving the right of self-determination of demands to the rank and file, top union leadership hoped to win back the loyalty of an extremely restless working class.

The right of self-determination of all local demands of course implied some kind of cultural revolution in the unions themselves: bureaucratic control of rank-and-file initiatives had to be broken; workers had to be given a chance to expel or to recall bureaucratic delegates and local leaders, and to elect younger leaders that had become popular during spontaneous outbreaks.

This cultural revolution in the unions was quite a success, and what top union leadership had expected came true: the workers initiated some extremely imaginative methods of struggling and, along with demands for higher wages, set out to demand or to enact workers' control over the work process by reorganizing the work process without anyone's permission.

Thus, for instance, at the Candi plant in the northeast of Italy, which makes washing machines and dishwashers and employs six thousand people, a strike broke out in which workers spontaneously enacted job rotation and job enlargement; they demanded equal wages for all since in certain shops there were fourteen different wage rates for jobs which the workers considered equivalent.

At the Fiat automobile plant in Turin (Fiat employs 120,000 workers), workers demanded the outright abolition of so-called unskilled work and a 30 to 60 percent wage increase for unskilled and semiskilled workers. They asserted that no worker is devoid of skill and that modern industry actually thrives on such social skills as adaptability, ability to adjust to varying working conditions, speeds and techniques, ability to perform a variety of simple jobs. Were workers not capable of doing more complex work than they are asked to do at any given moment and were they not taking initiative permanently, the factory would grind to a stop. This point was demonstrated in a spectacular way: repeatedly, thousands of Fiat workers in various departments decided to work to the rules and not to display skills they were not credited with nor paid for. In a matter of hours, bottlenecks developed all over the factory and production was paralyzed.

Self-determination of demands thus lead to a widespread revolt and attack against the social and technical division of labor and against the general oppressiveness of working conditions. In some key industries, foremen, technicians, and engineers were driven out of the shops by the workers who took over. Revolt against and general refusal to accept any kind of authority was so deep that even presently workers keep refusing to comply with orders and to bend to authoritarian regimentation and discipline. The true feeling of the workers was expressed in the summer of 1969 when, after several weeks of on-and-off work stoppages, the unskilled Fiat workers adopted the following slogan: "What we want is . . . everything!" At this point, the union clearly had lost control of the movement. The demands which sprang up in free assemblies were generally not negotiable since they aimed at total change and self-government from below. The struggle for workers' control spontaneously developed into the creation of organs of dual power which would refuse to enter compromises or to bargain with management.

Never had there been so clear a demonstration that genuine workers' control is a subversive and revolutionary demand and that it is compatible neither with institutionalized trade union organizations and mediations nor with the power of corporate management and of the corporate state. Genuine workers' control must lead to the formation of collective organs of workers' power, such as councils or soviets, and to an outright challenge of the power structure of society. This challenge, of course, cannot last for long; there can be no protracted truce between organs of workers' control and management. Nor can such organs of workers' control be institutionalized and coopted by management: they would immediately degenerate into new bureaucratic organs of mediation. Therefore, they have to wither away if the crisis brought about by the creation of workers' councils does not lead to total social change—to revolution.

The Italian May of 1969 and the French May of 1968 have further demonstrated that the working class as a whole and each worker individually have much more insight, skill, knowledge and creativeness than they are allowed to display in their jobs. An unbearable discrepancy has developed between the stupidity, fragmentation, irresponsibility, regimentation of work and the actual or potential creativeness of workers.

Some rather isolated attempts are being made in small plants [in the United States] to harness this potential creativeness through job enlargement, so-called participatory management, and methods such as Scanlon's Plan Y. The latter, as you know, gives the workers unlimited power to organize and to improve the work process and working conditions; it guarantees to them a so-called fair share of the reduction in costs which their inventiveness and initiative generate. We are told that in ten plants where Scanlon's Plan Y was implemented, the average yearly increase in productivity amounted to 23.1 percent, a fabulous figure indeed; and that, in a particular company, 408 out of 513 innovative ideas were successfully implemented because they brought real improvements to the productive process.

Revolution and Workers' Control

But we may then ask ourselves why Scanlon's Plan Y has not been adopted by any of the large corporations. And the answer to this question, I submit, is quite simply this: If you make the workers responsible for the efficiency and rationality of the process of production, they will tend to question the underlying decisions that have led to the production of this rather than that item, and they will wonder whether these decisions are rational, whether the allocation of the surplus generated is rational, and whether it is rational to produce with maximum efficiency things that are wasteful, useless, harmful or destructive. Furthermore, only marginal companies operating in new fields and looking forward to a long period of growth can give their labor force the kind of job security and stability that can breed team spirit in the factories and pride in workmanship.

In any large corporation, the limit to the pursuit of efficiency by workers in production is the limit which the market sets to the expansion of production. Any worker in a large corporation knows that increased productivity will generate lay offs, that the corporation will prefer to fire part of the work force while speeding up production for those who remain. Why then should the workers put their creativeness at the service of corporations if the more efficient they become, the greater the chance of becoming unemployed.

Workers' control, self-determination by the workers of the work process, is techni-cally feasible as of now. But politically and economically, it is not. As long as production will be geared to the market; as long as its goal will be maximum capital accumulation and not optimal satisfaction of the people's needs within work and outside of work; and as long as management will be a social function divorced from production work and holding distinct privileges over it, workers' control will be fought by corporate management as a direct attack on their prerogatives, on the power structure and on the logic of the system.[2] I do not want to imply thereby that the struggle for workers' control will by itself overthrow capitalism and the capitalist state. Much more is needed to achieve this. The struggle for workers' control can only help to build class consciousness and to clearly identify the nature of class contradictions and of the class enemy which has to be fought.

But, conversely, never will the destruction of the capitalist state and system lead up to a classless society unless the masses, in the very process of struggling, have learned to submit the process of production to their control, to their own needs and to their own goals, unless they have experienced the capability of self-determination and self-organization, and unless they have thus prepared the ground for the abolition of hierarchy, of bureaucracy, in one word, of social division of labor. To this end, workers' control, or rather the struggle for workers' control, is a self-educative means.

[2]William Foote White's *Money and Motivation* contains some striking examples (e.g. Chap. X) of workers' control and self-organization leading to stupendous boosts to productivity while at the same time running up against mounting management opposition because: (1) increased production had not been planned *by management* and cannot be marketed; (2) traditional management-labor relations are breaking down, the workers becoming unwilling to accept or to recognize the authority of bureaucrats; (3) managerial personnel rebel against a situation in which they are losing their power and hierarchical privileges.

Part II: Capitalist Relations of Production and the Socially Necessary Labor Force

During the last twenty years, the development of the productive forces in the advanced capitalist economies has led, apparently at an accelerating pace, to a qualitative change in the character of the labor force which, at every level, is socially necessary to the advance of the social process of production.

I hope, very briefly and rather schematically, to pinpoint some of the contradictions —dormant or explosive—which this current change has created for European capitalism and the way in which it attempts to disguise them, defuse them and prevent them.

A

The contradiction between the character and level of the training required by the development of the productive forces and the character and level of the training required, from the management's point of view, to perpetuate hierarchic relations in the factory and, more generally, the existing relations of production in society.

. . . Industry expects the universities to produce swarms of skilled workers, who can be put directly to work in production, applied research and management. However, the monopolies are perfectly well-aware of the danger for the existing order of a general upgrading of educational standards. For, once a certain level of culture has been reached, highly skilled workers feel the vital need for professional, intellectual and existential independence as much as workers in old-fashioned industry feel or felt the gnawing need for material satisfaction.

It is for this reason that the monopolies, although they are constantly clamouring for education "more in touch with real life," attempt to cut back the quality of higher education and the number of students enjoying it. For example, the chairman of Kodak-Pathé recently remarked: "It is a bad thing to be in a country where there is a surplus of highly skilled personnel, since, should a crisis arise, young people who have spent a long time in studying but without being able to get a suitable post at the end, are not merely a pointblank loss, from the point of view of wasted investment, but also a threat to the established order." The most extraordinary thing in this particular line of management argument is not only the expressed wish to restrict the number of "highly skilled personnel" to the number of "suitable posts . . . should a crisis arise," but also the utilitarian concept of culture (which is a "pointblank loss" if it does not lead to a "suitable post") and the cultural malthusianism motivated by fright at the thought that too much and too widespread culture might imperil "the established order" or, as we might choose to put it, the capitalist relations of production and the hierarchic relations of the firm.

In fine, the problem for big management is to harmonize two contradictory necessities: the necessity of developing human capabilities, imposed by modern processes of production and the—political—necessity of ensuring that this kind of development of capabilities does not bring in its wake any augmentation of the independence of the individual, provoking him to challenge the present division of social labour and distribution of power.

A solution is sought for—as we can see quite clearly in the French Fouchet reform —by backing specialization: educational reforms aim to set up, in contrast with traditional elite education, a stunted, utilitarian alternative, heavily biased towards technology. Frightened that an "over-rich" fostering of talents could lead to nonacceptance of discipline to work routines, an effort is made at initial mutilation: the end-product must be competent but blinkered; zestful but docile; intelligent as far as his immediate functions are concerned but stupid about everything else.

The cry is for specialists, for people who are not able to situate their knowledge in the general movement of science or their limited activity in the overall process of social praxis. It is with this in mind that the Fouchet reform splits education into two: the great majority of *lycée* and college students will receive a technical education, completely shorn of any advanced theoretical studies, such as philosophy, and—conversely—the teaching of philosophy, unaccompanied by any mathematics or science, will be nothing but an intellectual pastime; the point seems to be to deny access by people with a philosophical training to any jobs in which their critical turn of mind might endanger the established order. In other words, higher professional training will be separated off from authentic culture—by which I mean familiarity with the methods and proceedings of creative activity in the sciences and technology—and "culture" will be cut off from social praxis and knowledge of productive work. It ought to be pointed out that this choice really bears no relation to technological advance: indeed, it actually militates against it. It is completely untrue that modern technology demands specialization: quite the reverse. It demands a basic "polyvalent" education, comprising not a fragmentary, predigested and specialized knowledge, but an initiation—or, put more precisely, a faculty of self-initiation—into methods of scientifico-technological research and discovery. There is no purpose in cramming the student with immediately useful information and set-pieces; the important thing is to teach him to learn, to inquire and to develop his knowledge in an independent way, to dominate a whole field of activity and knowledge conceptually and synthetically in its connexions with adjacent fields. Only an education of this kind would enable the worker to maintain his standard of skills or, put another way, to master innovations which, given the rapid turnover of scien-

tific and technological developments, will threaten him—more than once in his productive life—with the redundancy of his store of knowledge and force him completely to overhaul and renovate his learning in order to avoid its depreciation and, in the last resort, his own loss of employment.

Hence, objectively technological development demands a solid and polyvalent education encompassing both methodology and theory and stimulating independence, which presupposes a total recasting of educational curricula and pedagogical methods. Management is against this not just because of the social cost of this kind of education—the rapid production of specialists is less burdensome and their loss of skills has to be carried by themselves—but also because specialists, predeprived of any true professional independence, will be more tame and ready to submit to the current division of labour and distribution of power.

It is instructive to examine the precedent of the United States in order to get some estimate of the chances of success of this education policy espoused by monopoly capitalism. The remedies adopted by European capitalism to cope with the crisis in bourgeois education are in many ways parallel to those essayed during the thirties in America, whose rotten fruits William H. Whyte described ten years ago—from a bourgeois humanist point of view, it must be admitted —in *The Organization Man*. He recounted there how theoretical studies, particularly in the natural sciences, were allowed to fall into discredit and decadence, while simultaneously, with monopoly encouragement, specialized studies (management, public relations, marketing, etc.) flourished handsomely, their curricula rigidly utilitarian and adjusted to the immediate needs of industry, attracting the great majority of students and teaching them "know-how" rather than a coherent complex of knowledge.

The advantages of this system for big business seemed astonishing: secondary schools kept piping in a labour force which was not only directly utilizable but actually preconditioned and preintegrated in the sense that the education given encouraged careerist ambition and discouraged habits of criticism. While the traditional universities of Europe stick to their old academic and mandarin ways, they too are leaving the field open to free enterprise in education, to private specialized schools, mushrooming everywhere, which give no proper technico-scientific or practico-theoretic culture but only formulae for making a successful career.

Yet, at the time when Whyte published his book, the educational system he denounced was already virtually over and done with. A report compiled by Allen Dulles, head of the CIA, on the comparative number of scientists and researchers in the U.S.A. and the Soviet Union, witnessed to Americans that they were in danger of building up a time-lag and provoked the government into taking measures to develop theoretical studies right across the board, through massive injections of funds and a vast programme of scholarships.

The fruits of this development programme are already visible: overcrowded universities, dispensing mass instruction to an unprecedented number of students, cut off from overloaded staff, seething in revolt, often with staff backing, protesting the lack of proper teaching; demands for a voice in creating curricula, in organizing courses, in fixing work methods and conditions; protests against authoritarian university administration; protests, more or less explicit, against the whole policy of American imperialism and the American way of life.

The general trend of this revolt, rather reminiscent of others in Italy (architectural students, for instance) or in France (at the Sorbonne or the IDES), is that, once a certain level of education has been reached, it becomes out of the question to try and limit the need for independence: it is impossible to teach knowledge and ignorance in the same breath, without those taught finally

grasping how they are being stunted; it is impossible to contain the independence inherent in cognitive praxis within tight limits, even by early specialization. In fine, it is impossible, in the long run, to bottle up independence. Monopoly capital dreams of a particular kind of specialized technician, recognizable by the coexistence in one and the same person of zest for his job and indifference about its purpose, professional enterprise and social submission, power and responsibility over technical questions and impotence and irresponsibility over questions of economic and social management. It is the task of the workers' movement to ensure that this dream really does prove a delusion, to bring the contradictions involved into the daylight and to counter the repressive and mystifying ideology of organization capitalism with the possibility, through struggle on every level, of a total alternative and a reconquest of man.

B

The contradiction between the growing— latent or actual—autonomy of productive work for an increasing number of workers and its plainly social character and the situation of work within the factory and within capitalist society. Or, in fact, in other words, the contradition, in a particular context, between the nature of the productive forces and capitalist relations of production.

During the era of Taylorism, capitalist relations of production found their natural extension and confirmation in work relations. For the vast majority of workers, labour power was merely a quantity of physiological energy, undifferentiatable between workers, and without any value in itself: it had value only when combined and utilized outside itself with other quantities of human energy. In other words, it was valorized only by management *fiat* and by being alienated into a product and production whose ultimate finality remained foreign to the worker. The worker was supposed to "work," not

"think"; other people had the job of thinking his work, and that of others, for him.
In short, his dehumanization and the alienation of his labour found their natural basis
in the division of labour and the process of
production.

But, for a growing number of workers,
this objective basis for the dehumanization
of the worker by capital—and for its single
possible form of negation: violent suppression of unhumanizable labour—is tending to
disappear. I am not claiming that new techniques, such as automation, are producing a
new working class and a generally greater
amount of individual autonomy at work. The
process is, in fact, very much more complex: previous individual grades of skill are
being rendered obsolete—a new kind of
semiskilled worker is ousting the old, who is
required on account of his technical responsibilities to have some qualification and,
most important, a general level of education
higher than that immediately required by his
tasks. His tasks, though they require a lesser
degree of individual qualification and direct
initiative, demand a much broader spectrum
of knowledge and involve control over a
much more extensive section of the production process. The personal involvement of a
worker supervising a multiple semiautomatic
lathe, for instance, is less than that of a
worker using a precision lathe, but his
position in the production process is less
restricted and he can gain a much more extensive understanding of it. The same thing
applies to a worker supervising an automated line or a technician in a refinery or a
petro-chemical or atomic energy plant, etc.
Individual skill and job qualification are sup-
planted by more directly social functions and
qualifications. Qualifications are no longer
centered round man's relations with inorganic nature but round social collaboration
with others—that is to say, harmonious
group action, collective team work, etc.
Briefly, the labor force is socially qualified
as a whole; relations are no longer the soli-
tary relations of the individual worker with

his material, mediated by his tools, but relations of groups of workers to the industrial
process, emerging from the conscious combination of human actions. Production no
longer requires combination imposed from
outside, by a third party—the combination
of labour as a quantity of raw physiological
energy; more and more, it is coming to require the reciprocal combination of those
who actually accomplish production—in
other words, cooperation within workteams,
in which traditional divisions between
worker, technician and engineer have disappeared.

Additionally, the natural basis of the industrial hierarchy tends to be dissolved in a
number of advanced sectors and the whole
traditional system of wages and grades,
based on individual work, productivity and
qualification, is thrown into crisis. The technical or scientific worker in automated industry is consigned to permanent underemployment as far as his individual tasks go, and
hence, as far as his level of consciousness
allows, he tends to transfer his interest from
his purely individual work to his social function and from his purely individual role in
production to the social significance and
purposes of management.

Furthermore, in scientific industries stimulated by automation (electronics, heavy
machinery, research, etc.) the work itself
takes on a potentially—or even actually—
creative character and there is a latent conflict between the teams of scientific and
technical workers, conscious of their abilities
and eager to valorize their labour power, and
the capitalist management of the firm, whose
policy subordinates—and often sacrifices—
this valorization to criteria of short- or long-
run profitability. In France, an interesting
example of this was the Neyrpic affair and,
even more striking, the vanguard role played
by the employees at Bull-Gambetta (technicians and engineers) who drew attention
to management errors and foresaw the 1964
crisis more than a year in advance, and
whose struggle ascended from the issue of

the firm to general political issues, denunciation of the management and demands for nationalization and the socialization of research, since the development of the productive forces and the valorization of "human capital" had proved impossible under the system of capital management.

In a key group of industries, scientific and economic pacesetters, the character of work —either on account of its social or its creative aspects—increasingly tends to enter into contradiction with capitalist management criteria and decision-making powers. It is more or less openly felt that tasks should be reorganized and reshuffled, that the command system should be recast and workers' control over the process of production be introduced, and that all this is quite within the bounds of possibility. And, at the same stroke, this very possibility demonstrates the true despotism of capital: it reveals that the alienation and mutilation of the worker has never been the necessary conclusion of the technology employed, but that capitalism actually needs shattered and atomized men and that, as long as it sustains the old system of traditional centralized and military hierarchies, arbitrarily limiting tasks and responsibilities even against the interests of greater productivity, it needs them, above all, in order to perpetuate its domination over men, not only as workers, but also as consumers and citizens. The natural basis of enslavement and dehumanization is replaced by deliberate techniques, gleaming with scientific chrome and dubbed "human engineering," "public relations," "management psychology" and so on. Oppression through the necessary division of labour is replaced, wherever it is on the way out, by indoctrination, ideological repression, smooth grimness and "cultural" conditioning, which starts at school, in the content and method of teaching, and which is prolonged and projected into public life through the degradation and diversion of genuine cultural needs in order to benefit needs (and merchandise) of personal consumption, comfort and escape.

It would be unrealistic to imagine that the objective contradiction between capitalist relations of production and the character of the labour force—its cost of production and reproduction, its mode of training and employment—will necessarily become conscious and explode. In reality, this contradiction is, as a rule, disguised in advanced capitalist societies, able to engage an enormous armoury of repression, conditioning and stupefaction; it will only explode at special moments of crisis. The importance of political and *cultural* work by the working class party must be kept in the forefront, to make these contradictions explicit and to weld together the scientific and technical neoproletariat, the students and the teachers with the working class, by demonstrating the character and prospects of the solutions to which their own specific problems will lead them, while taking the greatest care to respect them in their specificity and relative independence.

. . .

11.5 *Contradictions in Higher Education in the United States*

In several earlier sections[1] we saw how continued economic growth has required a complementary expansion of enrollments in secondary and higher education in the United States. In the following reading Samuel

[1]See Cohen and Lazerson, Section 4.6, p. 183, and Bowles, Section 5.2, p. 218.

Bowles briefly elaborates on this theme and argues that the role of education in reproducing the social relations of production is being undermined by the process of economic growth itself. Bowles contends that the rise in enrollments in higher education perforce raises expectations and aspirations that cannot be fulfilled. Schooling produces youth who demand interesting and socially useful work, but such jobs become increasingly scarce in the economy as capitalism increasingly bureaucratizes and "rationalizes" production. Furthermore, as enrollments at higher levels of schooling increase, it becomes increasingly difficult for the educational system to obfuscate and lend legitimacy to the class stratification that it engenders. As a result, the whole system of higher education in the United States is caught in a contradiction that promises to become increasingly serious over time.

Source: The following is excerpted from "Contradictions in U.S. Higher Education," by SAMUEL BOWLES. From *Political Economy: Radical Versus Orthodox Approaches*, edited by James Weaver. Copyright © 1971 by Samuel Bowles. Reprinted by permission of the author.

INTRODUCTION

The appearance of a radical student movement and the organization of radical professional and other white-collar workers in the late sixties and early seventies raises an important question: will this radicalism among the well educated play an important role in bringing about revolutionary changes in U.S. society? Will the movement be assimilated, bought off, isolated, or destroyed; or will it grow and spread into other sectors of society?

. . .

In this paper I will argue that the student movement and radicalism among young professionals is the manifestation of structural weaknesses endemic to the advanced capitalist system, that the continuing evolution of the capitalist system will exacerbate these weaknesses and thus help to create the opportunity for radical change in the U.S. Let me summarize the argument at the outset.

For at least a century, the growth of higher education in the U.S. has contributed to economic productivity and promoted stable political evolution within the context of a capitalist system. Until recently, colleges and universities have successfully produced the high-level labor and much of the advanced technology needed for economic growth. In addition, these institutions have given collective consciousness and legitimacy to groups occupying the peaks of the occupational and political hierarchy, while at the same time forestalling social discontent by maintaining the illusion of upward mobility through access to education. The expansion of higher education has served as once to enhance the material forces of production and to reproduce the social relations of production.

Yet a hundred years of economic growth and continued expansion of higher education have revealed some basic weaknesses. I will argue that the role of higher education in the further extension of the material forces of production has come into conflict with its role in the reproduction of the social relations of production. The internal consistency of the reproductive functions of higher education in the past was not rooted in any inherent versatility of our educational institutions. Rather, it was a consequence of the particular level of development of both the economy and the educational system. With continuing economic growth and college expansion, the reproductive functions and policies which were once complementary are rapidly becoming contradictory.

The imperatives of continued economic growth and the need both to obfuscate and to justify a system of social stratification based on hierarchy in the social relations of production have required an increasingly large enrollment of students and employment of faculty at colleges and universities. Yet the level of economic growth itself, and the process by which it has been achieved, have had contradictory consequences. Increasing numbers of students have little interest in doing the well paid but alienating work available. As high-level organizational skills and the capacity to handle new technologies have become increasingly important elements in economic growth, the culture of the college community has become anachronistic, dysfunctional, and particularly unsuited to the new role of colleges in training technicians and bureaucrats for the powerless middle levels of the production hierarchy. The expansion of enrollments has necessitated the reproduction *within* higher education of class distinction reflecting the hierarchical nature of production relations in the economy. As the internal structure of higher education has come to mirror the social relations of production, it has begun to expose the myth of mobility and at the same time to create a new, potentially radical political force in the society.

It seems likely that further growth of the system will not ameliorate, but intensify these problems. The assimilation of radical movements has in the past been achieved through a redistribution of the increases in output due to economic growth. Yet the crisis in higher education differs from most past challenges to stability: Economic growth does not provide the means for the solution of the problem. In very large measure it *is* the problem.

A slower or negative rate of economic growth would hardly solve the problem, for there are numerous groups in the society whose continued acquiescence to the capitalist system is purchased by the expectation of an economic payoff which can be provided only through the process of continued growth at a reasonably high rate. Moreover, even the most optimistic economists doubt that it would be possible to achieve full employment and high business profit, were the growth rate significantly reduced.

While some of the roots of student radicalism lie within the system of higher education itself, others have grown out of broader contradictions in the society as a whole. Attacks on campus racism arise less from the peculiarities of college life than from the nationwide movement for racial self-determination. The fight against ROTC and campus military recruiters is just a small part of the worldwide anti-imperialist struggle. Likewise, the radicalism of many young teachers, technicians, social workers, and other professionals is a response to the continuing failure to place the nation's productive capacities in the service of man.

The fact that the political manifestations of the movement are confined largely to the campuses and the professional societies should not obscure their broader social importance. The breakdown of the reproductive role of higher education represents an opportunity for radical change, not only on the campuses, where the contradictions are now most acutely felt, but also in other sectors of the society, where the crisis in higher education will help to destroy the mythology of opportunity and progress and thus reveal the shortcomings of the social institutions which regulate our lives. To take advantage of this opportunity requires some understanding of the ways in which the contradictory developments in higher education are likely to unfold and the defensive strategies likely to be followed by the dominant groups in the society.

It may be useful, then, to study the economic and social forces giving rise to the current crisis in higher education. . . . In section 2, I will survey the recent evolution of higher education and demonstrate that increasing enrollments have produced serious strains in the system. I will argue in section 3 that these strains are manifestations of fundamental weaknesses which have their origin in the structure of the U.S. economy. Some political implications of the analysis are suggested in the concluding section.

COPING WITH GROWTH: TECHNOCRACY AND THE JUNIOR COLLEGE BOOM

The fact that colleges and universities have often been centers of discontent should not obscure the fundamentally conservative functions of these institutions, namely, the reproduction of the social class system from generation to generation, and the legitimation of the resulting inequalities. The reproduction of class relations is facilitated by social inequalities in higher education. Acquiescence to class stratification is encouraged by maintaining the illusion that social mobility and personal betterment are possible through open access to higher education. Higher education further contributes to political stability through its contribution to a rapid rate of economic growth. Rapid growth in both the levels of enrollment and in the economy has been necessary for the performance of these functions. . . .

.   .   .

The expansion of enrollments . . . has brought about two important changes in the social role of higher education. First is the increasing scientific, cultural, and social role of the college community. Second is the frank recognition that colleges have become the training ground for much more than the economic elite; junior colleges and many four-year institutions have taken up the task

of training the middle-level bureaucrats and technicians of the future. While the adaptation to both of these consequences of growth has for the most part preserved the fundamental functions of higher education, the adjustments are far from perfect and have revealed some of the underlying weaknesses of the advanced capitalist system.

.   .   .

The process of college study itself undermines much of the legitimacy of the capitalist system, for it is simply impossible for higher education to transmit useful high level skills to students without at the same time developing some of the students' critical capacities and without transmitting some of the truth about how the society operates. Uncritical acceptance of the legitimizing myths of the capitalist system by the economic and political elites does not provide the intellectual basis for the extension and preservation of its main institutions. As long as the vast proportion of college students were destined for positions of leadership, the tradition of scholarship and unfettered inquiry was probably an appropriate context for college training. Yet with over half of each age cohort attending college, it is clear that both leaders and followers are being trained. The educational processes best suited to training an elite may be less successful in fostering quiescence among followers. Incompatibility of functions seems certain to arise as higher education is forced to play an increased role in the perpetuation of a conservative social mythology and the socialization of docility among middle-level workers.

.   .   .

The growth of two-year colleges and post-secondary technical institutes is another manifestation of the underlying problem, namely, the impossibility of accommodating one-half of each age cohort in "elite" institutions. In what follows I will argue that the junior colleges have served to create a class stratification *within* higher education, thus allowing an expansion of the number of students in higher education without undermining the elite status and function of the established institutions.

With a small fraction of each age group attending college, most could be accommodated at four-year institutions from which graduation assured a high chance of economic and social success. Of course there were always institutions which could not confer automatic status, but these were confined largely to a few fields (such as education and divinity) and to the South (particularly black colleges).

The idea that those who had made it into college had made it to the top could not survive the tremendous increase in enrollments. But it was not merely the expectation of success which had to change; the entire structure of higher education had become inadequate. A relatively uniform system of higher education enrolling such a large fraction of each age group would fail in a number of ways. The right to rule and the expectation of power would be extended to social groups who in their jobs and their political activities had previously exercised very little influence over their own lives or those of others. Unrealistic status and occupational expectations would be encouraged in lower- and lower-middle-class children; disappointment would undoubtedly result in discontent. Equally important, the social relations of the educational process itself—based on the notion that the colleges and universities were socializing an elite—would prove to be inappropriate when these institutions began training middle-level workers. Thus a uniform system of higher education would foster discontent and competition for power, for it would legitimize the power aspirations of much more than the old elite and fail to inspire the expectations and submissiveness appropriate to the future work roles of most of the newcomers to postsecondary schooling.

Structural change in educational processes has been necessitated by a shift in the occupational destinies of the students. Higher education in the 1960s and 1970s thus presents many parallels to secondary education around the turn of the present century, as working-class and immigrant children began to attend high school. They could not be kept out, for the economy apparently demanded a more thorough inculcation of skills and attitudes than was being provided in the elementary schools, and in any case, the ideology of the American system—including the mobility myth—had to be taught to these new participants in the political process. Yet if they were to sit in the same classrooms with the children of the privileged groups, education would cease to confer the badge of status, and, moreover, the newcomers might begin to expect to take up white-collar occupations for which the academic curriculum of the high school was ostensibly a preparation. These problems were perceived and debated during the first decades of this century.[1] The outcome, purportedly based on the best interests of all, was to accept the fact that working-class children would take up working-class jobs and to provide them with an education appropriate to their future work. This was the era that saw the beginnings of the industrial education movement, vocational tracks in high schools, and the development of class stratification within high school education.

The repetition of this process in higher education has been under way for some time, and for similar reasons. Concerns about poverty and racial discrimination and the desire to placate the previously excluded groups have given increased impetus to the movement. Enrollments in junior colleges are well over three times what they were ten years ago. Higher education has developed

[1]See Sol Cohen, "The Industrial Education Movement, 1906–17," *American Quarterly* 20 (Spring 1968): 95–110 and Lawrence A. Cremin, *The Transformation of the School* (New York: Vintage Books, 1964), Chapter 2.

a multitiered system dominated at the top by the ivy league institutions and the great state universities, followed by the state colleges, and ending with the burgeoning junior colleges. This system reflects both the social class structure of the families of the students and the hierarchy of work relations into which each type of student will move after graduation.

The results of a recent study of one of the more equalitarian systems—California's—illustrates this stratified system. As Table 11–A indicates, over 18 percent of the students at the University of California in 1964 came from families earning twenty thousand dollars or more, while less than 7 percent of the students in junior colleges came from such families. (Less than 4 percent of the children not attending higher education came from such families.) Similarly, while only 12.5 percent of the students attending the University of California came from families earning less than six thousand dollars, 24 percent of the students attending junior colleges and 32 percent of the children not enrolled in higher education came from such families.[2]

The segregation of students not destined for the top has allowed the development of procedures and curricula more appropriate to their future needs and actual life chances. The vast majority of students in junior colleges are programmed for failure, and great efforts are made—through testing

and counseling—to convince students that their lack of success is objectively attributable to their own inadequacies.[3] The magnitude of the task of lowering student expectations can hardly be exaggerated, as something like seven times as many entering junior college students plan to complete four or more years of college as actually succeed in doing so.[4]

Studies at junior colleges are, much more often than in four-year colleges, explicitly vocational, emphasizing such middle-level training as nursing, computer work, and office skills. The student is allowed less discretion in selecting courses or pursuing a liberal education. Systems of discipline and student management resemble those of secondary education more than those of the elite universities; some have called junior colleges "high schools with ash trays." The teaching staff is recruited heavily from the corps of high school teachers. Pressures from state legislatures seek to increase teaching loads and class sizes and in some cases, even to standardize curriculum and teaching methods.[5] Whatever the original educational in-

[2]Similar studies of Florida confirm this pattern (D. Windham, *Education, Equality, and Income Redistribution: A Study of Public Higher Education*, (Lexington, Mass.: D. C. Heath and Co., 1970) as does a nationwide census survey showing that college students from families earning less than five thousand dollars a year are over twice as likely to be enrolled in two-year (as opposed to four-year) colleges, compared to students from families earning fifteen thousand dollars and over. See Bureau of the Census, *Current Population Reports*, Series P-20, No. 183 (May 22, 1969). See also *National Norms for Entering College Freshmen: Fall, 1970* (Washington: American Council on Education, 1970).

[3]Burton R. Clark, "The 'Cooling Out' Function in Higher Education," *The American Journal of Sociology*, Vol. LXV, No. 6 (May, 1960), pp. 569–77.

[4]Though the proponents of junior colleges make much of the opportunity for students to transfer at the end of two years and receive a bachelor's degree from a four-year college, less than ten percent of the entering freshmen in California's junior colleges actually do this. See W. L. Hansen and B. Weisbrod, "The Distribution of Costs and Direct Benefits of Public Higher Education: The Case of California," *Journal of Human Resources*, Vol. IV, No. 2 (Spring, 1969), p. 180. Over three quarters of a large nationwide sample of entering junior college freshmen in 1970 stated that they intended to receive a B.A., B.S., or higher degree. [*National Norms for Entering College Freshmen: Fall, 1970* (Washington: American Council on Education, 1970).]

[5]We may expect to see resistance to these pressures from junior college faculties. Their professional status depends on their membership in the community of university and college teachers. Acquiescence to these pressures would not only make their work more difficult and less rewarding,

TABLE 11-A DISTRIBUTION OF FAMILIES BY INCOME LEVEL AND TYPE OF COLLEGE – UNIVERSITY OF CALIFORNIA, 1964

Income Class	All Families	Families Without Children in California Public Higher Education	Families With Children in California Public Higher Education			
			Total	Junior College	State College	University of California
$ 0– 3,999	16.1%	17.0%	6.6%	8.1%	4.1%	5.0%
4,000– 5,999	14.8	14.9	13.0	15.9	10.2	7.5
6,000– 7,999	18.9	19.0	17.6	19.6	17.0	11.1
8,000– 9,999	18.1	18.3	16.4	16.9	17.2	13.1
10,000–11,999	12.4	12.1	15.8	14.4	19.9	13.3
12,000–13,999	7.4	7.3	8.8	7.2	10.8	11.3
14,000–19,999	7.9	7.5	13.0	11.1	13.0	20.3
20,000–24,999	1.8	1.6	3.4	2.6	3.3	6.6
25,000 and over	2.6	2.3	5.4	4.2	4.5	11.8
Total	100.0%	100.0%	100.0%	100.0%	100.0%	100.0%
Median income	$8,000	$7,900	$9,560	$8,800	$10,000	$12,000

tent may have been, the social relations of the junior college classroom increasingly resemble the formal hierarchical impersonality of the office or the uniform processing of the production line.[6]

All this, of course, must not be seen as a failure of the junior college movement but rather as a successful adaptation to the tasks which they were set up to perform: processing large numbers of students to competently and happily fill the skilled but powerless upper-middle positions in the occupational hierarchy of the advanced capitalist economy.

But as the channeling of junior college graduates into these middle-level jobs becomes increasingly evident, these institutions lose the capacity to legitimize the class system which they so obviously reproduce. Increased access to junior colleges cannot reinforce the myth of mobility and personal betterment through education unless a junior

it would signal their descent into the mass of white-collar proletarians, following the route of the high school teachers some decades ago.

[6]This statement does not apply to the small number of exceptional liberal arts junior colleges. See Z. Gamson, J. Gusfield, and D. Riesman, *Academic Values and Mass Education* (New York: Doubleday 1970).

college education actually holds some promise of paying off in access to the high paying, high status jobs ordinarily held by college graduates. And this it does not do. First, it is clear from U.S. census data that the occupational opportunities and likely incomes of workers with less than four years of college fall far short of the opportunities open to four-year college graduates. Second, the monetary payoff to a junior college education is falling, particularly when compared to the monetary rewards of a four-year college degree.[7]

.   .   .

THE POVERTY OF EDUCATION: AN EMBARRASSMENT OF RICHES

The consequences of rapid growth in enrollments—the now anachronistic culture of the university community, the admission of an increasing portion of college students into institutions which effectively channel their graduates into the middle-level jobs in the occupational structure [and the growing tension between effective learning situations and

[7]See Tables 5 and 6 of the unexcerpted version of this paper cited in the source line.

the need to socialize workers for hierarchical production]—have produced serious strains in the structure of higher education. These strains are not simply the growing pains of a healthy organism, but they are instead evidence of fundamental contradictions.

The nature of the contradiction may be briefly summarized: the growth of both enrollments and the economy continues to be essential in legitimizing the class structure and allowing its reproduction from generation to generation. Yet economic growth has produced an incongruence between the job expectations of college students on the one hand and the manpower requirements of the economy on the other. The increasing discrepancy between jobs and expectations is no passing phenomenon, for both the change in student consciousness and the declining opportunities for rewarding work are firmly rooted in three aspects of the U.S. economy; namely, in the level of affluence; in the alienating social technology of production which is the price of affluence under capitalism; and in the pervasiveness of waste and irrational production necessitated by the difficulty in absorbing the surplus productive capacity of the economy.

The success of the economic growth process has itself undermined much of the rationale for higher education, for it has changed the way in which students value the economic payoff to their studies. The increased affluence of the families from which the students come, and the increased affluence which the students may expect in their adult life, tend to make the calculation of monetary gain secondary to other aspects of education. It is no longer enough that education pay off; college study must be interesting and enjoyable and must contribute to the individual's personal development in terms of more than just his productive capacities or likely future earnings. Thus while economic growth has led to an increasing dependence of the economy on the production of both a high level labor force and new

techniques in the universities, it has at the same time undermined the traditional bases of discipline and "rational" choice of "economically productive" specializations in the universities.

While the very success of the economy seems to lie at the heart of the problem, it might be thought that an advanced economy would generate tasks requiring a creativity and perspective which would justify a wholesale transformation of our schooling system toward a more liberating education. Yet the economy has little use for the products of a truly liberating education. The resort to production on a large scale and to efficient bureaucratic organization, in which both materials and personnel are molded into specialized parts, is a major source of our recent increase in output of marketable goods and services. Work tasks are fragmented, the mental processes associated with them are more specialized, and the social relations defined by work roles are more limiting. Increasingly, the rewarding work in the economy is eliminated in the interests of efficiency and hierarchical control of the production.[8]

In part this development may be explained by the elimination of hundreds of thousands of independent positions held in the past by small proprietors, self-employed professionals, and independent skilled craftsmen. Equally important, many previously rewarding jobs, while not eliminated, are transformed by the pervasive specialization and fragmentation of tasks.

The case of teaching provides a good example. Among all of the jobs available to college graduates, teaching is probably one of the more rewarding and least restrictive. The teacher is in direct contact with his material and has at least a modicum of control over his work; given a sufficiently vivid imagination, he may even entertain illusions of social usefulness. However, the teacher's

[8]See Edwards, Section 3.5, p. 115, and Keniston, Section 6.4, p. 269.

job has undergone subtle change, and it is probably true that work in education is less rewarding today than it was in the not-too-distant past. The educational efficiency binge of the 1920s led to the application of business management methods to the high schools. The concentration of decision-making power in the hands of administrators and the quest for "economic rationalization" had the same disastrous consequences for teachers that bureaucracy and "rationalization" of production had on most other workers. In the interests of scientific management, teachers lost control of curriculum, selection of texts, and, even to a major extent, methods of teaching. A host of specialists arose to deal with minute fragments of the teaching job. The tasks of thinking, making decisions, and understanding the goals of education were placed in the hands of educational experts and bureaucrats. Teachers, apparently, were not expected to be particularly intelligent. To facilitate administration and reap economies of large-scale production, schools became larger and more impersonal. The possibility of intimate or complicated classroom relationships gave way to the social relations of the production line.

The fragmentation of tasks and the demise of intimate personal contact has not been limited to teaching but rather has pervaded all of the "service" professions. In medicine, for example, the pursuit of efficiency has spelled the rise of large impersonal medical bureaucracies, the ascendency of specialists, and the demise of the general practitioner who once ministered to the health of the whole body and the whole family.

But the nature of the work task is not the only source of alienation. The product of work may be as alienating as the process. The waste and irrationality of what is produced in the U.S. is becoming increasingly evident; having a hand in producing it has little appeal to more and more college graduates. The growing number of young people who feel that we already produce too many commodities for private consumption balk at most work prospects available in a capitalist economy. Others, sensitive to concerns such as environmental issues, can feel nothing better than ambivalence about their work. And while employment in military and war-related work was not long ago seen as a social contribution, it is now taken on only with a sense of humiliation, embarrassment, or even contempt. Even work in the production of education itself has lost much of its appeal. The smug ideology which once celebrated the enlightening and equalizing mission of the teaching profession has given way under the pressure of radical political movements and recent scholarship to a more persuasive though less inspiring view of education, stressing its inegalitarian and repressive function.

As the elimination of rewarding work proceeds, the difficulty of finding a "good" job is exacerbated by the fact that the numbers of college graduates are growing much faster than the total labor force. Even if the number of "good" jobs were proportionally unchanged, there would not be enough rewarding work to go around. . . .

The most obvious vent for the surplus of highly educated workers is to plow them back into the educational system itself. At the present time, education is by far the largest field of study, constituting almost one-fifth of total enrollments at all colleges and a considerably larger number at four-year colleges. Another vent for the surplus is the graduate and professional schools, which now absorb a substantial portion of the graduating class of four-year colleges. But it can be seen at once that absorbing the surplus educated labor in the educational system, while alleviating the problem in the short run, exacerbates it in the long run, as it builds up the pressures for producing yet more higher education in later years.

For the above variety of reasons, the absorption of the surplus of educated labor through the schooling system itself is increasingly difficult. Expanded employment in other jobs of potential social usefulness does not seem to hold much more promise. The practice of medicine at all levels, because of its direct and obvious usefulness, would seem to be a likely outlet. But here we are confronted with the monopolistic power of the medical lobbies, particularly the American Medical Association, which, by restricting the supply of medical personnel, severely limits the capacity of the medical sector to absorb a greatly increased number of high-level workers.[9]

Of course some of the surplus can be absorbed outside the area labeled "social service."

The growing role of the U.S. in the world economy allows the "export" of some of the surplus educated labor. Direct U.S. foreign investment overseas and the operations of multinational corporations have resulted in an intensification of the international division of labor, with directing, coordinating, and innovating functions retained in the U.S. and functions requiring unskilled labor being shifted abroad.[10] Though considerable, the opportunities thus afforded for absorption of both high level labor and capital are limited, as much by nationalism and increasingly effective competition in the advanced countries as by the antiimperialist movement in the poor nations.

At home, the legal profession has devised a set of procedures and conventions which manage to use up the services of millions of

dollars more of lawyers than would probably be necessary in a more rational system. Some write tax laws and others become adept at tax evasion. In the spirit of Newton's third law, every new legal activity begets at least one opposing activity. But while contrived need may be a remunerative strategy, it must be transparently wasteful to many of those who participate in it, and it hardly appears as a rewarding way of life for many young people. Large legal firms of course recognize this and, to recruit today's top law students effectively, have allowed their young lawyers to work often as much as a day a week on company time serving ghetto organizations and other worthy causes. In other professions and industries, similar concessions are being made.

But there are limits to these concessions. Given what young people now want in a job, concessions may be the most profitable solution for firms, but nonetheless they are expensive. The day off a week and the productivity foregone through despecialization have to come out of somebody's pockets. With the present technological alternatives and social priorities, it seems doubtful that the demands for creative and rewarding work can be met by business without seriously impairing its ability to meet the political necessity of a rapid increase in output. Even major concessions in job content cannot obscure the pervasive waste and irrationality of *what* is being produced and *for whom.* . . .

While the hope of generating a sufficient amount of rewarding work in private employment seems dim, it might be thought that government programs to rectify the social ills of the nation would open up a virtually limitless number of creative and socially useful jobs. Similarly, it was once believed that the full utilization of the economy's capital stock and other productive resources could be insured by a federal commitment to decent housing, urban community development, and the like. Of course one can conceive of government social im-

---

[9]Other medical lobbies follow similar practices. The American Nurses Association recently sought to limit the supply of nurses by phasing out the current three-year nurse's training programs in favor of a four-year degree, despite the greatly increased expense to the student of the four year program and some evidence that four-year nurses are in no way professionally superior.

[10]S. Hymer, "The Multinational Corporation and the International Division of Labor" (mimeo, 1971).

provement programs which would at once absorb the surplus productive capacities of the nation and attract the enthusiasm and commitment of young people in pursuit of rewarding work. But while such programs are technically feasible, they seem to lack political viability.[11] The experience of VISTA, the community organizing aspects of the poverty program, and the Peace Corps illustrates how difficult it is to devise programs which sustain the commitment of idealistic young people and at the same time survive congressional scrutiny.[12]

The difficulty of finding rewarding work has sent shock waves from the labor market back into the schools. The urge to develop competence is undermined by the limiting and wasteful ways in which competence is used in the present economic system and by the very definition of competence which arises out of the alienating organization of work. Thus young people in increasing numbers reject "useful" studies in favor of less economically "productive" but more personally rewarding pursuits. Many leave college or choose not to go. Many more stay but reject much of the curriculum or turn away from intellectual activity altogether.

POLITICAL CONSEQUENCES OF CONTRADICTORY DEVELOPMENT

The immediate political consequences of the contradictions in U.S. higher education have been widely felt, particularly on the more elite campuses. Attempts to hitch up the intellectual community in more direct service to the state and the business community are met with ever more direct resistance. Attacks on ROTC and other campus war-related establishments have been widespread.

[11]Paul Baran and Paul Sweezy outline the political obstacles to such programs in *Monopoly Capital* (New York: Monthly Review Press, 1966) Chapter 6.

[12]Since 1967 an organization of ex-Peace Corps volunteers has called for its abolition.

Scientists at MIT initiate a symbolic strike. Young city planners and lawyers forego prestigious employment and dedicate their skills to radical community movements. Dozens of radical professional organizations have sprung up in medicine, sociology, the physical sciences, economics, engineering, law, city planning, Asian, African, and Latin American studies, to mention just a few. These groups give tangible political expression to a growing commitment among students, young teachers, and other intellectuals that their function is not to administer society but drastically to change it. Dr. Edward Teller's recent assessment of the strength of the movement is clearly extravagant but heartening nonetheless. He told a presidential commission that events in universities in 1969 and 1970 had "practically cut the connection between universities and defense related industries . . . . In twenty years," he warned, "the U.S. will be disarmed."[13]

Campus recruiters for business and the government are finding an increasingly cool reception and a narrower selection to choose from. Direct political action which originally focused on companies in the war business is now aimed at a much broader range of targets—General Motors, General Electric, and the Peace Corps, for example. Student attacks on campus recruitment by the USIS, Department of State, and companies with substantial international operations are indications of the repugnance felt by many students at being trained to administer the U.S. world empire. These political actions are but surface manifestations of a far more general problem. Business and government are being struck—more, it is true, by a wave of indifference to their pursuits than by open hostility—but struck nonetheless at a crucial point in their network of production and distribution: the source of supply of their skilled and professional labor.

[13]*New York Times*, 25 July 1970, p. 1.

Two long-run political manifestations of the contradictory development of U.S. higher education and the U.S. economy are less obvious, though no less important. First, by escalating serious class and racial inequalities from secondary to higher education, the expansion of enrollments has done much more than increase the awareness of the degree of inequity in our school system. It has created in the mass of nonelite college students a group of people who have had at least a taste of inequality and hardship, who are old enough to be politically active and yet young enough to have dreams and take chances, and who are brought together on a day-to-day basis through common experiences and in some cases common residence.

Recent campus political discontent outside the elite colleges may signal the beginning of a broad struggle for greater equality in higher education. Certainly events such as the strike at San Francisco State College in 1968 have brought into the open the shortsighted and narrow limits within which the dominant groups are willing to make concessions to Third-World and less affluent students. The conflicts have thus helped to clarify the fundamental role of the junior colleges and some state colleges in the class hierarchy of higher education, thereby undermining one of the central legitimizing beliefs of our social system.

A second source of potential radicalization arises from parallel contradictions in U.S. higher education and in the evolution of the class structure. Until recently, professional workers and white-collar labor have smugly accepted the comforting view that they constituted a privileged group—a modern aristocracy of labor. They had greater job security, greater control over their work and, of course, more money. They had little reason to be critical of the hierarchical social division of labor characteristic of capitalist production. Along with the substantially overlapping group of property owners, they were the main beneficiaries of the capitalist system and constituted the foundation of its political defense.

While the earnings of professional and other white-collar workers have recently kept pace with those of blue-collar workers,[14] the earnings distinction has become increasingly unimportant for many. And the working conditions of office and "brain" labor are increasingly coming to resemble those of the production line. The widespread unemployment and job insecurity of engineers, teachers, and technicians is symptomatic of these changes.[15] Since the late 1950s the difference between white and blue collar unemployment rates has steadily diminished.

Though the labor force remains highly segmented by occupational level as well as by race and sex, the continuing "rationalization of production" has greatly reduced the number of workers with a direct personal interest in maintaining the hierarchical division of labor. Just as the concentration of capital and the demise of the small property-owning producer has narrowed the base of support for private ownership of the means of production, the concomitant decreasing number of workers exercising independence and control in their work weakens the political defenses of hierarchy in production.[16] Continued growth in the advanced capitalist economy may belatedly create a common condition of work among all segments of the labor force, and thus give rise to a comprehensive working class consciousness.

Much will depend on the immediate objectives persued by students and by organizations of young white collar and profes-

[14]Evidence for the period 1959–1969 is contained in Bureau of the Census, *Current Population Report*, Series P-60, No. 73 (September 30, 1970). For the half century prior to the 1950s the earnings of white-collar workers fell in relation to those of skilled blue-collar workers (see Reich, Section 4.5, p. 174.

[15]Pressures for unionization among white-collar workers in part reflect an attempt to achieve at least the degree of job security held by unionized blue-collar workers.

[16]The argument concerning property ownership is from J. A. Schumpeter, *Capitalism, Socialism, and Democracy* (New York: Harper, 1942).

sional workers. If they seek to restore their lost privileges in the hierarchy of production—as independent decision makers and the directors of the labor of others—they will isolate themselves from other workers. Similarly, if they seek compensation for their lost independence in higher earnings, allies will be hard to come by. But if these backward looking goals are rejected in favor of demands for wider participation in control over production, the movement will find roots in a broad segment of the population, for it seems likely that over the next decades workers in all occupational categories as well as students will increasingly trace their frustrations to a common set of obstacles barring their pursuit of rewarding work and a better life. The capitalist economy—with its bias towards hierarchy, waste and alienation in production, and its mandate for a school system attuned to the reproduction and legitimization of the associated social division of labor—may then be seen as the source of the problem.

As the individual salvation once seemingly offered through access to higher education is shown to be an empty promise, the appeal of collective solutions will increase. With much of the legitimizing ideology of the capitalist system destroyed by everyday experience, the ground would be laid for a broad-based movement demanding participatory control of our productive and educational institutions and the development of a liberating education and its complement—a humane social technology of production.

11.6   *The Making of Socialist Consciousness*

In recent years the hegemony of capitalist ideology has been breaking down simultaneously in many of the advanced capitalist countries. Students, and youth in general, protest the Vietnam War and develop an international, anti-authoritarian youth culture; women challenge traditional sex roles; in the United States, blacks act increasingly on the assumption that meaningful black liberation is unattainable within the confines of existing economic institutions; blue-collar workers reject the wage agreements obtained by their union bureaucracy. The editors of the periodical *Socialist Revolution*, in a comprehensive editorial statement excerpted here, relate the development of these and other disparate protest movements to the need of capitalism both to expand the size of the work force and to increase the self-awareness and competence of the work force. The various oppositionist tendencies will continue to grow and have a common cause —opposition to capitalist relations of production—which can unite them to transform capitalist society. For though the proletariat is currently highly divided, it can achieve socialist consciousness if thought and practice "force the struggle into the primary contradiction . . . [of] alienated labor as a social relation." This reading contains an excellent and comprehensive synthesis of many of the ideas and arguments which we have attempted to present throughout the chapters of this book.

Source: The following is excerpted from "The Making of Socialist Consciousness" by the editors of *Socialist Revolution*. From *Socialist Revolution* 1, Nos. 1 and 2, (Jan.-Feb. and March-April 1970). Reprinted by permission of *Socialist Revolution*.

SOCIALIST REVOLUTION IN THE
DEVELOPED CAPITALIST COUNTRIES

. . .

A small, well-integrated, bourgeoisie—the corporate ruling class—dominates the developed countries. Its ruling practice of private accumulation has produced vast material wealth. It uses this record of economic growth and material abundance to sanction its claim to represent, in its own interests, the interests of society. Corporate capital has thus satisfied its own criterion of success. Because of this success, the world view of corporate capital has been rendered credible and ruling-class imperatives appear as basic morality, social decency and common sense. Alienated labor appears as the only kind of labor; consumption as the highest form of life activity. Poverty and exploitation are defined as minor, remediable concomitants of economic growth, which further growth will eliminate. In short, except in the underdeveloped "internal colonies," the corporate ruling class in developed societies rules primarily through ideological means, precisely because its root idea shaped and therefore corresponds with reality.

The material wealth that justifies capital's ideological domination has been produced by, and has in turn produced, a world proletariat characterized by a disparity of social condition and consciousness: capitalist exploitation and oppression reflects a disparity of evils. Worldwide, the social condition of the proletariat encompasses Rio de Janeiro *favelas*, South African mining towns surrounded by barbed wire, the shanty towns in capital's cheap labor havens in Hongkong, Formosa, Puerto Rico, the barracks of Caribbean sugar workers. Within the developed countries, the condition of the proletariat includes the shacks of Italian construction laborers in the Swiss Alps, the high rises outside of Paris, the new shopping centers in provincial Europe, the crowded streets of suburban Tokyo, the American subdivision, the black ghetto, the computerized factory and the sweat shop, the traffic jam, the new recreation-slums of the Yosemite floor. Is it any wonder that an international class consciousness has emerged only in erratic and self-contradictory ways?

The revolutionary task of our time is to unite this heterogeneity around opposition to the corporate ruling class and to develop its particularized grievances into explicit socialist consciousness and practice by demonstrating their common root in capitalist property relations. This in turn requires revolutionary theory that encompasses both the specific situation and the concrete, historial occasion of the entire world proletariat. Revolutionary theory mediates between and unites individual feelings, introspective understanding, social vision, historical consciousness, and political strategies and tactics.

Such theory is necessary for the proletariat to understand and fulfill its dual task: the abolition not only of the bourgeoisie but also of alienated labor and class society. In the process of revolution, the proletariat is not fulfilling its present existence as a class; it is repudiating itself.

For this reason, socialist revolution in developed countries requires both a degree of self-consciousness and a theory of history that was lacking in the bourgeois revolution, and in underdeveloped socialist revolutions in the Third World. There is nothing external to man that can lay the basis for developed socialist society in the way that private property lays the basis for capitalist society. Developed socialist society will be rooted in the only "property" proletarians have—their human capacities as social beings to rebuild and manage society. The revolution which finally establishes world socialism will be made by proletarians fully aware of themselves as *social* beings.

This historical self-understanding is necessary not only in the struggle to destroy the corporate ruling class but also capitalist production relations—alienated labor—which have still to be overcome in the underdeveloped socialist countries, and which define exploitation in capitalist society. And to win the socialist revolution, the struggle against the ruling class requires as well a struggle against those instrumental, manipulative, and oppressive social relations—racism, nationalism, chauvinism, and authoritarianism —as capitalism produces them in all spheres of life. It is the struggle against these capitalist social relations that provides the condition for a united movement toward a common destiny.

Bourgeois society, built upon the ideals of individualism and self-interest, has by its very nature turned people against each other. Integral to capitalist production relations, men and women are forced to dissemble, ideas are cut off from feelings, and direct intimate social relations put one at an economic, social, and political disadvantage. Historical self-understanding must therefore serve to uncover the social nature of man, the realization of which is impossible in bourgeois society, and upon the basis of which a proletarian revolution will be made. In the most profound sense, the proletariat has not one enemy but two—the ruling class and itself. In the absence of a humanizing militancy and a militant humanism, in the absence of a fierce common hatred for the common enemy, and a fiercer common love for the proletariat as a whole, history will degenerate into barbarism.

The revolutionary movement in developed capitalist societies inherits few guiding ideas from the past. Third World revolutionary movements know what they want, because they know what they need; economic development, the prerequisite for political and cultural development. In the developed countries, there are few existing guidelines for the socialist revolution; quite the contrary, the proletariat does not want what it needs today, does not need what it wants, and must discover what it wants to need.

In developed capitalist society, many still assume that capitalism is capable of meeting human needs. For people to comprehend the magnitude of this failure, to *feel* this failure without feeling anxiety and hopelessness, requires that concrete experience, including emotional experience, be informed by theoretical understanding. In societies in which production is quintessentially *social*, the social character of individual experience is extraordinarily complex and deep-rooted. Each individual act has a variety of social meanings, which many skills and much knowledge of history and of oneself are required to reveal. Because the ideological hegemony of the bourgeoisie depends upon the core idea of commodity accumulation, the prime requisite for socialist revolution is the redefinition of well-being, of abundance, in theory and practice. This requires historical comprehension: the synthesis of self-consciousness and social consciousness.

The task will not be easy. By virtue of its concentration of capital, the corporate ruling class has been able to concentrate ideological resources. A prime task of revolutionary organizing then consists of the struggle against the bourgeois world view, including the idea that it is in society's interest that the ruling class monopolizes these resources. Thus, the arena of struggle today is not only the streets and the factory. It is also the university, the public schools, the church, the labor union, the television stations, the publishing houses, the shopping center, the home —wherever men and women reproduce bourgeois ideas and bourgeois social relations.

In the past, opposition to bourgeois ideological rule has often been vaporous, sentimental, idealistic, utopian, divorced from the social existence of the proletariat: that is, opposition to the bourgeois world view has never risen from cultural dissent into revolutionary theory. The bourgeois idea—that capitalism would produce material wealth —proved largely correct, except during de-

CONTRADICTIONS OF ADVANCED CAPITALISM

pressions, especially during the Great Depression when the business classes lost much of their moral authority, and except for the condition of the subproletariat. Alternatives to bourgeois definitions of well-being and the good life that were glimpsed by only a few artists and intellectuals appeared utopian in the onrush of material production and were swept aside. The great majority of proletarians were too confined by the mundane struggle for survival to contemplate alternative world views and practice and to struggle for them.

Today, however, capitalist expansion faces a worldwide antiimperialist movement, which recognizes that capitalism has generated economic underdevelopment rather than development in the Third World, that has compressed the space for capitalist penetration. At home, the inability of capitalist production to expand without recourse to massive expenditures on objects for waste and destruction is now obvious, not only to a few Marxist economists, but to a large number of people. Further, there are signs that the basic economic contradiction of capitalism, which has extended beyond the factory and office, and has been partly displaced to the Third World, Europe, the state, and the subproletariat at home, is once again reappearing at the point of direct production.

Even more important, *the meaning of abundance and the good life themselves are being redefined by larger and larger sections of the proletariat.* Today, masses of people are repudiating the bourgeois definition of abundance—the very meaning of life under capitalism. They, and we, are thus engaged in a common project, and self-consciously or unselfconsciously are beginning to negate bourgeois ideological hegemony itself.

•   •   ○

REVOLUTIONARY POLITICS AND THE
REDEFINITION OF WELL-BEING

The imperatives of expanding and realizing surplus value are today generating social re-

lations within the proletariat and between capital and the proletariat that are experienced in ways that engender radical and potentially revolutionary politics. Capitalist development is producing a need for a politics oriented around the issue of alienated labor and around the revolutionary struggle for socialism.

This revolutionary potential is rooted in a proletariat which has been transformed according to the bourgeoisie's need to expand and realize surplus value [i.e., profits]. The expansion of surplus value has required both an expansion of the proletariat and the general technical and cultural upgrading of the proletariat. On the one hand, the quantitative growth of the labor forces has required the uprooting of the rural population, the mass migration of Southern black and poor white population to the cities, the destruction of small-scale industry and farming, and the mass entry of women into factory and office employment. In brief, the development of twentieth-century capitalism has been based on the proletarianization of the great majority of the population.

On the other hand, the expansion of surplus value has required rapid advances in productivity, which, in turn, has required an increasingly skilled proletariat. Advanced capitalism has produced not only a larger working class but also a new working class —not simply in the form of a stratum of technical workers or "mind workers" but rather in the form of an entire work force that compared to previous work forces in history is increasingly educated to complex techniques of production processes, communications, and economic and social control. Advanced capitalism has become more "rational," that is, more efficient, productive, and profitable. The need to expand surplus value has necessitated the development of new productive processes, new synthetic materials, new rational forms of work organization, efficient control of raw materials supplies, a "systems" approach to production, distribution, and economic control. These, in turn, require an upgrading of the technical level of the proletariat as a whole.

The *realization* of surplus value has required new, expanding markets, the substitution of values in exchange for values in use, and the creation of new needs, both domestically and internationally. Abroad, imperialism has transformed traditional, semifeudal, and semicapitalist modes of production. At home, commodity production has replaced pre- and semi-capitalist production in small-scale industry, on the farm, and in the home. In most of the nineteenth century, factory production replaced basic commodities traditionally produced by artisans and craftsmen; the problem of finding new markets for the products of large-scale industry was minimal. In the twentieth century, the market for traditional "wage goods"—food, clothing, shelter, and the related demand for capital goods—has been too thin to absorb the product of large-scale industry, To supplement the market for "wage goods," capital has been compelled to manipulate the production of the entire range of human needs.

The realization of surplus value requires the ruling class to direct the proletariat's search for the satisfaction of its needs, its unconscious motivations and desires, to the marketplace. Modern advertising exploits people's need for accomplishment, status, prestige, even affection and love; it focusses their awareness of these needs upon commodities in the market rather than upon their relations with one another. The ruling class is also compelled to manufacture new needs by increasing the general level of expectations and hammering away at the theme that commodities are indispensable for the "good life," a "happy home," "good marriage," and, in general, "success" in all spheres of life. And this requires product differentiation, advertising, sales, public relations, entertainment, commercial sports—industries and activities that are need-producing. The realization of surplus value depends upon surveys of consumer behavior,

motivational research, psychological depth studies, a greater emotional knowledge of the proletariat, the use of the mass media to educate the proletariat that commodities will satisfy their deepest emotional needs. Modern capitalism thus produces a kind of sensitivity, the sensitivity of the salesman, the copywriter, the sports promoter, the television director.

Both of these tendencies—the expansion and upgrading of the proletariat and the search for new markets—have led to the interpenetration of the economic base and superstructures, not merely in the form of an expanded role of government in the economy, but also in the integration of all secondary institutions and activities into production itself. The state, especially the education system, petty commodity production, the farm, and the home are all sources of labor power and exploitable markets. Recreation, leisure time, and cultural activity all constitute growing markets. And accompanying the spread of commodities and commodity culture into all spheres of life is the spread of instrumental social relations and new forms of social antagonism from the sphere of direct production into the secondary institutions.

Advanced corporate capitalism also requires the development of a political system designed to maintain the social order by politically containing and integrating the proletariat into a corporate liberal consensus. Keynesian and neo-Keynesian planning is impossible without cost-of-living indexes, budgetary control, balance-of-payments analyses. Production and distribution planning is impossible without an extended government apparatus that serves to coordinate corporate policies. Social planning is impossible without city planning, welfare departments, "humanistic" approaches to child care, education, family counseling, schools of psychology. Military planning is impossible without an elaborate science apparatus. And all of these activities rest on the development of an information industry, an information explosion, which includes "presentation depots" and "interpretation networks." The development and consolidation of the corporate liberal social order also engenders a kind of rationality and a kind of sensitivity—the rationality of the economist, urban planner, "systems" expert, and cost accountant, and the sensitivity of the social worker, public health nurse, psychotherapist, and teacher.

These changes taken together produce the conditions for a new kind of human being: first, "rational man," with an ability to conceptualize, analyze, and synthesize. By educating itself to the operation of the economy and society, the ruling class, at times deliberately and at times inadvertently, educates the proletariat as well. Second, "sensitive man," with an ability and need to empathize with others, to feel deeply. By educating itself to the emotional state of the proletariat, the ruling class also educates the proletariat, a proletariat that can potentially identify well-being with a social order in which both men and women can afford intimacy, spontaneity, and joy. Modern capitalism produces *awareness*—both of a cognitive and emotional kind—partial and distorted as it is, including the potential awareness of the irrational character of capitalism itself.

On the one side, capitalist society gives birth to a technically skilled, curious, aware, and understanding proletariat—a proletariat that is potentially equipped to rule. At the same time, the ruling class further consolidates its own rule by concentrating economic power, monopolizing the science apparatus, deepening its control over the education system and taking control of the state budget from the Congress.

Capitalism teaches that production is rational and then hires people to waste and destroy it. It programs students in school to perform as "human capital" and then hires them to design, build, program, and control machines and to create systems approaches to production, sales, and social problems. Capitalism educates people to new consumption horizons and then shortens these horizons by producing wasteful and destructive objects.

Material production is defined as well-being and then the bourgeoisie orders the production of objects whose usefulness is subordinated to the need to sustain aggregate demand, to maintain the corporate liberal social order at home, and to firm up the imperialist system abroad. Bourgeois thought teaches people to respect nature and then capitalist development wastes and destroys the productive forces by polluting the air and water, fouling the land, poisoning the food, the wild life, and man himself.

In these ways, advanced capitalism produces new experiences for which it has no satisfactory explanation, new promises of personal liberation and happiness that cannot be fulfilled, new hopes that it shatters, a new rational, sensitive man reproducing himself in a society that is increasingly irrational and insensitive. It teaches that men and women are historical subjects and treats them as objects. It defines people as ends and treats them as means. Needing historical understanding, the proletariat finds ideology, which constrains its intellectual development and historical consciousness. Needing emotional understanding, the proletariat finds manipulation, coercion, and oppression, which constrains its emotional development and self-consciousness.

Thus, people increasingly perceive and experience capitalist society as impoverished, not prosperous, as irrational, not rational, as insensitive, not sensitive. Capitalism produces the idea that well-being consists simply of material production and consumption, and an experience that contradicts this idea. Thus, there arises the possibility of a redefinition of well-being, the opposition of bourgeois ideology by critical thought, an opposition of bourgeois social relations by potentially socialist relations, and, ultimately, the opposition of bourgeois production relations by the struggle for socialist production.

CAPITALIST DEVELOPMENT IMPOVERISHES SOCIAL RELATIONS

Advanced capitalism has created a new proletariat and a new culture for that proletariat. It has spread into the home, leisure, recreation, culture, and education. The penetration of capital into spheres outside production and exchange has transformed the social relations, the needs, the expectations, and the values of the proletariat. In general, the proletariat experiences social relations as more impoverished, and alienated, in the sense that there exists a greater discrepancy between bourgeois thought and promise, and perceived reality. Capitalism has created a social and ecological environment in which people find themselves unable to establish trusting, loving, collective social relations.

The "traditional" proletarian cultures formed during earlier phases of capitalism in both urban and rural society have been replaced. The candy store gives way to the drive-in; the neighborhood block to the "strip"; the ethnic neighborhood to the homogeneous suburb; the rural sharecropping culture to the urban black ghetto; the village and town to the megalopolis. Modern capitalism has disintegrated earlier subcultures and reintegrated culture around commodity production and consumption.

For these reasons, fewer traditional avenues of escape from alienation in production are available. The milieus of the family, neighborhood, village, and town have been all but destroyed. The breakdown of neighborhood and community social structures and the growth of super-organizations of capital and the state and the social relations they create combine to atomize large sectors of the population; to transform associations, groups, and families into masses. At a time when individuals feel the heaviest pressures of alienation, escape from their situation becomes impossible in bourgeois daily life.

A vast, variegated proletariat lives under conditions of individual isolation, its life outside of work organized around commodity consumption. As capital offers more and more distractions in the form of new and different commodities, these distractions become less and less emotionally satisfying. As bourgeois ideology promises personal liberation and fulfillment through commodities, the proletariat becomes confused, irritated, and angry. Students rise up against authoritarian institutions; blacks burn the cities; street people reject alienated labor and attempt to establish their own turf in the streets; drop-outs seek escape in drugs, in the intimacy of personal encounters, mysticism, rural communes; the majority search for meaning in fantasy, in new sexual relations, escapist travel, televised heroism, controlled violence, and the military precision of professional sports. Antagonistic social relations, in the most chaotic, distorted, self-deceptive, and violent forms, are displaced from the factories and offices into the streets, the schools, and the home.

Capital tries to contain the chaos in the only way it knows how: by turning these forms of escape, these outbursts, these new experiments in living, into more capital. Eye drops are sold to counteract air pollution; depressants to relieve anxiety; speed to cure depression; "homemaking" objects for families in crisis; mace and machine guns to solve the problem of the black ghetto; teaching machines to control the schools; "psychedelic items," pro football, and films that begin and end with the individual "doing his own thing" to camouflage a barren culture. And simultaneously corporate ideology "explains" these outbursts and this disintegration in terms of new, mystified theories of human behavior—or as "problems," soluble in time, with compromise.

When the distractions no longer distract and the explanations no longer explain, the use of force becomes necessary, which still further dehumanizes social relations. The attacks against the institutions are extended into the courts, the jails, the army stockades, "corrections" systems, into relations with school principals, probation officers, social workers. Anger and rage become social products, which are countered by producing more commodities, and by producing fear to divert and suppress this anger and rage. The effect, however, deepens the anger and rage.

THE RISING OPPOSITION TO ALIENATED SOCIAL RELATIONS

The new proletariat as a whole experiences alienation in daily life as a tension between two competing perspectives, one established and developed by the bourgeoisie, the other struggling to be born. This tension exists between that part of the proletariat that is still afraid to question its own ideas, values, and needs, and to get closer to its feelings, and that part that is trying to subject its life to critical self-examination. These personal conflicts lead to new consciousness and create the possibility of transforming personal antagonisms into political conflicts. The divided self is then seen as the divided society, consisting of conflicting cultures, modes of thought, and structures of feeling. Such a society begins to reconstitute itself into political divisions—those who support imperialism and those who oppose it, racists and antiracists, male chauvinists and antimale chauvinists, authoritarians and antiauthoritarians.

These divisions run through the proletariat as a whole and between the proletariat and the ruling class. On the one side, the ruling class is relatively homogeneous, experiences daily life in similar ways, and has similar needs. On the other side, the proletariat is highly variegated, experiences daily life in many different ways. The ruling class develops diverse and conflicting needs in the proletariat, which lead the proletariat to engage in politics that divide it from itself, but that also contain the possibility of dividing the proletariat from the ruling class.

Revolution requires a united proletariat and a divided ruling class; yet today the ruling class is more united than divided and the proletariat is more divided than united. The point of revolutionary strategy, therefore, is to overcome the current divisions—between proletarian imperialists and antiimperialists, racists and antiracists, male-chauvinists and antichauvinists, authoritarians and antiauthoritarians—and to reconstitute them into the primary division: capitalists and anticapitalists.

In the forging of such a strategy, the working class will have to overcome deep-rooted social and ideological forces impeding the formation of revolutionary proletarian unity. The majority of Americans do not understand that they produce not only the objects they buy to satisfy their needs but also the needs that these objects are designed to satisfy. Their past wage struggles and wage advances have helped to force capital to raise productivity, introduce new commodity lines, new production processes, establish new location patterns—and, in general, to change the physical, ecological, and social environments. In other words, every advance in wages has been paralleled by an expansion of needs. The majority no longer feels certain that higher wages are the key to the "good life." Nevertheless, the majority of workers will strike for higher wages and continue to be preoccupied with quantitative issues until they understand fully that they are producing their own needs themselves, needs that they might not want to have. Only when they are made conscious of the discrepancy between bourgeois thought and practice and of the radical dissociation of their own thoughts and feelings by the further expansion of material production and increased social impoverishment by the practice of a revolutionary party will the majority of the proletariat begin to transform its consciousness.

The most important oppositionist practice today—the visible organized opposition—consists of the struggle against alienated social relations, instrumentalism, manipulation, and oppression in the secondary institutions around the issues of imperialism, racism, authoritarianism, and chauvinism. The traditional relations between black and white, women and men, and youth and age are disintegrating, and are being reintegrated along new lines.

The process of the disintegration of alienated social relations and their reintegration around new principles, values, and needs is rooted in the growth and structure of capitalist production in the twentieth century. Alienated labor and private property itself—the pillars of the capitalist mode of production—determine both the process of "de-alienation" in the secondary institutions and the limits on this process.

Imperialism

The first, and from a world perspective, the most important social relation that is being challenged is *imperialism*. Within the United States, imperialism is experienced by youth in obvious ways—the mobilization for war, the draft, the tracking system, the army, repression by the police and the courts, all forms of alienated social relations outside of production itself.

Capitalism produces imperialism because of its need to expand and realize surplus value. As capitalism spills over national boundaries and creates a world division of labor, more people and physical resources are integrated into world capitalism as a whole. Economic integration requires forms of social and political integration consistent with private property relations, such as the international conglomerate corporation, the modern state, international organizations, and a worldwide military network.

The creation of a world proletariat, economic underdevelopment, colonialism and neocolonialism become preconditions for revolutionary wars around the themes of national liberation and economic development. Revolutionary wars engender counter-revolutionary, imperialist attacks—that is, capitalism, in its final stages, produces a revolution of the weak against the strong, wars of the strong on the weak, wars in which the weak defeat the strong. Vietnam is the great watershed. Previous wars were fought between nations perceived as relatively equal. The Vietnamese war is fought between the army of the most developed nation and the people of a preindustrial country.

The youth of the advanced countries experience war, and the preparation and mobilization for war, not as a patriotic necessity but at the least as a drag and at the most as a crime. War is not seen as meaningless, old-fashioned but as meaningful only to capital.

These aspects of modern imperialism produce an antiimperialist political movement, revolts in the army, draft resistance, mass demonstrations, and insurgency in the schools. The revolt produces more repression, and repression produces more revolt. And, finally, the revolt, because it is informed neither by a high level of theoretical understanding (historical consciousness) or by emotional awareness (self-consciousness) begins to express the distortions of bourgeois society within itself—in the form of intolerance, insistence on the correct "line," the outburst of rage and anger against all symbols of authority irrespective of rational, strategic, or tactical considerations.

Racism

The present forms of racism, like super-imperialism, are specific to advanced capi-

talism. The expansion and realization of surplus value reshapes and reconstitutes the
black population in two important ways.
First, the mechanization of Southern agriculture provided new markets for Northern
capital and new efficiencies for capitalist
agriculture itself. Second, the Great Wars
produced a serious labor shortage, which led
to the uprooting of large sections of the
Southern proletariat, both black and white.
Blacks were pushed North by mechanization
and pulled North by war; in these ways,
capitalism proletarianized and ghettoized the
black population. Institutionalized racism
developed from its agrarian, slave forms into
corporate capitalist forms.

This development is crucial for any understanding of the black antiracist movement: black people have been socialized into
capitalist society, not in the earlier industrial capitalist stage but in the era of state
capitalism—the stage in which the proletariat as a whole has acquired an abundance
of expectations and needs. For blacks as a
race these needs cannot be satisfied, nor can
these expectations be fulfilled: first opportunities for upward mobility into independent business, professional, and farm careers
are few and far between in the present era
of corporate capital and corporate farming;
second, opportunities for geographical mobility, the acquisition of a little land, a home,
and a small savings account—opportunities
seized upon historically by the white proletariat, and ones that played an important
role in conservatizing the white proletariat
—are limited by institutionalized racism itself; third, opportunities for well-paid jobs in
the private sector of the economy are small
(in fact, the private sector provides fewer
and fewer jobs for blacks who, far more
than the working class in general, are dependent upon the state for employment, welfare, and material help of all kinds).

The black revolt against these conditions
produces brutal police repression, which, in
turn, produces more determined revolt.
Black leaders acquire the need for a higher
degree of historical consciousness and self-
consciousness, the only insurance against the
danger that the antiracist movement will itself reflect the distortions and impoverishment of bourgeois society. The development
of the Black Panther Party and the League
of Revolutionary Black Workers—antiracist
and anticapitalist movements—is a significant advance not only for the black movement, but also for the proletariat as a whole.

Antiauthoritarianism

Paralleling, and partly developing out of,
the antiimperialist and antiracist political
movements is *antiauthoritarianism*, which is
the guiding idea for the development of an
organized movement in the schools and
which is a strong tendency in the home.
Again, the ways in which authority is experienced today generate an organized, political movement, as well as personal and
cultural dissent.

As we have seen, expanded surplus value
has meant the creation of a new proletariat,
one which is socialized to capitalist society
not only in the factory, other places of work,
and the army but also in the schools and
colleges, which have become part of the productive apparatus. The schools retain their
older function of socializing individuals into
the acceptance of bourgeois values and
thought; they still try to structure experience
to produce a personality adaptable to bourgeois society. But they also take on two new
functions: first, a technical function—the
production of technical and administrative
knowledge, research and development, necessary for modern capitalist production. Second, the schools order experience to produce
a structure of feelings that are needed not
only for survival in bourgeois society as a
whole (for example, obedience, orderliness,

patriotism, racism), but also in work itself. In work, the manipulation of ideas, symbols, and people is increasingly important; in the "technostructure" of large corporations, in the state bureaucracy, in teaching and social work, in the hierarchy of labor unions, in sales and public relations, in entertainment and sports, modern employment requires men and women with advanced psychological and social skills.

To attain these goals, capitalism requires a high degree of efficiency and rationality in the schools. Time is rationed and programmed; the teacher's flexibility is lost, as are individuals and individual differences. The authorities see the student population in urban America as a problem in social control. The contradiction between the bourgeois idea of individualism and personal fulfillment and the open and subtle repression of the individual deepens. With the introduction of tracking, specialization of functions and division of labor, teaching machines, closed-circuit TV, and the rest of the paraphernalia of modern education introduced to control, mold, and produce a certain kind of personality, the school is transformed into a protofactory.

Like workers in the past, students are forced to organize themselves in radical unions and a host of other organizations, to realize their own individuality, a difficult and subversive act, because one of the main lessons of the school is that youth should look to authority to settle their differences and resolve their conflicts. Students experience this specific kind of authority, the synthesis between the authority of the parent and that of the factory, as a social phenomenon, not a personal one, and one that necessarily has social solutions. Again, however, without the corresponding development of historical and self-consciousness, the antiauthoritarian movement risks the danger of turning inward, recreating bourgeois social relations and defeat.

Male Chauvinism

Male chauvinism, like imperialism, racism and authoritarianism, today expresses itself in forms that engender an organized, antichauvinist movement. Capitalism requires an expanded proletariat and new markets; increasingly, women supply the first and the home provides the second.

On the one side, the development of capitalism in the twentieth century would not have been possible without the integration of women into higher education, the use of women in electronics and other industries in which the work process consists of light assembly operations, retailing, insurance, military, and other nonproductive sectors that demand masses of clerical and sales workers, and the state sector, which requires millions of teachers, social workers, and other nonmanual employees.

On the other side, the exploitation of women in production requires the substitution of mass-produced commodities for the use value traditionally produced in the home. Women have helped to produce the commodities that fill the home and leisure time and also have helped to produce the need for these commodities.

The expanded role of women in the labor force and the penetration of commodities into the home is one general process. Women enter the labor force from necessity or in search of "satisfaction in work," "creative jobs," or "the opportunity to acquire things for her home and herself," or all three. At the same time that women enter the labor force bourgeois society continues to sanctify the family and attempts to convince women that their basic social role consists of maintaining a happy, comfortable home. Women learn to be "high need achievers" and to adapt themselves to the male bourgeois ethic of personal ambition and competitiveness but simultaneously learn that they must subordinate their own aspirations to their primary role as homemaker. The mass media, the women's magazines, the government, and business propaganda promise "productive careers" and "creative homemaking" through commodities and simultaneously drum away at the theme of women as submissive to men and as the mainstay of the home. This theme repeats itself in the entreaties and demands of the husband, who wants to escape alienated labor in leisure, to be taken care of, but who also believes that he needs a passive, dependent mate.

Women experience life as a series of conflicting demands. They seek liberation in work but find alienation. Jobs for many women are temporary or part-time. For nearly all women these jobs are sex-typed— work that maintains and reinforces stereotypes of women that exist prior to their entering the labor force. These conditions inhibit the development of a proletarian consciousness and also force women to continue the search for their identities in their family role and through their social relations with men. Necessary household work diminishes and women feel ambivalent toward commodities and work-saving devices, wanting them and depending on them but resenting them because they threaten any creativity that women may have experienced in relation to their homemaking tasks.

These tendencies combine to produce a need for an awareness on the part of women of themselves as a definite, oppressed social group. The women's liberationist experiences male chauvinism as a social phenomenon, not only as an individual one, and learns that she can find her individuality only in a collective endeavor. Quarrels in the home, disappointment, hurt, self-hate, and rage— these emotions that follow the curve of the growth of material production—are experienced as feelings that demand social solutions. She replaces the older, social definition of herself with a new one. Free to leave her man and not starve, she seeks a total trans-

formation of her relations with men and of her dependence on the social milieu of the family. And this project again requires the further development of historical and self-consciousness—a transformation of all alienated relations, including alienated labor, or runs the risk of certain defeat.

All of these movements—by blacks, women, and youth—have already begun to link their opposition to alienated social relations with a critique of production. The draft resister opposes the allocation of the largest part of the Federal budget for military spending. The black militant begins to link racism with the utilization of public funds for business-oriented urban renewal, rather than for the needs of the black community. The women's liberationist sees male chauvinism in advertising, styles, and fashions.

The radical teacher opposes the fiscal deprivation of the school; the radical social worker, the fiscal starvation of the welfare budget; the radical scientist, the rape of nature; the radical industrial worker and technician, the production of unsafe, wasteful, useless objects. The opposition begins to mount demands for a reorientation of production—free abortions, free client-controlled child care centers, more classrooms, black-controlled ghetto redevelopment, curbs on the automobile industry, the oil industry.

When critiques of this depth and scope express themselves in action, the ruling class has difficulty containing the proletariat: social democracy and corporate liberalism begin to flounder. The proletariat's posing of alternatives to bourgeois social relations and ideological hegemony demonstrates the bourgeoisie's growing inability to rule on its own terms: through ideology. The coexistence of "orthodox" economic crises—in the form of inflation, unemployment, the fiscal crisis of the state, the imbalance in the international balance of payments—hurries the process along. The ruling class is thus caught between its own failures and the successes of the proletariat. At this point, it will be possible for the contradictions in the secondary institutions to be dissolved into the primary contradiction in production.

THE DEVELOPMENT OF ANTIBOURGEOIS CONSCIOUSNESS

All of these critiques, demands, and activities reflect a definite stage in the development of proletarian consciousness, *the* crucial issue for revolutionaries in advanced capitalist countries. Why is this the crucial issue? Because in the advanced capitalist countries, the bourgeoisie rules predominantly by ruling consciousness. On the one side, the ruling class has convinced the majority of the proletariat that well-being consists of commodity accumulation in a society that provides a high level of production. On the other side, the proletariat in advanced capitalist societies inherits no useful programs from the ruling class: the ends of the proletariat are not the ends of the bourgeoisie. The aims of the "movement" do not consist of economic development but rather the construction of a different society with different priorities and different social relations. The "movement" in the United States, unlike revolutionary movements in underdeveloped countries, does not seek to structure society in order to maximize the work effort, productivity, and production but rather to structure it to maximize the free development of the individual and social relations. It does this by identifying those activities that require the reintegration of social relations around dealienated principles, values, and needs, and building the movement around them.

A precondition for successful struggle is an understanding of how capitalism forms not only a bourgeois consciousness but also an antibourgeois consciousness. It is not that social relations today are "objectively" more brutal, cruel, and inhumane than those formed during and by the industrial revolu-

tion. It is rather that corporate capitalism has produced new needs and expectations that it cannot fulfill and that demand political solutions.

Individuals need to understand the process of formation of their needs, their social condition and social relation, and themselves. Advanced capitalism, which prides itself on its rationality and efficiency above all else, and which demands an explanation for everything, itself explains this need for understanding. And thus it attempts to explain the emptiness, boredom, deception and self-deception, coercion, and terror of modern life through psychoanalysis, mystified political theories and antiquated definitions of "human nature." These explanations run from Freud through Fromm and Spock, from Social Darwinism to modern social psychology, from the bohemian poets of the 1920s to Tim Leary. All of these explanations of the human condition are ideological.

The men who put these ideas into practice are trusted but prove to be untrustworthy. A Kennedy does not end imperialism but obfuscates it. A James Farmer does not end racism but frustrates efforts to understand and abolish it. Ben Spock does not alleviate the anxiety of parents about child raising but intensifies it. Madison Avenue and the women's magazines do not reduce the antagonism between men and women but perpetuate it.

Advanced capitalism produces still more needs, the need for more explanations and different practices, the need for trustworthy ideas and a trustworthy practice. Ultimately, capitalism produces the need for Marxism, a class analysis of alienation, production, and distribution, one that roots the experience of social relations in alienated labor itself and leads people to realize that social relations are impoverished not only because one is a youth, a woman, or a black, but because the individual is a proletarian—a person whose impoverished social existence is rooted in the mode of production itself. A person, no matter how successfully he or she fights alienated relations in the secondary institutions, still suffers under racism, authoritarianism, and male chauvinism in production itself, not only in the form of the "superexploitation" of black people and women, sex-typed jobs but in the form of racist, authoritarian, and instrumental personal relations with supervisors, managers, and the owners of capital. An individual who is saying "no" to those who oppress him or her in the secondary institutions is still compelled to say "yes" to those same people in production and the work experience.

THE MAKING OF SOCIALIST CONSCIOUSNESS

A theoretical critique of capitalism, ripped out of the context of practical, oppositionist activity, or vice versa, is at the least, irrelevant, and at the most, self-destructive.

. . .

Today, the movement against racism, male chauvinism, imperialism, and authoritarianism is acquiring a growing consciousness of itself as a historical category, as a historical subject. This is a promising development for the socialist revolution. Already there are signs that these movements may begin to aim their critiques of alienated social relations at production itself, that there is a growing understanding among youth, black people, and women that they cannot successfully fight instrumental and oppressive social relations in secondary spheres, so long as they subject themselves to instrumental relations in production.

Yet it is in the secondary institutions that instrumentalism and oppression can be fought without threatening the economic domination of capital. Capital resists the struggle against "managerial prerogatives" in direct production and the political fight to establish new priorities for overall economic planning more strongly than struggles for student power or community control. . . .

Socialist revolutionary thought and practice must widen and deepen the historical consciousness and self-consciousness being attained by a growing minority of the proletariat and acted upon in many ways in the secondary spheres. Revolutionary thought and practice must dissolve the secondary contradictions and force the struggle into the primary contradiction, not the contradiction between wages and profits, which merely *reflects* the primary contradiction, but the contradiction in alienated labor as a social relation. This requires the development of theoretical and live alternatives to a social order based on alienated labor—alternatives based on mass participation in social planning.

This also requires the giving back to capital the irritation, anger, and rage that blacks feel toward whites, women toward men, and youth toward age—the rage and anger that at present the proletariat has displaced and turns on itself but that should be expressed against capital in production.

This requires the opening up of psychic space, emotional space, for the development of new relations within the proletariat, in order that the struggle against capital intensifies, as the proletariat develops a capacity for more solidarity and more trust.

Socialist revolution is a process that negates bourgeois society and creates a new society, a process in which the struggle for humanity is inseparable from the struggle against the bourgeoisie.

SELECTIVE BIBLIOGRAPHY

The concept of a contradiction, the nature of the relationship among different contradictions and the view that strategy hinges on the correct handling of contradictions, are all discussed by Mao Tse-Tung [10]. Engels [2] presents the argument that the creation of a new society must be based on an understanding of the historical forces at work in the present. The essay by Althusser reprinted in Oglesby [9], argues that contradictions are always multidimensional, rarely reducible to narrow economic pheonomena, and their exact nature must be specified by concrete historical study in each circumstance. The international contradictions of imperialism, and the new factors introduced by the growth of a socialist world, beginning with the Bolshevik Revolution of 1917, are discussed by Horowitz [5]. The Mandel-Nicolaus exchange [7] examines the nature of contradictions produced by competition *among* the developed capitalist nations. Part II, "The Revolutionary Frontier," of Oglesby [9] contains essays that describe aspects of the revolutionary challenge from the Third World and from blacks in the U.S. Gorz [4] examines the domestic contradictions of developed capitalism and poses a strategy based on "nonreformist reforms." The essays in Cockburn and Blackburn [1] on the emergence of a student movement in the developed capitalist countries deepen and extend the essays by Gorz and by Bowles in Sections 11.4 and 11.5. Gintis [3] explores the role and potential of counter-culture. Finally, O'Connor [8] presents an overview and synthesis of the various contradictions, including a discussion of the growing revolts among blue-collar and public-sector workers, while Long [6] contains a number of essays on the practice of the "New Left."

[1] Cockburn, Alexander, and Blackburn, Robin, eds. *Student Power*. Baltimore: Penguin Books, 1969. See especially Jones, Gareth Stedman. "The Meaning of the Student Revolt"; and Adelstein, David. "Roots of the British Crisis."*

[2] Engels, Friedrich. *Socialism, Utopian and Scientific*. New York: International Publishers, 1935.*

[3] Gintis, Herbert. "Activism and Counter-culture." In *Party and Class-State and Revolution*. Edited by Raymond Franklin. (Forthcoming.)

[4] Gorz, Andre. *A Stragegy for Labor*. Boston: Beacon Press, 1967. Chapters 1 and 5.*

[5] Horowitz, David. *Empire and Revolution*. New York: Vintage Books, 1969.*

[6] Long, Priscilla, ed. *The New Left*. Boston: Porter Sargent, 1969.*

[7] Mandel, Ernest. "Where is America Going?" *New Left Review* 54 (March-April 1969): 3–15. See also the reply by Martin Nicolaus. "U.S.A.—The Universal Contradiction"; and Mandel's rejoinder. "The Laws of Uneven Development." In *New Left Review* 59 (Jan.-Feb. 1970): 3–38.

[8] O'Connor, James. "Some Contradictions of Advanced U.S. Capitalism." In *Economics: Mainstream Readings and Radical Critiques*. Edited by David Mermelstein. New York. Random House, Inc., 1970.*

[9] Oglesby, Carl, ed. *The New Left Reader*. New York: Grove Press, Inc. 1969. See especially Louis Althusser. "Contradiction and Overdetermination."*

[10] Mao Tse-Tung. *On Contradiction*. Peking: Foreign Language Press, 1964.*

*Available in paperback editions.

Visions
of a Socialist
Alternative

THROUGHOUT THIS BOOK WE HAVE CONCENtrated on the capitalist mode of production: its nature, its consequences for society, and the internal contradictions that may lead to its eventual demise. But what kind of society might replace capitalism? What is our vision of a more decent, humane, *socialist* society?

We cannot present a blueprint or an exact specification of how a socialist "utopia" would work; nor should we attempt to do so, since constructing imaginary utopias bears little relation to the actual task of building a decent society. Any *real* alternatives to capitalism will be historically linked to the forces and movements generated by the contradictions of capitalist society itself. New institutions which liberate rather than oppress can only be created by real people confronting concrete problems in their lives and developing new means to overcome oppression. The political movements arising from capitalism's contradictions therefore constitute the only means for society to move from its present condition to a new and more decent form, and only out of these movements will humane as well as practical new institutions be generated.

We can, however, explain what *values* would characterize a truly decent society and what *goals* should motivate the political movement for a more decent society. This brief chapter on socialism at the end of a long book on capitalism provides just a glimpse of some characteristics of a better society, and we consider the chapter's purpose to be suggestive rather than expositional. The bibliography at the end of the chapter offers guidance to a much fuller discussion of alternative socialist societies and institutions.

In a sense, the values underlying a decent society have been implicit throughout our analysis of capitalism. A truly socialist society would be characterized by equality: equality in sharing the material benefits of the society; equality rather than hierarchy in making social decisions; and equality in so-

ciety's encouragement to develop one's full potentials. Work must cease to be a means of "making one's living" and become nonalienated, a *part* of one's living. Arbitrary distinctions by race and sex (or language or eye color) would cease to be criteria for particular forms of oppression or for tracking people into limited opportunities. The irrationality of production for profits would be transformed into the rationality of production to satisfy people's needs, and the unequal relations of imperialism would be replaced by a cooperative ethic recognizing people's responsibility to each other.

But most importantly, socialism is more than a set of humane values; it is a *process*. And defining and describing this process is more difficult than defining the goals of a socialist society. Most fundamentally, socialism means democratic, decentralized and *participatory* control for the individual: it means having a say in the decisions that affect one's life. Such a participatory form of socialism certainly requires equal access for all to material and cultural resources, which in turn requires the abolition of private ownership of capital and the redistribution of wealth. But it also calls for socialist men and women to eliminate alienating, destructive forms of production, consumption, education and social relations. Participatory socialism requires the elimination of bureaucracies and all hierarchical forms and their replacement, not by new state or party bureaucracies, but by a self-governing and self-managing people with directly chosen representatives subject to recall and replacement. Participatory socialism entails a sense of egalitarian cooperation, of solidarity of people with one another; but at the same time it respects individual and group differences and guarantees individual rights. It affords to all individuals the freedom to exercise human rights and civil liberties that are not mere abstractions but have concrete day-today meaning.

These socialist values and process—and

the institutions which would encourage and promote them—must grow out of specific struggles against alienation and other forms of oppression. Hence one part of our struggle against concrete problems and forms of oppression that face us *now* must be to develop institutions which promote equality, nonalienating production, and the other requisites of a decent society.

We must stress that this development is not automatic: Just as the existence of oppression does not guarantee the emergence of oppositional forces (hence our analysis of contradictions), so oppositional forces do not inevitably lead to the creation of liberating institutions. The progression can occur only on the basis of a self-conscious and self-educated *political* movement. The two readings in this chapter provide some glimpses of a socialist society. They are not specific "how-to-do-it" manuals; instead they pose goals for the construction of new institutions.

12.1 *Marx's Concept of Socialism*

The central position that Karl Marx occupies in socialism's intellectual history would by itself make his thoughts on the nature of socialism important. But as Erich Fromm shows in this reading, Marx's concept of socialism is even more important because of what it was and remains: the vision of a humane society in which all men and women, no longer exploited, oppressed, and alienated, would be *free* to develop their own potentials to the fullest.

Source: The following is excerpted from Chapter 6 of *Marx's Concept of Man* by ERICH FROMM. Copyright © 1961 by Erich Fromm. Reprinted by permission of Frederick Ungar Publishing Co. Inc.

Marx's concept of socialism follows from his concept of man. It should be clear by now that according to this concept, socialism is *not* a society of regimented, automatized individuals, regardless of whether there is equality of income or not, and regardless of whether they are well-fed and well-clad. It is not a society in which the individual is subordinated to the state, to the machine, to the bureaucracy. Even if the state as an "abstract capitalist" were the employer, even if "the entire social capital were united in the hands either of a single capitalist or a single capitalist corporation,"[1] this would not be socialism. In fact, as Marx says quite clearly in the *Economic and Philosophical Manuscripts,* "communism as such is not the aim of human development." What, then, is the aim?

Quite clearly the aim of socialism is *man.* It is to create a form of production and an organization of society in which man can overcome alienation from his product, from his work, from his fellow man, from himself and from nature; in which he can return to himself and grasp the world with his own powers, thus becoming one with the world. Socialism for Marx was, as Paul Tillich put it, "a resistance movement against the destruction of love in social reality."[2]

[1] *Capital I*, l.c. p. 689.

[2] *Protestantische Vision* (Stuttgart: Ring Verlag, 1952), p. 6. [My translation—E.F.]

Marx expressed the aim of socialism with great clarity at the end of the third volume of *Capital*:

> *In fact the realm of freedom does not commence until the point is passed where labor under the compulsion of necessity and of external utility is required. In the very nature of things it lies beyond the sphere of material production in the strict meaning of the term. Just as the savage must wrestle with nature, in order to satisfy his wants, in order to maintain his life and reproduce it, so civilized man has to do it, and he must do it in all forms of society and under all possible modes of production. With his development the realm of natural necessity expands, because his wants increase; but at the same time the forces of production increase, by which these wants are satisfied. The freedom in this field cannot consist of anything else but of the fact that* socialized man, the associated producers, regulate their interchange with nature rationally, bring it under their common control, instead of being ruled by it as by some blind power; *they accomplish their task with the least expenditure of energy and under conditions most adequate to their human nature and most worthy of it.* But it always remains a realm of necessity. *Beyond it begins that development of human power, which is its own end, the true realm of freedom, which, however, can flourish only upon that realm of necessity as its basis.*[3]

Marx expresses here all essential elements of socialism. First, man produces in an associated, not competitive way; he produces rationally and in an unalienated way, which means that he brings production under his control, instead of being ruled by it as by some blind power. This clearly excludes a concept of socialism in which man is manipulated by a bureaucracy, even if this bureaucracy rules the whole state economy, rather than only a big corporation. It means that the individual participates actively in the planning *and* in the execution of the plans; it means, in short, the realization of

[3]*Capital* III, translated by Ernest Untermann (Chicago: Charles H. Kerr & Co., 1909), p. 954.

political and industrial democracy. Marx expected that by this new form of an unalienated society man would become independent, stand on his own feet, and would no longer be crippled by the alienated mode of production and consumption; that he would truly be the master and the creator of his life, and hence that he could begin to make *living* his main business, rather than producing the *means* for living. Socialism, for Marx, was never as such the fulfillment of life, but the *condition* for such fulfillment. When man has built a rational, nonalienated form of society, he will have the chance to begin with what is the aim of life: the "development of human power, which is its own end, the true realm of freedom." Marx, the man who every year read all the works of Aeschylus and Shakespeare, who brought to life in himself the greatest works of human thought, would never have dreamt that his idea of socialism could be interpreted as having as its aim the well-fed and well-clad "welfare" or "workers'" state. Man, in Marx's view, has created in the course of history a culture which he will be free to make his own when he is freed from the chains, not only of economic poverty, but of the spiritual poverty created by alienation. Marx's vision is based on his faith in man, in the inherent and real potentialities of the essence of man which have developed in history. He looked at socialism as the *condition* of human freedom and creativity, not as in itself constituting the goal of man's life.

For Marx, socialism (or communism) is not flight or abstraction from, or loss of the objective world which men have created by the objectification of their faculties. It is not an impoverished return to unnatural, primitive simplicity. It is rather the first real emergence, the genuine actualization of man's nature as something real. Socialism, for Marx, is a society which permits the actualization of man's essence, by overcoming his alienation. It is nothing less than creating the conditions for the truly free, rational, active and independent man; it is the fullfillment of the prophetic aim: the destruction of the idols.

That Marx could be regarded as an enemy of freedom was made possible only by the fantastic fraud of Stalin in presuming to talk in the name of Marx, combined with the fantastic ignorance about Marx that exists in the Western world. For Marx, the aim of socialism was freedom, but freedom in a much more radical sense than the existing democracy conceives of it—freedom in the sense of independence, which is based on man's standing on his own feet, using his own powers and relating himself to the world productively. "Freedom," said Marx, "is so much the essence of man that even its opponents realize it. . . . No man fights freedom; he fights at most the freedom of others. Every kind of freedom has therefore always existed, only at one time as a special privilege, another time as a universal right."[4]

Socialism, for Marx, is a society which serves the needs of man. But, many will ask, is not that exactly what modern capitalism does? Are not our big corporations most eager to serve the needs of man? And are the big advertising companies not reconnaissance parties which, by means of great efforts, from surveys to "motivation analysis," try to find out what the needs of man are? Indeed, one can understand the concept of socialism only if one understands Marx's distinction between the *true* needs of man, and the synthetic, *artificially produced* needs of man.

As follows from the whole concept of man, his *real needs* are rooted in his nature; this distinction between real and false needs is possible only on the basis of a picture of the nature of man and the true human needs rooted in his nature. Man's true needs are those whose fulfillment is necessary for the realization of his essence as a human being. As Marx put it: "The existence of what I

truly love is felt by me as a necessity, as a need, without which my essence cannot be fulfilled, satisfied, complete."[5] Only on the basis of a specific concept of man's nature can Marx make the difference between true and false needs of man. Purely subjectively, the false needs are experienced as being as urgent and real as the true needs, and from a purely subjective viewpoint, there could not be a criterion for the distinction. (In modern terminology one might differentiate between neurotic and rational [healthy] needs).[6] Often man is conscious only of his false needs and unconscious of his real ones. The task of the analyst of society is precisely to awaken man so that he can become aware of the illusory false needs and of the reality of his true needs. The principal goal of socialism, for Marx, is the recognition and realization of man's true needs, which will be possible only when production serves man, and capital ceases to create and exploit the false needs of man.

Marx's concept of socialism is a protest, as is all existentialist philosophy, against the alienation of man; if, as Aldous Huxley put it, "our present economic, social and international arrangements are based, in large measure, upon organized lovelessness,"[7] then Marx's socialism is a protest against this very lovelessness, against man's exploitation of man, and against his exploitativeness toward nature, the wasting of our natural resources at the expense of the majority of men today, and more so of the generations to come. The unalienated man, who is the goal of socialism as we have shown before, is the man who does not "dominate" nature but who becomes one with it, who is alive and responsive toward objects, so that objects come to life for him.

. . .

[4]Quoted by R. Dunayevskaya, *Marxism and Freedom*, with a preface by H. Marcuse (New York: Bookman Associates, 1958), p. 19.

[5]*Economic and Philosophical Manuscripts I*, Ia, p. 184.

[6]Cf. my *Man for Himself* (New York: Rinehart & Co., Inc., 1947).

[7]A. Huxley, *The Perennial Philosophy*, (New York: Harper and Brothers, 1944), p. 93.

12.2   *Socialism as a Pluralist Commonwealth*

The values and ideals of socialism will only be realized through socialist institutions—that is, through institutions that not only permit, but actively promote, these values by making them a part of life's everyday experience. But what can be said more specifically about institutions that will help build socialism in the United States?

Historically, the primary programmatic objective of the socialist Left has been to nationalize all major industry. This has led—most notably in the Soviet Union and Eastern Europe—to a system of *state-socialism* in which state bureaucracies run state industries in a centralized state economy. Whatever else it might accomplish, state-socialism obviously does not serve to promote the socialist values of egalitarian cooperation, participatory control, and individual freedom which we have held out as an important part of the socialist ideal. The tendency toward hierarchy and centralization reduces individual and social responsibility, thereby destroying the basis both for freedom and for a practice and ethic of voluntary cooperation. The Old Left objective of nationalization clearly is not sufficient to build socialism in its true sense.

In the following reading—drawn from the author's more comprehensive book entitled *A Long Revolution*—Gar Alperovitz addresses himself to the problem of developing viable and valid socialist institutions in the United States. After noting the problems of centralization inherent in state-socialist societies, Alperovitz reviews several of the historical traditions that have attempted to deal with these problems. He then turns to the problem of building socialism in the United States and describes some elements of a "pluralist commonwealth" that could serve as a new socialist alternative.

Source: The following is excerpted from *A Long Revolution* by GAR ALPEROVITZ, forthcoming. Copyright © 1971 by Gar Alperovitz. Printed by permission of the author.

The ideal of "socialism" suggests an encompassing set of values: justice, equality, cooperation, democracy, freedom. Yet socialism in practice has often meant state agencies running state industries in a dreary, authoritarian economy. Could socialism's basic structural concept—the common ownership of society's resources for the benefit of all—ever be achieved, institutionally, in ways which fostered and sustained—rather than eroded and destroyed—a cooperative, democratic society?

Although my primary concern here is with economic and social institutions, it is obvious there must also be discussion of political institutions capable of preserving (and extending) positive elements which, though badly corroded, still inhere in aspects of Western democratic traditions of freedom. . . . At this point, however, the central question is the structural organization of the economy. Achieve a valid solution, and various political alternatives may be possible (though by no means inevitable); without it, the power thrust of the economic institutions is likely to bypass whatever more narrowly political forms are created. . . .

CENTRALIZATION: CRITIQUES AND ALTERNATIVES

Socialism's historic authoritarian forms are often attributed either to the difficulties of capital accumulation in underdeveloped nations, to war and external threats, or to the legacy of previous Czarist or Asian feudal traditions. While such factors are not to be discounted, the structure of classical state-socialism itself also appears to have inherent tendencies toward hierarchy, away from participation and democracy. To the extent that nationalization centralizes decision making to achieve the planned allocation of resources, alienation appears: persons become ciphers in the calculus of technocrats; hope of a humanism based on the equality of individuals fades. Arbitrary party directives, or in some cases the worst forms of market competition, then naturally become dominant modes of administration —for there must be some way to regulate the often inefficient, irrational, and irresponsible practices of bureaucracies established to achieve "efficient," "rational," and "responsible" control of the economy. Nationalization has, historically largely precluded maintenance of an underlying network of local power groups rooted in control of independent resources—a political–economic substructure which might sustain a measure of control over central authority. . . .

Since a number of traditions have attempted to confront difficulties inherent in the centralizing tendencies of socialism, it is worth reviewing some of their criticisms and alternatives as a first approach to defining elements of a positive vision.

To begin with, it is helpful to acknowledge frankly that some traditional conservatives (as opposed to rightist demagogues) have long been correct to argue that centralization of both economic and political power leaves the citizen virtually defenseless, without any *institutional* way to control major issues which affect his life. They have objected to state-socialism on the ground that it destroys individual initiative, responsibility, and freedom—and have urged that privately held property at least offers a person some independent ground to stand on in the fight against what they term "statism." Most have held, too, that the competitive market can work to make capitalists responsible to the needs of the community.

Some conservatives have also stressed the concept of "limits," especially limits to state power, and like some new radicals have emphasized the importance of voluntary participation and individual, personal responsibility.[1] . . . Few traditional conservatives, however, have recognized the socialist argument that private property (and the competitive market) as sources of independence, power, and responsibility have led historically to other horrendous problems, including exploitation, inequality, ruthless competition, the destruction of community, expansionism, imperialism, war. . . .

A second alternative—also an attempt to organize economic power away from the centralized state—is represented by the Yugoslav argument for workers' self-management, i.e., decentralization of economic power to the social and organizational unit of those who work in a firm. This alternative may even be thought of as a way to achieve the conservative antistatist purpose—but to establish different, socially

[1] Karl Hess, Murray Rothbard, and Leonard Liggio, among others of the Libertarian Right, have recently reasserted these themes—as against old socialists, liberals, *and* more modern "statist" conservatives like William Buckley, Jr. The conservative sociologist, Robert A. Nisbet, has argued additionally that voluntary associations should serve as intermediate units of community and power between the individual and the state.

defined priorities over economic resources.

The Yugoslav model of decentralization raises a series of difficult problems: Though Yugoslavs proclaim themselves socialists and urge that the overall industrial system must benefit the entire society, the various workers' groups which actually have direct control of industrial resources are each inevitably only *one part* of society. And as many now see, there is no obvious reason why such (partial) groups will not develop special interests ("workers' capitalism") which run counter to the interests of the broader community.

Indeed, problems very much akin to those of a system based on private property have begun to develop in Yugoslavia. Overreliance on the market has not prevented inequality between communities and has led to commercialism and exploitation. An ethic of individual gain and profit has often taken precedence over the ideal of cooperation. Worker participation, in many instances, is more theory than practice. Meanwhile, as competitive tendencies emerge between various worker-controlled industries, side by side the need for some central coordination has produced other anomalies: The banks now control many nationwide investment decisions, several reducing local economic power; the Yugoslav Communist Party takes a direct and often arbitrary hand in both national and local decisions. In general, it has been extremely difficult for social units to develop a sense of reciprocal individual responsibility as the basis for an equitable community of mutual obligation.

The Yugoslav model recalls the historic themes of both guild socialism and syndicalism.[2] . . . Alternatives of this kind, un-

fortunately, suffer from a major contradiction: It is difficult to see how a political-economy based primarily on the organization of groups by function could ever achieve a just society, since such a structural alternative seems inherently to tend towards the self-aggrandizement of each functional group —*as against* the rest of the community.

The point may perhaps be most easily understood by imagining workers' control or ownership of the General Motors Corporation in America. It should be obvious that: (1) there is no reason to expect white male auto workers easily to admit more blacks, Puerto Ricans, or women into "their" industry when unemployment prevails; (2) no internal dynamic is likely to lead workers automatically or willingly to pay out "their" wages or surpluses to reduce the pollution "their" factory chimney might pour onto the community *as a whole*; (3) above all, the logic of the system militates against going out of "their" business when it becomes clear that the automobile–highway mode of transportation (rather than, say, mass transit) is destructive of the community as a whole though perhaps profitable for "their" industry.[3]

Were a socialist framework substituted for the capitalist market, such problems might in part be alleviated, but the Yugoslav experience (where both the commune and the nation have extensive powers) teaches that socialism does not automatically resolve the root contradiction inherent in a context which structurally opposes the interests of workers and society as a whole. Some basic

---

[2]It is also closely related to the "participatory economy" alternative recently offered by Jaroslav Vanek, and the model of workers' participation proposed by Robert A. Dahl. See, for instance: Vanek, Jaroslav, *The Participatory Economy* (Cornell University Press, 1971); *The General Theory of Labor-Managed Economics* (Cornell University Press, 1970); Dahl, Robert A., *After*

the Revolution? (Yale University Press, New Haven and London, 1970); See on other models of direct worker-based socialism: Coates, Kenneth, and Topham, Anthony, *Industrial Democracy in Great Britain* (MacGibbon & Kee, Great Britain, 1968).

[3]Dahl, for one, is aware of some of these shortcomings; he hopes through interest-group representation that somehow an "optimum combination" of worker and general community interests might perhaps be worked out.

distinctions must therefore be confronted: First, while workers' management of industry is important, the matter of emphasis is of cardinal importance; workers' control should be conceived in the broader context of, and subordinate to, the *entire community*. In order to break down divisions which pose one group against another and to achieve equity, accordingly, the social unit at the heart of any proposed new system should, so far as possible, *be inclusive of all the people*—minorities, the elderly, women, youth—not just the "workers" who have paid "jobs," and who at any one time normally number only some 40 percent of the population and 60 percent of the adult citizenry.

A second point: The only social unit inclusive of *all* the people is one based on geographic contiguity. This, in the context of national geography, is the *general* socialist argument; the requirement of decentralization simply reduces its scale. In a territorially-defined *local* community, a variety of functional groups must coexist, side by side. Day-to-day communication between them is possible and long term relationships can be developed; conflicts must inevitably be mediated directly by people who have to live with the decisions they make. There are, of course, many issues which cannot be dealt with locally, but at least a social unit based on common location proceeds from the assumption of comprehensiveness, and this implies a decision-making context in which the question "How will a given policy affect *all* in the community?" is more easily posed.

When small, territorially-defined communities own capital socially (as, for instance, in the Israeli kibbutz or the Chinese commune), unlike either capitalism or socialism, there is no built-in contradiction between the interests of owners or beneficiaries of industry (capitalist *or* local workers) *as against the community as a whole*. The problem of "externalities," moreover,

is in part "internalized" by the structure itself: Since the community as a whole controls productive wealth, *it*, for instance, is in a position to decide rationally whether to pay the costs of eliminating the pollution its own industry causes for its own people. The entire community also may decide how to divide work equitably among all its citizens.

. . .

Although small scale ownership of capital might resolve some problems, it raises others: The likelihood that if workers owned General Motors they might attempt to exploit their position—or oppose changes in the nation's overall transportation system —illuminates a problem which a society based on cooperative communities would also face. So long as the social and economic security of *any* economic unit is not guaranteed, it is likely to function to protect (and, out of insecurity, *extend*) its own special, status quo interests—even when they run counter to the broader interests of the society. The only long run answer to this basic expansionist tendency of all market systems is to establish some stable larger structural framework to sustain the smaller constituent elements of the political-economy. This poses the issue, of course, of the relative distribution of power between small units and large frameworks, and of precisely which functions can be decentralized and which cannot.

Some of the above questions may perhaps be explored most easily in the context of the alternative to centralization represented by the localized practice of cooperative community socialism in the Israeli kibbutz—an historically agricultural institution which is now rapidly becoming industrialized.[4] The

[4]The kibbutzim demonstrate, incidentally, that small industrial units can be highly efficient— contrary to theorists who claim that large scale is a technical necessity. The kibbutz movement has continued to grow in Israel, although the proportionate role of this sector has diminished as huge migrations have swelled the capitalist economy since 1948. The kibbutz experience is of course not transferable directly to advanced

many existing variations of the model suggest numerous alternative ways to make decisions involving not only workers' self-management but community (social) uses of both capital and surpluses. Some approaches have been successful, some obviously mistaken and wasteful. . . .

Within the best communities one major point deserves emphasis: Individual responsibility—to act, to take initiative, to build cooperation voluntarily—is a necessary precondition of a community of mutual, reciprocal obligation, and, ultimately, the only real protection against bureaucracy. When the ethic of an equitable, inclusive community is achieved, the efficacy of true "moral incentives" is dramatically revealed: Individuals are neither paid nor valued according to their "product," but simply because of their membership in the community. But there are huge problems even in the best settings, not the least of which is that small communities tend easily to become overbearing and ethnocentric. If they are to break out of conformity they must allow range for free individual initiative—without waiting for majority approval. And they must find ways to achieve flexibility and openness to prevent provincialism and antagonism against outsiders or (all) "others." . . . (Many of these issues are also emerging in the context of the Chinese

_____

industrial society. However, it is highly suggestive as an expression of a final major tradition which attacked centralization: Anarchism, a philosophical tendency in which there has historically been a long-standing debate about socialism—about whether it is possible to have individual freedom *without* a framework of state ownership of wealth, about whether it is possible to have it *with* state ownership. The most hopeful attempts to resolve the issue center on abstract formulations like Noam Chomsky's "libertarian socialism," but this idea has not been developed much beyond the level of generalization. Anarchist theory has always been aware of the danger of both a socialist "red bureaucracy" (in Bakunin's term) and *laissez faire* capitalism, but it has no fully developed program.

commune, a social and economic unit which, though more agrarian, large, and infused with a different ideology, is nonetheless structurally similar.)

The kibbutzim as a group have experimented with confederation, an idea which begins with democratic decentralization as a first premise and attempts to build a cooperative structure between small units yet responsible to them. (The Israeli confederation, with units dispersed throughout the geographically compact nation, hints at how small neighborhood communities might conceivably agglomerate into a larger, decentralized city on even more compact *local*, sites.) The confederate framework, in the Israeli context, in part—but only in part —also helps deal with the issue of economic insecurity and the self-aggrandizing expansionist logic of market systems. . . .

One may raise objections to practical failings of the existing models or to theoretical aspects of the various traditions, but it is hard to disagree with the judgment that centralization through corporate capitalism, fascism, or state-socialism has destructive implications for local communities—for all the people, that is, except the managing elites (and for them too, in more subtle, insidious ways). Accordingly, whether one accepts the conservative view that individuals must control capital, or the Yugoslav view that workers must, or the radical Israeli, Chinese, or anarcho-socialist view that "communities" smaller than the nation state must, we are compelled to come to terms with the general proposition that political power has in some way to be related to decentralized economic power.

A PLURALIST COMMONWEALTH

To review and affirm *both* the socialist vision *and* the decentralist ideal is to suggest that a basic problem of positive alternative program is how to define *community* economic institutions which are egalitarian and equitable in the traditional socialist sense of owning and controlling productive resources for the benefit of all, but which can prevent centralization of power, *and*, finally, which over time can develop new social relations capable of sustaining an ethic of responsibility and cooperation which a larger vision must ultimately involve.

A major challenge of positive program, therefore, is to create "Common-wealth" institutions through decentralization and cooperation, which might achieve new ways of organizing economic and political power so that the people (in the local sense of that word) really do have a chance to "decide" —and so that face-to-face relations establish values of central importance to the large units of society as a whole. . . .

Small units are obviously only part of the answer. My own view is (1) that it is necessary to affirm the principle of collective ownership or control of capital (and democratically planned disposition of surplus); and (2) extend it, at least initially, to local communities, the sub-units of which are sufficiently small so that individuals can, in fact, learn cooperative relationships *in practice*. These units might begin with the neighborhood in the city and the county in the countryside, but should be conceived only as elements of a larger solution—as the natural building blocks of a reconstructed nation of *regional commonwealths*.[5]

In place of the streamlined, socialist planned state which depends upon the assumption of power at the top, I would substitute an organic, diversified vision—a vision of thousands of small communities, each organized cooperatively, each working out its own priorities and methods, each generating broader economic criteria, and each

placing political demands on the larger system *out of this experience*. The locality should be conceived as a basis for (not an alternative to) a larger framework of regional and national coordinating institutions.[6]

A community which owned substantial industry cooperatively and used part of its surplus for its own social services would have important advantages: It could experiment, without waiting for bureaucratic decrees, with new schools, new training approaches, new self-initiated investments (including, perhaps, some small private firms). It could test various worker–management schemes. It would be free for a range of independent social decisions based upon independent control of some community economic resources. It could grapple directly with efforts to humanize technology. It could, through coordination and planning, reorganize the use of time, and also locate jobs, homes, schools so as to maximize community interaction and end the isolated prison aspects of all these presently segregated units of life experience.

Communities could work out in a thousand diverse localities a variety of new ways to reintegrate a community—to define productive roles for the elderly, for example, or to redefine the role of women in community. They could face squarely the problem of the "tyranny of the majority" and the concomitant issue of minority rights, and experiment with new ways to guarantee individual and minority initiative. The anarchist demand for freedom could be faced in the context of a cooperative structure. Communities might even begin to regard themselves as communities—communes, if you like—in the equitable, cooperative, humane sense of that term.

In their larger functions communities

---

[5]This poses as a research problem which industries—from shoe repair to steel refining—can usefully be decentralized and which cannot; and what scale—say, between 30,000 and 100,000—is appropriate for "communities."

[6]In its local form, such a vision is obviously greatly supportive of the ideal of community proposed by Percival and Paul Goodman in their book *Communitas*; see especially Schema II. *Communitas* (Chicago: University of Chicago Press, 1947).

would obviously have to work together, for both technological and economic reasons. Modern technology, in fact, permits great decentralization—and new modifications can produce even greater decentralization if that is a conscious objective. In cases where this is not possible or intolerably uneconomical (perhaps, for example, some forms of heavy industry, energy production, transportation) larger confederations of communities in a region or in the integrated unit of the nation state would be appropriate—as they would be for other forms of coordination as well.

The themes of the proposed alternative thus are indicated by the concepts of cooperative community and the Commonwealth of Regions. The program might best be termed "A Pluralist Commonwealth"— "Pluralist," to emphasize decentralization and diversity; "Commonwealth," to focus on the principle that wealth should cooperatively benefit all.

The vision, of course, is utopian, but in the positive sense of the word. It is a set of ideals to be discussed, a long-range forecast of ultimate objectives. Its purpose is not to blueprint the future but to help define areas for inquiry and experimentation, and to facilitate a serious dialogue about the relationship between present action and future consequences.

THREE LEVELS OF COMMUNITY

"The crux of the problem," Kenneth Boulding has observed, "is that we cannot have community unless we have an aggregate of people with some decision-making power. . . . It is easier for a relatively small unit to have some sense of community. . . ."[7] Although Boulding offered his argument in connection with management of traditional municipal services, in my opinion his point applies in many instances to economic mat-

[7]Boulding, Kenneth E., "The City as an Element in the International System," *Daedalus*, Fall, 1968, p. 1118.

ters as well—but it raises a host of very specific problems:

1. Could contradictions between interests within communities, for instance, be more rationally resolved by new cooperative principles of ownership without engendering *local* bureaucracies?
2. If each community were restructured so that it might engage its own development more directly, how, more specifically, might it establish a basis for cooperative trade between communities, and for control of larger industry?
3. How might large scale planning, investment, trade, economic balance, and ownership/control issues be wisely addressed?

There is no doubt that cooperative development proceeds best in communities sufficiently small so that social needs are self-evident. Voluntarism and self-help can achieve what centralized propaganda cannot—namely, engender group involvement, cooperative enthusiasm, spontaneity. This is a primary reason to emphasize small scale local structures *at the outset*—even if it may entail short term disadvantages. The hope is that thereafter, with the benefit of a real basis in some cooperative experience, it may be possible to transcend historical starting points in the longer development of a larger framework. . . .

A key question is how to prevent local centralization of power: Individuals as well as small groups must obviously retain some power as against the local collectivity as a whole. (And the organization of individuals and small groups *is* power—power to prevent bureaucratic domination, even in small settings.) One answer is self-conscious individual responsibility—and therefore another requirement is the achievement of local practices and relationships which build the experience of responsibility at the same time they constrain bureaucracy. This will require a further breakdown into smaller subgroupings organized both by function and neighborhood geography within communities. (A "city" would be understood as a confederation of smaller communities.) Another answer might be to distribute "vouchers" to individuals so they could freely choose different forms of such public services as education and medicine. This financial network would also permit substantial freedom of operation for a variety of semi-competitive, nonprofit service institutions.[8] . . .

The need for a larger scale framework becomes obvious when problems of market behavior are considered more closely: What if every community actually owned and controlled substantial industry? Even if each used a share of surpluses for social purposes as democratically decided, even if each began to evolve the idea of planned economic and social development, even if its people began to develop social experiences and a new ethic of cooperation—there would still be competition in the larger unit of the region or nation. Community industry would vie with community industry, neighborhood versus neighborhood, county versus county, city versus city. If communities were simply to float in the rough sea of an unrestricted market, the model would likely end in "community capitalism," trade wars, expansionism, and the self-aggrandizing exploitation—of one community by another. (And internally this would tend towards the exploitation of wage employees, as some kibbutzim exploit Arabs. . . .)

Such problems can ultimately never be resolved outside of a context of assured stability: The conditions of insecurity in which local expansionism arises as a defensive strategy, even when the best intentions prevail, must be eliminated. A larger structure capable of stabilizing the economic setting is necessary, and it will inevitably have to control substantially much wholesale market-

ing, longer term capital financing, and taxation, in order to rationalize the economic environment facing each community.

Other issues which cannot be resolved alone by one community, which point up further functions of a larger framework and a larger decision-making body, include: managing the ecology of a river system, deciding the location of new cities, establishing transportation between population centers, committing capital in large scale investments, and balancing foreign trade.

Since the socialist argument for a large unit appears to be correct in all these instances, the issues become: How large? And how might it be established without generating a new dynamic towards centralized power? A governing, continental scale "state" would be far too large for any hope of democratic management by localities— and totally unnecessary for technical efficiency save, perhaps, in continental transportation and some forms of power exploitation. (But cooperation *between* areas is feasible, as present international air transport or American tie-ins with Canadian energy sources illustrate.)

Accordingly, as William Appleman Williams and Robert Lafont have suggested, *regional* units organized on the principle of "commonwealth" become significant elements in a solution.[9] Some intermediate unit larger than a "community" but smaller than a nation of 300 million people (this country by the year 2000) appears to be required. For many economic matters the present states are too small and lack a tradition of direct economic responsibility. The unit must be capable of taking over (and decentralizing!) decisions now controlled by, say, the 500 largest economic corporations —without escalating to the scale of the entire social system. In America today, the

---

[8]A form of this approach (socialized surplus, Anarchist administration) is in use in Medicare payments and in some "transferable" higher education scholarships. It will surely be extended for health care. "Tuition vouchers" for elementary education have also been proposed.

[9]See Williams, William Appleman, *The Great Evasion* (Chicago: Quadrangle Books, 1964); Lafont, Robert, *La Revolution Regionaliste* (France: Editions Gallimard, 1967). For the idea of regionalism, also see the writings of the American anarchist Alexander Berkman.

most instructive example of a unit of approximate scale is the Tennessee Valley Authority, but one might begin to imagine a system in which this nation, by the end of the century, were broken into eight or ten confederated regions of 20 to 30 million people, each region made up of confederated communities (perhaps New England, Appalachia, Tidelands, Deep South, Mid-West, Plains and Mountain States, South-West, West Coast? In Canada, an independent or semiindependent Quebec might be another regional unit of appropriate scale.)

Part of the answer might also involve regional units of different sizes for different purposes. The metropolitan area as a unit, for example, might control certain heavy industries or specialized public services such as intra-urban transportation. A grouping of regions like New England and Appalachia might control electric power production and distribution; the Pacific Coast and the Mountain States might unite for a variety of functions, particularly for rational ecological planning and watershed control. In these instances, organization *across* regions is more rational: Black Americans and other minorities may for political reasons also wish to establish racially organized associations *across the nation*. The point of regional organization as a guideline is not to exclude higher order collaboration but rather to attempt to solve some problems of cooperation and power by building up units of rational scale which are still manageable by the localities implicit in a decentralist vision. . . .

PLANNING, POWER, AND PROCESS

Within the larger unit decisions should reflect the needs of real (that is to say, local) communities. But to avoid wastes and inequalities, planning is obviously also necessary. The issues then are: Who controls the planners? How are fundamental planning criteria determined? The thrust of the argument is that controlling criteria should in part be generated out of expressed community needs and experiences, out of specific demands for goods and services—over time, through stages—*and* that these must be bolstered by the development of independent local bases of power. At all levels, the appropriate unit's control of a local market through its direct receipt of some surpluses and its control of some capital, can offer economic leverage, just as its organization principles permit political leverage. The larger unit must have sufficient autonomous power, however, to balance the pressures from the strongest community (but not so much as to overwhelm them . . .).

In general, the difficult broader principle in a three-level vision of community, region, and nation is to anchor units in new social structures which preserve sufficient independence of decision and power (without which neither freedom nor responsibility is possible), but which are not so powerful as to produce unrestrained competition and deny the possibility of a substantial measure of rational planning. . . . The rule should be to leave as many functions as possible to localities, elevating only what is absolutely essential to the higher unit. . . .

A critical problem is to define *specific* ways in which people living in localities might constrain larger order systems without making it impossible for them to function. Here, some clues are available from modern American experience: In the Tennessee Valley Authority, for instance, local corporation farms (and other private business interests), rather than "communities," to a great extent keep the bureaucrats in line, serving *their* purposes—but T.V.A. authorities still retain sufficient power rationally to control much river development.[10]

[10]The way military contractors and the various services often *partially* "co-opt" the Federal civilian defense bureaucracy, paralleling the corporation farms of the T.V.A., is also instructive. Only in imagination do Defense Department bureaucrats simply "order" the corporations, the services, and their Congressional allies to do their bidding.

What if *communities* were the power base or building blocks of a new political-economy? They might reduce regional units to more limited roles, largely responsible to (in part "co-opted" by) the interests of the people—organized in new cooperative community forms. Given the proper social basis, a large unit (like a region) might be kept in check. Its ultimate role would then be partly simply coordination; its broad policy making and administrative functions would depend upon the development (and acceptance) of a rationally articulated political program. A two-chamber legislature might perhaps represent the organized communities, on the one hand, and the interests of the people at large, on the other. . . .

In this setting, several other basic questions could be addressed: What, for example, might be the best process for making decisions over such fundamental issues as *how much* of society's resources to allocate between consumption and investment (which entails a series of broad ecological considerations and also the matter of zero growth rates); *whether* to make major new society-shaping investments, as in one or another transportation system; *how* population should be dispersed; *how much* should be allocated to prevent the destruction of the environment (directly, or indirectly through time-using, voluntaristic methods)?

"Planning" is obviously required here too, but again it is important to recognize that in this sketch of an alternative program, the process of central "planning" would be quite different from that of the streamlined state or the Soviet "command economy." It would be much more organic: Social priorities would be developed in each community, first through local processes, and then subsequently in regional and national politics generated out of local experience. Ultimately,

In fact, the reverse is closer to a description of a reality which involves a complex interaction of centralized bureaucratic direction and sub-unit lobbying and pressure.

the central regional and national bodies would have to resolve conflicting claims about resource allocation through the more broadly representative political processes. . . .

To identify socialism with streamlined, computerized planning, as some do, is a fatal error. "Planning" would more likely be an "iterative" phenomenon, involving: first, information, priorities, and criteria generated at local levels; next an integration at a higher order "planning stage"; then the implications calculated; a return to smaller units for reconsideration; and finally back up again. (The Chinese call a similar process "two ups and two downs"; and some large U.S. corporations have developed sophisticated linear programming models for their decentralized internal management which are of relevance.)

One must recognize that decentralized, democratic planning inevitably involves inefficiencies and considerably more time. However, if successful, the gains in released energies, to say nothing of the quality of life, are likely to more than compensate what is lost. . . .

But this returns us to the question of whether the basic social units in which day-to-day life occur are, in fact, likely to sustain new, more humane experiences of community. It should again be clear why it is important to place priority on local social structures and processes which have a potential for developing and prefiguring a new ethic of cooperation, even if this may mean local communities initially function to an extent competitively as market operators. Staging is critical: Could social relationships within communities be strengthened so as to alter values and modify external relations *over time?* Could a cooperative development process permit the *subsequent* establishment of the necessary coordinating structures between communities and, in combination with national political efforts, the larger framework for the overall economy?

There are no easy answers to such questions and very little guidance available from foreign experience or past history. Chinese and Israeli developments suggest that communities may be able to sustain and deepen the quality of internal social relations while at the same time external relations involve both the use of market competition and a larger framework. The historical record also suggests that some limited form of market *and* planning both may be inevitable at certain stages of development under all types of socialism.[11] . . . One challenge, accordingly, is to recognize that competition can be a method of exploitation or a tool of rational administration; a second is to eliminate the former, and (if the social system is to overcome its origins in capitalism), to attempt shrewd trade-offs between competition and cooperation *at different stages of development*, as a new experiential basis emerges, as mutual needs develop, as larger national political possibilities open up, and as a new vision is created. . . .

In such a long process of development, as Martin Buber urged, the permissive environment which may be attainable if localities are not totally subservient to central agencies is more important, initially, than the apparent top–down rationality of centralized planning systems. The conservative, the Yugoslav, the Israeli, the Chinese, and the anarchist all seem right also to argue that a degree of local autonomy and a degree of competition must be assured if freedom and spontaneous innovation are to continue over time. . . .

EQUALITY?

One issue noted in passing deserves special consideration: Equality. Grant that communities might develop new cooperative ways,

[11]Marxist theoreticians as different as Charles Bettelheim and Paul Sweezy agree on this point. See, for instance, their exchange in *Monthly Review*, Vol. 22, No. 7 (December, 1970), pp. 1–21.

grant that they might begin to develop a different ethic, a different concept of the nature of community and cooperation, grant even that they might help each other to a greater extent than under capitalism; there is, nonetheless, no obvious reason why rich communities should be expected in practice to share their wealth with other communities. (In Yugoslavia, there are still regions of the nation in which workers earn one-fifth as much for the same work as in wealthier regions!) Globally, one need only compare the living standards of various socialist countries to be reminded that even when the rhetoric of equality is proclaimed, new social structures (in this case involving whole nations) do not automatically achieve it in practice.

There are, I think, two answers to the dilemma of equality: First (and this is crucial), America is so far advanced technologically that with different organization, it would not be a huge burden to raise the lagging areas of the nation. The society is not a Yugoslavia fighting to climb the steep hill of capital accumulation. Even now, at the top of the system, young people are falling away from the false affluence of consumerism. Were the waste of unemployment, militarism, and unnecessary consumption ended, the resources available would be enormous. Poor communities could be aided without intolerable cost. It would also be possible to allocate huge resources to other nations.

Second, politics would not die were the nation organized as a many-level Pluralist Commonwealth. (Indeed, what we are talking about might best be defined not as an *achieved*, static goal, but as a stage-by-stage *process* of increasing mastery of rational and irrational limitations on man's potential.) Even today, politics forces the creeping federal structure to reallocate funds in some programs, though it does so very erratically. In a new Commonwealth, local and regional bodies would have substantial influence on major decisions of investment and resource allocation which are now left to private corporations. Especially as a new vision and ethic develops, it is possible to imagine a considerably reinvigorated politics which could concentrate on helping underdeveloped communities—perhaps progressively narrowing the range of inequality by setting (and gradually lowering) maximum income ceilings, by setting (and gradually raising) minimum income floors, and by regularly introducing a greater share of such free goods as education, medical care, housing, and basic food stuffs.

But a progressive process of this kind is not the same as total equality, and the distinction is important: The only alternative to the process of politics is a central decision-making authority which *forces* its program upon all communities. *You simply cannot have it both ways.* A basic problem of both democracy and equality is when and what is to be centralized and what is not—and at which stages of development very specific trade-offs between conflicting values are made. There is trade-off at one level between equality and decentralization; place absolute priority on the former and you must have enormous power at the center to end variations between localities. On the other hand, if diversity and democracy are priorities, they bring with them a substantial degree of inequality between areas.

Other considerations make it appear that the nature of the trade-offs is even more complex. Although centralization in theory can establish equality *between areas*, most hierarchical systems have required highly stratified, unequal patterns of *individual incentives*. (The resulting inequality of state-socialist systems in practice is often ignored by their proponents and apologists.) Motivation is potentially different, however, in small units (which are the only historic examples of equality *between individuals*). Therefore, while centralization seems the short cut to general equality, it is likely in practice to be

a dead end. And while diversity and democracy seem to be antagonistic to equality, this appears to be the only way to build up different motivational patterns out of which an ethic of universal equality might eventually develop. . . .

Over the long haul the inevitable trade-offs between centralization and decentralization are likely to diminish as increasingly productive technology makes it easier to satisfy more needs—and as rational ecological judgments reduce the pressure for economic growth. If individual and community motivation for high living standards can be reduced by ending "consumerism," there will also be less need for the hierarchical and centralized controls that ever-expanding production seems to require. Finally, as true (and voluntary) *agreement with* the principles of a new vision of equality develops, centralized decision making to achieve it can, in fact, become more a matter of rational administration than of bureaucratic compulsion.

In the final analysis, therefore, the tension between the socialist vision and decentralist alternatives is best understood not as an ultimate contradiction but as a transitional problem of societies moving towards the postindustrial era. . . .

PRECURSORS

A variety of existing youth communes and collectives point in the direction of small scale cooperative community. Affluent white youths' need to transcend isolated individualism seems to be generated systematically out of the sterility of high income suburban (and nuclear family) life, out of the collectivizing experience of migration to the (university) ghetto, and out of the general contradiction between liberal expectations for fulfillment and American realities. Hesitant and beleaguered though they are, collectives and communes all over the country are experimental arenas in which some cooperative "commonwealth" values are being learned in practice—and in which the outlines of a new social vision are beginning, however falteringly, to emerge. . . .

Far more significant developments related to the concept of a Pluralist Commonwealth are to be found in parts of the black community, particularly in a few areas which are politically far ahead of the nation. Increasing numbers of black Americans today are attempting to articulate the idea of "the community" and are beginning to experiment with ways to institutionalize the notion that *its* interests should take priority. Here, the collective ideal and higher expectations seem rooted partly in earlier agrarian traditions, partly in collectivizing migrations to the (urban) ghetto, the experience of rising income levels (as compared with the rural South), and the contradiction between raised hopes and brutal denial and repression. All have been important (and are continuing) conditions out of which a new vision is slowly being forged.

If youth's experiments attempt to realize cooperative social values in isolated settings from New Mexico to Vermont, or the permissive but atypical atmosphere of a university town, in most ghettos the notion of "community" has been expressed as a demand for control of institutions in existing neighborhoods, like Harlem or Hough. The emerging concept of the "community corporation" is taking on increasing importance in this concept—and may become a critical element in an "alternative program" if it transcends the limitations of the inevitable initial compromises.

The mechanisms of a democratically controlled neighborhood corporation involve little more than drawing a legal line around a neighborhood or rural area to establish a geographically defined corporate entity which may undertake a variety of social, economic, and political functions. The crucial feature is democracy—either through the principal of one person, one vote, or through confederations of local block clubs, churches, and action organizations.

Though once conceived only as O.E.O. vehicles or instruments of "neighborhood government," such institutions become of much greater long-run interest when they assume ownership of industries and stores collectively in the name of the entire community, as they are now doing in many areas. The terms "community union," "community cooperative," or "community development corporation" (C.D.C.) are then more accurate descriptions. Instead of letting individual capitalists buy businesses and absorb the profits themselves, when a C.D.C. does so it either distributes small dividends to all members or, more significantly, it uses proceeds collectively for such community-building services as day care centers, recreational programs, or training activities.

Some C.D.C.'s (like FIGHT, in Rochester, New York) are already operating community-owned electrical manufacturing plants of substantial scale. In Los Angeles, Operation Bootstrap has established a cooperatively-owned toy factory; in the Chicano community of New Mexico there are a variety of cooperatively-owned industries ranging from farming and cattle feeding to furniture and wood products manufacturing; in Cleveland a rubber moulding factory is collectively-owned; in Philadelphia there is already a large community-owned shopping center (and one which is to be more broadly based in the community is in the planning stages in Cleveland).[12] . . .

In one or two instances, particularly in the New Communities, Inc., experiment in southwest Georgia, the vision of community has been developed much further, and has led to the purchase of land for a black,

[12]For information on these and other efforts, see: "Profiles in Community-Based Economic Development," available from The Cambridge Institute and the Center for Community Economic Development, 1878 Massachusetts Avenue, Cambridge, Massachusetts 02140.

collectively-owned city based on communitarian ideals—similar in hope, if not yet in practice, to the Israeli *moshav*. Obviously, none of the experiments represent the achievement of a fully developed alternative vision; their significance is only as the precursors of the possibility of a longer process which might conceivably transcend what must begin as "community capitalism." . . .

Two distinct ways of organizing power to bolster these community efforts have emerged: In many cities demonstrations, sit-ins, and other militant protests have successfully wrenched control of housing and even urban renewal from public bureaucracy—and placed ownership and control in the hands of community groups. Elsewhere, a more traditional form of power which attaches to the voting strength of well-organized groups has forced many concessions. In New Mexico, for instance, at one point state authorities were brought to direct state schools and hospitals to give preferential treatment to the purchase of vegetables from local community cooperatives.

The linkage between a local, community-owned vegetable cooperative and a higher order political authority is of special interest in that it illustrates in skeletal outline what might be thought of as a two tier Pluralist Commonwealth model. In this instance, the local community-based economic effort is fortified by political–economic decisions made by the higher unit—however, given the power relationships, it is forced to be responsive to a coalition of smaller scale units. . . .

The achievements of the Calumet Community Congress in Gary, Indiana, and the election of the radicals in Berkeley, California, could conceivably help open the way for a broadening of similar developments in white communities, beyond a few experiments which are just getting underway in Appalachia and Boston, Massachusetts. . . .

Such illustrations are only fragmentary local beginning points—and only partial aspects—of what might one day become "a long revolution" towards some form of Pluralist Commonwealth vision—if they are extended and combined with the development of regional and national alternatives, and if they become important in a longer term effort to build new political power.

SELECTIVE BIBLIOGRAPHY

Further reading is recommended both in Fromm, *Marx's Concept of Man*, and in Alperovitz, *A Long Revolution*, as cited in the source lines for Sections 12.1 and 12.2. There is a wide-ranging debate about what the term "socialism" means and what institutions might ensure a more decent society. Guevara [7] gives an inspirational account of the ideals of Cuban socialism and implicitly defines socialism in terms of socialist values—an excellent reading. Huberman and Sweezy [10] present the *classical* view of socialism as public ownership of the means of production. Lichtheim [11] contrasts socialism, defined as social ownership of the means of production, planning, and the gradual disappearance of the wage relation, with state capitalism, state socialism, and the welfare state. Mandel [12] provides a good analysis of production, distribution, and modes of living in a socialist society. He deals in particular with the socialization of production, choice in consumption, the "psychological revolution," and the possibilities for developing free, as opposed to alienated, labor. His emphasis on the psychological aspects of a more decent society counterbalances the limitations of his traditional Marxist view that socialism results from a society so affluent that scarcity ceases to be a problem; our analysis of consumerism, contrived needs, and the ecological damage associated with high levels of production suggests that the problems of scarcity will persist even in an affluent society until such time as Mandel's "psychological revolution" actually occurs.

Alperovitz (already cited) and Foley [4] argue for socialism as a *decentralized* social ownership of the means of production. Foley presents a careful analysis of the implications of decentralization for efficiency and incentives. Blumberg [2] shows, on the basis of extensive evidence, that even a limited degree of workers' management and participation reduces alienation; the implications for full worker control are obvious. Buber [3] sees the establishment of genuine communities of individuals as the only means for realizing the humanist values of socialism; "the socialist idea points of necessity to the organic construction of a new society out of little societies inwardly bound together by common life and common work." Goodman and Goodman [6] carry this theme to a concrete vision of the integrated work and consumption patterns that might characterize a socialist community. On another level, Goodman [5] argues that science and technology—what others call the "technological requirements of the industrial system"—are not in themselves inhumane; rather, "they have fallen willingly under the dominion of money and power." He argues that a prudent, ecologically minded, decentralized society would develop a humane technology that would greatly add to human welfare.

Robinson [13] stresses the importance of "cultural revolution" in creating a socialist society, drawing in particular on the Chinese experience. Gurley [8] contrasts capitalist development goals with Chinese development goals, which place great emphasis on equality and give priority to satisfying human needs over gains in material production. For case studies of current "socialist" countries, see Huberman and Sweezy [9], especially "the Lessons of Soviet Experience," on the Soviet Union; see the exchange in Sweezy [15] and Bettelheim and Sweezy [1] on Czechoslovakia; see Zeitlin [16], especially the preface, on Cuba; see Blumberg [2], Chapters 8 and 9, on Yugoslavia; and see Gurley [8], Robinson [13], and Snow [14] on China.

[1] Bettelheim, Charles, and Sweezy, Paul. "On the Transition Between Capitalism and Socialism." In *Monthly Rieview* 20, No. 10, (March 1969): 1–19; and "More On the Transition Between Capitalism and Socialism." In *Monthly Review* 22, No. 7 (December 1970): 1–21.

[2] Blumberg, Paul. *Industrial Democracy: The Sociology of Participation.* New York: Schocken Books, 1969.

[3] Buber, Martin. *Paths in Utopia.* Boston: Beacon Press, 1966.*

[4] Foley, Duncan. "On Replacing Capitalism." In Massachusetts Institute of Technology Economics Discussion Paper No. 64. Mimeo, 1970.

[5] Goodman, Paul. "Can Technology Be Humane?" In *New York Review of Books* (November 20, 1969): 27–34.

[6] Goodman, Paul, and Goodman, Percival. *Communitas.* New York: Random House, 1960.*

[7] Guevara, Ernesto "Che." "Man and Socialism in Cuba." Reprinted (among other places) in *Venceremos!* Edited by John Gerassi. New York: Simon & Schuster, Inc., 1968.*

[8] Gurley, John. "Maoist Economic Development: The New Man in the New China." In *The Review of Radical Political Economics* 2, No. 4 (Fall 1970): 26–38.

[9] Huberman, Leo, and Sweezy, Paul, eds. *50 Years of Soviet Power.* New York: Monthly Review Press, 1967.

[10] Huberman, Leo, and Sweezy, Paul. *Introduction to Socialism.* New York: Monthly Review Press, 1968.

[11] Lichtheim, George, "What Socialism Is and Is Not." In *New York Review of Books* (April 10, 1970): 41–45.

[12] Mandel, Ernest. *Marxist Economic Theory.*

2 vols. New York: Monthly Review Press, 1968.

[13] Robinson (Joan. *The Cultural Revolution in China*. Baltimore: Penguin Books, Inc., 1969.*

[14] Snow, Edgar. *The Other Side of the River*. London: Victor Gollancz, Ltd., 1963.

[15] Sweezy, Paul. "Czechoslovakia, Capital-ism, and Socialism." In *Monthly Review* 20, No. 5 (Oct. 1968).

[16] Zeitlin, Maurice. *Revolutionary Politics and the Cuban Working Class*. New York: Harper and Row, Publishers, Inc., 1970.*

*Available in paperback editions.

Biographical Notes

ACKERMAN, FRANK—is a graduate student in economics at Harvard University.

ALPEROVITZ, GAR—is a founder of the Cambridge Institute, a group exploring the prospect of decentralized socialism.

BARAN, PAUL—was the only Marxist economist to hold a professorship at a major American university in the last twenty years; he taught economics at Stanford University until his death in 1964.

BARON, HAROLD—is affiliated with the Urban Studies Institute of the Associated Colleges of the Midwest. He was formerly Director of the Research Department of the Chicago Urban League.

BIRNBAUM, HOWARD—is a graduate student in economics at Harvard University.

BLACKBURN, ROBIN—is an editor of the British bi-monthly Marxist periodical *New Left Review*. He has taught sociology at the London School of Economics.

BOGGS, GRACE—has taught in the Detroit public school system and is a long-time activist in the Black Liberation Movement.

BOGGS, JAMES—was born in Alabama, has worked in auto plants in Detroit since the 1940's and has written extensively on the Black Liberation Movement.

BONNEN, JAMES—teaches agricultural economics at Michigan State University.

BOOKCHIN, MURRAY—has written many books and articles on ecology and on libertarian anarchism.

BOWLES, SAMUEL—teaches economics at Harvard University.

CARMICHAEL, STOKELY—has been active for many years as a Black Power advocate and organizer in the North and the South.

COHEN, DAVID K.—teaches education at Harvard University, where he is director of the Center for Educational Policy Research.

DAVIES, MARGERY—is a graduate student in sociology at Brandeis University.

DOBB, MAURICE—is an eminent Marxist economist who recently retired from a Readership in Economics at Cambridge University, where he had taught since 1924.

EDWARDS, RICHARD C.—is an economist affiliated with the Center for Educational Policy Research at Harvard University.

ENGELS, FRIEDRICH—was a German-born socialist, manufacturer, and writer, best known for his life-long association and close collaboration with Karl Marx.

FINKELHOR, DAVID—studied at Harvard University and is at work on a book about communal living.

FRIEDAN, BETTY—is a prominent activist in the National Organization of Women.

FROMM, ERICH—was trained in psychoanalysis in Berlin and has written many books on social and psychological alienation.

GALBRAITH, JOHN KENNETH—has combined an academic career teaching economics at Harvard University with an active involvement in American politics. He served as Ambassador to India, 1961–1963.

GENOVESE, EUGENE—teaches history at the University of Rochester. He has written numerous articles on slavery in the Western Hemisphere from a Marxist perspective.

GINTIS, HERBERT—teaches economics and is affiliated with the Center for Educational Policy Research at Harvard University.

GOLDBERG, MARILYN POWER—is a graduate student in economics at the University of California at Berkeley.

GOODING, JUDSON—is an associate editor of *Fortune* magazine.

GORDON, LINDA—teaches history at the University of Massachusetts at Boston.

GORZ, ANDRE—is a well-known French Marxist and a member of the editorial board of *Les Temps Modernes*.

HAMILTON, CHARLES—teaches political science at Columbia University and is the author of many articles on black politics.

HERNDON, JAMES—has been a merchant seaman, a file clerk, a machinist, an oboe player and—most recently—a schoolteacher.

HOBSBAWM, ERIC—is an eminent Marxist historian and Reader in History at Birbeck College, University of London.

HOWE, FLORENCE—teaches humanities and women's studies at the State University of New York College at Old Westbury.

HYMER, BENNETT—has worked in the Research Department of the Chicago Urban League since 1964.

HYMER, STEPHEN—teaches economics at the New School for Social Research.

KATZ, ELIZABETH—lives in Cambridge, Massachusetts and is presently travelling in Central America.

KENISTON, KENNETH—teaches psychiatry at the Yale University Medical School.

LANGER, ELINOR—is a free-lance journalist whose writings have appeared in various periodicals including *Science* and the *New York Review of Books*.

LAUTER, PAUL—has taught English at Antioch College and is now on the staff of the United States Servicemen's Fund.

LAZERSON, MARVIN—teaches history of education at Harvard University, where he is affiliated with the Center for Educational Policy Research.

LONG, NGO VINH—is a Vietnamese graduate student at Harvard University who has been active in the peace movement. He edits and publishes a monthly bulletin, *Thòi-Báo Gà*, which carries news from Vietnam.

LUNDBERG, FERDINAND—was for many years a financial writer for *The New York Herald Tribune*. His first book on the super-rich became the subject of widespread public controversy in the 1930's.

MacEWAN, ARTHUR—teaches economics at Harvard University.

MAGDOFF, HARRY—is co-editor of the independent socialist journal, *Monthly Review*.

MARX, KARL—hardly needs an introduction. His writings have both contributed to the analysis of the capitalist system and have been a source of inspiration for revolutionaries throughout the world.

MEANS, GARDINER—an economist and long-time government adviser, is an expert on economic concentration.

MITCHELL, JULIET—is a member of the editorial board of *New Left Review*.

MORTON, PEGGY—is active in the Women's Liberation Movement in Toronto.

MUMFORD, LEWIS—has written numerous books about cities and the impact of modern technology on society.

O'CONNOR, JAMES—teaches economics at San Jose State College.

POLANYI, KARL—was born in Austria, educated in Europe, and emigrated to the United States in 1940 to teach economics and anthropology at Bennington College and Columbia University.

REICH, MICHAEL—teaches economics at Boston University.

SOCIALIST REVOLUTION is a bi-monthly journal whose purpose "is to help build the theoretical comprehension of advanced capitalism which is prerequisite to the development of mass socialist consciousness."

SWEEZY, PAUL—is a founder and co-editor of *Monthly Review*, in which he has written on numerous economic and political problems from a Marxist perspective. He has taught economics at Harvard University and the New School for Social Research.

TERKEL, STUDS—has a radio show in Chicago; he is a recognized master of the art of journalistic interviewing.

THERBORN, GORAN—is an editor of *Zenit*, a Swedish New Left journal.

WEINSTEIN, JAMES—is an editor of the journal *Socialist Revolution*; he has written several books on American history.

WEISS, JANICE—is a student at the Harvard Graduate School of Education.

WEISSKOPF, THOMAS E.—teaches economics at Harvard University.

WEISSKOPF, WALTER—is Chairman of the Department of Economics at Roosevelt University.

WETZLER, JAMES—is a graduate student in economics at Harvard University.

ZIMBALIST, ANDREW—is a graduate student in economics at Harvard University.